Proactive Policing

Effects on Crime and Communities

Committee on Proactive Policing:
Effects on Crime, Communities, and Civil Liberties

David Weisburd and Malay K. Majmundar, *Editors*

Committee on Law and Justice

Division of Behavioral and Social Sciences and Education

A Consensus Study Report of

The National Academies of
SCIENCES • ENGINEERING • MEDICINE

THE NATIONAL ACADEMIES PRESS
Washington, DC
www.nap.edu

THE NATIONAL ACADEMIES PRESS   500 Fifth Street, NW   Washington, DC 20001

This activity was supported by a Grant from the Laura and John Arnold Foundation and Grant No. 2016-IJ-CX-0001 with the National Institute of Justice of the U.S. Department of Justice, and with additional support from the National Academy of Sciences Presidents' Fund. Any opinions, findings, conclusions, or recommendations expressed in this publication do not necessarily reflect the views of any organization or agency that provided support for the project.

International Standard Book Number-13: 978-0-309-46713-1
International Standard Book Number-10: 0-309-46713-6
Library of Congress Control Number: 2017961947
Digital Object Identifier: https://doi.org/10.17226/24928

Additional copies of this publication are available for sale from the National Academies Press, 500 Fifth Street, NW, Keck 360, Washington, DC 20001; (800) 624-6242 or (202) 334-3313; http://www.nap.edu.

Copyright 2018 by the National Academy of Sciences. All rights reserved.

Printed in the United States of America

Suggested citation: National Academies of Sciences, Engineering, and Medicine. (2018). *Proactive Policing: Effects on Crime and Communities*. Washington, DC: The National Academies Press. doi: https://doi.org/10.17226/24928.

The National Academies of
SCIENCES • ENGINEERING • MEDICINE

The **National Academy of Sciences** was established in 1863 by an Act of Congress, signed by President Lincoln, as a private, nongovernmental institution to advise the nation on issues related to science and technology. Members are elected by their peers for outstanding contributions to research. Dr. Marcia McNutt is president.

The **National Academy of Engineering** was established in 1964 under the charter of the National Academy of Sciences to bring the practices of engineering to advising the nation. Members are elected by their peers for extraordinary contributions to engineering. Dr. C. D. Mote, Jr., is president.

The **National Academy of Medicine** (formerly the Institute of Medicine) was established in 1970 under the charter of the National Academy of Sciences to advise the nation on medical and health issues. Members are elected by their peers for distinguished contributions to medicine and health. Dr. Victor J. Dzau is president.

The three Academies work together as the **National Academies of Sciences, Engineering, and Medicine** to provide independent, objective analysis and advice to the nation and conduct other activities to solve complex problems and inform public policy decisions. The National Academies also encourage education and research, recognize outstanding contributions to knowledge, and increase public understanding in matters of science, engineering, and medicine.

Learn more about the National Academies of Sciences, Engineering, and Medicine at **www.nationalacademies.org**.

The National Academies of
SCIENCES • ENGINEERING • MEDICINE

Consensus Study Reports published by the National Academies of Sciences, Engineering, and Medicine document the evidence-based consensus on the study's statement of task by an authoring committee of experts. Reports typically include findings, conclusions, and recommendations based on information gathered by the committee and the committee's deliberations. Each report has been subjected to a rigorous and independent peer-review process and it represents the position of the National Academies on the statement of task.

Proceedings published by the National Academies of Sciences, Engineering, and Medicine chronicle the presentations and discussions at a workshop, symposium, or other event convened by the National Academies. The statements and opinions contained in proceedings are those of the participants and are not endorsed by other participants, the planning committee, or the National Academies.

For information about other products and activities of the National Academies, please visit www.nationalacademies.org/about/whatwedo.

COMMITTEE ON PROACTIVE POLICING: EFFECTS ON CRIME, COMMUNITIES, AND CIVIL LIBERTIES

David Weisburd (*Chair*), Department of Criminology, Law and Society, George Mason University; Institute of Criminology, The Hebrew University of Jerusalem
Hassan Aden, The Aden Group, Alexandria, VA
Anthony A. Braga, School of Criminology and Criminal Justice, Northeastern University
Jim Bueermann, Police Foundation, Washington, DC
Philip J. Cook, Sanford School of Public Policy, Duke University
Phillip Atiba Goff, John Jay College of Criminal Justice, The City University of New York; Center for Policing Equity, New York, NY
Rachel A. Harmon, School of Law, University of Virginia
Amelia Haviland, Heinz College of Information Systems and Public Policy, Carnegie Mellon University
Cynthia Lum, Department of Criminology, Law and Society, George Mason University
Charles Manski, Department of Economics, Northwestern University
Stephen Mastrofski, Department of Criminology, Law and Society, George Mason University
Tracey Meares, School of Law, Yale University
Daniel Nagin, Heinz College of Information Systems and Public Policy, Carnegie Mellon University
Emily Owens, School of Social Ecology, University of California, Irvine
Steven Raphael, Goldman School of Public Policy, University of California, Berkeley
Jerry Ratcliffe, Department of Criminal Justice, Temple University
Tom Tyler, School of Law, Yale University

Malay K. Majmundar, *Study Director*
Emily Backes, *Program Officer*
Leticia Garcilazo Green, *Senior Program Assistant*

COMMITTEE ON LAW AND JUSTICE

Jeremy Travis (*Chair*), Criminal Justice Department, Laura and John Arnold Foundation
Ruth D. Peterson (*Vice-Chair*), Criminal Justice Research Center, Ohio State University
Kimberlé W. Crenshaw, UCLA School of Law, University of California, Los Angeles
John J. Donohue III, Stanford Law School, Stanford University
Mark S. Johnson, Department of Community and Family Medicine, Howard University
Mark A.R. Kleiman, Marron Institute of Urban Management, Crime and Justice Program, New York University
James P. Lynch, Department of Criminology and Criminal Justice, University of Maryland
Daniel S. Nagin, Department of Public Policy and Statistics, Heinz College, Carnegie Mellon University
Anne Morrison Piehl, Department of Economics and Program in Criminal Justice, Rutgers University
Steven Raphael, Goldman School of Public Policy, University of California, Berkeley
Laurie O. Robinson, Department of Criminology, Law and Society, George Mason University
Cynthia Rudin, Computer Science Department and the Electrical and Computer Engineering Department, Duke University
Sally S. Simpson, Department of Criminology and Criminal Justice, University of Maryland
Susan B. Sorenson, School of Social Policy and Practice, University of Pennsylvania
Linda A. Teplin, Feinberg School of Medicine, Department of Psychiatry and Behavioral Sciences, Northwestern University
Bruce Western, Department of Sociology, Harvard University
Cathy Spatz Widom, Department of Psychology, John Jay College and the Graduate Center, The City University of New York

Kathi L. Grasso, *Board Director*
Malay K. Majmundar, *Associate Board Director*
Emily Backes, *Program Officer*
Tina M. Latimer, *Program Coordinator*
Leticia Garcilazo Green, *Senior Program Assistant*

Acknowledgments

This Consensus Study Report on the evidence regarding the consequences of different forms of proactive policing for crime and disorder, discriminatory application, legality, and community reaction and receptiveness was prepared at the request of the National Institute of Justice and the Laura and John Arnold Foundation. In response to that request, the National Academies of Sciences, Engineering, and Medicine appointed the Committee on Proactive Policing: Effects on Crime, Communities, and Civil Liberties (under the standing Committee on Law and Justice [CLAJ]) to carry out the task. Fifteen prominent scholars representing a broad array of disciplines—including criminology, law, psychology, statistics, political science, and economics—as well as two noted police practitioners were included on the committee, which met six times over a 2-year period.

This report would not have been possible without the contributions of many people. Special thanks go to the members of the study committee, who dedicated extensive time, thought, and energy to the project. Thanks are also due to consultants Joshua Correll (University of Colorado Boulder) and Jillian Swencionis (Center for Policing Equity) for their important contributions on issues relating to racial bias.

In addition to its own research and deliberations, the committee received input from several outside sources: academic experts who served as discussants for presentations by committee members; police practitioners and community representatives who participated in roundtables and webinars; and commissioned papers.

The committee's February and April 2016 meetings included open sessions at which experts commented on members' presentations. We thank

Claudine Gay (Harvard University), Amanda Geller (New York University), and Ruth Peterson (Ohio State University) for their discussant comments on "Evidence on Disparity/Discrimination/Racial Bias;" John MacDonald (University of Pennsylvania) and John Pepper (University of Virginia) for their discussant comments on "Evidence on the Impact of Proactive Policing on Crime and Disorder;" Robert Sampson (Harvard University) and Anne Piehl (Rutgers University) for their discussant comments on "Evidence on the Community Effects of Proactive Policing;" and David Sklansky (Stanford Law School) and Geoffrey Alpert (University of South Carolina) for their discussant comments on "Law and Legality."

The committee's April 2016 meeting also included an open session for a police practitioner roundtable and a community representatives' roundtable. For that practitioners' roundtable, we thank police chief Art Acevedo (Austin, Texas), police chief Debora Black (Glendale, Arizona), retired police chief Jane Castor (Tampa, Florida), sheriff Bob Gualtieri (Pinellas County, Florida), police commissioner Robert Haas (Cambridge, Massachusetts), and retired police superintendent Ronal Serpas (New Orleans, Louisiana).

For the community roundtable, we thank John DeTaeye, Collaborative Solutions for Communities (Washington, DC); Jin Hee Lee, NAACP Legal Defense and Educational Fund (New York City); Joseph Lipari, Citizen Review Board (Syracuse, New York); and Julia Ryan, Local Initiatives Support Corporation (Washington, D.C.).

The committee's two public webinars, held in June 2016, were on the topic of "Community Perspectives on Proactive Policing—Black Lives Matter." We thank Alicia Garza, National Domestic Workers Alliance, and Brittany N. Packnett, Teach for America, for their participation in and contributions to the webinars.

The committee also gathered information through several commissioned papers. We thank Geoffrey Alpert (University of South Carolina) for "Police Use of Force and its Relationship to Proactive Policing," Elizabeth Hinton (Harvard University) for "The Broader Context of Race and Policing," and Samuel Walker (University of Nebraska) for "History of Proactive Policing Strategies."

Several staff members of the National Academies also made significant contributions to the report. Emily Backes provided valuable research, writing assistance, and played an important role in helping to draft portions of the report. Leticia Garcilazo Green made sure that the committee meetings ran smoothly, assisted in preparing the manuscript, and provided key administrative and logistical support throughout the project. Thanks are also due to Kirsten Sampson-Snyder for managing the report review process; Yvonne Wise for managing the report production process; and Kathi Grasso, director of CLAJ, for providing overall guidance and oversight. We also thank Robert Katt for skillful editing.

ACKNOWLEDGMENTS

This Consensus Study Report was reviewed in draft form by individuals chosen for their diverse perspectives and technical expertise. The purpose of this independent review is to provide candid and critical comments that will assist the National Academies in making each published report as sound as possible and to ensure that it meets the institutional standards for quality, objectivity, evidence, and responsiveness to the study charge. The review comments and draft manuscript remain confidential to protect the integrity of the deliberative process.

We thank the following individuals for their review of this report: Robert D. Crutchfield, Department of Sociology, University of Washington; John F. Dovidio, Department of Psychology, Yale University; Lorraine Mazerolle, School of Social Science, The University of Queensland; John V. Pepper, Department of Economics, University of Virginia; Ruth D. Peterson, Department of Sociology (emerita), Ohio State University; Donald W. Pfaff, Laboratory of Neurobiology and Behavior, Rockefeller University; Sue Rahr, Criminal Justice Training Commission, Burien, Washington; Nancy M. Reid, Department of Statistical Sciences, University of Toronto; Jennifer Richeson, Department of Psychology, Yale University; Robert J. Sampson, Department of Sociology, Harvard University; Lawrence W. Sherman, Cambridge Police Executive Programme, Institute of Criminology, University of Cambridge and Department of Criminology and Criminal Justice, University of Maryland; Wesley G. Skogan, Institute for Policy Research, Northwestern University; Christopher Slobogin, School of Law, Vanderbilt University; Darrel W. Stephens, Major Cities Chiefs Association; and David R. Williams, Department of Social and Behavioral Sciences, T.H. Chan School of Public Health, Harvard University.

Although the reviewers listed above provided many constructive comments and suggestions, they were not asked to endorse the conclusions or recommendations of this report, nor did they see the final draft of the report before its release. The review of this report was overseen by John Monahan, School of Law, University of Virginia, and Ellen Wright Clayton, Center for Biomedical Ethics and Society, Vanderbilt University. They were responsible for making certain that an independent examination of this report was carried out in accordance with the standards of the National Academies and that all review comments were carefully considered. Responsibility for the final content rests entirely with the authoring committee and the National Academies.

David Weisburd, *Chair*
Malay K. Majmundar, *Study Director*
Committee on Proactive Policing:
Effects on Crime, Communities, and Civil Liberties

Contents

Summary		1
1	**Introduction**	15
	Charge to the Study Committee, 19	
	The Origins of Proactive Policing, 19	
	Professional Reform in the 20th Century, 23	
	The Challenge to the Standard Model of Policing, 25	
	The Emergence of Modern Proactive Policing, 29	
	The Committee's Definition of "Proactive Policing," 30	
	Assessing the Evidence, 33	
	Organization of the Report, 37	
	Conclusion, 39	
2	**The Landscape of Proactive Policing**	41
	Strategies for a Place-Based Approach, 43	
	Hot Spots Policing, 46	
	Predictive Policing, 49	
	Closed Circuit Television, 51	
	Strategies for a Problem-Solving Approach, 52	
	Problem-Oriented Policing, 53	
	Third Party Policing, 54	
	Strategies for a Person-Focused Approach, 57	
	Focused Deterrence, 58	
	Stop, Question, and Frisk, 60	

Strategies for a Community-Based Approach, 61
  Community-Oriented Policing, 63
  Procedural Justice Policing, 65
  Broken Windows Policing, 70
The Diffusion of Proactive Policing Across American Cities, 73
Conclusion, 79

3 **Law and Legality** 81
   Fourth Amendment, 83
     Legal Overview, 83
     Deterrence-Oriented Proactive Strategies, 85
     Place-Based Strategies, 90
     Third Party Policing, 93
   Equal Protection and Statutes Prohibiting Discrimination, 95
     Legal Overview, 95
     Deterrence-Oriented Proactive Strategies, 98
     Predictive Policing Strategies, 100
   Empirical Evidence on Proactive Policing and Illegal Police Behavior, 101
   Legal Mechanisms for Challenging Proactive Policing, 103
   Other Legal Standards and Values, 108
   Community-Based Policing, 111
   Conclusion, 116

4 **Impacts of Proactive Policing on Crime and Disorder** 119
   Mechanisms for Prevention, 119
   Place-Based Strategies, 122
     Hot Spots Policing, 122
     Predictive Policing, 129
     Closed Circuit Television, 132
   Problem-Solving Strategies, 135
     Problem-Oriented Policing, 135
     Third Party Policing, 139
   Person-Focused Strategies, 142
     Focused Deterrence, 142
     Stop, Question, and Frisk, 148
   Community-Based Strategies, 151
     Community-Oriented Policing, 151
     Procedural Justice Policing, 155
     Broken Windows Policing, 163
   Conclusion, 168
     Place-Based Proactive Strategies, 173

Problem-Solving Proactive Strategies, 174
Person-Focused Proactive Strategies, 175
Community-Based Proactive Strategies, 175

5   **Community Reaction to Proactive Policing: The Impact of Place-Based, Problem-Solving, and Person-Focused Approaches**   177
What Do We Mean By Community Impacts?, 179
A Model of the Effects of Proactive Policing on Community Outcomes, 179
Place-Based Interventions, 181
Problem-Solving Interventions, 188
Person-Focused Interventions, 195
Collateral Consequences for Society of Proactive Policing, 202
   Impact of Proactive Policing Practices on Health and Development, 203
   Impact of Proactive Policing on Civic and Institutional Engagement, 206
Conclusion, 208
   Place-Based Proactive Strategies, 208
   Problem-Solving Proactive Strategies, 209
   Person-Focused Proactive Strategies, 209

6   **Community-Based Proactive Strategies: Implications for Community Perceptions and Cooperation**   211
Community-Oriented Policing, 212
   Community-Oriented Policing's Impacts on Community Evaluations of the Police, 216
   Community-Oriented Policing Impacts on Orientations to the Police, 218
   Community-Oriented Policing Impacts on Cooperation and Collective Efficacy, 219
   Long-Term Effects of Community-Oriented Policing, 222
   Environmental Conditions, 223
Broken Windows Policing, 224
   The Impact of Broken Windows Policing on Fear of Crime and Collective Efficacy, 225
Procedural Justice, 227
   Antecedents of Perceived Legitimacy, 229
   General Evidence on the Procedural Justice Logic Model Outside of Policing, 232
   The Specific Features of Procedural Justice That Shape Perceived Legitimacy, 236

Evidence on Procedural Justice in Policing, 239
Procedural Justice and Police Practice, 245
Conclusion, 246

7 **Racial Bias and Disparities in Proactive Policing**   251
   Measuring Disparities, Bias, and the Motivations for Bias:
      Issues and Challenges, 254
      Counterfactual-Based Measures of Bias, 256
      Benchmark Measures of Bias, 256
      Outcome-Based Measures of Bias, 257
   Historical Background on Racial Disparities, Bias, and Animus in
      Policing, 263
      Racial Animus in Federal, State, and Local Policies, 265
      Racial Disparities in Federal, State, and Local Policies, 266
      Law Enforcement Resistance to the Civil Rights Movement, 268
      Racial Disparities in Criminal Justice Contact Driven by
         Federal Policy, 268
   Potential Reasons Why Modern Proactive Policing May Be
      Associated with Disparities and Bias, 275
   Evidence from Psychological Science on Racial Bias in Policing, 276
      The Psychological Science of Bias, 277
      Evidence from Studies of Racial Bias in Law Enforcement, 280
      Risk and Protective Factors for Bias in Proactive Policing, 283
      Risk Factors for Biased Behavior, 284
      Protective (bias-reducing) Factors for Biased Behavior, 286
   Evidence from Criminology, Economics, and Sociology on
         Racial Bias in Policing, 288
      Comparisons of Racial Composition of Police–Citizen
         Interactions to Alternative Population Benchmarks, 288
      Outcome Tests for Racial Disparities in Treatment, 294
   Conclusion, 297

8 **Conclusions and Implications for Policy and Research**   303
   Law and Legality, 305
   Crime and Disorder, 306
      Place-Based Strategies, 307
      Problem-Solving Strategies, 309
      Person-Focused Strategies, 310
      Community-Based Strategies, 312
   Community Impacts, 314
      Place-Based, Problem-Solving, and Person-Focused
         Interventions, 314
      Community-Based Interventions, 316

Racial Bias and Disparities, 318
Policy Implications, 321
Research Gaps, 325
 Improving the Quality of Data and Research on
  Proactive Policing, 326
 Proactive Policing and the Law, 329
 Crime-Control Impacts of Proactive Policing, 330
 Community Impacts of Proactive Policing, 331
 Racial Bias and Disparities in Proactive Policing, 332
The Future of Proactive Policing, 334

References   335

Appendixes

A Perspectives from the Field   375
B Biographical Sketches of Committee Members   383

Boxes, Tables, and Figure

BOXES

2-1 Hot Spots Policing in Sacramento, California, 49
2-2 Problem-Oriented Policing in Jacksonville, Florida, 55
2-3 Third Party Policing in Oakland, California, 56
2-4 Focused Deterrence in Boston: Operation Ceasefire, 59
2-5 Stop, Question, and Frisk in Philadelphia, 62
2-6 Community-Oriented Policing in Chicago, 67
2-7 Procedural Justice Policing in King County, Washington, 70
2-8 Broken Windows Policing in New York City, 73

6-1 The Elements of Procedural Justice, 230

7-1 The Infra-Marginality Problem, 259
7-2 Limitations of Outcome-Based Methodological Approaches, 262

TABLES

S-1 Four Approaches to Proactive Policing, 2

2-1 Four Approaches to Proactive Policing, 44
2-2 Percentage of Responding Agencies Using a Proactive Policing Practice, by Principal Crime Type Associated with a Hot Spot, 48

2-3 Prevalence of Use of Community-Policing Practices by North American Police Agencies Responding to the 2014 MCCA Survey, 66
2-4 Innovations Adopted by Departments, with and without Formal Policy, from the 2013 NPRP Survey ($n = 76$), 74
2-5 Prevalence of Use of Proactive Policing Strategies by Percentage of Agencies Responding to the 2012 Future of Policing Survey ($n = 200$), 75
2-6 Police Departments in 2007: (1) Using Computers for Hot Spot Identification, (2) Using Community-Policing Officers, (3) with Separate Full-Time Community-Policing Units, 76
2-7 Police Departments in 2013 with Community-Policing Mission Components, 77

4-1 Strength of Evidence on Crime-Prevention Effectiveness: Summary of Proactive Policing Strategies, 170

6-1 Community-Focused Elements in Community-Oriented Policing Interventions, 214

7-1 Racial/Ethnic Composition of Law Enforcement in the United States, 272

FIGURE

5-1 Logic model of proactive policing effects on community outcomes, 180

Summary

Proactive policing, as a strategic approach used by police agencies to prevent crime, is a relatively new phenomenon in the United States. It developed from a crisis in confidence in policing that began to emerge in the 1960s because of social unrest, rising crime rates, and growing skepticism regarding the effectiveness of standard approaches to policing. In response, beginning in the 1980s and 1990s, innovative police practices and policies that took a more proactive approach began to develop. This report uses the term "proactive policing" to refer to **all policing strategies that have as one of their goals the prevention or reduction of crime and disorder and that are not reactive in terms of focusing primarily on uncovering ongoing crime or on investigating or responding to crimes once they have occurred**. Specifically, the elements of proactivity include an emphasis on prevention, mobilizing resources based on police initiative, and targeting the broader underlying forces at work that may be driving crime and disorder. This contrasts with the standard model of policing, which involves an emphasis on reacting to particular crime events after they have occurred, mobilizing resources based on requests coming from outside the police organization, and focusing on the particulars of a given criminal incident.

Proactive policing is distinguished from the everyday decisions of police officers to be proactive in specific situations and instead refers to a strategic decision by police agencies to use proactive police responses in a programmatic way to reduce crime. Today, proactive policing strategies are used widely in the United States. They are not isolated programs used by a select group of agencies but rather a set of ideas that have spread across the landscape of policing.

TABLE S-1 Four Approaches to Proactive Policing

	Place-Based Approach	Problem-Solving Approach	Person-Focused Approach	Community-Based Approach
Logic Model for Crime Prevention	Capitalize on the evidence for the concentration of crime at microgeographic places	Use a problem-oriented approach, which seeks to identify problems as patterns across crime events and then identify the causes of those problems Draw upon solutions tailored to the problem causes, with attention to assessment	Capitalize on the strong concentration of crime among a small proportion of the criminal population	Capitalize on the resources of communities to identify and control crime
Policing Strategies	Hot spots policing, predictive policing, CCTV	Problem-oriented policing, third party policing	Focused deterrence; repeat offender programs; stop, question, and frisk	Community-oriented policing, procedural justice policing, broken windows policing
Primary Objective	Prevent crime in microgeographic places	Solve recurring problems to prevent future crime	Prevent and deter specific crimes by targeting known offenders	Enhance collective efficacy and community collaboration with police
Key Ways to Accomplish Objective	Identification of crime hot spots and application of focused strategies	Scan and analyze crime problems, identify solutions and assess them (SARA model)	Identification of known high-rate offenders and application of strategies to these specific offenders	Develop approaches that engage the community or that change the way police interact with citizens

SUMMARY

The United States has once again been confronted by a crisis of confidence in policing. Instances of perceived or actual police misconduct have given rise to nationwide protests against unfair and abusive police practices. Although this report is not intended to respond directly to the crisis of confidence in policing that can be seen in the United States today, it is nevertheless important to consider how proactive policing strategies may bear upon this crisis. It is not enough to simply identify "what works" for reducing crime and disorder; it is also critical to consider issues such as how proactive policing affects the legality of policing, the evaluation of the police in communities, potential abuses of police authority, and the equitable application of police services in the everyday lives of citizens.

To that end, the National Institute of Justice and the Laura and John Arnold Foundation asked the National Academies of Sciences, Engineering, and Medicine to review the evidence and discuss the data and methodological gaps on (1) the effects of different forms of proactive policing on crime; (2) whether they are applied in a discriminatory manner; (3) whether they are being used in a legal fashion; and (4) community reaction. The Committee on Proactive Policing: Effects on Crime, Communities, and Civil Liberties was appointed by the National Academies to carry out this task.

The committee made a decision to prioritize proactive policing strategies that are commonly applied in U.S. police agencies; cutting-edge strategies that, though not yet widely adopted, represent important new methods for preventing crime; and strategies that raise concerns about biased or abusive outcomes. In the context of this report, proactive policing is regarded as a strategic concern and refers to the policy decisions of departments regarding the means and goals of policing and not to the individual actions of officers.

Proactive policing has taken a number of different forms over the past two decades, and these variants often overlap in practice. The four broad approaches for proactive policing described in this report are (1) place-based interventions, (2) problem-solving interventions, (3) person-focused interventions, and (4) community-based interventions. Table S-1 summarizes the four approaches and the strategies they encompass. The rest of this summary discusses the consequences of these approaches for law and legality, crime and disorder, community reactions, and racial bias and disparities.

LAW AND LEGALITY

However effective a policing practice may be in preventing crime, it is impermissible if it violates the law. The most important legal constraints on proactive policing are the Fourth Amendment to the U.S. Constitution, the Equal Protection Clause (of the Fourteenth Amendment), and related statutory provisions.

Although proactive policing strategies do not inherently violate the Fourth Amendment, any proactive strategy could lead to Fourth Amendment violations[1] to the degree that it is implemented by having officers engage in stops, searches, and arrests that violate constitutional standards. This risk is especially relevant for stop, question, and frisk (SQF);[2] broken windows policing;[3] and hot spots policing interventions[4] if they use an aggressive practice of searches and seizures to deter criminal activity.

In addition, in conjunction with existing Fourth Amendment doctrine, proactive policing strategies may limit the effective strength or scope of constitutional protection or reduce the availability of constitutional remedies. For example, when departments identify "high crime areas" pursuant to place-based proactive policing strategies, courts may allow stops by officers of individuals within those areas that are based on less individualized behavior than they would require without the "high crime" designation. In this way, geographically oriented proactive policing may lead otherwise identical citizen-police encounters to be treated differently under the law.

The Equal Protection Clause guarantees equal and impartial treatment of citizens by government actors. It governs all policies, decisions, and acts taken by police officers and departments, including those in furtherance of proactive policing strategies. As a result, Equal Protection claims may arise with respect to any proactive policing strategy to the degree that it discriminates against individuals based on their race, religion, or national origin, among other characteristics. Since most policing policies today do not expressly target racial or ethnic groups, most Equal Protection challenges require proving discriminatory purpose in addition to discriminatory effect in order to establish a constitutional violation.

Specific proactive policing strategies, such as SQF and "zero tolerance" versions of broken windows policing, have been linked to violations of both the Fourth Amendment and the Equal Protection Clause by courts in private litigation and by the U.S. Department of Justice in its investigations

---

[1] The Fourth Amendment to the U.S. Constitution states: "The right of the people to be secure in their persons, houses, papers, and effects, against unreasonable searches and seizures, shall not be violated, and no warrants shall issue, but upon probable cause, supported by oath or affirmation, and particularly describing the place to be searched, and the persons or things to be seized."

[2] When carried out as a proactive policing strategy, an SQF program relies upon the legal authority granted by court decisions to engage in frequent stops in which suspects are questioned about their activities, frisked if possible, and often searched, usually with consent.

[3] In broken windows policing, the police seek to prevent crime by addressing disorder and less serious crime problems. Such police interventions are expected to reinforce and enhance informal social controls within communities.

[4] Hot spots policing efforts focus on "micro" units of geography where crime is concentrated. Microgeographic areas are commonly defined to include a single street or a cluster of street segments.

of police departments. Ethnographic studies and theoretical arguments further support the idea that proactive strategies that use aggressive stops, searches, and arrests to deter criminal activity may decrease liberty and increase Fourth Amendment and Equal Protection violations. However, empirical evidence is insufficient—using the accepted standards of causality in social science—to support any conclusion about whether proactive policing strategies systematically promote or reduce constitutional violations [Conclusion 3-1]. In order to establish a causal link, studies would ideally determine the incidence of problematic behavior by police under a proactive policy and compare that to the incidence of the same behavior in otherwise similar circumstances in which a proactive policy is not in place.

However, even when proactive strategies do not lead to constitutional violations, they may raise concerns about deeper legal values such as privacy, equality, autonomy, accountability, and transparency [Conclusion 3-2]. Even procedural justice policing and community-oriented policing, neither of which are likely to violate legal constraints on policing (and, to the extent that procedural justice operates as intended, may make violations of law less likely), may, respectively, undermine the transparency about the status of police-citizen interactions and alter the structure of decision making and accountability in police organizations.

CRIME AND DISORDER

The available scientific evidence suggests that certain proactive policing strategies are successful in reducing crime and disorder. This important conclusion provides support for a growing interest among American police in innovating to develop effective crime prevention strategies. At the same time, there is substantial heterogeneity in the effectiveness of different proactive policing interventions in reducing crime and disorder. For some types of proactive policing, the evidence consistently points to effectiveness, but for others the evidence is inconclusive. Evidence in many cases is also restricted to localized crime prevention impacts, such as specific places, or to specific individuals. Relatively little evidence-based knowledge exists about whether and to what extent the approaches examined in this report will have crime prevention benefits at the larger jurisdictional level (e.g., a city as a whole or even large administrative areas such as precincts within a city), or across all offenders. Furthermore, the crime prevention outcomes that are observed are generally observed only in the short term, so the evidence seldom addresses long-term crime prevention outcomes.

It is important to note here that, in practice, police departments typically implement crime reduction programs that include elements typical of several prevention strategies (as combining elements from multiple strategies may produce more positive outcomes for police agencies). Given this hybridization of tactics in practice, the committee's review of the evidence was often hindered by the overlapping character of the real-world proactive policing interventions evaluated in many of the published research studies.

The available research evidence suggests that hot spots policing strategies generate statistically significant crime reduction effects without simply displacing crime into immediately surrounding areas, though there is an absence of evidence on either the long-term impacts of hot spots policing strategies on crime or on possible jurisdictional outcomes (e.g., on crime in a city or in large administrative areas such as precincts). Hot spots policing studies that do measure possible displacement effects tend to find that these programs generate a diffusion of crime control benefits into immediately adjacent areas [Conclusion 4-1].

Another place-based strategy is "predictive policing," which uses sophisticated computer algorithms to predict changing patterns of future crime. At present, there are insufficient rigorous empirical studies to draw any firm conclusions about either the efficacy of crime prediction software or the effectiveness of associated police operational tactics. It also remains difficult to distinguish a predictive policing approach from hot spots policing [Conclusion 4-2].

A technology relevant to improving police capacity for proactive intervention at specific places is closed circuit television (CCTV), which can be used either passively or proactively. The results from studies examining the introduction of CCTV camera schemes are mixed, but they tend to show modest outcomes in terms of property crime reduction at high-crime places for passive monitoring approaches [Conclusion 4-3]. However, with regard to the proactive use of CCTV, there are insufficient studies to draw conclusions regarding its impact on crime and disorder reduction [Conclusion 4-4].

Despite its popularity as a crime-prevention strategy, there are surprisingly few rigorous program evaluations of problem-oriented policing. Much of the available evaluation evidence consists of non-experimental analyses that find strong associations between problem-oriented interventions and crime reduction. Randomized experimental evaluations generally show smaller, but statistically significant, crime reductions generated by problem-oriented policing programs. Program evaluations also suggest that it is difficult for police officers to fully implement problem-oriented policing. Many problem-oriented policing projects are characterized by weak problem analysis and a lack of non-enforcement responses to targeted problems. Nevertheless, even these limited applications of problem-oriented policing have been shown by rigorous evaluations to generate statistically significant short-term crime prevention impacts. These studies do not address possible jurisdictional impacts of problem-oriented policing and generally do not assess the long-term impacts of the evaluated interventions on crime and disorder [Conclusion 4-5].

Third party policing, which leverages nonpolice "third parties" (e.g., public housing agencies, property owners, parents, health and building inspectors, and business owners) who are believed to offer significant new resources for preventing crime and disorder, also draws upon the insights of problem solving. Though there are only a small number of program evaluations, the impact of third party policing interventions on crime and disorder has been assessed using randomized controlled trials and rigorous quasi-experimental designs. The available evidence suggests that third party policing generates statistically significant short-term reductions in crime and disorder; there is more limited evidence of long-term impacts. However, little is known about possible jurisdictional outcomes [Conclusion 4-6].

With regard to person-focused interventions, a growing number of quasi-experimental evaluations suggest that focused deterrence programs generate statistically significant short- and long-term areawide crime-reduction impacts. Crime-control impacts have been reported by controlled evaluations testing the effectiveness of focused deterrence programs in reducing gang violence and street crime driven by disorderly drug markets and by non-experimental studies that examine repeat individual offending. It is noteworthy that the size of the effects observed are large, though many of the largest impacts are in studies with evaluation designs that are less rigorous [Conclusion 4-7].

A more controversial person-focused intervention is SQF. Non-experimental evidence regarding the crime-reduction impact of SQF, when implemented as a general citywide crime-control strategy, is mixed [Conclusion 4-8]. A separate body of controlled evaluation research examining the effectiveness of SQF (combined with other self-initiated enforcement activities by officers) in targeting places with serious gun crime problems and focusing on high-risk repeat offenders reports consistent statistically significant short-term crime-reduction effects; jurisdictional impacts, when estimated, are modest. There is an absence of evidence on the long-term impacts of focused uses of SQF on crime [Conclusion 4-9].

The committee also reviewed the crime-prevention impacts of community-based crime-prevention strategies, including community-oriented policing, procedural justice policing (which seeks to impress upon citizens and the wider community that the police exercise their authority in legitimate ways), and broken windows policing. Although a large number of studies of community-oriented policing programs were identified, many of these programs were implemented in tandem with tactics typical of other approaches, such as problem solving. This is not surprising, given that typical implementations of community-oriented policing used by police departments often have included problem solving as a key programmatic element. The studies also varied in their outcomes, reflecting the broad range of tactics and practices that are included in community-oriented policing programs, and many of the studies were characterized by weak evaluation designs. With these caveats, the committee did not identify a consistent crime-prevention benefit for community-oriented policing programs [Conclusion 4-10].

There is currently only a very small evidence base from which to support conclusions about the impact of procedural justice policing on crime prevention. Existing research does not support a conclusion that procedural justice policing impacts crime or disorder outcomes. At the same time, because the evidence base is small, the committee also cannot conclude that such strategies are ineffective [Conclusion 4-11].

The impacts of broken windows policing are mixed across evaluations, again complicating the ability of the committee to draw strong inferences. However, the available program evaluations suggest that aggressive, misdemeanor arrest–based approaches to control disorder generate small to null impacts on crime [Conclusion 4-12]. In contrast, controlled evaluations of place-based approaches that use problem-solving interventions to reduce social and physical disorder provide evidence of consistent short-term crime-reduction impacts. Little is known about long-term or areawide impacts [Conclusion 4-13].

COMMUNITY REACTIONS

There is broad recognition that a positive relationship with the police has value in its own right, irrespective of any influence it may have on crime or disorder. Democratic theories assert that the police, as an arm of government, are to serve the community and should be accountable to it in ways that elicit public approval and consent. Given this premise and the recent conflicts between the police and the public, the committee thought it very important to assess the impacts of proactive policing on issues, such as fear of crime, collective efficacy, and community evaluation of police legitimacy.

Place-based, person-focused, and problem-solving interventions are distinct from community-based proactive strategies in that they do not directly seek to engage the public to enhance legitimacy evaluations and cooperation. In this context, the concerns regarding community outcomes for these approaches have often focused not on whether they improve community attitudes toward the police but rather on whether the focus on crime control leads inevitably to declines in positive community attitudes. Community-based strategies, in contrast, specifically seek to reduce fear, increase trust and willingness to intervene in community problems, and increase trust and confidence in the police.

There is only an emerging body of research evaluating the impact of place-based strategies on community attitudes, including both quasi-experimental and experimental studies. However, the consistency of the findings suggests that place-based proactive policing strategies rarely have negative short-term impacts on community outcomes. (There is virtually no evidence on the long-term and jurisdiction-level impacts of place-based policing on community outcomes.) At the same time, the existing evidence does suggest that such strategies rarely improve community perceptions of the police or other community outcome measures [Conclusion 5-1].

The research literature on community impacts of problem-solving interventions is larger. Although much of the literature relies on quasi-experimental designs, a few well-implemented randomized experiments also provide information on community outcomes. Studies show consistent small-to-moderate positive short-term impacts of problem-solving strategies on community satisfaction with the police; there is very little evidence available on the long-term and jurisdiction-level impacts of problem-solving strategies on community outcomes [Conclusion 5-2]. Because problem-solving strategies are so often implemented in tandem with tactics typical of community-based policing (i.e., community engagement), it is difficult to determine what role the problem-solving aspect plays in community outcomes, compared to the impact of the community engagement element. At the same time, there is little consistency found in problem-solving policing's impacts on perceived disorder/quality of life, fear of crime, and perceived police legitimacy. However, the near absence of backfire effects in the evaluations of problem-solving strategies suggests that the risk of harmful community effects from problem-solving strategies is low [Conclusion 5-3].

The body of research evaluating the impact of person-focused strategies on community outcomes is relatively small, even in comparison with the evidence base on problem-solving and place-based strategies. (Also, the long-term and jurisdictionwide community consequences of person-focused proactive strategies remain untested.) These studies involve qualitative or correlational designs that make it difficult to draw causal inferences about typical impacts of these strategies. Correlational studies show strong negative associations between exposure to such strategies and the attitudes and orientations of individuals who are the subjects of aggressive law enforcement interventions (SQF and proactive traffic enforcement) [Conclusion 5-4].The studies that measure the impact on the larger community show a more complicated and unclear pattern of outcomes.

The available empirical research on community-oriented policing's community effects focuses on citizen perceptions of police performance (in terms of what they do and the consequences for community disorder), satisfaction with police, and perceived legitimacy. The evidence suggests that community-oriented policing contributes modest improvements to the community's view of policing and the police in the short term. (Very few studies of community-oriented policing have traced its long-term effects on community outcomes or its jurisdictionwide consequences.) This occurs with greatest consistency for measures of community satisfaction and less so for measures of perceived disorder, fear of crime, and police legitimacy. Evaluations of community-oriented policing rarely find "backfire" effects from the intervention on community attitudes. Hence, the deployment of community-oriented policing as a proactive strategy seems to offer prospects of modest gains at little risk of negative consequences [Conclusions 6-1 and 6-2].

Broken windows policing is often evaluated directly in terms of its short-term crime control impacts. The logic model for broken windows policing seeks to alter the community's levels of fear and collective efficacy as a method of enhancing community social controls and reducing crime in the long run. While this is a key element of the broken windows policing model, the committee's review of the evidence found that these outcomes have seldom been examined. The evidence was insufficient to draw any conclusions regarding the impact of broken windows policing on community social controls [Conclusion 6-3]. Studies of the impacts of broken windows policing on fear of crime do not support the model's claim that such programs will reduce levels of fear in the community, at least in the short run.

While there is a rapidly growing body of research on the community impacts of procedural justice policing, it is difficult to draw causal inferences from these studies. In general, the studies show that perceptions of procedurally just treatment are strongly associated with subjective evaluations of police legitimacy and cooperation with the police. However, the extant research base was insufficient for the committee to draw conclusions about whether procedurally just policing causally influences either perceived legitimacy or cooperation [Conclusion 6-4].

Although this committee finding may appear to be at odds with a growing movement to encourage procedurally just behavior among the police, the committee thinks it is important to stress that a finding that there is insufficient evidence to support the expected outcomes of procedural justice policing is not the same as a finding that such outcomes do not exist. Moreover, although the application of procedural justice to policing is relatively new, there is a more extensive evidence base on procedural justice in social psychology and organizational management, as well as on procedural justice with other legal authorities such as the courts. Those studies are often designed in ways that make causal inferences more compelling, and results in those areas suggest meaningful impacts of procedural justice on legitimacy of the institutions and authorities involved. Thus, the application of procedural justice ideas to policing has promise, although further studies are needed to examine the degree to which the success of such implementations in other social contexts can be replicated in the arena of policing [Conclusion 6-5].

RACIAL BIAS AND DISPARITIES

Concerns about racial bias loom especially large in discussions of policing. The interest of this report was to assess whether and to what extent proactive policing affects racial disparities in police-citizen encounters and racial bias in police behavior. Recent high-profile incidents of police shootings and abusive police-citizen interaction caught on camera have raised questions regarding basic fairness, racial discrimination, and the excessive use of force of all forms against non-Whites, and especially Blacks, in the United States. In considering these incidents, the committee stresses that the origins of policing in the United States are intimately interwoven with the nation's history of racial prejudice. When the laws of the United States were designed to produce and maintain racial stratification, it was the job of police officers and sheriff's deputies to enforce those laws. Beginning in the 1960s and 1970s, as the country moved away from de jure systems of racial hierarchy, law enforcement tactics under the "War on Crime" and "War on Drugs" were characterized, if not by racial prejudice, then by racially disparate consequences. Although in recent decades, police have often made a strong effort to address racially biased behavior, there remain wide disparities in the extent to which non-White people and White people are stopped or arrested by police. Moreover, the U.S. Department of Justice has identified continued racial disparities and biased behavior in policing in a number of major police agencies.

As social norms have evolved to make overt expressions of bigotry less acceptable, psychologists have developed tools to measure more subtle forms of biased behavior. A series of studies in field settings with police suggest that negative racial attitudes may influence police behavior—although there is no direct research on proactive policing. There is a further growing body of research identifying how these psychological mechanisms may affect behavior, and what types of situations, policies, or practices may exacerbate or ameliorate racially biased behaviors. In a number of studies, social psychologists have found that race may affect decision making, especially under situations where time is short and such decisions need to be made quickly. More broadly, social psychologists have identified dispositional (i.e., individual characteristics) and situational and environmental factors that are associated with higher levels of racially biased behavior.

Proactive strategies often facilitate increased officer contact with residents particularly in high-crime areas involve contacts that are often enforcement-oriented and uninvited, and may allow greater officer discretion compared to standard policing models. These elements align with broad categories of possible risk factors for racially biased behavior by police officers. For example, when contacts involve stops or arrests, police may be put in situations where they have to "think fast" and react quickly. Social psychologists have argued that such situations may be particularly prone to the emergence of what they call "implicit biases."

Inferring the role of racial animus or other dispositional and situational risk factors in contributing to disparate impacts is a challenging question for research. There are likely to be large racial disparities in the volume and nature of police–citizen encounters when police target high-risk people or high-risk places, as is common in many proactive policing programs (though focused policing approaches may also reduce overall levels of police intrusion) [Conclusion 7-1]. However, studies that benchmark citizen–police interactions against simple population counts or broad measures of criminal activity do not yield conclusive information regarding the potential for racially biased behavior in proactive policing efforts. Identifying an appropriate benchmark would require detailed information on the geography and nature of the proactive strategy, as well as localized knowledge of the relative importance of the problem.

Such benchmarks are not currently available, and existing evidence does not establish conclusively whether and to what extent the racial disparities associated with concentrated person-focused and place-based enforcement are indicators of statistical prediction, racial animus, or other factors that may motivate biased behavior. However, the history of racial justice in the United States, in particular in the area of criminal justice and policing, as well as ethnographic research that has identified disparate impacts of policing on non-White communities, makes the investigation of the causes of racial disparities a key research and policy concern [Conclusion 7-2].

Per the charge to the committee, this report reviewed a relatively narrow area of intersection between race and policing. This focus, though, is nested in a broader societal framework of possible disparities and behavioral biases across a whole array of social contexts. These factors can affect proactive policing in, for example, the distribution of crime in society and the extent of exposure of specific groups to police surveillance and enforcement. However, it was beyond the scope of this study to review them systematically in the context of the committee's work.

THE FUTURE OF PROACTIVE POLICING

Proactive policing has become a key part of police efforts to do something about crime in the United States. This report supports the general conclusion that there is sufficient scientific evidence to support the adoption of some proactive policing practices, certainly if the primary policy goal is to reduce crime. Proactive policing efforts that focus on high concentrations of crimes at places or among the high-rate subset of offenders, as well as practices that seek to solve specific crime-fostering problems, show consistent evidence of effectiveness without evidence of negative community outcomes. Community-based strategies have also begun to show evidence of improving the relations between the police and public.

At the same time, there are key gaps in the knowledge base. As was discussed earlier, few studies to date have examined long-term outcomes, and there is typically little or no information about the larger areawide or jurisdictional impacts of these approaches. There are also significant gaps in the evidence that do not allow one to identify with reasonable confidence the effects of proactive policing on other outcomes. For example, existing research provides little guidance as to whether police programs to enhance procedural justice will improve community perceptions of police legitimacy or community cooperation with the police. Little is known about the impacts of proactive policing on the legality of police behavior and on racially biased behavior; these are critical issues that must be addressed in future studies.

Much has been learned over the past two decades about proactive policing programs. But, now that scientific support for these approaches has accumulated, it is time for greater investment in understanding what is cost-effective, how such strategies can be maximized to improve the relationships between the police and the public, and how they can be applied in ways that do not lead to violations of the law by the police.

1

Introduction

Over the past two decades, the police have often been the focus of praise for their innovations in policing strategies and their leadership in rolling back what seemed an inevitable rise in crime rates. In one of the earliest examples of this positive recognition of the role of the police in fighting crime, William Bratton, then commissioner of the New York City Police Department, was pictured on the cover of *Time*, one of the most important U.S. news outlets at that time, with a headline: "Finally, We're Winning the War against Crime. Here's Why" (*TIME*, 1996). Such headlines were common at the beginning of the new millennium, and they continue to be common as police agencies take credit for controlling crime in American cities (see, e.g., Youmans, 2000; Wood, 2001; Allen, 2002; Rashbaum, 2003; Williams, 2003; Cella, 2004; Dowdy, 2004). They express a more general acceptance by the public that the police play a key role in doing something about the crime problem.

It is worth noting that this confidence in the ability of police to address crime is of recent vintage. The conventional wisdom, at least from the 1960s until the mid-1990s in the United States, was that police had very little impact on crime rates (Bayley, 1994; Gottfredson and Hirschi, 1990). The origins of this view can be found in the 1967 report of the President's Commission on Law Enforcement and Administration of Justice, *The Challenge of Crime in a Free Society*, which detailed the relationship between so-called root causes and crime and raised questions regarding the practices common in U.S. policing (President's Commission on Law Enforcement and Administration of Justice, 1967). It was reinforced by a series of academic studies that challenged the crime-control effectiveness of standard police practices (see, e.g., Kelling et al., 1974; Levine, 1975; Spelman and Brown, 1984). If crime is rooted in poverty and deprivation, then what could police do to stop it? In turn, systematic study of the practices that dominated the efforts of the police to do something about crime did not yield positive results. It was thought that police should focus on other tasks such as bringing offenders to justice regardless of whether such work affected the crime rate, peacekeeping tasks such as intervening in domestic disputes, providing help and assistance to those in need by responding to emergency calls, and traffic control.

In part as a response to research that challenged the effectiveness of traditional policing strategies, the 1980s and 1990s saw the emergence of a series of innovative police practices. They could be contrasted with the "standard" models of policing in earlier decades by their focus on taking a proactive approach to crime problems. Most of the standard practices of policing simply reacted to the occurrence of a crime. They were part of the police role as first responders and agents responsible for bringing offenders to justice. The new strategies proposed by police and scholars were proactive, in that they went beyond the obligations of the police to respond to the occurrence of crime and to investigate and bring offenders to justice; instead, they focused on policing approaches that could be successful in crime prevention irrespective of whether they had been seen in the past as traditional components of police practice.

These innovative proactive policing strategies have now become part of the national lexicon. The growing perception that the police could prevent crime was buttressed by a National Research Council ([NRC] 2004) report, *Fairness and Effectiveness in Policing: The Evidence*. That report noted that research on the standard models of policing common in the United States at the time did not support claims for crime control. However, the report argued that evidence was beginning to emerge that promising new proactive policing strategies could prevent crime.

From the perspective of the police and police researchers, this was exciting news, but the evidence base reviewed in the 2004 NRC report was still developing and did not cover some important proactive approaches. A number of innovations in proactive policing were just beginning to be examined. While, for example, a series of randomized field experiments were found to support the effectiveness of hot spots policing, there was much less rigorous research at that time on problem-oriented policing, broken windows policing (which seeks to prevent serious crime by addressing disorder and minor offenses), and "pulling levers" or "focused deterrence" policing (which emphasizes identifying dangerous offenders and using multiple police and community pressures to reduce crime). Accordingly, while the 2004 NRC report provided a glimpse of the potential for proactive policing, the approaches and the research on their outcomes had only begun to be developed. This current report was commissioned because it was time to take a fuller look at whether proactive policing can reduce crime and disorder and, as important, which of the strategies developed have the greatest promise for crime reduction.

But the crime-control effectiveness of proactive policing should not be examined without consideration of its broader impacts on law and the community. Democratic societies require that police balance the provision of public safety from crime with other important values, such as police adherence to law, economy in the use of coercion, the provision of service, and attentiveness to fairness and the general welfare of citizens in the community (Bayley, 2006; Bittner, 1970; Manning, 2010; Muir, 1977). News reports over the past few years focusing on conflicts between the police and the public are a reminder that policing exists in a complex set of social contexts and that effectiveness in reducing crime and disorder is not the sole metric by which policing strategies should be evaluated. Americans have been confronted by difficult images of police brutality and even killings by police (Baker, Goodman, and Mueller, 2015; Buchanan et al., 2015; Dewan and Oppel, 2015; Graham, 2016). High-profile incidents of fatal violence directed at police officers in New York City and Dallas, Texas, have been interpreted as a response to those events (Achenbach et al., 2016; Mueller and Baker, 2014). Protests, and in some cases rioting, throughout the nation have focused on policing and often on what are perceived as unfair and abusive police practices (Domonoske, 2016; Lee et al., 2016; Nolan and Chokshi, 2016; Payne, 2014; *USA Today*, 2016). In particular, Blacks and other non-White groups have expressed concerns about how they are treated by the police and about the differential impacts of policing in non-White communities. The emergence of the Black Lives Matter group during this period suggests the heightened concerns of specific non-White communities to the policies and practices of the police (see Appendix A). This heightened discontent with policing, in a way reminiscent of the 1960s and 1970s, stimulated a blue-ribbon presidential task force to call for increased attention to strengthening the bonds between the police and the community (President's Task Force on 21st Century Policing, 2015).

The committee authoring this report was tasked with considering how proactive policing strategies bear upon these concerns. It is not enough simply to identify "what works" for reducing crime and disorder; it is also critical to consider how proactive policing affects the legality of policing, the evaluations of the police in communities, the potential abuses of police authority, and the equitable application of police services and police interference in the everyday lives of citizens.

Are the new proactive policing strategies the source of the growing challenge to the legitimacy of police in the United States? Some media commentators have made this connection directly. For example, Gloria Tso

(2016), in the Washington, D.C., newspaper *The Hill*, draws a direct connection between abusive and illegal police practices and hot spots policing, one of the proactive strategies that has emerged in the new millennium:

> The epidemic of police brutality—primarily affecting black males—can be linked to the history of a technique called hot spot policing. . . . a technique that stations many cops in areas with higher crime rates; these areas overlapped with areas inhabited by lower-class minorities. Police initially utilized this technique to prevent crimes from happening in hot spots, but the specific measures that would be taken to prevent crime were often left unclear; there were almost no boundaries to these officers' powers as authority figures who could stop at nothing in their crime-fighting efforts, which ironically led to many officers committing brutal crimes themselves.

Sarah Childress (2016), in an article for *Frontline*, argues similarly that broken windows policing has led to aggressive over-policing of non-White communities:

> Such practices can strain criminal justice systems, burden impoverished people with fines for minor offenses, and fracture the relationship between police and minorities. It can also lead to tragedy: In New York in 2014, Eric Garner died from a police chokehold after officers approached him for selling loose cigarettes on a street corner. Today, Newark and other cities have been compelled to re-think their approach to policing. But there are few easy solutions, and no quick way to repair years of distrust between police and the communities they serve.

Do specific types of proactive policing strategies lead to lawless behavior of the police? How do proactive policing strategies affect the communities served by the police? Do they lead to higher or lower evaluations of police legitimacy? Do they affect community cohesion more generally? Do they lead to inequitable policing practices that target specific ethnic or racial groups? These are key questions that have not been reviewed systematically across the range of proactive policing strategies. Moreover, these strategies vary widely and thus might be expected to have differential impacts on these outcomes.

This report addresses these questions regarding proactive policing. It reviews what is known about the consequences of proactive policing for crime control, communities, legality, and racial disparities and racial bias. Below we state the specific charge to the committee and then provide a historical review of proactive policing in order to place the report in context. We conclude this introductory chapter with a discussion of the specific definition of proactive policing used by the study committee in framing its report, followed by a summary of the organization of the report.

CHARGE TO THE STUDY COMMITTEE

In 2004, as noted above, the NRC published a report, *Fairness and Effectiveness in Policing: The Evidence*, which reviewed the existing evidence on police effectiveness and rebutted what had been a longstanding belief that the police had only a limited capacity to prevent crime. However, only a small number of proactive policing strategies were reviewed in that report, and since 2004 a substantial number of studies have assessed the effectiveness of proactive policing strategies. The time is right for a more comprehensive evaluation of proactive policing that includes not only its crime prevention impacts but also its broader implications for justice and U.S. communities.

The National Institute of Justice and the Laura and John Arnold Foundation asked the National Academies of Sciences, Engineering, and Medicine to review the evidence regarding the consequences of different forms of proactive policing for crime and disorder, discriminatory application, legality, and community reaction and receptiveness. The National Academies appointed the Committee on Proactive Policing: Effects on Crime, Communities, and Civil Liberties to carry out this task. Fifteen prominent scholars representing a broad array of disciplines—including criminology, law, psychology, statistics, political science, and economics—as well as two noted police practitioners were included on the committee, which met six times over a 2-year period. The specific charge to the committee was stated by the National Academies as follows:

> An ad hoc committee under the auspices of the National Research Council's (NRC's) Committee on Law and Justice (CLAJ) will review the evidence on: (1) the effects of different forms of proactive policing on crime; (2) whether they are applied in a discriminatory manner; (3) whether they are being used in a legal fashion; and (4) community reaction. The committee's review of the literature and the subsequent report will include a thorough discussion of data and methodological gaps in the research.

THE ORIGINS OF PROACTIVE POLICING

Attention to proactive policing as a broad-based police organization approach to reduce crime in communities is a relatively recent phenomenon in American policing. The use of the term "proactivity" did not develop until the 1960s, and a focus on the idea that the police would be proactive in efforts to do something about crime was not one to be found often in the policing literature until recent decades.[1] Indeed Sam Walker, a noted

---

[1] The discussion in this section relies heavily on Walker's (2016) review, prepared for the committee, of the history of proactive policing.

historian of the police, concluded that proactive policing "has almost no history prior to the late 1970s" (Walker, 2016, p. 1).

The term "proactive policing" was coined by Albert J. Reiss Jr. and David Bordua as part of a more general examination of the nature of police organization (Bordua and Reiss, 1966; Reiss and Bordua, 1967). They argued that different types of police organization would be needed to deal with different types of police activities. Reactive strategies were seen as those that required simply that the police respond to a citizen request for service. Such activities of the police were seen as more easily managed by a centralized command structure and enjoyed a measure of legitimacy because police were mobilized at the request of a citizen seeking police assistance (Reiss, 1971). However, because police practices that involved proactivity were initiated without a specific request for police involvement, they demanded a more professional and regulated style of police organization, since they involved a wider array of activities involving greater autonomy of police officers.

Of course, police proactivity, as defined by Reiss and Bordua, occurred long before scholars introduced it to the academic and practitioner lexicon. Some police have always been proactive on an individual level, as a matter of personal choice. In this context, many types of activities carried out by police officers throughout the past century have been proactive in that they have used proactive approaches to respond to identified problems. Moreover, as Bordua and Reiss (1966) pointed out in identifying the importance of proactivity, calls from citizens generate a reactive response, but vice offenses infrequently generate complaints, and so vice enforcement requires a degree of proactivity on the part of police officers. For example, when a 19th century foot patrol officer decided on his own to roust public inebriates because they might disrupt commerce on his beat, he was engaging in a proactive type of policing. But when Walker (2016) talks about the virtual absence of proactive policing from the landscape of American policing, he is referring to proactive policing as an *organizational* crime-prevention strategy, one that began to develop in the latter part of the 20th century, not as a tactic selected independently by a street-level officer or out of an informal culture of policing (see National Research Council, 2004; Weisburd and Braga, 2006a). Proactive policing has come to refer to an expansion of the practices of the police beyond simply responding to and investigating crime; and it takes a strategic approach to crime problems, meaning that these are strategies that were seen as *intentional policies of police organizations to develop effective crime control*.

Walker (2016) found that the available source material on policing in the 19th century is extremely limited. Nonetheless, the materials that do exist, with some exceptions, indicate an absence of any police organization–directed activities that might be considered even remotely proactive in the contemporary sense. Scholars are unanimous in characterizing U.S. police organizations in this period as dominated by politics, corrupt, inefficient in terms of crime control, and marked by uncontrolled abusive practices against people on the street (Miller, 1977; Fogelson, 1977; Walker, 1977).

It is important to understand that, despite the nominal quasi-military structure of police departments, U.S. police in the 19th century were in fact extremely *dis*organized in the sense of modern bureaucracy (Reiss, 1992). With little centralized direction from police chiefs, police commanders simply did not think about proactive efforts to address crime and disorder (and it should be remembered that U.S. cities in this period, with large numbers of recent immigrants and high rates of transiency, were extremely *dis*orderly). To the extent that police agencies in the United States were proactive, they showed initiative in helping to turn out the vote for machine politicians and in discouraging the vote for the opposition (Haller, 1976; Miller, 1975). In fact, much of the police proactivity that actually focused on offenses was intended to promote or protect crime, such as the regulation of thieves and selective law enforcement favoring some over others, all for the financial benefit of the police or the political benefit of their partisan machine allies. Beyond a simplistic belief that patrol deterred crime, there is no evidence of serious thinking about how the police might control crime and disorder more effectively. There was no effort devoted to professional police administration. The idea that the police were public servants, with a broad mission to serve and protect, did not crystalize until the early 20th century with the advent of the police professionalization movement. One manifestation of that development was the first book on police administration, which was published only in 1909 (Fuld, 1909).

Of course, this is not to say that proactivity in policing was absent. It was present in antebellum American policing even before the creation of unified municipal police accountable to a single authority (e.g., mayor) with full-time employees and a structure of internal hierarchical accountability. Levett's (1975) historical analysis shows that even in times and places where "entrepreneurial" forms (constables, city marshal, high constable, nightwatch, day/night police)[2] provided diffused modes of policing delivery,[3] the proactive control of "disorderly" people[4] constituted a significant portion of documented police activity. And following the unification of American

---

[2] Internal organizational hierarchy played a very limited role in regulating activities; officers competed for rewards, and work focused on protecting and recovering property for a fee (Reiss, 1992, p. 69).

[3] See Chadwick (2017) for a detailed accounting of the disarray of policing and its consequences in New York City.

[4] This included dealing with public drunkenness, prostitution, lewdness, vagrancy, vice, domestic disturbances, doing Sunday business, keeping an untidy house, workingmen strikes, and slavery runaways (Levett, 1975, pp. 52, 114).

municipal agencies, the number of arrests for such offenses, especially drunkenness, rose sharply.[5] Levett argues that following the unification of American policing into "political bureaucracies," local elites used the police to stigmatize and control immigrants and the lower classes, which were perceived to be the source of riotous, immoral, and disorderly behavior. Some might be tempted to draw connections between this and the emergence of "broken windows" as a proactive police management strategy that also focuses on disorders and that emerged in the 1980s. But the progenitors of the broken windows approach articulated a detailed logic model justified by crime prevention, not the control or suppression of "dangerous classes" (Wilson and Kelling, 1982).

Another important point is that the will and capacity of police administrators to impose strategies effectively was dependent upon the emergence of a "police civil service bureaucracy," which only began to emerge in the early 20th century and was characterized by a great reduction in the influence of political elites, replacement by an elaborated police hierarchy, and the codification of personnel policies (civil service) (Reiss, 1992, pp. 70–73). It took many decades for a truly legalistic, technocratic police bureaucracy to take hold in the United States (Reiss, 1992, p. 82) so that the prerequisites for strategic proactivity were feasible.

Other examples of proactivity in early American police departments include the corrupt methods of the police in organizing and regulating thieves and pickpockets. Indeed, public negativity about proactive crime detection by private entrepreneurs motivated the emergence of the modern police detective as an agent who is mobilized only in *reaction* to the reporting of a crime and who is controlled by the creation of the "case" as a structure of accountability (Klockars, 1985, Ch. 4). Creators of the new police detective in 19th century London were sensitive to the risks to police legitimacy posed by employing the proactive approaches embraced by entrepreneurial private detective agencies, such as the notorious Bow Street Runners. But American police agencies adopted many of these same proactive strategies. They developed networks of criminals as informers, offering immunity from arrest for information on others (Haller, 1976). Thief-taking (for financial reward) produced incentives for taking only cases with good prospects for a large reward, and it encouraged the development of close working relations with professional thieves and fences through whom police shared the rewards with favored criminals. In addition, the practice of "thief-making"

---

[5] American police of the late 19th and early 20th centuries were not only proactive in arresting drunks and the homeless (many of whom were migrants and immigrants), but also proactive in offering them shelter in police stations (Haller, 1976; Monkkonen, 1981). In a limited way, this presaged aspects of community and problem-oriented policing that emerged many decades later.

was publicly unpopular because it employed deceit to entrap or seduce people into engaging in criminal acts. Lincoln Steffens, as well as other muckrakers of the 19th and early 20th centuries, described how American police detectives resorted to these unpopular proactive methods to "license" certain thieves to operate (in exchange for a share of the proceeds of their work) while enforcing the law against others (Steffens, 1931, pp. 222–223). Con artists were required to pay bunco squad members a fee for non-enforcement. Another proactive tactic was to repeatedly harass a thief with a vagabond arrest until he left town (Haller, 1976). And dragnet arrests, made in response to a highly visible crime or crime wave, brought in many people innocent of the crime. While these methods were undeniably proactive, they can hardly be characterized as justified as primarily crime preventive, and they do not constitute a model or positive precursor to the sorts of contemporary proactive innovations the committee has targeted for evaluation.

Professional Reform in the 20th Century

The police professionalization movement that emerged in the early 20th century had a powerful and long-lasting impact in transforming local police departments and routine policing. The movement had a clearly focused reform agenda that included articulating a clear mission in society, as befits a profession; eliminating the direct political influence that had underpinned the corruption and inefficiency of the police in the 19th century; securing skilled administrators as police chief executives; introducing the principles of modern management to police organizations; and raising personnel standards with regard to recruitment, training, discipline, and retention.

By the end of the 1950s, after 40 to 50 years of reform efforts, most police departments were far more "professional" than they had been in 1900 or 1910 (Reiss, 1992).[6] Although significantly deficient by contemporary standards, they were better managed, with at least a nominal commitment to professional standards; better organized; and with rank-and-file officers who, despite many great deficiencies, were far more qualified than their earlier counterparts (Fogelson, 1977; Walker, 1977). Corruption, although still a problem, was no longer as blatant or pervasive as it had been. However, as the turmoil of the 1960s and beyond quickly demonstrated, many problems had not been addressed. The most serious included racial justice and the control of officer discretion, particularly with regard to the use of

---

[6] The committee uses the term "professional" largely in the sense that police reformers of the time used it: a combination of bureaucratic and professional occupation ideals.

deadly force and physical force and with regard to equal justice in stops, arrests, and employment practices.[7]

The great changes that occurred during the nearly half century of reform, with some notable exceptions, did not include the development of innovative approaches to the control of crime and disorder of the kind that are associated with proactive policing today. One noteworthy exception was the creation of the first police juvenile units, which also led to the employment of the first female police officers in the United States.[8] The new juvenile policing units, pioneered in Portland, Oregon, by Lola Baldwin, represented a proactive approach that sought at the outset to reduce juvenile crime with activities that disrupted the forces driving youths down the pathway to delinquency. The approach had a clear problem-oriented focus on juvenile delinquency, on young girls in particular, and in some instances on prostitution (then generally referred to as "White slavery"). It also involved nontraditional police tactics. Policewomen would patrol movie theaters, amusement parks, beaches, pool halls, and other locations or events that attracted young people, to look for juveniles who appeared to be engaging in or about to engage in illegal behavior (Walker, 1977, pp. 84–94). Their mandate was extremely broad. The head of the Detroit policewoman's unit explained that "a patrol problem may be defined as any situation, arising in a public place, that is potentially harmful to a woman or child" (Hutzel and MacGregor, 1933, p. 11). A few other innovative, proactive reform programs paralleled the new juvenile units.[9]

Some of the most notable efforts to promote innovative proactive approaches to crime came from the highly visible and influential progressive police leader, August Vollmer. He mobilized his small police force in Berkeley, California, to engage in raids of gambling and opium dens and later did the same during his short tenure as chief in Los Angeles (Oliver, 2017, pp. 169, 373). Ironically, late in his career, Vollmer (1936) wrote a controversial chapter in his book *The Police and Modern Society* in which he advocated

---

[7] See the findings and recommendations of both the President's Commission on Law Enforcement and Administration of Justice (1967) and the Kerner Commission (1968); also see Walker (1998, pp. 180–201).

[8] Women had been employed as police matrons in the 19th century, but they were primarily jail officials responsible for female inmates.

[9] Particularly notable was the Golden Rule policy initiated by Cleveland Police Chief Fred Kohler in 1908. Kohler was deeply disturbed by the high volume of arrests the police made each year, particularly for minor offenses. "I couldn't see that these wholesale arrests did any good," he declared. They not only "did not produce good results," he added, "they did harm." The Golden Rule involved what experts would recognize as diversion, de-escalation, and mediation. No juveniles would be taken to jail but instead would be taken home to their parents. Officers were directed to use "kindly efforts" to resolve domestic disputes. Finally, individuals who had broken the law because of "unfortunate circumstances" were to be given a reprimand rather than be arrested (see Walker, 1977, pp. 94–98).

a different form of police proactivity to deal with vice. In this book, he rejected the notion that the police should play a central role in dealing with prostitution, gambling, liquor, and narcotics. He argued that police were corrupted by involvement in enforcing laws against these vices and that these were appetites properly left to medical experts who draw upon insights from scientific research (Oliver, 2017, p. 486). Vollmer also devoted a chapter in his book to crime prevention, offering recommendations that presaged key features of the contemporary proactive strategies of community policing and problem-oriented policing. He advocated getting community leaders outside the police involved in crime prevention, drawing on an analysis of the problem (e.g., early childhood intervention), and working in partnership with other agencies. Even much earlier in his career, as chief of police in Berkeley, Vollmer showed a prescient concern for promoting the legitimacy of the police by what we now would call "procedural justice" in the way he himself dealt with offenders and police officers (Sherman, 2017, pp. xi–xii). But counterbalancing Vollmer's advocacy of a broader police role in some regards, his books and reports also repeated the standard agenda of police professionalization, especially the central mission of police as crime fighters (Vollmer, 1936; Vollmer and Parker, 1937). Two things are particularly worth noting. First, Vollmer's innovativeness was seasoned by and a part of the larger police professionalization movement. Second, Vollmer's innovative inclinations were remarkably exceptional (Sherman, 2017) and did not take hold as an active and vital, broadly based reform agenda until they emerged again about a half-century later.

The Challenge to the Standard Model of Policing

The emergence of the strategies reviewed in this report can be traced to challenges facing the police in the 1960s.[10] During the 1970s, criticisms of the police proliferated, as did criticism of the criminal justice system in general (Weisburd and Braga, 2006b; LaFree, 1998). This wave of criticism in part reflected the heightened level of social unrest experienced in the latter years of the 1960s, unrest that included race riots in urban centers and growing opposition to the Vietnam War, particularly among younger Americans. These forms of social unrest often put their young participants, even those from the middle class, as well as racial minorities, in conflict with the police. But the growing sense of a crisis in policing during this period also reflected fears that the criminal justice system was failing to combat crime in the United States effectively. In 1967, a presidential com-

---

[10] See Willis (2014) for a more detailed discussion of the emergence of several proactive police innovations as a recent historical phenomenon.

mission reinforced these doubts about the criminal justice system in its report, *The Challenge of Crime in a Free Society*:

> In sum, America's system of criminal justice is overcrowded and overworked, undermanned, underfinanced, and very often misunderstood. It needs more information and more knowledge. It needs more technical resources. It needs more coordination among its many parts. It needs more public support. It needs the help of community programs and institutions in dealing with offenders and potential offenders. It needs, above all, the willingness to reexamine old ways of doing things, to reform itself, to experiment, to run risks, to dare. It needs vision. (President's Commission on Law Enforcement and Administration of Justice, 1967, pp. 80–81)

Shortly thereafter, the National Advisory Commission on Civil Disorders (also known as the Kerner Commission) published a report that raised significant questions about the nature of criminal justice and the organization of policing in the United States. However, the central issue for policing raised in this report was the relationship between the police and racial and ethnic minorities in predominantly non-White communities. Although the report did not focus primarily on the police as responsible for patterns of discrimination against Blacks, it did present the police—as well as other criminal justice agencies—as contributing to those patterns, rather than helping to find solutions to the difficult social issues involved: "In Newark, Detroit, Watts and Harlem, in practically every city that has experienced racial disruption since the summer of 1964, abrasive relationships between police and Negroes and other minority groups have been a major source of grievance, tension, and ultimately disorder" (National Advisory Commission on Civil Disorders, 1968, p. 157).

In response to both the concerns documented in these two reports and the growing sense of alienation between the police and the public in the latter half of the 1960s, policy makers, the police, and scholars increasingly questioned the adequacy of how American policing was organized, particularly with respect to the strategies that had dominated American approaches to policing since at least World War II. The NRC has characterized these approaches as the "standard model" of policing:

> This model relies generally on a "one size fits all" application of reactive strategies to suppress crime, in contrast to more customized and proactive strategies. The standard model also emphasizes the role of arrests and the threat of punishment in achieving this objective, with less emphasis on other capabilities of the police. The standard model of policing has assumed that generic strategies for crime prevention can be applied throughout a jurisdiction, regardless of the level of crime, the nature of crime, or other possible variations. (National Research Council, 2004, p. 223)

General types of strategies that have been prominent in the standard model of policing include increasing the size of police agencies, random patrol across all parts of the community, rapid response to calls for service, generally applied follow-up investigations, and generally applied intensive enforcement and arrest policies (National Research Council, 2004, p. 224).

The standard model of policing was primarily a reactive model. Its focus on follow-up enforcement, rapid responses to citizen calls to the police, and investigation of crime and apprehension of criminals are directly responsive to the commission of a crime or citizen notification of crimes occurring. Even random preventive patrol, which was seen as a key method for deterrence of crime through the visible presence of police across a city (Repetto, 1976; Kelling et al., 1974), was rooted in the necessities of the rapid response system. With the advent of radio dispatch responses to emergency calls to the police, a key factor was having police cars spread in a jurisdiction to allow the police to respond to calls quickly. Accordingly, the standard model of policing was strongly rooted in the police reaction to a crime being committed.

Although important issues were being raised about the standard model of policing well before the end of the 1960s decade, there was at that time a relative dearth of academic research on the impacts of the policing strategies then in vogue on crime rates or on how the public viewed the police. The prevailing attitude was that post–World War II policing practices incorporated major improvements over policing strategies of prior decades and that these practices were effective not only in responding to specific crime events but also in having overall impacts on crime in the jurisdictions that police served. The crime control benefits were seen as resulting from the deterrence gained by police effectively identifying and investigating offenders, responding quickly to the scene of crimes, and being visible agents of control as they organized themselves for the new rapid response systems that radios and police cars enabled. But the issues identified during the 1960s showed the need for research on the standard model, and serious attention to that research began in the 1970s.

Since the founding of the London Metropolitan Police in 1829, modern policing had been grounded in Sir Robert Peel's principle that the police could effectively control crime through visible patrol dispersed through the larger community and organized by assigning officers to specific police beats and holding them accountable for patrolling those beats (Grant, 2010; Critchley, 1972). The assumption was that a visible police presence would deter criminals from offending. Additionally, dispersal of patrol throughout the community would make officers readily available to respond to problems they observed or were asked to deal with.

A large Police Foundation study in the 1970s sought to establish whether evidence actually supported these broadly accepted assumptions regarding visible police patrol. The study was one of the first large field trials in American policing. Although the design of this study was subsequently criticized (Larson and Cahn, 1985; Minneapolis Medical Research Foundation, Inc., 1976; Sherman and Weisburd, 1995), its results were to have lasting impact on assumptions regarding the impacts of policing on crime. Conducted in Kansas City, Missouri, preventive patrol was manipulated in large beat areas, with areas having higher, lower, or standard levels of police patrol vehicles. The study concluded that merely increasing or decreasing the intensity of routine preventive patrol by police officers in cars had no effect on crime, on delivery of police services to citizens, or on how community members felt about security in their communities.

Another large-scale study, conducted by Spelman and Brown (1984), challenged a core assumption of the standard model of policing: namely, that a more rapid response to calls for service would improve crime outcomes. A prior investigation in Kansas City had found little support for the crime-control effectiveness of responding more rapidly to calls for service (Kansas City Police Department, 1977), and the Spelman and Brown study was designed to test that assumption with greater rigor. With support from the National Institute of Justice, the research team interviewed 4,000 individuals who had been victims, witnesses, or bystanders in about 3,300 serious crimes committed in four U.S. cities. Based on the data they collected, these researchers challenged the crime-control effectiveness of rapid response to calls for service:

> Rapid police response may be unnecessary for three out of every four serious crimes reported to police. The traditional practice of immediate response to all reports of serious crimes currently leads to on-scene arrests in only 29 of every 1,000 cases. By implementing innovative programs, police may be able to increase this response-related arrest rate to 50 or even 60 per 1000, but there is little hope that further increases can be generated. (Spelman and Brown, 1984, p. xix)

Another element of the standard model, the use of follow-up investigations by police, was examined in a series of empirical studies in the 1970s and early 1980s. An assumption of the standard model was that general improvements in the methods used in police investigations would help to control crime for two reasons: more of the active offenders would be in prison, where they would no longer be committing crimes in the community; and the prospect of being discovered and arrested would deter potential offenders (National Research Council, 2004). However, the empirical studies during this period found that follow-up investigations had little effect on crime rates (Eck, 1983; Greenwood et al., 1975; Greenwood, Petersilia, and Chaiken, 1977; Skogan and Antunes, 1979).

In understanding the emergence of proactive policing, it is important to recognize the impact that these studies had on scholars and police at the time. In retrospect, however, many scholars overstated what could be learned from the findings about standard police practices (see, e.g., Goldstein, 1979; Gottfredson and Hirschi, 1990; Bayley, 1994). And some evaluations during this period reported more positive results from such standard police practices as routine preventive patrol (see, e.g., Chaiken, 1978; Press, 1971; Schnelle et al., 1977). Moreover, the body of research on the standard model of policing that has developed since these early studies provides a more nuanced portrait of that model's crime prevention outcomes.

This is especially the case in considering whether police staffing levels influence levels of crime. Econometric studies that make strong efforts to overcome key measurement and specification problems have begun to show significant crime-prevention gains for increases in the number of police in a city (see, e.g., Evans and Owens, 2007; Machin and Olivier, 2011). However, the conclusion that these studies reflect the impact of the standard model of policing has been criticized because they often examine the boost in police resources that comes from support for community policing or other proactive policing strategies (Lee, Eck, and Corsaro, 2016). At the same time, studies of police strikes conducted in periods when the standard reactive model of policing was dominant suggest that crime does go up in the absence of police (Sherman and Eck, 2002; Nagin and Weisburd, 2013). While the committee recognizes the importance of these studies as well as the more general questions raised regarding the impacts of the standard model of policing on crime, we do not draw a conclusion about its crime prevention outcomes. However, given the continued importance and dominance of the standard model of policing, we do think that this is an important area for future study.

The Emergence of Modern Proactive Policing

As the United States entered the 1990s, there appeared to be a scholarly consensus that traditional reactive police practices did not work in preventing or controlling crime (Weisburd and Braga, 2006b, p. 9). For example, Gottfredson and Hirschi stated in *A General Theory of Crime*, "No evidence exists that augmentation of patrol forces or equipment, differential patrol strategies, or differential intensities of surveillance have an effect on crime rates" (Gottfredson and Hirschi, 1990, p. 270). And a few years later, David Bayley made an even stronger assertion:

> The police do not prevent crime. This is one of the best kept secrets of modern life. Experts know it, the police know it, but the public does not know it. Yet the police pretend that they are society's best defense against

crime . . . this is a myth. First, repeated analysis has consistently failed to find any connection between the number of police officers and crime rates. Secondly, the primary strategies adopted by modern police have been shown to have little or no effect on crime. (Bayley, 1994, p. 3)

Official crime statistics, widely available to the public, seemed to reinforce this view of the ineffectiveness of policing strategies, as well as the general perception that the police were losing the "War on Crime." Even the established, professional police organizations in America's largest cities seemed unable to curtail the alarming rise in crime rates—especially violent crime rates, which doubled between 1973 and 1990 (Weisburd and Braga, 2006b, p. 10).

Proactive policing grew out of this period of crisis for American policing. Proactive policing was a product—one of many products, in fact—of an extraordinary convergence of several legal, social, and political crises that swept over American society in the tumultuous 1960s, profoundly affecting the police along with every other institution. The crises generated new demands on the police to improve both their capacity to address crime and disorder and their own internal standards of accountability. The crises of the 1960s were followed, as noted above, by several major research findings that undermined the basic principles that had guided modern policing since the founding of the London Metropolitan Police by Robert Peel in 1829. The result was a period of intellectual ferment as police chiefs, outside experts, and academics searched for new principles for police operations. This search generated numerous innovative responses, responses that came to be termed "proactive policing" and that are reviewed in this report.

THE COMMITTEE'S DEFINITION OF "PROACTIVE POLICING"

The committee believes its task must be seen in historical context and that its definition of proactive policing should be geared to innovations in police practices and policies that have been developed over the past few decades. In this report, the term "proactive policing" is used to refer to **all policing strategies that have as one of their goals the prevention or reduction of crime and disorder and that are not reactive in terms of focusing primarily on uncovering ongoing crime or on investigating or responding to crimes once they have occurred.** Specifically, the elements of proactivity include an emphasis on prevention, mobilizing resources based on police initiative, and targeting the broader underlying forces at work that may be driving crime and disorder. This contrasts with reactive policing, which involves an emphasis on reacting to particular crime events after they have occurred, mobilizing resources based on requests coming from outside the police organization, and focusing on the particulars of a given criminal incident. In practice, policing strategies range along a continuum between pure proactivity and pure reactivity. The more proactive elements that are present in a given strategy, the more proactive it is. The more reactive elements present in a given strategy, the more reactive it is.

The committee recognized at the outset that there is no accepted definition of proactive policing among scholars or the public. In the earliest references to proactivity (see Bordua and Reiss, 1966; Reiss and Bordua, 1967), scholars were focused primarily not on the strategies that were subsumed by the definition but rather on the implications of proactivity for the legitimacy of police intrusion in the lives of citizens (Black, 1971; Reiss, 1973). Proactivity was simply the situation where police powers were mobilized not as a result of citizen requests to the police but rather due to the decision, usually by street-level police officers or special units, to initiate enforcement or other policing powers. Proactive mobilization of police resources, as contrasted with reactive mobilization, was seen as creating additional challenges to the public acceptance of police powers because it meant that the police did not have the assent of the public before taking action.

Our definition of proactive policing is consistent with earlier conceptualizations of this idea in that we focus on situations where the mobilization of police resources comes as a result of the initiative of the police and not of citizens. Accordingly, proactive policing as we define it raises many of the questions about mobilization of police resources without citizen requests that interested these early policing scholars. However, proactive policing, in contrast to proactivity itself, refers to a group of strategies and programs, many of them initiated over the past three decades, for preventing crime.

As we noted above, the 2004 NRC report on police practices and policies proposed what it termed the "standard model of policing" to describe the common ways in which policing was organized before the 1980s. The study committee for that report drew from Herman Goldstein's classic critique of American policing in his article on problem-oriented policing published in 1979 (see also Goldstein, 1990). In that article, he tried to understand why a series of studies of American policing in the previous decades seemed to show that policing was ineffective in preventing crime. His conclusion was that policing had begun to focus more on the means of policing than its ends. Policing in this context had become focused on how fast the police could respond to calls for service, not how it could structure its responses to be most effective in reducing crime. Police managers had become concerned primarily with how to get enough officers on the street to meet their geographic patrol obligations and not upon how the allocation of patrol could be used most effectively to prevent crime.

The NRC study committee (National Research Council, 2004) identified two main ways in which innovative proactive strategies moved beyond the standard model of policing. The first is that many of the new strategies used "focus" in efforts to prevent crime. Many strategies identified specific geographic areas, for example crime hot spots, that would receive greater police attention. Other strategies capitalized on the fact that high-rate offenders were responsible for a large proportion of the crime problem. Accordingly, one key factor that distinguished innovative policing strategies was their approach to identifying how to focus resources on particular places and people. That study committee viewed this as one component of proactivity. In this case, the police do not simply comply with their reactive obligations to respond to and investigate crimes; rather, they purposely and strategically focus such resources to prevent crime.

The new proactive strategies went beyond the obligations of the police to respond to the occurrence of crime and to investigate and bring offenders to justice and focused instead on policing practices that could be successful in preventing crime irrespective of whether they had been seen in the past as traditional components of police practice. Because of this, the 2004 NRC report also identified an expansion of the tools of policing as an important innovation in police practices over the standard model (National Research Council, 2004, pp. 84–93, 232–251). The new proactive policing strategies pioneered a wide variety of new tools, ranging from community collaborations to the use of civil ordinances and to the introduction of innovative technologies that bring new information to enhance crime prevention.

But the new proactive policing strategies also reinterpreted traditional practices of policing to advance the crime control mission. For example, general preventive patrol is a key element of the standard model of policing. Innovative proactive policing strategies drew upon patrol methods but changed their mission through the development of hot spots policing (Sherman and Weisburd, 1995). In this case, police patrol in motorized vehicles, a key component of policing since the 1940s, was reallocated to specific places where crime was concentrated, in a conscious effort to be more successful in preventing crime. Stopping and questioning citizens had been a part of the standard practices of policing long before the Supreme Court specifically allowed it as a policing approach in *Terry v. Ohio* in 1968. However, this committee's interest in the practice called "stop, question, and frisk" develops not from the practice itself but rather from its use in some jurisdictions as a strategic proactive approach for anticipating and preventing crime.

There are likely scores of innovative proactive policing approaches that have been tried in police agencies in the United States and abroad. The committee could not review them all in depth, so we accordingly made a decision to give priority to certain types of proactive policing strategies. The first type includes strategies that have become commonly applied in American police agencies. It seemed important to us to provide insight into the effectiveness and potential intended and unintended impacts of proactive strategies that are already widely adopted in American police agencies. At the same time, we wanted to assess new and innovative practices and policies that may not yet have been widely adopted but seemed to the committee to represent important potential strategies for policing efforts to prevent crime. Finally, policing is in a period of tremendous community concern. Some of that concern is focused on proactive policing strategies that are seen as unfairly targeting some Americans over others and as leading to abusive policing practices. Accordingly, in selecting the specific practices and programs that would be examined by the committee, we agreed to focus particular attention on those that had been criticized for leading to biased or abusive outcomes or that sought to use positive community engagement as a method of enhancing crime control.

The committee decided not to examine innovations that were primarily technical in nature and did not include a clearly articulated goal of preventing crime. Some of these innovations—for example, computerized crime mapping—are often strongly linked to proactive policing innovations. These are included in our review in the context of those innovative strategies. But other new technologies being adopted by the police, such as body cameras or drones, do not as of yet have a specific strategic connection to crime control or proactive policing. We agree that such approaches should be assessed and reviewed (see, e.g., Lum, Koper, and Willis, 2016), but such a review goes beyond the scope of this report.

ASSESSING THE EVIDENCE

The committee included scholars from different disciplines, which sometimes emphasize different methodological and analytic approaches to developing evidence. Because of this, the committee took a broad approach in applying standards of evidence and included within its purview, for example, experimental studies, rigorous quasi-experimental approaches, econometric methods, and legal analysis. However, the committee also was in overall agreement regarding the characteristics of studies that would make the evidence persuasive for drawing conclusions.

A number of templates have been suggested for making systematic judgments about the strength of the statistical evidence in the case of a single evaluation or study, as, for example, the template incorporated in the What Works Clearinghouse established by the U.S. Department of Education's Institute for Education Sciences. Closely related are the templates for addressing the strength of evidence from a series of studies on the same sort of intervention, as with the Campbell Collaboration systematic reviews in education, crime control, parenting, and other areas. These reviews have been conducted for some categories of proactive policing (e.g., hot spots policing, problem-oriented policing, and focused deterrence policing), and they have informed the work of the committee. However, we have chosen not to rely upon a formal process of this sort in preparing this report. Instead, our approach focused on the committee reviewing the available evidence in each area and then providing an in-depth critique of studies' methods and conclusions. Here, we sketch the main considerations relevant to assessing the strength of evidence, considerations that guide both the committee's critiques and the statistical evaluation templates used elsewhere.

In considering the evidence from a single field test of an intervention, there are two main tasks. The first is to determine how informative the study is regarding the causal impact of the intervention on designated outcome variables in the current field test. The second is to determine the extent to which the results from this particular field test can be extrapolated to policing more generally. In the usual parlance, the first task concerns the *internal validity* of the impact evaluation, whereas the second task assesses its *external validity*. The statistical science associated with judging internal validity is well developed and is often easier for the committee to assess in our review. Yet the external validity of a finding or set of findings is particularly important in policy analysis, where the goal is to use the research evidence to shape policy development. In our review, we considered in a general way whether we can draw more general inferences about policing from specific studies. In some cases, that led us to note the limitations of, for example, using laboratory studies to make claims about police behavior in the field. In other cases, such as for hot spots policing studies, we note the large number of studies conducted in different contexts. A large group of experiments conducted in different places, in different types of police agencies, for example, provides a more convincing argument for the external validity of study findings than one or a small group of studies that have been conducted in one city. The limitations in the research base in policing means that we have to be cautious in drawing specific policy recommendations for police agencies. We return to this important issue in our detailed discussion of policy implications in Chapter 8.

The first task noted above, developing an internally valid estimate of the causal impact in a particular field test, requires outcome data of acceptable quality; both random and systematic errors in measurement are of concern. Next, a valid estimate of what levels those outcomes *would have taken* if the intervention were not implemented is required. These alternative values are called potential outcomes or counterfactuals. The "effects" of interest are defined as the difference between the observed values and the counterfactual values.

There are a variety of methods ("study designs") available for estimating the counterfactual values. In general, randomized controlled trials (RCTs) are seen as providing the strongest approach for creating such estimates. In an RCT, some units of observation are randomly assigned to the intervention and others are assigned to a control group receiving the alternative to which the treatment is being compared. The outcomes of the control group are then used to estimate the counterfactual for the treatment group. In principle, this approach ensures that the assignment of the treatment is not correlated with the potential outcome (which would impart bias to the estimated impact). A well-done RCT with reliable outcome data provides an unbiased estimate of the causal effect of the treatment, together with an estimate of how much statistical uncertainty is associated with that effect estimate.

In practice, an RCT may be difficult or even unethical to implement in a particular setting, or this design may engender administrative–fidelity problems that cloud the validity of the estimate of effect (e.g., cross-over from one condition to the other, noncompliance with treatment assignment, or treatment spill-over). There are alternative "quasi-experimental" research designs that in some cases may also produce trustworthy estimates and, indeed, share key statistical properties with high-quality RCTs (Nagin and Weisburd, 2013). These designs, when rigorous, identify methods for developing plausibly "as good as random" comparisons to use as the counterfactuals to the treatment condition. Natural experiments are examples of such research designs (Cook and Campbell, 1979), as are regression discontinuity designs (see, e.g., Berk, 2010). As another alternative to an RCT design, there are studies that use statistical controls as a primary method for providing valid estimates of the impacts of interventions. These are often termed multivariate methods, but they may mimic other types of quasi-experimental designs (e.g., propensity score matching, described by Rosenbaum and Rubin, 1983). These studies rely on high-quality data about the phenomenon under study, as statistical models are used to create equivalence of treatment and control conditions by including alternative confounding explanations of observed differences between treatment and nontreatment outcomes as statistical controls. Thus, assessing internal validity for all of these approaches requires a close understanding of the data-generating process. While the committee recognized the inherent advantages of randomized experiments, it assessed the strengths of specific studies in terms of how well threats to their internal validity had been addressed.

The second task (external validity) involves determining how relevant a particular finding or set of findings regarding an intervention's effectiveness is to estimating the potential effectiveness of similar interventions in other times and places. The challenge for this task is that while the new interventions are "similar" in some sense to those that were evaluated, they and the context in which they are implemented will not be identical to the evaluated cases. For example, if a hot spots policing intervention is effective in reducing robbery in a high-crime neighborhood in Chicago, would it also be similarly effective in reducing robbery in a high-crime neighborhood in Los Angeles? The implementing agency and the environment both differ in a variety of ways between these two neighborhoods. Does that negate the relevance of the Chicago finding? More generally, changes in the treatment details, the way in which it is implemented, the context of the implementation, and differences in the populations exposed can have considerable effects on the impact. Despite these potential pitfalls, for the purposes of policy design it is necessary to extrapolate from one time and place to a different time and place.

One way to strengthen the credibility of extrapolation is to show that the findings in that Chicago neighborhood can be replicated through high-quality evaluations in a number of other cities. That is, if the finding seems robust with respect to some other times and places, then it is more credible to extrapolate to still others. Alternatively, the intervention effect may vary, but in systematic ways. For example, if there is a reasonable presumption that certain factors (such as size and average education of the jurisdiction population) moderate the magnitude of the intervention effect, then the ideal evidence base would include high-quality evaluations conducted in a number of jurisdictions that differ with respect to those moderating factors. In principle that would provide a "predicted effect size" for any jurisdiction of particular size and education.

Another way to strengthen the credibility of extrapolation is by development of theory regarding the basic mechanisms on which a program innovation relies to influence behavior. What is learned from empirical studies of one or more interventions can then be framed as evidence not merely about the effectiveness of the specific interventions but rather about the effectiveness of the mechanisms underlying those interventions (Ludwig, Kling, and Mullainathan, 2011). That is, a series of empirical evaluations, perhaps taken together with other sorts of evidence, can allow evaluators to look inside the "black box" of a policing approach (e.g., hot spots policing) and interpret observed results in terms of the underlying mechanism (e.g., deterrence via the threat of punishment communicated by police presence). The accumulation of evidence supporting the strength and robustness of a particular mechanism enhances confidence that programs in new times and places that incorporate this mechanism will be effective.

These evidence-accumulation strategies rely on the intervention having homogeneous effects that are in fact not context dependent. If multiple studies result in conflicting evidence on effectiveness, new empirical work focusing on uncovering and testing contextual factors that aid or hinder treatment effectiveness is needed.

ORGANIZATION OF THE REPORT

This chapter has discussed the historical context of proactive policing, the charge to the study committee, the definition of proactive policing used in this report, and the standards used by the committee in evaluating evidence. Chapter 2 focuses more directly on the nature of the proactive policing strategies examined in the report. These strategies are divided into four broad categories: place based, person focused, problem solving, and community oriented. The logic for this division is presented in that chapter, as are the descriptions of the strategies that fall under each of those domains. As will become apparent, the real world is much messier than an academic effort to define and categorize proactive policing strategies. Nonetheless, the committee thought it important at the outset to try to identify strategies in terms of the broad mechanisms that are seen as contributing to crime prevention outcomes.

Policing strategies raise important issues regarding legality and lawfulness. Proactive approaches can involve, among other things, the gathering and aggregating of information, the use of algorithms (public and private) for decision making, the development of criteria for intervention beyond individual suspicion, and the concentration of interventions and resources. Such activities may create concerns about issues, such as privacy, arbitrariness or abuse (including arbitrariness or abuse with regard to arrests and the use of force), discrimination, accuracy, accountability, and transparency. These issues are the focus of discussion in Chapter 3.

The importance of reviewing the evidence of the effects of proactive policing on crime and disorder has already been noted. More than a decade has passed since the 2004 NRC report on police practices and policies (National Research Council, 2004), and many innovations in proactive policing had not been evaluated at the time of that study; other approaches, moreover, have yielded many new studies. These topics are the focus of Chapter 4.

As indicated above, even if the evidence were clear that proactive policing strategies are effective at reducing crime and disorder, the consequences of such strategies would need to be evaluated along additional dimensions. Police officers are some of the most visible representatives of law and government in most people's lives, and the fairness of policing has become a key issue today. The President's Task Force on 21st Century Policing, which was established by President Obama in December 2014, emphasized, "[b]uilding trust and nurturing legitimacy on both sides of the police/citizen divide is the foundational principle underlying the nature of relations between law enforcement agencies and the communities they serve" (p. 1). Proactive policing strategies can increase the points of contact and interaction between police and communities, and proactive approaches may also expand the police function beyond traditional law enforcement activities. The implications of proactive policing policy for community trust and legitimacy are therefore especially important.

Chapters 5 and 6 focus on the impacts of proactive policing strategies on communities and on community perceptions of the police. "Community outcomes" is a term used in this report to refer to how a group of people perceives and feels about its police, the policing that it receives, and the consequences of that policing. It also includes actions that community members take to assist police or to benefit themselves directly to deal with crime, disorder, and quality-of-life issues relevant to policing. We divide this discussion into two chapters to reflect the important distinction between strategies that are focused on crime control without a clear orientation to the community and its role in policing and those strategies seek to use community engagement to enhance crime control. Chapter 5 examines how proactive policing strategies that focus on places, people, or problem-solving impact the communities in which they are carried out. Chapter 6 examines proactive policing strategies, such as community policing and procedural justice policing, that seek not only to reduce crime but also to alter the fundamental relationships between the police and the communities they serve. Clearly, these proactive policing programs would be expected to have more direct, and at least in their logic model, more positive impacts on community perceptions of the police.

Concerns about racial discrimination loom especially large in discussions of policing. There are many historical reasons why non-Whites might distrust law enforcement. For instance, when the laws of the United States were designed to produce and maintain racial stratification, it was the job of police officers and sheriff's deputies to enforce those laws. Police across the nation were tasked with enforcing laws that disadvantaged Blacks, Native Americans, immigrants, and others who were targeted by laws designed to reinforce notions of racial superiority. From the Fugitive Slave Act of 1850, which regulated the movement of Black people before emancipation, to sundown towns that required all non-Whites to leave a jurisdiction before the sun set, and to segregated schools, water fountains, and lunch counters, it was the job of law enforcement to regulate *de jure* racial hierarchies (Hinton, 2016a, 2016b).

Beginning in the 1960s and 1970s, law enforcement tactics under the "War on Crime" and "War on Drugs" were characterized, if not by racial animus, then by racially disparate consequences (Hinton, 2016a, 2016b). More generally, even scholars trying to reform the police often seemed to neglect the question of race and the impacts of policing on non-White communities (Williams and Murphy, 1990). And this concern with discrimination and disparate consequences for non-White communities has continued through the new millennium. We review in Chapter 7 not only the evidence on explicit biases against Black and other non-White people but also implicit biases that may play a role in policing even when the police have no specific policies to target non-White individuals.

A parallel (if less prominent) critique of police and race in the United States is that Black neighborhoods suffer from under-policing. Anything that reduced crime—especially violent crime—in non-White neighborhoods would be a boon to those communities. This was precisely the argument advanced by the Clinton administration in support of the 1994 Omnibus Crime Bill that poured federal resources into municipal policing (Brickey, 1995; Hinton, 2016a, 2016b).

This report does not answer a series of questions at the heart of tension between non-Whites and the police across the United States: Is policing biased against the poor, Blacks, or other non-Whites? Are they more likely to be shot and killed than advantaged groups? These are key questions that need to be answered. The focus of this report, however, is more modest. The committee's main interest is whether and to what extent proactive policing affects racial disparities in police–citizen encounters and racial bias in policy behavior.

Chapter 8 summarizes the main findings for each of the four areas on which the report focuses: law and legality, crime control, community impacts, and racial disparities and racial bias. It then explores the broader policy implications of the report. Finally, it lays out the committee's suggestions for filling research gaps in order to strengthen the knowledge base regarding proactive policing and its impacts.

During the course of this study, the committee also gathered information through roundtables and webinars open to the public. The purpose of these activities was to explore topics and issues relevant to the study charge from the perspectives of both the police carrying out proactive policing and the communities that experience proactive policing. These sessions, which helped to inform the committee's deliberations, are summarized in Appendix A.

CONCLUSION

Proactive policing, as the committee defines it, is a relatively new phenomenon in American cities. Although there were historical precedents for police proactivity in 19th and 20th century America, its current form developed from a crisis in confidence in policing that emerged because of social unrest, rising crime rates, and growing skepticism regarding the standard model of policing that had been dominant in the latter half of the 20th century. The chapters that follow answer the specific questions with which the committee has been charged: What are the consequences of proactive policing for legality, crime, communities, and racial disparities and racial bias?

2

The Landscape of Proactive Policing

The previous chapter provided a broad historical context and specific definition of proactive policing. But, having delineated a broad concept of proactive policing, the committee also notes that the various programs and interventions undertaken in the name of proactive policing differ greatly in terms of both what the police do and the theoretical models that inform their activities. Any description of proactive policing is made even more difficult by the fact that police activities span a wide array of responsibilities, many of them shared with state or federal law enforcement. For example, the committee decided not to examine proactive policing approaches to white collar crime, which are primarily carried out by federal law enforcement agencies. Similarly, we did not consider law enforcement efforts to deal with organized crime, international drug trafficking, or trafficking in human beings. The committee decided that while such activities are often proactive and may involve local law enforcement, they were not a part of the landscape of proactive policing that has come to be associated with municipal policing in American cities, which was the main focus of our discussions. This means, to a great extent, that the policing strategies reviewed in this report refer to those public, frontline policing strategies that have been applied to prevent or reduce ongoing, street-level crime and disorder harms.

In focusing on this range of proactive policing, we faced an additional problem. How could such a broad array of approaches be linked in ways that would help to draw broader conclusions about the broad mechanisms underlying prevention? The committee decided that an approach that identified what the key logic models of prevention were at the outset would provide for the greatest insights into understanding whether proactive policing was effective and whether and how it affects communities, the lawfulness of policing, and racial disparities and racial bias. Taking this approach meant that we recognized at the outset that policing in the real world would not conform simply to the prevention models we identified. In the real world of policing, practices may draw upon a variety of logic models for prevention. This makes sense when the goal is preventing crime rather than identifying the underlying theoretical mechanisms that create preventive outcomes. What this means in practice is that specific programs carried out in policing often fall across the categories defined by the committee.

The committee identified four broad approaches to crime prevention that summarize the directions that proactive policing has taken over the past few decades: place-based approaches, problem-solving approaches, person-focused approaches, and community-based approaches (see Table 2-1). While the police practices described in this report may include elements of multiple models of prevention, it is generally the case that they develop primarily as a response to the insights of one logic model in particular. For example, hot spots policing and predictive policing developed primarily in response to the insights underlying the logic model of place-based prevention (described below), whereas community-oriented policing and procedural justice policing rely primarily on a logic model emphasizing the key role played by communities in crime prevention. This does not mean that specific programs do not also draw from other logic models of prevention. Rather, it is possible to think about the broad directions of proactive policing in reference to these categories and, more generally (as we do in later chapters), to draw broader conclusions about why programs or practices have the impacts observed.

The *place-based approach* seeks to focus policing resources more efficiently and effectively by capitalizing on the concentration of crime incidents at certain locations, or microgeographic places, within a department's entire jurisdiction. Policing strategies that take a place-based approach include hot spots policing, predictive policing, and use of closed circuit television (CCTV).

A second approach, referred to here as the *problem-solving approach*, seeks to take a scientific approach to diagnosing the problems that underlie a pattern of crime incidents. After identifying the causes of these problems, it attempts to tailor solutions to the problems by addressing their causes, thereby preventing (or reducing) future crime. Strategies that take this approach include problem-oriented policing and third party policing.

The third approach focuses on deterring crime by capitalizing on the insight that a small proportion of the crime-committing population commits a disproportionate share of the crimes. Strategies that employ this *person-*

focused approach include focused deterrence; repeat offender programs; and stop, question, and frisk (SQF).

The fourth approach, which we call the *community-based* approach, focuses on involving the community in defining the key problems of policing and on fostering the community's role (as understood by a strategy's logic model) in maintaining order and public safety. Strategies that take a community-based approach include community-oriented policing, procedural justice policing, and broken windows policing.

These four approaches have different implications for the outcomes of policing, whether those outcomes be crime control, a community's evaluation of its police, the lawfulness of policing, or potential disparities or bias in the application of policing. To understand why and how these approaches have been used in actual policing programs and interventions, we will ask three questions for each approach:

1. What factors underlay its emergence as a proactive policing approach?
2. What are the main types of policing practices (here called *strategies*) that use this approach?
3. What is the underlying logic model, and the evidence for that model, that informs strategies that adopt this policing approach?

Before applying the conceptual framework and its taxonomy of policing approaches and strategies to the real world and the research literature about it, two caveats are in order. First, as already noted, actual policing programs and implementations of proactive practices often incorporate elements that fall under two or more of the approaches as defined above; even more frequently, they combine elements from several strategies, as these are defined in this chapter. To aid comprehension, we reserve the terms "approach" and "strategy" for the taxonomic elements of the framework summarized in Table 2-1. We reserve "logic model" for the rationale underlying an approach or a strategy implementing an approach. Second, although the committee has adopted terminology in common use in the research literature and in policing practice, we recognize that the strict characterizations given in this report will sometimes conflict with how these terms are used in one study or another. For purposes of our discussion, the committee has interpreted whatever terminology the original authors used into the terminology of our conceptual framework.

STRATEGIES FOR A PLACE-BASED APPROACH

Policing has always had a geographic or place-based component, especially in how patrol resources are allocated for emergency response systems

TABLE 2-1 Four Approaches to Proactive Policing

	Place-Based Approach	Problem-Solving Approach	Person-Focused Approach	Community-Based Approach
Logic Model for Crime Prevention	Capitalize on the evidence for the concentration of crime at microgeographic places	Use a problem-oriented approach, which seeks to identify problems as patterns across crime events and then identify the causes of those problems Draw upon solutions tailored to the problem causes, with attention to assessment	Capitalize on the strong concentration of crime among a small proportion of the criminal population	Capitalize on the resources of communities to identify and control crime
Policing Strategies	Hot spots policing, predictive policing, CCTV	Problem-oriented policing, third party policing	Focused deterrence; repeat offender programs; stop, question, and frisk	Community-oriented policing, procedural justice policing, broken windows policing
Primary Objective	Prevent crime in microgeographic places	Solve recurring problems to prevent future crime	Prevent and deter specific crimes by targeting known offenders	Enhance collective efficacy and community collaboration with police
Key Ways to Accomplish Objective	Identification of crime hot spots and application of focused strategies	Scan and analyze crime problems, identify solutions and assess them (SARA model)	Identification of known high-rate offenders and application of strategies to these specific offenders	Develop approaches that engage the community or that change the way police interact with citizens

(Sparrow, Moore, and Kennedy, 1992). In order for officers to respond quickly to citizen calls, police organizations developed geographically based systems that took into account the crime levels in particular areas. Under the standard model of policing, which emphasized shortening response times, police resources were organized using macrogeographies, which refers to areas the size of patrol officers' beats, an organization's precincts, or other relatively large administrative areas. In contrast to the standard model, proactive place-based policing (see Weisburd, 2008) focused on smaller, "micro" units of geography, often termed "crime hot spots." Such a hot spot might be a single building or address; street segments or the faces of a street block; or clusters of addresses, block faces, or street segments with common crime problems.

Since the 19th century, scholars have found evidence that crime is more prevalent in some places than others (Guerry, 2002; Quetelet, 1842; Mayhew, 1968). However, research emerging in the late 1980s showed that this concentration of crime occurred at a very microgeographic level. Place-based proactive policing developed in response to this growing body of evidence (Sherman, Buerger, and Gartin, 1989; Sherman and Weisburd, 1995; Weisburd and Green, 1995). Its logic model was based on the research findings that crime incidence was highly concentrated in crime hot spots. As Sherman and Weisburd (1995, p. 629) remarked in the first large-scale test of effectiveness of hot spots policing in Minneapolis, Minnesota, if "only 3 percent of the addresses in a city produce more than half of all the requests for police response, if no police are dispatched to 40 percent of the addresses and intersections in a city over one year, and, if among the 60 percent with any requests the majority register only one request a year (Sherman, Buerger, and Gartin, 1989), then concentrating police in a few locations makes more sense that spreading them evenly through a beat."

Important to the development of place-based policing are theoretical perspectives that also emerged during this period (Braga et al., 2011; Weisburd and McEwen, 1997; Weisburd and Telep, 2010). Key to the standard model of police patrol had been the idea that opportunities for crime were common throughout the urban landscape (see Repetto, 1976). But with the entry of economists into the analysis of crime (Becker, 1968; Ehrlich, 1973; Cook, 1986), the assumption that the crime rate was somehow determined by the number of "offenders" was challenged. The economic theory of crime conceptualized criminal behavior as a choice available to everyone, influenced by the perceived costs and benefits of available criminal opportunities. The crime rate, from this perspective, is determined both by the potential payoff to exploiting an opportunity (amount of "loot" in the case of property crime) and by the probability of arrest and punishment. The availability of attractive criminal opportunities is thus one determinant of crime and is itself heavily influenced by private behavior of potential victims.

Routine activities theory (Cohen and Felson, 1979), situational prevention (Clarke, 1995), and crime pattern theory (Brantingham and Brantingham, 1993) challenged the idea that criminal opportunities were unending and raised the question of whether specific places have characteristics that attract or generate crime. These perspectives, which are often termed "opportunity theories" (see Cullen, 2010; Wilcox, Land, and Hunt, 2003), suggested that reduction of crime opportunities at specific places would likely prevent crime without displacing it to other locations.[1] Using this theoretical background, advocates of place-based policing argued that traditional objections to targeting microgeographic hot spots—objections that assumed crime displacement—would be unlikely to offset the crime prevention gains generated by focusing policing on hot spots.

The underlying logic model of place-based policing—that police can capitalize on the strong concentration of crime at microgeographic places—has been confirmed in a large number of studies over the past few decades (see Andresen and Malleson, 2011; Braga, Papachristos, and Hureau, 2014; Brantingham and Brantingham, 1999; Crow and Bull, 1975; Curman, Andresen, and Brantingham, 2015; Pierce, Spaar, and Briggs, 1988; Roncek, 2000; Sherman, 1997; Sherman, Buerger, and Gartin, 1989; Weisburd and Amram, 2014; Weisburd et al., 2004; Weisburd and Green, 1995; Weisburd, Morris, and Groff, 2009; Weisburd, Maher, and Sherman, 1992; Weisburd, Groff, and Yang, 2012; Weisburd, 2015). These studies confirmed that microgeographic concentrations of crime do not necessarily conform to traditional ideas about crime and communities. In particular, neighborhoods that are considered troubled often have discrete locations that are free of crime, and crime hot spots do occur in neighborhoods that are generally viewed as advantaged and not crime prone (see, e.g., Weisburd, Groff, and Yang, 2012). A number of studies also suggested that hot spots of crime are often stable over long periods of time (see, e.g., Weisburd, Groff, and Yang, 2012; Andresen and Malleson, 2011).

Hot Spots Policing

Sherman and Weisburd (1995) developed the strategy of hot spots policing in the Minneapolis Hot Spots Patrol Experiment. Hot spots policing covers a range of police responses, but they all focus resources on locations where crime incidents have been highly concentrated. By focusing on microgeographic locations with high concentrations of crime, hot spots policing

---

[1] The four main dimensions of opportunity theory are (1) motivated offenders, (2) suitable targets, (3) guardianship, and (4) accessibility/urban form.

aims to increase the *general* deterrence of police actions, in this case by increasing perceptions of the certainty of enforcement action (Durlauf and Nagin, 2011). There may also be a *specific* deterrent impact of hot spots policing, if offenders who are arrested because of increased patrols are thereby dissuaded from future offending. In addition to specific and general perceptual deterrence, police can also alter the situational opportunities that exist at hot spots by altering the environmental design of places (see, e.g., Clarke, 1997), engaging "place guardians" such as building managers or store owners (Eck and Weisburd, 1995), and engaging communities at the hot spots (Weisburd, Davis, and Gill, 2015).[2]

Once a hot spot is identified, police may implement a range of tactics appropriate to the particular type of hot spot to prevent crime in the given microarea, and these tactics often incorporate elements typical of one or another of the other three proactive policing interventions discussed above (refer to Table 2-1). In 2008, the Police Executive Research Forum (PERF) conducted a survey on hots spots policing that was distributed to its general members.[3] The results of the survey indicate that when police engage in hot spots policing, they implement aspects of general patrol/enforcement strategies, an offender-oriented strategy, problem-oriented and community-oriented strategies, or a general investigative strategy.[4] Table 2-2 shows the use of each policing practice by the principal type of crime associated with

---

[2] As noted earlier, actual policing practice often combines elements from two or more of the approaches. A hot spots policing practice that seeks to engage the community could easily become a hybrid of place-based and community-based approaches.

[3] PERF agencies represent an important and influential group of the nation's largest police forces. To be eligible for PERF general membership, one must be the executive head of a state or local police agency that has 100 or more employees and/or serves a jurisdiction of at least 50,000 persons. The survey discussed here was completed by 191 PERF agencies, representing a response rate of 63 percent. "The responding agencies were predominantly large, with a mean of 997 officers and a median of 315. Their service populations averaged nearly 460,000 and had a median size just below 161,000. Eighty-three percent of the [agencies] were municipal agencies, while the remainder consisted primarily of county [agencies] (13 percent)." The U.S. agencies in the sample represented all four primary regions of the United States (as defined by the U.S. Census Bureau), and their jurisdictions accounted for 21 percent of the country's population in 2006 (Koper, 2014, pp. 126–127).

[4] A general patrol/enforcement strategy can include such practices as directed patrol, traffic stops and field interviews, order maintenance, foot patrol, overtime saturation patrol, fixed police presence, and use of mobile suppression or saturation units. An offender-oriented strategy may consist of interventions that target known offenders, execute warrant services, and check on probationers and parolees. Problem-oriented and community-oriented strategies include problem analysis and problem solving, intervening at problem locations, community policing partnerships, and multiagency task force operations. General investigative strategies consist of interventions such as surveillance, decoy operations, buy-bust/reverse stings, and the use of technologies like surveillance cameras or gunshot detection systems (Koper, 2014).

TABLE 2-2 Percentage of Responding Agencies Using a Proactive Policing Practice, by Principal Crime Type Associated with a Hot Spot

Proactive Policing Practice	Range Across Crime Types	Robbery	Assault	Homicide/ Shooting	Gang	Drug
Problem Analysis and Problem Solving	77–93	93	82	77	86	89
Targeting Known Offenders	63–90	80	63	69	89	90
Community Policing/Community Partnerships	73–89	89	76	73	85	85
Directed Patrol	61–91	91	61	65	86	86
Enhanced Traffic Stops and Field Interviews	59–84	80	59	69	84	84
Intervening at Problem Locations	64–85	74	74	64	82	85
Surveillance Operations	45–88	86	45	59	82	88
Mobile Suppression or Saturation Unit	46–79	72	46	63	79	72
Warrant Service	59–74	68	59	62	71	74
Checks on Probationers and Parolees	58–72	72	58	62	72	71
Use of Overtime for Saturated Patrol	48–78	78	48	61	69	65
Order Maintenance (broken windows)	56–77	64	56	56	76	77
Multiagency Task Force Operations	36–84	59	36	58	81	84
Foot Patrol	42–59	53	43	42	59	59
Use of Technology (e.g., cameras, gunshot detection)	39–58	56	39	47	56	58
Buy and Bust/Reverse Stings	11–87	18	11	17	36	87
Fixed Police Presence	26–46	43	26	34	43	46
Decoy Operations	11–46	29	11	12	16	46

NOTE: n = 176 agencies.
SOURCE: Koper (2014, p. 130).

> **BOX 2-1**
> **Hot Spots Policing in Sacramento, California**
>
> The Sacramento Police Department (SPD) implemented a hot spots policing program in 2011. In coordination with researchers, the SPD engaged in hot spots policing for 90 days from February to May.
> The SPD's crime analysis unit determined that about 5 percent of street segments in Sacramento accounted for one-half of crime calls for service, in line with theories regarding the concentration of crime in particular locations. To identify hot spots, the SPD analyzed citizen-generated calls for service in those districts that met the criteria to receive the hot spots program. Forty-two hot spots were identified that met three criteria: (1) not larger than one standard linear street block, (2) not extending for more than one-half block from either side of an intersection, and (3) not within one standard linear block of another hot spot.
> Officers were assigned one to six hot spots in their patrol area and were given a random order in which to visit each, giving the SPD a great deal of control over officer activities. The officers visited each of their hot spots for 12 to 16 minutes apiece. Through their in-car computers, officers received suggestions on proactive activities to engage in while at hot spots, including making traffic stops, street checks, and business contacts. Officers also were encouraged to initiate citizen contacts while present in the hot spot.
>
> SOURCE: Adapted from Telep, Mitchell, and Weisburd (2014).

a hot spot.[5] As these results illustrate, there is often overlap between tactics used in hot spots policing and tactics typically associated with the other proactive policing approaches in Table 2-1. Box 2-1 describes a hot spots policing program in Sacramento, California, further demonstrating that police departments often use a range of tactics from different approaches at hot spots.

Predictive Policing

Predictive policing is a strategy for proactive policing that uses predictive algorithms based on combining different types of data to anticipate where and when crime might occur and to identify patterns among past criminal incidents. Predictive policing tends to focus on geospatial predic-

---

[5] The underlying logic model of hot spots policing does not limit police to implementing only these practices. For example, the police could engage in community policing (foot patrol being one tactic often associated with community policing, another being door-to-door getting-to-know-you police interventions) or procedural justice.

tion of crime activity, and many police departments who adopt predictive policing approaches use computer software to generate maps of predicted crime activity.[6]

Predictive policing takes data from disparate sources (both real-time crime data and frequently other noncrime data) and identifies patterns in the aggregated dataset. Police then use those patterns to anticipate, prevent, and respond more effectively to future crime. Predictive policing overlaps with hot spots policing but is generally distinguished by its reliance on sophisticated analytics that are used to predict likelihood of crime incidence within very specific parameters of space and time and for very specific types of crime.

Predictive methods can be used to predict crime incidence by type, predict offenders, predict perpetrators' identities, or predict victims of crime. For geospatial prediction of crime activity, many police departments use computer software to generate maps of predicted crime activity. Methods used to identify likely perpetrators of past crimes use available information from crime scenes to automatically link suspects to crimes; methods predicting potential victims of crimes identify at-risk groups and individuals, such as those in proximity to at-risk locations, individuals at risk of victimization, and individuals at risk of domestic violence (Perry et al., 2013).

Making predictions is only half of predictive policing; the other half is carrying out interventions that act on the predictions (Perry et al., 2013). Police combine predictions (and crime analysis more generally) with strategies and tactics at predicted locations. For example, in Shreveport, Louisiana, the police department used monthly predictions of locations of future crimes to drive a strategic decision-making model that included increasing officer awareness of hot spots in roll call and using predictions to implement a broken windows intervention (Hunt, Saunders, and Hollywood, 2014).

Predictive policing as a strategy for proactive policing has its origins in the National Institute of Justice's first predictive policing symposium, held in 2009 in Los Angeles. Participants at that meeting identified numerous

---

[6] According to Ferguson (2012, p. 265), predictive policing is a "generic term for any crime fighting approach that includes a reliance on information technology (usually crime mapping data and analysis), criminology theory, predictive algorithms, and the use of this data to improve crime suppression on the streets." Ratcliffe (2014, p. 4) defines predictive policing as "the use of historical data to create a spatiotemporal forecast of areas of criminality or crime hot spots that will be the basis for police resource allocation decisions with the expectation that having officers at the proposed place and time will deter or detect criminal activity." However, predictive policing methods may at times also focus on predicting individuals who may become offenders or on predicting perpetrator identities using regression and classification models that include risk factors, statistical modeling to link crimes, and computer-assisted queries and analysis of intelligence and other databases (Perry et al., 2013).

potential applications of predictive policing, but the primary actual use was the description of the time and location of future incidents in a crime pattern or series. For example, police in Richmond, Virginia, used predictive policing methods to analyze random gunfire incidents. Using this analysis to make predictions, they were able to anticipate the time, location, and nature of future incidents (Uchida, 2009).

There are a number of companies that sell commercial predictive policing software (e.g., PredPol and HunchLab 2.0) as well as one program funded by the National Institute of Justice and available without charge.[7] These software programs require access to real-time crime data (and, sometimes, other noncrime data) that are geocoded, reliable, and fit for the analytic purpose. The software must also have an appropriate algorithm that can produce viable predictions when needed and produce them in a format that is easily translated to operational personnel. Beyond the software, in order to implement predictive policing, a decision-making system in the operational environment capable and willing to make resource allocation decisions based on the predictions is necessary, along with the adoption of appropriate tactics tailored to the crime problem (see Ratcliffe, 2014). We note, however, that a software program is not necessary to produce results akin to those produced by predictive policing software programs; with sufficient knowledge and under the right circumstances, a well-trained crime analyst could perform the activities of a dedicated software program.

Because the concept of predictive policing is relatively recent, there is a lack of clarity with regard to both the specifics of operationalization of these definitions and the specifics of the police strategies applied (Santos, 2014). The effectiveness of predictive policing is difficult to establish because, to be a bona fide new policing strategy, it may require combining two components. The first is a software algorithm or prediction regime that is able to better predict future criminality than any existing alternative mechanisms (such as current software for crime mapping and/or the abilities of a crime analyst). Second, predicted grids should incur an operational response that is identified specifically with predictive policing.

Closed Circuit Television

CCTV is a surveillance technology comprising one or more video cameras connected in a closed circuit to a monitoring system. A CCTV system for proactive policing usually includes a number of cameras that can pan, tilt, and zoom in various directions; a mechanism to convey the real-time images to a monitoring location; a range of other elements that store,

---

[7] The PROVE software utility is available at https://www.hunchlab.com/tools/prove [July 2017].

display, or otherwise monitor the camera live feed; and a human element whereby someone monitors the images either in real time or in response to an incident (Ratcliffe, 2006). Though CCTV may be used reactively, the committee examines here the uses of CCTV for proactive policing; that is, when CCTV is used to view suspicious situations or disorders, to which police might be able to respond before the situation deteriorates into a crime incident.

How cameras are monitored varies significantly among police departments. When used proactively, CCTV cameras are actively monitored, requiring a person who watches the camera feed and can deploy personnel to the incident in real time. Some CCTV systems, such as in the town of Malmö, Sweden, are actively monitored only during weekend nights from midnight to 6 a.m. (Gerell, 2016). Some systems may also have such high camera-to-operator ratios that doubt is cast as to the level of "active" monitoring actually taking place (Smith, 2004; Piza et al., 2015).

CCTV cameras are used to increase the risks for offenders of committing crime and specifically comprise a formal surveillance mechanism that enhances or replaces the role of police or security personnel (Welsh and Farrington, 2008; Clarke and Eck, 2005). In other words, prevention occurs if a potential offender is aware of the camera and makes the decision that the risk of capture outweighs the benefits of the imminent offense (Ratcliffe, 2006). CCTV cameras placed overtly are hypothesized to generate a general deterrence mechanism that increases the perceived risk of capture among the general potential offender population, should a crime be committed. They also raise the possibility of specific deterrence by which any offenders who are captured through use of the camera scheme are dissuaded from future offending. This *perceptual deterrence* is therefore rooted in the certainty, severity, and celerity of punishment, where "deterrence is maximized by sanctions that are perceived as inexorable, burdensome, and expeditious" (Apel, 2016, p. 59). CCTV aims to heighten the last of these: perception of the celerity of enforcement action.

STRATEGIES FOR A PROBLEM-SOLVING APPROACH

Herman Goldstein argued in 1979 that the police could be more effective in reducing crime if they took a more "problem-oriented" approach. Goldstein noted that the police had become so concerned with the means of policing that they had neglected the goals of policing. He called on police to refocus on those goals, which in his view could be defined as solving problems in communities (Goldstein, 1979, 1990). The logic model of problem solving assumes that if the police focus on specific problems, they will be more successful at reducing crime and other community problems. Strategies for a problem-solving approach, such as problem-oriented policing and third party policing emerged from Goldstein's work.[8] These problem-solving strategies seek to identify causes of problems and draw upon innovative solutions with attention to assessment.

Problem-solving strategies, with their analytic focus, often incorporate policing practices characteristic of other approaches. For example, in practice there is often overlap of problem-solving practices with practices typical of a place-based approach and a person-focused approach. As will be discussed below, interventions that primarily take a community-based approach often explicitly include elements characteristic of the problem-solving approach as well.

Problem-Oriented Policing

Problem-oriented policing is an analytic method for developing crime reduction tactics. This strategy draws upon theories of criminal opportunity, such as rational choice and routine activities, to analyze crime problems and develop appropriate responses (Clarke, 1997; Braga, 2008; Reisig, 2010). Using a basic iterative process of problem identification, analysis, response, assessment, and adjustment of the response (often called the scanning, analysis, response, and assessment [SARA] model), this adaptable and dynamic analytic method provides a framework for uncovering the complex mechanisms at play in crime problems and for developing tailor-made interventions to address the underlying conditions that cause crime problems (Eck and Spelman, 1987; Goldstein, 1990). Depending on the nuances of particular problems, the responses that are developed—even for seemingly similar problems—can be diverse. Indeed, problem-oriented policing interventions draw upon a variety of tactics and practices, ranging from arrest of offenders and modification of the physical environment to engagement with community members.

Historically, most police departments engaged in incident-driven crime prevention strategies. These departments sought to resolve individual crime incidents instead of addressing recurring crime problems (Eck and Spelman, 1987). In his seminal article that challenged existing police policy and practice, Herman Goldstein (1979) proposed an alternative: police should search for solutions to the recurring problems that generated repeated calls. Goldstein described this strategy as the "problem-oriented approach" and envisioned it as a departmentwide activity. He intended for problem-oriented policing to also address the problem of unguided police discretion

---

[8]Proactive partnerships with other organizations (such as code or liquor enforcement agencies, schools, probation, and private businesses), situational crime prevention, and crime prevention through environmental design are also commonly used as practices for a problem-solving approach. These are generally included in our review as third party policing practices.

(which could give rise to negative consequences such as improper use of force, ineffective crime reduction procedures, corruption, and discriminatory practices) and the "means-over-ends syndrome" (meaning an overemphasis on means, without appropriate attention to the goals, or ends).

Goldstein also emphasized from the outset that police engaged in problem-oriented policing should focus their efforts on problems the community cares about and that practices typical of a community-based approach should be among those considered in trying to reduce any given problem. Eventually the Office of Community Oriented Policing Services (COPS Office) in the U.S. Department of Justice formally hybridized problem-oriented policing and community-oriented policing by making problem-oriented policing a key element of its community-oriented policing strategy (discussed below). Thus, like many of the strategies discussed in this chapter, problem-oriented policing is in practice often implemented in practice in conjunction with practices characteristic of other policing approaches.

Problem-oriented policing requires police to be proactive in identifying underlying problems and to develop an array of tactics to address the problem, not just a particular police tactic (Goldstein, 1990; see also Weisburd et al., 2008, p. 10). However, research suggests that it is often difficult for police officers to fully implement a problem-oriented policing strategy (Cordner, 1998; Eck and Spelman, 1987; Clarke, 1998; Braga and Weisburd, 2006). Indeed, the research literature is filled with cases where problem-oriented policing programs tend to fall back on traditional methods and tend to have weak problem analysis components (Buerger, 1994; Capowich and Roehl, 1994; Cordner and Biebel, 2005; Read and Tilley, 2000). Box 2-2 describes a problem-oriented policing program in the Jacksonville, Florida, Sheriff's Office.

Third Party Policing

Third party policing draws upon the insights of problem solving but also leverages "third parties" who are viewed as significant new resources for preventing crime and disorder. The argument for third party policing asserts that the police cannot successfully deal with many problems on their own. Thus, the failures of the standard model of policing are inherent in the limits on police powers, and crime prevention requires police engagement with third parties. Using civil ordinances and civil courts or the resources of private agencies, police departments engaged in third party policing recognize that much social control is exercised by institutions other than the police (e.g., public housing agencies, property owners, parents, health and building inspectors, and business owners) and that crime can be better managed through coordination with these institutions, using means other than the criminal law.

> **BOX 2-2**
> **Problem-Oriented Policing in Jacksonville, Florida**
>
> Problem-oriented policing can be operationalized in many different ways. The Jacksonville Sheriff's Office implemented a problem-oriented policing program directed at microgeographic crime hot spots in order to reduce violent crime. Officers identified and analyzed specific crime and disorder problems in these places in order to develop effective responses. To this end, officers (in conjunction with a crime analyst) were encouraged to explore the "root causes" of violence in identified locations and to propose solutions for those causes. In some cases, officers focused their tactics on the offenders present in the locations or the community; in others they opted for environmental crime prevention tactics that could reduce violent crime. In still other cases, officers worked with residents and city agencies to develop custom responses to particular problems. In each case, a high degree of importance was placed on creativity and officer discretion.
>
> The officers spent their full shifts engaging in problem-oriented policing at their assigned location. Working closely with community partners and using the SARA model, officers undertook a range of activities at the various locations. The most common were situational crime prevention measures, such as repairing fences, installing or improving lighting, and erecting road barriers. In addition, officers frequently engaged business owners and rental property managers in improving security measures, business practices, and other forms of prevention and collaboration. Other activities aimed at solving causes of problems included community organizing (e.g., conducting community surveys and other forms of citizen outreach), social services (e.g., improving recreational opportunities for youth), code enforcement, aesthetic community improvements (e.g., removing graffiti or cleaning up a park), and nuisance abatement (Taylor, Koper, and Woods, 2011, p. 158).

Mazerolle and Ransley (2006, p. 192) suggested that the growth of third party policing may be part of a larger transformation of governance in Western democracies away from state sovereignty and control and toward "networks of power." Meares (2006, p. 207) similarly suggested that third party policing bears similarities to certain forms of civil regulation (e.g., of accountants, lawyers, employers, and sports leagues) and that, given the pervasive forms of civil regulation today, it is not surprising that third-party efforts are becoming common in the enterprise of street crime control.

Again, there is often overlap in practice between third party policing and the other strategies examined by the committee. The focal point of third party policing can be people, places, or situations. Third party policing efforts are sometimes directed specifically at categories of people—such as young people, gang members, or drug dealers—and at other times at specific places, such as crime hot spots (Mazerolle and Ransley, 2006,

> **BOX 2-3**
> **Third Party Policing in Oakland, California**
>
> This description of the Beat Health Program, initiated by the Oakland Police Department, is adapted from the researchers' report on the program (Mazzerole and Roehl, 1999, pp. 1–3). The program used civil remedies to control drug and disorder problems by focusing on the physical decay and property management conditions of specific commercial establishments, private homes, and rental properties. Police officers worked with city agency representatives to inspect targeted properties, coerce landowners to clean up blighted properties, post "no trespassing" signs, enforce municipal regulations and health and safety codes, and initiate court proceedings against property owners who failed to comply with civil law citations. Although the ultimate targets of the Beat Health program were offending individuals living or socializing in identified zones, program staff interacted primarily with nonoffending third parties—landlords, business owners, and private property owners—responsible for the property.
>
> The mandate of the Beat Health Unit was to reduce drug and disorder problems throughout Oakland. The Beat Health Unit made preliminary visits to sites that came to its attention due to a large number of calls for service, narcotics arrests on the property, special requests from community groups for police assistance, or citizen complaints. During the preliminary site visit, a Beat Health team sought to establish a relationship with the site manager or with anyone who was thought to have a stake in improving conditions at the location.
>
> In addition to working closely with city agencies during inspections, the Beat Health teams often worked with police department neighborhood service coordinators, community groups, merchant associations, and other units of the Oakland Police Department. A substantial portion of the intervention activity involved working with and pressuring third parties (primarily owners, parents of grown children, and property managers) to make changes to properties that had drug and disorder problems. Although much of the contact with property owners was to gather information, many property owners were directly involved in problem-solving interventions.
>
> Beat Health teams suggested ways to increase security, made referrals to city agencies for assistance, discussed relevant legal ordinances and safety code responsibilities (including landlords' rights and tenants' responsibilities), encouraged owners to voluntarily fix and clean up properties, and supported owners in their intervention and prevention efforts. The Beat Health Unit also offered training to landlords and owners in screening tenants and effectively managing rental properties. The officers maintained contact with property owners throughout the intervention period (about 6 months) to ensure that problems were mitigated. In these ways, police analyzed the problem and implemented a solution that posed an alternative to conventional crime-control strategies
>
> SOURCE: Adapted from Mazerolle and Roehl (1999, pp. 1–3).

p. 197). For example, police in southern California used regulatory policy to promote responsible management among operators of nuisance motels (Bichler, Schmerler, and Enriquez, 2013). In Oakland, California, police implemented the "Beat Health" third party policing program to abate drug and disorder problems (see Box 2-3). Still other third party policing programs may seek to engage business improvement districts in crime prevention activities, such as coordinating private security services to complement public security (Cook, 2011; Cook and MacDonald, 2011).

Third party policing interventions (and the problem-solving policing approach more generally) could also include strategic partnerships with private security entities. For example, there are now approximately 1,000 private Business Improvement Districts in the United States, funded by special assessments on owners within the boundaries of the district, that supplement public services.

STRATEGIES FOR A PERSON-FOCUSED APPROACH

In the standard model of policing, the primary goal of police was to identify and arrest offenders *after* crimes had been committed. But beginning in the early 1970s, research evidence began to suggest that the police could be more effective if they focused on a relatively small number of chronic offenders (Pate, Bowers, and Parks, 1976). Similar to the research showing a concentration of crime at certain microgeographic locations, Wolfgang, Figlio, and Sellin (1972) found that a large proportion of crime was committed by a small proportion of offenders: just 6 percent of the juveniles they studied were responsible for 55 percent of juvenile arrests. These findings—the existence of a substantial, identifiable group of chronic offenders—were replicated in a series of other studies of criminal behavior (see, e.g., Farrington and West, 1993; Howell et al., 1995; Blumstein, Farrington, and Moitra, 1985).

These studies led to innovations in policing based on the logic model that crime prevention outcomes could be enhanced by focusing policing efforts on the small number of offenders who account for a large proportion of crime. From this perspective, the standard model of generalized investigation and prevention was deficient because it spread resources too broadly across the general criminal population. Specific deterrence could be gained by focusing on very high rate offenders who are responsible for a large part of the crime problem, and general deterrence would be enhanced by the message that high rate offenders are the focus of concentrated police activities. Such programs, at least in their development, rely not on the social or demographic characteristics of offenders as a method of allocation of police resources but rather on official data about crime.

Focused Deterrence

Offender-focused deterrence, also known as pulling levers, is a strategy that attempts to deter crime among a particular offending population and is often implemented in combination with interventions typical of a problem-solving approach (Braga and Weisburd, 2012). Focused deterrence allows police to increase the certainty, swiftness, and severity of punishment in innovative ways. The first focused deterrence intervention, Operation Ceasefire, was implemented to reduce youth homicide in Boston during the mid-1990s (Braga et al., 2001; Kennedy, Piehl, and Braga, 1996). This well-known program was designed to prevent violence by reaching out directly to gangs, saying explicitly that violence would no longer be tolerated, and backing up that message by "pulling every lever" legally available when violence occurred (Kennedy, 1997). Box 2-4 gives a more detailed description of Operation Ceasefire. Central to the strategy is direct interaction with offenders and communication of clear incentives for compliance and consequences for criminal activity. Most offender-focused deterrence interventions target various criminally active groups and networks, including gangs and drug crews.

Focused deterrence interventions target specific behaviors by the relatively small number of chronic offenders who are viewed as highly vulnerable to criminal justice sanctions. The strategy aims to directly confront offenders—for example, by telling them that continued offending will not be tolerated and informing them how the system will respond if they violate behavior standards. An important aspect of the strategy is often the use of face-to-face meetings with offenders. McGarrell and colleagues (2006) suggested that these types of direct communication, followed up with appropriate enforcement responses to continuing violations, may cause offenders to reassess the risks of committing crimes. It is likely that other complementary crime-control mechanisms are at work in a focused deterrence strategy (see, e.g., Braga, 2012). Focused deterrence typically is incorporated in a hybrid intervention or program with elements of both the problem-solving and community-based approaches. According to Braga and Weisburd (2012, pp. 349–350), "the emphasis is not only on increasing the risk of offending but also on decreasing opportunity structures for violence, deflecting offenders away from crime, increasing the collective efficacy of communities, and increasing the legitimacy of police actions."

There have also been examples of focused deterrence applied to street drug markets and individual repeat offenders. In High Point, North Carolina, the Drug Market Intervention aimed focused deterrence at eliminating public forms of drug dealing such as street markets and crack houses by warning dealers, buyers, and their families that enforcement was imminent (Kennedy and Wong, 2009; Corsaro et al., 2012; Saunders et

> **BOX 2-4**
> **Focused Deterrence in Boston: Operation Ceasefire**
>
> Operation Ceasefire was implemented by the Boston Police Department during the mid-1990s in an effort to tackle rising youth gun violence. A small population of chronic offenders involved in neighborhood-based groups was identified as responsible for more than 60 percent of youth homicide in Boston.
>
> As part of the Operation Ceasefire Program, the police and their law enforcement, social service, and community partners reached out directly to the identified gangs, explicitly warning them that violence would no longer be tolerated. The warnings were given teeth by applying every legally available enforcement response when violence occurred. For example, the police and other law enforcement agencies sought to:
>
> > . . . disrupt street drug activity, focus police attention on low-level street crimes such as trespassing and public drinking, serve outstanding warrants, cultivate confidential informants for medium- and long-term investigations of gang activities, deliver strict probation and parole enforcement, seize drug proceeds and other assets, ensure stiffer plea bargains and sterner prosecutorial attention, request strong bail terms (and enforce them), and bring potentially severe federal investigative and prosecutorial attention to gang-related drug and gun activity. (Braga and Weisburd, 2015, p. 57)
>
> At the same time, gang members were offered constructive help from youth workers, probation and parole officers, and in time even from churches and other community groups. But these service partners also reinforced the message that violence was no longer acceptable to the community and that gang members' typical justifications for violence were wrong. The partners in Operation Ceasefire delivered these messages across multiple venues for contact with gang members, including formal meetings (known as "forums" or "call-ins"), the contacts that individual police officers and probation officers had with gang members, meetings with gang members in detention at juvenile facilities, and service partners who worked directly through outreach to the gangs. In this way, the police focused on a narrow problem (gang violence) by targeting specific offenders (gang members).

al., 2015). This intervention targeted individual "overt drug markets" and established a joint police-community partnership that identified individual offenders and notified them of the consequences they faced if they continued dealing in drugs. This partnership also provided support services for these individuals through a community-based resource coordinator, while conveying the message that there now was an uncompromising community norm opposed to drug dealing.

In a focused deterrence intervention in Chicago, parolees who had been involved in gun- and gang-related violent crimes and were returning to one of the highly dangerous neighborhoods selected for the intervention were required to attend "offender notification forums." The forums informed them that as convicted felons, they were vulnerable to federal firearms laws with stiff mandatory minimum sentences. The forums also offered social services and included talks by community members and ex-offenders (Papachristos, Meares, and Fagan, 2007). The communications process at these forums was intentionally designed to promote positive normative behavior change by engaging the parolees in ways they were likely to view as procedurally just, rather than simply threatening.

Stop, Question, and Frisk

SQF has become one of the most controversial proactive policing strategies because police directly interact with citizens, using intrusive police powers. The legal authority to perform individual SQF is grounded in the landmark 1968 Supreme Court decision *Terry v. Ohio*. *Terry v. Ohio* and related decisions have concluded that police may stop a person based upon a "reasonable suspicion" that they are about to commit, are in the process of committing, or have committed a crime.[9] If a separate "reasonable suspicion" that the person is armed and dangerous exists, the police may conduct a frisk of the stopped individual. Given this standard, although situational factors are also relevant, *Terry v. Ohio* stops cannot be conducted lawfully without reference to the behavior of the individual being stopped. When carried out as a proactive policing strategy, an SQF program relies upon the legal authority granted in *Terry v. Ohio* and its progeny to engage in frequent stops in which suspects are questioned about their activities, frisked if possible, and often searched, usually with consent.[10]

Stops, frisks, and arrests, whether reactive or proactive, are subject to the same legal standards. Traditionally, stops, frisks, and arrests are tools police use reactively as a means to address a particular crime they witness or have reported to them or to investigate specific suspicious behavior. In this context, harmless or ambiguous conduct often will not justify the resources that would be necessary to address it, and officers leave such conduct unaddressed rather than intrude on individuals. By contrast, as a proactive policing strategy, departments often employ coercion more expansively and to promote forward-looking, preventative ends. This strategic use of Fourth Amendment doctrine is legal (*Whren v. United States* 517

---

[9] The Supreme Court has not ruled as to whether *Terry v. Ohio* can be used to investigate a completed misdemeanor, and it has suggested that it might not be permissible. However, *Terry* can be used as the legal justification for police to investigate a completed felony (*United States v. Hensley*, 469 U.S. 221 [1985]); see also *Navarette v. California* (572 U.S. ___ [2014]).

[10] Police may perform a frisk (or pat-down) on an individual if, during a lawful stop, they have reasonable suspicion that the person is armed and dangerous. A frisk is a limited search of the person's outer clothing for the purpose of discovering weapons (*Terry v. Ohio*, 392 U.S. 1 [1968]).

U.S. 806 [1996]). See Chapter 3 of this report for a full discussion of the legality of SQF. Nevertheless, in this way, some deterrence-oriented proactive strategies generate incentives for officers to conduct more frequent and intrusive, and therefore liberty-reducing, searches and seizures, aided by the rules developed by the U.S. Supreme Court for reactive policing, than reactive policing would generate.[11] Today, police executives regard SQF as an important crime prevention tool (see, e.g., Terkel, 2013).

SQF programs often involve blanketing areas within a city with pedestrian stops to reduce violent crime, as was the case in Philadelphia (see Box 2-5). It is often assumed in these programs that such stops play a key role in deterring potential offenders, as it raises the probability of being stopped and searched by the police. Other cities have used SQF programs in an attempt to change perceived risks of engaging in particular crimes, such as gun and drug crimes.

Although we have categorized SQF as a strategy for a person-focused approach because of the legal requirement that police focus on the behaviors of specific people to undertake a stop, SQF has also been used as a proactive policing tactic aimed at controlling and preventing crime at specific places. For example, Weisburd, Telep, and Lawton (2014) found that SQF in New York City had been implemented as a type of hot spots policing tactic, where SQF stops were concentrated on specific high-crime streets. Kansas City, Pittsburgh, and Indianapolis have used SQF practices to address gun crime at hot spots (see Sherman, Shaw, and Rogan, 1995; Cohen and Ludwig, 2003; McGarrell et al., 2001).

Some scholars argue that the SQF strategy has negative consequences for communities (see Chapter 5 of this report; see also Fagan et al., 2010), and it has been criticized for targeting the young, non-Whites, and specific neighborhoods (see Gelman, Fagan, and Kiss, 2007; Ridgeway, 2007; Stoud, Fine, and Fox, 2011; see also Chapter 7 of this report). In New York City, a court found the SQF program of the New York Police Department (NYPD) to be unconstitutional and restricted the NYPD's use of the strategy. See Chapter 3 of this report for a discussion of SQF's legality.

STRATEGIES FOR A COMMUNITY-BASED APPROACH

The community-based approach seeks to enlist and mobilize people who are not police in the prevention of crime and the production of public safety. However, in this approach, the focus is generally not on specific actors such as business owners but the community more generally. While community-based strategies may incorporate practices typical of the other

---

[11] Proactive strategies that emphasize narrowly focused deterrence are unlikely to have this effect.

> **BOX 2-5**
> **Stop, Question, and Frisk (SQF) in Philadelphia**
>
> In 2008, Mayor Michael Nutter ordered the Philadelphia Police Department (PPD) to increase its use of SQF, arguing that the program of frequent stops would remove guns from the streets and combat a "crime emergency" in certain Philadelphia neighborhoods. In 2009, the police made 253,276 pedestrian stops in a city of 1.526 million—a ratio of one SQF stop for every six inhabitants (Goode, 2012).
>
> After complaints of police abuse, the American Civil Liberties Union of Pennsylvania (ACLU-PA) filed suit against the city in 2010. The suit argued that the PPD was using race and ethnicity to stop individuals without sufficient individualized reasonable suspicion. The lawsuit resulted in a settlement in 2011 between the ACLU-PA and the city, requiring the PPD to make changes to its SQF policy including recording data on stops and frisks (including recording where the stop occurred, the reason for the stop, and the outcome of the stop), creating a monitoring system to review the data, and refraining from certain problematic SQF practices (La Vigne et al., 2014).
>
> Following the settlement agreement, the ACLU-PA has continued to monitor the PPD's use of SQF and has released a series of court-mandated reports on its findings. Each quarter, the ACLU-PA is provided data from approximately 3,200 randomly selected pedestrian and car stops but reviews only the pedestrian stops. ACLU-PA counsel and trained law students independently review each pedestrian stop and frisk under guidelines incorporating standards set by the U.S. Supreme Court. The reviewers take at face value whatever reason for a stop and frisk is stated by the police officer who made the stop, but they assess whether the stated reason comports with legal standards. Using this procedure, in its sixth and most recent report released on March 22, 2016, the ACLU-PA reported that for the first and second quarters of 2015, 33 percent of all stops and 42 percent of all frisks were still being conducted without reasonable suspicion.*
>
> ---
> *See *Bailey v. City of Philadelphia*, Plaintiffs' Sixth Report to Court and Monitor on Stop and Frisk Practices: Fourth Amendment Issues. Available: https://www.aclupa.org/download_file/view_inline/2674/198 [December 2017].

proactive policing approaches, such as problem-solving or place-based policing, their key orientation is toward the community. In some cases, community-based strategies rely on enhancing the community's ability to engage in collective action to do something about crime. This is often referred to as the "collective efficacy" of the community (Sampson and Raudenbush, 1999). In other cases, the strategy seeks to change community evaluations of the legitimacy of police actions (Tyler, 2004). These objectives are often intertwined.

Much of 20th century police reform attempted to assign the police the core responsibility for crime control (Fogelson, 1977; Kelling and Moore, 1988; Walker, 1977), whereas community policing reformers sought to encourage the clientele of the police to become "coproducers" of crime control, dealing not only with the immediate concerns of a specific incident but also with underlying issues that may aggravate crime problems. As the 2004 National Research Council report on policing stated, "community policing may be seen as [a] reaction to the standard models of policing. . . . While the standard model of policing has relied primarily on the resources of the police and its traditional law enforcement powers, community policing suggests a reliance on a more community-based crime control that draws not only on the resources of the police but also on the resources of the public" (National Research Council, 2004, p. 233).

The impetus for community-based policing strategies came in part from conflicts between the police and the public that emerged in the 1960s and 1970s, especially among non-White and disadvantaged communities (see Chapter 1). The approach's logic model developed from a growing research base that suggested that the community was key to crime control (Reiss and Tonry, 1986; Skogan, 1992). One early indication that community involvement was important for controlling crime came from a large-scale study conducted in the late 1970s of rapid response to emergency calls to the police (Spelman and Brown, 1981). Although the study overall found that increasing police response time would not lead to crime reductions, the researchers also concluded that citizen willingness to call the police was key to any potential crime prevention gains. Similarly, a series of studies in the 1970s and 1980s pointed to the importance of citizen cooperation in increasing police effectiveness (see, e.g., Reiss, 1971; Spelman and Brown, 1984).

Community-Oriented Policing

At its outset, community policing did not originate as a proactive approach to solving *crime problems*. In its original formulation, its proponents sought to give greater priority to a wide range of order maintenance and public service functions that had not been given priority during the "professional" reform era (Goldstein, 1987; Greene and Mastrofski, 1988; Kelling and Moore, 1988; Rosenbaum, 1994).While it may be argued that service to citizens was always an important part of American police work (see, e.g., Wilson, 1968), community-based policing legitimated a set of roles for the police that had previously been unrecognized or underappreciated, especially in the way that governments measured police performance (crime, arrest, and clearance rates). In short, community-based policing at the outset did not necessarily define crime reduction, at least in terms of traditional measures, as a central element of its success (see, e.g., Klockars,

1988; Skolnick and Bayley, 1986). However, crime control became a key goal of community policing over time, making it attractive to national, state, and local community leaders sensitive to the high political priority crime control had assumed in the 1980s and 1990s.

As a strategy focusing on a community-based proactive crime prevention approach, community-oriented policing tries to address and mitigate community problems (crime or otherwise) for the future and to build social resilience, collective efficacy, and empowerment to strengthen the infrastructure for the coproduction of safety and crime prevention. These objectives reflect a variety of program theories (variants of the approach's logic model as stated in Table 2-1) about the crime-prevention mechanism at work in community-oriented policing. For example, with practices such as neighborhood watch or police–citizen patrols, increased guardianship may create a deterrent effect. Guardianship may also be the result of building collective efficacy in neighborhoods, so that citizens feel empowered to apply informal social controls to risky behavior, suspicious incidents, or unsupervised youth. Skogan (1986, 1990) discussed community-oriented policing as playing an important role in reducing fear and thereby lowering the chances of citizen withdrawal and isolation—two factors that, when left unchecked, may lead to further crime and disorder (see also the discussion below of broken windows policing).

Community-oriented policing has been described as both a philosophy of policing and an organizational strategy (National Research Council, 2004; Greene, 2000) in which police agencies embrace a vision of their function that is larger than just reacting to and processing crime (Skogan and Hartnett, 1997). This vision generally entails the inclusion by police agencies of community groups and citizens in coproducing safety, crime prevention, and solutions to local concerns. Despite its longevity as a reform—it dates back more than three decades—there is still considerable variation in how community-oriented policing is defined. Nevertheless, a degree of consensus seems to have formed around treating it as an organizational strategy that embraces three core processes and structures (Skogan, 2006b): (1) citizen involvement in identifying and addressing public safety concerns, (2) the decentralization of decision making to develop responses to locally defined problems, and (3) problem solving. Each of these three elements of community-oriented policing could be implemented independently. What gives problem solving and decentralization a *community-oriented policing* character is when these elements are embedded in the community engagement (often called "partnership") element. The inclusion of problem solving as an element again points to the overlap across the committee's four approaches to proactive policing (refer to Table 2-1).

Early manifestations and research on community-oriented policing focused on tactics such as foot patrol, neighborhood watch, and community meetings or newsletters. However, as noted above, the definition expanded to include practices from the problem-solving approach. More recently, community-oriented policing has encompassed such notions as building collective efficacy and empowerment (see Sampson, 2011); procedural justice and legitimacy (see Tyler, 1990);[12] and efforts to increase police accountability through citizen review boards, body-worn cameras, and improved complaint processes.

In 2014, the Major Cities Chiefs Association (MCCA), whose membership represents the largest police agencies in North America and the United Kingdom, conducted an electronic survey to better understand the community policing practices of its members. Of the 75 North American member agencies, 42 responded to the survey. Table 2-3 shows the number and percentage of departments who reported that they engaged in specific community-oriented policing practices. Some of these practices fall under the committee's definition of proactive policing, but others do not. It should be noted that this list is not exhaustive of the sorts of tactics and activities that have been characterized as "community-oriented policing" (see Roth, Roehl, and Johnson, 2004).

Departments define and deploy what this committee means by a strategy of community-oriented policing in different ways; some view it as the responsibility of a special community-policing unit, while others view it as an organizational philosophy. Many agencies do both. (See Box 2-6 for a description of community-oriented policing in Chicago.) According to the 2014 MCCA survey, responding departments allocated personnel to perform community-oriented tasks using centralized, decentralized, or hybrid structures. Seventeen percent of agencies ($n = 7$) used a centralized structure where only full-time community policing officers were deployed to conduct community-oriented policing activities; 21 percent ($n = 9$) used a decentralized structure, which considered community-oriented policing exclusively a part of patrol officer duties; and the majority of respondents (62%; $n = 26$) used a hybrid structure with a combination of dedicated full-time staff, patrol officers, and special units engaging in activities aimed at community-oriented policing objectives (Scrivner and Stephens, 2015, p. 9).

Procedural Justice Policing

A more recent organizational innovation with a focus on the community-based approach is procedural justice policing. Like community-oriented policing, this strategy also assumes that the police cannot succeed in their efforts to control crime without the support of the public. However, in its efforts to change the public's relationship with the police, procedural

---

[12] Procedural justice and legitimacy are discussed in the next section.

TABLE 2-3 Prevalence of Use of Community-Policing Practices by North American Police Agencies Responding to the 2014 MCCA Survey

Community-Policing Practices	Number of Departments	Percentage of Departments
Problem Solving	42	100.0
Officer Representation at Community Meetings	42	100.0
Community Engagement	41	97.6
Bicycle Patrols	39	92.9
Citizen Volunteers	36	85.7
Training—Recruit	35	83.3
Foot Patrols	34	81.0
Citizen Ride-Along	32	76.2
Citizen Police Academy	32	76.2
Training—In-Service	31	73.8
Block Watch	28	66.7
POP Projects Assigned/Monitored at Precinct/Division Level	26	61.9
Neighborhood Store Front Offices	19	45.2
Citizen Neighborhood Patrols	19	45.2
Other Special Units	16	38.1

NOTE: MCAA = Major Cities Chiefs Assocation, POP = problem-oriented policing.
SOURCE: Scrivner and Stephens (2015, p. 10).

justice policing focuses on how the police treat the public as individuals in everyday encounters.[13] Whereas community-oriented policing often focuses on giving the community the *outcomes* that it wants (e.g., more safety, more noncrime services, greater responsiveness to personal needs), procedural justice focuses on giving citizens police decision *processes* that manifest demonstrations of police fairness and regard for a person's dignity. Fair and considerate police processes are presumed to render even unpleasant outcomes (an arrest or citation) less objectionable to the person on the receiving end.

Also, unlike community-oriented policing, procedural justice policing does not seek to enlist the public in coproductive activities during these routine encounters but rather seeks to impress upon the citizen and the

---

[13] Conceivably, this strategy could include many other occasions when police and public interact, such as neighborhood association meetings attended by the police.

> **BOX 2-6**
> **Community-Oriented Policing in Chicago**
>
> Chicago engaged in a departmentwide community policing effort that was monitored by outside researchers from the mid-1990s until 2004 (Skogan, 2006b). In this effort, the entire city and all of the people in the department were integrated into the community policing plan. A key feature was the decentralization of service delivery to the neighborhood level to establish a "turf orientation" (e.g., keeping officers working in the same beat rather than dispatching them out of the beat). Another was stimulation and reinforcement of community involvement (through police-coordinated "beat meetings" with neighborhood residents and campaigns to increase citizen participation in a variety of civic activities). The problem-solving element was introduced by providing training for both officers and neighborhood residents, and officers were expected to set aside time from answering calls for service to work on broader problems identified as priorities. A strong underlying theme of these problem interventions incorporated the "broken windows" perspective (discussed below) of giving priority to the reduction of physical and social incivilities in the neighborhoods. Finally, the Chicago plan called for police to play a key role in initiating and facilitating teamwork with other city service-delivery agencies to alleviate neighborhood problems and address priority issues.
>
> The Chicago Police Department faced many challenges in implementing key elements of the community policing program. This was due to things, such as insufficient resources, rank-and-file culture, skepticism of middle managers, bureaucratic inertia, the competing demands of a new management system (Compstat), and so on. For example, the department attempted to keep community policing "beat team" officers mostly in their assigned beats so that they could develop greater knowledge of their beat and stronger relations with its residents (Skogan, 2006b, pp. 61–62). However, it took several years for the department even to have the capacity to measure the implementation of this tactic. By 1998, the department had established that it was falling slightly short of the 70 percent target for dispatches of beat team officers to calls within their own neighborhood (66% accomplished).
>
> Another challenge was keeping officers assigned to the same beat over an extended time period, rather than rotating them to other beats or job assignments. Skogan (2006b, p. 64) judged that only 36 percent of Chicago's beats had sufficient officer assignment stability to repeatedly show up at the monthly neighborhood beat meetings and to be a familiar face to the community members in attendance.

wider community that the police exercise their authority in legitimate ways.[14] According to the logic model of this strategy, when citizens feel that policing is legitimate, they are more inclined not only to defer to police

---

[14]Legitimacy, within the context of the procedural justice literature, is "a property of an authority or institution that leads people to feel that authority or institution is entitled to be deferred to and obeyed" (Sunshine and Tyler, 2003, p. 514).

authority in the present instance but also to collaborate with police in the future, even to the extent of being more inclined not to violate the law. That is, procedural justice policing is based upon the idea that police shape the evaluative judgments citizens make about police performance (i.e., whether it is effective, fair, lawful), and these evaluations shape general orientations toward the police (i.e., police legitimacy). Legitimacy then shapes the behavior of citizens in terms of law abidingness, cooperation with authorities, and engagement in the community (see Chapter 5 of this report; see also Tyler, 2003). Therefore, when police engage in activities that promote procedural justice, they are presumed to enhance their perceived legitimacy not only among those who experience police contacts directly but also from a broader communication of their actions to the community more generally.

Procedural justice policing tries to encourage four main characteristics of police behavior that are viewed as affecting perceptions of police legitimacy: (1) Do they provide opportunities for voice, allowing members of the public to state their perspective or tell their side of the story before decisions are made? (2) Do they make decisions in ways that people regard as neutral, rule-based, consistent, and absent of bias? (3) Do they treat people with the dignity, courtesy, and respect that they deserve as human beings and as members of the community? (4) Do people believe that their motives are trustworthy and benevolent—that is, that the police are sincerely trying to do what is good for the people in the community?

The key to understanding the procedural justice strategy is that its elements focus on how people experience policing: whether they feel they have voice, whether they think the procedures are neutral, whether they feel respected, and whether they infer that the police are trustworthy. Trustworthiness is the key to accepting discretionary decisions, according to this logic model. The argument underlying the strategy is that the way people perceive these features of police action shapes whether people do or do not judge the police to be legitimate.

In deciding to include procedural justice as a proactive policing strategy, the committee recognized that many of the behaviors connected to procedural justice may also more generally be seen as a standard part of democratic policing (Nagin and Telep, 2017). Although the committee agrees with this position, it recognizes that procedural justice policing has been presented by its advocates not only as "good police behavior" but also as a strategic approach to policing that should increase police legitimacy, citizen compliance, order, and safety in police-public encounters and should reduce crime in the long run (see, e.g., Tyler, Goff, and MacCoun, 2015).

While it may be true that treating people with respect and fairness can be seen as part of overall good practice, in procedural justice policing the police modify their actions to consciously and deliberately mold the attitudes of the community in advance of events that might create conflict or crisis. Under the logic model informing this strategy, the police are instructed to do this in order to proactively influence what happens later. For example, the strategy may aim to create a climate in which the public is more willing to defer to police authority, in which people more willingly obey the law and help to solve crimes, and in which the public accepts that the police are acting with good intentions and should be given the benefit of the doubt in ambiguous situations. Sometimes such activities may come as a response to citizen calls for police service, and in this sense they may be seen as reactive. But they also may occur in community meetings or with other proactive contacts with the police. Moreover, even in responses to citizen requests for police service, under procedural justice policing police officers should seek to apply procedural justice principles not only to initiators of police responses but also to bystanders and offenders.

In this sense, the police act proactively by engaging in many types of actions designed to build a "reservoir of trust" in the community. Whatever the fit of procedural justice with democratic principles, procedural justice policing seeks to develop longer-term gains in terms of police legitimacy and crime. Advocates of this approach argue that an overarching focus on the principles of procedural justice is key to prevention and other outcomes. Indeed, it is sometimes presented as an alternative to other proactive policing strategies that focus on short-term crime-prevention gains:

> We argue that these changing goals and style reflect a fundamental tension between two models of policing: the currently dominant proactive risk management model, which focuses on policing to prevent crimes and makes promises of short-term security through the professional management of crime risks, and a model that focuses on building popular legitimacy by enhancing the relationship between the police and the public and thereby promoting the long-term goal of police community solidarity and, through that, public-police cooperation in addressing issues of crime and community order. (Tyler, Goff, and MacCoun, 2015, p. 603)

Until recently, procedural justice practices were not explicit objectives of particular policies and programs but rather were simply observed in their "natural" state as the product of discretionary choices made by individual police officers in specific police–public interactions (Mastrofski et al., 2016). The report of the President's Task Force on 21st Century Policing (2015) argued that procedural justice is an important aspect of building trust and legitimacy in communities, and therefore the task force called on departments to adopt procedural justice as a guiding principle. This call

> **BOX 2-7**
> **Procedural Justice Policing in King County, Washington**
>
> In 2012, the King County Sheriff's Office developed a procedural justice policing intervention in the context of its community-oriented policing program. The procedural justice training program sets expectations for how officers should communicate and interact with each other and the public. Using the L.E.E.D. model (Listen and Explain with Equity and Dignity), the training curriculum uses scenarios, discussions, and group exercises to demonstrate how principles of procedural justice can be applied to various interactions, not only with the public but also with other officers and colleagues.
>   Through the training program, the King County Sheriff's Office sought to make the concepts of procedural justice part of its culture by embracing the use of procedural justice principles both internally and externally. The agency began to actively engage employees in setting expectations; addressed employee performance concerns through student-centered training instead of exclusively through discipline; and refocused its hiring, training, and promotion policies to emphasize procedural justice and to reward those officers who embody its principles. During all interactions with the public, officers are required to apply the principles of procedural justice, using the L.E.E.D. model, as a method for gaining voluntary compliance and strengthening legitimacy (McCurdy and Bradley, 2013).

has led to the development of a larger number of programs and policing interventions that explicitly promote procedural justice.[15]

Box 2-7 describes how the King County, Washington, Sheriff's Office has implemented principles of procedural justice in its work.

Broken Windows Policing

Another strategy of the community-based approach uses a very different logic model for the problem of crime control. Broken windows policing sees the key to crime prevention as operating in the informal social controls within communities (Wilson and Kelling, 1982). Its focus, accordingly, is on how the police can reinforce and enhance such social controls, especially where informal social controls have become weak (see Weisburd et al.,

---

[15] Procedural justice policing can follow both an internal and external model. Internal procedural justice refers to practices within an agency and the relationships officers have with their colleagues and leaders. It follows the logic model that those officers who feel respected by their organization are more likely to bring this respect into their interactions with the public. External procedural justice focuses on the ways officers interact with the public and how the characteristics of those interactions shape the public's trust of the police (Tyler, 1990; Sunshine and Tyler, 2003; Haas et al., 2015).

2015). It shares with community-oriented and procedural justice policing a concern for community welfare and envisions a role for police in finding ways to strengthen community structures and processes that provide a degree of immunity from disorder and crime in neighborhoods. Unlike community-oriented policing, this strategy does not emphasize the co-productive collaborations of police and community as a mode of intervention; rather it focuses on what police should do to establish conditions that allow "natural" community entities to flourish and promote neighborhood order and social/economic vitality.

The concept of broken windows policing developed out of a Police Foundation study, the Newark Foot Patrol experiment (Police Foundation, 1981). The police officers walking patrol in the study were engaged in activities (e.g., closing down a bar early after being called twice to end brawls in that same bar) that might be seen as part of the policing task in the standard model of policing. However, from this study's results and drawing on earlier studies by Zimbardo (1969) and Zimbardo and Ebbesen (1969), Wilson and Kelling (1982) identified a link between social disorder and crime and suggested that the police ought to pay attention to many problems that may be seen as peripheral to the police function under the standard model. The broken windows hypothesis held that "untended" behavior (e.g., abandoned property, unruly youth behavior) could lead to the breakdown of community controls and that serious crime developed because the police and citizens did not work together to prevent urban decay and social disorder (Weisburd and Braga, 2006b, pp. 14–15).

According to Wilson and Kelling (1982, p. 31), "at the community level, disorder and crime are usually inextricably linked, in a kind of developmental sequence." The broken windows logic model posits an indirect pathway from disorder to crime through increased fear and, subsequently, the breakdown of informal social controls in the community. The fear-of-crime literature at the time provided fairly consistent support for a strong linkage between disorder and fear (Garofalo, 1981; Garofalo and Laub, 1978; Hunter, 1978; see Hinkle, 2013 for a review), and early studies in this area can in some sense be seen as supporting the broken windows logic model.

Diminished informal or community social controls are thus a key component of the logic model underlying the broken windows concept of crime control. Wilson and Kelling (1982) argued that disorder problems, and the resulting increased levels of fear, lead to withdrawal from the community. This withdrawal takes two forms: people moving away and the remaining residents becoming less likely to intervene in community affairs. "Untended" behavior also leads to the breakdown of community controls (Weisburd et al., 2015):

> A stable neighborhood of families who care for their homes, mind each other's children, and confidently frown on intruders can change, in a few years or even a few months, to an inhospitable and frightening jungle. A piece of property is abandoned, weeds grow up, a window is smashed. Adults stop scolding rowdy children; the children, emboldened, become more rowdy. Families move out, unattached adults move in. Teenagers gather in front of the corner store. The merchant asks them to move, they refuse. . . . Such an area is vulnerable to criminal invasion. Though it is not inevitable, it is more likely that here, rather than in places where people are confident they can regulate public behavior by informal controls, drugs will change hands, prostitutes will solicit, and cars will be stripped. (Wilson and Kelling, 1982, pp. 31–32)

The nature of police "broken windows" interventions varies from informal enforcement tactics (warnings, rousting disorderly people) to formal or more intrusive ones (arrests, citations, SQF), all intended either to disrupt the forces of disorder before they overwhelm a neighborhood's capacity for order maintenance or to restore afflicted neighborhoods to a level where community sources of order can now sustain it. The two most commonly implemented (separately or in combination) forms of broken windows policing have been the use of aggressive policing that uses misdemeanor arrests to disrupt disorderly social behavior to prevent crime (often referred to as "zero tolerance"[16]) (see Taylor, 2006; Cordner, 1998; Eck and Maguire, 2006; Skogan, 2006b; Skogan et al., 1999) and the use of problem-oriented or community-oriented policing methods to address disorderly conditions that might contribute to crime (see Kelling and Coles, 1996). Box 2-8 describes a zero tolerance version of broken windows policing that was implemented in New York City.

A broken windows strategy may also be used in conjunction with other proactive policing strategies. For example, in Jersey City, New Jersey, officers used aggressive order maintenance as a tactic to reduce violent crime at hot spots (Braga et al., 1999). Similarly, a broken windows strategy was used in Los Angeles, through the Los Angeles Police Department's Safer Cities Initiative, to target homeless encampments in the downtown "skid row" area that were believed to be linked to high rates of street crime and disorder. The tactics implemented for this initiative included breaking up encampments, issuing citations, making arrests, and maintaining a visible police presence in the area (Berk and MacDonald, 2010).

---

[16] However, Kelling and Sosa (2001) argued that the term "zero tolerance" is often used derisively to describe broken windows policing interventions in which officers consistently use discretion and routinely assess the circumstances surrounding offenses, and therefore, they argue, the use of the term may be inaccurate for these interventions.

> **BOX 2-8**
> **Broken Windows Policing in New York City**
>
> A broken windows policing strategy is sometimes called "zero tolerance policing." Zero tolerance policing was implemented in New York City in 1993 by Police Commissioner William Bratton. The goal of the policy was to prevent crime by stopping low-level disorder and petty offenses before they flourished and invited more serious crime.
>
> Using the broken windows logic model, Bratton instituted an aggressive citywide campaign to apprehend perpetrators of quality-of-life crimes, a campaign designed to "reclaim the public spaces of New York" (Bratton and Knobler, 1998, p. 228). To restore order in New York City, officers were instructed to make arrests for minor offenses, such as approaching a vehicle in traffic to wash its windshield, littering, panhandling, prostitution, public intoxication, urinating in public, vandalism, school truancy, and a variety of other misdemeanor public-order offenses (Eck and Maguire, 2000, p. 225). As part of the strategy, the NYPD's drug enforcement efforts targeted low- and middle-level drug dealers and encouraged drug enforcement arrests by patrol officers, allowing officers to seek warrants, make narcotics arrests, and target suspected drug dealers for quality-of-life violations (Bratton and Knobler, 1998, p. 227).
>
> Under this strategy, proactive enforcement increased dramatically. Misdemeanor arrests by the NYPD rose from 133,446 in 1993 to 205,277 in 1996, while misdemeanor complaints rose only slightly (Harcourt, 1998, p. 340).

THE DIFFUSION OF PROACTIVE POLICING ACROSS AMERICAN CITIES

To what extent have these four proactive policing approaches spread across the landscape of American policing? To answer that question, the committee drew on data collected from the National Police Research Platform (NPRP), PERF, and MCCA. The PERF and MCCA surveys have already been described earlier in this chapter.

Overall, it is clear that many departments claim to be using multiple proactive policing innovations. The NPRP, the most comprehensive and representative survey gathering this information, uses a diverse national sample of approximately 100 municipal police and sheriff's agencies, of which the majority are agencies that have between 100 and 3,000 sworn officers. Between October and December 2013, the NPRP conducted a survey of its participating agencies, asking knowledgeable persons within the organization to indicate whether specific innovations had been adopted, whether department policy regarding an adopted innovation had been established

TABLE 2-4 Innovations Adopted by Departments, with and without Formal Policy, from the 2013 National Police Research Platform (NPRP) Survey ($n = 76$)

Innovation	Departments Adopting with Formal Policy	Departments Adopting without Formal Policy	Total Departments Adopting (with or without formal policy)
Broken Windows Policing	59.2% ($n = 45$)	19.7% ($n = 15$)	78.9% ($n = 60$)
Problem-Oriented Policing	68.4% ($n = 52$)	13.2% ($n = 10$)	81.6% ($n = 62$)
Procedural Justice Policing	81.6% ($n = 62$)	7.9% ($n = 6$)	89.5% ($n = 68$)
Hot Spots Policing	75.0% ($n = 57$)	15.8% ($n = 12$)	90.8% ($n = 69$)
Community-Oriented Policing	90.8% ($n = 69$)	6.6% ($n = 5$)	97.4% ($n = 74$)

NOTE: The NPRP survey asks departments if they are engaged in "community policing." The survey's use of "community policing" is equivalent to the committee's articulation of "community-oriented policing."
SOURCE: Adapted from Mastrofski and Fridell (n.d., p. 2).

and, if so, in what year.[17] Seventy-six of the 100 police agencies completed the questionnaire.[18] Interestingly, the survey results suggest that there is very wide use of proactive policing in medium-to-large police agencies in the United States. Mastrofski and Fridell (n.d., p. 3) reported that three-quarters of the responding departments adopted at least 8 to 10 "innovations."[19] Table 2-4 lists the findings relevant to proactive policing.

The most commonly employed proactive policing innovation according to this survey was community-oriented policing, which more than 90 percent of agencies claim to be employing, supported by formal policy. Using the taxonomy adopted for this report, 9 of 10 local law enforcement agencies with more than 100 sworn officers reported in 2013 that they had adopted community-oriented policing with supporting formal policies (Mastrofski and Fridell, n.d.). Community-oriented policing became popular among police leaders in the 1990s (Roth, Roehl, and Johnson, 2004)

---

[17] The median number of sworn officers for the entire NPRP was 274; the median for the 2013 department-characteristics survey was 255.

[18] Although 24 NPRP agencies did not complete the survey, the profile of survey respondents did not differ markedly from the total NPRP sample (Mastrofski and Fridell, n.d., p. 1).

[19] The 2013 NPRP survey designated the following as innovations: evidence-based policing, video recording (CCTV), CompStat, broken windows policing, early intervention systems, problem-oriented policing, procedural justice policing, hot spots policing, crime analysis, and community policing (Mastrofski and Fridell, n.d., p. 3).

and was especially attractive because of the availability of federal grants, issued by the COPS Office, to support community-oriented policing programs (Reisig, 2010, p. 20). The popularity of this strategy has seemingly been sustained despite declining funding in the latter part of the 2000s.

Perhaps surprising, given the relatively later emergence of procedural justice policing on the American police reform agenda, an almost equal number of departments (89.5%) claim to have implemented practices for this strategy in their department. While the depth of involvement and commitment to these strategies cannot be gauged by the surveys, the data suggest that police agencies across the United States are concerned about police legitimacy (as defined in the procedural justice logic model) and view community-based policing interventions as key to their work.

Ninety-one percent of departments surveyed claimed to use hot spots policing, again pointing to very high penetration of this strategy in American policing. Problem-oriented policing was also widely noted, with about 82 percent of responding NPRP departments claiming to use this strategy. Use of broken windows policing was claimed by 79 percent of NPRP respondents.

PERF conducted the Future of Policing Survey in 2012. The survey instrument was distributed to 500 police departments across the country, and nearly 200 police departments responded. While the PERF Survey was directed at its membership, which generally consists of larger and more progressive police agencies, the results provide a picture of the use of proactive policing strategies similar to the NPRP results (see Table 2-5). In this case, community-oriented policing, problem-oriented policing, and directed patrols/focused deterrence were the strategies most commonly used. Targeting known offenders and hot spots policing were also common, with almost

TABLE 2-5 Prevalence of Use of Proactive Policing Strategies by Percentage of Agencies Responding to the 2012 Future of Policing Survey ($n = 200$)

Strategy	Current Use (%)
Community-Oriented Policing	93.7
Problem-Oriented Policing	88.9
Hot Spots Policing	79.9
Directed Police Patrols/Focused Deterrence	92.1
Targeting Known Offenders	79.3
Predictive Policing	38.2

SOURCE: Police Executive Research Forum (2014, p. 50).

TABLE 2-6 Police Departments in 2007: (1) Using Computers for Hot Spot Identification, (2) Using Community-Policing Officers, (3) with Separate Full-Time Community-Policing Units

Population Served	Percentage of Departments Using Computers for Hot Spot Identification	Percentage of Departments Using Community-Policing Officers	Percentage of Departments with Separate Full-Time Community-Policing Units
All Sizes	13	47	14
1,000,000 or More	92	100	85
500,000–999,999	100	97	61
250,000–499,999	80	98	61
100,000–249,999	66	94	61
50,000–99,999	56	87	58
25,000–49,999	31	69	33
10,000–24,999	19	50	17
2,500–9,999	9	42	7
2,499 or Fewer	5	39	9

SOURCE: Reaves (2010).

80 percent of departments claiming to use these strategies. Not surprisingly, predictive policing, which is a newer innovation, was less commonly employed.[20] Although the agencies affiliated with PERF do not constitute a representative sample of all U.S. police agencies or of any subset thereof (e.g., large agencies), they may serve as a good indicator of likely trends in the use of strategies among larger police agencies (see Koper, 2014, p. 126).

The largest and most representative of the surveys to provide information on proactive policing is the Law Enforcement Management and Administrative Statistics (LEMAS) Survey, administered by the Bureau of Justice Statistics (BJS). BJS collects data from a representative sample of local police departments and provides national estimates on a variety of agency characteristics. The survey is completed every 3 years. Table 2-6 displays the 2007 survey findings on hot spots and community policing,

---

[20] In addition, to date, most departments implementing predictive policing must first purchase predictive policing software. This upfront cost may slow adoption of the strategy.

TABLE 2-7 Police Departments in 2013 with Community-Policing Mission Components

Population Served	Percentage of Departments with Mission Statements with a Community-Policing Component
All Sizes	68
1,000,000 or More	86
500,000–999,999	97
250,000–499,999	91
100,000–249,999	87
50,000–99,999	91
25,000–49,999	87
10,000–24,999	81
2,500–9,999	74
2,499 or Fewer	50

SOURCE: Reaves (2015).

and Table 2-7 presents the 2013 survey findings on community policing.[21] One advantage of the LEMAS survey is that it allows one to look at the variability in policing strategies by department size—and the overall story that emerges from these findings is that the claimed use of proactive strategies declines as the size of departments declines.

The prevalence of SQF is not examined by any of the above surveys, possibly because few departments created formal policies or structures to implement it, or possibly because of the controversy surrounding use of this strategy.[22] However, one relevant survey data source, the 2011 BJS Police-Public Contact Survey, found that of the 62.9 million people ages 16 and older with one or more police contacts in 2011, 7.3 percent (4.59 million) reported the contact was an involuntary street stop or arrest or other involuntary contact (not an involuntary traffic stop).[23] Among those individuals reporting an involuntary contact, 19.1 percent (72,083 indi-

---

[21] BJS uses the term "community policing," which corresponds with the committee's use of the term "community-oriented policing," as both emphasize collaboration with communities, support through agency management structures, and problem solving (see Reaves, 2010, p. 26).

[22] Though SQF is not a formal strategy in most police departments, it is used by all police departments in response to reasonable-suspicion observations or calls for service.

[23] The Police-Public Contact Survey does not identify the police department with which the person interacted.

viduals) reported being searched or frisked (Langton and Durose, 2013, pp. 2, 11–12). Between 2003 and 2010, reported SQF stops in New York increased almost four-fold from 160,851 to about 600,000 (Weisburd, Telep, and Lawton, 2014). At its peak in 2011, the NYPD reported 685,000 SQFs (for a population of 8.5 million).[24] Philadelphia and Los Angeles also saw substantial increases in pedestrian stops made by the police in the first decade of the 21st century. In Philadelphia, police reported 250,000 stops (in a city of 1.5 million) in 2009, double the number in 2007. Los Angeles reported 244,038 stops (in a city of 3.85 million) in 2008, double the number of stops in 2002 (Jones-Brown, Stoudt, and Moran, 2013).

These data tell us that many of the proactive policing approaches described in this chapter are not isolated programs used by a select group of agencies but rather a set of strategies that have been diffused across the landscape of American policing. Although the surveys are informative and present a general picture of American policing, especially among large departments, they do not offer a complete picture. For example, it is not known with certainty what motivates police organizations to embrace these innovations. One hypothesis is that these adoptions are motivated by "technical" concerns, such as a desire to reduce crime and to create and maintain safe communities (Mastrofski and Uchida, 1993; National Research Council, 2004, pp. 308–312). Police departments may also be motivated by federal funding incentives or in response to federal litigation (see Chapter 3 for a discussion of the U.S. Department of Justice's litigation strategy).[25] Still another perspective, sometimes termed "institutional theory," suggests that the motivation is the pursuit of legitimacy among one's peers and support from an organization's stakeholders. According to this hypothesis, police leaders may adopt strategies in the absence of hard evidence that they work in a technical sense (or even in the face of evidence that they do not work) simply because they perceive that their peers, especially high-visibility leaders in the field, are touting those strategies or using them. And this motivation, according to institutional theory advocates, can account for the rapid diffusion of certain police innovations in the past few decades (Weisburd et al., 2003; Willis, Mastrofski, and Weisburd, 2007). Where institutional pressures are strong for adoption, there can be a tendency to garner the benefits of "being on board" with the innovation without having fully implemented it.

---

[24] That figure declined to 191,851 SQF incidents in 2013, and further declined to 22,565 SQF stops in 2015, as a result of court challenges and a changing political environment. See http://www.nyclu.org/content/stop-and-frisk-data [May 2017]. Chapter 3 of this report discusses *Floyd v. City of New York* (2013).

[25] As described above, for example, community-oriented policing was an especially attractive innovation for police departments because of the availability of federal grants, issued by the COPS Office, to support community-oriented policing programs (Reisig, 2010, p. 20).

These surveys of police agencies also do not collect information relevant for determining with confidence the fidelity with which each strategy was implemented, how frequently it is actually used, or the scope of its use (how many people use it) within the department (Maguire and Mastrofski, 2000). Moreover, it is unclear whether departments consistently report their practices across surveys. Systematic data are lacking on how many resources (e.g., staffing levels) are devoted to each proactive strategy; also lacking are systematic data on how they are targeted.

Further complicating researchers' ability to estimate the prevalence of proactive policing approaches is that the standard way to calculate staffing levels for a given proactive strategy is to tally the number of officers assigned to a unit charged with that strategy. However, the problem with this estimation is that usually the officers assigned to engage in that proactive strategy are also charged with engaging in many other activities, and agency records do not readily distinguish proactive-program efforts from other efforts. For example, officers assigned to specialist community-based policing or problem-solving units also may have responsibilities for responding to calls for service (reactive policing). And officers whose basic job assignment is traditional reactive patrol in the same neighborhood may also take opportunities during their discretionary time to engage in community policing and problem solving.

Even thoroughly researched proactive projects (e.g., Skogan, 2006b, pp. 59–64) do not provide much information on the "dosage" of staff time and activities (Mastrofski and Willis, 2010, p. 83). In the few instances where detailed time-management studies have been executed via systematic observation by researchers, the finding is that although community-policing specialists spent more time on community-policing and problem-solving activities than generalist patrol officers in the same department, the norm for community-policing specialists remained the traditional, reactive encounter (Parks et al., 1999; Smith, Novak, and Frank, 2001). Surveys that simply gather department staffers' general impressions of how much officers engage in a given strategy are vague or even misleading. New methods are therefore necessary to determine the prevalence, scope, and frequency of the use of various policing innovations throughout law enforcement agencies in the United States. We return to this issue in our concluding chapter, where we discuss the committee's recommendations for new data collection on proactive policing.

CONCLUSION

Each of the four approaches to proactive policing identified by the committee is derived from a different logic model, each focusing on a different method for preventing crime and disorder. A place-based approach seeks to capitalize on empirical findings about the concentration of crime in small microgeographies. A problem-solving approach assumes that when the police focus on solving specific problems, rather than applying broadly defined generalized strategies, greater crime-prevention gains will be achieved. In a person-focused approach, empirical data on the concentration of crimes among a small part of the criminal population form the key element of the logic model. And finally, with a community-based approach, the importance of the community in solving crime problems is the primary logic model of prevention. In practice, these approaches often entail overlapping police strategies and programs in the field, an issue that we will turn to in later chapters, as the committee assesses the impacts of proactive policing that are more difficult to isolate and examine. One conclusion that can be drawn from reviewing these approaches is that they are, overall, used widely in American policing. The widespread use of proactive policing practices makes careful assessment of their consequences for crime, communities, legality, and bias and discrimination particularly important.

3

Law and Legality

This chapter examines the relationship between proactive policing and the law. Supporters of proactive policing strategies that are intended to build community relationships, such as community-oriented policing and procedural justice policing, suggest that these strategies will help protect legal values and lead to less law-breaking by police. Critics sometimes argue that proactive policing—through strategies such as hot spots policing; stop, question, and frisk (SQF); and broken windows policing—lead police officers and departments to violate the law (see, e.g., Rosenbaum, 2006; Kochel, 2011). In either case, law is a critical constraint on policing; however effective a policing practice may be in reducing or preventing crime, it is impermissible if it violates the law.

Proactive policing, as defined in Chapter 1, is rarely forbidden by law. The proactive policing practices discussed in this report generally are law enforcement strategies or tactics, and occasionally, higher-level philosophies of policing.[1] Law primarily regulates individual acts by officers and the decisions and policies set by municipalities and departments that guide these acts; the law neither encourages nor discourages particular strategies or philosophies. Nevertheless, since some proactive policing strategies are implemented through common sets of policies and acts, and those policies and acts are governed by federal, state, and local law, the law governs proactive policing strategies indirectly. Since different kinds of proactive strate-

---

[1] The logic models discussed in Chapter 2 for the four proactive policing approaches, including the associated primary objective and key ways to accomplish the objective shown in Table 2-1, are examples of philosophies of policing.

gies may be implemented with similar police action, and proactive strategies are often implemented in a variety of ways, proactive strategies based on the same logic model may raise disparate concerns, and strategies based on different logic models may raise similar issues. Moreover, proactive strategies may vary in how much they raise legal concerns, depending on what activities are used to implement them. In light of these considerations, this chapter highlights proactive strategies with significant legal implications rather than considering each proactive strategy by its logic model.

The committee considered several ways that law and proactive policing might interact. First, since constitutional and statutory law regulates police activities that might be used to implement a proactive strategy, a strategy could cause violations of law by increasing the probability that police action falls outside the boundaries of existing legal constraints. Second, legal rules concerning permissible conduct, or legal consequences for violations such as those arising from civil suits and criminal prosecutions of officers, could shape departmental and officer decision making about whether and how to conduct proactive policing. Third, even if police action pursuant to proactive policing does not violate the law, it may undermine legal values and principles such as privacy, bodily integrity, autonomy, or accountability, or it may foster inequality in ways that generate public concern. This public concern could in turn be the basis for changing the law to expand regulation of proactive policing. Fourth, some proactive strategies could *reduce* opportunities for lawbreaking by the police or increase incentives for police compliance with the law.

There are other ways that proactive policing and law interact that were not central to the committee's charge and therefore were not considered by the committee. Most notably, law sometimes promotes particular proactive policies. The U.S. Department of Justice (DOJ), for example, promotes community policing through litigation by its Civil Rights Division against police departments for patterns and practices of constitutional violations, leading to enforceable settlements that mandate implementing community policing. The Office of Community Oriented Policing Services (COPS) in DOJ also awards grants promoting community-oriented policing and procedural justice policing pursuant to federal legislation.

This chapter comprises several parts. Since the most important legal constraints on proactive policing are the Fourth Amendment and the Equal Protection Clause of the U.S. Constitution, the first two sections of the chapter describe ways proactive policing interacts with these constitutional rights and related statutory provisions. This discussion of legal rights and proactive policing is largely based on court decisions, federal investigations, and non-empirical legal scholarship because the limited existing empirical research does not permit strong conclusions about whether proactive strategies lead to constitutional violations. The third section considers the implications of the major remedial mechanisms the law uses to induce police compliance with constitutional rights, in order to consider the effects legal consequences might have on the means by which proactive policing strategies are implemented. In addition to Fourth Amendment and Equal Protection law, proactive strategies must comply with a diverse array of other federal, state, and local law that regulates the police. The fourth section therefore considers some of these other rules and, more broadly, discusses ways that proactive policing strategies may violate legal values even when they are implemented in ways that comply with the law. The fifth section discusses the relationship between law and community-based proactive policing strategies, namely, community-oriented policing and procedural justice policing, which raise different issues than do other proactive policing strategies.

FOURTH AMENDMENT

Legal Overview

The Fourth Amendment to the U.S. Constitution states: "The right of the people to be secure in their persons, houses, papers, and effects, against unreasonable searches and seizures, shall not be violated, and no warrants shall issue, but upon probable cause, supported by oath or affirmation, and particularly describing the place to be searched, and the persons or things to be seized." Under the Fourth Amendment, a police officer *seizes* a person when he restricts his liberty, either by a show of government authority to which the individual submits or by physical force (*Terry v. Ohio*, 392 U.S. 1 [1968]; *Hodari D. v. California*, 499 U.S. 621[1991]). Thus, arrests, pedestrian stops, traffic stops, and all uses of force by the police constitute seizures within the meaning of the Fourth Amendment. Fourth Amendment *searches* occur when the government intrudes upon an individual's reasonable expectation of privacy (*Katz v. United States*, 389 U.S. 347 [1967]) or when it physically trespasses onto a person's property for the purpose of gathering information (*United States v. Jones*, 565 U.S. __ [2010]; *Florida v. Jardines*, 569 U.S. 1 [2013]). Searches include both physical searches, such as looking in a car trunk or frisking a suspect, and electronic searches, such as listening in on a phone call or placing and monitoring a GPS [global positioning system] unit on a suspect's car.

Under the terms of the Fourth Amendment, a government search or seizure must be *reasonable*. Fourth Amendment reasonableness often requires that the police possess a quantum of evidence about an individual's involvement in a criminal offense before initiating a search or seizure. In some cases, the amount of suspicion required to engage in a stop or search is tied to the intrusiveness of the activity. Thus, a stop, which is a brief detention of a person short of a full arrest, requires that an officer have evidence rising to a "reasonable suspicion" that the person stopped is currently involved in criminal activity or has just committed or is about to commit an offense.[2] In order to lawfully conduct a frisk, which involves patting down a person's body outside his or her clothes for weapons, the officer must reasonably suspect that a person with whom an officer is interacting is armed and dangerous (*Terry v. Ohio*, 1968; *Adams v. Williams*, 407 U.S. 143 [1972]). Since arrests are more intrusive than stops, the U.S. Supreme Court requires that an officer have "probable cause" to believe that a person has committed a crime, a higher level of justification than "reasonable suspicion" (*Draper v. United States*, 258 U.S. 307 [1959]; *Atwater v. City of Lago Vista*, 432 U.S. 318 [2001]). Many types of searches other than frisks, such as searches of homes, also require probable cause to believe that a suspect or evidence of a crime will be found in the location searched, and these searches sometimes require a warrant, which ensures that a police officer establishes probable cause to a neutral magistrate before the search takes place.

For some searches and seizures, including some that may be used in proactive policing, it does not make sense to measure reasonableness by whether there is individualized suspicion because the police actions in these instances are not carried out primarily because someone is suspected of a crime. These actions include, for example, uses of force, DNA sampling of arrestees, and immigration checkpoints. Courts evaluate whether these activities are reasonable by balancing the severity of the intrusion on the individual against the interests of the government (*Graham v. Connor*, 490 U.S. 386 [1989]; *Indianapolis v. Edmond*, 531 U.S. 32 [2000]; *Maryland v. King*, 569 U.S. ___ [2013]).

While stops, searches, and arrests are all regulated by the Fourth Amendment, the Fourth Amendment case law defining what constitutes a search or seizure also puts many common policing activities used in proactive policing strategies beyond the scope of the Fourth Amendment's restrictions. Most critically, the doctrine governing consensual encounters, the third party doctrine, and the doctrine concerning movements in public permit police to gather information and monitor individual action in several ways without engaging in a search or seizure within the meaning of the Fourth Amendment. First, unlike encounters that would communicate "to a reasonable person that the person was not free to decline the officers'

---

[2] As noted in Chapter 2, the U.S. Supreme Court has not ruled as to whether *Terry* can be used to investigate a completed misdemeanor, and it has suggested that it might not be permissible. However, *Terry* can be used as the legal justification for police to investigate a completed felony (*United States v. Hensley* (469 U.S. 221 [1985]); see also *Navarette v. California* (572 U.S. ___ [2014]).

requests or otherwise terminate the encounter" (*Florida v. Bostick*, 501 U.S. 429 [1991]), consensual encounters between police officers and pedestrians do not constitute a seizure. Similarly, searches to which a subject voluntarily consents—even if the action is a search within the meaning of the Fourth Amendment—are considered reasonable (*Schneckloth v. Bustamonte*, 412 U.S. 218 [1973]). Second, under the third party doctrine, police may obtain, without probable cause or a warrant, information an individual has revealed to a third party, though the police would have had to comply with these requirements if the information had not been previously disclosed. This is true even if the information was disclosed on a limited basis or for a limited purpose, such as to one's bank through bank transactions (*United States v. Miller*, 425 U.S. 435 [1976]; *Smith v. Maryland*, 442 U.S. 735 [1979]). Third, the police may also watch a person's movements in public, including through technological means, unless they engage in a physical trespass to do so, without triggering the Fourth Amendment (*United States v. Knotts*, 460 U.S. 276 [1983]; *United States v. Jones*, 2012). Finally, the decision to investigate is not itself an activity regulated by the Fourth Amendment, though it can lead to searches and seizures that are regulated. When a police activity does not constitute either a search or a seizure within the scope of the Amendment, it need not be reasonable and does not require probable cause or a warrant under the Fourth Amendment, though it may still be subject to other law.

Deterrence-Oriented Proactive Strategies

As Chapter 2 suggests, several proactive policing strategies work to maximize the perceived consequences of criminal activity to potential criminals as a means to discourage that activity. One way some departments pursue this aim is to engage in frequent searches and seizures to deter criminal activity. Thus, SQF promotes stopping and frisking pedestrians as a means of discovering weapons and drugs and deterring people from carrying them. Similarly, hot spots policing often involves intensive patrols, including stops, frisks, and arrests within the microgeographical high-crime locations, and zero tolerance policing includes frequent stops, searches, and arrests, often for minor offenses (Mastrofski, Worden, and Snipes, 1995). Although both reactive and proactive stops, frisks, and arrests are subject to the same legal standards, deterrence-oriented proactive strategies interact with the Fourth Amendment in distinctive ways. Specifically, proactive practices often take significant advantage of Fourth Amendment discretion generated by the U.S. Supreme Court in reactive contexts, and there is some indication that in doing so these proactive practices may produce constitutional violations.

The Court frequently crafts Fourth Amendment rules that are simpler and more permissive than a determination of government need and individual interests in individual cases might otherwise warrant, in order to ensure that law enforcement has guidance and yet adequate flexibility to address the myriad, and sometimes unpredictable, circumstances that officers face (*Atwater v. Lago Vista*, 532 U.S. 318 [2001]) (Harmon, 2012b). More specifically, the rules governing stops, frisks, and arrests permit officers generous discretion. Thus, lower courts following constitutional case law permit officers to stop a suspect on the street based on reasonable suspicion of criminal activity rather than probable cause; to make a frisk based on reasonable suspicion that a suspect that has been stopped is armed and dangerous (*Terry v. Ohio*, 1968); and to make a warrantless custodial arrest, even for a very minor offense, such as a seat belt violation, that is punishable only by a fine (*Atwater v. Lago Vista*, 2001).

In justifying giving officers clear rules and flexibility, the U.S. Supreme Court has reasoned in part that officers usually have weak incentives to use intrusive means to address minor or equivocal conduct. As a result, officers are most likely to use the full zone of flexibility permitted by Fourth Amendment doctrine only when circumstances most warrant it (*Atwater v. Lago Vista*, 2001; cf. *Hudson v. Michigan*, 547 U.S. 586 [2006]). Notably, this reasoning assumes conventional policing: traditionally, stops, frisks, and arrests are tools police use reactively as a means to address a particular crime they witness or have reported to them or to investigate specific suspicious behavior. In this context, harmless or ambiguous individual conduct often will not justify the resources that would be necessary to address it, and officers are assumed to leave such conduct unaddressed rather than intrude on individuals.[3] By contrast, in proactive policing, departments often employ coercion more expansively to promote forward-looking, preventative ends rather than merely to investigate or enforce criminal law. Thus, proactive policing may encourage legal stops, frisks, and arrests even for equivocal or minor individual conduct.

This strategic use of Fourth Amendment doctrine for proactive policing is legal: the U.S. Supreme Court has repeatedly resisted considering subjective officer motives in evaluating searches and seizures for reasonableness, and it has permitted the pretextual use of legal authority to engage in searches and seizures (*Whren v. United States*, 517 U.S. 806 [1996]). Nevertheless, deterrence-oriented proactive strategies that rely on stops, frisks,

---

[3] This assumption about the frequency with which police do not take formal enforcement action even when there is sufficient evidence to do so ("leniency") is generally supported by empirical research (National Research Council, 2004, pp. 115–116). Legal factors (e.g., strength of evidence) are among the more powerful predictors of police use of formal enforcement, but they are hardly determinative. However, this literature does not compare police practices under high and low levels of proactivity, and many of the studies were conducted at times when proactive practices were not strategically promoted.

and arrests generate incentives for officers to conduct more frequent and intrusive, and therefore liberty reducing, searches and seizures than reactive policing would generate, and those strategies are aided by the legal rules developed for reactive policing.[4] Moreover, some scholars and critics argue that using these tools proactively potentially affects the legality of the police activities that result because departments encourage stops, frisks, and arrests for reasons other than the individual suspicion that provides the legal basis for the activities (Meares, 2015). Departments need to employ strong incentives for officers to engage in only those searches and seizures that satisfy the demands of the Fourth Amendment. Otherwise, encouraging stops, frisks, and arrests could easily result in searches and seizures that do not comport with constitutional standards. Without a strategy to ensure that officers comply with the Fourth Amendment, when departments encourage aggressive and frequent use of stops, summonses, and arrests pursuant to proactive strategies, they also increase the frequency of *illegal* stops, summonses, and arrests both in absolute numbers (because they conduct more) and in relative terms (because more of the additional stops, summonses, and arrests conducted are illegal).

The litigation against the New York City Police Department's (NYPD's) SQF program illustrates some of these issues. For many years, the NYPD claimed that its SQF and broken windows policing policies encouraged—except for occasional mistakes—only stops, frisks, and arrests that satisfied the Fourth Amendment's reasonable suspicion requirement. Plaintiffs contended, by contrast, that the program resulted in many stops and frisks without adequate suspicion. In *Floyd v. City of New York* (959 F. Supp 2d 540 [2013]), the district court declared the program unconstitutional in part because it agreed with the plaintiffs, finding that many of the stops pursuant to the program violated the Fourth Amendment. According to the *Floyd* decision, the pressure to conduct stops as part of the program, when combined with inadequate training about the constitutional standard, led officers to engage in a practice of routine, unconstitutional stops that violated both the Fourth and Fourteenth Amendments.

DOJ has similarly contended that proactive policing that utilizes widespread stops and arrests for minor crimes causes constitutional violations. In its investigation of the New Orleans Police Department, for example, DOJ found that an organizational focus on arrests and statistical measures of productivity, in combination with poor training and policies, contributed to illegal stops, pat downs, and arrests (U.S. Department of Justice, 2011).

More recently, in its investigation into the Baltimore Police Department, DOJ found that the police department emphasized "an aggressive,

---

[4] Proactive strategies that emphasize narrowly focused deterrence are unlikely to have this effect.

'zero tolerance' strategy that prioritized making large numbers of stops, searches, and arrests—often for misdemeanor street offenses like loitering and disorderly conduct." This strategy was conducted "with minimal training and insufficient oversight from supervisors or through other accountability structures" (U.S. Department of Justice, 2016, p. 17). According to DOJ, the consequences were "repeated violations of [] constitutional and statutory rights, further eroding the community's trust in the police" (U.S. Department of Justice, 2016, p. 5). Moreover, according to DOJ, the strategy had long-term effects. Even though Baltimore no longer formally uses a zero tolerance policing strategy, zero tolerance "continues to drive policing in certain Baltimore neighborhoods and leads to unconstitutional stops, searches, and arrests" (U.S. Department of Justice, 2016, p. 5).

Several scholars have argued that it is unlikely that any programmatic use of stops, frisks, and arrests could be effective in preventing crime and still survive proper constitutional scrutiny (Bellin, 2014; Meares, 2015). If so, then no department should adopt these strategies. That said, courts have not forced many departments to give up SQF, broken windows, or zero tolerance policing. And other scholars assume that a legal version of these strategies is possible, if departments aggressively use the legal authority to conduct stops or arrests (by encouraging officers to make all possible legal stops and arrests) and still train and supervise officers to avoid unconstitutional conduct (Harmon, 2012b). Either way, legal scholars conclude that deterrence-based strategies that employ aggressive stops, frisks, and arrests raise the prospect of increased constitutional violations, and the litigation surrounding these programs supports that conclusion.

The committee identified little systematic empirical research documenting either exactly how large the problem of unconstitutional behavior resulting from programmatic action is or exactly why it occurs. In finding the NYPD's use of SQF unconstitutional, the court was strongly influenced by an expert report by Fagan and Macdonald (2012), which found that many of the stops apparently violated the Fourth Amendment. Analyzing the reasons officers provided for stops and frisks in the reports they were required to make when they conducted stops, the authors found that at least 7 percent of the stops conducted by the NYPD during the program lacked legal justification and another 24 percent lacked sufficiently detailed documentation to support a conclusion that the stop was legal.

Fagan and MacDonald's report offers a rare window into the justifications for police action on a large scale. Still, it only provides limited evidence either about how many illegal stops occurred or, more importantly, whether any individual policy or menu of department policies caused them to take place. The findings by the court in *Floyd* and by DOJ are grounded in legal evidence, rather than social science evidence that satisfies the standards for attributing causation as used by this committee. Fagan and McDonald

(2012) do not undertake the mathematical exercise of statistically evaluating whether or not the 7 percent rate of illegal stops was larger, smaller, or indistinguishable from the rate of illegal stops that would have occurred in the absence of SQF.[5] Similar problems arise with the evidence discussed in other court decisions and legal commentary. Whether there is "evidence" that a particular policy is associated with constitutional violations from a legal perspective is not the same issue as whether there is "evidence" that the policy causes constitutional violations in the sense of statistical causation. In acknowledging this distinction, the committee is not giving priority to either the legal or the social science definition of evidence. Rather, the purpose of credibly testing a previously defined null hypothesis against an alternative hypothesis (the social science assessment of causal connection) is, quite plainly, different from the goal of establishing a legal finding that an unconstitutional act occurred.

Further, even as a basis for describing how common illegal stops were during the period they studied, there are important limitations to the kind of data available to Fagan and McDonald (2012), namely, the self-reports of stops generated by NYPD officers. As the court pointed out in its decision, the reports on which the authors relied likely overestimated the legality of the stops conducted because officers may overstate the legal grounds for stops and may fail to document illegal stops more often than legal ones. In addition, the study intentionally estimated the legal sufficiency of the reports generously. As a result, many more of the NYPD's stops under SQF could have been illegal. However, the court did not mention an alternative way in which the reports could understate legal stops. Fagan and McDonald (2012) considered merely whether the stops are "apparently unjustified," a standard designed to capture those stops for which the reports indicated inadequate grounds for the purposes of the litigation. However, an officer's conduct is legal if an objective basis for the stop exists, regardless of whether he or she provides adequate documentation of that basis. Since the criminal code is vast, and reasonable suspicion requires only "a minimal level of objective justification for making the stop" (*Illinois v. Wardlow*, 528 U.S. 119 [2000]), it is possible that some proportion of the stops found to be "apparently unjustified" by Fagan and McDonald (2012) could have had a legal basis that the officer had not stated in the documentation (Bellin, 2014). Given the weak scrutiny the NYPD gave to the reports, officers might have had little incentive to take care to include all of the grounds that justified the stops. Thus, it is difficult to know to what degree Fagan and McDonald (2012) estimates overstate or understate the proportion of SQF stops that were in fact illegal.

---

[5] See the Chapter 1 section on "Assessing the Evidence" for additional discussion of the points made here about assessing evidence of causal relationships.

Yet Fagan and McDonald (2012) provide far more information about proactive policing and legality in the NYPD context than exists with respect to proactive policing efforts in most other cities.[6] It is not easy, using existing data sources, for empirical researchers to count constitutional violations or develop meaningful proxies for them, and quantitative and qualitative criminological research often does not evaluate policing in terms that align with legal categories (Harmon, 2017). As a result, the limited empirical research about how proactive strategies change the frequency of constitutional violations does not provide a basis for concluding that proactive strategies either increase or reduce constitutional violations, according to the standards of causality used by the committee. The empirical evidence on whether SQF policies affect crime rates does not further clarify the issue (Meares, 2014).

Place-Based Strategies

Place-based strategies focus resources on locations where crime is concentrated in order to prevent and to respond more effectively to crime. To a substantial degree, the Fourth Amendment implications of a high-crime-area strategy depend on the kind of efforts police departments take to deter crime in the identified areas. If, for example, a department uses closed circuit television to deter crime at a particular street intersection or in a public park, it may do so without triggering Fourth Amendment scrutiny because that policing practice monitors individual movements only in public places and therefore does not constitute a search within the meaning of the Fourth Amendment. By contrast, if predictive policing or hot spots policing leads a department to engage in intensive stops, frisks, and arrests in a limited geographic area, these strategies will raise many of the same concerns as do the deterrence-based strategies discussed above. However, in addition to the Fourth Amendment issues raised by policing practices within specified areas, place-based strategies raise a distinctive set of Fourth Amendment issues by identifying specific microgeographic areas as locations of intensive recent or likely future criminal activity.

In *Illinois v. Wardlow* (2000), the U.S. Supreme Court held that unprovoked flight in a "high-crime area" can constitute reasonable suspicion justifying a pedestrian stop. Although lower courts have been slow to refine what constitutes a high crime area, a police department's designation that a location is a hot spot is relevant to the legal analysis in which courts

---

[6]The spreading use of body-worn cameras may provide the opportunity to study whether or not stops are constitutional, an approach that may yield better data on the proportion of SQFs that are illegal.

engage in making that determination.[7] As a result, hot spots policing can have consequences for the legal rights of those who interact with the police in a hot spot location.

Under *Illinois v. Wardlow*, courts consider the fact that a suspect's actions occurred in a "high-crime area" in evaluating whether the officer's suspicion was sufficient to warrant a stop by the officer. Courts may permit stops in high crime areas on the basis of weaker suspicious behavioral cues by individual suspects than would be permissible in other areas because those cues can be taken to have additional meaning in a neighborhood with higher levels of criminal activity. As an extension of this logic, some scholars have suggested that courts in the future could include conclusions drawn from predictive policing technologies in assessing whether adequate suspicion exists to justify a traffic or pedestrian stop (Ferguson, 2012, p. 263). Thus, by lowering the amount of evidence of criminal activity (other than a department's designation or prediction) necessary to make an officer's intrusion constitutional, the department's implementation of the policing strategy can now, and might further in the future, affect the scope of the rights of citizens to act free from interference. In doing so, all other things being equal, the strategy will also reduce the likelihood that an officer's actions in conducting a stop will violate the Constitution because it is not justified by adequate suspicion.

A department's characterization of an area as one of high crime can be consequential even when it is wrong. First, courts are unlikely to uncover or reveal a conflict between police assertions about an area and crime rates in that area. The vast majority of stops are never challenged legally because they result in no criminal charge, and a motion to suppress evidence in a criminal case is the primary mechanism by which the constitutionality of stops is contested. Moreover, in the absence of a clear legal standard about what constitutes a high-crime area, even when a stop is challenged, courts often defer to police assessments of the status of a neighborhood, sometimes without requiring specific evidence to support the designation. (Ferguson, 2011; Harris, 1998; see also, e.g., *United States v. Smith*, 594 F. 3d 530 [6th Cir. 2010]; *United States v. Ruidiaz*, 529 F. 3d 25 [1st Cir. 2008]). If such a designation is made without adequate basis, then the inferences a court draws about whether adequate suspicion exists within that area could be similarly unfounded.

Analogously, if predictive policing strategies that generate conclusions about the area are unreliable or nontransparent, they may produce predictions that are either unjustified or unfair and similarly lead to unsupported

---

[7]Hot spots are often very small geographically, as small as a single intersection. Although courts have not clarified the size of a high-crime area within the meaning of *Illinois v. Wardlow*, cases seem to suggest that it may be substantially larger than a hot spot might be.

judgments that stops and frisks defended on the basis of those predictions are constitutional as a result. The discretion awarded to departments in designating hot spots may itself raise Fourteenth Amendment issues. Although not legally or empirically tested, ethnographic research has argued that the race and nationality of local residents and business people can play a role in labeling an area as "high crime" (Brunson and Miller, 2006; Chesluk, 2004; Muniz, 2012, 2014; Quillian and Pager, 2001; Sampson and Raudenbush, 2004).

Even if a court scrutinizes a department's designation of a high-crime area and eventually concludes that the department erred in classifying the area as one of high crime at the time an officer conducted a stop, the department's designation would make it reasonable for an individual officer to *believe* that it was a high crime area and therefore to believe that he had a greater basis for suspicion then he had in fact.[8] Even if an officer lacks reasonable suspicion, making the stop unconstitutional, his reasonable mistake would change the consequences of his illegal act. Several remedies for constitutional violations, including the exclusionary rule and civil suits for damages under § 1983, are mostly unavailable against officer conduct that is unconstitutional but based on an officer's reasonable mistake about the legal status of his actions (*Herring v. United States*, 555 U.S. 135 [2009]; *Harlow v. Fitzgerald*, 457 U.S. 800 [1982]; *Mullenix v. Luna*, 577 U.S. ___ [2015]). Assuming that the likelihood of civil damages or evidentiary exclusion shapes an officer's incentives to ensure that reasonable suspicion exists before engaging in a stop, a proactive policing strategy in which high-crime areas are sometimes erroneously designated could cause additional, albeit unknowing, constitutional violations by officers.

The law governing high crime areas also has implications for the deterrence-oriented policing strategies discussed above. In place-based proactive policing, hot spots are designated in advance by departments. But individual police officers may equally use a history of crime in a location as part of the circumstances that justify a stop under *Illinois v. Wardlow* even when an agency has not previously labeled the area. Officers encouraged to engage in aggressive enforcement pursuant to deterrence-oriented proactive strategies need legal reasons to justify their activities, and the history of crime in the area often provides one (Fagan and Geller, 2015). Thus, for example, Fagan and Geller (2015) found in a study of 4.7 million stops by NYPD officers that police officers asserted that more than one-half of the stops took place in an area with a high incidence of crime. Weisburd, Telep, and Lawton (2014) showed that stops were indeed concentrated in specific loca-

---

[8] As discussed in Chapter 7 of this report, social psychological processes of implicit bias and discrimination may affect policing in minority neighborhoods (see also Sampson, 2012, and Sampson and Raudenbush, 2004).

tions and that those high-SQF locations were strongly correlated with crime hot spots. Used in this way, deterrence strategies, combined with *Illinois v. Wardlow*, can have significant distributional consequences, exposing individuals to additional scrutiny because of perceived or actual neighborhood characteristics, which often correlate with race and economic status. The committee did not find causal empirical research to date that adequately engaged with this question, in spite of the psychological, ethnographic, and correlational social science literature documenting this phenomenon.

Third Party Policing

Third party policing leverages the actions of third parties in deterring and reducing the opportunities for targeted offenders or criminal conduct. For example, as described in Box 2-3 (see Chapter 2), as a means to indirectly control drug and disorder problems the Oakland, California, Beat Health Program focused on civil remedies for addressing conditions of physical decay and property management problems of specific commercial establishments, private residences, and rental properties. As this program illustrates, departments often take advantage of existing civil laws and regulations in implementing third party policing because these laws provide much of the leverage to demand third-party participation in crime prevention and control. Nevertheless, departments can also utilize third parties to prevent or reveal crime in another way, one that three aspects of Fourth Amendment doctrine facilitate: officers may use information obtained through third parties that would otherwise be unavailable without establishing individualized suspicion or obtaining a search warrant.

First, the Fourth Amendment does not apply to information that a person voluntarily provides to a third party when the third party makes that information available to the government (*United States v. White*, 401 U.S. 745 [1971]; *United States v. Miller*, 425 U.S. 435 [1976]; *Smith v. Maryland*, 442 U.S. 735 [1979]). Thus, when police officers secure information about individuals from third parties, their conduct is not subject to the Fourth Amendment protection, whereas efforts to obtain the information directly from the suspect may involve protected searches and seizures.

Second, when a third party shares or reasonably appears to share common authority over a location or over property, he or she may consent to a search by government actors (*United States v. Matlock*, 415 U.S. 164 [1974]). Although that consent is not valid against an objecting co-occupant who remains present during the search (*Illinois v. Rodriguez*, 497 U.S. 177 [1990]; *Georgia v. Randolph*, 547 U.S. 103 [2006]), it otherwise has the potential to permit police access to locations unavailable without the cooperation of the third party.

Third, the Fourth Amendment applies only to government conduct, and any exposure of private information usually negates the argument that an individual has a reasonable expectation of privacy against the government. This means that private searches by third parties can limit the applicability of the Fourth Amendment to subsequent searches made by law enforcement of the same locations or the same information. This third avenue is illustrated by the U.S. Supreme Court decision in *United States v. Jacobsen* (466 U.S. 109 [1984]). In that case, Federal Express employees examined a package damaged during transport and discovered a white powdery substance they suspected was contraband. They reassembled the package and called the Drug Enforcement Administration (DEA). When the DEA agents arrived, they reopened the package and subjected the powder to a field chemical test that indicated the substance was cocaine. In upholding the government's use of the cocaine in a criminal case against the package's recipients, the U.S. Supreme Court held that since private actors had already opened the package, the government's re-inspection of the contents uncovered nothing new and therefore did not constitute a search within the meaning of the Fourth Amendment. In its decision, the court noted that even an illegal private search can undermine the reasonableness of an expectation of privacy with respect to the information discovered (*United States v. Jacobsen*, 1984).

There are limitations on the use of private searches by the government. Most notably, if a private actor is an agent of the state or if government actors are deeply entangled in private searches, the search he or she conducts may be a public rather than private one, and therefore fall within the scope of the Fourth Amendment (*Coolidge v. New Hampshire*, 403 U.S. 443 [1971]). Similarly, if a police officer or department compels, encourages, endorses, or participates in a search or seizure by a third party, the action may be subject to Fourth Amendment protections (*Skinner v. Railway Lab. Execs. Ass'n*, 489 U.S. 602 [1989]). Thus, while a proactive strategy that takes advantage of third party access to private information would likely permit officers to gather evidence without triggering Fourth Amendment scrutiny for that evidence gathering, a proactive strategy that *induces* searches by private parties may be subject to constitutional regulation.

Even with these limitations on private searches, it might be said that in each of the circumstances described above—voluntary disclosure, consent by a third party, and involuntary exposure—proactive policing that leverages the cooperation of private third parties may narrow the applicability of Fourth Amendment protection to police efforts to obtain information. Ceteris paribus, officers who are able to obtain information from third parties (and thus without searches and seizures), are likely to conduct fewer searches and seizures and therefore have less opportunity to violate the Fourth Amendment. In this way, third party policing may reduce constitutional violations. At the same time, if third party policing gives police officers an incentive to strongly encourage private searches, it may lead to more frequent violations of the rules limiting the use of private searches by the government. In addition, to the degree that proactive policing encourages information gathering outside the scope of the Fourth Amendment, it may increase intrusions on privacy that are unregulated by Fourth Amendment law in ways that raise concerns about private invasion, even if the intrusions comply with constitutional law. The committee knows of no empirical literature assessing these risks.

As the Beat Health example suggests, police departments can also leverage searches designed to enforce civil regulatory laws, such as health and safety codes, building codes, and environmental regulations. Although administrative searches are governed by the Fourth Amendment, the Supreme Court has not usually demanded individualized suspicion or warrants for them (*Camara v. Municipal Court*, 387 U.S. 523 [1967]). Instead, the Court's doctrines permit civil government inspections, such as housing code inspections, so long as they are reasonable, which often requires nothing more than that reasonable legislative or administrative standards govern them. This is therefore another mechanism by which proactive policing may allow police to avoid standards governing individualized suspicion that might otherwise limit access to the information in the absence of an administrative search regime. As with third-party searches, although such a strategy might be construed to limit protection for privacy, it also reduces the opportunities for constitutional violations against the same individuals. Under existing law, police officers may attend, or use information discovered during, such searches when they are carried out by other government officers, or they may conduct administrative searches themselves, consistent with the Fourth Amendment (*New York v. Burger*, 482 U.S. 691 [1987]), so long as the primary motive for the search is not to uncover ordinary criminal wrongdoing (*Indianapolis v Edmond*, 531 U.S. 32 [2000]).

EQUAL PROTECTION AND STATUTES PROHIBITING DISCRIMINATION

Legal Overview

Unlike the Fourth Amendment, the Equal Protection Clause of the Fourteenth Amendment applies to all police activities, including policy decisions by departments to investigate suspects or to search or seize them. It guarantees equal and impartial treatment by government actors under the law. A policy or police action may violate the Equal Protection Clause either because it expressly singles out individuals for disfavored treatment on the basis of their race or other impermissible classification or because, though facially neutral, the policy is selectively enforced against members of one race or other impermissible classification in an intentionally discriminatory manner.

However, not all policies involving racial classifications or creating racial disparities in investigation or enforcement violate the Equal Protection Clause. Laws or policies that draw express racial or ethnic classifications among citizens do not violate the Equal Protection Clause if they are narrowly tailored to serve a compelling state interest (*Wayte v. United States*, 470 U.S. 598 [1985]). This test, known as "strict scrutiny," is difficult to pass. Facially neutral laws and policies that are selectively enforced in a discriminatory manner violate the Equal Protection Clause only if they are also motivated by a discriminatory purpose (*Washington v. Davis*, 426 U.S. 229 [1976]).

Proving discriminatory effect requires establishing that an individual received less favorable treatment because of his race or other classification. Plaintiffs often establish this disfavored treatment with statistical evidence. Chapter 7 considers further the difficulties of establishing unfavorable treatment, including the difficulties of establishing the proper comparison populations. As with the Fourth Amendment, however, the legal concept of causation in Equal Protection law does not necessarily satisfy the criteria social scientists use to identify causal relationships. For instance, federal courts are divided as to whether plaintiffs claiming that police officers selectively enforced the law against them because of their race must demonstrate that "similarly situated individuals of a different race" did not have the law enforced against them in order to demonstrate discriminatory effect. This standard, which is always required for plaintiffs attempting to establish selective prosecution (*United States v. Armstrong*, 517 U.S. 456 [1996]; *United States v. Davis*, 793 F.3d 712 [7th Cir. 2015]; *United States v. Mason*, 774 F.3d 824 [4th Cir. 2014]), makes selective enforcement by the police exceptionally difficult to establish (*United States v. Whitfield*, 649 F. App'x 192 [3d Cir. 2016]).

In contrast to some of the historical practices discussed in Chapter 7 of this report, most policing policies today do not expressly target racial or ethnic groups, so most Equal Protection challenges require proving discriminatory purpose as well as discriminatory effect. The concept of discriminatory intent in Equal Protection law is distinct from the concepts of racial bias used in the psychological literature and discussed in Chapter 7 of this report. Proving discriminatory purpose requires showing (1) that the government intended to treat an individual unequally because of his or her classification, and (2) that it acted *because* of the harmful effect on a chosen group, not merely *in spite of* that effect. In other contexts, Equal Protection strictly scrutinizes government conduct even if the plaintiff does not prove that the desire to treat a group unequally was the only purpose guiding an activity, so long as it is demonstrated to be one motivating factor behind the harm. However, some lower courts have refused to apply law enforcement on race unless the decision was based solely on race (e.g., *United States v. Travis*, 62 F. 3d 170, 174 [6th Cir. 1995].[9] Discriminatory intent can be proved through direct evidence, such as admissions by a policy maker or officer, or circumstantially, using statistical evidence of discrimination to show that discriminatory intent likely exists (*Washington v. Davis*, 1976), including the kind of statistical evidence discussed in Chapter 7.

Though the legal concept of discriminatory intent is distinct, efforts to prove that intent in lawsuits are plagued by many of the same evidentiary challenges, discussed in Chapter 7, that affect social scientists' efforts to establish the reasons for racial disparities. In addition, assessing the legal adequacy of evidence of discriminatory intent is complicated both by the social and historical context in which law enforcement operates also discussed in that chapter and by the subtle and nonobvious ways racial bias and animus may operate in society. For instance, symbolic racism, as defined in Sears (1988), involves the belief that prejudice against Black people is no longer a problem in U.S. society today, that the overrepresentation of Black Americans in low-income, low-educated, and high-crime groups is primarily due to their own personal shortcomings, and that Black people in general demand too much from society at large and have also "gotten more than they deserve." A core part of symbolic racism, as described by Sears (1988), is therefore the belief that if a Black person received less favorable treatment, it was likely because they objectively deserved less favorable treatment. Holding such a view would presumably influence whether one believed that indirect evidence established the discriminatory purpose necessary to prove an Equal Protection violation.

In addition to the Equal Protection Clause, federal statutes, including Title VI of the Civil Rights Act of 1964 and the Omnibus Crime Control and Safe Street Act of 1968, also prohibit discrimination by police departments that receive federal funding. These statutes provide protection against discrimination that significantly overlaps with Equal Protection law, but they also sometimes permit liability for unintentional discrimination when Equal Protection does not (28 CFR § 42.104(b)(2); 28 CFR § 42.203).

---

[9]This view finds some support in the Supreme Court's Fourth Amendment jurisprudence. The Court has suggested that seizures in the context of an immigration checkpoint based solely on ethnicity are arbitrary and therefore unreasonable under the Fourth Amendment (*United States v. Martinez-Fuerte*, 428 U.S. 543, 554 [1976]), but that seizures largely on the basis of ethnicity may be permissible at least where ethnicity is relevant to the law enforcement interest at stake (*United States v. Brignoni-Ponce*, 422 U.S. 873 [1975]). Nevertheless, the Supreme Court has also indicated that "the constitutional basis for objecting to intentionally discriminatory application of law is the Equal Protection Clause not the Fourth Amendment" (*Whren v. United States*, 517 U.S. 806, 813 [1996]), raising questions about the relevance of this analysis to the Equal Protection context.

They also allow federal agencies to address noncompliance by terminating federal financial assistance to the offending agency, a remedy unavailable under Equal Protection law.

Deterrence-Oriented Proactive Strategies

Proactive policing strategies that use frequent stops, frisks, and arrests to prevent future crime often raise Equal Protection concerns as well as Fourth Amendment issues. Many critics have argued that such strategies cause unwarranted racial disparities, and both the district court's decision in *Floyd* and DOJ's analyses in its pattern-and-practice investigations in New Orleans and Baltimore found that the proactive policing strategies at issue caused discriminatory policing in violation of the Equal Protection Clause.

For example, in *Floyd*, Judge Scheindlin found that, in carrying out SQF, the NYPD violated the Equal Protection Clause by disproportionately and discriminatorily stopping non-Whites. Specifically, she noted that officers likely targeted Blacks for stops based on a lesser degree of objectively founded suspicion than they applied in stopping Whites, and officers subjected them to different treatment during stops, including more frequent use of force, despite the fact that Whites who were stopped were more likely to be found with weapons or contraband (*Floyd v. City of New York*, 2013). She also found that the NYPD had an unwritten policy of targeting "the right people" in carrying out SQF, which encouraged subjecting young Black and Latino men to heightened police enforcement on the basis of their race, and that the department had shown deliberate indifference in the face of evidence that the program was carried out in a discriminatory manner.

In Baltimore, DOJ linked the Baltimore Police Department's (BPD's) zero tolerance policy—which was implemented in the early 2000s and included frequent stops, searches, and arrests—to "overwhelming statistical evidence of racial disparities in BPD's stops, searches, and arrests," in violation of Title VI and the Safe Streets Act (U.S. Department of Justice, 2016, p. 48). DOJ concluded that the evidence was sufficient to establish discriminatory impact under the Equal Protection Clause. DOJ also found evidence suggesting that the discrimination against Blacks was intentional because of the magnitude of the statistical relationship between race and stops, because the proactive strategy focused on Blacks and Black neighborhoods, because of statements by officers and supervisors indicating that the program was being carried out in a discriminatory fashion, and because of the department's failure to act in the face of evidence of discrimination. For example, one supervisor allegedly instructed officers to carry out the zero tolerance strategy by arresting "all the Black hoodies" in a neighborhood (U.S. Department of Justice, 2016, p. 66). In the course of DOJ's investigation, at least some top BPD officials shared the view that its proactive policing strategy had discriminatory effects. One told DOJ that "stop and frisk killed the hopes and dreams of entire communities" (U.S. Department of Justice, p. 63). DOJ contended that even after zero tolerance was no longer the formal policy of the police department, supervisors within the department continued to implement this form of proactive policing, with its discriminatory and other consequences.[10] Other DOJ and private civil suits resulting in settlements have alleged that the frequent use of stops, frisks, and arrests in other cities has also violated the Equal Protection Clause but have drawn less express connection between the enforcement practices and proactive policing strategies.

More broadly, concerns about discrimination in proactive policing are often framed as concerns about racial profiling. Racial profiling usually refers to police decisions to engage in vehicle or pedestrian stops, searches, or arrests or to take other law enforcement actions based at least in part on an individual's race, ethnicity, religion, or national origin, outside of the context in which officers target an individual because he satisfies a specific description of a criminal suspect or other person of interest. For instance, officers implementing a deterrence-oriented proactive strategy might use race as a factor in choosing which people to stop, frisk, or arrest because they believe that the targeted race is overrepresented in the criminal population the strategy is intended to deter, and they would thereby engage in racial profiling. Even if their belief were accurate and hit rates or deterrence could be improved using race as a criterion, this use of race may not pass constitutional scrutiny. The overwhelming number of people selected would still likely be innocent in the sense of needing no deterrence from the targeted conduct; those selected on the basis of their race would suffer additional harm from being selected for this reason; and courts applying strict scrutiny would be unlikely to find this use of race "narrowly tailored" to serve a "compelling state interest."

Although legal claims about unwarranted racial disparities have focused on stops, frisks, and arrests, other kinds of intensive enforcement resulting from proactive policing may also raise questions about disparate impacts, including third party enforcement of civil regulatory codes, specifically "nuisance violations." These violations, which are filed against landlords whose tenants contact 911 frequently, require the landlords to take steps to reduce the frequency of these calls. In practice, the steps taken frequently involve evicting tenants who request police assistance by calling 911. Desmond and Valdez (2013) documented a positive correlation between the use of third-party enforcement and the fraction of neighborhood

---

[10]Legal claims that proactive policing led to discrimination often remain unadjudicated either because procedural barriers bar suit or the parties settle, making a court ruling unnecessary.

residents who are Black. Similar to Fagan and MacDonald's (2012) analysis of the geographic incidence of SQF in New York, documenting such a pattern may constitute legal evidence of Fourteenth Amendment violations in the use of third-party enforcement.[11]

The difficulties of assessing and understanding racial disparities and racial bias are discussed further in Chapter 7. It remains an open question whether any tendency that proactive policing strategies have to cause Fourth and Fourteenth Amendment violations are linked, though some theorists suggest that such linkage is likely (Meares, 2015; Bellin, 2014). To be clear, this is not due to mixed or null conclusions of credible evaluations of the causal impact of proactive policing strategies on the incidence of Fourth or Fourteenth Amendment violations; it is because the empirical social science literature that could establish such causal effects has not adequately engaged with the question.

Predictive Policing Strategies

As noted in Chapter 2, predictive policing strategies seek to anticipate, prevent, and respond more effectively to crime by collecting information and identifying patterns in aggregated data about past crime and other information. To the degree that these predictions focus on individuals or groups who may commit or fall victim to crime, rather than to places where crimes may be committed, they could raise Equal Protection concerns. First, predictive strategies or the law enforcement interventions based on the resulting predictions may be implemented by departments with discriminatory effect and intent. Doing so would violate the Equal Protection Clause, just as implementing SQF or broken windows policing with discriminatory effect and intent violates the law. Second, these strategies are sometimes directed intentionally at members of a particular religion or national origin and therefore contain an express classification that singles out members for unfavorable treatment. This raises a distinctive kind of Equal Protection claim, one only touched upon above.

When predictive policing is targeted at members of a religion or national origin, they are likely to be subject to heightened scrutiny, requiring that the government prove a strong justification between the governmental interest and the means used to achieve it. In *Hassan v. City of New York* (2015), for example, plaintiffs alleged that the NYPD adopted a long-term

---

[11]Desmond and Valdez (2013) do not do a counterfactual analysis of whether or not the rate at which Black residents were denied emergency response service or evicted changed as a result of the adoption of third-party enforcement. As a result, their study does not address the question of whether third party policing in this instance exacerbated racial disparities in victimization or simply relabeled an existing phenomenon.

program of extensive surveillance and investigation of Muslim individuals, businesses, and institutions after the terrorist attacks of September 11, 2001. Among other claims, the plaintiffs contended that this selective investigation violated Equal Protection law. Though this claim has not yet been fully litigated, the U.S. Court of Appeals for the Third Circuit permitted the case to go forward for discovery and trial because the allegations, if true, could establish a constitutional violation, even if the NYPD was motivated by a legitimate law enforcement purpose in establishing the program. Specifically, the Third Circuit panel ruled that allegations of religious discrimination are subject to heightened Equal Protection scrutiny, even if the program containing them was motivated by national security and public safety concerns.

Although the program challenged in *Hassan* would not fall within the bounds of proactive policing as described in this report because it sought to uncover rather than prevent criminal activity, it raises the same legal concerns as would a proactive strategy that is similarly directed at members of a particular religion or national origin and is thus illustrative. Similar legal analysis might have applied, for example, to the Los Angeles Police Department's 2007 plan to identify and map Muslim communities in Los Angeles to help them avoid the influence of extremist elements that might lead to terrorism had criticism not led the department to abandon the plan (Roush, 2012).

EMPIRICAL EVIDENCE ON PROACTIVE POLICING AND ILLEGAL POLICE BEHAVIOR

There are relatively few empirical studies that credibly examine whether or not proactive policing is causally related either to police behavior that is likely to raise constitutional challenges or to legal findings of constitutional violations. Two challenges make such research exceptionally difficult. First, researchers have limited data about the kinds of police conduct that often raise constitutional challenges. Unlike serious crime and arrest rates, there is little nationwide data collection on many kinds of police behaviors, including stops, searches, and uses of force, that may trigger a constitutional challenge. Individual agencies often have different standards for how police conduct is reported internally, including, for example, different standards for definitions of what constitutes force (Alpert, 2016), and for whether data concerning police conduct is available for research. To the extent that many proactive policies may alter the legality of police behavior and that there is value in social science evaluation of this possibility, systematic and standardized collection of data on relevant police outcomes is necessary.

Second, even with such data, constitutional violations are difficult for researchers to define and to measure. Such violations require fact-specific analysis and legal judgments, and different observers are likely to come to differing conclusions about whether a violation occurred (Harmon, 2017). Unless and until a court has given a final judgment on the question, there is no authoritative basis for concluding that a researcher's determination about whether a constitutional violation occurred is accurate. Nor do easy proxies for legality exist. For example, citizen complaint rates might vary for reasons independent of the constitutional violations that might spur them, including agency-specific methods of taking (or resisting) complaints. Lawsuit rates might vary with the strength of the local bar and with settlement practices (Harmon, 2017). And, in the extreme, it is possible that the majority of residents could be very satisfied with a department that regularly violated the constitutional rights of a small minority of the population, making community satisfaction surveys a similarly weak measure.

The committee conducted a systematic search of peer-reviewed publications examining the relationship between proactive policing and the legality of police officer actions. The committee found notably less research on the impact of proactive policing strategies on legality than it found on the implications of proactive policing for crime control or community satisfaction. The few studies that were found generally assessed satisfaction with the police or perceptions of police legitimacy; this literature is reviewed systematically in Chapters 5 and 6 of this report as part of the committee's examination of community impacts.

Fagan and colleagues (2010) used a modified pre-post design to attempt to identify the impact of broken windows policing on officer SQF behavior in New York City. To the extent that this deterrence-oriented strategy led to unequal treatment of people of different races or ethnicities, this could be interpreted as evidence that SQF led to an increase in violations of the Equal Protection Clause. The authors found a sharp increase in stops of Blacks and Latinos in the "late" period of broken windows policing relative to the early period, from 27 and 15, respectively, per 1,000 people to 131 and 64 per 1,000 people. For White people, the comparable change was from 4 per 1,000 in the early period to 18 per 1,000 in the late period. These findings are consistent with, but by no means evidence of, the proactive SQF policy causing a large increase in illegal racial targeting by the NYPD. That said, comparing officer behavior in New York City to stop behavior in a different city, or making a comparison with a "pre" period that is not defined by the low level of stops, would make this evidence more convincing.

In essence, the calculation by Fagan and colleagues (2010) assumes that, in the absence of the broken windows policing policy in New York City, the rate at which Blacks or Hispanics would be stopped by the NYPD would have been constant over time. Potentially alternate explanations include demographic change, variation in the taste of residents and police officers, or changes in recording practices. Fagan and colleagues, (2010) further demonstrated that the percentage of neighborhood residents who are Black was a strong predictor of the number of stops, conditional on crime rates, but they did not explore whether the increased use of broken windows policing had changed the relationship between the racial composition of a neighborhood and the frequency with which police make (potentially illegal) stops.

LEGAL MECHANISMS FOR CHALLENGING PROACTIVE POLICING

Police departments and officers have myriad complex reasons for following the law, including the costs and consequences of litigation challenging the constitutionality of police conduct. As a general matter, departments may, in part, determine if and how proactive strategies are employed in response to their perceptions about this litigation and the remedies likely to be imposed as a result. However, given the substantial limitations on constitutional remedies for police misconduct in the context of proactive policing and the limited information departments collect about lawsuits and their connection to police practices, these legal consequences may provide only limited incentives for departments and officers with respect to proactive strategies. To the degree this occurs, the law may not substantially discourage even those proactive strategies that result in provable constitutional violations.

Several kinds of legal actions can be brought against police conduct. Individuals whose rights have been violated by the police can bring civil suits under federal and state law for damages, for a declaration of the rights of the parties, or for a command to adopt particular reforms. The federal government (and occasionally states) can also bring civil suits against police departments who have engaged in a "pattern or practice" of rights violations, seeking reform.[12] In addition, criminal defendants whose rights have been violated can challenge police conduct by moving to exclude illegally obtained evidence from criminal trials in which the government would

---

[12] The use of the term "pattern" by DOJ also diverges from the social science meaning of the term. Identifying a pattern in, say, use of force, in social science research would imply identifying some measure (e.g., time, officer, or place) that was correlated with that variable. Claiming to have identified a correlation would require statistically distinguishing the estimated correlation from zero, which involves mathematical calculations. However, with regard to legal findings of a pattern, the U.S. Court of Appeals for the Fifth Circuit has found that "The number of [violations]...is not determinative.... In any event, no mathematical formula is workable, nor was any intended" (*United States v. Peachtree Tenth Corp.*, 437 F.2d 221, 227 [5th Cir. 1971], cited in June 28, 2013, DOJ Findings Letter regarding the Investigation of the Los Angeles County Sheriff's Department Stations in Antelope Valley).

introduce it, and federal and state prosecutors can bring criminal charges against police officers for their actions.

Title 42 U.S.C. § 1983 was passed in its original form as part of the Civil Rights Act of 1871. It permits a civil suit against any person, agency, or municipality that, while acting under color of law, deprives another of his or her constitutional rights; and it is frequently used to challenge police practices (*Monell v. Dept. of Soc. Serv.*, 436 U.S. 658 [1978]). When successful, these suits typically result in settlements or other judgments against individuals and municipalities for monetary damages, though they can also lead to equitable relief in the form of a court declaration that a policy or act is unconstitutional or a command to an agency either not to engage in some conduct or to carry out particular reforms to prevent future constitutional violations.

Under 42 U.S.C. § 1983, governments act by making policies or decisions or by permitting practices that are so persistent and widespread that they function as policy or law. A municipality or police department can only be sued under section 1983 if a departmental policy, custom, or practice causes—in the sense of being the moving force behind—a constitutional violation by an officer (*Monell v. Dept. of Soc. Serv.*, 1978). Thus, a city will only be directly liable for harms associated with a proactive policing strategy if the policies, decisions, or practices that implement that strategy cause constitutional injury (*Monell v. Dept. of Soc. Serv.*, 1978). For example, a federal district court found New York City liable for the NYPD's program of aggressively stopping, questioning, and frisking suspects because the program resulted in a widespread practice, amounting to a policy, of conducting unconstitutional stops and frisks and targeting racially defined groups in a disproportionate and discriminatory manner (*Floyd v. City of New York*, 2013). The court did not bar the proactive goal of deterring weapons possession, nor the practice of using stops and frisks aggressively to achieve it, so long as the policy as implemented did not cause constitutional violations or otherwise violate the Equal Protection Clause.

Plaintiffs can also bring civil suits against individual officers for violating clearly established constitutional rights while acting under color of law (42 U.S.C. § 1983). Where prior law makes clear that an officer's conduct under the specific circumstances violates the Constitution, the officer can be liable for the injuries that result. If an officer violates a right that is not clearly established under existing law, he is entitled to qualified immunity, which protects him against being sued or held liable for his actions (*Pearson v. Callahan*, 555 U.S. 223 [2009]). A right is not clearly established unless preexisting court decisions squarely govern the question, such that every reasonable officer would have understood that the particular conduct violated the law. For example, in one recent U.S. Supreme Court case, *Mullenix v. Luna* (2015), the court held that existing precedent had not put "beyond debate" the conclusion that an officer who shot "a reportedly intoxicated fugitive, set on avoiding capture through high-speed vehicular flight, who twice during his flight had threatened to shoot police officers, and who was moments away from encountering an officer" had acted unreasonably (*Mullenix v. Luna*, 2015). Thus, it found the officer entitled to qualified immunity, shielding him from liability and suit.

While suits against officers might seem less relevant to influencing departmental decision making than suits against municipalities or police departments, they may have similar effects on policy. Even when an individual officer(s) is named as a defendant and not the department or municipality, municipalities almost inevitably indemnify officers, meaning that they pay the costs of damages actions against them. Thus, municipalities bear the financial burden for judgments for damages in section 1983 suits even when the judgments operate formally only against individual officers (Schwartz, 2014). Given indemnification, civil judgments could, at least in theory, deter cities from adopting policies that give rise to unconstitutional conduct that might lead to liability, and cities that pay frequent civil judgments might be encouraged to reform strategies that tend to produce constitutional violations. However, municipalities only infrequently collect and analyze information about civil suits or the police practices that give rise to them. In departments that do not use the information provided by civil suits to manage their liability risk, damages actions may have limited effect on decision making about continuing proactive strategies that lead to such suits (Schwartz, 2010).

Sometimes monetary damages are inadequate to repair an injury to a plaintiff. In those circumstances, private plaintiffs may seek equitable relief instead. Equitable relief can include a judicial order to do something, an order not to do something, or a declaration about the rights of the parties, among other remedies. Though equitable relief is less common than damages, it can operate powerfully on the government agency against which it is levied. If damage actions incentivize reform, it is by making reform a cost-effective alternative to costly future judgments. By contrast, equitable relief can mandate immediate policy change and imposes stark legal and reputational consequences for those who refuse to comply.

While private suits for equitable relief have played an historic role in efforts to promote civil rights in many other arenas, including housing, school desegregation, and prison conditions, the U.S. Supreme Court has established notable obstacles to civil lawsuits for equitable relief against police departments, mostly importantly in the form of limits on standing (*City of Los Angeles v. Lyons*, 461 U.S. 95 [1983]; *Rizzo v. Goode*, 423 U.S. 362 [1976]). In general, unlike a plaintiff seeking only damages, a plaintiff asking for forward-looking relief must demonstrate that there is a "real and immediate threat" of future injury. In *City of Los Angeles v. Lyons* (1983), the U.S. Supreme Court applied this standard with special vigor to plaintiffs seeking injunctive relief against a police department, holding that it cannot be satisfied by demonstrating a past injury by the police or by speculation that the police might injure the same plaintiff. Thus, Adolph Lyons, who had sought to challenge the chokehold policy of the Los Angeles Police Department after he had been choked to unconsciousness during a traffic stop, did not have standing because he could not show that he would likely be stopped again, and then either that he would illegally resist, resulting in a chokehold, or that officers would subject him to a chokehold without provocation. Although the "real and immediate threat" standard applies to all plaintiffs seeking injunctive relief, given the vagaries of police–citizen interactions, the standard has proven to be an especially high bar for plaintiffs challenging police policies.

Though *Lyons* has stymied many suits against departments, plaintiffs challenging proactive policing may have a somewhat easier time bringing equitable relief claims than plaintiffs challenging traditional policing methods. The same qualities that make preventative policing policies proactive—their forward looking, strategic focus—can make the threat of future injury more "real and immediate." For instance, courts are more likely to find standing for equitable challenges under *Lyons* when a policy targets relatively innocent or common conduct—as proactive policing sometimes does when it encourages stops based on minimal suspicion or arrests for very minor offenses—because the risk to the plaintiff of being targeted under such a policy is less dependent on his own future wrongdoing and therefore less speculative (*United States v. Chang*, Civ. Action No 02-2010, Memorandum Op., D.D.C. [Sep. 9, 2010]; *National Congress for Puerto Rican Rights v. City of New York*, F. Supp. 2d 154 [S.D.N.Y. 1999]). Similarly, plaintiffs are likely to have an easier time showing that they are likely to be injured in the future when a department engages in the challenged conduct frequently or when the policy targets a subpopulation of which they are a part (*United States v. Chang*, 2010; *National Congress for Puerto Rican Rights v. City of New York*, 1999). Strategies that depend on widespread use of stops, frisks, and arrests, like SQF, broken windows, and zero tolerance, often encourage a large volume of police-citizen encounters and are often accused of disproportionately focusing police action against particular racial or ethnic groups. They therefore may make it more likely that the burdens of the policy will fall on a particular plaintiff attempting to establish standing (*Floyd v. City of New York*, 2013; U.S. Department of Justice, 2016). Strategies that expressly concentrate resources on identifiable activities, places, or defendants, such as problem-oriented, hot spots, and focused deterrence policing, are similarly more likely than are general patrol strategies to create a realistic risk that plaintiffs who fall within those parameters will be subject to the allegedly unconstitutional police intervention.

Section 1983 suits are the primary method for challenging the consequences of proactive strategies in court, but they are not the only one. Title 42 U.S.C. § 14141 permits DOJ to bring suit for equitable relief against police departments that engage in a pattern or practice of constitutional violations. DOJ is not subject to the standing requirements of *City of Los Angeles v. Lyons* and therefore can bring cases seeking forward-looking remedies that could not be brought by private individuals.

In most of the early efforts to pursue pattern and practice suits against police departments, DOJ focused on policing acts rather than on strategies. However, in some recent suits DOJ has expressly linked proactive policing strategies to constitutional violations. Most recently, as noted above, DOJ found that zero tolerance policing as implemented by the BPD caused a pattern of constitutional violations (U.S. Department of Justice, 2016). "Pattern-and-practice" suits are usually settled through consent decrees, in which the city and DOJ agree to reforms the department will adopt in order to prevent future constitutional violations. In these decrees, DOJ sometimes expressly promotes one proactive strategy, community-oriented policing, as well as other mechanisms for encouraging transparency, accountability, and community participation in determining policing policy. DOJ can similarly demand that departments not engage in proactive strategies it views as linked to violations. To the extent that police departments look to prior consent decrees for information on what activities might get them sued, this linkage could discourage some departments from adopting zero tolerance policing or similar proactive strategies that DOJ has previously described as facilitating constitutional violations.

Other legal remedies for police misconduct, such as the exclusionary rule, are much less likely to affect police department use of proactive policing strategies. The exclusionary rule prohibits the use in any criminal trial of evidence obtained unconstitutionally, and it is often labeled the primary remedy for deterring Fourth Amendment violations (*Utah v. Strieff*, 579 U.S. ___ [2016]). However, the exclusionary rule cannot deter constitutional violations that do not produce evidence or do not result in a criminal prosecution of the individual whose rights were violated (*Terry v. Ohio*, 1968; *Rakas v. Illinois*, 439 U.S. 128 [1978]). Many proactive strategies do not emphasize prosecuting criminal conduct, or if they do, they focus on minor crimes that may not involve physical evidence or extensive motions practice. Even beyond these limitations, U.S. Supreme Court cases have notably limited the circumstances in which the exclusionary rule applies (*Utah v. Strieff*, 2016; *Herring v. United States*, 2009). Thus, even if a proactive strategy leads to illegally obtaining evidence and introducing it in criminal trials, the expected value of the strategy is unlikely to be undermined significantly by the increasingly remote threat of evidentiary exclusion. Finally, as with civil rights lawsuits, departments often do not gather sufficient information about evidentiary suppression to effectively internalize the expected costs of exclusion for policies that might trigger the exclusionary rule.

Criminal prosecutions of police officers are similarly unlikely to notably affect proactive policing, both because such prosecutions are relatively rare and because the costs of those prosecutions are borne heavily by the individual officers who are prosecuted, so are far less likely to be internalized by departments in a manner that prompts reform (Harmon, 2012a).

OTHER LEGAL STANDARDS AND VALUES

In addition to the Fourth and Fourteenth Amendments, a wide variety of federal, state, and local statutes constrain proactive policing. The federal Electronic Communications Privacy Act, for example, which incorporates the federal Wiretap Act, Stored Communications Act, and Pen Register Act, restricts how police may gather private information and how they collect information from third parties, such as Internet or cell service providers. State constitutions and statutes, along with local charters and ordinances, determine how police executives are hired and fired and how budgets are formulated. They determine when police are disciplined and what kinds of judicial or administrative review disciplinary mechanisms receive. And they determine what kinds of information about police activities are collected by departments and made available to the public. As these examples suggest, the entirety of law that could influence proactive strategies is extensive and diverse and cannot be easily summarized.

Even when proactive policing does not violate constitutional law or this array of additional legal constraints, or does so in unenforceable ways, proactive strategies sometimes violate deeply held legal values, such as privacy, bodily integrity, equality, autonomy, accountability, and transparency. Threats to these values may subject policing strategies to political responses that can, in turn, push municipalities and states to more aggressively impose additional regulation on policing. For instance, the Maryland State Police engaged in an extensive and intrusive undercover operation to investigate political activists in 2005 and 2006, which led to public outrage when it was revealed in 2008. In response to the public reaction and an investigation of the surveillance program, the Maryland General Assembly passed the Freedom of Association and Assembly Protection Act of 2009. The law sets additional controls over police surveillance activities, even when those activities comply with the Constitution, and requires local law enforcement agencies in Maryland to adopt policies implementing those controls (Roush, 2012). Similarly, after concerns about privacy and accountability were raised about the city's use of drones and video cameras, Seattle passed an ordinance setting up new political checks on law enforcement acquisition and use of surveillance equipment.[13] In light of potential legislative responses to concerns that proactive policing strategies violate traditional legal values, even when the strategies comply with existing law, some of these concerns are considered here.

For example, even assuming that SQF, broken windows, and zero tolerance policing can comply with Equal Protection and antidiscrimination law, many have argued that these strategies undermine equality and have unfair distributional consequences (Sekhon, 2011; Colb, 2001). Critics also contend that the practices used in these strategies invade bodily integrity and privacy in ways Fourth Amendment law cannot fully address (Harmon, 2012b). To address these concerns, legal scholars often advocate changing constitutional doctrine to forbid the strategies (Stuntz, 2002; Colb, 2001; Capers, 2010), but they might as easily argue that departments should give up the strategies preemptively or that other legal avenues be used to prohibit them.

Similarly, though focused deterrence (a person-focused strategy) and place-based strategies often comply with constitutional law, when departments identify chronic offenders or high-crime neighborhoods, they do so based on criminal histories and crime data. Blacks are likely to be overrepresented in criminal history data (Snyder, 2011; Kaeble, Maruschak, and Bonczar, 2015; Raphael and Stoll, 2013) and to live in neighborhoods in which crime is more likely to take place (Lofstrom and Raphael, 2016). To the degree that the data reflect earlier discriminatory criminal justice policy or historical housing discrimination, proactive strategies that seem neutral and may survive legal challenge can nevertheless have the effect of compounding earlier discrimination. In this way, proactive strategies can, in effect, "launder" racial disparities that result from prior government decision making: they can make the disparities appear to be driven by reasonable and legitimate policy goals rather than preexisting discrimination.

Similar concerns are often raised about using predictive policing methods, including the power of "big data" and crime analytics techniques, to isolate patterns among past criminal incidents. These methods can replicate discrimination and provide it with a superficially neutral justification. Such concerns are often aggravated by the absence of transparency and accountability for the algorithms used to identify patterns and predict future crime incidence (see, e.g., Joh, 2017). One of the most commonly used recidivism risk assessment tools, the Correctional Offender Management Profiling

---

[13] Seattle, WA, Municipal Code 14.18.20 (2013); Seattle, WA., Ordinance 124142 (2013).

for Alternative Sanctions, or COMPAS, is based on calculations that are considered proprietary by its creator, Northpointe (Angwin et al., 2016).[14]

More generally, concentrating policing on particular problems or neighborhoods is likely to have important distributional consequences, including focusing the costs of police and prosecutorial power more heavily on places where specific groups are overrepresented. For instance, a decision to interrupt open-air drug markets, rather than targeting doctors who run prescription drug mills, will mean that some culpable offenders are more likely to suffer criminal justice consequences than others. David Weisburd (2016) argued that such focusing of policing can reduce overall harm. A focused policing approach, for example, at crime hot spots will not lead to large-scale police intrusion in a neighborhood overall. But such focusing can have negative consequences in the form of reduced liberty for some when people who live in identified hot spots suffer additional police stops or arrests.

Beyond distributional effects, although some types of focused policing may reduce overall harm, other proactive strategies may increase individual and aggregate negative consequences of policing. Even when legal, and even when effective in preventing crime, each additional stop and arrest imposed constitutes a significant intrusion on individual interests in liberty, autonomy, bodily integrity, and privacy and potentially constitutes an erosion in perceptions of the police, at least among some in the community. The negative consequences can be both financial, in the form of lost income, and intangible, such as the dignity harms of being frisked in public. Yet these various harms are sometimes overlooked in existing assessments of policing policies (Harmon, 2015).

Some scholars have suggested that the risk of unfair policing that many proactive strategies entail indicates that those proactive strategies should be replaced with a "newer policing" that focuses on changing public perceptions of the police (Tyler, Goff, and MacCoun, 2015). Others have argued that the negative consequences resulting from some proactive strategies can be mitigated by programs designed and implemented with an emphasis on public participation, legitimacy, and fairness (Braga and Weisburd, 2010). For instance, an ongoing test program in Brooklyn Park, Minnesota, proactively focuses additional policing on hot spots but also seeks to establish effective and trusting relationships between police and residents of the hot spots and shared expectations for the program (D. Weisburd, 2016).

---

[14] At the same time, increased availability of administrative data on police activity may allow police departments to prevent, and others to better assess, potential Fourth or Fourteenth Amendment violations, as demonstrated by Goel, Rao, and Shroff (2016).

COMMUNITY-BASED POLICING

The heterogeneity of policing programs under the rubric of community policing makes it difficult to assess credibly the relationship between such programs and legal constraints and values. Activities associated with the approach, this report calls "community-based policing" (see Chapter 2), such as engaging in foot patrols or attending community meetings, have no significant legal implications. They are not governed by the Fourth Amendment, the Equal Protection Clause, or by federal or state statute. Nevertheless, in addition to encouraging officers to engage in particular activities, community-based policing also changes the allocation of discretion and responsibility within police departments and alters the mechanisms by which the department hears the concerns of the community. Whatever the positive benefits for legitimacy, community satisfaction, and crime control, these organizational changes can also limit traditional pathways of accountability in policing.

Traditionally, elected mayors and city councils and appointed city managers influence policing through police chiefs and other top commanders, whom they often hire and fire.[15] Police executives make and implement policy and priorities through a hierarchical command staff that oversees street-level officers. Thus, chiefs operate at the fulcrum of an external accountability mechanism by which voters, through elected officials and more directly, influence police executives and an internal accountability mechanism in which chiefs operate through a hierarchical command staff to shape officer action through rules governing officer conduct, professional rewards for good behavior, and sanctions for noncompliance. State and municipal law often draws the outer boundaries of this system of accountability in multiple ways: (1) through laws determining the form of the local government and the local electoral process, (2) by requiring departments to collect and disclose some kinds of information to the public, (3) by setting qualifications and powers for police executives, and (4) by regulating administrative investigation and discipline of officers.

Though community-based policing strategies are unlikely to violate the structural parameters set by state law, a community-based approach nevertheless changes the nature of both internal and external accountability in police departments. First, with respect to internal accountability, community-based policing often includes devolving authority down the organizational hierarchy to frontline officers, whose patrol assignments are geographic areas (Skogan, 2006c). Communities are encouraged to provide input directly to street-level officers. Those officers in turn are given discre-

---

[15] Most sheriffs are elected, meaning that unlike police chiefs, they are directly accountable to voters.

tion to allocate policing resources and shape problem solving, pursuant to that input, without as much command approval as is often required in traditional policing. These direct lines of communication and additional discretion can enable officers to act quickly and reactively to community input and can enable officers to develop valuable problem-solving skills (Weisburd, McElroy, and Hardyman, 1988; Bittner, 1983). However, the process concomitantly weakens the traditional power that command staff has over policy and officer action. For example, in an early study of a community-oriented policing strategy, Weisburd, McElroy, and Hardyman (1988) found that pilot community-policing units in the NYPD engaged in aggressive patrol tactics against low-level drug dealers, activities that were otherwise discouraged for patrol officers (as contrasted with specialized drug enforcement units) because of corruption hazards.

In concept, the additional officer discretion generated by the community-oriented policing strategy could permit additional violations of law and policy by individual officers. The potential problems here are highlighted in systematic social observations of police departments, which found higher rates of illegal searches among officers who embraced community-oriented policing than among those who did not (Gould and Mastrofski, 2004).

However, departments sometimes develop alternative means of supervising officers to replace traditional rules, monitoring, and sanctions. For example, in one study, supervisors of patrol officers engaged in community-based policing developed alternative metrics for productivity, such as assessing whether the officers made progress on priority problems in the neighborhood, rather than looking at arrests or response times. They also used supervisor approval for patrol strategies, careful selection of officers, and positive reinforcement of values to encourage law-abiding conduct by officers while they were out on patrol (Weisburd, McElroy, and Hardyman, 1988). These alternative supervision mechanisms may mitigate or eliminate effects on legal compliance by individual officers. For instance, a positive relationship between documentation and legality was noted by Gould and Mastrofski (2004), who observed the constitutionality of more than 100 searches in a single agency. In addition, whether decentralizing discretion results in a net increase or decrease in legal violations depends on several additional factors, including whether the counterfactual, more hierarchical, structure effectively promotes legal compliance. There is little empirical research about the comparative effectiveness of these alternative supervisory strategies, and therefore no way exists at present to assess the net accountability effects of community-oriented policing or similar strategies.

Second, with respect to external accountability, proactive policing strategies frequently emphasize informal community involvement in identifying, prioritizing, and solving problems through neighborhood meetings or through collaboration with business, religious, and neighborhood leaders, rather than either formal processes of aggregating community will, such as elections, or individual methods for providing input into police priorities, such as 911 calls (Skogan, 2006c). Replacing traditional means for collective input allows departments to respond more precisely (e.g., at the neighborhood or street corner level) and more thoroughly to more local concerns, and it allows voices that may get drowned out in the political process to be heard. But it may also make departmental choices less representative of broader community values. Moreover, since neighborhoods often lack elected leaders designated to represent their specific areas, officers have less structured and clear guidance about how to balance competing views. In addition, when departments replace other traditional, individual, forms of input, such as citizen calls, to set priorities, they move departments away from the classic account of policing by Reiss and Bordua (1967), which holds that "[i]n a democratic society, the major volume of police work derives from an external source, the citizen complaint, rather than from an internal organizational source." In this way, the community-based policing approach can change the basis for the legitimacy of police departments.

Like community-oriented policing, procedural justice policing operates both as a philosophy and as a strategy in police departments. As described in Chapter 2, in procedural justice policing, police officers give citizens voice, make decisions neutrally, treat people with dignity and politeness, and convey concern and benevolence, in order to promote perceptions of police legitimacy and thus achieve greater public cooperation with and deference to the police and increased compliance with the law.

Though the four pillars of procedural justice—giving voice, acting neutrally, treating citizens with dignity and respect, and conveying trustworthy motives—could reduce constitutional violations, procedural justice strategies may nevertheless sometimes exist in tension with other legal values. For example, one important principle in liberal legal regimes is that citizens should be able to limit their cooperation with law enforcement to no more than what is legally required of them. To that end, the law's commands should be clearly defined in advance and ascertainable to those subject to them, a principle known in some contexts as legality.

Outside of the context of *Miranda* warnings (384 U.S. 436 [1966]), police officers are not usually required by constitutional law to tell citizens that they may refuse consent in order for their consent to be found knowing and voluntary (*Schneckloth v. Bustamonte*, 412 U.S. 218 [1973]; *United States v. Drayton*, 536 U.S. 194 [2002]). Procedural justice practices often seek to facilitate compliance by having officers request cooperation, both in circumstances when the officers might have no power to compel cooperation and in circumstances where they could issue an order enforceable either by force or by the threat of an arrest. Given that an invitation to cooperate is ambiguous, procedural justice practices can comply with the law while making it harder for people to distinguish requests from commands that they are legally obliged to follow. Doing so can thereby make it harder for citizens to enforce fully their legal rights, if they wish to comply with the law but do not wish to cooperate with police requests that are not legally obligatory. The empirical literature studying the effects of procedural justice policing largely fails to distinguish cooperation with optional requests from compliance with legally mandatory commands, which makes it harder to assess the effects of procedural justice practices on populations with different preferences about cooperation versus compliance. There is some empirical evidence that suggests that police officers themselves may not fully understand the difference between a citizen's failure to comply with an optional request and resistance to a lawful order. While not examining the distinction between requests and orders per se, Heffernan and Lovely (1991) presented police officers, lawyers, and lay people with hypothetical search and seizure scenarios and found that, on average, officers were better at identifying constitutional violations than lay people but worse than lawyers.

More broadly, the logic model underlying procedural justice emphasizes the centrality of citizen feelings about policing and deemphasizes the significance of the legal or normative status of police conduct (Meares, 2013). This logic model emphasizes the importance of community satisfaction with the police and the benefits that may accrue from the perception that the police are trustworthy and legitimate. Thus, procedural justice scholars define terms such as legitimacy and fairness differently than legal and political philosophers do. In these latter perspectives, procedural justice is a virtue of the decision-making process, not a quality of how that process is perceived (Solum, 2004). Similarly, legitimacy is a quality of political institutions, not of perceptions of those institutions. In legal and political philosophy, perceptions of how an institution functions may be considered in deciding whether it lives up to the normative demands of procedural justice and political legitimacy, but those demands have content independent of how the institution is perceived.

Criteria for police action based on perceptions that were developed in accordance with the procedural justice logic model often align closely with criteria based on deep legal values such as fairness and accountability. But there could be some distance between the normative standards by which policing might be meaningfully assessed from an objective perspective and standards based on subjective perceptions—the yardsticks by which police departments are encouraged to measure themselves under this logic model. By contrast, to the degree that procedural justice policing operates as intended, it may make violations of the law less likely. For example, procedural justice policing tries to induce citizens to comply voluntarily with officers. If an officer invites a person to talk to police on the street, and the person cooperates, then the officer may avoid a seizure that triggers Fourth Amendment scrutiny (or custody that triggers the need for *Miranda* warnings and a waiver by the person in custody before asking questions). Similarly, if an officer invites a citizen to turn out his pockets, and the individual voluntarily complies, the Fourth Amendment requires no individualized suspicion for the search. Fewer rules for officers to follow in carrying out their duties could, mechanically, mean fewer legal violations by police. Less directly, if procedural justice policing increases citizen compliance and reduces conflict between citizens and officers, it may limit the situational factors that can lead to escalation, such as arrests and use of force, and therefore reduce the opportunities for making an arrest illegally or using excessive force (Owens et al., 2016).

In addition, procedural justice may include changes within the police department, namely, the application of procedural justice principles internally to how officers are treated by their organization and those who oversee it. Thus, for example, a department might seek to give officers voice, treat them neutrally and with dignity, and display trustworthy motives before imposing administrative discipline. Or it might solicit input for policies and priorities that affect an officer's work. If adopting procedural justice policing increases the legitimacy of internal rules to officers, and thereby increases their compliance with departmental policies regarding treatment of civilians, then procedural justice policing could decrease officers' legal violations, including Fourth Amendment violations.

This argument was made by Wolfe and Piquero (2011) and by Tyler and colleagues (2007), who surveyed groups of law enforcement officers about their perceptions of procedural justice in their agency and their willingness to follow their supervisor's orders. Both studies found that perceptions of fairness and procedural justice were positively correlated with various measures of rule compliance by officers. Wolfe and Piquero (2011) found that officers who felt that they were treated fairly within the Philadelphia Police Department were less likely to engage in misconduct on the job and were also less likely to be the subject of an internal affairs investigation. Since all officers work for the same organization, in the absence of further information on the supervisory strategies to which each officer was subject, it is difficult to attribute this finding to changes in procedural justice. For example, it seems highly plausible that officers developed poor opinions of their employers because they were subject to investigation. Similar concerns apply to the findings by Tyler, Callahan, and Frost (2007), who surveyed officers in multiple agencies and estimated the correlation between the officer's perceptions of legitimacy and procedural justice with their self-reported propensity to violate department rules. Without a better understanding of why, exactly, individual officers vary in their perceptions of legitimacy, it is difficult to draw causal conclusions from these studies about the impact of introducing procedural justice–oriented policies on the legality of officer actions. In short, given their research design, the existing literature does not provide evidence supporting or refuting the hypothesis that procedural justice principles applied internally and that officers' perceptions of the legitimacy of the police organization will increase the likelihood that officers follow department rules.

CONCLUSION

However effective a policing practice may be in preventing crime, it is impermissible if it violates the law. The most important legal constraints on proactive policing are the Fourth Amendment and the Equal Protection Clause (of the Fourteenth Amendment) of the Constitution, along with related statutory provisions. Several proactive practices are made possible by particular aspects of contemporary Fourth Amendment doctrine: SQF, broken windows, and hot spots policing strategies take advantage of the low level of individualized suspicion required for stops and frisks. Closed circuit television depends on the doctrine that puts most movements in public beyond the scope of the Fourth Amendment. Third party policing sometimes uses doctrine that permissively allows police to use information gathered from third parties.

Empirical evidence on the relationship between particular policing strategies and constitutional violations is insufficient to draw any significant conclusions about the likelihood that particular proactive strategies increase or decrease constitutional violations. Research about whether proactive policing leads to constitutional violations is hampered by inadequate data on police conduct that raises constitutional concerns, including stops, searches, and uses of force; the absence of accurate objective measures of constitutionality or proxies for constitutional violations; and studies that do not adequately engage in counterfactual analysis. Nevertheless, there are case-specific evidence and ethnographic and theoretical arguments consistent with the hypothesis that proactive strategies that use aggressive stops, searches, and arrests to deter criminal activity may decrease liberty and increase Fourth Amendment and Equal Protection violations. In addition, proactive policing strategies can affect the Fourth Amendment status of policing conduct.

Community-oriented policing and procedural justice policing strategies differ from other proactive policing strategies in that there are plausible mechanisms by which they may decrease constitutional violations rather than increase them. However, there is insufficient empirical evidence to support the existence of these effects (especially given the heterogeneity of these approaches and the activities used to pursue them), and both community-oriented policing and procedural justice policing sometimes may disrupt traditional mechanisms of accountability by changing how departments make decisions or how demands and requests are conveyed to individuals with whom the police interact.

Civil lawsuits for damages and equitable relief are likely to be both the most common and most successful legal mechanisms for enforcing constitutional rules when police departments engage in proactive policing. While civil lawsuits for equitable relief have more direct effect, such suits face practical and legal obstacles that sometimes make them difficult to bring successfully. Civil lawsuits for damages face different obstacles and are unlikely to encourage constitutional compliance unless departments collect information about the number and kinds of lawsuits they face, enabling the departments to identify and mitigate sources of constitutional violations within them. DOJ has also sought to limit some kinds of proactive policing, such as zero tolerance policing, and encourage other kinds of proactive policing, such as community-oriented policing, in its pattern and practice lawsuits against departments.

Even when proactive policing does not violate or encourage violations of the law, it may implicate important legal values such as privacy, equality, and accountability that are of substantial public concern. In doing so, proactive policing strategies can raise substantial distributional and equality concerns and can sometimes spur local and state law changes, adding to existing regulation of the police.

Compared to the other outcomes examined in this report, there is relatively less empirical evidence on the impact of proactive policing policies on the legality of officer actions. This is at least in part due to the nature of legality itself, which is intrinsically determined in an ex post, individual manner relative to evolving case law, rather than a more objective, a priori, standard such as the standards for determining assault, racial disparities, or community satisfaction. The committee drew the following overarching conclusions regarding law, legality, and proactive policing:

CONCLUSION 3-1 Factual findings from court proceedings, federal investigations into police departments, and ethnographic and theoretical arguments support the hypothesis that proactive strategies that use aggressive stops, searches, and arrests to deter criminal activity may decrease liberty and increase violations of the Fourth Amendment and Equal Protection Clause; proactive policing strategies may also affect the Fourth Amendment status of policing conduct. However, there is not enough direct empirical evidence on the relationship between particular policing strategies and constitutional violations to draw any conclusions about the likelihood that particular proactive strategies increase or decrease constitutional violations.

CONCLUSION 3-2 Even when proactive strategies do not violate or encourage constitutional violations, they may undermine legal values, such as privacy, equality, and accountability. Empirical studies to date have not assessed these implications.

4

Impacts of Proactive Policing on Crime and Disorder

As noted in Chapter 1, proactive policing developed as part of an important set of innovations in American policing, growing out of concerns in the late 20th century that the police were not achieving crime prevention goals through standard approaches. Many of the proactive policing strategies that are the focus of this report began with the primary goal of doing something about problems of crime and disorder. Even approaches that included other key aims, such as community-based policing, shared as an important concern the solving of community problems such as crime. In this chapter, we turn to the crime and disorder control impacts of proactive policing strategies. The chapter begins by reviewing the mechanisms through which these strategies are seen to affect crime and other problems. It then discusses each of the four general approaches to prevention described in Chapter 2 and reviews the evidence regarding the specific proactive policing strategies that fall under each approach. Research on the relationship between proactive policing and crime is substantially more developed than the other outcomes addressed by the committee. In light of that, we discuss a selection of highly influential research findings in detail and summarize the other key literature. Finally, the chapter lays out the committee's key conclusions about these findings and the strength of the evidence for crime prevention outcomes.

MECHANISMS FOR PREVENTION

The diverse array of programs that are included under the "proactive policing" rubric all seek to harness one or more crime-prevention mechanisms. We review below three basic mechanisms: reduction in criminal opportunities, deterrence, and increases in perceived legitimacy of the law and law enforcement.

The environment for potential offenders may be viewed as consisting of an array of criminal opportunities, some enduring (a gas station that could be robbed) and some transitory (a heated argument in a bar). Each opportunity is characterized from the potential offenders' perspective in terms of the effort, potential reward, and likelihood of apprehension and punishment (Clarke, 1980; Cook, 1979, 1986; Clarke and Cornish, 1985; Nagin, 2013; Nagin, Solow, and Lum, 2015). Problem-solving interventions often focus on attending to these opportunities (or potential crimes) to stop offending before it occurs. At the most basic level, some proactive programs seek to limit criminal opportunities, such as when police assist in making the case for closing a nightclub that tends to have a high rate of violence or when officers are involved in negotiating gang conflicts before the shooting starts. Other proactive programs address crime opportunities directly by "hardening" them, or increasing the cost and effort it would take for an offender to take advantage of a potential target. Such actions might include problem-solving activities by the police, including using situational crime-prevention measures (Clarke, 1997; Cornish and Clarke, 2003) or crime prevention through environment design (Jeffrey, 1971; Newman, 1972). For example, the police can encourage residents to use locks, doors, gates, guards, or cameras. The police can also work with businesses to make potential criminal opportunities more visible to guardians (e.g., removing obstructions that block police view of an alley or the interior of a neighborhood store). The police can also proactively try to reduce the potential for criminal opportunities to emerge by adjusting the routines of individuals so that potential offenders and victims do not meet (or at least do not meet without the presence of a guardian). For example, the police might request that schools release children at different times to reduce opportunities for bullying or fights. This type of opportunity-reduction strategy arises from routine activity and crime-pattern theories (see Cohen and Felson, 1979; Brantingham and Brantingham, 1993, respectively).

In addition to removing or hardening opportunities for crime, police may proactively try to prevent crime by changing an offender's risk perception of being apprehended if the offender takes advantage of a crime opportunity. For example, police agencies may choose to proactively increase foot patrol in a crime hot spot in an effort to reduce the rate of vandalism, car theft or break-ins, burglaries, robberies, assaults, or other crimes. The heightened police presence and visibility aims to increase an offender's perception that he may be apprehended if he takes advantage of crime opportunities at that hot spot. Although individual offenders at a hot spot may vary in their perceived risk of apprehension (and that perception may also vary for different types of crimes, times, locations, or situations), hot spots policing is believed to alter offenders' average perceived risk of apprehension, resulting in fewer offenders exploiting opportunities at that hot spot and lowering the crime rate at that location.

This adjustment in a would-be offender's perceived risk of detection or apprehension is hypothesized to occur through the prevention mechanism of deterrence (Nagin, 2013). The crime reduction value of deterrence is influenced not only by the perceived risk of apprehension (a cost), but also relatedly from a rational calculation of a multitude of costs and benefits associated with that criminal opportunity (see Clarke, 1997; Clarke and Cornish, 1985). An offender's calculation may be constrained by many factors (intoxication, lack of available information, cognitive deficits, etc.) that are specific to the offender. As a result, the outcome of proactive policing deterrence efforts may be partially stochastic. But in terms of aggregate criminal behavior, deterrence is hypothesized to occur when offenders perceive their risk of apprehension to be high and the perceived benefits do not outweigh those risks.

Deterrence is the primary prevention mechanism in the logic models underlying the place-based and person-focused approaches to proactive policing.[1] In hot spots policing, for example, deterrence is created by increasing police presence in places with high levels of concentrated opportunities or routines for criminal offending, thus conveying an increased sense of apprehension and discouraging offenders from taking advantage of those opportunities. Or police may increase the number of pedestrian or traffic stops on a street with high levels of gun violence. Police officers often exercise discretion and do not take enforcement actions against all illegal activity. However, a decrease in discretion with a concomitant increase in lawful stops supported by reasonable suspicion can have a corollary benefit of increasing a would-be offender's perception that she might be stopped and possibly searched for a weapon (as well as apprehended for carrying the weapon), thus deterring her from carrying that weapon (and, in turn, using that weapon in a crime). In focused deterrence policing, a strategy for the person-focused approach, authorities make direct contact with potential high-risk offenders in an attempt to transform a vague and generalized threat of arrest into an explicit, personalized, and highly salient warning that arrest is imminent if the individuals persist in offending. Other examples of deterrence may be less direct, as we will discuss below.

---

[1] Chapter 2 defines the four approaches identified by the committee and discusses typical proactive policing strategies that focus on each approach. Table 2-1 summarizes the committee's conceptual framework of broad approaches and the strategies for them. The logic model that informs an approach is summarized in that table and discussed in more detail in the section of Chapter 2 for that proactive policing approach.

Aside from deterrence (and in some cases related to deterrence), community-based policing activities are believed to prevent crime not necessarily because they increase the perceived risk of apprehension among potential offenders (although they could) but because they help to increase social and informal control through collective efficacy and increased guardianship (i.e., a community's or citizens' willingness to step in to control the behavior of others in the community) (see Sampson, 2011). Some mechanisms typical of the community-based approach attempt to reduce citizen fear and uncertainty and stop citizen withdrawal from aspects of community life that may create informal social control (see Skogan, 1988). Other proponents for a community-based approach have hypothesized that police can prevent future offending by increasing community members' perceptions of the legitimacy of the law and legal authorities such as the police and the courts. Tyler (2006), for example, hypothesized that the use of procedural justice during officer and citizen exchanges (i.e., how officers treat and interact with an individual) will increase citizens' compliance with the law in the future.

As discussed in Chapter 2, the police engage in many proactive crime prevention practices that are grounded in these prevention mechanisms. We now turn to a review of the scientific evidence for these interventions and close with a critical assessment of this body of evidence. Note that deterrence mechanisms, as well as related mechanisms that make criminal opportunities less attractive, have the advantage that they do not necessarily entail the imposition of additional punishment, such as arrest or prosecution. Further, if potential offenders perceive a higher risk of arrest, greater potential for detection and disapproval by other community members, or the reduction and availability of opportunities (and rewards) for crime, then both arrests and crime may actually decrease (Nagin, 2013).

PLACE-BASED STRATEGIES

Hot Spots Policing

Emerging theoretical paradigms and empirical findings on the concentration of crime and disorder at small "hot spot" locations (see Brantingham and Brantingham, 1982, 1984; Sherman, Buerger, and Gartin, 1989) led Sherman and Weisburd (1995) to explore the practical implications of police proactively targeting crime hot spots with preventive patrol. With cooperation from the Minneapolis Police Department they developed a large experimental field study to challenge the conclusions of the well-known Kansas City Preventive Patrol Experiment (Kelling et al., 1974) that varying the levels of police patrol at places has little value in preventing or controlling crime. They also sought to show that proactively focusing police efforts on crime hot spots presented a new and promising approach for preventing crime.

The Minneapolis field study addressed two limitations of the earlier Kansas City experiment. The design of the earlier experiment, which involved just 15 patrol beats, had limited the statistical power of the results. A second limitation was that the treatment condition was diffused across relatively large areas—entire police patrol beats—which meant that the level of treatment intervention applied at hot spots within these beats may have been too diluted to generate the hypothesized deterrent effect. In the Minneapolis redesign, the researchers first analyzed the addresses of calls for police service and then set appropriate boundaries, based on the researchers' observations, to define "microgeographical locations" where service calls clustered. Each of the resulting 110 crime hot spots was considerably smaller than a patrol beat (refer to Box 2-1 in Chapter 2 for the definition of hot spot areas). The 110 hot spots were grouped into five statistical blocks based on natural cutting points within the distribution of "hard crime" calls for service frequencies. The within-block randomization procedure created two equal groups of 55 hot spots in the treatment group and 55 hot spots in the control group. Changes in the number of calls for service between the treatment year and a baseline year were calculated for each hot spot, then the statistical differences in the year-to-year changes were compared between the set of hot spots in the treatment condition and the set of control hot spots.

Based on the observations of trained researchers, the treatment hot spots received two to three times as much police patrol presence when compared to the control hot spots. The study authors noted that there was some breakdown in the treatment applied during summer months due to officer vacations and peak calls for service to the police department. They therefore conducted a sensitivity analysis with varying comparison dates to account for the lack of dosage during the summer months. Using a series of analysis-of-variance models, the authors reported that the police patrol treatment generated between 6 percent and 13 percent reductions in calls for service in the treatment hot spots relative to calls for service in control hot spots. These reduction percentages passed tests for statistical significance. Analyses of systematic social observation data on disorderly behavior in both treatment and control hot spots, collected by trained researchers during the treatment year, found that observed disorder was only half as prevalent in treatment hot spots relative to control hot spots (Koper, 1995).

The Minneapolis Hot Spots Patrol Experiment established the potential importance of crime hot spots for policing (see below for confirmatory evidence in later studies), and it challenged the conventional logic that had assumed that police patrol could not be effective. However, the question remained whether concentrating on such places would merely shift crime from place to place (e.g., see Reppetto, 1976). The first hot spots study to examine the problem of displacement directly was the Jersey City Drug Market Analysis Experiment (Weisburd and Green, 1995). The study identified 56 drug hot spots of varying sizes, ranging from a group of addresses to a group of street segments evidencing similar drug activities. These were then randomly allocated either to a treatment group that received a systematic problem-oriented response to drug crime or to a control group that received the normal reactive responses typical of drug enforcement at the time. The randomized controlled trial compared calls for service at the treatment and control drug hot spots during a 7-month pre-intervention baseline period to calls for service during a 7-month post-intervention assessment period. The analysis revealed statistically significant differences in the pre- and post-intervention levels of calls for service between the treatment and control groups; in treatment drug markets, calls for service for disorder increased 8 percent, whereas calls for service in the control drug markets increased 20 percent.

The research team also used a randomized design method to compare calls for service over the same experimental periods at the two-block buffer zones surrounding the treatment and control drug hot spots. The analysis revealed that for public morals and narcotics calls, the level of calls in the buffer catchment areas for the experimental sites decreased, compared with the level of calls in buffer catchment areas for control sites, and the decrease was statistically significant. Calls regarding public morals declined by 34 percent in experimental catchment areas and increased by 3 percent in catchment areas for control sites. For narcotics, calls in the experimental site catchment areas declined by 12 percent while in control site catchment areas the level of calls for narcotics increased by 57 percent. To assess drug market activity in the area surrounding each treatment or control hot spot, the Jersey City Drug Market Analysis Experiment research team replicated the initial drug market identification process to identify drug markets in the area surrounding each hot spot in the original set. They estimated that drug market activity was half as likely to occur in areas surrounding treatment-condition hot spots as in areas surrounding the control condition hot spots.

The Police Foundation and the Jersey City Police Department subsequently collaborated on a controlled study to determine whether proactive policing targeted at two high-activity crime hot spots would result in immediate spatial displacement of crime incidents to areas surrounding the targeted location or would instead lead to diffusion of crime-control benefits into surrounding areas (Weisburd et al., 2006b). The study used crime mapping and database technologies, supplemented with observations from police officers and researchers, to identify two hot spots for the treatment condition: one location with active street prostitution and another with an active street-level drug market. To measure possible crime-displacement or benefit-diffusion effects associated with the proactive policing in these targeted hot spots, the researchers demarcated one- and two-block buffer zones around the hot spots as "catchment areas." The treatment interventions at the targeted hot spots comprised mostly traditional enforcement tactics (including police crackdowns), along with some situational responses.

The outcomes measured in this experiment were prostitution and drug events as observed by trained members of the research team during 20-minute observation periods in the targeted hot spot and its two catchment areas. More than 6,000 such observation periods were compiled over the course of the study. For the prostitution hot spot and its catchment areas, the research team used a quasi-experimental design in which trends in observed prostitution events were analyzed for a 9-month period and then adjusted for citywide *disorder call* trends. For the drug-market hot spot and its catchment areas, the quasi-experimental design involved analysis of trends in observed drug-behavior events for a 9-month period, but these trends were adjusted for citywide *drug call* trends. Pre-test versus post-test changes in the hot spots and catchment areas were evaluated using difference-of-means tests, after the trends in observed events had been adjusted for the citywide trend in the relevant call category.

For the prostitution hot spot, the analysis found a statistically significant 45 percent reduction in observed prostitution events at the location targeted for proactive policing, a statistically significant 61 percent reduction in such events in catchment area 1 (the one-block buffer zone), and a statistically significant 64 percent reduction in catchment area 2. For the drug-crime hot spot location, the analysis found a statistically significant 58 percent reduction in observed drug behavior within the hot spot, a 33 percent reduction (statistically not significant) in catchment area 1, and a statistically significant 64 percent reduction in catchment area 2. Consistent with these findings, ethnographic research in the neighborhoods and interviews with arrested offenders suggested that the intensified policing in the hot spot did not simply displace potential offenders into surrounding areas. Displacement did not occur, this ancillary research suggested, because the diminished opportunities and increased risks associated with moving were judged by potential offenders to exceed potential gains from moving their criminal behavior to areas immediately adjacent to the hot spot location.

A number of reviews of hot spots policing evaluations have consistently documented that this strategy has reduced crime in hot spots without displacing crime incidence to other locations. In fact, many of the evaluations reported a diffusion of crime-control benefits from targeted areas to the proximate areas (see, e.g., Sherman and Eck, 2002; Weisburd and Eck, 2004). Relative to other crime-prevention programs oriented toward intervening at larger geographic aggregations, such as neighborhoods and cities, rigorous evaluations of hot spots policing program are facilitated by the relative ease through which an adequate number of specific hot spot locations can be randomized to treatment and control conditions. In the 2004 report *Fairness and Effectiveness in Policing: The Evidence*, a National Research Council (NRC) study committee was unambiguous in its conclusions regarding the effectiveness and importance of hot spots policing, concluding that "studies that focused police resources on crime hot spots provide the strongest collective evidence of police effectiveness that is now available" (National Research Council, 2004, p. 250).

An ongoing, systematic review of hot spots policing studies, conducted under the auspices of the Campbell Collaboration, provides a detailed analysis and summation of the research results on how this strategy affects crime. The most recent report from this Campbell review covered results from 19 rigorous studies involving 25 evaluations of hot spots policing interventions (Braga, Papachristos, and Hureau, 2014). Of the 19 studies reviewed, 10 used quasi-experimental research designs to evaluate the effects of hot spots policing, and 9 were randomized controlled trials. A majority of the 25 evaluations concluded that the hot spots policing practices studied had generated statistically significant crime control benefits in the treatment areas, compared to control areas. Twenty of the 25 evaluations (80%) reported substantial gains in crime control that were associated with the hot spots intervention evaluated.

This Campbell meta-analysis was able to calculate effect sizes for just 20 main effects tests and 13 displacement and diffusion tests, due to limited information in the original research reports. For the main effect sizes, the meta-analysis calculated a moderate and statistically significant positive overall mean effect. Nine of the 13 displacement/diffusion tests reported effect sizes that favored benefit-diffusion effects over crime-displacement effects. The displacement/diffusion meta-analysis suggests a small but statistically significant overall "diffusion of crime control benefits effect" (Clarke and Weisburd, 1994) generated by the hot spots policing strategies. However, all but one of the crime-displacement and benefit-diffusion tests were limited to examining spatial displacement and diffusion effects that were proximal to the targeted area in space and time. That is, they evaluated whether the more intensive policing in the targeted hot spots was associated with an increase or decrease in crime incidents occurring in the immediately adjacent area during the test period. (Only the Jersey City Drug Market Analysis Experiment examined whether offenders displaced to distal locations beyond areas immediately surrounding the study hot spots.)

An important point about hot spots policing programs that have been evaluated is that the policing practices used in the targeted crime hot spots can vary considerably. These strategies and tactics can include practices typical of a problem-oriented policing strategy and practices typical of zero tolerance policing such as more frequent arrests for misdemeanors, as well as increased patrol, focused drug enforcement, pedestrian and traffic stops, increased gun searches and seizures, and the use of surveillance technologies (e.g., license plate readers). The Campbell review categorized these varied programs into two different strategies (consistent with the conceptual framework developed in Chapter 2 and summarized in Table 2-1) to control crime in hots spots (Braga, Papachristos, and Hureau, 2014). Programs more typical of a problem-oriented policing strategy involved police-led efforts to change the underlying conditions at hot spots that are perceived to be factors contributing to recurring crime problems (Goldstein, 1990). Consistent with this strategy (as described in Chapter 2 of this report), in these programs the police are not the sole implementers of the selected proactive practice. Instead, city services, businesses, and other stakeholders may partner with the police to address the conditions targeted in the hot spot. The second strategy identified by the Campbell review as characteristic of hot spots policing interventions relied on increasing traditional policing activities in the targeted hot spots, with the intention of preventing crime through general deterrence and increased risk of apprehension.

The meta-analysis included in the Campbell review used these two category types as an effect-size moderator to compare the evaluated programs. Of the 20 tests for main effects size, the review's authors characterized 10 as evaluating problem-oriented practices applied to hot spots policing and 10 as evaluating intensified traditional policing tactics in the targeted hot spots. Their analysis found that the programs applying problem-oriented policing practices had an overall mean effect size (average effect size across all 10 studies) that was twice the overall mean effect size for the 10 programs that applied increased traditional policing practices.

Hot spots policing has been criticized for having only a short-term impact (Rosenbaum, 2006). As is the case for other proactive policing strategies reviewed below, little is known about the long-term impacts of this strategy. At the same time, if the mechanism for crime control is the visible presence of police (see Nagin, 2013), then the main gains expected would be short-term and police should expect to continue to manage such places in the long term. This was confirmed in a reanalysis of the Philadelphia Foot Patrol Experiment. During the initial experiment, teams of four foot patrol officers, concentrated in 60 violent crime hot spots of Philadelphia, Pennsylvania, were able to reduce violent crime by 23 percent over a 3-month period, compared to equivalent control locations (Ratcliffe et al., 2011). Subsequently Sorg and colleagues (2013) found that the deterrent effect identified during the experiment dissipated rapidly; differences in violent crime between control and experimental areas were no longer present within a short time after the experiment finished. More long-term gains might be expected in the case of problem-oriented hot spots interventions, which seek to solve underlying problems, or in cases where a hot spots intervention was maintained over a long period of time. But beyond the Philadelphia Foot Patrol Experiment, little evidence exists in the research literature regarding these questions.

Another question for which solid empirical studies are lacking is whether hot spots policing will produce areawide or jurisdictional impacts on crime (e.g., in a city as a whole, or even large administrative areas such as precincts within a city). In some sense, the large number of well-controlled studies, often randomized experiments, within jurisdictions hampers the ability to draw jurisdictional inferences about crime. Randomly allocating hot spots within jurisdictions necessarily makes it very difficult to gain estimates of an overall program effect across the jurisdictions. Hot spots policing programs have generally compared gains in crime hot spots in treatment and control conditions; they have not estimated the potential large-area impacts of this approach. The logic model of the strategy implies there should be such impacts, given the effects on hot spots and the diffusion-of-benefits impacts noted in a series of studies. Of course, the level of jurisdictional impacts would depend on the scope of the hot spots policing program. However, the possibility of distal displacement of crime makes the investigation of jurisdictional impacts particularly important.

The importance of considering the jurisdiction-level effects of a hot spots policing approach, as well as other geographically focused policing approaches, also follows from consideration of the possible opportunity costs of concentrating police presence. The additional officers that are assigned to the hot spots would otherwise be patrolling lower-crime areas or perhaps engaged in other productive activities that would presumably reduce crime. So the reduction in crime in hot spots logically comes at a cost to other policing activities, assuming that overall police resources are fixed. The case for a hot spots model requires a demonstration not only that additional policing of hot spots reduces crime in those areas but also that in effect, the additional police are more productive assigned to hot spots than they would be in their alternative assignment. None of the evaluations of hot spots policing has measured this sort of opportunity cost as it relates to jurisdictional outcomes.

Weisburd and colleagues (2017) used an agent-based model to compare overall crime prevention impacts in a simulated borough of a city with four beats. The model produced meaningful areawide crime-prevention benefits in the experiments with hot spots patrol as compared to randomized patrol in a jurisdiction. For instance, high-intensity hot spots policing, where half of the police officers assigned to a beat spent all of their time in the top five hot spots in that beat, reduced the incidence of robbery by 11.7 percent at the borough level, 11.5 percent at the police-beat level, and 77.3 percent at the hot-spot level in comparison to random police patrol. That study did identify distal displacement to areas farther from hot spots, though the distal displacement impacts were small. While these results follow the general logic model for hot spots policing, actual field experiments are needed to draw strong inferences about areawide impacts of the approach.

Summary. A large number of rigorous evaluations, including a series of randomized controlled trials, of hot spots policing programs have been conducted. The available research evidence suggests that hot spots policing interventions generate statistically significant crime-reduction impacts without simply displacing crime into areas immediately surrounding the targeted locations. Instead, hot spots policing studies that do measure possible displacement effects tend to find that these programs generate a diffusion-of-crime-control benefit into immediately adjacent areas. Our knowledge base on the crime-reduction impacts of hot spots policing programs is still developing, however. The available evaluation literature has generally not analyzed crime displacement and diffusion effects beyond areas proximate to targeted hot spot locations. Moreover, the research literature does not provide estimates of the systemwide or large-area impacts of hot spots policing when implemented as a crime-control strategy for an entire jurisdiction. The long-term crime-reduction benefits of this approach have also not been established, as hot spot policing program evaluations have focused on estimating short-term crime prevention impacts.

Predictive Policing

Predictive policing, as discussed in Chapter 2, is—in terms of crime and place—"the use of historical data to create a spatiotemporal forecast of areas of criminality or crime hot spots that will be the basis for police resource allocation decisions with the expectation that having officers at the proposed place and time will deter or detect criminal activity" (Ratcliffe, 2014, p. 4). However, predictive policing is a relatively new strategy, and policing practices associated with it are vague and poorly defined (Perry et al., 2013; Santos, 2014). Additionally, because the forecasts (and crime analysis more generally) need to be combined with effective practices and tactics targeted at predicted locations or to predicted individuals, there are few studies to date that have tried to parse out the effects of the analysis or forecast itself as a proactive activity. While predictive policing has gained considerable name recognition as a new policing strategy, it is difficult to distinguish predictive policing in any meaningful way from hot spots policing, with the exception that the predictive policing forecasts are usually generated using sophisticated software programs that claim a predictive capability. This raises two questions: First, does the software significantly enhance the ability of existing analytical approaches in the identification of crime hot spots? Second, are there police tactics employed in predicted areas that are more effective than or different from patrol tactics usually employed in hot spots policing?

One example to consider is a study by Hunt, Saunders, and Hollywood (2014), which examined the impact of predictive modeling on preventing property crimes. Predictions on locations of future crimes were derived monthly for the Shreveport, Louisiana, Police Department, which were then used to drive a strategic decision-making model that included increasing officer awareness of hot spots in roll call and using predictions to implement a broken windows approach (see Wilson and Kelling, 1982). Four selected high-crime districts were randomly allocated to experimental and control groups (two each), and two medium-crime districts were also randomly assigned. Control areas used traditional hot spot mapping of past property crimes to direct an existing operational unit for proactive activities. Hunt and colleagues found no evidence that crime was reduced more when police used the software-driven predictive modeling, compared to control areas that used more traditional crime-mapping techniques to direct operations to crime hot spots. However, the authors suggested a number of possible explanations for their null findings, including concerns regarding the selected policing tactics, the implementation of the strategy, low statistical power due to the small sample size, and a lack of resources in the experimental group.

Mohler and colleagues (2015) conducted one of the few other known published studies of the crime prevention impact of predictive policing technology in Los Angeles, California, and in Kent, England. Rather than comparing fixed experimental and control crime hot spots, they compared days in which directed patrol was deployed using predictive policing algorithms to days in which conventional forms of crime mapping and analysis were used, randomly allocating days to either predictive policing or conventional mapping and analysis. Contrary to the findings of Hunt, Saunders, and Hollywood (2014), Mohler and colleagues (2015) found that use of their predictive forecasting led to an average 7.4 percent reduction in crime compared to the days officers used hot spots derived from conventional crime mapping by analysts, which showed no statistically significant reduction in crime.

These two studies present a common challenge in evaluating the impact of technology on police crime-control effectiveness, especially in proactive contexts. Although both studies attempted to directly test and compare the impact of one analytic technology with another, the effects were still mediated by the agencies implementing the approach. This is one important limitation of drawing inferences from only a few evaluation studies. Mohler and colleagues' (2015) study in two locations might be considered stronger in this regard, although officers in Los Angeles and Kent still had to act upon the technology to create the effect. Both sets of maps in this study looked identical despite their underlying data and analysis being different, which suggests that predictive algorithms are not substantially more precise in directing traditional police proactivity than more conventional forms of crime mapping.

One clear problem in assessing the outcomes of these studies is to determine the baseline of "traditional" crime analysis against which to draw conclusions regarding the efficacy of newer predictive algorithms. The ability of crime analysts varies substantially from place to place, along with the software and data quality they can access. They are rarely, if ever, asked to identify small square grids of only a few hundred feet on each side in their normal work day. So determining whether predictive algorithms are a significant enhancement to existing methods of hot spot detection is hampered by variability in the existing approaches. The findings may be different in these studies because standard practice differs.

Another limitation of these studies is that the policing tactics adopted appear to be in most locations a traditional patrol response. In other words, rather than new practices and tactics emerging from predictive policing, to date the strategy has consisted of more-honed spatial resource allocation models whose location forecasts are then linked to traditional crime-prevention policing activities.

A study that presents some insights into the impact of predictive and crime analytic technology is Kennedy, Caplan, and Piza (2011). The authors examined the use of a different predictive crime analytic approach—risk terrain modeling—in enhancing a place-based proactive policing approach in five jurisdictions. This quasi-experimental study compared street segments and intersections that received police proactivity using results of risk terrain modeling with control segments derived from propensity score matching that did not receive extra police effort. The analysis found positive effects of this hot spots policing strategy; however, the control segments did not receive targeted patrols, thereby begging the question whether the technology or the directed patrols caused the observed crime reduction. In other words, was the crime reduction caused by standard police patrols that were no different than a traditional hot spots policing approach, or was value added by the software over and above what could be normally achieved by a combination of existing analytical and operational approaches? In short, whether risk terrain modeling either predicts crime or facilitates proactive policing better than other predictive policing models remains to be tested.

Other predictive analytical approaches may be useful, especially the near-repeat techniques that use short-term event patterns to forecast probabilities of future events (Johnson et al., 2009; Gorr and Lee, 2015) or processes such as the Epidemic Type Aftershock Sequence method (a nonparametric self-exciting point process [see Mohler et al., 2011]). These approaches could be more effective at predicting short-term crime hot spots than traditional crime mapping approaches, though the methods to assess predictive accuracy have not yet been generally agreed upon and different approaches often produce different types of crime forecast from different data sources—further confounding comparisons.

Some of the studies of computer algorithms designed to predict the spatial pattern of crime have been conducted by the same researchers who designed the algorithms. Some of these algorithms and programs have been subsequently commercialized. The possibility of bias in the reported findings from the evaluations cannot be ruled out. Furthermore, the breadth (and arguably, the vagueness) by which predictive policing has been defined means that many studies of it will likely be unique with respect to what they are studying. It may be some time before there is sufficient replication to draw reasoned conclusions about any policing activities targeted to crime prediction areas.

At present, the newness of many predictive policing technologies is such that their accuracy is difficult to determine; moreover, the base rate of crime activity or other benchmark against which these new technologies should be measured has not been established. If the predictive technologies are deemed to be more accurate than, say, a heat map of the previous year's crime or the manually estimated predictions of a crime analyst, how much should a computer-generated prediction affect the actions of police? In other words, how much influence should a prediction have in the totality of circumstances for reasonable suspicion and for changing the balance of suspicion in predicted crime areas (Ferguson, 2012)? While the advent of big data might increase the accuracy of crime prediction of both crime-prone individuals (whether as perpetrators or as victims) and crime-prone areas, data quality will become an issue (Ferguson, 2015) and "blind reliance on the forecast, divorced from the reason for the forecast, may lead to inappropriate reliance on the technology" (Ferguson, 2012, p. 316).

Summary. At present, there are insufficient robust empirical studies to draw any firm conclusion about either the efficacy of crime-prediction software or the effectiveness of any associated police operational tactics. Furthermore, it is as yet unclear whether predictive policing is substantively different from hot spots policing.

Closed Circuit Television

Another technology believed to improve police capacity for proactive intervention at specific places is closed circuit television (CCTV). CCTV is thought to create a general deterrent effect on crime by increasing an offender's perceived risk of being identified or apprehended for criminal activity. CCTV can also be used proactively by the police to monitor suspicious situations or disorders that might turn into criminal events. In this way, the police might be able to respond before a tense situation deteriorates into criminality or to use information learned from remote observing of criminal activity to direct street officers where to conduct searches or apprehension of suspects. These are two different applications of CCTV technology, with the general deterrence application conveying a threat of police intervention simply through the presence of the camera, whereas the proactive use involves more specific deterrence through the active direction of officers to imminent or observed criminality.

Prior reviews of controlled evaluations of passively monitored CCTV systems suggest mixed crime-control impacts of CCTV. However, these studies evaluated the effects of CCTV in its general deterrence capacity; they did not specifically evaluate proactive police use of CCTVs. For instance, Welsh and Farrington (2008) completed a meta-review of studies in which CCTV was the main intervention in an area that had at least 20 crimes prior to the CCTV implementation. Also, each study had to involve at least one experimental area and one reasonably comparable control area and, at a minimum, had an evaluation design comprising before-and-after measures of crime in both the experimental and control areas. They concluded that "CCTV has a modest [16 percent] but significant desirable effect on crime, is most effective in reducing crime in car parks, is most effective when targeted at vehicle crimes (largely a function of the successful car park schemes), and is more effective in reducing crime in the U.K. than in other countries" (Welsh and Farrington, 2008, pp. 18–19; see also Gill and Spriggs, 2005).

Over the past decade, a number of additional studies have taken place. The largest U.S. study examined the crime-reduction effects of CCTV use by law enforcement and municipal authorities in Baltimore, MD, Chicago, IL, and Washington, DC (La Vigne et al., 2011). The design was relatively strong because it used pre-post measures and matched comparison areas that were identified on the basis of a variety of place characteristics. However, the definition of treated and control areas introduced measurement error related to the physical placement of the camera, since this study defined a treated area as the entire area within 200 feet of the camera's location, rather than defining an area as "treated" if it was in the area the camera could actually see (called a "camera viewshed"). Use of actual camera viewsheds to define the treated area has become more common over the past decade, avoiding this problem (see, e.g., Ratcliffe, Taniguchi, and Taylor, 2009; Gerell, 2016; Piza, Caplan, and Kennedy, 2014). La Vigne and colleagues (2011) found that, in the downtown Baltimore area, both property and violent crimes declined by large percentages (between 23% and 35%) in the months following camera implementation. In Chicago, their analysis indicated that crime was reduced in some areas but not in others. Cameras alone did not appear to have an impact on crime in the District of Columbia. Overall, the results indicate that cameras have the most impact when they are highly concentrated, actively monitored, and integrated into a broader law enforcement strategy. Consistent with previous studies as well as a recent study from Schenectady, New York (McLean, Worden, and Kim, 2013), La Vigne and colleagues (2011) indicated that CCTV cameras are not universally effective; there are factors at each place that contribute to the effectiveness of the CCTV strategy.

As with the use of other technologies such as predictive policing software or license plate readers, it is difficult to disentangle the technology from the efficacy of the associated policing response to the technological stimuli. For example, even if police never respond to crime in the viewshed of a camera, the deterrent effect of CCTV may still be effective for transient offenders new to the area but ineffective in deterring resident criminals who learn by experience about the absent police response. With all of the CCTV studies mentioned, whether and exactly how police were proactively using these cameras was unknown. Given that these evaluations of CCTV systems did not explicitly cite a specific and proactive differential response from police in their discussion of the project implementation, the committee concluded that any response from police services was probably reactive and not a proactive engagement using a team dedicated to responding to CCTV-identified incidents, as was the case with the next study discussed.

Piza and colleagues (2015) used a randomized controlled trial to explicitly test the use of CCTV to support proactive policing in Newark, New Jersey. In the treatment group, 19 cameras were monitored by a dedicated camera operator; two patrol cars had exclusive responsibility for responding to incidents identified by the camera operator. In the control group, 19 cameras were used "normally," that is, with monitors reporting suspicious activities through the computer-aided dispatch system to patrol officers. The researchers' experimental analyses suggested that the treatment condition produced "tangible and meaningful crime reductions of violent crime and social disorder" relative to the control condition (Piza et al., 2015, p. 62). Results varied between time periods measured, but they found 40–48 percent reductions in violent crime and 41–49 percent reductions in social disorder—substantively large effects, which they estimated would have occurred less than 10 percent of the time under the null hypothesis of no relationship between CCTV and crime.

As with other studies involving technology, camera systems are often implemented in combination with other initiatives, so parsing out the individual impact of the cameras is difficult. Research designs also vary considerably, and CCTV schemes have been operationalized in myriad ways, making it difficult to identify an optimal configuration of camera installation and operational support.

Summary. The results from studies examining the introduction of CCTV camera schemes into relatively passive monitoring systems are mixed, but they tend to show modest outcomes in terms of property crime reduction at high-crime locations. The evidence suggests that the use of CCTV systems *without* a dedicated police operational response may be effective at reducing vehicle crime and less effective at combating violence, although the way the system is implemented and used appears to be important in achieving any crime reduction. CCTV may also be more effective when bundled with other crime-prevention measures. With regard to the use of an operational police presence in the field and dedicated to responding to active monitoring of a reasonable number of cameras, the evidence appears promising. However, the strength of conclusions about this proactive use is constrained because the evidence base consists of a single study.

PROBLEM-SOLVING STRATEGIES

Problem-Oriented Policing

Problem-oriented policing seeks to identify the underlying causes of crime problems and to frame appropriate responses using a wide variety of methods and tactics (Goldstein, 1979, 1990; Braga, 2008; see Chapter 2 of this volume). Depending on the nature of the crime and disorder problem being addressed, problem-oriented policing interventions may engage a diversity of enforcement, situation prevention, and community engagement strategies. The 2004 NRC report concluded that problem-oriented policing is a promising approach to deal with crime, disorder, and fear; it recommended additional research to understand the organizational arrangements that foster effective problem solving (National Research Council, 2004). This section discusses the evidence showing that even an imperfect implementation of problem-oriented policing—so-called "shallow" problem solving—generates crime-prevention gains (Braga and Weisburd, 2006). However, the committee believes that improvements to the process of problem-oriented policing could produce even stronger crime control effects.

Many evaluations of problem-oriented policing interventions use weaker evaluation designs,[2] such as one-group-only pre-post comparisons

---

[2] We use "weaker" here to refer to the relative strength of findings as evidence. For discussion of standards of evidence and how the committee assessed the research literature, see the Chapter 1 section, "Assessing the Evidence."

of crime and disorder indicators. For instance, in the influential Newport News, Virginia, test of problem-oriented policing, Eck and Spelman (1987) used time series models to evaluate the effectiveness of three problem-solving initiatives. Their analyses suggested that the implemented interventions were associated with varying, statistically significant crime reductions for the targeted crime problems: residential burglaries in an apartment complex, thefts from vehicles parked downtown, and street prostitution–related robberies. However, the strength of these results is limited by very short time series lengths (marginally longer than $n = 50$ observations), no comparison areas, and no consideration of possible crime-displacement effects. However, there have also been more rigorous tests of the crime-control efficacy of problem-oriented policing.

Researchers from the Center for Crime Prevention Studies at Rutgers University teamed with the Jersey City Police Department to evaluate a problem-oriented policing intervention targeting locations with high rates of violent crimes (Braga et al., 1999). The team identified 24 locations with a high incidence of violent crime, using computerized mapping and database technologies to rank areas, defined by street intersections, with high levels of service calls for, or incidents of, assault and robbery, as well as police and researcher perceptions of more-violent areas. In the randomized block-field design for this experiment, the 24 violent-crime areas were matched into 12 pairs, with one member of each pair allocated to the treatment condition and the other member randomly allocated to the control condition. The treatment condition, which was applied over a 16-month period, combined several practices typical of a problem-oriented policing strategy, including aggressive enforcement against disorder incidents and some situational responses.

The main analyses of effect used count-based regression models to calculate statistical differences for a number of crime activity indicators at each location between a 6-month pre-test period and a 6-month period after the intervention (post-test period). These pre-post differences were then compared for the locations in the treatment condition against their matched control location. The analyses found that locations in the treatment condition had a statistically significant 21 percent reduction in total calls for service, relative to their matched controls, and a 42 percent reduction in reported crime incidents. There were also varying levels of reduction in calls for service and crime incidents for all the crime-type subcategories. Systematic observations were made of social and physical disorder in the 24 locations during the pre-test and post-test periods, and analysis of the data on these observations found that social and physical disorder had been reduced. The research team also analyzed data on measures for displacement of crime behavior and diffusion of crime-control benefits in the two-block catchment areas surrounding each treatment and control location.

These analyses did not find statistically significant support for either crime displacement into the catchment areas or diffusion of crime-control benefits outside the targeted locations.

In another collaboration, researchers from Harvard University teamed with the police department in Lowell, Massachusetts, on a randomized controlled trial to test a problem-oriented policing strategy in reducing crime and disorder incidence at hot spots in Lowell (Braga and Bond, 2008). The researchers used spatial analyses of service calls involving crime or disorder, supplemented by observations on appropriate hot spot boundaries from both police officers and the research team, to identify 34 hot spots. Pairing of hot spots was based on matching for the numbers and types of calls for service, neighborhood demographics, and other location characteristics. In the randomized block field design for the trial, one member of each pair was randomly allocated to treatment, with the other member allocated to the control condition. The problem-oriented policing intervention, which continued for 12 months, consisted mainly of aggressive disorder enforcement tactics but also included some situational responses.

The main analysis used by Braga and Bond (2008) applied count-based regression models to the pair-wise differences between a number of crime and disorder indicators measured during the 6-month pre-test and post-test periods before and after the 12-month intervention. The pre-post differences for the matched pairs were then analyzed for overall mean differences between the treatment condition and controls. (The same design was used in the Jersey City trial described above.) The authors found that the problem-oriented intervention resulted in a statistically significant 19.8 percent reduction in total calls for service, relative to the control condition. They also found varying levels of reductions for all their crime-type subcategories. Systematic observations were made during the pre-test and post-test periods for measures of both social disorder and physical disorder, and analysis of the data from these observations found that both types of disorder decreased at treatment hot spots relative to their matched controls. A mediation analysis of the core treatment elements suggested that the crime and disorder gains were driven by situational responses, such as razing abandoned buildings and securing vacant lots, rather than increased misdemeanor arrests or police-led social service actions.

Both the Jersey City and Lowell experiments documented proactive policing interventions similar to the usual practices in the field for a problem-oriented policing strategy; that is, the problem-solving component involved only weak or "shallow" problem analysis, with only limited development of responses to address the problems after analysis. Despite this gap between the ideal for a problem-solving approach and these actual implementations, the problem-oriented policing strategy was found to be effective in reducing crime and disorder in the treated hot spots in both cities. These findings suggest that it may not be essential for achieving crime reduction outcomes to implement problem-oriented policing interventions exactly as the strategy was defined by Goldstein (1979, 1990). It may be enough to focus police resources on risks that the problem-oriented policing project identifies, such as risks typically associated with crime hot spots (Braga and Weisburd, 2006).

Taylor, Koper, and Woods (2011) implemented a randomized controlled trial comparing the effectiveness of both directed patrol and problem-oriented policing interventions at hot spots of viclent crime in Jacksonville, Florida. The authors identified 83 hot spots of nondomestic violence and randomly assigned them into three conditions: directed patrol, problem-oriented policing, and the control condition. In the problem-oriented intervention, teams of officers and crime analysts conducted problem analysis and problem solving at selected hot spots, employing such situational crime-prevention measures as installing or improving lighting, erecting road barriers, and repairing fences. The police officers typically worked with business owners and rental property managers to improve security measures and business practices, along with other means to collaborate on crime prevention. Many of these collaborative activities, such as conducting surveys in the community and various modes of outreach to community members, can be viewed as community organizing. Other responses to the problems identified included providing social services (such as improved youth recreational opportunities), stricter enforcement of municipal codes, nuisance abatement, and even aesthetic improvements in the community, such as cleaning up parks and removing graffiti. Across the 22 locations assigned to the problem-oriented policing condition, the participating teams implemented 283 discrete problem-solving measures. The researchers found that this problem-oriented policing intervention was associated with a 33 percent drop in street violence during the 90-day assessment period after the intervention, relative to control areas. Statistically nonsignificant reductions in crime were associated with the directed patrol intervention relative to the control condition.

A review of evaluations of problem-oriented policing by Weisburd and colleagues (2008) for the Campbell Collaboration examined findings on crime and disorder outcomes (see also Weisburd et al., 2010). Although this review covered a large number of empirical evaluations, it identified only 10 as having randomized experimental or quasi-experimental study designs. The reviewers' meta-analysis found that the problem-oriented policing programs tested by these 10 more rigorous evaluations had produced a combined modest but statistically significant decrease in outcome measures for crime and disorder. Similar results were obtained when the randomized experiments and the quasi-experimental evaluations were analyzed separately.

This review also reported on crime reduction effects found in evaluations with just a pre-post comparison design, which did not include a comparison group and were therefore less rigorous in methodology than the random experiments and quasi-experimental studies. Of the 45 pre-post evaluations reviewed, 43 had reported beneficial crime-prevention effects attributed to the problem-oriented policing intervention evaluated. Furthermore, the crime-reduction effects found by these pre-post comparisons were much larger than the effects found by the 10 evaluations with more rigorous research designs.

Finally, it is important to note that evaluations of problem-oriented policing have looked at the impacts of the approach on the specific problems examined, often at specific places. There is often an absence of assessment of possible displacement outcomes, and there has not been study of whether a problem-oriented approach used widely in a city would reduce overall crime in that jurisdiction.

Summary. Despite the popularity of problem-oriented policing as a crime-prevention strategy, there are surprisingly few rigorous program evaluations of it. Much of the available evaluation evidence consists of non-experimental analyses that report finding strong impacts on crime. The far fewer randomized experimental evaluations generally show smaller, but statistically significant, crime reductions generated by problem-oriented policing interventions relative to the control condition. Program evaluations largely examine the short-term impacts of problem-oriented policing on crime and disorder outcomes, and there is little evidence regarding displacement or possible jurisdictional impacts of this approach. Program evaluations also suggest that it is difficult for police officers to fully implement problem-oriented policing. Many problem-oriented policing projects are characterized by weak problem analysis and a lack of non-enforcement responses to the problems identified. Nevertheless, even these limited applications of problem-oriented policing have generated crime prevention impacts.

Third Party Policing

While regarded by some as a distinct approach to crime prevention (Buerger and Mazerolle, 1998), the committee views third party policing as aligned with a problem-solving approach, since police using this strategy seek to persuade or coerce organizations or nonoffending persons, such as public housing agencies, property owners, parents, health and building inspectors, and business owners, to take some responsibility for preventing crime or reducing crime problems. Community organizations have long advocated for the use of civil remedies to control crime and disorder problems (Roehl, 1998), and some observers suggest that code enforcement and nuisance abatement strategies represent important mechanisms for residents and the police to "coproduce" public safety (Blumenberg, Blom, and Artigiani, 1998).

The first direct evaluation of third party policing occurred with the Oakland Police Department's Beat Health Program (refer to Box 2-3 in Chapter 2). This intervention took a problem-solving approach designed "to control drug and disorder problems, in particular, and restore order by focusing on the physical decay conditions of targeted commercial establishments, private homes, and rental properties" (Mazerolle, Price, and Roehl, 2000, p. 213). This randomized controlled trial compared the Beat Health intervention (the treatment condition) with the routine policing practices of a regular patrol division as the control condition (Mazerolle, Price, and Roehl, 2000). A street block that included a residential or commercial property referred to the Beat Health police unit as having a drug problem or other indicators of blight became eligible for inclusion in the trial. For the trial, 100 such street blocks were randomly assigned to either the Beat Health intervention or the control condition ($n = 50$ for each condition). A difference-of-differences design was used for the analysis of effect, with a pre-test period of 21.5 months before the 5.5-month intervention period and a post-test period of 12 months after the intervention. In addition to the indicators of effect within the street-block units, crime displacement and control-benefits diffusion effects were assessed in catchment areas extending 500 feet out from the problem address on each street-block unit. The analysis showed that the units in the Beat Health program had a statistically significant 7 percent reduction in drug calls relative to units in the control condition (in which drug calls actually increased by 55%), but there were no statistically significant differences in other categories of service calls. The effects were also more prominent in residential treatment blocks than in commercial areas. The analysis of effects in catchment areas showed an overall (across all catchment areas in the treatment condition) diffusion of crime-control benefits, compared to catchment areas for the control condition (Mazerolle, Price, and Roehl, 2000).

In San Diego, the police worked with the Code Compliance Department (the third party in this intervention) to encourage property owners to fix drug-related problems—for example, by evicting offending tenants (Eck and Wartell, 1998). When the police identified a property as having persistent drug activity, the Code Compliance Department could use San Diego's nuisance abatement legislation to fine the property owners or close their properties for up to 1 year. To evaluate this intervention, Eck and Wartell (1998) used a randomized controlled trial in which properties identified by the police as having a drug-related problem were randomly assigned to one of two treatment groups ($n = 42$ and $n = 37$) or to the control condition ($n = 42$). Property owners in one treatment group received a letter from police describing enforcement action and offering assistance;

property owners in the other treatment group met with a narcotics detective and were threatened with nuisance abatement. The main outcome for this trial was incidence of post-intervention official crime at each problem property, measured as the aggregate of five 6-month consecutive periods (a total of 30 months post-intervention). Property owners in the meeting treatment group experienced large reductions (declines of almost 60%) in reported crime, whereas the property owners in the letter-receiving group experienced smaller crime reduction effects (a decline of 13%).

As we noted in Chapter 3, third party policing's use of coercive mechanisms to influence business and housing owners may raise privacy concerns. Descriptive research also suggests that overly coercive applications of third party policing strategies may produce unintended harmful consequences for community members (Desmond and Valdez, 2013).

A related approach to third party policing is the development of Business Improvement Districts (BIDs). BIDs rely not only on policing resources but also on private security, often including guards and CCTV. A quasi-experimental evaluation of 30 BIDs created in Los Angeles during the 1990s found that expenditures on private security were effective in creating a sustained reduction in crime (Cook and MacDonald, 2011). The authors found the data closely fit a linear dose-response curve: on average, an additional $100,000 spent on private security annually resulted in an incremental reduction of six robberies, four assaults, and five burglaries. Given standard estimates of the social cost of these crimes, the benefit-cost ratio exceeded 20. The crime-reduction effects were coupled with reductions in the numbers of arrests for these crimes, thus providing a further cost savings to the criminal justice system in Los Angeles County. The authors found no evidence of geographic displacement of crime to areas outside the BID resulting from the private security within the BID (Cook and MacDonald, 2011).

Summary. There are only a small number of evaluations of third party policing programs, but these evaluations have assessed the impact of third party policing interventions on crime and disorder using randomized controlled trials and rigorous quasi-experimental designs. The available evidence supports a conclusion that third party policing generates statistically significant short-term reductions in crime and disorder; there is more-limited evidence of long-term impacts in evaluations of BIDs. Implementations of this strategy, whether measured in an experimental evaluation of Oakland's Beat Health Program or in a quasi-experimental evaluation of BIDs, did not displace crime incidence to nearby areas outside the intervention boundary. Indeed, the Oakland evaluation showed a diffusion of crime-control benefits to nearby areas (i.e., crime measures decreased in the nearby area). However, little is known about possible jurisdictional impacts of adopting these approaches.

PERSON-FOCUSED STRATEGIES

Focused Deterrence

Focused deterrence strategies have been implemented to halt ongoing violence by gangs and other criminally active groups, disrupt disorderly and violent drug markets (known as Drug Market Intervention or DMI), and prevent continued criminal behavior by individual repeat offenders.[3] The 2004 NRC policing report described the then-available scientific evidence on the crime reduction value of focused deterrence practices as "promising" but "descriptive rather than evaluative" (National Research Council, 2004, p. 241), and the 2005 NRC report on firearms violence suggested the evidence was "limited" but "still evolving" (National Research Council, 2005, p. 10). A recent Campbell Collaboration systematic review identified 24 evaluations of focused deterrence strategies that used comparison groups (Braga, Weisburd, and Turchan, in press). The Campbell review meta-analysis suggested that focused deterrence strategies were associated with an overall, statistically significant, moderate crime-reduction effect. However, program effect sizes varied by program type, with gang violence reduction strategies generating larger crime-reduction impacts and drug market intervention smaller impacts.

In an earlier Campbell review, Braga and Weisburd (2014) noted that existing evaluations of focused deterrence programs used quasi-experimental tests, and many of these had weaker study designs that depended upon non-equivalent comparisons. The reviewers expressed concern over the lack of randomized controlled trials and called for more rigorous evaluations of focused deterrence programs. As of the writing of this report, their call for more rigorous research on this strategy has not been answered. However, many of the quasi-experimental evaluations completed since the first iteration of the Campbell review have employed more rigorous methods. The evolution in rigor of quasi-experimental evaluation techniques is evidenced by the difference in the study designs used to evaluate separate implemen-

---

[3] The committee decided not to review repeat offender programs for two reasons. First, these programs were common in the 1980s but have generally been replaced by programs using a focused deterrence strategy as reviewed here. Second, there has been no additional research evidence on repeat offender programs beyond the research reviewed in the 2004 NRC report. That report concluded that available studies represent "only indirect examinations of their effect on reducing crime, and conclusions about their crime reduction effectiveness rely on ancillary assumptions about the effectiveness of selective incarceration and incapacitation" (National Research Council, 2004, p. 241).

tation periods of the well-known Boston Operation Ceasefire Program (described in Chapter 2, Box 2-4, of this volume): one in the 1990s, the second in the mid-2000s.

The initial evaluation of Operation Ceasefire in Boston, sponsored by the U.S. Department of Justice (DOJ) in the 1990s, used a quasi-experimental design to compare youth homicide trends in that city with trends in other major U.S. cities and in other large cities of New England. (Braga et al., 2001). The main outcome variable for assessing the program's impact was the average number of homicide victims per month, ages 24 and under, between January 1, 1991, and May 31, 1998. Supplementing this assessment of outcome were analyses of Operation Ceasefire's effect on citywide, monthly counts of gun assault incidents and service calls reporting gunshots fired, as well as monthly gun assault incidents by youths in one high-risk policing district. The effect of Operation Ceasefire on these outcome variables was analyzed using Poisson and negative binomial regression models that controlled for potential confounders (covariates) such as secular trends, seasonal variations, youth population trends and employment rate trends in Boston, robbery and adult homicide trends, and youth drug arrest trends. Program impact was estimated using a dummy variable in the regression models, with June 1996 through May 1998 as the post-implementation period.

The analyses in this first Operation Ceasefire evaluation found that the program was associated with statistically significant reductions not only in the youth homicide rate but also in the other indicators of serious gun violence. The regression models estimated, after controlling for the potential covariates, that a 63 percent reduction in the monthly count of youth homicides could be attributed to the program. The regression modeling also attributed to the intervention a 25 percent reduction in citywide gun assault incidents, a 32 percent reduction in citywide shots-fired calls for service, and a 44 percent reduction in the monthly count of gun assaults by youth in the high-risk district (Braga et al., 2001).

As noted, this evaluation of Operation Ceasefire also compared the youth homicide trend in Boston with the trends in 39 major U.S. cities, as well as 29 New England cities with populations greater than 60,000 (Braga et al., 2001). After controlling for the covariates listed above, the regression analysis found only three cities—Dallas, Texas; Jacksonville, Florida; and Virginia Beach, Virginia—that had statistically significant reductions in youth homicide trends (monthly counts) during the Operation Ceasefire implementation period. In four other cities—Los Angeles, California; New York City, New York; Philadelphia, Pennsylvania; and Tucson, Arizona—reductions in monthly counts of youth homicides were statistically significant at some point in the entire time series but not during the implementation of the Boston intervention. However, for all these other major U.S. cities, the researchers concluded that for corresponding time periods, the trajectories of the youth homicide time series were distinct from the youth homicide trajectory in Boston. Based on these findings, Braga and colleagues (2001) concluded that the trend in youth homicide reduction associated with implementing Operation Ceasefire was distinct from the trends in most other major U.S. cities.

To assess whether implementation of Operation Ceasefire coincided with the start of the 63 percent decrease in Boston monthly youth homicides, a companion study by Piehl and colleagues (2003) analyzed in more detail the time series of youth homicide counts. They applied an econometric model to evaluate all possible monthly break points in the time series, while controlling for trends and seasonal variations, for the maximal monthly break point associated with a significant change in the series' slope (trajectory). This analysis found that the "optimal break" in the time series occurred during the summer months of 1996, after Operation Ceasefire was implemented in January of that year.

This first evaluation of Operation Ceasefire has been reviewed by a number of researchers who have made their own assessments of the relationship between the implementation of the intervention and the trend in the youth homicide rate in Boston during the 1990s. One reviewer suggested that some of the decrease in youth homicides may have occurred without the intervention because violence in general was decreasing in most major U.S. cities during this period (Fagan, 2002). To illustrate his point, Fagan graphed the time series for youth gun homicide in Boston and other Massachusetts cities, showing that a general downward trend in gun violence was occurring even before Operation Ceasefire.

Shortly after Fagan's review, Rosenfeld, Fornango, and Baumer (2005) used a growth-curve analysis to examine predicted homicide trend data for the 95 largest U.S. cities during the 1990s. This analysis produced some evidence that the reduction in the youth homicide rate in Boston after Operation Ceasefire began was steeper than elsewhere, but the authors concluded that given the small number of youth homicide incidents, their statistical models did not support any strong conclusion about Operation Ceasefire effectiveness. However, a review of the Rosenfeld, Fornango, and Baumer (2005) analysis by Berk (2005) raised a number of concerns about their statistical and methodological analysis. Yet another reviewer agreed with the original evaluation that Operation Ceasefire was associated with a substantial reduction in the youth homicide rate in Boston but concluded that uncertainty remained about the extent of the intervention's (causal) effect on youth violence throughout Boston, given the complexities of analyzing citywide data on homicide rates (Ludwig, 2005).

A 2005 report by an NRC study committee concluded that the Operation Ceasefire evaluation was compelling in associating the intervention with the subsequent decline in youth homicide. However, that study committee agreed with other reviewers in suggesting that many complex factors affect youth homicide trends, making it difficult to specify the nature (i.e., a statistical association versus a causal connection) of the relationship between the Operation Ceasefire intervention and subsequent changes in youth offending behaviors (National Research Council, 2005). Because the evaluation was not a randomized, controlled experiment, the design does not rule out the possibility that alternative factors, including complex interactions among the covariates that were considered in the regression analysis, may have been more important causal factors in the observed trend in youth homicides in Boston than the Operation Ceasefire intervention.

Braga, Hureau, and Papachristos (2014) conducted a quasi-experimental evaluation of a reconstituted Boston Ceasefire program implemented during the mid-2000s in response to a growing problem of gang violence. Propensity scores were used to match treated Boston gangs ($n = 16$) to untreated Boston gangs ($n = 37$) that were not connected to the treated gangs through rivalries or alliances. The impact of the Ceasefire program was assessed using difference-in-differences estimators calculated from growth-curve regression models to compare gun violence trends during the 2006–2010 study period for the gangs in the treatment condition to their matched untreated gang. This evaluation found that total shootings involving the directly treated gangs were 31 percent less than total shootings in which the untreated gangs were involved. Braga, Apel, and Welsh (2013) used a similar evaluation methodology and found that the Ceasefire treatment condition also was associated with spillover deterrent effects on untreated gangs that were socially connected to treated gangs by rivalries or alliances. Total shootings involving these socially connected but untreated gangs decreased by 24 percent relative to total shootings by matched comparison gangs.

Other versions of the focused deterrence strategy have also employed rigorous quasi-experimental approaches. For instance, the seminal focused deterrence strategy, the Drug Market Intervention, was implemented to control disorderly and violent drug markets operating in High Point, North Carolina. In a recently completed quasi-experimental evaluation, Corsaro and colleagues (2012) analyzed longitudinal data to estimate the intervention's effects by comparing violent crime trends in treated neighborhoods with trends in matched comparison neighborhoods, also in High Point. This evaluation reported modest 12–18 percent reductions in violent crime in the treated areas relative to control areas (Corsaro et al., 2012). More recently, Saunders and colleagues (2014) applied a synthetic control group quasi-experimental design to evaluate the High Point Drug Market Intervention Program and reported a 21 percent reduction in general crime rates in treated areas with little evidence of spatial displacement of crime incidence to nearby areas.

The Project Safe Neighborhoods (PSN) intervention was implemented to test the hypothesis that Chicago's homicide and gun violence problem could be improved by intervention tactics targeting the population at high risk of being either a victim or offender of gun violence (Papachristos, Meares, and Fagan, 2007). To test this hypothesis, the researchers selected two adjacent police districts on Chicago's West Side to receive the intervention (the treatment districts). In these districts, the rates of murder and gun violence in 2002 were more than four times the city average. Two other of Chicago's 25 police districts were selected via propensity-score matching as controls. Thus, neither the treatment nor the control districts were randomly selected. The PSN intervention, which began in May 2002, followed two principles: (1) Enforcement activities should be highly specific and targeted to those most at risk of being a gun-violence victim or offender. (2) Serious effort had to be made toward changing attitudes of those at risk with the law and law enforcement and toward changing the thinking by young men that would justify using a gun (the "normative side" of gun violence).

The PSN intervention comprised four component policing practices: (a) increasing federal prosecution for convicted felons who carried or used a firearm, (b) seeking longer sentences for successful federal prosecutions, (c) activities to curtail the supply of illegal firearms (gun recoveries by special teams composed of officers from both the U.S. Bureau of Alcohol, Tobacco, and Firearms and the Chicago Police Department), and (d) offender notification meetings—a practice associated with the procedural justice strategy—to communicate messages about deterrence and social norms to the potential offender population. The offender notification meetings were directed at recently released former prison inmates who had involvement in gun or gang violence and were returning to the treatment districts. These randomly selected offenders were informed that as convicted felons, they were vulnerable to federal firearms laws that carried mandatory minimum sentences if they were apprehended carrying a gun. On the constructive side, returning offenders were also offered social services and were encouraged by community members and other former offenders to change their life pattern.

In the quasi-experimental design used to evaluate the PSN intervention, monthly and quarterly counts of homicide incidents between January 1999 and December 2004 were the measures used to quantify the key outcome variable (Papachristos, Meares, and Fagan, 2007). Other outcomes included monthly and quarterly counts of gun homicide incidents, gang homicide incidents, and aggravated assault incidents in the treatment districts, relative to the control districts.

The research team analyzed not only the overall effects of the PSN treatment but also the effectiveness of the four component interventions. Through regression modeling on individual outcome growth curves, they estimated that the overall PSN intervention in the two treatment districts was associated with a statistically significant 37 percent reduction in homicides, compared with the control condition. They also found that the PSN intervention as a whole was associated with statistically significant decreases in gun-related homicides and aggravated assaults. There was also a decrease in gang-involved homicides, but this decrease was not statistically significant.

Of the four PSN component practices, the offender notification meetings were associated with the largest, statistically significant effect on homicide reduction, relative to the control condition. That is, the treatment districts with higher proportions of offenders who attended a forum experienced larger declines in homicides relative to control districts. The study also found modest but not statistically significant reductions in homicide rates, relative to the control condition, for two other components: intensifying federal prosecutions of felons apprehended with a firearm and curtailing the supply of illegal guns (quantified as the number of guns recovered by the special teams). The regression analysis did not show an association between declines in homicides in the treatment districts and the fourth PSN component, increasing the length of sentence associated with federal prosecutions (Papachristos, Meares, and Fagan, 2007).

In a supplemental analysis of the PSN intervention (described further in the procedural justice section of this chapter), Wallace and colleagues (2016) studied recidivism among former offenders who attended an offender notification meeting. The authors applied a survival analysis technique to the data on offender recidivism and found that offenders who attended one of the PSN meetings were 30 percent less likely to be arrested again, compared with a similar group of recently released former offenders from the same neighborhood who had not attended a meeting. Furthermore, the analysis found that the PSN treatment condition was associated with reduced recidivism rates for prior offenders, whether or not they were gang members, but the reduction in recidivism was greater for offenders who had only one felony conviction when they attended a PSN meeting.

Summary. A growing number of quasi-experimental evaluations have found that focused deterrence programs generate statistically significant crime reduction impacts in areas under the treatment condition. Unfortunately, there have been no randomized experimental evaluations of focused deterrence interventions, and although there are some noteworthy exceptions, the overall methodological rigor of focused deterrence evaluations needs to be strengthened. However, consistent crime-control impacts have been reported both for short- and longer-term outcomes—not only by controlled evaluations that tested program effectiveness using outcomes such as reductions in gang violence and street crime driven by disorderly drug markets but also by non-experimental studies that examined repeat offending by individuals.

Stop, Question, and Frisk

One of the first studies to examine whether the increase in the use of a stop, question, and frisk (SQF) strategy in New York City reduced crime was carried out by Smith and Purtell (2008). They used an interrupted time series, lagging SQF stop rates to crime rates. Their analysis found that SQF may have dissimilar effects across different types of crime or locations. The SQF strategy seemed to be associated with citywide reductions in incidents of robbery, murder, burglary, and motor vehicle theft but not with reduction in incidents of assault, rape, and grand larceny. Smith and Purtell (2008) also examined impacts of SQF in precincts with "impact zones" in which stop and frisk activity was concentrated. In those precincts, stops were found to be associated with reductions in robbery, assault, and grand larceny, although the authors point out that there are declining returns to scale for both the city and for precincts with impact zones.

Rosenfeld and Fornango (2014) critiqued Smith and Purtell's (2008) methods, arguing that other factors may have contributed to their findings. Unlike the earlier Smith and Purtell study, Rosenfeld and Fornango (2014) used yearly rates of crime and SQF stops across all 75 precincts in the New York Police Department and limited their analysis to robbery and burglary. Per their critique of Smith and Purtell (2008), they included measures of precinct-level economic disadvantage, immigration, and residential stability. Their results indicate that there are no statistically significant correlations between SQF and burglary or robbery and only marginally significant negative relationships between stops lagged 2 years behind precinct burglary rates (Rosenfeld and Fornango, 2014, p. 11). Both of these studies were based on non-experimental data and are therefore vulnerable to all the problems inherent in the use of such data to make causal inferences.

Perhaps the most important of these problems is separating cause from effect. One way of disentangling cause from effect in non-experimental data is through the use of instrumental variable (IV) regression. The valid use of IV regression requires the identification of a source of variation in the application of SQFs that affects the crime rate only through its effect on the frequency of use of SQF. This approach is one of the two analyses used by Weisburd and colleagues (2016), who drew from an earlier study showing that SQFs in New York were used as a hot spots policing strategy (Weisburd, Telep, and Lawton, 2014). Employing an adaptation of Bartik's

Instrument (see Bartik, 1991), they used frequency of stops occurring in the same borough but in different precincts as an instrument and found a deterrent effect of SQFs at a microgeographic level. Interpreting their results in terms of numbers of SQF stops, they found that in the year with the highest number of SQF stops (686,000), their models predicted a reduction of 11,771 crimes, or a 2 percent decrease in crime at the city level, attributable to SQF.

The second analysis used by Weisburd and colleagues (2016) was a space-time interaction model known as bivariate Ripley's K (see Diggle et al. [1995]; this analysis was also used by Wooditch and Weisburd [2016]) to examine the daily impact of SQF on crime. Similar to the Bartik (1991) analysis, they found that SQFs had a deterrent effect on crime, at least within a limited time frame (less than 5 days).

There is also a separate body of research on the effectiveness of SQF in targeting places with serious gun crime problems and focusing on high-risk repeat offenders. Koper and Mayo-Wilson (2006, 2012) have reviewed studies of police tactics intended to reduce firearms violence. In these studies, the police employed various aggressive enforcement approaches ranging from traffic and pedestrian stops to car checks at locations with high concentrations of gun crime. But unlike zero tolerance tactics that depend on indiscriminate arrest for even minor offenses, the enforcement tactics were tailored to increase the risks for carrying firearms illegally in crime hot spots, and the evaluations found that such tactics had positive crime-prevention outcomes (see, e.g., McGarrell et al., 2001; Sherman, Shaw, and Rogan, 1995).

A recent study of an intervention to reduce gun crime in St. Louis, Missouri, reported similar crime-reduction outcomes (Rosenfeld, Deckard, and Blackburn, 2014). This study evaluated the effect of directed patrol and self-initiated enforcement efforts conducted at firearm violence hot spots in St. Louis. Thirty-two violent crime hot spots were randomly allocated to two different treatment conditions (directed patrol only, directed patrol with enforcement activities), as well as one control condition (no special treatment). For the directed patrol with enforcement activities, officers were asked to remain in a hot spot for approximately 15 minutes each time, following the Koper Curve principle (see Koper, 1995), and to engage in a variety of self-initiated activities. These included making arrests; conducting vehicle, pedestrian, and business checks; carrying out foot patrol; and other problem-solving techniques. The researchers found that directed patrol with these self-initiated activities reduced total firearm violence by 20 percent at the treatment area relative to the control areas. Firearm assaults decreased by about 55 percent, but there was no significant change in robbery using a firearm. However, the authors attributed their findings to the increased certainty of arrest and the increase in occupied-vehicle checks that resulted from the self-initiated activities, not specifically from pedestrian checks or SQF.

Two randomized experiments in Philadelphia to examine the effects of foot patrol in small, violence-prone hot spots generated some valuable insights into the link between pedestrian stops (also called field investigations, many of which included frisks) and violent crime. While neither the Philadelphia Foot Patrol Experiment (Ratcliffe et al., 2011) nor the subsequent Philadelphia Policing Tactics Experiment (Groff et al., 2015) were designed to explicitly test the impact of SQF or pedestrian stops in particular, the association between pedestrian stops conducted by the foot patrol officers in both experiments is illuminating. In the first experiment, after 3 months violent crime was reduced by 23 percent in 60 randomly selected crime hot spots. The authors noted that whereas pedestrian stops changed by less than 1 percent in control areas, the intervention sites that had two groups of officers patrolling in pairs for 16 hours a day, 5 days a week, saw a 64 percent increase in pedestrian stops. In the intervention areas that demonstrated the clearest evidence of crime reduction, there was a "substantial jump in proactive activity for foot patrol officers" (Ratcliffe et al., 2011, p. 821).

In contrast, during the Philadelphia Policing Tactics Experiment, foot patrol officers in violent crime hot spots were unable to replicate the gains demonstrated in the Philadelphia Foot Patrol Experiment. The authors (Groff et al., 2015) noted a number of differences related to implementation and dosage. The later experimental areas were larger, foot patrol officers were veterans rather than rookies, and most of the foot patrol sites were only patrolled for 8 hours a day compared to 16 in the earlier experiment. All of this translated to differences in pedestrian stops, with no significant increases in police activity in foot patrol areas and a suggestion that "the veterans were less aggressive in their enforcement than the officers with less experience from the Philadelphia Foot Patrol Experiment who increased pedestrian and vehicle stops" (Groff et al., 2015, pp. 44–45). Thus, while there were implementation differences between the experiments, the first experiment's foot patrol areas had substantial increases in pedestrian stops and proactive activity and were associated with significant crime-reduction gains.

Summary. Non-experimental analyses of SQF programs implemented as a general, citywide crime control strategy have found mixed outcomes. A separate body of experimental and quasi-experimental evaluation research examines the effectiveness of SQFs and other self-initiated enforcement activities by officers in targeting places with serious violence or gun crime problems and focusing on high-risk repeat offenders. Often, these studies do not specifically isolate the impact of SQF on crime. Evaluations of these focused uses of enforcement tactics that have included pedestrian stops report meaningful and statistically significant crime reductions at targeted locations, though the estimated jurisdictional impact (when measured) has been modest.

COMMUNITY-BASED STRATEGIES

Community-Oriented Policing

As a proactive crime prevention strategy, community-oriented policing tries to address and mitigate community problems (crime or otherwise) for the future and build social resilience, collective efficacy, and empowerment to strengthen the infrastructure for the coproduction of safety and crime prevention. There can be overlap between community-oriented and problem-oriented policing programs, given that the community can be involved in specific problem-solving efforts. This overlap is not surprising, as the basic definitions of community policing used by police departments often include problem solving as a key programmatic element (see, e.g., Trojanowicz and Bucqueroux, 1994; Skogan and Hartnett, 1997).

Three extensive reviews of the crime-control impacts of community-oriented policing are worth mentioning. In an update to an earlier comprehensive review of crime-prevention programs (see Sherman, 1997), Sherman and Eck (2002) reviewed 23 studies on the effects on crime and victimization of community-oriented policing programs such as neighborhood watch, community meetings, door-to-door contacts, police storefronts (substations in the community), increasing information flow to citizens, and legitimacy policing (which is reviewed in the next section). The authors concluded that some community-oriented policing efforts were "promising" in reducing crime and victimization, such as those that increased community participation with planning and priority setting about specific crime problems or from door-to-door visits by the police. However, many other community-oriented policing approaches did not appear to be effective, such as monthly newsletters, education programs, or community meetings. The strongest research, which used randomized controlled trials to examine monthly community newsletters, education efforts, and home visits after domestic violence, found no statistically significant effects on crime reduction in the treatment condition compared with the control condition (Sherman and Eck, 2002).

The 2004 NRC study on policing (National Research Council, 2004) also reviewed the research on community-oriented policing and concluded that broad-based, community-oriented policing programs (i.e., community meetings, newsletters, education programs) generally do not reduce crime but may improve other important outcomes, such as citizen views of the police (see Chapter 5 of this report). Any observed crime-prevention impacts were more directly associated with other strategies such as problem-oriented policing, implemented within a community-based policing approach. That NRC study also included foot patrol as a community-based policing tactic.

A Campbell systematic review sponsored by the UK National Policing Improvement Agency identified 25 eligible studies, which evaluated 65 controlled tests of community-oriented policing programs (Gill et al., 2014). This review collected 114 eligible outcome measures across five types of outcome categories—citizen satisfaction, legitimacy of police, citizen perceived disorder, citizen fear of crime, and official crime and victimization. Forty-seven official crime and victimization outcomes across the 25 studies were identified. This systematic review only included studies with at least one comparison group or lengthy pre- and post-time series analysis, and only one study was identified as a randomized controlled trial. Of the 65 controlled tests of community-oriented policing programs, the authors were able to calculate odds ratios for 37 tests to be included in a meta-analysis. Their conclusion from this meta-analysis was that community-oriented policing programs had limited effects on crime.

These three reviews, across a period of more than two decades, seem to have arrived at similar conclusions. The direct impact of a community-oriented policing strategy (that is not focused necessarily on problem solving as discussed above) on crime prevention and control remains questionable. Further, evaluation studies on community-oriented policing continue to be carried out with only moderate levels of methodological rigor. Many of these studies compare nonrandomly constituted, large, and often noncomparable geographic areas with and without the program. Such studies suffer from low internal validity and insufficient statistical power, reducing the committee's confidence in their results.

The committee confirmed these findings, based on the three major reviews discussed above, when we examined research in the Evidence-Based Policing Matrix (the "Matrix"), a continually updated tool on policing intervention studies (see Lum et al., 2011; Lum and Koper, 2017).[4] The Matrix only includes evaluations that measure crime-control effects of policing interventions and uses inclusion criteria that are slightly more restrictive than the Gill et al. (2014) review. For example, the Matrix includes neither evaluations that use time series studies without comparison groups nor studies that compare an intervention in a neighborhood with larger, noncomparable units, such as the rest of the jurisdiction (see, for example, Esbensen [1987], which is included in the Gill et al. [2014] review but not in the Matrix). The Matrix also includes only those studies that show at

---

[4] See also http://cebcp.org/evidence-based-policing/the-matrix/ [October 2017].

least some police involvement (so community activities to prevent crime that do not involve the police are not included).

We found 12 studies in the Matrix that meet the definition of community policing described by Gill and colleagues (2014) and that fall under our description of community-oriented policing as described in Chapter 2. The interventions evaluated by these studies included: (1) organizing residents and increasing community involvement in both setting priorities and determining responses to specific problems (Connell, Miggans, and McGloin, 2008; Giacomazzi, 1995; Lindsay and McGillis, 1986; Pate, McPherson, and Silloway, 1987; Tuffin, Morris, and Poole, 2006); (2) general increases in police contact with citizens, including door-to-door contacts, business checks, newsletters, and storefronts (Pate and Skogan, 1985; Wycoff et al., 1985); (3) community-based anti-gang initiatives (Cahill et al., 2008); (4) neighborhood watch (Bennett, 1990); and (5) a combination of many of these practices and tactics (Chicago Community Policing Evaluation Consortium, 1995). Of these 12, two studies used a randomized controlled experimental design (Pate et al., 1985a, in both Newark and Houston) and another two used rigorous quasi-experimental designs (Lindsay and McGillis, 1986; Pate, McPherson, and Silloway, 1987).

Pate and colleagues (1985a) examined two randomized controlled experiments, one in Newark, New Jersey, and one in Houston, Texas, on the impact of community newsletters on fear of crime and residents' perceptions. Although this may not necessarily be a "community-involved" interaction, it does involve the police increasing communication with citizens, which is one of the foundations of community-oriented policing. In the case of Newark, three conditions were tested using random assignment: households that received a newsletter with local crime statistics, households that received a newsletter without local crime statistics, and households that were not mailed any newsletter. Findings indicated that those who were sent newsletters without crime statistics took significantly fewer crime prevention actions than those not sent a newsletter at all. In Houston, respondents in households that were sent newsletters regardless of whether crime information was included perceived a greater increase in crime than respondents not sent newsletters. Those who were given statistics also had increased levels of worry about victimization than those receiving newsletters without statistics. The study by Pate and colleagues (1985a) thus indicates that increased information to the community, in particular information about crime, may lead members to be less satisfied with police services and more fearful of crime. However, these studies did not measure the impact of newsletters on objective measures of crime or victimization; they only measured community perceptions thereof.

Two additional studies in the Matrix used quasi-experimental designs (Lindsay and McGillis, 1986; Pate, McPherson, and Silloway, 1987), while the other eight studies were more modest in methodological rigor. With regard to the two quasi-experimental studies, Pate, McPherson, and Silloway (1987) examined an intervention that used community block clubs, recruitment of community leaders, and other tactics for involving the community. In their evaluation, 21 neighborhoods were first matched on demographic and socioeconomic characteristics and then randomly allocated to one of three conditions: (1) police helping to organize block clubs and recruit community leaders; (2) in addition to organizing clubs and recruiting leaders, police officer activity included tactics such as officers attending block meetings, engaging in special control, and providing further services; and (3) an untreated control group. Neither of the two treatments were found to have a statistically significant impact on burglary. Lindsay and McGillis (1986) also attempted a relatively rigorous quasi-experimental design, in which they matched census tracts in Seattle, Washington, based on preprogram burglary rates. One tract in each matched pair received a community crime prevention program; the other tract did not. Their analysis of outcomes in treated and control tracts found that whereas paired tracts were very similar on burglary rates prior to the intervention, those that received the crime prevention program had significantly lower burglary rates post-intervention (2.45% in treated tracts versus 5.65% in controls). The pre- and post-burglary rates amounted to a 61 percent decline in burglary in treatment tracts, compared to 5 percent in control tracts. The authors also measured the impact of the intervention on displacing crime into adjacent census tracts and found no evidence of such displacement.

Of the eight studies that were more modest in methodological rigor, all but two found positive impacts on crime. These studies commonly compared one large area that was selected for treatment with another that was not selected. Whereas Bennett (1990) found no statistically significant impact of neighborhood watch on crime, and Cahill and colleagues (2008) found mixed results of the impact on crime of a gang reduction program, the other six studies all showed that the interventions reduced crime. However, as with previous reviews of evaluation studies, less confidence should be placed in these findings, given their less rigorous evaluation designs.

The difficulty in evaluating and assessing the evaluation research evidence on the crime prevention impacts of community-oriented policing interventions continues to stem from a number of challenges. Most importantly, studies on community-oriented policing are often carried out using less rigorous evaluation designs. This is likely due to many reasons, the first of which is that agencies often implement interventions before an evaluation plan can be properly designed, or they have less interest in evaluation than in implementation. Second, because community-oriented policing is both a general philosophy (logic model) of proactive policing and a strategy that is decentralized and locally shaped, it has resulted in a variety of activities—sometimes vague—that can be defined as "community oriented." Interventions may include multiple components, the dosages of which may be difficult to identify, measure, and track when the intervention is evaluated. Further, because of the multifaceted characteristic of community-oriented policing, identifying the mechanism(s) or activity(ies) that contribute to a finding is also difficult. Was it, for instance, the community collaboration component that created the effect, or simply the police presence and crackdown? In some studies such as that by Koper and colleagues (2010; see also Koper, Woods, and Isom, 2016), which was included in the Campbell review (Gill et al., 2014) but was not among the 12 Matrix evaluations, the enforcement aspect of the intervention was more prominent, which likely led to the statistically significant findings, although the intervention could be considered community oriented. The size of the unit of analysis further complicates evaluations of community-oriented policing. Hot spots studies indicate that police can create deterrent effects when focusing on much smaller geographic units of analysis and tailoring efforts to those crime concentrations. Community-oriented policing, on the other hand, tends to be implemented in larger areas and neighborhoods, which might dilute its effects.

Summary. Overall, the committee did not identify a consistent crime-prevention benefit for programs using a community-oriented policing strategy, as that strategy is defined in Chapter 2. Research evaluations of such programs found mixed effects. Moreover, programs that showed significant outcomes often included tactics typical of other crime-prevention strategies, such as problem-oriented policing, that have been found to reduce crime outcomes. Empirical studies on community-oriented policing also tend to be characterized by relatively weak evaluation designs, although that is not true for all the evaluations reviewed here.

Procedural Justice Policing

The manner in which police interact with citizens may have important consequences for citizen evaluations of whether they were treated fairly and with dignity and, more generally, for their trust in the police. These perceptions may in turn have behavioral consequences. One is whether citizens comply with any requests or orders made by police officers during encounters. There may also be behavioral outcomes beyond the immediate encounter. Among these is future willingness to cooperate with the police—for example, in providing information about crimes witnessed or reporting such crimes. This section examines the evidence on one specific but very important outcome: whether procedurally just treatment of citizens by the police increases the likelihood of citizens' subsequent legal compliance. Although, as we noted in Chapter 2, procedural justice advocates also argue that this approach will produce long-term crime-prevention gains in the community, such jurisdiction-level outcomes have not been examined to date. While procedural justice policing might be characterized as a person-based strategy, we include it among the community-based strategies because of its overarching objective of building community trust.

The largest part of the research on procedurally just treatment by the police and legal compliance is based on survey research in which people are asked questions about their perceptions of their procedurally just treatment by police on some or all of the dimensions delineated above, their overall perceptions of police legitimacy, and indicators of criminal offending. Offending is measured by either self-reports of past offending or future intentions to offend. Most surveys are cross-sectional, but a few are panel surveys, usually over two waves. Surveys also measure demographic characteristics of the respondents and their perceptions of factors that might also be associated with perceptions of procedurally just treatment, legitimacy, and/or indicators of offending. An example is respondents' perceptions of sanction risk. These survey-based studies consistently find that perceptions of procedurally just treatment are positively associated with perceptions of legitimacy, generally of police themselves, net of association of other predictor variables in regression-based studies (Tyler, Schulhofer, and Huq, 2010; Wolfe et al., 2016; Hinds, 2007). With few exceptions (Augustyn, 2015; Cavanagh and Cauffman, 2015) these studies also find that perceptions of legitimacy are negatively associated with self-reported offending or intentions thereof (Fagan and Piquero, 2007; Reisig, Bratton, and Gertz, 2007; Jackson et al., 2012).

Do these associations credibly demonstrate a causal relationship whereby more procedurally just treatment by the police results in improved perceptions of that treatment, which in turn improves perceptions of police legitimacy, which in its turn increases legal compliance? Nagin and Telep (2017) point to four important shortcomings in the survey-based studies and the procedural justice literature more generally that stand in the way not only of credible inferences about causal connections down this envisioned chain of consequences but also the effectiveness of policies to promote procedural justice. These shortcomings can be stated as four limitations in the evidence for causation throughout the above set of hypothesized consequences: (1) The associations observed among the "links" in this supposed chain of consequences may be a reflection of third common causes (sometimes called "confounders"), of reverse causality, or of both. (2) Evidence for a causal link to perceptions of procedurally just treatment from actual treatment in procedurally just ways is very limited, and the constrained body of research draws contradictory conclusions. (3) Evidence on the effectiveness of policies such as training for promoting procedurally just treatment by police is limited. (4) Evidence that such policies are effective in achieving their ultimate objective—crime reduction—is even more limited. These four shortcomings are discussed in turn below, drawing substantially from the more extended discussions in Nagin and Telep (2017). Following this discussion, the committee discusses earlier reviews by Mazerolle and colleagues (2012b, 2013b) that reach a somewhat different conclusion about the evidence, and we attempt to reconcile the difference in conclusions.

With respect to the first shortcoming, it is important to recognize that perceptions of procedurally just treatment by the police cannot be directly manipulated in a social science experiment. What can potentially be manipulated for the sake of experimentation is the way police treat citizens. This principle has fundamental implications for both causal inference and policy. Concerning causal inference, a key requirement for making credible causal inferences about the effect of procedurally just treatment on legal compliance is that treatment including policy manipulation can credibly be assumed to be exogenous: for example, a policy change as a treatment condition within a randomized experiment or a policy change that is not a direct response to a spike in citizen dissatisfaction with the police or an uptick in crime. Without such exogenous change, the statistical associations observed among perceptions of procedurally just treatment, legitimacy, and legal compliance may reflect third common causes and/or reverse causality, rather than the causal effect of procedurally just treatment on legal compliance that is assumed by the logic model for the procedural justice policing strategy.

Two examples of credible third common cause explanations for statistical associations among procedural justice treatment, legitimacy perceptions, and legal compliance involve social control–based theories and community context. Individuals with larger "stakes in conformity" (Toby, 1957) or with investments in conventional social bonds (Hirschi, 1969) may not only be more legally compliant but may also perceive that agents of the criminal justice system treat them more fairly and are more legitimate. No study we know of accounts either for the independent effect of such factors on legal compliance or, more generally, for the compliance effect of moral commitments to abide by the law. Likewise, the legacy of ill treatment of disadvantaged non-Whites, particularly Blacks, compared to Whites by the police may negatively affect their perceptions of their treatment by the police, independent of their personal experience with police who are trying to be procedurally just. Again, parsing out the effect of procedurally just treatment from the independent effect of legal socialization arising from community context is extraordinarily difficult.

Reverse causality may also account for the measured associations: for example, it may be that legal compliance affects perceptions of legitimacy and procedurally just treatment, rather than the reverse. One possible form of reverse causality is referred to as "neutralization" (Sykes and Matza, 1957), a situation in which offending is rationalized by the offender as a justified response to poor treatment by the police. More generally, police-community relations are bilateral, with each side affecting the behavior of the other. Just as citizens are reacting to their treatment by the police, so the police are responding to the behavior of citizens. Sorting out the extent to which each party is reacting to the other in this context is extremely difficult.

The committee identified only one study that assessed the association between perceptions of procedurally just treatment and actual treatment as assessed by third parties. Worden and McLean (2014) compared citizen perceptions of their treatment in 539 recorded encounters with the police that were later assessed by trained observers. The correlation of citizen perceptions of procedurally just treatment (e.g., was the citizen given the opportunity to explain themselves?) and the observer's assessment of such treatment as just was only 0.12. Interestingly, the correlation of perceptions and observers' assessments of *unjust treatment* (e.g., was the citizen treated disrespectfully?) was much larger and negative, –0.31. The latter finding is consistent with a small body of studies involving third-party observers of police–citizen encounters in which Mastrofski, Snipes, and Supina (1996, p. 296) conclude: "Our police may be able to do little to enhance their cause but a great deal to hurt it."

Experimental work by Mazerolle and colleagues (2012b, 2013b), MacQueen and Bradford (2015), and Sahin and colleagues (2016) involved manipulation of officer behavior through a script or protocols that were randomly assigned to the officers for use during traffic stops or in an airport screening process. These studies thus provide an opportunity to compare citizen perceptions with what officers were *supposed* to do in encounters. In each study, the experimental script/protocol was infused with concepts from procedural justice theory, whereas the control script/protocol was "business as usual."

These studies reached conflicting conclusions. Mazerolle and colleagues (2012b, 2013b) concluded that the experimental treatment increased citizen perceptions of the fairness of their treatment at the encounter and police legitimacy overall. Sahin and colleagues (2016) found a salutary effect for the encounter itself but not for overall confidence in the police. MacQueen and Bradford (2015) found a backfire effect in which the experimental treatment resulted in more negative views of the encounter and the police more generally. We also note that these experiments were conducted in a very controlled setting in which the potential for hostile interaction was low and that response rates to post-treatment surveys mailed to study participants in the Mazerolle and colleagues (2012b, 2013b) and MacQueen and Bradford (2015) studies were less than 10 percent.

With respect to the third shortcoming listed above, research on the effectiveness of policy intended to promote procedurally just practice by police pertains mostly to training. Rosenbaum and Lawrence (2013) report the findings of a randomized experiment involving Chicago police officers that tested the effectiveness of the Quality Interaction Program (QIP). Results based on pre and post surveys of study participants found no statistically significant impact of the training on officer respect toward civilians or on perceptions of the importance of quality of treatment at traffic stops. By contrast, officer behavior in the videotaped scenarios showed a statistically significant treatment effect in which officers receiving the additional training were more likely to demonstrate respectful and supportive behavior. However, the post-training sample of videotaped officers was very small ($n = 34$).

Skogan, Van Craen, and Hennessy (2015) examined the effects of the Chicago Police Department's day-long training program on procedural justice. The program, distinct from the QIP but based on similar principles, included five modules that focused on legitimacy, procedural justice, cynicism, and race. More than 9,000 officers received the in-service training. Based on a comparison of pre- and post-training survey data of participating officers, post-training officer endorsement of various indicators of procedurally just treatment increased. A second, less rigorous analysis found evidence that these effects were sustained longer term.

Robertson and colleagues (2014) examined the effectiveness of a program in Scotland similar to Chicago's QIP program. The study examined a nonrandomized group of 95 police recruits who received nine sessions of procedural justice training over 12 weeks and 64 control-group officers. The survey-based findings were mixed; the treatment group officers had improved scores in communication skills but decreased score on the item "people should be treated with respect, regardless of their attitude." In scenarios, officers receiving treatment were more likely to score "good" than the control group officers in terms of their use of procedural justice in practice, but the difference was not statistically significant.

None of these studies examined actual officer behavior in the field, but two recent randomized trials do so. One took place in Manchester, United Kingdom, where Wheller and colleagues (2013) randomly allocated officers to one of three treatment groups differing in the duration and content of procedural justice training or to a comparison group receiving no procedural justice training. Small sample sizes made it difficult to differentiate among treatments. As with the Chicago evaluations, after training, officers in the treatment group significantly improved on some indicators of interest (e.g., building empathy and rapport, fair decision making), but not others (e.g., perceived value of procedural justice and perceived level of public cooperation). This study went on to evaluate behavior in the field, but only toward victims, not suspected perpetrators. There were some positive impacts of the training on victim perceptions, although these effects were neither consistent across measures of procedurally fair treatment nor large in magnitude. Owens and colleagues (2016) examined the impact of randomly assigned procedural justice–infused training on officer behavior. Officers assigned the treatment were less likely to resolve incidents with an arrest and were less likely to be involved in incidents where force was used.

In summary, knowledge about the effectiveness of procedural justice training is limited and findings are not consistent across studies. However, the results of the Wheller and colleagues (2013) and Owens and colleagues (2016) studies provide encouraging signs of effectiveness in altering officer behavior in the field. Evidence of such effectiveness is important because unless policies can be devised that reliably change behavior of police officers in their delivery of procedurally just treatment, the predicted benefits of such treatment will be out of reach.

Finally, with respect to the fourth shortcoming in the evidence base, only two studies provide indirect tests of the effect of procedurally just treatment on those citizens' legal compliance. One is an outgrowth of a domestic violence experiment; the other involves a gun violence intervention in Chicago. The domestic violence study by Paternoster and colleagues (1997) used data from the Milwaukee domestic violence experiment (Sherman et al., 1992), in which police responding to misdemeanor domestic violence calls for service randomly assigned suspects between mandatory arrest and non-arrest conditions. For those who were arrested, Paternoster and colleagues (1997) created a survey based on indicators of perceived procedurally just treatment and administered the survey at the time of their booking of the suspects from either treatment group who were arrested. They found that individuals who perceived greater procedurally just treatment were less likely to recidivate for domestic violence.

There are two important limitations of this study that stand in the way of interpreting this finding as a causal association. Both follow from the prior discussion. First, procedurally just treatment was not randomly assigned or exogenously manipulated in any way. Second, there were no third-party observers assessing officer treatment. Measures of procedurally just treatment were based solely on the arrestees' perceptions, which, for reasons previously discussed, may not be closely tied to actual treatment and may also be related to recidivism due to unobserved characteristics of the arrested individual.

Wallace and colleagues (2016) examined the impact on recidivism of offender notification forums infused with procedural justice. The forums were implemented as part of a Project Safe Neighborhoods intervention in

Chicago. The forums lasted 1 hour and sent a message to individuals recently released from prison with a history of violence that further violence would no longer be tolerated. The message was explicitly designed to focus not only on deterrence but also on emphasizing individual choice, respect, and fairness. The evaluation of this intervention compared re-incarceration rates between parolees in two police districts receiving forums to parolees in two comparison districts where there were no forums. Hazard models suggest a significant intervention effect both within neighborhoods (i.e., comparing forum attenders to non-attenders in the same precinct) and between neighborhoods (i.e., comparing forum attenders to non-attenders in comparison precincts). Parolees attending a forum had a longer time on the street (and out of prison), on average, than non-attendees (as described above, a 30% reduction in recidivism). Additionally, forum attendees had lower hazards of committing weapons offenses or murder compared to non-attendees. Effects for violent crime overall and violent property crime were less consistent.

This study (Wallace et al., 2016) is important because it analyzed the impact of an actual policy intervention that addressed a serious crime problem and that was directed at individuals with extensive criminal histories. The difficulty of interpretation involves extracting the contribution of procedural justice to a multipronged intervention involving focused deterrence and access to social service components as other prominent features of the intervention package. Interventions such as this are exemplars of the more general challenge of parsing out the contribution of any one component of a complex intervention, especially in circumstances where the component parts are so heterogeneous. We also note that because participation in the forums was not randomly assigned, the observed associations may be contaminated by selection bias.

The conclusion of our review with respect to the four shortcomings in the evidence base is that the well-documented *association* of perceptions of procedurally just treatment by police and/or perceptions of police legitimacy with legal compliance, while consistent with a causal linkage across these factors, has many other possible noncausal interpretations that the evaluation designs do not rule out. Further, from a policy perspective, evidence is extremely limited for the effectiveness of training or other policy levers in affecting police behavior vis-à-vis procedural justice.

Our conclusions differ from the more affirmative conclusions of Mazerolle and colleagues (Mazerolle et al., 2012a, 2013a; Higginson and Mazerolle, 2014). We attribute the difference to several factors. First, the reviews by Mazerolle and colleagues examined studies only through April 2010.

Second, they included any study that met other technical inclusion criteria and that stated that one of its purposes was to improve police legitimacy or that articulated an objective consistent with Tyler's conception of procedurally just treatment.[5] Their expansive inclusion criteria for studies that constitute a test of procedural justice policing (as this committee uses the term) have several important consequences. One is that their meta-analysis leaves unspecified the sources of perceptions of legitimacy. Definitions of what constitutes procedurally just treatment vary across studies. For example, Bottoms and Tankebe (2012, p. 129) argue that it is the quality of dialogue between the citizen and the police officer that is crucial: "legitimacy needs to be perceived as always dialogic and relational in character." Such a difference in emphasis is important because that difference is crucial not only to pinning down and testing the sources of perceptions of legitimacy but also to designing policies that are effective in promoting legitimacy.

A second consequence of an expansive inclusion criterion is that the legitimacy enhancement objective was only one among many objectives of the interventions included in the review. Thus, while the committee's discussion above focused on interventions designed to enhance procedural justice through scripts or training, the reviews by Mazerolle and colleagues (2012a, 2013a) included a variety of intervention types, including community-oriented policing, Weed and Seed programs (which include a variety of elements design to "weed" a community of criminal and disruptive influences such as gangs and "seed" pro-social influences), and restorative justice (see Higginson and Mazerolle, 2014). These practices include elements of procedural justice policing but also cover a far broader range of activities than is implied by the definition of procedural justice used by this committee. As a consequence, it is difficult to sort out what part of program benefits are attributable to the procedural justice component of the intervention or practice (Cook, 2015).

Summary. There is a lack of rigorous program evaluations that directly test whether procedural justice policing can reduce crime and disorder. Prior reviews of impact evaluations have included multifaceted programs comprising a broad range of other crime prevention activities that go well beyond procedural justice policing. It is therefore difficult to isolate any crime prevention benefits associated with this approach.

---

[5]Tyler's (1990) hypothesis about the effect of procedural just treatment in improving citizens' compliance with the law is noted at the beginning of this chapter, in the initial discussion of the logic model for procedural justice policing.

Broken Windows Policing

As described in Chapter 2, broken windows policing is a strategy for a community-based approach to proactive policing that developed from Wilson and Kelling's (1982) propositions about the relationship between disorder and crime. Disorder includes social incivilities (e.g., public drinking, loitering, and prostitution) as well as physical incivilities such as trash accumulations in public areas, vacant lots, and abandoned buildings. If disorder is a *cause* and not just a correlate of serious crime, Wilson and Kelling (1982) argued, then proactive suppression of disorder would yield another even more important benefit than just improving social order: it would reduce serious crime. This line of reasoning became the rationale, or logic model, supporting broken windows policing tactics.

Broken windows policing is controversial for two reasons. First, the underlying hypothesis of a causal linkage between disorder and serious crime was unproven, even as it spawned an era of greatly expanded policing against disorder in New York City and many other large U.S. cities. Second, the most common implementation of the strategy has been aggressive policing against disorder that involved making large numbers of arrests for minor crimes and expanding the issuance of summons for even less serious legal infractions.

Since the appearance of the Wilson and Kelling (1982) paper, a modestly sized body of research has been conducted addressing the causal linkage between disorder and serious crime or the effectiveness of aggressive policing against disorder in reducing serious crime. We review the research on these two facets of the logic model in turn.

With regard to the causal relationship between disorder and crime hypothesized by Wilson and Kelling (1982), the evidence is mixed. While there is strong evidence that places that have more disorder also tend to have more serious crime, what is uncertain is whether the correlation of crime and disorder across places and also over time is a reflection of a common set of underlying causes, such as poverty, social disorganization, or even ineffective policing,[6] or whether the relationship is causal—specifically in the direction that disorder begets serious crime. Empirically distinguishing these alternative explanations for the correlation of crime and disorder has proven difficult.

Studies of the effect of urban blight or disorder on crime have yielded differing conclusions. For example, Skogan (1990) examined the association of neighborhood disorder with robbery victimization and concluded there was a causal relationship, but Harcourt's (2001) reexamination of

---

[6]This issue is thus another instance of the "third common cause" or confounder problem that we discussed with respect to the evidence base for the causal linkage presumed in the logic model for procedural justice policing (see previous subsection).

Skogan's data found no comparable association for other crimes such as assault, burglary, or rape. He concluded, therefore, that there was no causal relationship. Eck and Maguire (2006) critiqued Harcourt's findings, suggesting that they were based on removing those neighborhoods in Skogan's analyses that had high disorder and crime relationships. Another study by Keizer, Lindenberg, and Steg (2008) that used a number of field experiments found a causal link from disorder conditions to crime, especially when disorder conditions were allowed to spread or linger. Freedman and Owens (2011) used plausibly exogenous changes in the funding formula for the Low Income Housing Tax Credit program as a source of controlled variation in neighborhood disorder. They found that improving the quality of housing in low-income places can cause reductions in violent crime (homicide, rape, robbery, and assault) at the county level, although they found no substantive impact on property offenses (burglary, larceny, auto theft, and arson).

Taylor (2001) used a longitudinal analysis of disorder and crime in 66 Baltimore neighborhoods to support a conclusion similar to Harcourt (2001). Similarly, Sampson and Raudenbush (1999) found that once neighborhood characteristics were taken into account, the association between crime and disorder, including the association for homicide, vanished. This finding is notable because disorder was measured in their analysis based on systematic observation by trained observers. They concluded: "Rather than conceive of disorder as a direct cause of crime, we view many elements of disorder as part and parcel of crime itself" (Sampson and Raudenbush, 1999, p. 638). They also observed that "Attacking public order through tough police tactics may thus be a politically popular but perhaps analytically weak strategy to reduce crime" (Sampson and Raudenbush, 1999, p. 638). Yang (2010), using a longitudinal approach, also questioned a direct and consistent causal link from disorder to crime.

A different conclusion is reached in an evaluation of a citywide blight-reduction project in Philadelphia to remediate abandoned buildings and clean up abandoned lots during the period from 1999 to 2013. More than 5,000 buildings and lots were remediated during that time, and the effect on crime was evaluated by Branas and colleagues (2016). They described the lot clean up this way:

> Remediation involves removing trash and debris, grading the land, planting grass and trees to create a park-like setting, and installing low wooden post-and-rail fences with walk-in openings around each lot's perimeter to show that the lot was cared for, permit recreational use, and deter illegal dumping. Landscapers return approximately once each month to perform basic maintenance. (Branas et al., 2016, p. 2159)

The authors compared changes in local assault rates in treated places with a matched sample of places that were eligible for treatment but did not receive it. The results for the remediation over the first year were a 4.5 percent reduction in gun assault and 2.2 percent reduction in overall assault rate, both highly significant statistically. The remediation treatment also conveyed social benefits that exceeded costs. Nonetheless, drawing inferences from this quasi-experiment is limited because the assignment of the treatment was not in any sense exogenous but rather a choice made by owners (for private lots and buildings). It is unfortunate, in retrospect, that the treatment condition was not assigned in a fashion that would permit stronger inferences about causation. Nonetheless, the findings support a finding that there needs to be stronger experimental research done in this area before one can draw strong conclusions about the causal direction of the disorder/crime relationships.

Alongside this literature of mixed findings about a causal relationship between disorder and crime, just as important in the police context is how the broken windows logic model has translated into police practice and whether those practices are effective in reducing crime. (This is the second facet of the broken windows logic model on which limited evidence exists.) As Braga, Welsh, and Schnell (2015) pointed out, policing to counter disorder can take various forms. The two most common (separately or in combination) have been the use of aggressive policing that uses misdemeanor arrests to disrupt disorderly social behavior and the use of problem-oriented or community-oriented policing practices to address disorderly conditions that are hypothesized to contribute to crime.

With regard to the effect of increased misdemeanor arrests in reducing violent crimes, Kelling and Sousa (2001) used precinct-level data from New York City to examine whether higher rates of misdemeanor arrest were associated with lower levels of crime, after taking account of other characteristics of the precincts. They concluded that aggressive misdemeanor arrests prevented more than 60,000 violent crimes between 1989 and 1998, or a statistically significant 5 percent reduction in violent crime. Kelling and Sousa (2001, p. 9) noted, "the average NYPD [New York City Police Department] precinct during the ten-year period studied could expect to suffer one less violent crime for approximately every 28 additional misdemeanor arrests made." Corman and Mocan (2005), who also analyzed New York City data, reached a similar conclusion.

Balanced against these findings is a study by Rosenfeld, Fornango, and Rengifo (2007), which found smaller effects of increased misdemeanor arrests on crime incidence, and studies by Fagan and Davies (2003) and Harcourt and Ludwig (2005) that found no evidence of a statistically significant effect. The Harcourt and Ludwig (2005) study is notable because it includes an analysis of data that uses a similar regression technique on the same dataset used by Kelling and Sousa (2001). Specifically, both studies examined police precinct–level data from New York City for the years 1989 to 1998 and used panel regression methods to estimate the causal contribution of misdemeanor arrest rates to violent crime rates. Harcourt and Ludwig concluded that the substantial crime prevention effect identified by Kelling and Sousa (2001) may be no more than regression to the mean.[7] Specifically, they found that the largest increases in misdemeanor arrest rates occurred in those precincts with the largest increase in violent crime in the 1980s and that subsequently these same precincts experienced the largest decrease in crime for reasons unrelated to intensive misdemeanor policing. We note that this Harcourt and Ludwig (2005) critique of Kelling and Sousa (2001) pertains to all the studies based on non-experimental data: the misdemeanor arrest rate in some time period may be driven by the overall crime rate prior to that period, which makes it difficult to distinguish whether the association is a reflection of increased arrest rate causing decreased crime rate, a change in crime rate causing a positively correlated change in arrest rate, or neither of these causal connections occurring consistently over times and places.

Another important shortcoming of these types of studies is that they do not account for the intensity of use of other policing tactics that may also be affecting crime and thereby biasing the estimated impact of the misdemeanor arrest rate in unknown ways. We note that this shortcoming is not the fault of the authors of these studies because data measuring the intensity of use of other policing tactics is not available.

The relationship between misdemeanor arrests and crime has also been studied using experimental and quasi-experimental methods. Two recent meta-analyses of the studies by Braga, Welsh, and Schnell (2015) and Weisburd and colleagues (2015) reach the conclusion that broken windows policing based on increasing the misdemeanor arrest rate is not effective in reducing serious crime. The Braga, Welsh, and Schnell (2015) review also includes studies of interventions that aimed to reduce disorder not by aggressive policing against disorder but by tactics typically used for community-based and problem-solving approaches and designed to change social and physical disorder conditions at particular places. The review authors found that these tactics did have a modest crime-reduction effect.

The Braga, Welsh, and Schnell (2015) review is important because it also speaks to different approaches to policing practices aimed at reducing

---

[7] In this context, regression to the mean refers to the police responding to a random increase in crime at a specific location by increasing the intensity of misdemeanor arrest activity at that location. If crime subsequently subsides at that location, the decline may be in whole or in part attributable to crime randomly returning to its normal level (regressing to the mean) rather than to the increased police activity.

disorder, practices that this report considers as exemplifying the community-based and problem-solving approaches (see Chapter 2). The authors identified a diverse group of 30 controlled tests of police-led interventions to control crime by reducing social and physical disorder, 21 of which used quasi-experimental designs (70%), while 9 used randomized experimental designs. Units of analysis included small places (such as crime hot spots and problem buildings; 46.7% of the tests), small police-defined administrative areas such as patrol beats (26.7% of the tests), neighborhoods and selected stretches of highways (13.3% of the tests), and larger police-defined administrative areas such as precincts and divisions (13.3% of the tests). Twenty evaluations tested the impact of community-based/problem-solving interventions largely designed to change disorderly conditions in places; 10 evaluations tested the impact of aggressive order-maintenance tactics intended to control problem behaviors of disorderly individuals in the areas targeted for treatment. Given the broad definition of "policing disorder" (i.e., policing that is intended to decrease disorder) used by the authors, it is important to note that many of the studies they reviewed appear in other sections of this chapter (e.g., Braga and Bond [2008] is discussed in the problem-oriented policing section; Pate and Skogan [1985] is discussed in the community-oriented policing section; Weisburd et al. [2006b] is discussed under hot spots policing).

We noted above that an important limitation in the studies on the effect on crime rate of increased misdemeanor arrests is that those studies lacked controls for other policing tactics and practices that were being used in conjunction with the tactic of increasing misdemeanor arrests and that might also be affecting the crime rates observed. Interpretation of the results found in the experimental and quasi-experimental studies reviewed by Braga, Welsh, and Schnell (2015) is complicated by another form of this problem: how to parse out the causal contribution of the "broken windows" component of the intervention from the contribution from other components of an intervention intended to reduce disorder. Further complicating matters, as Weisburd and colleagues (2015) emphasized, is that discerning the mechanism by which order-maintenance policing might reduce the more-serious crimes is extremely difficult. We also note that studies included in the Braga, Welsh, and Schnell (2015) meta-analysis are very heterogeneous in terms of the character of interventions and the size of the city or town in which they took place. As that review's authors suggest, such heterogeneity raises concerns about the interpretability of an effect size that is an amalgam of results from such diverse studies (Braga, Welsh, and Schnell, 2015, pp. 572–573).

Summary. The scientific evidence on the effects of broken windows policing on crime is mixed. In general, the available program evaluations suggest that aggressive practices based solely on increasing the misdemeanor arrest rate to control disorder generate small to null impacts on crime. The better-controlled evaluations of hybrid interventions that incorporate practices typical of place-based and problem-solving approaches in order to reduce social and physical disorder have found consistent short-term crime-reduction effects from the entire intervention. However, the study designs do not allow the contributions of specific tactics to be parsed out from the overall effect of the hybrid intervention.

CONCLUSION

This review has focused on the effectiveness of several policing strategies that are proactive in the sense that they are anticipatory responses to problematic crime patterns, rather than routine and reactive responses to calls for service. The primary goal of proactive policing is crime prevention, and assessing the evidence that these strategies reduce crime has been the focus of this chapter. Other potential outcomes, such as improving the public's perception of the police, are considered in the chapters that follow.

The committee's review of the evidence base focused on evaluations of real-world interventions that were developed and conducted by police departments. While the evidence generated by these interventions is far from complete or definitive, the past three decades have been something of a "golden age" for the production of systematic evidence on what works. The police, more than other criminal justice agencies, have been amenable to running field experiments, and even non-experimental interventions are better documented than in the past, due to the increasing quality and quantity of data on crime and police activities. Although the available evidence still has important gaps and contradictions, this recent trend in research is favorable to the ultimate goal of evidence-based crime policy.

One challenge in developing or reviewing this evidence base is the overlap of the approaches as we defined them in Chapter 2. These approaches were defined to distinguish the key underlying logic models for different strategies. In practice, the broad approaches and the strategies for them, as delineated here and in Chapter 2, are not mutually exclusive, and each of them has fuzzy boundaries when it comes to classifying specific actual programs and interventions used by police organizations. For example, a project to clean up vacant lots that facilitate drug dealing may originate from an intervention plan that could reasonably be said to involve community-oriented policing, problem-oriented policing, or broken windows policing—three proactive policing strategies with separate sections in this chapter. Our review acknowledges these potential ambiguities and overlaps.

A second challenge in assessing the evidence, as discussed above, is that most real-world interventions are quite complex and may include elements of several strategies, as those strategies are defined in this report. For example the Weed and Seed programs funded by DOJ have been used to assess the impact of "legitimacy policing" on crime, but each of those programs has also included elements of community-oriented policing, neighborhood restoration, and stepped-up law enforcement (Higginson and Mazerolle, 2014; Cook, 2015). Separating out the effect of the "legitimacy" element from the others is not possible, given that each program was implemented as a bundle.

Many of the evaluations to date have been short term, examining crime-prevention outcomes for no more than 1 or 2 years, and often less. Some proactive policing programs have had only short-term goals, for example, suppressing crime in high-crime areas such as hot spots. However, others do not have just short-term goals, but our knowledge base is focused on short-term, rather than long-term, gains among people, places, or communities. Similarly, many of the interventions in the literature examined by the committee are focused on places, and place is a key feature of some interventions whose underlying logic model comports more closely with a community-based, person-focused, or problem-solving approach (as these approaches are defined in this report). In this context, issues of whether crime is displaced to areas *nearby* are common in evaluations and are reflected in their study designs. However, very little is known about *distal* displacement of crime across a jurisdiction. Nor are there estimates of jurisdictional impacts for key strategies such as hot spots policing, problem-oriented policing, third party policing, and procedural justice policing. In Chapter 8, the committee provides suggestions on filling these and other knowledge gaps.

Finally, while the evidence base has grown dramatically over the past decade, the interventions that the committee examined are often limited to specific contexts. In some cases—for example, hot spots policing—we had a large enough number of evaluations to draw more general conclusions that are likely to apply in different types of cities in different circumstances. Accordingly, by necessity our discussion of the quality of evidence in this chapter has referred more to the credibility of the design in drawing causal statements about a program's outcomes than to reasonable extrapolation of those outcomes across different settings. As we note in Chapter 8, much more work needs to be done before one can provide specific policy prescriptions about the use of the approaches this committee reviewed.

With these challenges and caveats as context, the committee has drawn a series of conclusions about the effectiveness of proactive policing strategies in reducing crime and disorder, offered with the proviso that the state of the art is constantly developing. We summarize the key findings below in Table 4-1. Note that "broken windows" and "stop, question, and frisk" are divided into two subcategories, reflecting broad differences in practices

TABLE 4-1 Strength of Evidence on Crime-Prevention Effectiveness: Summary of Proactive Policing Strategies

Policing Strategy	Principal Mechanism[a]	Strength of Evidence (study design, replication)[b]	Do Strong Studies Find Significant Positive Effects?	Concerns
PLACE-BASED STRATEGIES				
Hot Spots Policing Example: Concentrated patrol of microgeographic high-crime places	Deterrence	Strong	Yes	
Predictive Policing Example: Data-intensive algorithm for predicting near-term crime in hot spots	Deterrence	Weak	Mixed	Not yet well defined
CCTV (type I) Example: Passive monitoring of cameras in high-crime area	Deterrence (general)	Medium	Mixed	
CCTV (type II) Example: Proactive camera surveillance linked to dedicated operational police response	Deterrence (specific)	Weak	Yes (but only one study)	Only one intervention studied
PROBLEM-SOLVING STRATEGIES				
Problem-Oriented Policing Example: Close taverns that have frequent violence	Opportunity Deterrence	Medium	Yes	Only a small number of potential implementations have been studied

Third Party Policing Example: Police coordinate with private security in a Business Improvement District	Opportunity Deterrence	Medium	Yes	
PERSON-FOCUSED STRATEGIES				
Focused Deterrence Policing Example: Police department "calls in" a gang and delivers a personalized "carrot and stick" message	Deterrence	Medium	Yes	No RCTs, but evidence base includes strong quasi-experiments
Stop-Question-Frisk (type I) Example: High-volume *Terry* stops throughout jurisdiction	Deterrence	Medium	Mixed	No RCTs
Stop-Question-Frisk (type II) Example: High-volume *Terry* stops in violent-crime hot spots	Deterrence	Strong	Yes	Studies are confounded with hot spots policing practices, one RCT
COMMUNITY-BASED STRATEGIES				
Community-Oriented Policing Example: Neighborhood watch, newsletters, and community meetings	Collective efficacy	Weak	No	Broad category, not well defined

Continued

TABLE 4-1 Continued

Policing Strategy	Principal Mechanism[a]	Strength of Evidence (study design, replication)[b]	Do Strong Studies Find Significant Positive Effects?	Concerns
Procedural Justice Policing Example: Train police to improve interactions with public	Legitimacy	Weak	Mixed	Evaluated interventions typically include tactics from other strategies, so effect of procedural justice component is not determinable
Broken Windows Policing (type I) Example: High-volume arrests for certain misdemeanors	Deterrence	Medium	Mixed	No RCTs
Broken Windows Policing (type II) Example: Clean up vacant lots	Deterrence, Opportunity, Collective efficacy	Strong	Yes	Evaluations to date do not allow identification of whether impact is due to collective efficacy or deterrence

NOTES: RCT = randomized controlled trial.
[a]Principal mechanisms:
  Deterrence: Increase perceived and/or actual likelihood of arrest if an offense is committed.
  Opportunity: Curtail availability of attractive opportunities to commit crime.
  Legitimacy: Improve community perception of the legitimacy of police actions or of the police force generally.
  Collective efficacy: Increase the willingness of citizens to intervene and accordingly strengthen informal social controls.
[b]Strength of causal evidence:
  Weak: Available evaluations have weak design and/or are sparse.
  Medium: A few well-done studies done in different contexts with research designs that provide a strong basis for drawing causal conclusions.
  Strong: A number of well-done studies conducted in varying contexts with research designs that provide a strong basis for drawing causal conclusions.

within these strategies that lead to differing impacts. Each strategy is described according to which of three mechanisms, hypothesized to potentially reduce crime rates, may apply to that strategy: (1) an increase in the perceived or actual probability of arrest, which would potentially reduce crime rates through deterrence or incapacitation; (2) a reduction in access to or profitability of criminal opportunities; and (3) increases in collective efficacy or police legitimacy. Each strategy-category is then assessed according to the strength of the evidence that at least some of the real-world programs in that category have reduced crime. That assessment is a one-word summary of the much more nuanced discussion in the chapter text and the numbered conclusions below. The last two columns of the table note whether studies found significant positive outcomes for the strategy and any specific concerns of the committee regarding the studies' designs or results.

Place-Based Proactive Strategies

The committee found particularly strong evidence for proactive policing programs that take advantage of the strong concentration of crime at crime hot spots. A number of rigorous evaluations, including a series of randomized controlled trials, of hot spots policing programs have been conducted.

> CONCLUSION 4-1 The available research evidence strongly suggests that hot spots policing strategies produce short-term crime-reduction effects without simply displacing crime into areas immediately surrounding targeted locations. Hot spots policing studies that do measure possible displacement effects tend to find that these programs generate a diffusion of crime-control benefits into immediately adjacent areas. There is an absence of evidence on the long-term impacts of hot spots policing strategies on crime and on possible jurisdictional outcomes.

In contrast, we could not draw a strong conclusion regarding predictive policing, which draws directly on the insights of hot spots policing but seeks to develop more sophisticated predictive tools.

> CONCLUSION 4-2 At present, there are insufficient rigorous empirical studies on predictive policing to support a firm conclusion for or against either the efficacy of crime-prediction software or the effectiveness of any associated police operational tactics. It also remains difficult to distinguish a predictive policing approach from hot spots policing at small geographic areas.

The evidence suggests that the use of CCTV, absent a dedicated operational response on the ground, may be more effective at reducing vehicle crime and less effective at combating violence, though the way the system is implemented and used appears to be important in achieving any crime reduction. There are insufficient studies with regard to proactive use of CCTV with dedicated operational resources to draw any firm conclusions.

CONCLUSION 4-3 The results from studies examining the introduction of closed circuit television camera schemes are mixed, but they tend to show modest outcomes in terms of property crime reduction at high-crime places for passive monitoring approaches.

CONCLUSION 4-4 There are insufficient studies to draw conclusions regarding the impact of the proactive use of closed circuit television on crime and disorder reduction.

Problem-Solving Proactive Strategies

There is promising evidence regarding problem-oriented policing programs. Much of the available evaluation evidence consists of non-experimental analyses that suggest strong effects in reducing crime; randomized experimental evaluations generally show smaller, but statistically significant, crime reductions generated by problem-oriented policing programs.

CONCLUSION 4-5 There is a small group of rigorous studies of problem-oriented policing. Overall, these consistently show that problem-oriented policing programs lead to short-term reductions in crime. These studies do not address possible jurisdictional impacts of problem-oriented policing and generally do not assess the long-term impacts of these strategies on crime and disorder.

While there are only a small number of program evaluations of third party policing, the impact of third party policing interventions on crime and disorder has been assessed using randomized controlled trials and rigorous quasi-experimental designs.

CONCLUSION 4-6 A small but rigorous body of evidence suggests that third party policing generates short-term reductions in crime and disorder; there is more limited evidence of long-term impacts. However, little is known about possible jurisdictional outcomes.

Person-Focused Proactive Strategies

The results from evaluations of these offender-focused proactive policing programs, which capitalize on the concentration of crime among a subset of criminals, indicate that this approach does reduce crime rates. A growing number of quasi-experimental evaluations suggest that focused deterrence programs generate statistically significant crime-reduction impacts. While there have been no randomized experiments, and only a few of the quasi-experimental designs are rigorous, the programs from the stronger (as well as the weaker) designs show consistent outcomes.

> CONCLUSION 4-7 Evaluations of focused deterrence programs show consistent crime-control impacts in reducing gang violence, street crime driven by disorderly drug markets, and repeat individual offending. The available evaluation literature suggests both short-term and long-term areawide impacts of focused deterrence programs on crime.

SQF programs have generated much controversy. Non-experimental analyses have examined the impact of SQF when implemented as a general, citywide crime-control strategy. A separate body of controlled evaluation research examines the effectiveness of SQF in targeting places with serious gun crime problems and focusing on high-risk repeat offenders.

> CONCLUSION 4-8 Evidence regarding the crime-reduction impact of stop, question, and frisk when implemented as a general, citywide crime-control strategy is mixed.

> CONCLUSION 4-9 Evaluations of focused uses of stop, question, and frisk (SQF) (combined with other self-initiated enforcement activities by officers), targeting places with violence or serious gun crimes and focusing on high-risk repeat offenders, consistently report short-term crime-reduction effects; jurisdictional impacts, when estimated, are modest. There is an absence of evidence on the long-term impacts of focused uses of SQF on crime.

Community-Based Proactive Strategies

The committee's findings regarding community-based interventions provide less optimism for the impacts of strategies using this approach to reduce crime and disorder. Overall, we did not identify a consistent crime-prevention benefit from community-oriented policing programs. Studies report mixed effects, and community-oriented policing programs often include tactics typical of other crime-prevention strategies, such as problem-oriented policing, that can be seen to generate crime control impacts when they are observed in isolated application. The empirical studies to date on community-oriented policing also tend to have weak evaluation designs. There are even fewer rigorous program evaluations that directly test whether procedural justice policing is associated with crime and disorder reductions. Prior reviews of impact evaluations have included multifaceted programs comprising a broad range of tactics typical of other crime prevention strategies; such programs go well beyond just procedural justice policing. As with community-oriented policing, it is difficult to isolate any crime-prevention benefits specifically associated with the procedural justice policing strategy.

> CONCLUSION 4-10 Existing studies do not identify a consistent crime-prevention benefit for community-oriented policing programs. However, many of these studies are characterized by weak evaluation designs.

> CONCLUSION 4-11 At present, there are an insufficient number of rigorous empirical studies on procedural justice policing to draw a firm conclusion about its effectiveness in reducing crime and disorder.

Although the available program evaluations suggest that generalized aggressive use of increased misdemeanor arrests as a means to controlling disorder in a broken windows strategy generates small to null impacts on crime, controlled evaluations of place-based practices that use problem-solving interventions to reduce social and physical disorder, another implementation of a broken windows strategy, have consistently reported crime-reduction effects. However, it is unclear whether these effects are due to the reinforcement of community social controls or to the deterrence and opportunity reduction generated by police activities.

> CONCLUSION 4-12 Broken windows policing interventions that use aggressive tactics for increasing misdemeanor arrests to control disorder generate small to null impacts on crime.

> CONCLUSION 4-13 Evaluations of broken windows interventions that use place-based, problem-solving practices to reduce social and physical disorder have reported consistent short-term crime-reduction impacts. There is an absence of evidence on the long-term impacts of these kinds of broken windows strategies on crime or on possible jurisdictional outcomes.

5

Community Reaction to Proactive Policing: The Impact of Place-Based, Problem-Solving, and Person-Focused Approaches

The purpose of this chapter and the one that follows is to describe what is known about community reactions to various forms of proactive policing. We treat these outcomes as a distinct category, separate from the outcome of efforts by the police to manage proactively the rate and type of crime. There is broad recognition that a positive relationship between the police and the community has value in its own right, irrespective of any influence it may have on crime, disorder, or public safety (National Research Council, 2004, p. 291; Lum and Nagin, 2017). This view has gained traction in the recent public discussion of policing. As an example, the President's Task Force on 21st Century Policing (2015) labeled popular legitimacy (i.e., public trust in the police) the "first pillar" of policing. This perspective was also echoed in the discussions that the committee had with representatives from various community organizations, as well as police practitioners (see Appendix A). Police leaders consistently emphasized that community perceptions and feelings about their police and the practices of those police were essential criteria for selecting policing strategies and judging police performance. Representatives of community organizations observed that members of a community give high priority to a broad range of performance issues extending well beyond the relatively narrow confines of crime and disorder control. They argued that those members of the public most alienated from and resistant to the police are profoundly motivated by perceptions of long-term police disrespect and inattention to the broader welfare of communities.

Such judgments derive from philosophical valuations of what is prized in a democratic society and the role of police in pursuit of those goals.

Democratic theories assert that the police, as an arm of government, are here to serve the community and should be accountable to it in ways that elicit public approval and consent. Specific notions of precisely what constitutes democratic policing vary, but most are built on a foundation of "trust, equality, and legitimacy" (Manning, 2010, p. 3; see also Sparrow, 2016), with restraint and the minimization of harm, responsiveness to what people want, accountability to legal institutions, and the reduction of inequality as frequent themes of what is essential to the creation and preservation of democratic policing (Manning, 2010, Chs. 1 and 11). It is easy to see why a democratic society wants authorities who strive to meet these expectations, and it has been claimed that public feelings about the trustworthiness, equality, and perceived legitimacy of policing have played a key role in fueling the intense public dissatisfaction and scrutiny experienced by American police organizations in recent years (President's Task Force on 21st Century Policing, 2015).

The proactive policing strategies reviewed in this report have as one of their primary goals the reduction of crime and disorder. The initial motivating force behind some of these approaches was this goal of reducing crime and disorder, with the potential for negative community outcomes constituting collateral concerns (Rosenbaum, 2006). Place-based, problem-solving, and person-focused approaches fall into this category. However, strategies falling into the broad category of a community-based approach were launched first and foremost as a corrective to community alienation from the police, with subsequent interest growing in their capacity for crime and disorder control as well (Skogan, 2006b). Hence, this chapter focuses on the community impacts of the three approaches that give primacy to crime and disorder control. Chapter 6 considers the community effects for strategies that were launched with improving community effects as the initial rationale.

This chapter is organized as follows. First it discusses the key types of community impacts on which it focuses. It then provides a preliminary model that links the key elements of community effects: a model that underlies much of the research that is relevant to tracing the impacts of proactive policing on the community. We then organize our discussion of findings into three separate sections, one each for the three broad proactive policing approaches that give primacy to controlling crime and disorder: the place-based, problem-solving, and person-focused approaches as defined in Chapter 2. Each section includes a description of the presumed mechanisms by which the intervention affects community outcomes and a discussion of limitations of the extant research. In addition to these more-or-less proximal community reactions to proactive strategies, we discuss the small and diffuse literature on the indirect, or "collateral," effects of proactive strategies on societal conditions such as public health and civic engagement. In the chapter's final section, we present and briefly discuss the conclusions we have drawn.

WHAT DO WE MEAN BY COMMUNITY IMPACTS?

The committee considers three types of community reactions or outcomes: evaluations, orientations, and behaviors. First, how do proactive strategies affect the way people *evaluate* their experiences with and impressions about what police do? Do they judge that police behave effectively (e.g., in reducing crime and disorder; in responding to calls for help)? Are the police fair and considerate toward the public? Do the police apply their authority and distribute their services equitably? Are the members of the community content with the nature of police service?

Second, how do proactive strategies affect the way people *orient* toward the police as an institution? Do people have trust and confidence in the police—that is, view them as legitimate? Much of the recent public discussion of policing has focused on public trust, which is one aspect of what is more generally called perceived legitimacy. The other aspects of perceived legitimacy are the perceived obligation to defer to the police, which motivates a willing acceptance of police authority, and normative alignment, the belief that the police and community share common values (Tyler and Jackson, 2014).

Third, how do proactive strategies affect the ways that people *behave* toward the police, the law, and their communities? Do people become more cooperative with police and other legal institutions? The legal system relies upon members of the community to report crimes, identify criminals, act as witnesses in court, and serve on juries. More broadly, do the police behave in ways that strengthen the community's collective efficacy[1] and thereby facilitate the creation of social capital among members of the community?

A MODEL OF THE EFFECTS OF PROACTIVE POLICING ON COMMUNITY OUTCOMES

For assessing community outcomes in this and the following chapter, the committee relies on a logic model that has framed much of the research on community effects, one that links community evaluative judgments to community orientations and ultimately to behaviors. The model begins with *formal police policies*, which are presumed to shape *police officer actions on the street* that are relevant to the community. The policies are

---

[1] Sampson, Raudenbush, and Earls (1997) coined the term "collective efficacy" to refer to the degree to which people who live in communities trust their neighbors and are willing to intervene in community affairs.

also assumed to affect community practices where community involvement with police is part of the intervention (e.g., community participation in collaborative efforts with the police). Police and community actions, in turn, are hypothesized to shape the sort of evaluative judgments community members make about police performance (effective, fair, lawful). And these evaluations are seen to shape the general orientation toward the police (perceived police legitimacy). Perceived legitimacy in turn is hypothesized to shape the *behavior* of community members in terms of law abidingness, cooperation with authorities, and engagement in the community. Figure 5-1 depicts this linkage.

We label this a logic model to make clear that it depicts a theoretically postulated flow of effects. The validity of this flow as a causal description is something that must be separately evaluated and will be discussed in our review of the evidence. In addition, it is important to recognize that although this logic model proposes a linear progression through stages 1 to 5, it is possible that there are reciprocal influences, an expectation recognized by arrows pointing in the reverse direction in Figure 5-1. Also, there could be other factors ("third variables") that are a part of this model. These issues need to be considered when determining whether this logic model is empirically supportable as a causal model for any particular policing strategy or fielded intervention.

The stage numbers in Figure 5-1 are intended to convey a temporal sequence. Policies are the purposive, official acts of public figures with responsibility for directing the practices of the police. Policies will vary in the nature and extent to which they promote or emphasize a given proactive strategy. Indicators of police practice reveal the fidelity of actual police actions to the ideal established by policy—or the extent or dosage of the implementation. Community evaluations reflect how members of the community rate the performance of the police on relevant criteria. A variety of criteria for evaluating police performance have been proposed, including crime-control effectiveness, equity in the distribution of services, palatability of the experience of contact with the police, the perceived procedural justice of police actions, and satisfaction with police services. These are judgments about what people believe that police officers actually do or accomplish while on the job, particularly within their own communities.

| Police policies 1 | → ← | Police/community practices 2 | → ← | Community evaluations 3 | → ← | Community orientations 4 | → ← | Community behavior 5 |

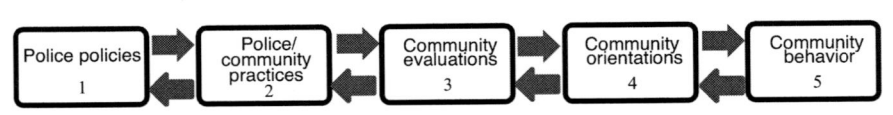

FIGURE 5-1 Logic model of proactive policing effects on community outcomes.

Community evaluations are hypothesized to develop from people's personal experiences, the experiences of their family and friends, and what they see occurring within their community.[2] Community orientations indicate how community members feel about the police: their trust, confidence, or deference to police authority. And, finally, community behavior refers to actions community members take that are relevant to levels of crime, disorder, and manifestations of civic virtue or societal economic contributions. In later sections, we will consider some limitations to this model as a representation of the causal process.

Before beginning the review of findings in this and the following chapter, we reiterate an earlier point about the geographic level of impacts of the approaches examined. As with studies of crime effects, units of analysis for community effects in the literature we reviewed were usually areas much smaller than the entire jurisdiction: typically neighborhoods, police beats, districts (multiple beats), census blocks, or hot spots. We know surprisingly little about whether and to what degree proactive policing strategies influence community outcomes in the larger urban areas within which such strategies are implemented. Without estimates of the areawide impacts of proactive policing strategies, it is difficult to assess whether these strategies, applied broadly in jurisdictions, would have meaningful effects across entire jurisdictions.

PLACE-BASED INTERVENTIONS

Place-based interventions concentrate police efforts at the micro-geographic spaces where crime or disorder concentrates. Hot spots policing is the most common strategy for this proactive policing approach, but that speaks only to the concentration of police resources according to the concentration of crime or disorder. The content of such interventions can vary widely, drawing on tactics also used in one or more of the other strategies considered in Chapters 2 and 4, such as police patrol, crackdowns, or practices typical of problem-oriented policing. In this section, we consider the full variety of such hot spots interventions as place based.

One of the earliest tests of hot spots interventions on community perceptions is provided by Shaw (1995), who conducted a matched comparison group quasi-experiment in Kansas City, Missouri, comparing residents' reactions to gun-detection patrols in a target area to a comparison area. The two-phased, person-focused hot spot intervention involved a door-to-door consultation with the community preceding the proactive patrols. The precise nature of the proactive tactics, all involving officer-initiated contacts

---

[2] Of course, people may observe these events directly, but their impressions may also be shaped via news and social media.

with the public, was left to officer discretion. Car checks, frequently involving a traffic violation, were the most frequent occasions to look for illicit weapons. Field observations of unknown reliability[3] and the absence of complaints and lawsuits suggested a "general absence of excess in police encounters" (Shaw, 1995, p. 700). The study found that there was no appreciable difference between the target beats and control beats in terms of support for proactive police interventions (high portions of both saying it was "good for the neighborhood") (p. 704).[4] It also found that target-area residents observed a higher quality of neighborhood life following the intervention (for both social disorder and fear of crime), but both areas experienced similar reductions in crime. The panel design of this study suffered from a relatively low sample size, so that, with attrition, the time 2 samples were relatively small for both the treatment and comparison groups (64–71 respondents per group).

A subsequent randomized controlled trial (RCT) used an interesting approach to measuring community reactions to place-based problem-oriented policing in a hot spots framework by interviewing 52 "key community residents" who shaped the way a public space is used at some point during the day in treatment and control areas (Braga and Bond, 2009; see reference to this study in the section below on "Problem-Solving Interventions"). The specific problem-solving practices (in Lowell, MA) included aggressive enforcement, but many also used social service tactics to disrupt underlying conditions. The outcome analysis revealed that the key residents in the treatment areas observed heightened police presence[5] and a decline in perceived disorder. But they did not note changes in policing strategy, inclination of the police to work with residents, police demeanor toward the public, or fear of crime. Hence, there were some positive community reactions and no significant "backfire" collateral effects of the crime-prevention strategies.

Two other studies examined the impact of police crackdowns, one with a disorder reduction approach. A quasi-experiment reported by Hinkle and Weisburd (2008) found that in Jersey City, New Jersey, intensive police crackdowns meant to reduce crime and disorder at a drug market increased

---

[3] The study was written and published posthumously by the author's colleagues, who were unable to access some of the field observation material.

[4] Eighty-eight percent of treatment-area residents rated this type of enforcement as good for the neighborhood; 82 percent of the control-area residents gave the same rating. The difference was not statistically significant.

[5] It is difficult to know how to interpret this indicator, inasmuch as it covered the complete array of possible reasons to have contact with the police.

fear of crime, and the effect size was substantial (odds ratio = 3.12).[6] Residents exposed to a crackdown strategy had more than three times the odds of developing fear of crime compared to people not exposed to a crackdown. The researchers speculated that the greatly heightened police presence and visibility created by the enforcement crackdowns may have increased residents' sense that their neighborhoods were not safe. However, a later block randomized experiment by Weisburd and colleagues (2011) looked at typical broken windows practices for disorder reduction applied to hot spots policing in three medium-sized California cities. They found no statistically significant effects across a broad range of community indicators, including fear of crime, perceived police legitimacy, collective efficacy, and perceptions of crime. Higher levels of perceived physical disorder, which were marginally statistically significant, were found in hot spot treatment areas compared to control areas, but these perceptions had not manifested themselves in more fearful or unhappy residents. So overall, the results appeared not to confirm concerns some have expressed about potentially negative consequences of hot spots policing on community outcomes (Kochel, 2011; Rosenbaum, 2006).

Weighing the differences between these two studies of the impact of place-based use of broken windows tactics is important for drawing conclusions. The intervention in Jersey City was not designed to undertake a full broken windows strategy; rather, its tactics included an intensive crackdown on drugs, prostitution, and social/physical disorder and the removal of violent offenders, tactics shared with the broken windows strategy. Evaluators of hot spots policing in the three California cities examined a program specifically designed as a broken windows strategy but incorporating more measured police interventions than sometimes used in that strategy (e.g., warnings and explanations for first offenders, citations and arrests for repeat offenders). The Jersey City intervention took place in high-crime, high-violence neighborhoods; the California city intervention took place in three smaller cities with lower levels of serious crime and disorder. And the researchers noted that both the duration/dosage of the treatment and the short-term measurement of outcomes may have been inadequate to engender and measure a range of community effects.

Using an RCT, Weisburd, Morris, and Ready (2008) reported the effects of a different place-based intervention: a community policing/problem-solving combination that targeted risk and protective delinquency factors.

---

[6] See Lipsey and Wilson (2001) and Wilson (n.d.) for guidelines on interpreting odds ratio effect sizes. Guidelines based on Cohen's "Rules-of-Thumb" thresholds are small (1.50), medium (2.50), and large (4.30). They note that these guidelines do not consider the intervention's context. For example, a small effect could be impressive if it requires few resources or other costs. Smaller effects could also be interpreted as substantial where the problem at issue is severe or impervious to change.

The principal policing tactic was increasing positive contact between police and the juveniles living in selected block groups. Notably, this intervention used a much larger geographic unit (a census block) than would qualify as a microgeographic space (e.g., an address, street segment, or small cluster of street segments). The study found no appreciable, statistically significant difference between treatment and control groups in the students' perceptions of police legitimacy (a composite of ratings of police respectfulness, trust, fairness, and honesty).

Another study examined the effects of hot spots policing in Philadelphia under three experimental conditions: foot patrol, person-focused policing (repeat offenders), and problem-oriented policing (Ratcliffe et al., 2015).[7] Control hot spots maintained the usual random patrol between calls for service. (Only the person-focused condition yielded statistically significant crime reductions compared to the control condition.) Survey data of community outcomes were analyzed using a quasi-experimental design. None of the three experimental interventions showed statistically significant effects across seven community outcome indicators: perception of violent crime, satisfaction with police services, perceptions of property crime, perceptions of physical disorder, perceptions of social disorder, perceptions of safety, and perceptions of procedural justice. The mailed citizen survey had a low (9%) response rate that could be attributed in part to underestimates of unoccupied addresses; area weighting of census data was used to adjust for over- and under-representation of different demographic groups in the sample (Ratcliffe et al., 2015, p. 402).[8] This study is noteworthy in part because the city studied had higher treatment duration levels than other studies and took place in a higher-crime urban area.

The most recent of this group of studies was an RCT reported by Kochel and Weisburd (2017). This study assessed the effects of hot spots policing on police legitimacy and collective efficacy in St. Louis County, Missouri. Two types of hot spots interventions were evaluated—doubling time spent in hot spots (directed patrol) and problem solving in hot spots—with both treatment conditions compared to standard police practice. A diverse array of community outcomes was measured in three waves of resident surveys, the last wave occurring 9 months after treatment ended. Outcomes included assessment of police competence and satisfaction with

---

[7] This is a truly hybrid approach that implemented a place-based strategy with tactics typical of both person-focused and community-based strategies.

[8] Research indicates that nonresponse by itself is a weak, and sometimes even negative, predictor of nonresponse bias. (See Pickett, 2017, for a recent overview of this literature as it pertains to criminal justice research.) The comparison of survey respondents to 2010 census data showed that White and older female respondents, as well as those with more education, were a little overrepresented, compared to their presence in the general population. The researchers concluded that the sample of respondents closely approximated that of the actual population.

police, police legitimacy, procedural justice and trust, perceptions of police misconduct, feelings of personal safety, cooperation with police, and collective efficacy.

Community impacts were diverse. Directed patrol and problem solving did not affect perceptions of police competence or resident satisfaction with police. There were initial declines in perceived legitimacy for directed patrol and problem solving, but by 9 months there were no differences (there were statistically significant increases in perceived legitimacy between the 6th and 9th month). Directed patrol dampened increases in procedural justice/trust from wave 1 to 2, but the effect evaporated by the last wave. Directed patrol did not generate resident concerns about aggressive policing. Residents in problem-solving areas experienced negative results regarding feelings of personal safety, but these dissipated over time. Both directed patrol and problem solving generated long-term improvements in residents' willingness to cooperate, and there were long-term benefits for collective efficacy delivered by directed patrol.

Overall, then, this study showed no "long-term" (9 month) effects for most community indicators and improvements in a couple of them (cooperation with the police and collective efficacy). Given that the analysis also showed crime reduction for both treatment groups, one might interpret these results as encouraging; there appear to be no tradeoffs in the longer term. But an important lesson taken from this study is that place-based directed patrol and problem solving did generate some initial community negativity on some indicators, but over a relatively short time these effects were either nullified or reversed. This temporal effect reinforces the notion that outcomes are dynamic and that it matters how far out from the intervention they are measured. This RCT measured those dynamics over the course of a relatively short time period. It would be useful to know temporal patterns over a time period of several years.

These studies of place-based strategies have centered on interventions in hot spots, but the diversity of police tactics employed is remarkable: gun detection patrols, broken windows enforcement, focusing on repeat offenders, directed patrol, and problem-oriented policing. Despite this diversity, there has been relatively little variation in findings about the community consequences of the interventions: for the most part, researchers do not find statistically significant effects. One evaluation of a Jersey City crackdown did yield a fairly substantial increase in fear of crime, one that was not replicated in a later RCT in three small California departments, an intervention that may not have been as intense in the sorts of enforcement activities that are visible to the public. Statistically significant beneficial effects were also relatively rare: a Kansas City, Missouri, gun detection patrol project and a problem-oriented hot spots approach in Lowell, Massachusetts, both registered some statistically significant reductions in fear of crime or perceptions of disorder. And directed patrol and problem solving in St. Louis County, Missouri, yielded statistically significant improvements in collective efficacy and cooperation with police (though no statistically significant outcomes across the many other community impacts measured). Tellingly, none of the five tests of outcomes that could be classified as citizen satisfaction with the police or perceived police legitimacy yielded statistically significant effects.

The committee concluded that the extant research suggests that a place-based policing strategy rarely leads to negative community outcomes among those measured. Caution is warranted, however. First, the available evaluations concentrate on relatively short-term effects, leaving unexamined the possibility of multiyear accretions of community effects. For example, it may take much longer for the informal community networks of a geographic area to embed a cumulative and incrementally created positive or negative perspective that could exert a powerful indirect influence over how residents evaluate their recent experiences with the police (Gau and Brunson, 2010; Rosenbaum et al., 2005; Weitzer and Tuch, 2002). Also unexamined are several important forms of community reaction going beyond attitudes toward the police, such as legal cynicism (Desmond and Valdez, 2013) and crime reporting (Desmond, Papachristos, and Kirk, 2016). Also, possible jurisdictionwide effects are rarely examined.

One concern about the rarity of observed negative community outcomes from place-based proactive strategies is that they could be concentrated in places where the police–community climate is already so negative at the outset that the strategies have little margin to make matters worse (i.e., to have a backfire effect). The committee was able to review the pre-treatment outcome levels for four of the six studies showing null effects. In all of these studies, the pre-treatment outcome levels fell in the middle to positive side of the outcome scales, allaying concerns that in these communities the state of police–community affairs was so bad they could not be made worse by a place-based proactive strategy.

The committee notes that the evaluations report little about what police officers in these programs actually did. There is a general absence of a detailed, systematic monitoring of the interventions that are most likely to affect community reactions, especially those pertaining to citizen satisfaction and perceived police legitimacy. For example, most evaluations only describe the training protocol and report the amount of time spent in the hot spot or a count of incidents handled. But citizens likely react to more than mere police presence. They care about the risk of being stopped, questioned, and searched, and they care *how* those activities are executed. If community impacts are a concern, then evaluators need to include assessments of what police organizations did to control police discretion, to limit abuses, and to promote quality service. In effect, the street-level police practices generated by place-based programs (stage 2 in the logic model depicted in Figure 5-1) are black-boxed (i.e., not examined in the research as reported) so that the study report fails to provide readers with a good grasp of the character of the intervention as the community experienced it.

The logic models proposed for how place-based proactive practices are expected to affect community outcomes are diverse, which complicates interpretation of the pattern of results across studies. Some research seems animated primarily by concerns about the collateral damage that place-based strategies could produce by more effectively concentrating law enforcement efforts in a small geographic space than other approaches, such as the reactive "standard model" of patrol, which shows a weaker link between police resource deployment and where crime and disorder are distributed (Weisburd et al., 2011). The collateral damage approach simply examines whether the public is troubled by the place-based intervention, regardless of the possible causal linkages among different outcomes, such as those displayed in Figure 5-1.

Other research begins with hypotheses of more positive community outcomes, and some of this research does explore causal linkages across various community outcomes. A brief exposition of this rationale is given in Kochel and Weisburd (2017). Place-based directed patrol and problem solving are expected to increase police visibility, increase police-public interactions, increase both negative and positive experiences with police, and increase particular kinds of police activities (more enforcement for directed patrol and more efforts to change routine activities in places targeted for problem solving). The first three of these first-order effects (visibility, police-public interaction, and positive/negative interactions) are not reflected in the logic model displayed in Figure 5-1; they fall between stages 2 and 3 of that model and might be termed "direct experiences of policing." They in turn are expected to affect public perceptions about police service and conduct (community evaluations), which in turn affect third-order effects of perceived police legitimacy, perceptions of safety, and collective efficacy. The enforcement and problem-solving first-order effects are expected to affect public perceptions about police service and conduct indirectly by the intermediating effects on crime at places of concern. Unfortunately, Kochel and Weisburd (2017) presented all community outcomes as direct effects and did not offer estimations of the strength of intervening process pathways. While this is consistent with the experimental design of their project, estimations of these pathway effects would promote a better understanding of assumptions about place-based effects. However, it is easily conceivable that a reordering of effects could be justified, which is of particular concern for non-experimental studies. For example, engaging in acts of collective efficacy could easily be viewed as a cause of reduced crime levels (Sampson, 2002), as well as a downstream consequence.

A clearer exposition of the causal process by which place-based interventions affect community outcomes—and a focused empirical testing of that process—would be especially helpful in trying to explain why the evaluations of place-based strategies have shown few community effects of any sort. A model for such an exposition is given by Weisburd and colleagues (2015), who develop and evaluate the mechanisms by which broken windows policing is presumed to reduce crime. The authors outline an underlying causal sequence tracing effects from police reducing social and physical disorder to reduction of residents' fear of crime to increases in community social control to crime reduction. They offer a narrative review and meta-analysis to assess what empirical research shows about this process. They note significant variation in the impact of broken windows policing tactics (some place based and some not) on fear of crime. Of six experimental/quasi-experimental studies, three found no change, two found a significant reduction, and one showed a backfire effect. Only one tested for impact on informal social control, finding no effect. A meta-analysis reinforced the sense that fear reduction and collective efficacy were not attributable to the broken windows tactics, yet the authors cautioned that there were various limitations in the research: for example, the confounding of a broken windows strategy with many other proactive strategies, the failure to measure and model informal social control, and the specification of a theoretically reasonable follow-up time period to assess program impacts (years longer than most available studies).

Summary. There is only a small, emerging body of research evaluating the impact of place-based strategies on community attitudes, including both quasi-experimental and experimental studies. Place-based policing tactics were often co-implemented and integrated with tactics typical of other approaches, such as problem solving, community based, and person focused, making it difficult to know how much of an intervention's effects were due to its place-based character. The available research is also limited in its focus on outcomes measured as attitudes toward police and on short-term and less-than-jurisdictionwide effects. However, the consistency of the findings of the available studies leads the committee to conclude that place-based policing strategies rarely have negative impacts on short-term, police-focused community outcomes; at the same time, such strategies rarely improve community perceptions of the police or other community outcome measures. Caution about the broad generalizability of this finding is therefore warranted.

PROBLEM-SOLVING INTERVENTIONS

For this report's purposes, problem-solving interventions have been defined as strategies that try to identify causes of problems, select innovative solutions (backed by scientific evidence wherever possible), assess the effects of the intervention, and adjust future interventions accordingly. The most prevalent strategy for this approach is problem-oriented policing, but also included is third party policing.[9] Our analysis focuses on 18 reports that offered some evidence on problem-solving strategies using experimental or quasi-experimental designs (sample compiled mostly from the Evidence-Based Policing Matrix [Lum, Koper, and Telep, 2011][10] and from Gill et al. [2014]).[11] These reports have generated 26 independent tests that assess one or more indicators of community reactions to a problem-solving strategy.

The method for problem solving among the projects studied has been remarkably similar, while the nature of particular problems targeted has been diverse. Most projects designated one or more geographic areas (neighborhoods, beats, precincts, public housing area, microplaces) and leave it to the assigned police and residents of the areas to identify the problem to solve, drawing on some version of the scanning, analysis, response, and assessment (SARA) process. The range of problems targeted for intervention has been wide, although addressing neighborhood social and physical disorder in its various manifestations has been a popular choice. A few studies were launched with a much narrower mandate, such as targeting juveniles with a high risk for delinquency (Weisburd, Morris, and Ready, 2008), architectural design to reduce crime (Armitage and Monchuk, 2011), drug crime in public housing (Giacomazzi, McGarrell, and Thurman, 1998), or juvenile crime in a park (Baker and Wolfer, 2003). We do not know how representative our sample is of the population of problems that are targeted by problem-solving practices in American police agencies in general.

Evaluations of the community reactions to problem solving have concentrated on four types of outcome measures: perceived disorder or quality of life of the respondent, fear of crime or perception of crime risk, satisfaction with the police, and the perceived legitimacy of the police. Simply looking at the statistical significance of study results, respondent satisfaction is the only indicator that shows a positive impact with strong consis-

---

[9] To a lesser extent, proactive partnerships with other organizations (such as code or liquor enforcement agencies, schools, probation, and private businesses) may also be considered as a problem-solving intervention.

[10] The Evidence-Based Policing Matrix focuses on interventions that are "primarily" police interventions; scored a 3 or higher on the Scientific Methods Scale (Sherman et al., 2002) and included at least a well-matched comparison group, multivariate controls, or rigorous time series analysis.

[11] Armitage and Monchuk (2011); Baker and Wolfer (2003); Bond and Gow (1995); Braga and Bond (2009); Breen (1997); Collins et al. (1999); Giacomazzi, McGarrell, and Thurman (1998); Graziano, Rosenbaum, and Schuck (2014); Jesilow et al. (1998); Kochel and Weisburd (2017); Pate et al. (1986); Segrave and Collins (2005); Chicago Community Policing Evaluation Consortium (1995); Skogan and Hartnett (1997); Tuffin, Morris, and Poole (2006); Ratcliffe et al. (2015); Weisburd, Morris, and Ready (2008); Wycoff and Skogan (1993).

tency across evaluations (14 significantly positive, 4 no significant effect). Virtually all of the others show mixed results with respect to direction of statistically significant effect or any significant effect: perceived disorder/quality of life (7 significantly positive, 1 significant backfire,[12] and 5 no significant effect), fear of crime (6 positive, 9 no significant effect), and legitimacy (6 significantly positive, 6 no significant effect). Notably only 1 of the 26 evaluations produced a statistically significant backfire effect, and that was only for a single community outcome. The size of intervention effects in these studies tends to be modest or moderate. For example, Skogan and Hartnett (1997, p. 210) matched comparison-group evaluation of five Chicago police districts employing problem-oriented policing in a community-based policing framework yielded an assessment of mostly consistent positive effects that were "not overly dramatic" on citizen satisfaction (a combined index of police responsiveness, demeanor, and effectiveness in dealing with crime).[13] Similarly, small-to-moderate effect sizes were recorded for reductions of citizen perceptions of gun/drug problems in these districts (Gill et al., 2014, p. 415).[14] A comparable pattern emerged in the six-site matched comparison-group evaluation of "reassurance" policing in the United Kingdom, an intervention that also embedded problem-oriented policing in a community-based approach (Tuffin, Morris, and Poole, 2006; Gill et al., 2014, pp. 416-417).

Only a handful of the evaluations relied on randomized experimental designs. Two (Kochel and Weisburd, 2017; Weisburd, Morris, and Ready, 2008) showed no significant effects on the four indicators commonly studied in quasi-experimental evaluations: perceived disorder, fear of crime, citizen satisfaction, and perceived police legitimacy. One evaluation (Graziano, Rosenbaum, and Schuck, 2014) showed significant positive effects on citizen satisfaction and on police legitimacy with the community as perceived by officers.

One RCT (Braga and Bond, 2009) of a problem-oriented practice, embedded in a place-based policing strategy, showed consistent pretest-posttest improvements across a range of community outcomes (see detailed discussion of this study above, in the section on place-based interventions). However, statistically significant positive effects were observed only on perceived social and physical disorder and on frequency of contact with

---

[12] This was a comparison of a single treatment in a single neighborhood and control area in a small Connecticut city, which generated a large, significant backfire finding, a distinct outlier in a body of studies that showed much smaller effects. Given the small number of observations in this study, this finding should be interpreted with caution.

[13] The odds ratios calculated for these interventions were in the small to very-small range (Gill et al., 2014, p. 416).

[14] All of the five sites recorded odds ratios in the "small" range (below 2.5). See Lipsey and Wilson (2001) on interpreting effect sizes.

police; no statistically significant changes were found in perceptions of policing styles and strategies, demeanor toward citizens, police willingness to collaborate with the public on crime and disorder control, and fear of crime. Effect sizes fell in the small range (odds ratios below 2.5), except for the number of contacts with police, which showed a large effect (odds ratio well above 4.3). This study was especially noteworthy for its employment of surveys of "key community residents" who were in a good position to know and shape what was going on in the studied hot spot in which they resided or worked (e.g., an apartment complex manager).[15]

One RCT found an increase in residents' sense of efficacy in problem solving (Graziano, Rosenbaum, and Schuck, 2014), and the other found a positive trend in collective efficacy over time, but it was not statistically distinguishable from the control condition (Kochel and Weisburd, 2017). Finally, only one RCT assessed the impact of problem-solving efforts on the community's inclination to cooperate with police, finding a small, but statistically significant increase over the course of 9 months (Kochel and Weisburd, 2017, p. 162).[16] Perhaps the most extensive exploration of problem solving's effects on collective efficacy and other forms of citizen self-help and supportive behavior toward police is the evaluation of reassurance policing in the United Kingdom, a program that incorporated problem solving as a key element of a community-based policing approach in six jurisdictions (Tuffin, Morris, and Poole, 2006). This matched comparison-group evaluation found little evidence to support an effect for this program on these indicators.[17]

It is worth considering why community satisfaction should emerge as a fairly reliable consequence of practices typical of a problem-solving approach but not other outcomes such as perceived disorder, fear of crime, or perceived police legitimacy. One possibility is that problem solving may be perceived to reduce crime sufficiently to satisfy community members with the police effort but still insufficient to reduce fear of crime and perceptions of disorder. Another possibility is that the effect is due not so much to the problem-solving aspect (especially the problem analysis and customizing of the solution to the problem diagnosis) of the intervention as it is to the community outreach aspect that so often is also a feature of this policing approach (see the community-oriented policing section of the next chapter).[18] Nearly all of the interventions evaluated for the problem-solving approach

---

[15] The number of cases in treatment and control groups was small (26 each), but the evaluators argued that the careful selection of this small sample of informants increased the power of the statistical analysis to detect effects.

[16] Over the "long-term" (9-month) period, problem solving showed a 6 percent increase in residents' willingness to cooperate, compared to a 2 percent decline for "standard practice."

[17] See the "Impacts on Community Behavior" section of Chapter 6 for details.

[18] See Kochel and Weisburd (2017, pp. 165–166) for an exposition of this argument.

in this chapter included one or more elements of community-oriented policing (heightened police–community engagement). It is possible that variation in the execution of the community engagement element of these interventions accounts for the pattern of variation in citizen satisfaction. One might anticipate that the more substantial the community engagement in the problem-solving process, the more likely that police effort and performance will concentrate on community priorities, the better "advertised" the results, and the more positive the community spin on those results among community members when they (or some community representatives) had a hand in the process. This was in fact a key feature of the focused deterrence ("pulling levers") strategy first introduced in Boston as part of a problem-solving tactic (applied within a person-focused policing approach) to deal with gang violence in the 1990s (Braga, 2001; Kennedy, 1997). Yet researchers have also observed that the norm for community engagement in problem solving tends to be the identification of problems and the assessment of outcomes, not the analysis of those problems or "coproductive" involvement with the community in the intervention strategy itself (Braga and Bond, 2009). Nonetheless, it is possible that community satisfaction from problem-solving experiences is due not to technical success in reducing problems but to the public's observation of and even limited participation in the process itself, afforded by activities that incorporate tactics from community-oriented policing. In the research to date, these two possible mechanisms are confounded and cannot be isolated for analysis.

Regardless of the resolution of the role of community-oriented policing practices in problem solving's apparent capacity to satisfy the public, one might still wonder why the other community impact measures did not reflect a similar positive effect with much consistency. The possibilities are numerous. The most straightforward explanation is the absence of evaluations that assess problem-solving interventions that have the reduction of community alienation as *the* targeted problem, instead of reduction of crime or disorder. In this regard, the true capacity of focusing the SARA process of problem-oriented policing to improve most community outcomes remains untested.

Another explanation is that some effects take longer than others and that they depend on demonstrating the success of certain indicators in a causal chain. Given that the vast majority of these studies relied upon evaluations of effects within a year or two after the intervention's onset, there may simply have been insufficient time to register effects. One underlying logic model that fits the observed pattern is that community satisfaction with the police is a necessary precursor to community cooperation with successful problem-solving interventions, which will later yield reductions in the targeted problems, and those in turn will reduce fear, increase perceptions of disorder, and enhance perceived legitimacy (Gill et al., 2014). This logic model may be contrasted with one that presupposes that the community's judgments of the police are driven by their perceptions of the police's success in problem solving, which Skogan (2009) termed an "accountability" model and which is consistent with the sequence displayed in Figure 5-1. A third possibility—and the one the committee considers most likely—is that both causal processes are at work simultaneously.

Testing the process of community outcomes to establish causation would require long-term, multiyear studies with extensive longitudinal measurement of community members' perceptions, attitudes, and behaviors. An example of short-term longitudinal measurement is given in a three-wave RCT evaluation of a St. Louis County, Missouri, project that included a problem-solving component among the interventions compared (Kochel and Weisburd, 2017; see also the description earlier in the "Place-Based Interventions" section of this chapter). This evaluation used a large assortment of community and crime/disorder outcome indicators. Extending the longitudinal impact analysis across waves of much longer duration than 3 months would allow an empirical assessment of the possible underlying causal processes.

Variation in effects across evaluations of problem solving may also reflect variations in the fidelity or intensity of the problem-solving component of the intervention. The challenges of problem-solving implementation are widely acknowledged by researchers and police leaders (Braga and Weisburd, 2006; Braga, 2010; Weisburd et al., 2010) but are typically discussed in the context of evaluating crime and disorder outcomes, not community outcomes. Achieving insufficient rigor in the SARA process is frequently mentioned as a limitation, which yields at best shallow problem solving (i.e., weak problem analysis and constrained or uncreative responses) (Braga, 2010; Braga and Bond, 2009; Braga and Weisburd, 2006). Perhaps shallow problem solving should not be a great surprise when considering the typical low intensity of the organizational efforts to enable and promote these activities. For example, training in problem-solving techniques typically lasts only a few days.

Most studies do not report implementation with enough detail to make comparisons across studies. One that does go into considerable depth suggests the complexity of measuring problem-solving implementation, which could involve the following aspects of the program: problem identification, development and implementation of solutions, community organization involvement, involvement of other government and private organizations, and police involvement (Skogan and Hartnett, 1997, pp.184–193). As we note in the community-based policing discussion in Chapter 6, the onsite evaluators gave the Chicago Police Department's problem solving a grade of C, illustrating how difficult it can be to align all of the strategy's elements on a citywide scale (Skogan and Steiner, 2004, pp. viii–x). Another onsite process analysis of the National Reassurance project in the United Kingdom went a step further and found a correlation across six sites between the extent of problem-solving implementation (community involvement, specification and delineation of the problem's nature) and one of the community outcomes: public perceptions of juvenile-caused nuisances (Tuffin, Morris, and Poole, 2006, pp. 80–82). It would be especially helpful for comparing the effects of problem-solving efforts to develop a comprehensive rating system for determining the extent of implementation, notwithstanding the challenges of rating so diverse a set of interventions (Eck, 2006).

While accounting for the implementation of interventions in a "mediation" analysis is an important consideration in evaluating the technical crime-control efficacy of a problem-solving approach (Braga, 2010, p. 176), there is a second aspect that is probably far more relevant to assessing *community* reactions. This aspect concerns the tactics and strategies actually employed (Braga and Bond, 2009; Braga, Hureau, and Papachristos, 2014). There is a world of difference in how a group of juveniles and their family/friends will likely react to stop, question, and frisk (SQF) compared to midnight basketball. Hence, researchers' capacity to predict community outcomes will be heightened to the extent that evaluators take into account differences in the tactics selected for an intervention and differences in the efforts by the police to achieve community acceptance of those tactics. No such analysis is currently available for community effects evaluations.

Evaluations of problem solving are concentrated in large urban communities. About two-thirds are in American communities, and the remainder are in the United Kingdom or Australia. Chicago, the third most populous American city, accounts for 23 percent of the evaluations, although 27 percent of the evaluations were conducted in communities of under 115,000 population. No clear differences in community reactions to problem solving have been reported across these geographic and demographic ranges.

Summary. The available evidence on the short-term community outcomes of interventions using a problem-solving approach shows an intriguing and somewhat encouraging pattern. (There is little evidence available on the long-term impacts of problem-solving strategies on community outcomes or on jurisdictionwide impacts.) Most of the quasi-experimental or experimental evaluations of community satisfaction register small or moderate, positive short-term effects, while other community outcome measures show at best mixed findings. There is no obvious single factor to account for this variation. The virtual absence of backfire effects should reassure practitioners that problem-solving tactics have not obviously undermined police-community relations.[19] The principal challenge here is knowing what to do with these findings, since there are a number of possible explanations, one of them being that positive community effects derive primarily from the *processes* of community engagement, which are virtually always a part of the interventions that have been evaluated, and not from the reduction of the targeted problems.

PERSON-FOCUSED INTERVENTIONS

Person-focused strategies attempt to capitalize on the strong concentration of crime among a small portion of the criminal population. Two types of community outcomes seem relevant to person-focused interventions (Shaw, 1995, p. 708). First, there is interest in how the targeted offenders or offender groups (e.g., gang members in a focused deterrence intervention) react to this strategy, not only in terms of the degree to which they are ultimately deterred from crime but also in how they evaluate their experience with the police and its consequences, especially the procedural justice–perceived police legitimacy linkage. These are involuntary "clients" of the police. Knowledge of their reactions would help researchers establish the extent to which alternative mechanisms to deterrence, such as procedural justice, play a role in mitigating negative outcomes and promoting positive ones. Second, there is interest in the effects on the broader community in which any person-focused intervention is implemented. Here the interest is in the community as "citizenry" with a stake in how their society is policed, with "community" usually defined operationally as the residents of a study area. A focused deterrence strategy in particular attempts to secure broad community support for the interventions, involve members of the community in the intervention, and thereby secure acceptance of the fairness and ultimate perceived legitimacy of a process that includes a highly targeted punishment element. How does the broader community feel about the focused deterrence process? How have their feelings about the police been affected? What were their views about the quality of life in the community as a consequence of the focused deterrence intervention?

Evaluations need to be conducted from the perspectives of both the offenders being targeted and the larger community. It is important to distinguish them because the experiences and perspectives of the two groups may be strikingly different (Braga, Hureau, and Papachristos, 2014). One would expect that if the person-focused program is successful in concentrating police enforcement interventions on a particular targeted group,

---

[19] This must be qualified by the notation that evaluations of problem solving have virtually ignored certain collateral effects measures, such as physical and mental health, employment, and legal cynicism. See the "Collateral Consequences" section of this chapter below.

then the people experiencing that intervention first-hand will show greater negativity about the police than those toward whom the police enforcement practices are not concentrated. On the other hand, the general (e.g., residential) population in areas experiencing person-focused policing, who are the presumed primary beneficiaries of that program, may be more inclined to evaluate the results positively—if they are aware of the intervention.

Unfortunately, empirical research on person-focused interventions has concentrated heavily on crime control outcomes and has largely left community outcomes unexamined. The absence of experimental evaluations of community outcomes of person-focused strategies is also noteworthy. And notably, the available empirical research looks at SQF, traffic stops, and repeat offender practices, but the committee could locate no research assessing the impact of the focused deterrence strategy on community outcomes.

Several studies relying on correlational analysis of cross-sectional data and qualitative field observation show, with consistency, the expected negative correlation formed by citizens who experience SQF and aggressive traffic enforcement. The Police–Public Contact Survey of 2011 provides broad insights into the scope of police actions nationwide and their relationship to perceptions of citizens who experience those actions (Langton and Durose, 2013, p. 3). Less than 1 percent of 241 million U.S. residents ages 16 and older reported experiencing a street stop (not in a moving motor vehicle) as their most recent contact with police in 2011. Ten percent of 212 million drivers ages 16 and older reported being stopped while operating a motor vehicle during that period as their most recent contact with police. Twenty-nine percent of respondents subjected to street stops felt that police had not behaved properly, while 12 percent of stopped drivers made that assessment of their experience. Thus, although large majorities of those stopped did not find police actions improper, substantial numbers of citizens across the nation had formed negative judgments about the propriety of police actions. Only 3.5 percent of drivers stopped by police received a personal or vehicular search, but 39 percent of those searched felt that police had not behaved properly, while only 11 percent of those stopped but not searched felt that way (Langton and Durose, 2013, p. 9). The survey found that the likelihood of Black drivers being stopped was significantly higher than for Whites and Hispanics and that there were no statistically significant differences by race/Hispanic origin for street stops. Other studies have offered more in-depth analyses of high-risk populations defined by race, gender, and age.

A study of 45 young Black males (13–19 years old) living in disadvantaged St. Louis, Missouri, neighborhoods used a survey and in-depth interviews to learn their impressions and reactions to the policing they and others received in their neighborhoods (Gau and Brunson, 2010). Nearly 8 in 10 respondents had been stopped at least once during their lifetime, the average number of stops being nearly 16. This study and other analyses of the same data (Brunson, 2007) paint a picture of Black youths who perceived police order-maintenance practices in their predominantly Black neighborhoods as frequently experiencing police stops as harassment (about 8 in 10) and knowing someone who was harassed or mistreated (about 9 in 10), the most common complaints being harsh, illegal, and disrespectful police treatment (Brunson, 2007, pp. 78–95). Two-thirds of respondents indicated that police were not easy to talk to, and a frequent theme was that the police gave their neighborhoods low-quality service (slow response times and ineffective crime prevention and case solving). While acknowledging the need for police to deal with crime and disorder, respondents felt that officers were too narrowly focused on drugs and gangs, with insufficient attention to other problems, especially the needs of crime victims.

Two types of perceived police misconduct strongly shaped respondents' negative views toward police: being stopped with insufficient evidence and police violence or threat of violence in excess of what circumstances required (experienced directly and vicariously through second-hand accounts of family, friends, and neighbors). For both types, respondents were turned off by the failure of police to conform their practices to the requirements of law. And in the first type of misconduct, respondents were especially frustrated by the irrelevance of their own adherence to the law to inoculate them from unwarranted police attention. Finally, an especially disliked practice was when officers who were frustrated by failing to find evidence to support an arrest drove the respondents to a hostile or unfamiliar neighborhood and released them to get home on their own, knowing that this put the youths' safety at great risk. Many respondents attributed the concentration of these policing practices in their neighborhood to their being predominantly Black and disadvantaged.

A large, cross-sectional survey of young persons in New York City found similarly negative associations of respondents' perceptions of SQF experiences. Tyler, Fagan, and Geller (2014) found a strong inverse correlation between the number of stops experienced or observed by young people in New York City and the legitimacy they accord the police.[20] In their analysis it is neither the frequency nor amount of intrusiveness of the stops that strongly affects these feelings but rather the lawfulness and fairness they perceived to have occurred during those stops, similar to the outrage expressed by adolescent Blacks in distressed St. Louis, Missouri, neighborhoods. Though this pattern suggests there might be a "right" way to conduct stops that minimizes the risk of negatively affecting perceived

---

[20] See Fratello et al. (2013) for a description of similar findings from a randomly drawn street sample of 474 young people (ages 18–25) at risk for SQF experiences in several hot spots of SQF policing in New York City in 2011.

legitimacy, the researchers also found that repeated-stop experiences of the same person were associated with declines in perceived legitimacy over time, irrespective of how people were treated. In New York City during the time of this study, the overwhelming majority of stops were of young people who were not engaged in criminal activity at the time they were stopped. Hence, it is easy to see how a person repeatedly stopped while innocent would over time come to view the police as acting unfairly and inefficiently.

A qualitative study of involuntary encounters with the police in the Kansas City, Missouri, metropolitan area focused on traffic stops and found different results depending upon the reason for the stop—as perceived by the driver (Epp, Maynard-Moody, and Haider-Markel, 2014). Those perceived as traffic safety stops (e.g., speeding, traffic light, driving under the influence) were distinguished from investigatory stops (where the officer was looking to acquire evidence of a more serious criminal offense). Motorists inferred from the officer's stated reason for the stop which sort of situation they were encountering. Safety stops were inferred when officers stated a safety offense; investigatory stops were inferred when the officer gave a reason that was a minor violation (license plate light out, turning too wide, driving too slow) or offered no reason at all.

Black motorists had a higher probability of being subject to presumed investigatory stop than White drivers, whereas there was a general absence of race effects for the presumed traffic safety stops. Black drivers and White drivers indicated that they experienced similar levels of impolite demeanor during traffic stops, but Black drivers were much more likely than Whites to report impolite police behavior during investigatory stops, and they were less likely to accept as legitimate the officer's decision to pull them over. The researchers noted that it was not only the difference in treatment shown by the police during the stop that mattered here but also (as with previously reviewed studies) the feeling that there was no justifiable reason for the investigatory stop.

Some studies conducted in the United Kingdom point to the negative effect on ratings of the police when someone has experienced a police search (see Miller and D'Souza, 2016, for a review). Searches in general (Miller, Bland, and Quinton, 2000; Skogan, 1994), and pedestrian searches in particular (Clancy et al., 2001), are associated with lower levels of satisfaction with and confidence in the police. While these studies do not measure the effect of proactive policing as the product of a *strategy*, they offer a broader empirical base to generalize beyond studies of policing in the United States.

The above studies point to a consistently pronounced negative association of citizens' experiences with SQF and traffic (investigatory) stops with assessments of the police. However, because they are just correlational and qualitative studies, they have limited capacity to support causal inferences about the contribution of these person-focused practices to the views of those who experience them. For example, research suggests that evaluations of the police in specific situations are strongly influenced by the broader orientations that citizens bring to those encounters; in fact, much more so than the influence of an individual encounter on the citizen's general orientation to the police (Brandl et al., 1994; Worden and McLean, 2017b). Furthermore, these broader orientations are not merely a summation of the consequences of the citizen's past personal experiences with the police but are shaped by a variety of socialization sources among friends, family, coworkers, etc. Not taking these "global" orientations toward police into account risks overstating the contribution to individuals' perception of a given experience with a person-focused encounter.

A few studies examine the effects of person-focused interventions on the *residential population at large*, and they do not show negative effects. A recent quasi-experiment explored the impact of a person-focused (repeat offenders) practice imbedded in a hot spots policing intervention in Philadelphia (Ratcliffe et al., 2015). The police developed a list of active repeat offenders living or operating in the treatment areas. Officers had discretion in selecting interventions, which could include merely talking to the offenders, performing field interrogations, or serving criminal warrants. Researchers reported that officers actively pursued this focused offender tactic over an 8-month period. The study found that residents living in areas exposed to that strategy had no statistically different ratings of seven community outcomes than did those in the control areas (see above discussion of this study in the place-based interventions section).

Another study examined the impact on public confidence in the police from both direct personal exposure to SQF and from indirect sources (e.g., coming from second-hand accounts and general impressions or transmitted by word of mouth) (Miller and D'Souza, 2016). The researchers asked whether SQF experiences in a given geographic area affected the attitudes of residents besides those immediately involved in these events, a useful question because most people rarely have contact of this sort with the police. The study employed a multilevel longitudinal multiple regression analysis of the survey responses of nearly 108,000 London residents in 32 boroughs between 2006 and 2013. The first analysis refers to the direct impact of first-hand SQF experience compared to those who have not had such an experience in the last year. The second analysis refers to the impact of the SQF rate in the entire area (borough) in which the respondent resided. Consistent with prior research, respondents who had been stopped in the last year or searched or arrested in the last year were less likely to rate the police as fair/responsive or effective (difference was statistically significant). These effects were larger than those of various personal characteristics (e.g., age, socioeconomic status, ethnicity) but not as large as the visibility of foot or bike police patrol to respondents, which showed the expected positive relationship to confidence in the police. Controlling for respondents' personal SQF experiences, personal characteristics, and crime/disorder rates in the borough, the analysis also examined the impact of borough-level exposure to two sorts of SQF search rates determined from police records ($n = 224$ borough-months). One type of search was covered by the Police and Criminal Evidence Act of 1984 (PACE), governing searches that require "reasonable grounds" for suspicion. The other type of search was covered by Section 60 of the 1994 act: searches not requiring such grounds for suspicion (e.g., weapons searches at sporting events). Using both lagged and unlagged estimates, there was only one statistically significant effect: for Section 60 searches on perceptions of police effectiveness (a positive correlation statistically significant for lagged effects only).[21] There was some indication of variable effects across subgroups of the respondents. Blacks and persons with low socioeconomic status perceived lower levels of fairness and responsiveness where Section 60 search rates were higher and at the same time were more positive in their perceptions of police effectiveness under those conditions (both differences were statistically significant). However, the meaning of this pattern is not entirely clear, since the statistically significant effects were lagged for the effectiveness dependent variable (hence taking longer to show an effect) and unlagged for the fairness and responsiveness dependent variable. The authors accounted for this pattern by speculating that "negative stories about searches move quicker through social networks than positive stories or that the interpretation becomes more positive with the lapse of time" (Miller and D'Souza, 2016, p. 472).

Two features of this analysis of Black and low-socioeconomic status subgroups are particularly noteworthy. When one outlier borough that had very high and variable search rates was excluded, the effects were no longer statistically significant. Also, the size of these effects was quite small. The average effect of Section 60 searches on Black respondents' perceptions of police fairness and responsiveness was only 0.024 points on a 4-point scale, with a standard deviation of 0.6. Effects were even smaller for respondents of low socioeconomic status. Hence, the evidence from this study of wider effects of SQF, excluding the study's results from direct exposure to SQF, does not support a finding that this SQF proactive strategy generated a strong reaction in the general public. Finally, the authors acknowledged that boroughs may be too large a unit of analysis to capture variation in

---

[21] The researchers speculated on reasons for the absence of effects for PACE searches (Miller and D'Souza, 2016, p. 472). One possibility is that because Section 60 searches are executed in specific locations, they may yield a greater sense of safety for some residents but not others. Another explanation is that PACE searches, which require reasonable grounds, may generate weaker positive or negative effects than Section 60 searches, which require no grounds. Finally, the PACE searches displayed much less annual variation than Section 60 searches, which may make it more difficult for residents to perceive changes in PACE search levels.

SQF rates that is meaningful to residents and that the high daily mobility of urban dwellers, coupled with heightened use of social media, may simply render geographic-based exposure to SQF less relevant.

The pattern among this handful of studies is suggestive but insufficient to state with confidence what the effects of person-focused strategies are on community views. All of the four studies looking at the impact of person-focused strategies on those directly targeted (one focusing on SQF of Black youths living in high-crime St. Louis neighborhoods, one of SQF in New York City, one of traffic stops in Kansas City, Missouri, and one of SQF searches in London) illuminate consistent and fairly strong negative reactions. Only two studies examined the larger residential (stakeholder) community's response to these practices. A quasi-experiment in Philadelphia found no community effects. The London study found that the general community response depended upon the citizen's race, but this association disappeared when a single outlier geographic area was dropped from the analysis.

One might infer from these results that communities at large have no predictable reaction to person-focused interventions. But two studies are a precarious basis for drawing such a conclusion at this point. Especially important for future research is to compare the profile of personal characteristics of the targeted offenders to that of the larger community of stakeholders. In that context, much more needs to be known about the public's tolerance/enthusiasm for such interventions. Here are propositions worth testing from this small body of research. The more indiscriminately and intensively person-focused proactive policing is practiced in a given community area, one presumes the smaller the population of those residents who embrace or tolerate such practices. Regardless of their own personal experiences, the more that residents of a given community group feel at risk for person-focused proactivity by virtue of their personal characteristics (e.g., race), the less likely they are to accept those practices and the police who practice them. However, the negative impact of this practice may be mitigated by police taking care to clearly articulate the legitimacy of each stop (e.g., reasonable suspicion; see the discussion of procedural justice in Chapter 6).

As with place-based and problem-solving strategies, empirical research on person-focused strategies would benefit from illumination of the community elements that may accompany those person-focused strategies. For example, while much has been made of the importance of community leaders' involvement and support of focused deterrence strategies (Braga, 2001; Kennedy, 1997), it is not known how important that is in promoting broad community acceptance of these strategies, especially for those community members most proximate or similar to those who are actually targeted for proactive intervention. Further, there is considerable variance in the sorts of law enforcement and community activities employed. How much do those differences affect community reactions, and does that in turn depend upon which segments of the community are at greatest risk of being the targets of the person-focused tactics? And, as noted previously for place-based and problem-solving strategies, the absence of measures of long-term (multiyear) effects of person-focused strategies means that the evidence base lacks results from tests of the potential cumulative impact of such methods on community outcomes. For example, the cumulative consequences of individuals' exposure to SQF may couple the intensification of broader community hostility toward the police resulting from diffusion of negative views through informal community networks. The absence of empirical research on these issues precludes offering evidence-based answers to such questions. However, given the positive findings regarding the impact of focused deterrence strategies on crime (see Chapter 4), tracking community effects seems an especially worthwhile endeavor for future study.

Summary. The body of research exploring the impact of person-focused strategies on community outcomes is relatively small, even compared to the evidence for problem-solving and place-based strategies. There are only a handful of studies on interventions that primarily used SQF, traffic stops, or repeat offender practices; there are none on focused deterrence interventions. Most of the studies involve qualitative or correlational designs, making it hard to draw causal inferences. In evaluating person-focused strategies, it is important to distinguish effects on the person targeted for these interventions (suspects and offenders) from effects on the larger stakeholder community that is intended to benefit from the intervention. The studies that measure impacts on targeted persons all show marked negative associations between experiencing a given strategy and the attitudes and orientations of those who experienced the interventions. The studies that measure the impact on the larger community do not indicate a clear pattern of outcomes. The long-term and jurisdictionwide community consequences of person-focused proactive strategies remain untested.

COLLATERAL CONSEQUENCES FOR SOCIETY OF PROACTIVE POLICING

As discussed above (and in the next chapter), much of the literature assessing community reactions to proactive policing strategies focuses on community evaluations, orientations, and behavior toward the *police*. However, an emerging body of literature examines the indirect, or *collateral*, consequences of proactive policing practices on community characteristics such as public health and civic and institutional engagement. Although most of this literature is correlational, it nevertheless raises important questions regarding the impact of proactive policing policies on communities.

Moreover, much of this literature examines the implications of such practices for poor and non-White communities. Because of the concentration of proactive policing tactics in these neighborhoods, the literature stresses the importance of exploring these effects further, as these collateral consequences may be especially salient for particular neighborhoods and communities. We note that a large literature exists in the criminal justice field that assesses the consequences of arrest, imprisonment, and other criminal justice contact for health and mental health; employment and earnings; and families, communities, and society writ large. For example, incarceration is strongly correlated with negative social, economic, and health outcomes not only for prisoners and former prisoners but also for their families (National Research Council, 2014). Moreover, a number of collateral consequences have been documented for people who are arrested and convicted of crimes but not incarcerated. These consequences include effects on people's employment and business opportunities and on access to government benefits, including student loans and housing (see, e.g., Colgate-Love, Roberts, and Klingele, 2013). To the extent that proactive policing practices foster criminal justice contact and involvement, such consequences may also be said to derive indirectly from proactive policing.

Impact of Proactive Policing Practices on Health and Development

As noted above, many scholars have suggested that the criminal justice system adversely affects physical and mental health (see, e.g., Golembeski and Fullilove, 2005; Johnson and Raphael, 2009; Western, 2006). Less well studied is the specific effect of proactive policing practices on health and development. However, an emerging public health literature suggests that involuntary police contact may threaten the health of individuals stopped by the police—for instance, in SQF stops. The adverse health effects may arise from the physical nature of some stops, which present risks of physical injury; from emotional trauma associated with unwarranted accusations of wrongdoing; and from contacts associated with racism, which may cause stigma and stress responses and depressive symptoms (see, e.g., Bylander, 2015; Garcia and Sharif, 2015; Nordberg et al., 2015; Shedd, 2015). Alternatively, people targeted for such interventions may also be at greater risk for health problems due to "third variable" vulnerabilities, such as limited wealth and education. On the other hand, much of this literature also acknowledges that policing may improve individual and population health by improving public safety and building feelings of security.

Geller and colleagues (2014) conducted a population-based survey of young men in New York City in 2012–2013 to understand the extent and nature of their experiences with the New York City Police Department's SQF tactics and the association between these contacts and dimensions of respondents' mental health. The survey found that young men who reported police contact also reported higher anxiety scores (controlling for demographic characteristics and criminal involvement). Anxiety symptoms were correlated to the number of times the young men were stopped and to how they perceived the encounter, and these correlations were statistically significant. Those respondents who reported more police intrusion also tended to have greater anxiety levels. The statistical associations between respondents' experiences with the police and their mental health were strong and largely robust (consistent) across samples and models—particularly among respondents reporting stops carried out in an intrusive fashion. Geller and colleagues (2014) concluded that such associations between police intrusion and mental health, as observed in a population-based sample of young men reporting high rates of contact with the police, raise public health concerns for the individuals and communities most aggressively targeted by the police. However, the authors are careful to note that the cross-sectional nature of the data analyzed does not lend itself to causal claims and that the causal direction of the relationship is in fact uncertain. That is, it is possible that the respondents' mental health influenced their perception of their interactions with the police and that those prone to the greatest anxiety and stress tended to exaggerate their experiences, or that respondents displaying mental health symptoms might have attracted greater reasonable suspicion or may have responded to police questions in ways that escalated their encounters.

Another study examined the impact of proactive policing practices on adolescent development. Jones (2014, p. 36) argued that targeted policing practices do more than shape young men's perceptions of the police; they also shape their "life space, affecting what they do, where, and with whom." This ethnographic study of adult and adolescent Black men in a San Francisco neighborhood, where police implemented problem-oriented policing interventions along with other targeted law enforcement practices, found that routine exposure to proactive policing practices had the potential to influence normative adolescent development. Pointing to areas where future research is needed, Jones (2014) questioned whether the penetration of police practices into young men's peer and family networks gives neighborhood youth a criminalized identity, keeping them linked to the juvenile or criminal justice system and to peers who are more deeply committed to delinquency or criminal behavior. The question, in other words, is whether policing practices make it more difficult for young people to drift out of delinquency.

In addition, a study by Desmond and Valdez (2013) focused on the harm to the urban poor associated with the application of coercive third party policing strategies. The authors examined the use of Milwaukee's nuisance-property ordinance that charged or threatened landlords with a substantial fine for repeated tenant behavior that police authorities deemed to be a nuisance (e.g., noise, domestic violence, frivolous use of 911, family trouble). Analyzing all nuisance property notifications (identifying a property as a nuisance, the property owner's abatement response, and the police response to the owner's response) and all nuisance-eligible properties over a 2-year period, and controlling for a variety of neighborhood socioeconomic factors, property code violations, and the crime rate, researchers found that properties in predominantly Black neighborhoods were disproportionately likely to get cited for nuisances and those located in integrated Black neighborhoods were most likely to be judged a nuisance. A substantial portion of citations (almost one-third) for nuisance incidents were based on domestic violence, and the typical property owner response was eviction, a response encouraged by the police who reviewed landlord responses to threats to punish them. In addition, landlords threatened and discouraged tenants from summoning police assistance and instead encouraged them to solve the problem themselves (e.g., by making the abusive party in the domestic relationship move out) or to refer the problem to the landlord or another nonpolice entity. Most of the landlords who received a nuisance citation for domestic violence responded with efforts to evict, either formally or informally, or they threatened eviction if the tenant summoned the police again. The researchers noted, "the nuisance property ordinance has the effect of forcing abused women to choose between calling the police on their abusers (only to risk eviction) or staying in their apartments (only to risk more abuse)" (Desmond and Valdez, 2013, p. 137).

Noting that Milwaukee's ordinance was similar to ordinances of other American cities, the authors argued that this coercive form of third party policing was implicated in "the reproduction of racial, economic, and gender inequalities" (Desmond and Valdez, 2013, p. 137) that disproportionately exposes women in poor Black neighborhoods to higher rates of eviction, which in turn causes homelessness, loss of wealth, residential instability, unemployment, and a variety of mental health problems. But because this descriptive study lacked a comparison to the distribution of harms where no such coercive third party policing program was present, the results do not provide evidence confirming a causal impact of third party nuisance abatement programs on these important societal outcomes.

Similarly, other scholars have considered the health impacts of racism and perceived racism on individuals and communities. This literature is important because much of the discussion surrounding proactive policing strategies has focused on its targeting of non-White communities. The public health literature indicates that racism as a social condition is a cause of health and illness (Link and Phelan, 1995; Ford and Airhihenbuwa, 2010; Gee and Ford, 2011; Jones, 2001; Williams and Mohammed, 2013; Brondolo et al., 2009; Dressler, Oths, and Gravlee, 2005). For example,

Lewis and colleagues (2006) found a positive association between discrimination and coronary artery calcification in Black women, while McLaughlin, Hatzenbuehler, and Keyes (2010) found that experiences of discrimination were correlated with elevated levels of psychological distress. Therefore, if proactive policing strategies are implemented in a discriminatory fashion or are perceived to be discriminatory (see Chapter 7 of this report), there may be resulting public health consequences for the communities experiencing that discrimination or perceiving policing activity to be discriminatory.

Summary. The committee concluded that existing studies of the collateral consequences of more aggressive policing styles are informative in suggesting the importance of focusing more research on potential public health consequences of proactive policing strategies. However, the research to date does not allow the committee to draw evidence-based conclusions regarding these potential consequences. Future studies of proactive policing should include measures that examine potential negative consequences of policing interventions on physical and mental health for both individuals and the communities where such interventions are implemented.

Impact of Proactive Policing on Civic and Institutional Engagement

Another emerging body of literature considers the indirect effect of proactive policing practices on civic and institutional engagement and political life. In this area, scholars have suggested that involvement with the criminal justice system may have an impact on levels of civic engagement. Justice and Meares (2014), for example, hypothesized a link between policing and political life by arguing that the criminal justice system, through encounters between police officers and citizens, educates those it contacts in what it means to be a citizen. This "education," they suggested, has the potential to incite radicalization, resistance, and solidarity, as well as anger, insecurity, and despair. And Weaver and Lerman (2010) concluded that contact with the criminal justice system is associated with weakened attachment to the political process and increased negative perceptions of government.

In another study, which examined the consequences of SQF tactics on civic engagement by assessing non-emergency calls for service or information requests ("311 calls") from 2010 to 2011 in New York City, Lerman and Weaver (2014a) showed that the concentration of police stops, at the block-group level, was associated with higher levels of community engagement. However, there was also a negative correlation between the number of stops that featured searches or the use of force, especially if the stop did not result in an arrest, and incidence of neighborhood-level outreach to local government. These results suggest that the nature and perception of policing practices may affect levels of civic engagement in urban communities.

In a subsequent study, Lerman and Weaver (2014b) estimated the magnitude of the relationship between encounters with law enforcement, Americans' attitudes toward government and democratic values, and their likelihood of voting or engaging in other forms of citizen participation. Using a nationally representative survey and in-person interviews, they assessed the relationship between increased use of SQF tactics and citizens' attitudes and behavior that were associated with their experiences with police. For example, the authors found that people who had been arrested but never convicted were 16 percent less likely to "feel like a full and equal citizen" and were 20 percent less likely to believe that "everyone in the U.S. has an equal chance to succeed." Moreover, people who had been stopped and questioned by police or arrested for a crime but never convicted were about 10 percent more likely to express distrust of government. Lerman and Weaver (2014b) concluded that these attitudes contribute to disengagement from the democratic process, an action that is not passive but rather is a conscious effort at non-engagement. That is, these respondents believed non-engagement to be the best strategy against intrusive law enforcement—to intentionally stay invisible, to actively avoid authorities, and to keep a low profile.

Though not focused specifically on proactive policing strategies, Brayne (2014) assessed the impact on institutional engagement of being stopped by the police or of being arrested but not convicted. The study found that individuals who had been stopped by police, arrested, convicted, or incarcerated were less likely to interact with surveilling institutions, including medical, financial, labor market, and education institutions, than their counterparts who had not had criminal justice contact. That is, they exhibited behaviors of "system avoidance": the practice of individuals avoiding institutions that keep formal records and therefore heighten the risk of surveillance and apprehension by authorities. Using data from the National Longitudinal Study of Adolescent Health and controlling for sociographic, behavioral, and other pertinent factors (e.g., possession of medical insurance), the study found that individuals who had been stopped by the police had 33 percent higher odds of not obtaining medical care when needed and that those who had been arrested (but not convicted) had 29 percent higher odds. The results also showed that arrest (without conviction) or conviction were statistically significant negative predictors of institutional attachment (obtaining medical care, possessing a bank account, and being in school/working), but being stopped by police was not a significant predictor of bank account ownership or of being in school or working. Thus, Brayne (2014) concluded that fear of surveillance and subsequent system avoidance, rather than sociodemographic characteristics or behavioral characteristics, may shape individuals' behavior and involvement with institutions that are consequential for future outcomes. Most notably, her "difference-in-differences" identification strategy has a plausibly causal interpretation, as she found no such change in avoidance behavior with regard to social groups that did not keep records, such as attending church or participating with volunteer groups, avoidance behaviors one might expect if people were becoming generally less active in the community, rather than specifically avoiding record-keeping institutions.

Summary. The impact of policing on civic and institutional engagement is an emerging area of study, and the committee did not have an evidence base adequate for drawing conclusions. But the limited number of studies to date do suggest the potential for research to offer insights into the impacts of proactive policing approaches, and policing more generally, on civic participation. Again, we think this area should be a more widely examined subject of research in the future.

CONCLUSION

Throughout this chapter, we have noted the limitations of the existing research base for assessing the community outcomes of proactive policing strategies that have developed primarily as crime-fighting strategies. The modest number of studies assessing the impact of problem-solving, place-based, and especially person-focused proactive strategies on community outcomes calls both for caution at present in drawing conclusions and for more research. These implications are emphasized in Chapter 8. Nonetheless, the extant research does allow the committee to draw several specific, narrow conclusions regarding the impacts of proactive policing approaches that focus on crime control.

Place-Based Proactive Strategies

There is only an emerging body of research evaluating the impact of place-based strategies on community outcomes, including both quasi-experimental and experimental studies. Place-based strategies in the studied interventions were often co-implemented and integrated with tactics typical of other approaches (such as problem solving, community based, and person focused), making it difficult to know how much of the effects were attributable to their place-based character. However, the consistency of the findings of these studies leads the committee to draw the following conclusion:

CONCLUSION 5-1 Existing research suggests that place-based policing strategies rarely have negative short-term impacts on community outcomes. At the same time, such strategies rarely improve community perceptions of the police or other community outcome measures. There is a virtual absence of evidence on the long-term and jurisdiction-level impacts of place-based policing on community outcomes.

The committee notes that its conclusion regarding the absence of negative short-term effects on community outcomes is in contrast to a growing narrative that presumes or expects such strategies will have community impacts (see Chapter 1).

Problem-Solving Proactive Strategies

The research literature on community impacts of problem-solving proactive policing interventions is relatively large compared to the other approaches reviewed in this chapter. Much of this literature relies on quasi-experimental designs. However, a few well-implemented randomized experiments also provide information on community outcomes. Because problem-solving strategies are so often implemented in tandem with practices typical of community-based policing (i.e., community engagement), it is difficult to determine what role the problem-solving aspect plays in community outcomes, relative to the impact of the community engagement practices in the intervention. Nevertheless, the committee was able to draw the following conclusions:

> CONCLUSION 5-2 Studies show consistent small-to-moderate, positive impacts of problem-solving interventions on short-term community satisfaction with the police. There is little evidence available on the long-term and jurisdiction-level impacts of problem-solving strategies on community outcomes.

> CONCLUSION 5-3 There is little consistency found in the impacts of problem-solving policing on perceived disorder, quality of life, fear of crime, and police legitimacy, except for the near-absence of backfire effects. The lack of backfire effects suggests that the risk is low of harmful community effects from tactics typical of problem-solving strategies.

Person-Focused Proactive Strategies

The body of research evaluating the impact of person-focused interventions on community outcomes is relatively small, even when compared to the evidence base for problem-solving and place-based strategies. There are a handful of studies on SQF, traffic stops, and repeat offenders but none on focused deterrence. Most of the studies involve qualitative or correlational designs, making it hard to draw causal inferences. In evaluating person-focused strategies, it is important to distinguish effects on the person targeted for these interventions (suspects and offenders) from effects on the larger stakeholder community that is intended to benefit from the interventions. The studies that measure impacts on targeted persons all show marked negative associations between exposure to the strategy and the attitudes and orientations of those who experienced the interventions. The studies that measure the impact on the larger community show a more complicated pattern, but overall do not indicate a clear pattern of outcomes.

> CONCLUSION 5-4 Studies evaluating the impact of person-focused strategies on community outcomes have a number of design limitations that prevent causal inferences to be drawn about program effects. However, the studies of citizens' personal experiences with person-focused strategies do show marked negative associations between exposure to stop, question, and frisk and proactive traffic enforcement approaches and community outcomes. The long-term and jurisdictionwide community consequences of person-focused proactive strategies remain untested.

6

Community-Based Proactive Strategies: Implications for Community Perceptions and Cooperation

Community-based proactive strategies recognize and promote the community's active role in the crime-prevention process. They seek to define the relationship or mode of interaction between the police and the community in a way presumed to reduce crime or disorder. As we mentioned in Chapter 5, unlike the other proactive policing approaches considered in this volume, police often employ strategies for a community-based approach with an explicit hope that they will not only reduce crime but also improve people's assessments of police performance, increase community perceptions of police legitimacy, and enhance cooperation and community engagement to secure public order and safety (Skogan, 2006b). Not surprisingly, then, one might expect to see more research on how community-based strategies affect community outcomes than on how the other three proactive approaches affect community outcomes (the subject of Chapter 5 of this report). This is indeed the case, but even here the research on the community impacts of community-based interventions has concentrated heavily on two strategies: community-oriented policing and procedural justice policing, with much less attention to the community impacts of broken windows policing. Consequently, the bulk of our discussion is skewed to the first two strategies for a community-based policing approach.

While community-oriented policing and procedural justice policing are both strategies that take a community-based approach, their places in the landscape of proactive policing are distinct. The concept of what this report calls "community-oriented policing"[1] has been central to discussions of policing for several decades, and many departments have developed various policing policies that come under the committee's concept of a community-oriented policing strategy. Consequently, there is a large prior literature on evaluations of community-oriented policing. In contrast, the concepts informing procedural justice policing are comparatively new to the field of proactive policing, at least as policy-level interventions. The broader concept of procedural justice developed within the field of social psychology, in theory-driven studies exploring why people trust authorities, view them as legitimate and entitled to be obeyed, and consequently defer to their authority. Research has subsequently studied procedural justice and perceived legitimacy in work organizations and with court procedures. However, these concepts have only recently been directly applied to policing.

COMMUNITY-ORIENTED POLICING

As noted in Chapter 2, community-oriented policing (also called community policing) is widely acknowledged to have many meanings, sometimes as a set of specific tactics, sometimes a set of program-level interventions, and sometimes a general philosophy of how police should relate to the community (Cordner, 2014). Despite its longevity as a reform (at least three decades), as noted in Chapter 2, there is still considerable variation in how community-oriented policing is defined. We follow Gill and colleagues (2014, p. 405) in requiring that, to qualify in this review as community-oriented policing, an intervention must include "some type of consultation or collaboration between the police and local citizens for the purpose of defining, prioritizing, and/or solving problems." As is the case with other proactive policing strategies, practices typical of a community-oriented strategy are often implemented in combination with practices and tactics typical of other strategies, including strategies that focus on a different policing approach. For instance, some community-oriented policing interventions include practices typical of problem-oriented policing, broken windows policing, hot spots policing, or focused deterrence. As noted many times already in this report, this hybrid character of real-world interventions makes it more difficult to draw conclusions from evaluations of these hybrid interventions regarding the impacts of community-oriented policing, as a distinctive strategy, on community outcomes.

---

[1] The research literature has often used the term "community policing" for what we mean here by community-oriented policing. We have applied our term in reporting on the literature where the topic addressed by the author(s) seemed closer to our *strategy* of community-oriented policing, as presented in Chapter 2, than to the broader concept of any community-based *approach* to proactive policing.

As discussed in Chapter 2, it is well established that community-oriented policing became very popular among American police leaders in the 1990s. What is not so well acknowledged is the variable character of community-oriented policing that exists among these police agencies. For the purpose of assessing the community impact of community-oriented policing, it is a significant limitation that the research literature often lacks clear distinctions not only among the different varieties of community-oriented policing but also with respect to their scope and intensity (Cordner, 2014). There currently is no metric for making comparisons across different community-oriented policing programs; therefore, it is difficult to know how appropriate it is to compare results across impact studies.

One indication of the challenges presented in summarizing the effects of community-oriented policing is to consider the difficulties in generalizing about it from the available empirical research. A useful tool in this regard is the data provided in an appendix of a systematic review of 45 studies of the impact of community-oriented policing (Gill et al., 2014). This appendix provides a brief description of each of the community-oriented policing interventions described in the study reviewed. Table 6-1 shows the frequency of those that involve community engagement or collaboration. As is apparent, there are a wide variety of practices used in these interventions, ranging from foot patrols to collaboration with community groups and community newsletters. Clearly this range of practices will influence the nature and intensity of community-oriented policing's impact on community outcomes. And these 45 studies did not attempt to determine the independent contribution of different program elements in the community-oriented policing interventions they evaluated.

Furthermore, the outcome measures employed in studies are inconsistent, making it even more difficult to draw direct comparisons (Gill et al., 2014, p. 422). To this point, the committee adds that these inconsistencies arise in how given measures are conceptualized, operationalized, or interpreted. An example of this is given in the classification of "legitimacy" outcome measures (measures of what this report calls "perceived legitimacy"). A single research project by Tuffin, Morris, and Poole (2006) accounted for 6 of the 10 comparisons we examined on perceived-legitimacy outcomes. The actual survey question (of residents) used for this item was, "Taking everything into account how good a job do you think the police in your local area are doing?" (Tuffin, Morris, and Poole, 2006, p. 51). Excellent or good responses were interpreted as showing confidence in the police. However, it is not clear why that item has more in common with other outcome indicators used by the meta-analysis to assess perceived legitimacy (e.g., "police are fair," "trust in police," "treating people politely") (Gill et al., 2014, p. 417, Fig. 7) than it does with some of the indicators used for assessing the community outcome of "citizen satisfaction": "good job

TABLE 6-1 Community-Focused Elements in Community-Oriented Policing Interventions

Intervention Number	Intervention	Number of Studies
	Decentralization of Police Organization	
1	Decentralization (unspecified)	1
2	Permanent beat assignment	10
3	Community substations/storefronts	3
4	Special community-policing unit created	1
5	Change management philosophy	1
	Community Engagement/Collaboration	
6	Foot/bike patrol	4
7	Resident contact (one-on-one): e.g., door-to-door surveys	9
8	Collaboration with community groups (unspecified)	7
9	Beat/neighborhood organization meetings	18
10	Crime-prevention education for citizens	1
11	Neighborhood/Block Watch	3
12	Community volunteers	3
13	Community newsletter	9
14	Community relations training for police	1
15	Community rallies, unspecified mobilization	4
16	Increase positive police–citizen contacts (e.g., on the street, recreation programs)	2
	Problem Solving	
17	Problem solving (general)	15
18	Agency partnerships	2
19	Broken windows (clean up physical and social disorder)	3
20	Household security inspections	1
21	Environmental change for crime control, improve neighborhood infrastructure	1
22	Enforcement-oriented interventions (crack downs, hot spot patrol)	1

NOTE: Data from Gill et al. (2014, App. A). The number of defined interventions per study varied from 1 to 4.

to prevent crime," "evaluation of police," or "quality of police service." The last of these, "quality of police service," is a scale comprising ratings of items that seem good candidates for perceived legitimacy, not satisfaction: police politeness, helpfulness, and perceived fairness (Gill et al., 2014, p. 416, Fig. 6).

Another source of variation across studies to which insufficient attention has been paid is the way in which the targeted community population is defined (Gill et al., 2006, p. 422). Most evaluations of community-oriented policing tend to aggregate "community" as a general population of residents, and this undoubtedly masks what are potentially striking differences. "Community" is most often operationalized as people who live in proximate geographic areas, typically within the boundaries of a police beat or a neighborhood. Residents of a neighborhood presumably have a stake in how their neighborhood is policed, but that stake is not necessarily uniform. The context of how people relate to police—their role—can vary profoundly. Victims and suspected offenders can be expected to hold different concerns or priorities about what they want police to do and accomplish. Those who own and work in businesses may have different priorities from those who reside near them. Those who frequent parks and recreational facilities will have a different framework for evaluating police than those who live near those facilities. And people of different ethnicity may have different histories with the police that produce different evaluation frameworks. Regardless of their role in a particular encounter with the police, people who have frequently been the object of enforcement activity possess a different set of sensitivities from others whose experiences have been as service recipients (see, for example, Brunson and Weitzer, 2007).

Much of the original impetus for community-oriented policing came from groups of citizens who were disgruntled because they felt abused as objects of enforcement or underserved as victims of crime (Kelling and Moore, 1988), and there is currently much interest in community-oriented policing as a way to deal with both of these groups who are more likely to experience contact with the police or to desire their assistance (President's Task Force on 21st Century Policing, 2015; App. A of this volume). Yet the extant research on community-oriented policing typically fails to distinguish these "high-intensity" populations and thus offers little to enlighten policy and practice for the parts of society that were key to animating the movement for change.

A notable exception to the tendency to ignore high-intensity subgroups within a studied community is the evaluation of Chicago's community policing program across three different racial groups (Skogan, 2006b). Comparing trends in confidence in the police[2] across Blacks, Latinos, and Whites between 1994 and 2003, the researcher noted that improvements were

---

[2] In this study, "confidence" was measured as a composite of three scales, which were constructed from neighborhood resident surveys: perceived demeanor of officers, responsiveness to neighborhood concerns, and perceived effectiveness in controlling crime/disorder and helping victims.

observed across all measures for each racial group but added a caveat that highlights the importance of disaggregating "community" into subgroups:

> In the end, however, the contrast between the general optimism of whites and the still-widespread pessimism of African Americans was almost as large in 2003 as it had been in 1994 when CAPS was still in development. Things got better between African Americans and the police, but confidence had also grown among whites, keeping the gap just as wide. "The glass was only half full" when it came to healing the breech between police and the public, for while Chicagoans were more confident in the police, they were still deeply divided by race. (Skogan, 2006b, p. 322)

Finally, most of the studies of community-oriented policing that focus on community outcomes do relatively little to establish the strength of the causal connection between policy and practice. They tend to test the extent to which either policy or practice leads directly to each of the types of outcomes depicted in Figure 5-1 (see Chapter 5 of this report) as stages 3, 4, or 5. The correlations and/or causal links between stages 3 (community evaluations), 4 (community orientations), and 5 (community behavior) have not been a topic of systematic exploration. This presents numerous challenges for testing the validity of efforts to use community-oriented policing to promote desirable community outcomes.

We begin with these caveats in order to emphasize the difficulty in drawing conclusions regarding the effects on community outcomes of community-oriented policing. We find this surprising in some sense, given the very strong focus of community-oriented policing on changing the relationship between police and the public (Kelling and Moore, 1988; National Research Council, 2004, pp. 85–90; Skogan, 2006c; Skolnick and Bayley, 1986). Despite this focus, the extant research literature makes it difficult to draw very strong conclusions about precisely those outcomes that community policing was meant to influence. The following sections outline what these studies show and what they are unable to show.[3]

Community-Oriented Policing's Impacts on Community Evaluations of the Police

Studies of the impact of community-oriented policing on community evaluations of specific aspects of police performance have focused on citizen perceptions of disorder (e.g., severity of drug problems, social disorder), citizen fear of crime, and citizen satisfaction with police performance). Gill and colleagues (2014) provided a detailed comparison of these effects

---

[3] We rely heavily in the next sections on a recent systematic review of community-oriented policing's impact (Gill et al., 2014).

with 16 independent comparisons of perceived disorder, 18 comparisons of fear of crime, and 23 comparisons on citizen satisfaction, but fewer of these comparisons had sufficient information to calculate odds ratios (11 disorder, 10 fear, and 17 satisfaction outcomes). The meta-analysis produced only one statistically significant effect—citizen satisfaction increased—although all three outcomes showed small average effects in the expected positive direction. Satisfaction with police was characterized as a "moderate" effect (odds ratio of 1.37; Gill et al., 2014, p. 415). This effect qualifies as "small" according to some standard rules of thumb (see, e.g., Lipsey and Wilson, 2001), but many communities and their leaders might consider a 37 percent improvement in the odds of citizen satisfaction to be substantial. While perhaps insufficient to change very negative evaluations to very positive ones, it could arguably yield a discernible difference in a community.

Across individual studies in all three types of community-evaluation indicators, effect sizes were in the small range. Similarly, Skogan and Hartnett (1997, p. 210) concluded regarding Chicago's community-policing efforts, "To be sure, the successes wrought by the program were not overly dramatic." Returning to the full range of 17 evaluations of citizen satisfaction in the meta-analysis by Gill and colleagues (2014), very few (just two) yielded a small effect in a negative direction (odds ratios of 0.827 and 0.479), neither statistically significant. This pattern of infrequent backfire effects was repeated with the other community outcomes assessed in the meta-analysis.

The authors concluded that there was "robust evidence that community policing increases citizen satisfaction with the police" (Gill et al., 2014, p. 418), and "no evidence that community policing decreases citizens' fear of crime" (p. 419). Of course, the potential synergy between program elements is not captured by this simple analysis, so the committee also considered a comparison of programs that had all three elements of community policing present in "strong" form: organizational decentralization (beat integrity), community engagement (regular community meetings, foot/bike patrol, or positive police–citizen contact), and problem solving. Six of the 17 comparisons had all three elements but showed only a small and not statistically significant differences from those that did not. Of course, the small number of cases for comparison makes this exercise tenuous, so the available evidence provides no guidance about how best to proceed with the particular policies and practices that will promote citizen satisfaction most effectively.

Community-Oriented Policing Impacts on Orientations to the Police

The Gill and colleagues (2014) meta-analysis included 10 independent comparisons of the effect of community-oriented policing on perceived legitimacy. The most frequent measure of perceived legitimacy was confidence in the police (six comparisons). Other indicators included perceived "trust in police," "procedural justice," "treating people politely," and "police fairness." On average, the odds that people living in areas where the local police had a community-oriented policing policy viewed those police as legitimate were about 1.28 times the odds for someone living in an area where local police had no such plan. This difference was marginally statistically significant ($p = .077$) (Gill et al., 2014, pp. 415–416).

A noteworthy feature of the sample of study comparisons in this meta-analysis is the large portion of comparisons that came from the same project. The evaluation by Tuffin, Morris, and Poole (2006) of the National Reassurance Policing Program (NRPP) in the United Kingdom accounted for 6 of the 10 comparisons. One advantage of this common origin is ease of comparability of design and measures across the six sites, which reduces the risk of variability in effects due to evaluation methodology differences in different studies. In this NRPP evaluation, there was some variability in effects across sites. Four showed stronger effect sizes (odds ratios of 1.66–3.34), and two showed much weaker changes (close to null effects). The evaluation report attributed differences in program performance to variation across sites in implementation, not to the socioeconomic characteristics of the sites (Tuffin, Morris, and Poole, 2006, pp. 88–90).

As with evaluations of police performance, the meta-analysis revealed only 2 of 10 studies showing a backfire effect on perceived police legitimacy. The most striking of these was a study of El Centro, California, which focused its intervention on a predominantly Mexican area of the city (Sabath and Carter, 2000).[4] Although the treatment district showed statistically significant improvements in citizens' familiarity with the police and perceptions of crime-control effectiveness, it showed no gains in trust toward the police, while the comparison district did show a statistically significant increase in trust.

---

[4]The intervention included establishing a community center with a police substation to improve police-community relations, youth programming, permanent beat assignment of officers, and knock-and-talk visits using bilingual officers. The evaluation used a two-wave panel survey design with a matched comparison group and compared approximately 150 households in each of the treatment and comparison districts. The odds ratio calculated by the meta-analysis for the intervention's effect was 0.440 and was statistically significant (Gill et al., 2014, p. 417).

Community-Oriented Policing Impacts on Cooperation and Collective Efficacy

Do citizens behave differently as a consequence of being exposed to a community-oriented policing intervention? Chapter 4 speaks to the impact of community-oriented policing on criminal and disorderly behavior. Our concern here is with two types of related behaviors: whether citizens are willing to cooperate with the police, and, as noted in Chapter 5, what Sampson, Raudenbush, and Earls (1997) termed "collective efficacy," which refers to the degree to which people who live in communities trust their neighbors and are willing to intervene in community affairs. Both types of behavior speak to the ability of communities to enhance informal social controls either through alerting the police to community problems or working together directly to intervene in those problems.

Many expect that community-oriented policing should bring police and citizens closer together in common cause and should strengthen communication among various community groups as well as between police and the public. It should invest residents with the necessary skills, resources, and sense of empowerment to mobilize against neighborhood problems (Renauer, 2007; Sargeant, Wickes, and Mazerolle, 2013; Slocum et al., 2010; Velez, 2001). Much of the available research on policing precursors of collective efficacy focuses on the degree of police crime-control effectiveness or perceived legitimacy (reviewed below in the section on procedural justice policing). Research seeking to test the relationships, either associational or causal, between community-oriented policing and collective efficacy is limited (Sargeant, Wickes, and Mazerolle, 2013). Scott (2002) found in 77 Indianapolis neighborhoods that greater resident access to the police was associated with higher levels of social capital (not the same as collective efficacy, but sharing a concern for acting on behalf of community interests). However, other key measures of community policing failed to display a statistically significant association with social capital (e.g., frequency of police involvement in community events and activities). Renauer (2007) found evidence to support a backfire effect; increased police presence at community meetings was associated with *less* informal social control in 81 Portland, Oregon, neighborhoods. He speculated that low–socioeconomic status neighborhoods attracted more police attention. Sargeant, Wickes, and Mazerolle (2013), using qualitative interviews of key informants in two Brisbane suburbs, did not find the expected association between community-oriented policing and each community's collective efficacy. In the suburb with low collective efficacy before the intervention and a high immigrant population, police efforts to reach out to residents did not yield the expected gains because those efforts were not perceived as legitimate (i.e., were not seen as fair or effective). Nor did residents possess the knowledge and skills needed to act effectively to mobilize organizations on their behalf. In the wealthier suburb, which had high collective efficacy prior to the intervention, the relative absence of problems disinclined police to invest much community-oriented policing effort there, nor were residents particularly desirous of such police interventions.

The strongest evaluation of community-oriented policing's impact on collective efficacy is the assessment of the NRPP in the United Kingdom (Tuffin, Morris, and Poole, 2006). This policing program had several elements: focusing policing activity on those "signal" crimes expected to have a disproportionate impact on public feelings of safety, community involvement in identifying priorities for targeting interventions and participation in the interventions, and making locally known authorities and police officers readily accessible to the community. This pre-post, matched comparison group design used a two-wave panel (1 year apart) to study program effects in one area for each of six different UK police forces.[5] The study found evidence of desired changes attributable to the NRPP for many of the outcomes measured (decreases in crime and in perceptions of antisocial behavior, increases in feelings of safety and in confidence in the police), but virtually absent was a statistically significant change relative to comparison sites in measures of social cohesion, feeling trust in other members of the community, collective efficacy, or involvement in voluntary/community activity. Of the five outcome indicators used, only one (trust in the community) had a statistically significant (but modest) positive increase when pooled across all sites,[6] but there were no statistically significant changes in measures of willingness of neighbors to intervene or of voluntary activity. At the individual site level, the difference in perceived legitimacy across treated and untreated groups was statistically significant in only 3 of the 30 tests. The evaluators speculated that the development of social capacity may take longer than changing community perceptions of conditions in their neighborhood and feelings about the police.

To summarize, most of this small number of studies on community-oriented policing's record in promoting collective efficacy are cross sectional in nature. Given their designs, these studies can only establish whether there is the expected statistical relationship; they cannot distinguish how much of any association found is due to the effects of community policing on collective efficacy and how much is due to the effects of collective efficacy on community policing (the issue of potential reverse causality). Nor can they rule out the possibility of third common causes (confounders). On the

---

[5] The number of respondents available from both waves varied between 170 and 205 for each community outcome assessed.

[6] There was a 5 percentage point difference between treatment and control sites (Tuffin, Morris, and Poole, 2006, p. 57).

other hand, these studies can provide credible information about people's feelings about their experiences, as well as suggestions about how those feelings are associated with their views about the police. The exception to this limitation is the evaluation of the NRPP, but that study found only small differences that were not statistically significant, using conventional measures of confidence.

There is a significant body of research on the correlates and predictors of citizens' crime reporting behavior, but very little empirical research that explicitly examines the causal linkage between community-oriented policing and crime reporting (Schnebly, 2008).[7] One study examined the effects of police department resource commitment to community-oriented policing on the willingness of victims and third parties to report victimizations to the police or other nonpolice third parties (apartment manager, school administrator) for 2,379 assault and robbery incidents recorded by the National Crime Victimization Survey from 1997 through 1999 (Schnebly, 2008).

Controlling for other factors known to influence reporting behavior (victim and city characteristics), Schnebly found that in cities with a larger percentage of the force working in full-time community-oriented-policing assignments, third parties were more likely to report victimizations to a police official. Further, victims in cities served by police agencies with higher portions of the force working as community-oriented policing officers were more inclined to notify nonpolice third parties than to make a report to the police. Additional analyses showed that the amount of training of police *recruits* and of residents in community-oriented policing showed no statistically significant relationship to victimization reporting behaviors. However, the proportion of *current* officers who had received community-oriented policing training showed a statistically significant positive relationship to the likelihood of residents reporting their victimization. The study also examined whether community-oriented policing's relationships with the community were conditioned by either victim or event-related characteristics and found some associations of this sort. For instance, residential instability reduced the strength of the negative relationship of full-time community-oriented policing staffing to the likelihood of police notification. The study speculated about the apparent contradictions and complexities of the findings. However, it is difficult to draw conclusions from a single study, particularly one with a number of self-acknowledged limitations. The measures of community-oriented policing staffing did not distinguish between different approaches to community-oriented policing, nor did they consider the degree to which officers who were not community-oriented-

---

[7] We exclude from consideration here the research that examines the effects of procedural justice policing and perceived legitimacy on crime-reporting behavior, which we cover in the section below on procedural justice policing.

policing specialists engaged in community-oriented policing activities. Further, variation in the degree of community-oriented policing effort within a given city may vary tremendously from neighborhood to neighborhood, but only city-level measurement was possible. And as is true with the literature on community-oriented policing and collective efficacy, this study was cross sectional, measuring all variables during the same time period.

In summary, the available literature on the relationship between community-oriented policing and community behavior consists predominantly of studies of collective efficacy and crime reporting. Three aspects of this literature are important: the number of studies is small, the findings across them are mixed, and there are many methodological limitations, particularly with interpreting study results as evidence for causal connections. These aspects make it inappropriate to draw conclusions about the effects of community-oriented policing on citizen cooperative behavior.

Long-Term Effects of Community-Oriented Policing

In addition to enhancing perceived police legitimacy, an important goal of community-oriented policing is to build, improve, or sustain communities. Such transformations rarely take place in the span of months or even a few years. Yet most studies of community-oriented policing's effects (and associations with outcomes) use a time frame that is short term, generally a year or less. The sources of such temporal bias are many, but three are particularly powerful: (1) Research funding cycles tend to support short-term projects. (2) American police organizations experience a high rate of turnover at the top, which makes for greater program instability as new chiefs tend to be "new brooms," sweeping out their predecessors' innovations to make room for their own (Mastrofski, 2015). (3) It is difficult to sustain experimental and even quasi-experimental research protocols for extended time periods.

How long does it take for a policing innovation to register an effect and sustain it? One might expect that the longer an intervention has been operating, the greater its prospects for showing an effect. For example, it has been suggested that the changes to organizational structure that are part of community-oriented policing (e.g., decentralization and reduced hierarchy and specialization) may simply take many years to accomplish and to yield organizational transformation (Mastrofski and Willis, 2010, p. 71). Alternatively, some interventions may realize their successes early, and others may even decline over the long run because they are insufficiently flexible to respond to changing conditions.

One of the few exceptions to the bias toward short-term research is the decade-long evaluation of community-oriented policing in Chicago (Skogan,

2006b, Chapter 10).[8] Between 1994 and 2003, fear of crime declined under this community-oriented policing intervention (at the greatest rate for Blacks and at the lowest rate for Latinos). During that same period, perceptions of disorder declined significantly for Blacks while increasing significantly for Latinos. And trends in evaluations of police "confidence" (demeanor, responsiveness, and performance) increased for all three racial groups. Interestingly, the generally increasing year-to-year level of these indicators (combined into a single quality-of-service index) plateaued for all ethnic groups after about 6 years, with the group scoring the lowest percentage of positive responses (Blacks) at 40 percent and the highest group (Whites) scoring more than 60 percent, with Latinos in the middle at nearly 50 percent (Skogan, 2006b, p. 280). Unfortunately, because community-oriented policing was implemented citywide for most of that time period, there were no comparison groups to help rule out the effects of other influences.[9]

Finally, it is worth noting that the study of long-term community effects calls for a consideration of the long-term history of police "treatments." Neighborhoods with a long history of receiving one or more elements of community-oriented policing may respond differently from those with little or no such experience, and the response over time may vary with the duration of the treatment. Whether neighborhoods that have experienced several years of positive police outreach are more responsive to a new community-oriented policing program than those for whom there is no history of such outreach is an open question. Neighborhoods with a history of fraught relations with the police may take longer to respond positively than neighborhoods with a more positive history.

Environmental Conditions

Because community-oriented policing requires interaction between the police and the community for it to achieve effective outcomes, the environment in which a community-oriented policing intervention is delivered is particularly important for its success. This means that one should approach generalizing about the effects of community-oriented policing with a healthy respect for the possibility that it will depend upon the character of the community where it is employed (Reiss, 1992; Klinger, 2004). At what sorts of

---

[8] Another study that offered a slightly longer-term evaluation of a community-oriented policing program was a follow-up to the UK's NRPP, which added a 2nd-year evaluation to the original 1-year study (Quinton and Morris, 2008). The follow-up found a continuation in the second year of the desirable impacts observed in the original evaluation by Tuffin, Morris, and Poole (2006).

[9] It is difficult to determine whether the plateauing pattern was due to program features or how they were implemented, other features of the organization (e.g., the growth in Compstat's potentially antagonistic influence), or a variety of external factors.

jurisdictions have community-oriented policing studies been conducted? It is instructive to consider the sample produced by the systematic review by Gill and colleagues (2014), the review used above for its outcome showing that the strongest outcome association with community-oriented policing interventions was citizen satisfaction. Of the 17 comparisons, 6 were made in UK areas of large size or served by large police departments, at least by American standards (e.g., Leicester, Surrey, Bexley, Thames Valley); 5 were conducted in Chicago, 2 in Australia, 1 in Newark, 1 in Houston, 1 in Madison, and 1 in a small California city. While in some respects this represents a diverse sample, it clearly ignores or grossly underrepresents rural, small town, and suburban agencies in the United States. The strong representation of the United Kingdom and Chicago in particular make it hazardous to formulate a basis for generalizing results broadly.

It is also appropriate to reiterate the point that studies of community-oriented policing mostly focus on effects at a level below the jurisdiction (police beat, neighborhood, or district/borough). The prospects of jurisdictionwide effects remain virtually unexamined.

Summary. The available empirical research on community-oriented policing's community effects focuses on citizen perceptions of police performance (in terms of what they do and the consequences for community disorder), satisfaction with police, and perceptions of police legitimacy. There is considerable variability of findings within and between types of community outcome measures. Overall, community-oriented policing programs show a tendency to increase citizen satisfaction and have positive but weaker effects on perceptions of police legitimacy. Nonetheless, there are a number of limitations in the extant research that limit the committee's capacity to draw firm conclusions about what this means.

BROKEN WINDOWS POLICING

As we noted in Chapter 2, the committee considers broken windows policing to be a strategy for a community-based approach. Our reasoning is that the mechanism that underlies the original formulation of the community-based approach is rooted in making changes in the community. Such changes are driven in part by changes in policing, but it remains the case that the long-term goal of broken windows policing is to enhance the ability of the community to exercise informal social controls presumed to play a central role in the nature and extent of community order and safety (Weisburd et al., 2015; Wilson and Kelling, 1982).

There are two specific outcomes relevant to our discussion that are predicted by the broken windows logic model. The first is that fear of crime is a key causal factor in increasing crime rates. A key purpose of broken windows policing is to reduce fear of crime, which should lead in the long run to stronger informal social controls in urban communities. Wilson and Kelling (1982, p. 31) noted in discussing the Newark Fear of Crime Experiment:

> First, outside observers should not assume that they know how much of the anxiety now endemic in many big-city neighborhoods stems from a fear of "real" crime and how much from a sense that the street is disorderly, a source of distasteful, worrisome encounters. The people of Newark, to judge from their behavior and their remarks to interviewers, apparently assign a high value to public order, and feel relieved and reassured when the police help them maintain that order.

The second outcome is similar to that which was discussed above in regard to community-oriented policing. Broken windows policing would be expected to increase the degree to which citizens are willing to intervene in doing something about community problems. For Wilson and Kelling (1982), social and physical disorder are key factors in the decline of communities. As discussed in Chapter 2, broken windows policing, with its focus on reducing disorder, is expected to reverse the decline of collective efficacy in communities, thereby preventing a breakdown in community social controls.

The Impact of Broken Windows Policing on Fear of Crime and Collective Efficacy

In assessing the impacts of broken windows policing, the committee drew heavily from a recent systematic review conducted by Weisburd and colleagues (2015). They examined studies that used either a control/comparison group design (experimental or quasi-experimental) or a before-after assessment of outcomes, and each study had to report impacts on fear of crime and/or informal social control. Overall, they identified just six studies that examined the impact of disorder policing on fear or collective efficacy/informal social control. One of the studies was a randomized experiment. Four studies used quasi-experimental designs with comparison groups, and one study used a before-after design. All six examined impacts on fear, while only one examined impacts on informal social control (defined as collective efficacy). The committee's review did not identify any additional studies.

The earliest studies that examined the impact of disorder policing on fear were a pair of Police Foundation studies by Pate and colleagues (1985b, 1985c). The first examined a police program in Newark, New Jersey, that aimed to reduce fear of crime by reducing the signs of crime (Pate et al., 1985a). Findings were mixed across different measures, but as a whole, the authors concluded that the program was ineffective in reducing fear in the targeted area relative to the comparison area. The second Newark study involved an order-maintenance program as part of the police intervention, and it found that fear of property crime was significantly reduced, relative to the comparison area (Pate et al., 1985b).

Research by McGarrell, Giacomazzi, and Thurman (1999) examined the impact of a community policing program that involved elements of broken windows policing (improving physical conditions, targeting drug and social disorder problems) in the area surrounding a public housing facility. Fear of crime was significantly reduced relative to the comparison area, even though there were no statistically significant reductions in crime. On the other hand, a pre-post case study of a partnership policing program in two villages in Wales found no statistically significant impacts on fear (Rogers, 2002).

Finally, two more recent and related studies also produced mixed findings. (These findings are also reviewed in Chapter 5, as they both are also hot spots policing initiatives.) Using data from the Police Foundation Displacement and Diffusion study conducted in Jersey City, New Jersey, Weisburd and colleagues (2006b) and Hinkle and Weisburd (2008) found that aggressive police crackdowns on social and physical disorder appeared to increase fear of crime in the target areas relative to the surrounding catchment areas that did not receive any extra police attention. However, a randomized experimental evaluation of the impacts of broken windows policing in three cities in California, designed in part as a follow-up to the Police Foundation study, found that a 6-month police intervention that focused on reducing social and physical disorder but encouraged police use of discretion (see Kelling, 1999) had no impact on fear of crime or collective efficacy (Weisburd et al., 2011). An important point is that this study is the only one identified by the committee that evaluated the impact of broken windows policing on any measure of informal social control. The authors suggested that the differing findings across these two studies were due to the differing nature of the interventions. While both police programs were consistent with the broken windows strategy of targeting disorder, the Jersey City intervention involved a very aggressive crackdown on disorder that included sweeps, a violent offender removal program, and intensive enforcement aimed at street-level drug sales and use and at prostitution. The intervention in California used a less heavy-handed approach to broken windows policing. It emphasized rapid repair of physical disorder and a discretionary approach to handling social disorder through mediation and warnings.

In this regard, recall also the differing findings in the two studies by Pate and colleagues (1985b, 1985c) discussed above. The intervention that attempted to reduce fear by cleaning up disorder (reducing the signs of crime) showed no impact on fear, while the policing program that had a disorder abatement component was found to reduce fear by a statistically significant amount. Thus, it may be that how the police design and deliver a disorder-focused program may affect the extent to which the mechanisms of broken windows policing are confirmed.

Weisburd and colleagues (2015) provided in their meta-analysis a quantitative summary of the evidence of these disorder policing programs on fear of crime. (They did not provide a quantitative summary regarding collective efficacy because only one study reported on these outcomes.) Using a random effects model because of the variability of treatments and outcomes, they found a slightly negative, albeit statistically not significant, impact. This suggests, if anything, a very slight backfire effect in the samples examined, but the authors concluded that the data do not, in general, support or refute any clear impact. We think their conclusion is reasonable, given the small number of studies available.

All in all, the committee simply does not have enough evidence to draw a solid conclusion regarding the impacts of broken windows policing.

Summary. The committee is not able to draw a conclusion regarding the impacts of broken windows policing on fear of crime or on collective efficacy. This is due in part to the surprisingly small number of studies that examine the community outcomes of broken windows policing and in part to the mixed effects observed. The committee notes how little attention has been paid to community processes in this area, given the emphasis on enhancing community social controls in the original logic model for this strategy as proposed by Wilson and Kelling (1982). The importance of informal social controls in their logic model would imply that collecting data on collective efficacy is critical. But we found only one study that attempted to assess collective efficacy. With regard to fear of crime as an outcome of interest to the model, there are more studies, but they differ considerably in the observed change in fear of crime, based on the policing tactics carried out in the intervention under study. Overall, it appears that softer approaches that focus on community engagement and utilization of police discretion are more effective in reducing fear. Such approaches are also more consistent with Kelling's suggestions for how police should address disorder (Kelling, 1999; Kelling and Coles, 1996).

PROCEDURAL JUSTICE

For a variety of reasons the question of perceived legitimacy has become more central to proactive policing in the United States over the past several years. Perceived legitimacy may be defined as the belief that the police are entitled to exercise authority within the community and that as a consequence their directives ought to be accepted and receive deference. Recent events involving police shootings in different U.S. communities and subsequent public protests have led national police leaders to be concerned about the issue of public trust and to seek information about how to increase trust. An example of that effort is the recent report of the President's Task Force on 21st Century Policing (2015), which made perceived legitimacy a core theme in its discussion of policing. Because of this concern about their legitimacy, police departments have increasingly developed proactive efforts to engage in policies and practices that promote and sustain their perceived legitimacy among the people in the communities they police. As we detail below, these efforts have typically focused on enhancing procedural justice in police-citizen encounters. Our main question is whether proactive policing programs based on a procedural justice model improve attitudes toward the police and cooperation with the police.

Perceptions of police legitimacy are subjective and must be studied by interviewing people and discerning their orientations toward the police. Hence, by definition, efforts to understand perceived legitimacy need to focus on people's perceptions about the police and their subjective reactions to police actions. The model outlined in Figure 5-1 in Chapter 5 of this report presents a logic flow that incorporates these subjective responses to policing. It moves from police policies and practices to what is actually going on in the community (police behavior) to the subjective evaluations and orientations of the people within that community (police legality/perceived fairness; popular legitimacy). To the degree that this logic model is accepted as a causal model, it suggests that those perceptions, in turn, feed into law-related behaviors in the community (cooperation, engagement).

One key question is whether changes in police behavior do in fact change the law-related behavior of people in the community. A second question is why that change occurs, which is an issue of mediating mechanisms. The presumed mechanism in procedural justice models is that outlined in Figure 5-1 (perceived procedural justice shapes perceptions of police legitimacy). While some of the connections outlined in that model have been tested in prior studies that have been based upon the assumption that the logic model presented is a causal model, there has been no single study that tests this entire model. Nor have there been efforts to explore issues of bi-causality. In a similar case, Chapter 4 of this report outlines research that associates hot spots policing with crime rate changes. The presumed mediating (causal) mechanism in that case is deterrence. However, as is the case here, there are no studies that directly test whether hot spots policing changes the crime rate because it changes people's perceptions about the risk of being caught. It could be the case that hot spots policing changes the popular legitimacy of the police. In other words, in both cases there is indirect evidence to support the presumed causal connection in the underlying logic model, but in neither case has there been a direct test of that causal mechanism in a proactive policing intervention. In part, this lacuna reflects the inherent difficulties of testing mediating mechanisms.

One important aspect of this overall logic model is the linkage between evaluations, orientations, and behaviors—that is, the aspect of the model that begins with people's subjective evaluations of the police and flows to their behaviors. This element in the logic model reflects the fact that perceived legitimacy of policing represents people's evaluations and orientations, rather than objective realities. Therefore, it must be studied through interviews with members of the community.

Antecedents of Perceived Legitimacy

Within the psychological literature on the antecedents of perceived legitimacy, a number of studies suggest that perceptions of the procedural justice of police actions are strongly related to perceived legitimacy.[10] Procedural justice in policing refers to an interrelated cluster of evaluations of different aspects of the way police officers behave when dealing with the public. These non-experimental studies support a logic model that says that when people deal with authorities, their evaluations of the perceived fairness of the procedures through which authority is exercised influence their perceptions of police legitimacy more strongly than does the perceived outcome of the encounter (Tyler, 2006; Tyler, Fagan, and Geller, 2014; Tyler and Jackson, 2014). Similarly, when people are making overall assessments of the legitimacy of a criminal justice institution in their community, they appear to focus on how members of that institution generally deal with the public (Sunshine and Tyler, 2003; Tyler, 2006; Tyler, Fagan, and Geller, 2014; Tyler and Jackson, 2014).

The psychological literature on perceived procedural justice has identified four elements of experience that are linked to whether people evaluate institutions as being procedurally just. Those dimensions are not derived from prescriptive norms identified and defended by legal scholars and political philosophers. Rather, they have been drawn from research on the criteria that community members themselves use to rate their experiences (Tyler, 1988). Studies suggest that there is substantial agreement across race, gender, and income levels in the criteria that define a fair procedure

---

[10] Abuwala and Farole (2008); Bradford (2011); Elliott, Thomas, and Ogloff (2011); Farole (2007); Hasisi and Weisburd (2011); Hinds (2007); Hinds and Murphy (2007); Jonathan-Zamir and Weisburd (2013); Kitzmann and Emery (1993); Mazerolle et al. (2013b); Myhill and Bradford (2012); Tor, Gazal-Ayal, and Garcia (2010); Tyler (2006); Tyler, Casper, and Fisher (1989); Tyler and Fagan (2008); Wemmers (1996).

> **BOX 6-1**
> **The Elements of Procedural Justice**
>
> **Decision Making**
>
> **Voice.** People believe that they should be given an opportunity to tell their side of the story, state their case, and explain their point of view before decisions are made.
>
> **Neutrality.** People want police decisions to be made based upon facts and the impartial and consistent application of rules and policies across people. Explaining why people are being stopped and/or how the police pursue particular policies helps people to feel that police actions are neutral. People also want to understand what the rules are and what these rules require them to do during interactions with legal authorities and afterwards. Authorities need not only to be fair but also to be seen as fair. This means that they need to have transparent procedures and to explain those procedures and the decisions that develop through them in ways that allow people to understand both what they need to do before and after the decision and how the decision will be made.
>
> **Treatment**
>
> **Respect.** The police are authorities, and people use their treatment as signals of their worth as people and of their standing in the community. Therefore, it is important to respect people and their rights. Treating people with dignity and courtesy validates them as a human being and affirms their status as members of the polity.
>
> **Trustworthiness.** Police actions require discretion. In granting the police discretion people want to believe that the police are sincere and benevolent. In other words, people what to believe that the police are acting in good faith to consider the needs and concerns of the various people involved in a situation and/or of the broader community. People infer trustworthy motives when the police express care and concern for citizen's welfare, when they see the police making efforts to provide them with assistance, and when officers show sensitivity to legitimate societal interests.

(Tyler and Huo, 2002). Those criteria, noted in Chapter 2 of this report, are listed in Box 6-1.

Two of the criteria shown in Box 6-1 are linked to how police officers are perceived to make decisions: (1) whether they provide opportunities for voice, allowing members of the public to state their perspective or tell their side of the story before decisions are made and (2) whether they make decisions in ways that people regard as neutral, rule-based, consistent, and without bias. Two other criteria are linked to how the police are viewed as treating people: (1) whether they treat people with the dignity, courtesy, and respect that they deserve as human beings and as members of the community and (2) whether people believe that their motives are trustworthy and benevolent: that is, that the police are sincerely trying to do what is good for the people in the community. The model suggests that perceived trustworthiness is the key to community acceptance of discretionary decisions.

The key to understanding this model is that the criteria focus on how people *experience* policing, that is, whether they feel they have voice, whether they think the procedures are neutral, whether they feel respected, and whether they infer that the police are trustworthy. The underlying argument of procedural justice is that the way people perceive these features of police action shapes whether people do or do not judge the police to be legitimate.

Procedural justice as defined by these four criteria has been typically assessed in one or both of two ways. The first is to ask people how fairly "decisions were made" or how "they were treated." The second is to ask about the four aspects of procedural justice that emerge from studies of the meaning of procedural justice (Tyler, 1988). When studies assess subjective voice, neutrality, respect, and trust, they typically find that these dimensions are highly correlated and that all four dimensions correlate strongly with evaluations of overall justice in decision making and treatment (Tyler, 1988; Tyler and Fagan, 2008; Worden and McLean, 2014).

These findings suggest that it is possible to view perceived procedural justice as an overall concept by asking people questions such as "were decisions made fairly" and/or "were you treated fairly"? It is equally possible to distinguish four component dimensions contributing to it. Empirical studies indicate that people distinguish more strongly among these four dimensions when they are evaluating their personal experiences than when they are making ratings of general police behavior in their community (Tyler, 2006).

In addition to perceptions of police treatment along the four dimensions that contribute to perceived legitimacy, researchers have also observed and coded officer conduct to determine how officer actions relate to those perceptions. That is, rather than relying upon a research participant's personal perceptions and judgments about how the police treated her, researchers can construct a protocol for observing and classifying officer behavior that conforms to the definition of procedural justice, such as behavior showing those features listed in Box 6-1. Such a protocol requires sufficiently clear and detailed instructions to create reliable measures of officer conduct that trained third-party observers can replicate reliably (and in that sense, objectively) from situation to situation and across observers. Using this approach Worden and McLean (2014) coded officer conduct in the areas predicted to influence perceived procedural justice that fall into the category of "police practices" in the logic model portrayed in Figure 5-1.

Some type of coding of officer behaviors that are distinct from the subjective evaluations of either the people involved or the officers involved is essential for translating the concept of perceived procedural justice into terms that police officers can use to conform their behavior to the requirements of that concept. Interestingly, the relatively few studies that have explored objective measures of the components of perceived procedural justice have found that, unlike subjective measures (community members' perceptions), the four elements portrayed in Box 6-1 are only modestly related, suggesting that they are best conceived as a formative index (Jonathan-Zamir, Mastrofski, and Moyal, 2015; Worden and McLean, 2014). Further, the only study (Worden and McLean, 2014) to have compared objective and subjective measures of officer conduct along these dimensions found that the two measures are themselves related but the magnitude of that connection varies across dimensions (see discussion below). An important emerging area of research uses the coding of police videos to establish the objective features of police behavior under different circumstances and the connection of that behavior to people's experiences with the police (Voigt et al., 2017).

Given the relatively recent interest in the procedural justice model of proactive policing, there is, as we note below, a limited literature that examines whether perceived procedural justice is a key factor in explaining perceptions of legitimacy. At the same time, there is a large research literature that has been developing over the past century in social psychology, and more recently, in criminal justice outside policing. The committee thought it important to summarize this literature in drawing conclusions more generally about the relevance of the procedural justice model for policing.

General Evidence on the Procedural Justice Logic Model Outside of Policing

What empirical evidence supports the procedural justice model? The theoretical underpinnings of perceived procedural justice are from social psychology (Leventhal, 1980; Thibaut and Walker, 1975), so initial evidence in this area comes from research in that field. The first research program in this area was that of John Thibaut and Laurens Walker (1975) and is summarized in their book *Procedural Justice*. Their research is reviewed in *The Social Psychology of Procedural Justice* (Lind and Tyler, 1988). The hallmark of these studies is that they are well-designed randomized controlled trials. Their context is variations in courtroom procedures, and they demonstrated that different procedures are rated differently in terms of perceived procedural justice. Procedural variations also shape a variety of types of evaluations of judicial procedures and/or authorities.

These procedural justice findings were replicated in a series of studies conducted within the Thibaut-Walker research group (Houlden et al., 1978; LaTour, 1978; Lind, Thibaut, and Walker, 1973; Lind et al., 1978; Thibaut, Walker, and Lind, 1972; Thibaut, Friedland, and Walker, 1974; Thibaut and Walker, 1975; Walker et al., 1974). The strength of these studies is their high internal validity, while their weaknesses include their laboratory context (Damaska, 1975; Hayden and Anderson, 1979), their lack of measurement of perceived legitimacy as an outcome of personal experiences, and—in the context of this report—their lack of focus on the police.

The theoretical elements in the psychological literature on procedural justice have been reviewed by Miller (2001) and MacCoun (2005). Miller identified two behavioral consequences of procedural *injustice*. The first is a marked disinclination to comply with authorities. The second is a diminished willingness to pursue group goals and concerns. He also noted the absence of any negative consequences of fair procedures and that a focus on using procedures for exercising police authority that are experienced by the public as fair valuably expands the universe of goals beyond compliance to include enhancing the viability of organizations.

When MacCoun (2005) conducted his review, the social psychology literature had more than 700 articles on the topic of procedural justice. MacCoun's review suggests that, across the wide range of types of authority considered in this literature, experimental variations in actual procedural justice and differences in perceived procedural justice in different settings are both consistently found to shape compliance and cooperation with authorities. In particular, these effects were found with both experimental and correlational research designs. MacCoun (2005, p. 173) noted that "the sheer heterogeneity of tasks, domains, populations, designs, and analytic methods provides remarkable convergence and triangulation" in support of the core propositions of the procedural justice model.

The central arguments of procedural justice models have subsequently been tested in management settings, and a distinct literature on procedural justice has developed within the sub-disciplines of organizational psychology/organizational behavior. An early example is from Earley and Lind (1987), who reported on a study in which workers were randomly assigned to work under different procedures. These differences were found to influence the workers' perceptions of fairness and performance on the job. The subsequent literature on procedural justice in work settings has expanded broadly to include variations in many aspects of work organizations and their association with a number of dependent variables, including but not limited to adherence to rules and work requirements. Some studies are conducted in ways that provide support for a causal connection between these variables, while others more appropriately support the demonstration of an association.

Cohen-Charash and Spector (2001) reviewed 190 studies (148 field studies and 42 laboratory studies) and found that variations in workplace characteristics reliably shaped perceived fairness. Procedural justice was reliably related to a number of workers' evaluations, including satisfaction with one's job, pay, supervisor, management, and performance appraisal procedures (Cohen-Charash and Spector, 2001, Table 7, p. 299). It was further associated with commitment to the job, normative commitment, trust in the organization, trust in one's supervisor, and the employee's intention to remain at or leave their job (Table 7, p. 300). Variations in the workplace characteristics associated with differences in perceived fairness were found to have an uneven relationship with required workplace behaviors. Studies found an association with workplace performance for field studies but not for lab studies. The studies consistently found an association with voluntary cooperation (organization citizenship behavior) and counterproductive work behavior (more perceived fairness leads to less shirking, sabotage, etc.). Many of these studies are experiments, and their results support the argument that these connections are not only associations but also reflect causal connections.

Colquitt and colleagues (2001) reviewed the organizational justice[11] literature, and Colquitt and colleagues (2013) re-reviewed the original set of studies, as well as the subsequent literature. In the 2013 re-review, in which the authors identified 493 distinct studies, they found statistically significant overall influences of procedural justice on trust, organizational citizenship behavior, task performance, and (negatively) on counterproductive work behavior. The review found equally strong relationships for studies that focus upon particular events and those that make overall workplace evaluations. Perhaps most significantly, in terms of the model outlined, Colquitt and colleagues (2013) conducted a mediational analysis and found that the relationship between the organizational justice of the organization and relevant employee behaviors is partially mediated by "social exchange quality" (see Colquitt et al., 2013, Fig. 1, p. 217).[12] Social exchange quality is quantified as an index that combines measures of trust, mutual respect, perceived management support, and commitment. In many respects, it is similar to the concept of perceived legitimacy in a management context. This type of mediating role has also been identified in more recent studies

---

[11] Studies of procedural justice in organizational settings often use the term "organizational justice" to consider three interrelated aspects of what is here being called "procedural justice": organizational justice, interactional justice, and informational justice.

[12] The term partial mediation refers to a situation in which the direct relationship between two variables is significantly reduced when a mediator is introduced, but there is still a significant direct relationship.

of management settings (Ma, Liu, and Liu, 2014).[13] Many of the studies reviewed are laboratory or field experiments that provide evidence not merely of statistically significant association but also of causal connection.

In the case of compliance, several studies illustrate the influence of the procedural justice of the climate of an organization as evaluated by employees and their compliance with rules and rulings, which is treated in this literature as an aspect of task performance. Greenberg (1994) manipulated the objective fairness of the enactment of smoking bans in a work setting and found compliance variations. Greenberg (1990) varied the objective fairness of pay changes and found an impact on employee theft. Lind and colleagues (1993) conducted a field study involving interviews with disputants and found that perceived fairness shaped the acceptance of arbitration awards. Dunford and Devine (1998) and Lind and colleagues (2000) interviewed employees and found that variations in the perceived fairness of termination procedures predicted whether terminated workers filed lawsuits. In a multinational setting, Kim and Mauborgne (1993) conducted a non-experimental survey-based study and found that rule following was linked to perceived management fairness.

In recent years there has been a series of studies of the association of procedural justice with the perceived legitimacy of the court system. Several studies deal with the courts. They find a significant association between trust and confidence in courts and their perceived procedural justice (Abuwala and Farole, 2008; Baker, 2016; Dillon and Emery, 1996; Farole, 2007; Kitzmann and Emery, 1994; Shute, Hood, and Seemungal, 2005; Tyler, 2001; Wemmers, Van der Leeden, and Steensma, 1995; Wemmers, 2013). A significant association was also found between perceived procedural justice and the willingness to accept court decisions (Baker, 2016; MacCoun et al., 1988; Tyler and Huo, 2002). Some of these studies are experiments, and their findings support an argument for the causal influence of procedural justice on these elements of perceived legitimacy in legal proceedings.

In summary, the logic model underlying the procedural justice policing strategy has been widely supported in studies varying in their focus and methodology. What is particularly striking is the convergence of these findings. Many studies, including those with experimental variations in pro-

---

[13] This literature was also reviewed by Chang (2015), who concluded that there are statistically significant associations between organizational justice and task performance (Chang, 2015, Table 2) and between ratings of organizational justice and organizational citizenship behavior (Table 3). He suggested that both procedural justice (fair decision making) and interactional justice (fair interpersonal treatment of employees) are significantly associated with task performance and cooperative workplace behaviors (Chang, 2015, p. 34). Interestingly, this review found equally strong relationships irrespective of whether employee behavior was self-rated or assessed by independent third parties. Again, many of these studies are experiments.

cedures, suggest that it is possible to reliably create policies and practices that influence perceived procedural justice. Studies also suggest that such variations shape not only perceived procedural justice but also compliance, cooperation, and a variety of other types of organizationally relevant behaviors.

The Specific Features of Procedural Justice That Shape Perceived Legitimacy

The large literature in social psychology establishes that it is possible to create settings that reliably influence perceived procedural justice (Lind and Tyler, 1988). The most replicable manipulations of procedural justice have involved variations in two procedural elements: voice (of those being acted upon) and neutrality (of those conducting the procedure). Voice manipulations typically vary whether or not people have input into legal decisions, while neutrality is manipulated through variations in whether or not the decision maker explains what facts or rules were used in making the decision.

The original Thibaut and Walker (1975) research varied court procedures between adversarial and inquisitorial, a variation which shapes whether people do or do not have (indirect) voice. Other studies varied whether or not the procedure produces decisions that are explained to participants. One element of procedural justice is whether or not authorities explain the basis for their decisions. In work-related studies conducted in experimental settings, there are often experimental variations introduced in terms of whether the supervisor does or does not explain how compensation was determined. Subsequent studies in this organizational justice literature have varied several aspects of work conditions in work organizations and then tested for any impact upon perceived justice. For example, variations of work conditions would include whether people are allowed to participate in a performance appraisal session at which their pay is determined or whether the reasons for job layoffs are explained to them. The study participants might participate in a performance task and receive or do not receive an explanation for the way their performance was rated when compensation was determined. The experimental variation might involve differences in how the basis for compensation was explained (or if it was explained at all) or, where appropriate, whether or not the participants had voice and could advocate for the quality of their work. These studies have found that a variety of types of human resource practice variations have a systematic impact (either positive or negative) with perceptions of procedural justice (Tremblay et al., 2010). Because these studies are experiments, they suggest evidence that variations in objective work conditions influence perceptions of procedural justice. Similarly, elements of leader behavior are associated with procedural justice (Koivisto and Lipponen, 2015).

The court system is one type of organization in which organizational justice has been studied. An empirical literature evaluating the structure of the courts provides guidance concerning the features of courts that shape the nature of the interactions people have with authorities in courts. As an example, a substantial body of studies of restorative justice conferences have found that such conferences have a statistically significant association with later levels of recidivism, and are also experienced by participants as having more features of positive procedural justice than do the features of traditional case disposition (Hipple, Gruenewald, and McGarrell, 2014). Studies also have considered what happens in a courtroom. Greene and colleagues (2010) coded objective features of courtroom atmosphere and found that they were systematically related to litigants' perceptions of justice.

The role of arbitrators is similar to the role of police officers in that they do not seek voluntary consent. However, both arbitrators and mediators (who do need the consent of the parties they deal with) want to craft solutions that will not be resisted and undermined by the two opposing parties, so they benefit from following the principles of procedural justice. There have been studies of the features of mediation and other alternative dispute resolution procedures that lead to their perceived fairness in the eyes of all of the parties in an interaction (Tyler, 1989). As with restorative justice conferences, those features can serve as the basis for procedural designs. Core features include giving both parties the ability to present their side of the story, having a neutral decision maker (the third party), believing that the third-party decision maker is listening to and considering each party's arguments, and feeling that the third party is sincerely trying to reach a solution that is responsive to both opposing parties' concerns.

Effective third parties in these informal proceedings know to treat the opposing parties with courtesy, to listen to and acknowledge their issues, and to account for those concerns when presenting proposed solutions (Tyler, 1987, 1988, 1989). They are aware that evidence of favoritism or bias undermines their authority. Because mediation focuses upon gaining voluntary acceptance, mediators involved in dispute resolutions learn from their experience to follow the principles of procedural justice.

Utility of employee training is another area in which the management literature helps in identifying impacts of procedural justice. To test the impact of training union officers in procedural justice, Skarlicki and Latham (1996) used a quasi-experimental design comparing union leaders who received procedural justice training with leaders who did not receive training. After 3 months of training, workers who were working under trained leaders reported greater procedural justice in their workplace and engaged in more peer-assessed union citizenship behavior. These behavioral changes were found to be mediated by employee evaluations of procedural justice. Skarlicki and Latham (1997) replicated their first study and found similar outcomes, but they were only partially mediated by procedural justice. Cole and Latham (1997) replicated this training program and found that trained supervisors were rated by outside experts as solving problems more fairly. Another study conducted by Nakamura and colleagues (2016) randomly assigned managers to receive brief 90-minute training and found an impact 3 months later on the fairness of trained managers as perceived by lower-performing employees. Richter and colleagues (2016) designed a procedural justice training program for framing the delivery of bad news and found that trained managers were viewed as fairer and mitigated negative reactions associated with receiving bad news.

The workplace literature (see, e.g., DeCremer and Tyler, 2005) also identifies individual characteristics that are reliably associated with variations in perceived procedural justice. When people are more centrally focused upon their status and identity or when they draw more of their sense of themselves from membership and status in a group (e.g., because they strongly identify with it), they are more affected by their treatment. An explanation proposed to account for this association is that treatment communicates information about status and standing. Social scientists label such information relational because it communicates information relevant to social identity (Tyler and Lind, 1992).

The literature on social identity (Abrams and Hogg, 1988; Tyler and Blader, 2000) indicates that identification can be directly shaped by organizational structures and leader actions, suggesting another avenue for potential change management. In other words, these individual characteristics reflect variations in the nature of people's connection to their community and to institutions in the community. Such connections are malleable and can be changed in a variety of ways.

When people receive feedback indicating either that their standing in a community is high or that the status of the community itself is high (or both), they are more likely to identify with that community. And as people identify more strongly with the community, they are more affected by whether or not they are treated justly, since such treatment communicates social identity–relevant information and their identities are more strongly intertwined with the community. Hence, a general approach to amplifying the role of procedural justice in the evaluation of community authorities is to strengthen the identification of residents with their community. This logic model also highlights the reciprocal influences of procedural justice and social identification upon one another. Procedural justice promotes identification of community members with both authorities and institutions (Tyler and Blader, 2000). Identification, in turn, leads to a greater emphasis on procedural justice when reacting to authorities. Both of these processes evolve and interact over time.

Evidence on Procedural Justice in Policing

Many of the ideas mentioned in the community-oriented policing literature reviewed above in this chapter are similar to ideas in the procedural justice research literature, in the sense that the focus is on the experiences of people in the community and on their behavior toward the police. Despite these similarities in conceptualization, studies of community-oriented policing have, as noted above, seldom directly assessed perceptions of procedural justice or injustice of different aspects of community-oriented policing programs. Hence, one clear limitation of the existing studies is the lack of examination of the connection between actual police policies and practices and measures of the different intervening psychological constructs outlined in the logic model. The committee therefore cannot draw upon the large community-oriented policing literature for guidance in this area.

On the other hand, in comparison to community policing studies that measure procedural justice, there is a larger policing literature that begins with perceived procedural justice and looks at its consequences (Donner et al., 2015). Although issues of causality and third (potentially confounding) variables remain open questions, a number of studies that measure associations among perceptions, either through a cross-sectional design or using panel designs involving interviews with members of the public, find statistically significant correlations between perceived procedural justice, perceptions of legitimacy, compliance, and cooperation.[14]

Several studies of policing suggest that procedural justice policing is

---

[14] There have been a wide variety of approaches used to assess compliance, with most studies relying upon self-report of behavior. Cooperation has also been studied in a variety of ways. A typical approach has been to ask people if they would cooperate in an appropriate situation if one arose. For example, if called, would they serve on a jury? If they witnessed a crime, would they report it? See Bates, Allen, and Watson (2016); Bond and Gow (1996); Bradford (2011); Bradford et al. (2014, 2015); Casper, Tyler, and Fisher (1988); Dai, Frank, and Sun (2011); Elliott, Thomas, and Ogloff (2011); Fagan and Piquero (2007); Fagan and Tyler (2005); Gau and Brunson (2010, 2015); Goff, Epstein, and Reddy (2013); Hinds (2007, 2009); Hinds and Murphy (2007); Hasisi and Weisburd (2011); Jackson et al. (2012, 2013); Jonathan-Zamir and Weisburd (2013); Kane (2005); Mastrofski, Snipes, and Supina (1996); McCluskey (2003); Murphy (2005, 2013); Murphy, Hinds, and Fleming (2008); Myhill and Bradford (2012); Myhill and Quinton (2011); Norman (2009); Piquero, Gomez-Smith, and Langton (2004); Reisig and Lloyd (2009); Reisig, Tankebe, and Mesko (2014); Stott, Hoggett, and Pearson (2012); Sunshine and Tyler (2003); Tankebe (2013); Taylor and Lawton (2012); Tyler (1988, 2000, 2006, 2009, 2011); Tyler and Blader (2005); Tyler, Casper, and Fisher (1989); Tyler and Fagan (2008); Tyler, Fagan, and Geller (2014); Tyler and Huo (2002); Tyler and Jackson (2014); Tyler et al. (2007); Tyler, Schulhofer, and Huq (2010); Tyler and Wakslak (2004); Ward et al. (2011); Watson and Angell (2013); Wolfe et al. (2016).

strongly correlated with community members' perceptions of legitimacy and their cooperation with police. For example, Donner and colleagues (2015) reviewed 28 studies and concluded that police interactions with the public that are informed by concepts of procedural justice are positively correlated with public views of police legitimacy and with trust in the police. This conclusion is supported by studies that use either subjective (i.e., citizen-experienced; see Mazerolle et al., 2013b; Wolfe et al., 2016) or objective (researcher-assessed) measures (Dai, Frank, and Sun, 2011; Mastrofski, Snipes, and Supina, 1996; Mazerolle et al., 2013a) of citizen cooperation. It also correlates positively with deference to police authority as reported in surveys (Tyler and Huo, 2002; Tyler and Fagan, 2008). At the same time, there is little evidence of correlation between objective procedural justice behaviors and citizen outcomes (Nagin and Telep, 2017). Indeed, only one study (Worden and McLean, 2014) compared objective versus subjective measures of procedural justice behaviors, and it found only a small, albeit statistically significant, correlation.[15] That study also found that procedurally unjust behavior is more critical to evaluations than procedurally just behavior. These findings are consistent with Skogan's (2006a) work suggesting that negative citizen/police encounters are far more consequential for citizen attitudes toward the police than positive encounters.

This is not to say that positive encounters cannot build trust; studies show that they can. Tyler and Fagan (2008) used a panel study design to demonstrate that fair contacts were found to be statistically significantly associated with increased trust among those with contact with the New York City Police Department, although negative contacts had a stronger influence. Tyler, Fagan, and Geller (2014) used a similar panel design but focused upon 18 - to 26-year-olds in New York City. They found that both fair and unfair contacts were associated with changes in perceived legitimacy, and both were equally influential.

Several recent experimental studies explore the impact of procedurally just treatment on citizen attitudes toward the police, as well as their cooperative behavior. These studies do not at this time provide a clear conclusion regarding whether procedural justice policing improves perceptions of police legitimacy and cooperation. Mazerolle and colleagues (2013b) conducted one such study focusing upon police stops in Australia. They found that a single-stop experience that the civilian viewed as reflecting procedural justice or injustice generalized to shape trust in the police in the community. This study, called the Queensland Community Engagement Trial, was a randomized controlled trial that delivered an experimental treatment to each

---

[15] In this study, the categories used by observers were drawn from theories about procedural justice. Similarly, the dimensions of citizen perception assessed were drawn from those same theories.

stopped civilian in the form of a scripted set of officer statements during traffic checks for drunk driving. Randomly chosen officers were trained to follow a detailed protocol designed to maximize the procedural justice of the brief interactions occasioned by random breath testing (RBT). Reactions to those officers were compared with the reactions to officers not trained using this special script. Scripts were designed to incorporate the elements of procedural justice into officers' statements during the stop. During 30 of 60 RBT operations, officers were directed to use the experimental script, and senior officers monitored their compliance with the statements listed in the protocol. These police-citizen encounters were quite brief: ordinarily (i.e., in the control condition), they were "very systematic and often devoid of anything but compulsory communication" (Mazerolle et al., 2013b, p. 40). The control-condition encounter was about 20 seconds in duration and did not have the procedural justice statements. The scripted, procedurally just encounters were longer, at 97 seconds on average, but still quite brief. Each driver who was stopped during these 60 RBT encounters was given a survey to complete later and return to the researchers. The procedural justice treatment had the hypothesized impact on civilians' judgments. However, response rates, for both experimental and control drivers, were only about 13 percent. This low rate of return raised concerns about the strength and generalizability of the findings.

The design of the Queensland Community Engagement Trial, but not its results, has been replicated in other settings (MacQueen and Bradford, 2015; Sahin, 2014). MacQueen and Bradford (2015) used a block-randomized design with pre- and post-test measures built around a similar type of police-civilian experience. Their treatment was also a stop procedure that involved the presentation of key messages and subsequent distribution of a leaflet to motorists, through which they evaluated their experience. The study found no significant improvements in general trust in the police or in perceived police legitimacy.[16] Similarly, a recent experiment using traffic stops in Turkey (Sahin et al., 2016) found that officer behavior during traffic stops shaped views about the particular police officers involved but did not generalize to overall perceptions about the traffic police as an organization. And Lowrey, Maguire, and Bennett (2016), who studied street stops by having observers view video clips of police and civilian actions and verbal statements during traffic stops, found an impact upon specific evaluations of the stop, including obligation to obey the particular officers and having trust and confidence in those officers, but not on generalizations to broader attitudes about the police as an organization.

---

[16] The committee notes that the failure of the study may be due to implementation errors and does not necessarily suggest that the theory informing procedural justice is wrong (MacQueen and Bradford, 2016).

These particular forms of police contact are all highly scripted and therefore do not vary in the ways that other forms of police contact do. They do reflect the highly scripted nature of traffic stops. Worden and McLean (2016, p. 34) commented: "Traffic checkpoints that involve very brief encounters between police and citizens are susceptible to such prescriptions, but police–citizen encounters in most domains of police work—and especially in those with the strong potential for contentious interactions—do not lend themselves to such experimental or administrative manipulation." Studies of the police emphasize that the police normally deal with a wide variety of situations many of which are less scripted, and different officers have very different styles of addressing each type of situation (Muir, 1977). More specifically, Epp, Maynard-Moody, and Haider-Markel (2014) argued that it is investigatory street stops, not traffic stops, that are central to creating feelings of injustice among community residents, since traffic stops are routinized and linked to understandable violations of known laws, whereas citizens stopped on the street are often confused about what, if anything, they have done to justify the stop. Hence, traffic stops are much less likely to create variations in perceived unfairness in treatment on the part of civilians who have contact with police officers and hence are less likely to have an impact on perceived legitimacy.

In the case of assessing impact on cooperation, Mazerolle and colleagues (2013c) created a combined measure of self-reported behavioral ongoing compliance and future willingness to cooperate. They evaluated five experimental studies that provided eight outcome measures. In three of eight cases there is a statistically significant influence of police intervention upon compliance/cooperation. Mazerolle and colleagues (2013c, p. 261) concluded that the results suggest that the "interventions had [a] large, significant, positive association with a combined measure of compliance and cooperation." Another study by Mazerolle and colleagues (2014) contains an extended meta-analysis on procedural justice effects. In reviewing community policing efforts with procedural justice elements, the authors found four studies exploring influence upon compliance/cooperation and reported three statistically significant relationships in the expected direction (Mazerolle et al., p. 28). Experiencing fairness promotes compliance and cooperation. For restorative justice conferencing, they found four studies that examined influence on compliance/cooperation and four statistically significant relationships (Mazerolle et al., p. 29). The authors concluded that procedural justice has positive effects upon perceived legitimacy and that procedural justice and perceived legitimacy jointly shape self-reported compliance/cooperation.[17]

---

[17] Other studies also find an influence on cooperation (Hinds, 2009; McLean and Wolfe, 2016; Murphy, 2013; Sunshine and Tyler, 2003; Tyler and Fagan, 2008; Tyler, Goff, and MacCoun, 2015; Van Damme, Pauwels, and Svensson, 2015; White, Mulvey, and Dario, 2016).

This relatively optimistic conclusion was questioned by Nagin and Telep (2017), who reviewed the same and also more recent studies. In particular, as has been noted, several recent efforts have failed to replicate the Mazerolle study on traffic stops. In addition, the reviews by Mazerolle and colleagues took a more expansive view of studies that constitute tests of the effects of the perceived legitimacy of the police. They included any study that met other technical inclusion criterion (e.g., reported data required to measure effect sizes) and that either had as one purpose improving perceived police legitimacy or articulated an objective that was consistent with Tyler's conception of procedurally just treatment.

In light of these issues affecting the evidence base, the committee agreed that a strong conclusion regarding the impacts of procedural justice policing on people's evaluations of police legitimacy (i.e., on perceived legitimacy) or on people's cooperation with the police could not be drawn from existing studies on the police.

Recent studies suggest that perceived procedural justice may impact identification with the community, social capital, and engagement in the community (Kochel, 2012; Tyler and Jackson, 2014). Kochel (2012) studied the police in Trinidad and Tobago through interviews with 2,969 people in 13 police districts and found that the nature of police-citizen interactions was associated with collective efficacy. Collective efficacy is particularly strongly and positively associated with judgments about the quality of police services, a combined measure that includes satisfaction with services and judgments about whether the police are competent, respectful, capable of maintaining order, and willing to help citizens with their problems.[18] Tyler and Jackson (2014) conducted a national survey and found that procedural justice and perceived legitimacy of policing are associated with identification with the community, collective efficacy, and behaviors, such as likelihood of shopping in the community and participating in local politics. These findings suggest that the perceived fairness of policing has an impact beyond the arena of crime and criminal justice—it more broadly affects communities and their well-being.

This literature has several problems. First, it generally begins with community perceptions and evaluations of what the police are doing, rather than using objective, researcher-assessed first-hand accounts of actual police actions. A small number of studies directly connect police actions to perceptions about the police (Worden and McLean, 2014). For example, Mazerolle and colleagues (2013a) conducted a meta-analysis that considers six experimental studies; they concluded that interventions are found to be associated with "large, significant increase in perceptions of procedural

---

[18]Unfortunately, this study does not cleanly distinguish procedures from outcomes because it combines process and outcome measures.

justice" (Mazerolle et al., 2013a, p. 261). However, the specific police actions associated with this impact are often not clear. This is an important area for further research.

Another example is given by Jonathan-Zamir, Mastrofski, and Moyal (2015). This field observation of police–citizen interactions measured the relationship between researcher-established measures of the degree of police procedural justice behavior and the observable attitude of the citizen toward the police at the end of the encounter. Observers noted that in half of the 156 observed encounters, citizens manifested behaviors that signaled an attitudinal orientation to the police. They found a strong, statistically significant difference: "encounters in which the officer displayed higher levels of procedural justice were significantly likely to yield overall satisfaction with the police handling of the situation at the encounter's conclusion" (Jonathan-Zamir, Mastrofksi, and Moyal, 2015, p. 862). Of course, displayed attitudes may not reflect how a citizen actually feels, and the study was unable to detect any attitudinal valence for half of the observed citizens.

Worden and McLean (2014) rectified this problem. They compared different aspects of overt police officer behavior, as identified by observers, to citizens' self-reported perceptions of procedural justice. Using multiple regression analysis, they estimated that the objective ratings could account for only around 10 percent of the variance in subjective perceptions. Procedural injustice had a greater effect on subjective experience. This asymmetry is found to stem not from the relatively strong effects of negative experiences but rather from people's tendency to overestimate the procedural justice with which the police are acting, as compared to researchers' objective judgments of how the police are acting. People who deal with the police are generally positive in their ratings of police performance, even when the degree of procedural justice, as rated by observers, is low. The authors suggested that reactions to a specific experience reflect both what happens in that experience and the general attitudes toward the police that people bring into the situation.

Interestingly, the Worden and McLean (2014) findings also indicate that people's judgments about the propriety of police action are correlated more strongly to perceptions of the procedural justice of police actions than to the actual legality of officers' behavior. This echoes the results of a recent experimental study that presented people with videos of police-citizen interactions varying in procedural justice (Meares, Tyler, and Gardener, 2016). That study provided contextual information indicating that the officers acted legally or illegally. Also, respondents were presented with scenarios varying in the actual legality of police conduct. These variations had little impact upon judgments about the appropriateness of police actions. Instead, the results indicate that these citizen judgments of police propriety were primarily driven by the procedural justice of police actions, not by their actual legality.

Finally, Worden and McLean (2014) speculated that the relationship between the police and the public is a reciprocal one. They postulated that if the citizen is disrespectful or resistant, then that can lead the police to use physical force, and when the police use physical force they are then evaluated as less procedurally just. This suggests the potential limitation of studies that do not consider reciprocal influences—a possible limitation in any non-experimental study. The type of contact people have (traffic stop, investigatory stop, call for help, etc.) also shapes ratings of the police. Searches are associated with low ratings of procedural justice.

Procedural Justice and Police Practice

As this review has noted, there have been very few studies in the area of policing that connect police policies and practices and/or the actions of police officers to the perceptions of people in the community about the police. Despite the current lack of direct evidence in the policing arena, evidence exists in other literatures that suggests that developing procedural justice approaches may be possible in the arena of policing. One such area is a substantial body of research consistent with, but by no means conclusive proof of, the hypothesis that procedural justice training may change police behavior in the field. For example, there is research consistent with the idea that officers trained in the principles of procedural justice express more support for using procedural justice when dealing with people in the community than do officers without this training. The trained officers also express stronger commitment to the goals and standards of the organization they work for. Some of this evidence is the result of experimental evaluations of training programs, which can be interpreted as causal evidence (e.g., Schaefer and Hughes, 2016; Skogan, Van Craen, and Hennessy, 2015). However, the majority of this research is based on correlational analyses of the results of officer surveys, sometimes augmented with objective or third-party performance evaluations (Bradford et al., 2014; DeAngelis and Kupchik, 2007, 2009; Farmer, Beehr, and Love, 2003; Taxman and Gordon, 2009[19]; Trinkner, Tyler, and Goff, 2016; Tyler, Callahan, and Frost, 2007; Wolfe and Piquero, 2011). One should therefore be careful to not attribute a causal interpretation to these findings.

There are also a handful of studies that suggest that officers trained in procedural justice concepts may be more successful at incident de-escalation

---

[19] Taxman and Gordon (2009) survey correctional officers, and we include this study because of the strong relationship between the oversight and enforcement aspect of police and correctional officer's professional tasks.

in the field (Wheller et al., 2013; Owens et al., 2016). One approach to changing police officer behavior is through training officers to use procedural justice in their policing activities. A second approach is to make internal department dynamics more consistent with procedural justice, on the assumption that, as a consequence, officers will adopt these fairer approaches as a general aspect of how they police, without the need for explicit training programs. There is evidence consistent with the suggestion that changes in the internal dynamics of police departments lead to changes in police behavior. When officers experience their superiors in their own departments as being procedurally fair, they are perceived to be fairer in their actions when dealing with the public, they express more support for using procedural justice when dealing with people in the community, and they are less likely to engage in actions such as the use of force (Bradford et al., 2014; DeAngelis and Kupchik, 2007, 2009; Farmer, Beehr, and Love, 2003; Harris and Worden, 2014; Taxman and Gordon, 2009; Trinkner, Tyler, and Goff, 2016; Tyler, Callahan, and Frost, 2007; Wolfe and Piquero, 2011).

CONCLUSION

The research literature on interventions that take a community-based approach concentrates on three main strategies for proactive policing: community-oriented policing, broken windows policing, and procedural justice policing. The committee reviewed each of these strategies in terms of the evidence for associations with and causal impacts on community outcomes. Given the focus in the logic model for each of these strategies on altering community perceptions and behavior, there is a surprisingly limited research literature on community outcomes.

Of these three strategies, community-oriented policing has had the most extensive examination of the association of police practices with community outcomes. Nonetheless, as we noted in the beginning of the chapter, it is difficult to draw very strong conclusions from this literature. The nature of the benefits of community views of police and policing is ambiguous because there is inconsistency across studies in the conceptualization and measurement of different community outcomes. For example, measures that are presented as indicators of citizen satisfaction with police practices in one study are considered indicators of perceived legitimacy in another. This ambiguity makes the synthesis of findings across studies challenging because researchers do not apply a consistent or standardized set of measures for a given outcome.

A fundamental challenge for understanding the implications of evaluations of community-oriented policing is the great variation exhibited in the *content* of community-oriented policing elements (or tactics) that comprise the actual intervention evaluated. The range of elements, how they are specifically accomplished, and the intensity with which they are implemented vary tremendously from study site to study site. Many evaluations give short shrift to the implementation issue, yet those that have examined it in depth have found such challenges to be profound, implicating this as a source of the heterogeneity of effects that have been observed. The absence of a standardized framework for developing a meaningful taxonomy of community-oriented policing practices employed in actual interventions prevents the committee from identifying with confidence specific features, much less combinations of features, that contribute to stronger positive community impacts. Moreover, very few studies of community-oriented policing have traced its long-term effects (beyond a year) on community outcomes or its jurisdictionwide consequences. Therefore, it is difficult to say with confidence what long-term exposure to community-oriented policing produces in community reactions across the full jurisdiction. Understanding and explaining long-term trajectories of community impacts requires monitoring program implementation fidelity over time, as well as monitoring an array of forces and events that originate outside the program and the police organization.

With these limitations in mind, the committee drew the following conclusions from its review of the community-oriented policing research literature.

CONCLUSION 6-1 Community-oriented policing leads to modest improvements in the public's view of policing and the police in the short term. (Very few studies of community-oriented policing have traced its long-term effects on community outcomes or its jurisdictionwide consequences.) These improvements occur with greatest consistency for measures of community satisfaction and less so for measures of perceived disorder, fear of crime, and police legitimacy. Evaluations of community-oriented policing rarely find "backfire" effects on community attitudes. Hence, the deployment of community-oriented policing as a proactive strategy seems to offer prospects for modest gains at little risk of negative consequences.

CONCLUSION 6-2 Due to the small number of studies, mixed findings, and methodological limitations, no conclusion can be drawn about the impact of community-oriented policing on collective efficacy and citizen cooperative behavior.

Broken windows policing is often evaluated directly in terms of its short-term crime-control impacts. We have emphasized in this report that the broken windows policing model seeks to alter the community's levels of fear and collective efficacy as a method of enhancing community social controls and reducing crime in the long run. While this is a key element of the broken windows policing model, the committee's review showed that these outcomes are seldom examined. In the case of collective efficacy, only one study reported an outcome on this issue, and the committee did not believe that this evidence was persuasive enough to draw a conclusion. In the case of fear of crime, a larger number of studies were available.

> CONCLUSION 6-3 The committee is not able to draw a conclusion regarding the impacts of broken windows policing on fear of crime or collective efficacy. This is due in part to the surprisingly small number of studies that examine the community outcomes of broken windows policing and in part to the mixed effects observed.

Procedural justice policing relies on a logic model that posits that perceptions of police legitimacy are primarily responsive to community members' evaluations of the procedural justice that people experience when dealing with authorities. Procedural justice involves judgments about how fairly: (1) decisions are made and (2) people are treated. The procedural justice model of perceived legitimacy has received empirical support in psychological studies conducted in laboratory settings. The procedural justice model has also received empirical support from studies conducted by organizational psychologists in work settings. The key question for the committee is whether the relationships found in these domains can be extended to the domain of proactive policing practices in real-world communities. While there is a rapidly growing body of research on the community impacts of procedural justice policing, it is difficult to draw causal inferences from these studies because most existing studies rely on cross-sectional or correlational designs, and there are very few field experiments to clarify the causation underlying observed statistical associations. The committee therefore reached the following general conclusions regarding this question:

> CONCLUSION 6-4 In general, studies show that perceptions of procedurally just treatment are strongly and positively associated with subjective evaluations of police legitimacy and cooperation with the police. However, the research base is currently insufficient to draw conclusions about whether procedurally just policing causally influences either perceived legitimacy or cooperation.

> CONCLUSION 6-5 Although the application of procedural justice concepts to policing is relatively new, there are more extensive literatures on procedural justice in social psychology, in management, and with other legal authorities such as the courts. Those studies are often designed in ways that make causal inferences more compelling, and

results in those areas suggest that the application of procedural justice concepts to policing has promise and that further studies are needed to examine the degree to which the success of such strategies in those other domains can be replicated in the domain of policing.

While Conclusion 6-4 may appear to be at odds with a growing movement to encourage procedurally just behavior among the police (see, e.g., President's Task Force on 21st Century Policing, 2015), the committee stresses that a finding that we did not have evidence to support the expected outcomes of procedural justice policing is different from finding that such outcomes do not exist. The extant literature in this area is sparse and has only begun to develop in recent years, and the evidence from this small group of existing studies is simply not consistent enough for the committee to draw a stronger conclusion. At the same time, the principles of procedural justice are likely to be consistent with many of the goals of policing in democratic societies, a subject discussed further in Chapter 3 of this report. What is missing to date is information on the extent to which these principles will affect community attitudes toward the police as well as individuals' cooperation with the police. On the other hand, studies generally do not find negative effects of pursuing procedural justice strategies, suggesting that there is little likelihood of undermining existing trust in the police or otherwise undermining policing through implementing these approaches (although, as we suggested in Chapter 3, they may raise other concerns about legality and transparency not yet explored in the empirical literature).

7

Racial Bias and Disparities in Proactive Policing

The high rates at which non-Whites are stopped, questioned, cited, arrested, or injured by the police present some of the most salient criminal justice policy phenomena in the United States (Kochel, Wilson, and Mastrofski, 2011; Lytle, 2014). Because these kinds of police contact are associated with at least some forms of what is known as proactive policing, recognition of this reality is an important starting point for this chapter. Additionally, because many proactive policing strategies by design increase the volume of interactions between police and the public, such strategies may increase the overall opportunity for problematic interactions that have disparate impacts.

Concerns about the interaction between race and policing are not new. For example, researchers have been studying differential stop and arrest rates across demographic groups—and more generally, racial disparities in criminal justice involvement, offending, and the likelihood of becoming a crime victim—for several decades (see, e.g., Sampson and Lauritsen, 1997; Tonry, 1995). Nonetheless, several recent high-profile incidents of police shootings and other police–citizen interactions caught on camera and viewed widely have made questions regarding basic fairness, racial discrimination, and the excessive use of force of all forms against non-Whites in the United States a pressing national issue.

In considering these incidents, it is important to note that the origins of policing in the United States are intimately interwoven with the country's history of discrimination against non-White people, particularly toward Black people. From the tracking and kidnapping of enslaved Black people (Campbell, 2012) to the regulation of Black movement (Loewen, 2005) and the criminalization of Black bodies for the purpose of economic exploitation (Lichtenstein, 1996), police officers have often been the enforcement arm of both explicitly racist and tacitly discriminatory norms and laws. Although some of the more egregious historical practices ended a long time ago, others ended later and within the living memory of many Americans—and all are remembered as part of the collective history shared by Black and other non-White communities. From this perspective, it is easy to see how the nation's history is intrinsically linked to misgivings some non-White Americans continue to have about possible police animus and racial bias. And it is by no means clear that explicit animus-driven biases against non-Whites, or examples of racial animus by the police, are a thing of the past. There are certainly many examples of such problems in specific police departments, and some police agencies, as we noted in Chapter 3, have entered consent decrees to address U.S. Department of Justice findings of racial disparities in outcomes and racial bias in police practices.

The purpose of this chapter is to explore whether and to what extent proactive policing policies are deployed in a racially disparate way, if racial differences in implementation are due to racially biased behavior, and if so, what the motivation is for the bias. But before examining the evidence on these questions, we begin by defining and discussing the terminology used throughout the chapter.

Racial Disparity Racial disparities refer to objective differences that exist in the real world. The report uses the term *racial disparity* to denote outcomes that differ by race or ethnicity. For example, if in a certain community, Black people experience greater levels of poverty than White people and per capita, Black people are arrested more frequently for violent crime than White people, then these would be racial disparities in poverty and in arrest rates for violent crime. A critical point is that these differences can be discussed without assuming that race, per se, gives rise to the observed differences. For example, Black people may be arrested more frequently in part because they experience greater poverty.

Racially Biased Behavior As used in this report, the term *racial bias* refers to a difference in a person's behavior that is attributable to the race or ethnicity of another person. For example, if a police officer decides to stop and frisk Person A (who is Black), but does not stop Person B (who is White), and if the officer bases that decision entirely or in part on race, that behavior would constitute racial bias. Racial profiling is a subset of racially biased behaviors, as defined by the committee (see Chapter 3).

To be clear, racial bias refers only to behavior and as used in this report is entirely agnostic as to the psychological motives or other causes that gave rise to that behavior. Potential causes include racial animus, statistical prediction, or other risk factors (see below).

Racial Animus The report will use the term *racial animus* to describe negative attitudes toward a racial or ethnic group or toward members of such a group. For example, an officer may dislike Black or Latino people, and this attitude may lead to the racially biased behavior of an officer stopping Black or Latino people more frequently than White people with otherwise identical characteristics to those stopped. Racial animus thus refers to an internal, mental evaluation of individuals or groups based on race. Note that racial animus may give rise to racial bias in behavior, but it is certainly possible that an individual who harbors racial animus does not act on it. In such a case there would be racial animus but not racial bias in behavior. This report will use the phrase "racial animus" synonymously with "racial prejudice," although social psychologists differentiate between the two dispositions.

Statistical Prediction The report will use the term *statistical prediction* to identify racially biased behavior that is due to individual or group predictions of behavioral outcomes. For example, statistical prediction occurs in the case where there is racial bias in the choice of individuals to stop on the street because of an assessment that Blacks and Latinos have different likelihoods of carrying weapons. Economists call such prediction "statistical discrimination."

Situational Risk Factors for Racially Biased Behavior Racially biased behaviors may arise from racial animus, statistical prediction, or features of situations that facilitate differential treatment based on group membership. For instance, social psychologists argue, as we detail later in the chapter, that persons who are forced to act "quickly" may act consistent with their implicit biases, resulting in racially disparate behaviors.

With regard to motivations for racially biased behaviors, we want to briefly address the distinction between explicit and implicit attitudes. The term *explicit* is often used to describe attitudes and beliefs that are consciously and intentionally endorsed by the individual. By contrast, *implicit* is often used to describe subtle responses that are not necessarily consciously accessible to the individual and (if they are accessible) may not be endorsed. Racial animus and statistical prediction may both exist as conscious or "explicit" processes. An officer may knowingly dislike Latino people or may consciously believe that Black people commit more crime. But these processes may also operate without conscious awareness. For example, an officer may consciously espouse the idea that Black people are as good as White people and may sincerely believe that, for example, a Black and a White person in the same neighborhood wearing the same type of clothes are equally likely to be carrying weapons (meaning that there is no statistical prediction that would cause biased behavior). Still, that officer may encounter a young Black man on the street and experience a momentary negative "gut" reaction or somehow think that the individual looks suspicious. The psychology literature often refers to these kinds of reactions as implicit biases; in the terminology adopted by this committee, they are examples of racial animus or prediction. By whatever name, they are attitudes that may affect behavior.

The chapter begins by discussing the challenges involved in measuring racially biased behavior and identifying its causes. It then acknowledges the high levels of police distrust found in some non-White communities—particularly Black communities. This distrust is discussed in the context of the historical relationship between police and Black communities, through which current perceptions of legitimacy and concerns about racial animus have been forged. The next section discusses reasons that proactive policing may be associated with racial disparities or racially biased behavior. The chapter then examines the relevance and possible implications for proactive policing of racially biased behavior driven by racial animus, identity threats, and other psychological processes. Finally, the chapter focuses on economic, statistical, and sociological studies, reviewing the research on racial profiling (a subset of biased behaviors that is of particular importance for policing) and outlining a framework for thinking about the potentially racially disparate consequences of proactive policing strategies.

In reviewing each of these issues, the concern of the committee is with evaluating available evidence on whether and how issues of race are intertwined with the policies and practices of proactive policing. In many cases there is little informative quantitative data on whether the use of proactive policing is influenced by the racial or ethnic identity of citizens in a causal sense. We call attention to this lack of data because it is especially troubling, given the importance of these issues in American society and the evidence of racially disparate policing in the ethnographic and descriptive literature.

MEASURING DISPARITIES, BIAS, AND THE MOTIVATIONS FOR BIAS: ISSUES AND CHALLENGES

Identifying the role of race in someone's decision-making process is a complicated task, and determining the motive(s) behind another person's observable action is even more complicated. For example, a police officer may decide to stop and question or frisk a Black citizen but may decide not to question a White citizen, creating a racial disparity in stops. Indeed, many police departments across the country collect data on officer-citizen interactions, including characteristics of the individual stopped such as race, ethnicity, gender, and age; consequences of the interaction whether it be a citation, arrest, or a warning; information on whether the individual was searched; and in some instances the consequences of searches. Using these incident-level data, it is easy to tabulate the racial composition of those stopped, searched, arrested, cited, and so on. Studies that do such tabulations tend to find that non-White people comprise a large share of stops.

For example, in Harcourt's (2007) review of this research, the author noted studies of Maryland in the late 1990s where Blacks comprised 63 percent of all stops along Interstate 95, a study in Missouri in 2001 where Blacks and Latinos accounted for 75 percent of stops, and a study of Volusia County, Florida, where non-Whites accounted for 70 percent of stops and 80 percent of searches along Interstate 95. See also all the studies discussed in McMahon and colleagues (2002).

Based solely on measures of officer's behavior, however, it is impossible to know whether this behavior was actually racially biased.[1] If the Black and White pedestrians, for instance, acted differently as the officer approached (e.g., nervous versus calm), or if the officer encountered them in different surroundings (at night in an alley versus at noon in the park), or if the officer was searching for a suspect described as Black, an objective observer might conclude that the officer was simply responding to the situation at hand—that is, the officer was not behaving in a different way toward each citizen because of their different races.

Given the various sources of racial disparities in police–citizen interactions, how does one assess whether a disparity in outcomes reflects racially biased behavior and then identify the motivation for a bias assessed to exist? The existing empirical research on racially biased behavior answers this question in one of three ways. First, researchers have identified situations where the only plausible difference in encounters is the race of the citizen. This can be accomplished through randomized trials in a laboratory setting or by using observational data in a regression analysis framework where researchers attempt to statistically adjust for other factors that are correlated with race and may also influence an officer's decision. A second approach, benchmark analysis, involves comparisons of policing disparities to various population and/or behavioral benchmarks. Third, researchers attempt to disentangle biased behavior that is motivated by statistical prediction from

---

[1] The racial composition of stops tells us little about whether there is evidence of racial disparities. For example, the proportion of stops that are of Black people effectively reveals the likelihood that a person is Black among those who are stopped by the police. A more relevant statistic is the likelihood that Black people are stopped by the police and how this likelihood compares to those for members of other racial groups. Moving from what can be estimated with police stop data (e.g., the likelihood of being Black conditional on being stopped) to the more relevant stop rate (e.g., the likelihood of being stopped by police conditional on being Black) requires additional information. To be specific, suppose that the variable B equals 1 for individuals who are Black and 0 (zero) otherwise and that the variable S equals 1 when an individual is stopped by the police and 0 otherwise. The likelihood that a stopped individual is Black is thus given by the conditional probability $P(B = 1|S = 1)$. We want to learn the likelihood that a Black person is stopped, given by the conditional probability $P(S = 1|B = 1)$. To do so, we need additional information; specifically the unconditional probability of being stopped ($P(S)$) and the unconditional probability of being Black ($P(B)$). With this information, the likelihood that a Black person is stopped can be calculated via Bayes's theorem.

other sources using an assessment of the "productivity" of police-citizen interactions, where productivity is measured by whether contraband or some other indication of illegal activity is uncovered.

Counterfactual-Based Measures of Bias

Studies of behavior in a simulated laboratory environments offer the benefit of studying how people make decisions in situations where, by construction, the only variable that differs across encounters is the race of the subject. By manipulating the images and information given to subjects, social psychologists are potentially able to separate different motives for biased behavior. This is rarely possible in nonlaboratory regression-based analyses, which attempt to quantify the role of other, nonrace-based factors in an officer's decision and use the magnitude of those estimated relationships to extract an estimate of the influence of race.

That said, laboratory experiments suffer from problems of external validity. Even in the best, most immersive video simulation of an interaction with a hostile suspect, officers do not fire actual bullets at an actual human being, and no suspect really fires back. Further, officers are aware of the fact that they are in a simulation, and they know they are being monitored, so their behavior in an experimental study may differ from their behavior on the street.

Benchmark Measures of Bias

Benchmark studies effectively compare interracial differences in the likelihood of being stopped, employing data on the underlying racial composition of the population at risk of being stopped in conjunction with police stop data to estimate these conditional probabilities. Of course, there is much debate regarding what constitutes the appropriate population benchmark, with broad benchmarks subject to the criticism that the researcher is not properly identifying the population at risk and overly narrow benchmarks subject to the criticism that the definition of who is at risk may itself be a function of racial animus.

For example, suppose the outcome of interest was arrest-related deaths. One might argue that those at risk were those who were arrested by the police, making the race of the arrested population the relevant benchmark. However, differential arrest rates across races may reflect geographic differences in enforcement or racial bias in arrest decisions of law enforcement. To the extent that different enforcement practices contribute to racial disparities in arrest rates, using the racial composition of arrests to benchmark deaths in custody would understate the racial disparities in the risk of dying while being arrested, independent of any racial disparity in offending.

If one were interested in inequality more broadly, inclusive of how differences in poverty, educational resources, geographic segregation and isolation, and the nation's social history contribute to disparities in adverse outcomes, one might prefer the broader benchmark based on representation of the general population. However, this broader benchmark would be inappropriate for isolating the degree to which racial disproportionality in the outcomes of interest is due to disparate treatment by the police, since the societal and environmental factors included in the broader, general population benchmark will contribute to racial disparities in offending that are independent of policing practice.

Outcome-Based Measures of Bias

The third common methodological approach to studying biased behavior tests for differences in the outcomes of police–citizen interactions by the race of the citizen. Researchers performing outcome-based tests reason that, to the extent that the productivity of stopping, and perhaps searching, an identified demographic group differs from the productivity associated with other groups, the police would enhance public safety by either diverting resources away from the group in question (if the productivity rate for the group is below the average for all stops) or policing this group more intensively (if the productivity rate is above the average).

For example, suppose that an analysis of searches conducted for a given municipality reveals that drugs or other contraband are discovered in 10 percent of searches in which the citizen is Hispanic but 20 percent of searches in which the citizen is (non-Hispanic) White. Using the productivity argument outlined above, one might infer that the police are searching too many Hispanic and not enough White people to "maximize productivity"; reallocating enforcement resources from Hispanic stops to White stops would uncover more contraband. An implication of this line of reasoning is that if the rate at which contraband is discovered is equal across the two groups, then the police are not "overpolicing" one group relative to the other. In other words, the outcome test offers an empirical prediction under the null hypothesis of no bias: hit rates should be equal across racial groups. In this context, an unequal hit rate is frequently interpreted as evidence of animus-driven biased behavior; the assumption here is that statistical prediction (by the police) would generate disparities in treatment that improve the allocation of police resources, whereas racially biased behavior that is not driven by statistical prediction is likely to be driven by animus (although, as noted above, there are other causes of racially biased behavior).

Of course, this line of reasoning is too simplistic because it glosses over the potential illegality of such a biased enforcement scheme and masks a key methodological weakness of the outcome test. Regarding the first point, police practices that generate equal hit rates may prove to be unconstitutional to the extent that they are based on a strategy that targets members of a specific racial group for enhanced scrutiny. For example, suppose that young Black men are objectively more likely to carry prohibited drugs than young White men. Suppose further that young men of all races are less likely to carry drugs when the likelihood of being stopped by the police is high. Local police may rationally choose to stop Black men at a higher rate than White men and to do so until the "hit rate" (the rate at which stops and searches uncover contraband) is equal across these two groups. Doing so would minimize the amount of drug carrying, and perhaps distribution, for a given level of enforcement. However, this policy ultimately would generate a higher probability that young Black men who are not carrying are stopped and searched by the police, with the disparate treatment of Black men having a measurable disparate impact. Moreover, to the extent that officers act on an a priori assessment that Black males are more likely to be carrying, this may engender differential and perhaps less respectful and even abusive treatment of the group that is presumed guilty. The interviews of poor Black teenagers in St. Louis conducted by Brunson (2007) revealed that these young people perceived that police officers often assumed they were up to something, regularly stopped and searched them without probable cause, and often used unjustifiable violent force. In other words, even if profiling to equalize hit rates increases efficiency in terms of making arrests that generate contraband discoveries, it may certainly generate unconstitutional searches and abuse in the process, and with disparate impact.

The methodological problem associated with the empirical prediction under the null hypothesis of no bias is what some economists have deemed the "infra-marginality" problem. The outcome test for bias in treatment is essentially a test of whether the contraband discovery rate differs across groups. If the hit rate for stops made of Black people is lower than that for stops made of White people, then the common interpretation is that Black people are being held to a less stringent or lower evidentiary standard by police officers when making decisions whether to stop and search an individual. However, it is easy to generate a simple hypothetical example where suspects differ in their observable signals of culpability, where there are differences across race in the proportions that display these signals, where officers hold one group to a differential evidentiary standard, yet where the hit rates are equal across groups (see Box 7-1).

Further, if the average propensity to offend is higher among one racial group and the distributions of the offending propensity vary across racial groups, one cannot predict a priori what hit rates would be in the presence of racial animus (see Box 7-2). For example, if Black people are more likely to offend than White people, animus-driven, racially biased treatment by the police may generate higher hit rates for Blacks, equal hit rates across

BOX 7-1
The Infra-Marginality Problem

Suppose that the police stop and search people with the aim of discovering narcotics and that Black and White people encountered in the street fall into one of four categories. First, there are people who display no detectable evidence of carrying narcotics. Suppose that 1 percent (or as a probability fraction, 0.01) of people in this category are carrying narcotics. Second, there are people who, when they encounter the police, exhibit furtive movements. Suppose that 10 percent of these individuals are carrying. Third, there are people who smell like marijuana, and 20 percent of them are carrying. Finally, there are people who both exhibit furtive movements and smell like marijuana. Suppose that 50 percent of suspects encountered who display these two external signals are carrying narcotics. These four categories of individuals and the associated probabilities that a randomly chosen person within each group is carrying are summarized in the first two columns of the table below.

External Signal of Carrying Contraband	Probability of Carrying if Exhibiting Signal	Distribution of Encountered Black Suspects with Signal	Distribution of Encountered White Suspects with Signal
No Signal	0.01	0.70	0.70
Furtive Movements	0.10	0.15	0.15
Marijuana Odor	0.20	0.10	0.15
Furtive Movements & Marijuana Odor	0.50	0.05	0.00
Implied Hit Rate	-	0.20	0.20

Suppose that among both Black and White people encountered by the police, 70 percent exhibit no evidence of carrying and 15 percent exhibit furtive movements only. Hence, 85 percent of the individuals of each group exhibit lesser evidence of carrying and are similar in the proportions of the group that exhibit external signals of carrying. Suppose, however, that among the remaining 15 percent, Black suspects are more heavily distributed toward the highest culpability category. The example in the table assumes that the remaining 15 percent of White suspects smell like marijuana only. For the remaining Black suspects, we assume that 10 percent are in the "smells like marijuana" category while 5 percent are in the highest category of external signals: they both smell like marijuana and exhibit furtive movements. The distributions across these categories imply a higher average propensity to carry among Black people; that is, the likelihood of discovering contraband by randomly stopping a Black person is higher than the likelihood of randomly stopping a White person. This difference is driven entirely by the small difference in the distribution of people across the top two categories (note that the distribution across the four categories is equal for 95 percent of both groups).

Now suppose that the stopping decisions of police are racially biased in the following manner. The police stop and search all Black people who exhibit

continued

> **BOX 7-1 Continued**
>
> furtive movements or any signal with higher average culpability. They also stop and search all white people who either smell like marijuana or both smell like marijuana and exhibit furtive movements. In other words, the police apply a lower evidentiary standard to Black people than White people. In this example, the police stop 15 percent of White people, and all White people who are stopped and searched smell like marijuana. Given the assumptions shown in the table, the proportion of White stops that yield contraband will be 20 percent (the probability of carrying for individuals that exhibit this signal).
>
> By contrast, the police stop 30 percent of Black people due to the lower evidentiary standard. However, the composition of who is stopped varies in terms of the likelihood of carrying. One-half of Blacks who are stopped and searched exhibit furtive movements only, one-third of those stopped smell like marijuana, while one-sixth of those stopped exhibit both furtive movements and smell like marijuana. The hit rate for searches of Black suspects will be the weighted average of the hit rates for these three groups, calculated as 1/2(.1) + 1/3(.2) + 1/6(.5) = 0.20. Therefore, despite the differential treatment of Black people, the hit rate of Black stops in this example equals the hit rate for White stops. An outcome test applied to this case would fail to uncover the racially biased difference in evidentiary standard for a stop.
>
> The infra-marginality problem follows the fact that the hit rate observed for the average person stopped and searched does not necessarily equal the hit rate for people who are on the margin of being searched. In our example, White people who are searched are homogenous in that they all fall in the category of "smells like marijuana," and thus the average hit rate for this group identifies the hit rate for the group just above the evidentiary line drawn by the police. However, for Black people in our hypothetical example the evidentiary line is drawn at furtive movements. The average hit rate averages the carrying behavior of a heterogeneous group of suspects, which includes the hit rate for those who fall in the

racial groups, or lower hit rates for searches of Black people.[2] With this in

---

[2] An early and seminal contribution to this literature by Knowles, Persico, and Todd (2001) addressed the infra-marginality problem by offering a theoretical model whereby the search rates and carrying propensities are endogenously determined by strategic interaction between police and potential suspects. A key aspect of their theoretical model is that they assume that officers can always increase the likelihood of detection to 100 percent by focusing enforcement efforts on a specific group, a condition that forces both officers and suspects to play "mixed strategies" whereby officers search suspects at a given rate and individuals carry contraband with a given probability. In this model, the likelihood of carrying is ultimately determined by the cost to officers of searching a suspect while the likelihood of being searched is determined by the relative benefits of carrying contraband for the group in question. Bias is introduced into the model via a lower cost to officers of searching Black suspects and, in turn, a lower equilibrium carrying rate for Black citizens. Dharmapala and Ross (2004) extended the model of Knowles, Persico, and Todd (2001) to allow for imperfect observability of citizens by the

marginal category (furtive movements only) as well as the hit rates for suspects in the infra-marginal categories (smells like marijuana and both smells like marijuana and exhibits furtive movements). Hence, the average hit rate of 0.20 is higher than the hit rate of the marginal category at the evidentiary threshold applied by the police (0.10 for exhibiting furtive movements only) and cannot be used to detect the hit rate at the margin.

The numbers in this example can easily be modified to generate either relatively higher hit rates for Black stops or lower hit rates for Black stops, even when Black people are subject to racially biased treatment. For example, if the distribution of White suspects does not change but the proportion of Black suspects in the "smells like marijuana" category is reduced to 0.05 and the proportion in the most culpable category is increased to 0.10, the hit rate for Black stops now exceeds that for White stops. This second example generates a higher hit rate for Black suspects even though police behavior is assumed to be racially biased in a way that is not obviously consistent with statistical prediction. Moreover, one could not justify the differential treatment of Blacks based on this higher hit rate. The marginal Black suspects impacted by the differential treatment carry drugs at a rate similar to the White suspects who are, in a relative sense, given a pass by the police (i.e., those White suspects whose behavior falls just below the evidentiary standard that the police in this example apply to White people).

Alternatively, if the distribution of White people across these categories is held constant, the proportion of Black people in the highest culpability category is zeroed out, and the Black proportion in the "smells like marijuana" category is increased to 0.15 (making the distribution for carrying the same for Black people and White people), the hit rate for Black stops would be lower than that for White stops. In short, even in the presence of racially biased behavior, one can generate a relatively lower hit rate for Black stops, a relatively higher hit rate for Black stops, or hit rates that are equal across races.

---

mind, it is likely that any comparison of hit rates across groups provides a somewhat asymmetric test for animus against Blacks. Specifically, lower hit rates imply disparate treatment. However, equal or even higher hit rates for Blacks cannot rule out bias or animus (see Dharmapala and Ross, 2004, for an alternative development of this argument).

---

police. The innovation here is to admit the possibility that for most individuals, the police cannot increase the likelihood of detection to 100 percent given resource constraints. With this extension, there will be some individuals for whom the relative benefits of carrying are high and for whom the pure strategy of always carrying dominates. To the extent that the fraction of the population for whom this pure strategy is optimal differs across racial groups, the inframarginality problem reemerges and the strong predictions from Knowles, Persico, and Todd (2001) regarding the consequences of bias for relative hit rates disappears.

> **BOX 7-2**
> **Limitations of Outcome-Based Methodological Approaches**
>
> Implicit in both the outcome-based and benchmarking methodological approaches are conceptualizations of whether observable racial disparities are justifiable; these conceptualizations are partial and overly narrow. Neither is based on a clear articulation of the social objectives that society hopes to achieve through the delegation of coercive power to local police departments. For example, suppose that the proper objective of the police is simply to respond to and investigate crimes that occur. In this instance, a comparison of racial disparities in arrests to racial disparities in offending would be informative as to whether the arrest disparities are unwarranted. On the other hand, suppose that the social objective is to minimize the social costs caused by criminal victimization. In this instance, policing resources should be devoted toward those activities that generate the highest level of general deterrence and offender incapacitation and focus on crimes that are particularly socially costly. Whether a racial disparity is unwarranted or not would then depend on racial disparities in susceptibility to deterrence, in the prospects of incapacitation through policing efforts, and in the severity of crimes typically committed. As a further alternative, suppose the objective that society wishes the police to pursue is to minimize the total social costs associated with both criminal victimization and the criminal justice system, inclusive of social tensions between the police and citizens created by frequent coercive encounters. To the extent that the latter (social tensions between police and citizens) is a byproduct of activity that reduces crime, local police departments confront a trade-off in deciding whether a given level of enforcement efforts targeted at a specific community is warranted.
>
> A more fundamental problem with the outcome test concerns the actual objectives that police are pursuing or should be pursuing. The discussion of outcome-based tests presumes that police are seeking to maximize the detection of contraband net of the costs of search. One might contend that discovering contraband should be pursued only insofar as pursuing this objective minimizes the social costs of crime and punishment. Manski (2006) offers a more general framework for analyzing optimal enforcement strategies, in which the social costs of completed offenses, punishment, and searches are considered in allocating enforcement resources and determining the optimal rates to stop and search individuals from different demographic groups. Optimal enforcement strategies depend on the degree to which the criminal behavior of individuals can be deterred and the degree to which deterrence effects vary across individuals. Social costs are minimized by concentrating enforcement on groups whose offending is more responsive to changes in the search probability. In the face of such heterogeneity, an optimal strategy may certainly result in differential ex-post offending (i.e., hit rates) among members of different groups. With this alternative framing of society's objectives, there are no clear predictions regarding how hit rates should vary in the presence of biased treatment targeted at one demographic group.

HISTORICAL BACKGROUND ON RACIAL DISPARITIES, BIAS, AND ANIMUS IN POLICING

There is a large and persistent gap in the level of trust that non-White people have in law enforcement as compared to White people, a longstanding phenomenon that is a function of the history reviewed below. This difference is highlighted in a recent study from the Cato Institute (Ekins, 2016). That study found that 68 percent of White respondents viewed the police favorably, while 40 percent of Black respondents reported favorable views. Black respondents (73%) were more likely to say that the police are too quick to use force than were White respondents (35%), and Black respondents were more likely to say that police tactics are generally too harsh (56% versus 26% for White respondents). Similarly, 43 percent of Black respondents, but 62 percent of White respondents, say the police are courteous; 31 percent of Black respondents, but 64 percent of White respondents, believe that the police treat everyone equally; and about 4 in 10 Black respondents rate the police highly in terms of enforcing the law, protecting them from crime, and responding quickly to calls for help, as opposed to approximately 6 in 10 White respondents.

In recent years, gaps have also developed between White people and Hispanic people; in 2015, there was a 5 percentage-point difference in the fraction of White respondents (57%) and Hispanic respondents (52%) who placed "a great deal" or "quite a lot" of confidence in the police (Jones, 2015). The Cato Institute study discussed above finds even larger gaps between White people and Hispanic people in the views held about the police (Ekins, 2016). We note that the more frequently measured racial gap between White people and Black people in views about the police is generally unchanged over recent decades and that overall trust in the police as measured by national polls, such as the Gallup Poll, has remained more or less constant over the past 30 years, with between 50 and 60 percent of adult Americans expressing trust in the police (Balz and Clement, 2014; Jones, 2015).

A representative survey of police officers in the United States revealed similar differences in how White and Black police officers viewed treatment of non-White people (Weisburd and Greenspan, 2000). More than half of Black officers, compared with just 17 percent of White officers, agreed or strongly agreed that Whites received "better treatment" than Blacks. A recent evaluation of video-recorded traffic stops made in Oakland, California, during April 2014 provides empirical support for the Black officers' self-reports (Voigt et al., 2017). That study found that officers were more likely to speak to Black drivers in informal familiar language (e.g., "man" versus "sir"), while also using more harsh legal terms (e.g., arrest versus registration), and fewer explanatory terms (e.g., "the reason . . ." or ". . . because . . .") (Voigt et al., 2017).

These differences extend to how officers feel about the need for police reform, particularly with respect to how the police interact with people in non-White communities. For example, a recent survey of police officers conducted by the Pew Research Center (Morin et al., 2017) found that 27 percent of White officers, but 69 percent of Black officers, said that the protests that followed fatal encounters between police and Black people were motivated to at least some extent by a genuine desire to hold police accountable, whereas 92 percent of White officers, but only 29 percent of Black officers, said that the country has made the changes needed to ensure equal rights for Black people.

The response of people from different communities to a particular police incident or policing strategy is a function not only of the contemporary actions of the law enforcement but also of the historical relationship between those communities. The historical record provides the framework for how those contemporary actions are viewed. In this section, we begin with a historical context for thinking about how changes in policing practices may be viewed in different communities, particularly non-White communities, in the United States.

This section largely focuses on the relationship between Blacks (and Black communities) and the police. Blacks have been the largest non-White group for most of American history, whereas the Hispanic population in the United States was relatively small for most of the 20th century. It was only in the mid-1980s that the Hispanic population began to grow at the pace typical of recent years. In 1970, Blacks represented 11 percent of the population of the United States, while Latino/Hispanics represented 4.6 percent. By 2013, Blacks comprised 12.3 percent of the population and Latino/Hispanics represented 17.1 percent (National Academies of Sciences, Engineering, and Medicine, 2016). Though there are some portions of the Hispanic community that have long histories with the police, such as Mexican Americans in the Southwest and Puerto Ricans in New York City, there is relatively less historical analysis of these policies. A notable exception is Garcia's (1980) documentation of the extent of cooperation between federal immigration officials and local police departments during the 1950s; Perea and colleagues (2014) also include considerable material on the police and Latinos.

Before we review key moments in the history of race and policing in the United States, three important points of clarification are necessary. First, the purpose of this short summary is not to document the specific history of each of the roughly 18,000 law enforcement agencies in the United States. Rather, we will describe policies, both federal and more local, that potentially influenced all local agencies because of their national character or that were commonplace in areas where most Black people lived (the "Black Belt" South and northern urban centers) (see North, 1981; Hagan, Shedd, and Payne, 2005; Walker, Spohn, and DeLone, 2007).

Second, this is not a history of racial animus or bias in the formation and application of proactive policing strategies in particular (about which relatively little is known). Rather, the discussion focuses on the role of racial bias in general, and animus in particular, in police practices in general and the resultant disparate impacts on members of specific racial and ethnic groups. Current proactive policing policies have developed and have been implemented in an era in which the police are widely credited with having made considerable improvement in their behavior when dealing with Black Americans and with predominantly Black communities (National Research Council, 2004). But the form, impact, and perception of these policies are certainly affected by this history.

Third, in this account the committee has sought to highlight how the structure of criminal justice policies, both in the past and today, can have the effect of both creating and perpetuating racial inequality in the absence of explicit racial animus or racially biased behavior. Thus, while some policies might plausibly be considered to be grounded in "race neutral" reasons, it is critical to understand that these policies can have important negative economic, social, and health impacts on non-White people in society. As discussed in Chapter 3, this makes systematic bias in policing policies particularly difficult to identify and potentially address in both a legal and social science sense.

Racial Animus in Federal, State, and Local Policies

Police are charged with enforcing laws and ordinances in the communities they serve. For the majority of people living in the United States, the police are the visible face of the government and certainly of the criminal justice system. This means that police officers historically, in the course of their jobs, were tasked with enforcing rules that in some instances, as in the case of vagrancy laws, explicitly disadvantaged non-White people (Goluboff, 2016; Douglas, 1960).

There are plenty of examples from American history of policies that were explicitly the product of racial animus and deliberately disadvantaged Black people. These policies often relied on local police for the force of law. For example, the Fugitive Slave Act of 1850 specifically instructed local judges to issue warrants for the arrest of people who had fled across state boundaries despite being "held to service." The act required those warrants to be acted upon by local law enforcement and also introduced criminal penalties for interfering with the apprehension of slaves who had escaped to free territory.

Even after the passage of the Fourteenth Amendment, local governments continued to pass laws that specifically required police officers to arrest Black people or people who engaged in certain economic transactions with Black people. In cities throughout the country, Black people were prohibited from otherwise public spaces that were reserved for White people, including but not limited to swimming pools, lunch counters, restrooms, water fountains, and public schools. People who entered these spaces in violation of local ordinances were arrested by the police (Hinton, 2016a, 2016b; Goluboff, 2016; Branch, 1998).

Prior to 1948, communities could freely adopt racially restrictive covenants that criminalized the leasing of property to non-White people or to members of certain religious groups (Brooks and Rose, 2013). Many of these restrictive covenants were adopted in what became known as "sundown towns": municipalities that had either formal or informal policies that regulated when Black people could move freely in the town. Specifically, Black people were permitted to travel to town, to work, and to shop, but they had to leave "before the sun went down" (Loewen, 2005). Punishment for disobeying these rules could be violent and was often delivered by police officers or sheriff's deputies. Because these sundown-town policies often were informal, it is difficult to determine when the practice ended—or whether it completely has. In his archival and ethnographic research, Loewen (2005) found formal signs demarking sundown towns as late as the 1970s, with officials in some jurisdictions still admitting to informal enforcement as recently as 2001.

Racial Disparities in Federal, State, and Local Policies

In addition to the criminal justice system being used for explicitly racist purposes, U.S. history is replete with examples of changes to the criminal justice system that have, at minimum, disparate impacts on non-White communities. These examples are particularly relevant, as modern proactive policies are often implemented in a manner that can be justified legally in race-neutral terms (although important concerns about the extent to which proactive policies interact with enforcement of the Fourteenth Amendment are discussed in Chapter 3). For the purpose of providing historical context, we highlight some particularly salient examples of policy changes that, despite having as a touchstone the seemingly objective goal of crime reduction, are now commonly understood both to have had serious negative implications for non-White people and to have enhanced, rather than mitigated, racial inequality in the United States (Alexander, 2012; Garland, 2001b; Hinton, 2016a, 2016b; Pager, 2003; Holzer, Raphael, and Stoll, 2006; Raphael and Stoll, 2013). A direct implication of this history is that, in the absence of clear evidence to the contrary, the historical record does not support the assertion that changes in policing policies should be "given the benefit of the doubt" in terms of the relative harm they cause to White and non-White people.

The Thirteenth Amendment to the U.S. Constitution prohibited slavery "except as punishment for crime." In other words, forced labor was still allowed, as long as the laborer had been convicted of a crime. As documented by Ransom and Sutch (1977), Foner (1988), Lichtenstein (1993, 1996), Mancini (1996), Ingram (2014), and LeFlouria (2015), after the ratification of the Thirteenth Amendment, southern state and county governments quickly enacted a series of laws known collectively as the "Black Codes" (Ransom and Sutch, 1977). While technically race neutral, these laws in practice were applied almost exclusively to Black people and were actively used to control and limit the newly freed population. Georgia, for example, criminalized hunting on Sundays and letting cattle roam free, but only in counties with large Black populations (Foner, 1988). A key feature of all of these laws was a vagrancy statute requiring individuals to prove, on demand and in writing, that they were employed. Failure to do so would result in arrest and fine, incarceration, or both (Ransom and Sutch, 1977). In spite of the fact that late 19th century employment rates appeared to be higher among Black adults than White adults (Higgs, 1977), vagrancy laws were almost exclusively used to arrest non-White people and continued to be used to arrest "uppity" non-White people and "radicals" through the 1960s (Lichtenstein, 1993; Goluboff, 2016).

Once arrested and convicted (Black Codes also tended to prohibit non-White people from serving on juries), Black people were no longer protected by the Thirteenth Amendment. In fact, state penitentiaries and county jails would charge private citizens for the privilege of "leasing" the labor of incarcerated individuals. The practice was lucrative for states, with several states drawing more than 50 percent of their annual state income from such revenue at the so-called "nadir" of American race relations in 1901 (Lichtenstein, 1996). Although the Panic of 1907 made convict leasing less profitable, the Federal Aid Road Act of 1916 allowed states to use the value of convict labor as part of their "match" for federal highway funding, reinvigorating the process (Schoenfeld, 2014). This produced a perverse incentive for states to arrest individuals from vulnerable populations— overwhelmingly Black people—to serve as revenue engines for the state (Larsen, 2016; Lichtenstein, 1993). This practice, although formally abolished by Alabama (the last state) in 1928, persisted in less formal ways until it was finally outlawed in 1941, a mere 75 years ago (Blackmon, 2009).

Law Enforcement Resistance to the Civil Rights Movement

Specific actions of individual police officers, along with policies and practices ordered by mayors or governors, created a situation in which law enforcement was used to deny or limit the social, economic, and legal rights of Black people during the Civil Rights Movement. Central components of modern U.S. history are the images of state and local law enforcement officers using force against Black men, women, and children engaged in either acts of peaceful protest (as in the Selma to Montgomery March led by the Student Nonviolent Coordinating Committee on March 7, 1965) or exerting their federally protected rights (as in the state-controlled Arkansas National Guard prohibiting nine Black students from entering Little Rock's Central High School during September 5–20, 1957). As suggested by the events that led up to and followed the trial leading to the Supreme Court's decision in *United States v. Price* (383 U.S. 787 [1966])—better known as the Mississippi Burning case—local law enforcement sometimes interfered even more violently with civil rights efforts. In that incident, members of the Neshoba County Sheriff's office and a Philadelphia, Mississippi, police officer were eventually convicted by federal prosecutors for conspiring with members of the Ku Klux Klan and others to murder three civil rights workers who had gone to Philadelphia to register Black voters in the summer of 1964.

Racial Disparities in Criminal Justice Contact Driven by Federal Policy

This active resistance by law enforcement to the Civil Rights Movement coincided with federal government policies that expanded the physical presence of officers in places where many Black people lived, resulting in greater entanglement of Black people in the criminal justice systems of states and cities. Two weeks after President Johnson signed the Civil Rights Act of 1964 into law, the killing of an unarmed Black 15-year-old boy by New York City police sparked the Harlem uprising and a wave of other disturbances that summer—prompting President Johnson to call for a "War on Crime." One of the major components of the War on Crime was the enactment of the Law Enforcement Assistance Act of 1965 and the Omnibus Crime Control and Safe Streets Act of 1968. Both bills created new federal grant programs that directed federal funds to local law enforcement agencies through the Justice Assistance Grant (JAG) Program. This program increased the level of policing in areas that recorded more violent crimes, which in many areas has led to greater policing of poorer and/or more predominantly Black communities.

The "War on Drugs" that developed during the presidency of Richard Nixon provides another example of the criminal justice system being used in a way that disproportionately impacted non-White communities. As the federal government expanded the War on Drugs through the 1980s, the disparity in implementation manifested itself in two notable ways. First, Black people were arrested for drug use in proportions, as a percentage of group population, that were much higher than survey data on drug use would predict. By the early 1990s, Black adults made up only 13 percent of drug users (according to survey data) but constituted 40 percent of those arrested for drug violations (Langan, 1995).

Second, federal penalties for drug violations put in place by the Anti-Drug Abuse Act of 1986 were substantially more severe for drugs that Black people were more likely to use. In 1993, the National Household Survey on Drug Abuse found that 12 percent of White people over the age of 12 reported any lifetime use of cocaine, compared with 9.5 percent of Black and Latino people. The same survey found that cocaine in its processed, "crack" form was more popular among Black and Hispanic people than among White people: 3.4 percent of Black and 2.0 percent of Hispanic people over the age of 12 admitted to ever using crack cocaine, compared to 1.6 percent of White people. With little debate, the Anti-Drug Abuse Act imposed a 5-year mandatory minimum sentence for possession of only 5 grams of crack cocaine, while it imposed the same mandatory minimum punishment for possession of 500 grams of powder cocaine. Although the social settings of typical transactions for crack and powder cocaine are different and the faster absorption of processed crack cocaine leads to different consumption experiences (Nestler, 2005; National Institute on Drug Abuse, 2016), the 100:1 weight ratio in thresholds for punishment for crack and powder put in place in 1986 is difficult to justify using objective measures of social harm (Bobo and Johnson, 2004; Tonry and Melewski, 2008). Despite repeated recommendations by the U.S. Sentencing Commission to revise the crack quantity thresholds upward, to lessen the disparity between the sentencing scheme for the two forms of the drug, and several legislative efforts to mitigate the difference, Congress did not act to reduce the sentencing disparity between crack and powder cocaine until the Fair Sentencing Act of 2010.

Finally, the Violent Crime Control and Safe Streets Act of 1994, which itself contained no explicit mention of race, was enacted in the context of fears of "super-predators": understood to be young people with "absolutely no respect for human life and no sense of the future," who were overwhelmingly from "[B]lack inner-city neighborhoods" (DiLulio, 1995). This law implemented mandatory life sentences for people convicted of serious federal crimes if they had previously been convicted of drug or violent offenses at the federal or state level. While race-neutral on their face, such repeat-offender sanctions and "three strikes" laws, which impose longer punishments on people who have had more frequent interactions with the criminal justice system, have led to racial disparities in punishment. In part supported by federal funding programs designed to increase local policing, police departments serving cities with more than 250,000 people have more police per capita (around 22 per 1,000 people in 2014) than departments in other places (about 16 per 1,000 people in 2014) (U.S. Department of Justice, 2014). To the extent that the Black population of the United States is more likely to live in larger cities than the White population,[3] Black people are more likely to come in contact with the police, all other things being equal, simply because they live in places where there are more police officers.

Pointing out the instances in which criminal justice policies, and policing in particular, have differentially impacted Black people does not invalidate the observation that Black and other non-White communities have benefited from some policies that have brought greater focus on crime within their communities. Policing, like clean water, good street lighting, and public transportation, is a public good designed in principle to help victims of crime and, more generally, support community members in achieving their goals and projects. During the same period that birthed these social policies and proactive policing, many Black communities expressed a desire for both harsher punishments of criminal behavior and more responsive policing (Fortner, 2015; Kennedy, 1997). In fact, a parallel (if less prominent) critique of police and race in the United States is that Black neighborhoods have historically suffered from under-policing (Kennedy, 1997; Forman, 2017).

There is a growing body of evidence that exposure to violence and crime is an important component of persistent poverty (Sharkey and Torrats-Espinosa, 2017; McCoy et al., 2015; Sharkey et al., 2014), and scholars have also found that segregated Black neighborhoods have historically suffered from under-policing (Kennedy, 1997; Meares, 1998). Taken together, these findings imply (although they do not prove) that reductions in crime may reduce some forms of racial inequality. It is certainly the case that the spectacular declines in U.S. crime rates since their peak in the early 1990s were disproportionately concentrated in the nation's largest cities (and in particular, in the central cities of metropolitan areas), in which the population is disproportionately non-White (Kneebone and Raphael, 2011). These declines greatly reduced the disparity in crime rates relative to suburban cities. Within cities, there is also evidence suggesting that these declines in crime accrued disproportionately to non-White neighborhoods (Lofstrom and Raphael, 2016).

While this link has not been conclusively and explicitly proven, the

---

[3] Based on the 2014 American Community Survey, 20 percent of Black people versus 7.6 percent of White people live in cities with more than 250,000 residents (Ruggles et al., 2015).

crime reductions associated with proactive policies may place downward pressure on one component of inequality in the United States. Over the past 40 years, police departments across the country have become more diverse (Sklansky, 2005), a phenomenon that has been credibly shown to reduce one potential measure of bias in policing—the relative arrest rates of Black and White adults—without affecting official crime rates (McCrary, 2007). Table 7-1 presents tabulations from various sources on the racial composition of police and other law enforcement entities. Panel A shows data on local sworn officers for the period 1987 through 2013 from the Law Enforcement and Administrative Statistics Survey (LEMAS). Panel B shows similar estimates from the Decennial Census for the period 1950 through 2015 on the racial composition of individuals who self-report their occupation as "Police Officers and Detectives." Panel C presents similar tabulations from the Decennial Census for those who self-report as "Sheriffs, Bailiffs, Correctional Officers, and Jailers."

While there are some discrepancies between these different measures, the underlying trends are quite clear. In the 1950s, law enforcement officers were largely White. By 2015, over a quarter of police officers and detectives were from non-White groups, as were roughly a third of sheriff's deputies and correctional officers. This finding is consistent with data from LEMAS according to which law enforcement agencies overall have become more diverse since 1987 and departments serving larger jurisdictions have become even more diverse (Reaves, 2015; see also Equal Employment Opportunity Commission, 2016, p. 13). However, a study analyzing police personnel data for 269 police departments in jurisdictions with more than 100,000 residents also found that (1) there are still substantial gaps between the representation of non-Whites within law enforcement agencies and their demographic representation in communities, and (2) the representation of non-Whites in police departments has not kept pace with changing demographics (*Governing*, 2015; see also Equal Employment Opportunity Commission, 2016, p. 13).

In summary, while there have been important changes in the scope for racial bias and animus in policing, with respect to the impact of proactive policing on racial bias and disparate outcomes, law enforcement in the United States does not start with a clean slate. As noted by Chief Terrence M. Cunningham in his presidential address to the International Association of Chiefs of Police, "this dark side of our shared history has created a generational—almost inherited—mistrust between many non-White communities and the law enforcement agencies that serve them" (Jackman, 2016).

This perspective is echoed in the discussions that the committee had with representatives from Black Lives Matter (see Appendix A). The committee was urged repeatedly by community advocates to avoid a narrow

TABLE 7-1 Racial/Ethnic Composition of Law Enforcement in the United States

Panel A: Minority Representation Among Local Police Officers, 1987–2013, from the Law Enforcement Management and Administrative Statistics Survey

Year	Non-Hispanic White	Non-Hispanic Black	Non-Hispanic Other	Hispanic	Non-White (Total)
1987	0.85	0.09	0.01	0.05	0.15
1990	0.83	0.11	0.01	0.05	0.17
1993	0.81	0.11	0.02	0.06	0.19
1997	0.79	0.12	0.02	0.08	0.22
2000	0.77	0.12	0.03	0.08	0.23
2003	0.76	0.12	0.03	0.09	0.24
2007	0.75	0.12	0.03	0.10	0.25
2013	0.73	0.12	0.04	0.12	0.27

Panel B: Racial and Ethnic Composition of Police Officers and Detectives, 1950–2015, Tabulated from the Integrated Public Use Microdata Samples

Year	Non-Hispanic White	Non-Hispanic Black	Non-Hispanic Other	Hispanic	Non-White (Total)
1950	0.97	0.02	0.00	0.01	0.03
1960	0.94	0.04	0.00	0.02	0.06
1970	0.91	0.06	0.01	0.02	0.09
1980	0.86	0.09	0.01	0.04	0.14
1990	0.82	0.10	0.02	0.06	0.18
2000	0.77	0.11	0.04	0.09	0.23
2010	0.74	0.10	0.04	0.12	0.26
2015	0.73	0.10	0.05	0.12	0.27

Panel C: Racial and Ethnic Composition of Sheriffs, Bailiffs, Correctional Officers and Jailers, 1950–2015, Tabulated from the Integrated Public Use Microdata Samples

Year	Non-Hispanic White	Non-Hispanic Black	Non-Hispanic Other	Hispanic	Non-White (Total)
1950	0.95	0.01	0.00	0.03	0.05
1960	0.94	0.03	0.00	0.02	0.06
1970	0.92	0.05	0.01	0.02	0.08
1980	0.79	0.15	0.01	0.05	0.21
1990	0.77	0.15	0.02	0.06	0.23
2000	0.69	0.20	0.03	0.08	0.31
2010	0.69	0.19	0.03	0.09	0.31
2015	0.67	0.18	0.04	0.11	0.33

SOURCES: Panel A data from Reaves (2015) and Panels B and C data from Integrated Public Use Microdata Samples.

framing of proactive policing and to frame the ways in which communities experience policing. For instance, Brittany Packnett, a leader in the Black Lives Matter movement and a national figure in the wake of the Ferguson, Missouri, protests, advised the committee to include the full context that shapes community experiences, from history to broader social constructions of race (see Appendix A). She elaborated:

> I think the tactic [of proactive policing] doesn't feel neutral when it's divorced from the other realities. . . . Folks in those neighborhoods are saying "Why aren't you doing anything to invest in the reasons why this is a hot spot in the first place?" When it feels divorced from other realities it feels like every single time there is going to be some level of bias attached. . . . Because you are coming over here because we're poor. Well, why are we poor? . . . Why is it all Black and Latino over here? . . . It is impossible to divorce those realities when you live in this skin and when you live in our zip code . . . [proactive policing will always feel biased] because they require a need to ignore *why* things are the way they are and simply address *that* things are the way they are. . . . That lack of context always feels biased.[4]

The committee views this perspective as important to keep in mind throughout the remaining sections of the chapter. Because the focus of our study task is on policing, we do not examine the broader social forces that lead to the outcomes that police address. As Ms. Packnett suggested to the committee, an alternative approach would be to employ social rather than policing interventions to address crime problems. Although such approaches have been suggested to address, for example, crime hot spots (see Weisburd, Telep, and Lawton, 2014), they have not been developed broadly as crime prevention approaches in recent years. The choice of policing as a response to crime problems is in itself a policy decision that has implications for communities. This issue is beyond the scope of the committee's deliberations but one that we think is important for policy makers to consider as they explore crime prevention approaches.

The historical and contemporary social context of policing plays a role in how communities perceive police behavior, and one cannot assess the motivation for or effect of disparate treatment or racially biased behavior without recognizing that proactive policing is nested in the more general historical context of racial disparities and bias in policing. This context must include attention to the experiences of Black and other non-White Americans, with due consideration to the impacts on Black and other non-White communities.

---

[4] We should note that Ms. Packnett may not have been using "bias" in the way in which the committee has defined the term for the purposes of this report.

POTENTIAL REASONS WHY MODERN PROACTIVE POLICING MAY BE ASSOCIATED WITH DISPARITIES AND BIAS

The committee identified four components of many proactive policing strategies that are plausibly related to an increase in racially disparate criminal justice outcomes. These features of proactive policing may lead to racial bias in department policy in general, as well as in individual officers' decisions about stops and arrests. As discussed in later sections, only a limited body of research has empirically tested the causal connections between these potential mechanisms and changes in racial disparities and racial bias.

First, if non-White people are more likely to commit criminal offences, racial disparities in police-citizen interactions are likely to occur. Earlier reviews of the empirical literature did indeed document relatively higher offending rates among Black people in the United States (Sampson and Lauritsen, 1997; Tonry, 1995), rates that were likely influenced by a range of factors known to increase crime, including differences in income, education, social networks, discrimination, neighborhood characteristics, and many others. More recently, O'Flaherty (2015, Chapter 11) reviewed empirical trends from homicide statistics and victimization surveys, which revealed a higher offending rate among Black people for homicide and robbery. Hence, a proactive effort to combat robbery may generate a racial disparity in arrest rates to the extent that members of one group commit this offense at a higher rate than the comparison group.

Disparities in the historical relationship between law enforcement and residents of difference races and ethnicities can manifest not only as differential crime rates across demographic groups but also as different behaviors on the part of citizens interacting with police. Extensive research demonstrates that, compared to White people, Black people are more distrustful and nervous (even scared) when interacting with a police officer (e.g., see Najdowski, Bottoms, and Goff, 2015). To the officer, this nervousness may appear suspicious (Najdowski, 2011), and the officer may stop and question the Black person based, in part, on this "suspicious" behavior. As a second example, U.S. neighborhoods are generally still segregated by race, and areas with more Black residents tend to have lower income and more crime. Accordingly, officers are statistically more likely to encounter Black citizens in high-crime neighborhoods. An officer may decide to question a Black suspect partly because the encounter occurs in a high-crime area (Terrill and Reisig, 2003). In both of these cases, a dimension that rightfully influences an officer's decision (the citizen's nervous behavior or the perception of greater danger at the location) is related to the suspect's race.

Second, police departments may prioritize enforcing ordinances and laws that non-Whites are more likely to violate. For example, if Black and Latino drug users are more likely to purchase narcotics on street corners or in open air markets, whereas White drug users are more likely to conduct transactions in private spaces, local drug enforcement that prioritizes "buy busts" will generate racial disparities in arrests. Disparities may also result from explicit or implicit priorities communicated by police leadership to officers on patrol. Certainly a proactive departmentwide policy of targeting, say, young Black men would be unconstitutional. Nonetheless, in a nation with nearly 18,000 independent law enforcement agencies, it is possible that such policies articulated from the top govern law enforcement practice in some jurisdictions.

Third, policing efforts may be geographically concentrated. This may result naturally from the geographic concentration of calls for services and calls to report a crime that initiate investigations. Alternatively, disparities may result from proactive strategies that target specific neighborhoods. To the extent that high-crime areas that disproportionately generate calls for service are more likely to become the focus of proactive strategies and more likely to be located in non-White neighborhoods, racial disparities in the incidence of police–citizen interactions will result. More focused geographic programs, such as hot spots policing, may reduce overall police intrusion in larger neighborhoods by focusing on the small number of streets that have high-crime rates (D. Weisburd, 2016). Nonetheless, non-White people may in turn be overrepresented on the targeted streets.

Finally, proactive policies that target high-activity offenders or those with more extensive criminal histories are likely to involve non-White suspects disproportionately. As previously discussed, non-White, and particularly Black, Americans are more likely to live in areas with more police per capita. This will likely result in more contact with the police, and thus an increased probability of being identified as a high-activity offender for Black people relative to otherwise identical White people.

EVIDENCE FROM PSYCHOLOGICAL SCIENCE ON RACIAL BIAS IN POLICING

This section attempts to evaluate the contribution contemporary psychological science can make to understanding the role of racial bias in proactive policing. A central focus of the relevant research is disaggregating the causes of biased behavior into two factors: "dispositional factors," which are individual differences that tend to predict an individual's relative tendency to engage in biased behaviors, and "situational factors" that tend to provoke such behaviors. Further, when psychologists discuss dispositional factors in the literature, they tend to refer to individual differences in "stereotyping" and "prejudice" (Stangor and Crandall, 2013). While not identical, these terms are similar to "statistical prediction" and "animus" as defined by the committee, and in the interest of simplicity we will use the committee's terms in reviewing the literature. A broad term some social psychologists use for situations that can tend to facilitate disparate treatment—regardless of the presence or absence of dispositional factors associated with bias—is "identity traps" (Goff, 2013, 2016; Goff and Godsil, 2017).

The Psychological Science of Bias

Studying racial animus and statistical prediction has been a central concern of American psychology since nearly the start of the 20th century. During that era in American history, negative racial attitudes were more openly expressed than is typical today. Overt, non-anonymous expressions of racial animus have declined markedly in American society because social norms have evolved to prohibit them (Dovidio, 2001; Dovidio and Gaertner, 2004). For example, self-reports of so-called "old-fashioned racism" in which people took pride in their anti-Black feelings, have decreased over time, and Whites' stated support for integration and interracial marriage has increased. Similarly, evaluations of the police have suggested that there have been important gains in professionalism, leading to less racial animus among law enforcement officers (National Research Council, 2004).

Although overt expressions of biased behavior have declined in society and among police, racial animus has not disappeared. Rather, it has evolved.[5] Researchers have developed a variety of tasks that measure animus and statistical prediction indirectly or implicitly. While this research has had little direct translation to the field of policing, it does establish basic findings about factors and situations where people are more likely to express, and act upon, negative racial attitudes. These findings have potential implications for how the actions of individual police officers, and policing policies more generally, may be shaped by attitudes such as racial animus or prediction.

For example, in one influential study, participants sat at a computer and completed a series of trials on which a face appears briefly and is quickly followed by a word (Fazio et al., 1995). Regardless of the face, participants are asked to classify each word as either "positive" or "negative." But participants are typically influenced by the face. When a Black face precedes the word, participants are often faster to identify a negative word and slower to identify a positive word; when a White face precedes

---

[5] It is important to note that social psychology has largely focused on studying Black/White racial biases. Although several researchers have acknowledged this limitation, such acknowledgment does little to counteract the limits on the field's ability to generalize across interracial groups. Consequently, much of the literature reviewed here will necessarily be limited to a discussion of Black/White biases.

the word, they are often faster to classify a positive word and slower to classify a negative word. The evidence from this task (and many others like it) suggests that participants associate Black people (more than White people) with negativity. Similar work suggests that Blacks (more than Whites) are associated with weapons and with the general concept of danger (Payne, 2001). These implicit measures are potentially valuable tools in exploring racial attitudes because they have the potential to uncover attitudes that participants are unwilling to report when asked directly. These measures may even show associations of which the participants, themselves, are unaware. Critically, these forms of animus may influence real-world behavior, including interracial interactions (Dovidio, Kawakami, and Gaertner, 2002; McConnell and Leibold, 2001).[6]

There is, to our knowledge, no peer-reviewed work in psychology examining how any motivating factors, implicit or explicit, held by police influence their behavior toward subjects in the real world. There are, however, several studies examining the effects of different causes of racially biased behavior on interpersonal interactions more generally. For example, McConnell and Leibold (2001) asked White participants to complete an implicit measure of negative attitudes toward Black people (akin to racial animus). The participants also had brief interactions with one White experimenter and one Black experimenter. These interactions were videotaped and later coded. The results suggest that participants with greater animus had more awkward and uncomfortable interactions with the Black experimenter. They demonstrated more speech hesitation, more speech errors, and were less likely to smile when interacting with the Black experimenter. Moreover, the Black experimenter felt worse about interactions with these same participants.

Dovidio, Kawakami, and Gaertner (2002) measured attitudes toward Black people using both an explicit measure (a questionnaire) and an implicit measure. They found that explicitly measured attitudes were related to participant's deliberate behavior: participants who expressed less positive attitudes on an explicit measure tended to say fewer nice things to a Black interaction partner. But implicit measures were related to nonverbal behavior, leading to more blinking and less direct eye contact. Finally, Richeson and Shelton (2003) showed that, when interacting with a Black person, participants with higher levels of implicitly measured negative at-

---

[6] Implicit measures of animus include skin conductance, essentially a physical measure of sweating (Rankin and Campbell, 1955), other physiological measures (e.g., measuring facial muscle movements with EMG), brain imaging (EEG, fMRI) (e.g., Phelps et al., 2000; Hart et al., 2000), indirect self-reports (e.g., completing a word with blank letter-spaces with negative instead of positive words), subliminal priming, sequential priming (e.g., Fazio, 1995), implicit association tests (Greenwald, McGhee, and Schwartz, 1998), and the go/no-go association task (Nosek and Banaji, 2001).

titudes suffered cognitively—as if they were working harder to control their behavior. Though these studies do not involve police or law enforcement scenarios, they clearly have relevance for officers interacting with members of different racial groups, and they raise a host of questions: Are officers inadvertently communicating a sense of discomfort when interacting with Black or Latino citizens? Does an initial sense of discomfort alter the course of the interaction, potentially evoking greater hostility from the citizen? These questions have direct relevance for how proactive policing may influence racial disparities.

It is worth noting that one implicit measure of social cognition, the Implicit Association Test (IAT), has sparked vigorous debate. Questions have been raised about whether certain aspects of the measurement procedure (e.g., the cognitive demands of the task or the differential salience of categories, like Black and White), can create an illusion of biased behavior, racial animus, or the unconscious process psychologists refer to as "implicit bias" on the IAT, even when the participant does not harbor negative views toward Black people. Questions have also been raised about the reliability and validity of the measure. The task typically demonstrates good internal reliability (if a person completes the task and researchers compute a score based on the odd-number trials, it correlates well with a score based on the even-number trials), but the task does not show acceptable test-retest reliability: that is, if a person takes it today, he or she may get one measure of their racial attitudes; if that person does the task again tomorrow, he or she may get a very different measure. While some have argued that this nullifies the utility of the IAT-based measure, others hypothesize that the nature of racial attitudes is simply more labile than previously imagined (Cunningham, Preacher, and Banaji, 2001). Finally, in terms of construct validity, there is disagreement about what the IAT actually measures. Arguments persist regarding how well it predicts behavior (Oswald et al., 2013, 2015; Nosek, Greenwald, and Banaji, 2007), why there are relatively low correlations between different implicit measures of animus (Ito et al., 2015), and whether or not the attitudes being studied are conscious (Fiedler, Messner, and Bluemke, 2006; Hahn et al., 2014). Each side of these debates is supported by experimental laboratory research. Still, there is relative consensus that implicit measures of attitudes—including but not limited to the IAT—predict racially biased behaviors under some range of conditions (Greenwald et al., 2009; Oswald et al., 2013). Under which conditions, how well, why, and for which people, is less clear, given the current state of the research.

Evidence from Studies of Racial Bias in Law Enforcement

There are a number of studies that directly examine the question of racial bias in law enforcement, using evidence collected in both the real world and in the laboratory. This review is organized topically, focusing first on domains that seem most relevant to the question of proactive policing, then discussing a few domains that are broadly related to the justice system even if they do not bear directly on proactive policing.

Perceptions of Suspicion

Eberhardt and colleagues (2004) conducted a series of studies with both undergraduates and police officers in which they subliminally presented images related to crime (this preliminary exposure is called "priming"). They then presented a pair of faces: one White and one Black. When thinking about crime, where would people look? The study showed that students and officers both paid greater attention to Black faces. In a follow-up study, the researchers again tested police officers. Some were primed with the idea of crime, while others were not. Then the officers were presented with a picture of a suspect, who was either Black or White. After viewing the suspect, officers were given a surprise memory task that involved identifying the suspect from a lineup of other suspects of the same race. In both the Black-suspect lineup and the White-suspect lineup, some of the suspects had more stereotypically Black or Afrocentric features, whereas others had more stereotypically White or Eurocentric features. In other words, even though all the faces were persons of the same race (e.g., Black), some of the individuals had facial features that were more typical of Black people in general (i.e., similar to the stereotype of a Black face, e.g., darker skin tone), whereas others had facial features that were less typical of Black people and more typical of White people (i.e., similar to the stereotype of a White face, e.g., lighter skin tone). Crime-primed officers who viewed a Black suspect systematically misremembered the suspect: in the lineup, they typically identified a suspect with more stereotypical Black features. By contrast, the crime-primed officers who saw a White suspect showed a weak tendency to identify a less stereotypical White suspect. In other words, when the officers were thinking about issues of crime and criminality, they tended to ascribe the crime to suspects with more stereotypical Black or Afrocentric (less Eurocentric) faces.

Racial Bias in the Use of Force

One real-world investigation of the role of race in an officer's decision to use force comes from Terrill, Mastrofski, and their colleagues (Terrill and

Mastrofski, 2002; Terrill and Reisig, 2003). Researchers analyzed reports from observers who rode with police officers in two cities for almost 6,000 hours, coding interactions with roughly 12,000 citizens. Among other variables, the observers recorded the gender, race, and age of the citizen; the citizen's level of disrespect and resistance toward the officer; whether the citizen had a weapon, and critically, the officer's use of force along a continuum from none to verbal commands to physical restraint to physical strikes with the body or "external mechanisms."

In their analysis, the researchers sought to statistically control for variables that a reasonable police officer should be expected to use when making decisions about how much force to employ. For example, officers might be expected to use more force with someone who resisted arrest or someone who was engaged in conflict when the officer arrived. To the extent that their statistical models, which included these variables, captured the actual decision rules of the officers, the researchers could also examine whether a citizen's race (or gender or apparent wealth) could explain additional variation in use of force. The data suggest that, under the statistical modeling of the role played by an extensive set of factors, police used greater force with non-White suspects (Terrill and Mastrofski, 2002).

In a follow-up analysis, Terrill and Reisig (2003) suggested that much of the apparent effect of a suspect's race on police use of force can be explained by the neighborhood in which the encounter took place. This result suggests that discrepancies in behavior (racial bias) may be driven by statistical prediction on the basis of the environment. The authors suggested that the tendency to use greater force with non-White suspects may be driven by the fact that, in certain parts of town, officers expected greater levels of danger or reduced accountability. This suggestion is consistent with laboratory-based evidence on when people are most likely to be behave in a way that is consistent with racial animus.

Additionally, Kahn and colleagues (2016) examined individual variation in suspects' faces, particularly whether racial stereotypicality is related to police use of force. In a random sample of booking photos, Kahn found that, controlling for type of arrest, reported level of resistance, and the presence of drugs and alcohol in a suspect's system, ratings of White suspects' phenotypic stereotypicality were negatively associated with likelihood and severity of force. That is, the more stereotypically "White" a suspect looked, the less force was used (statistically controlling for all the other variables). Interestingly there was no relationship between the stereotypicality of Black suspects' faces and use of force in the same sample.

Racial Bias in the Decision to Shoot

Concern about the impact of suspect race on officer-involved shootings has sparked a flurry of work, using both real-world data and laboratory simulations. In what is probably the most sophisticated of the real-world analyses, similar conclusions have been drawn by the vast majority (but not all) of the work on this domain.

In laboratory experiments, several researchers have used video game simulations to explore racial bias in the decision to shoot. These simulations present a target (usually male) who is either White or Black. On some trials the target is armed, and on some trials the target is unarmed. The participant is instructed to shoot the armed targets but not to shoot the unarmed targets; not shooting in these experiments usually requires a response distinct from inaction—for example, pressing a button labeled "don't shoot."

In studies of undergraduates, these studies reveal consistent evidence of racial bias in both response time and accuracy (Correll et al., 2002, 2007; Greenwald et al., 2003; Plant, Peruche, and Butz, 2005; see Payne, 2001, for similar results from a somewhat different task). When responding to an unarmed target, the student participants are typically slower to indicate "don't shoot" and more likely to incorrectly shoot if the target is Black (rather than White); when responding to an armed target, participants are typically slower to shoot and more likely to incorrectly choose "don't shoot" if the target is White (rather than Black).

Results with police officers in similar experiments are somewhat mixed. Plant and Peruche (2005) found that officers showed bias in their behavior (at least initially). By contrast, Correll and colleagues (2007) found that police outperformed lay people—though they still showed bias in the speed of their responses (e.g., shooting armed Black targets more quickly), they showed no appreciable evidence of bias in their actual decisions (e.g., they were no more likely to shoot an unarmed Black target than to shoot an unarmed White target). After a number of additional studies with police, these researchers suggested that, when faced with a potentially hostile suspect, police probably activate some potential source of bias, but that police (unlike undergraduates) are able to overcome those potential sources and use diagnostic information (is the target armed?) to formulate their ultimate response (e.g., see Sim, Correll, and Sadler, 2013).

More recently, James and colleagues sought to develop a more realistic and immersive simulation (James, James, and Vila, 2016; James, Klinger, and Vila, 2014; James, Vila, and Daratha, 2013). These researchers used a deadly-force simulator, similar to those used by law enforcement agencies for training. The results were counterintuitive. Participants (both officers and lay people) were slower to shoot armed Black suspects than armed

White suspects, and they were less likely to shoot unarmed Black suspects than unarmed White suspects. While no explanation of the results is evident from the data, the researchers emphasized in explaining the data that all simulations have liabilities. Participants were typically aware that the research involved race, and in the work by James and colleagues, there was reason to suspect that officers and lay people responded strategically, intentionally attempting to act without racial bias (Wegener and Petty, 1997). This concern is compounded because, in these studies, participants had several seconds to respond. Given sufficient time, the desire to respond in an egalitarian fashion can override factors like racial animus or statistical prediction when individuals are aware that race may influence behavior (Fazio et al., 1995; Gaertner and Dovidio, 1986; Neely, 1977; Payne, Lambert, and Jacoby, 2002).

Several laboratory studies have also examined the effect of variability in racial stereotypicality on decisions to shoot—for example, does it matter if Black targets have lighter versus darker skin? Targets with greater racial stereotypicality seem to induce greater bias in the decision to shoot in computer simulations, and this pattern holds for both undergraduates and police (Kahn and Davies, 2011; Ma and Correll, 2011).

Risk and Protective Factors for Bias in Proactive Policing

In addition to innovations regarding the measurement and effect of dispositional factors that reflect internal characteristics of the individual, there is a sizable psychological literature identifying situations that tend to provoke racially biased behaviors, even absent negative racial attitudes, as well as situations that reduce the likelihood that racial animus will lead to biased behavior or (racially) disparate outcomes. Associations between race and concepts such as danger, crime, and negativity are notoriously difficult to "undo" in a permanent sense (Lai et al., 2014; Plant, Devine, and Peruche, 2010). In turn, statistical prediction that takes into account ethnic or racial characteristics may be accurate at times (e.g., in identifying the likelihood of individuals being involved in terrorist activities), although given the country's normative commitment to equality, the legal standard for allowable statistical prediction is quite high. Recognizing the challenges of permanently changing attitudes, researchers have increasingly focused on identifying features that affect expression of attitudes as biased behavior; that is, they have focused on factors that increase or decrease the likelihood that any existing animus will result in biased behavior. It is particularly important to consider these factors in light of the nature of proactive policing, which may increase the frequency and extent of an officer's contact with citizens and which may also rely heavily on officer discretion. To the extent that some proactive policies may increase the scope

Risk Factors for Biased Behavior

In a series of studies by Fein and Spencer (1997), high-performing students were brought into a laboratory and given a challenging academic test. The students then received either false-positive or false-negative feedback on their test performance. Finally, students were presented with a woman whom they were led to believe was either Jewish (a stigmatized group in this context) or Italian (a nonstigmatized group in this context) and asked to rate her in terms of her overall personality and qualifications for a job. Students who received false-positive feedback rated the Italian and Jewish targets the same. However, students who received false-negative feedback rated the Jewish target much worse than the Italian one.

Across the literature, what social psychologists define as "threats to self-concept" tend to produce biased responses when: (1) the threat is in a domain that is important (Branscombe et al., 1999; Fein and Spencer, 1997); (2) a stigmatized individual is an appropriate target for negative behavior (Frantz et al., 2004; Goff, Steele, and Davies, 2008; Richeson and Sommers, 2016); and (3) negative behavior does not violate anti-racist norms (Dovidio, 2001; Dovidio, Gaertner, and Abad-Merino, 2017). For instance, in experimental laboratory studies, researchers have demonstrated that the mere presence of a stigmatized group member often causes White participants to experience concerns with appearing racist (Goff, Steele, and Davies, 2008; Richeson and Shelton, 2007, 2013; Shelton and Richeson, 2005, 2006, 2015; Shelton, Richeson, and Vorauer, 2006; Trawalter, Richeson, and Shelton, 2009; Vorauer et al., 2000; Vorauer and Kumhyr, 2001; Vorauer, Main, and O'Connell, 1998). Subsequently, this concern predicts social distancing behaviors (Goff, Steele, and Davies, 2008), negative evaluations of interracial interactions (Vorauer, Main, and O'Connell, 1998), and even negative evaluations of stigmatized group members (Frantz et al., 2004).

More broadly, psychology has identified robust sets of dispositional (individual characteristics) and situational (related to the environment) factors that are associated with higher levels of racially biased behavior. A dispositional risk factor for bias is a relatively enduring personal trait that puts an individual at risk of biased behavior. For example, *social dominance orientation*[7] measures individuals' support for hierarchies that disadvantage

---

[7] While many forms of explicit animus have declined over time, social dominance orientation continues to exert an influence on behavior without the expression of this attitude having been diminished by prevailing social norms.

members of lower social strata; individuals who self-report higher levels of social dominance orientation are more likely to engage in biased behavior (Sidanius and Pratto, 1999). One study revealed that social-dominance orientation tends to be relatively higher in police officers compared to members of the general public, college students, and also public defenders, even after controlling for differences in gender, income, social class, age, education, and ethnicity (Sidanius et al., 1994).

Another dispositional risk factor identified in this literature is *aversive racism*. In this case, egalitarian values are explicitly stated, but unacknowledged negative racial attitudes and/or negative affective responses to members of stigmatized groups are found (Dovidio and Gaertner, 2004; Gaertner and Dovidio, 1986). To the extent that proactive policing places officers and residents in more frequent interactions that feature asymmetric power, it may be a risk factor for contemporary forms of behavioral bias, such as social dominance orientation or aversive racism (Gaertner and Dovidio, 1986; Sidanius and Pratto, 2001). However, this hypothesis has not been directly tested.

A third dispositional risk factor identified by social psychologists is *executive function*, which is a kind of flexible cognitive capacity that allows people to pay attention, follow rules, and use different intentional strategies. Unlike social dominance orientation and aversive racism, executive function is a protective factor for biased behavior. A variety of studies clearly demonstrate that participants with greater executive function may harbor animus, but the animus is less likely to influence their behavior (Amodio et al., 2008; Ito et al., 2015; Payne, 2005).

A *situational* risk factor for biased behavior is an aspect of a person's physical or social surroundings that serves as a cue, making biased behavior more likely (Goff, 2016). One situational risk factor that may be relevant to policing is *task complexity*. When faced with a complex situation requiring difficult decisions, people often rely on superficial cues, hunches, and intuitions, which increases the likelihood of biased behaviors (e.g., Macrae et al., 1994; Miller, Bland, and Quinton, 2000; Robinson, Schmeichel, and Inzlicht, 2010). This influence is plainly reflected in much of the work reviewed above (e.g., Bodenhausen and Lichtenstein, 1987; Richeson and Shelton, 2005; Sommers and Ellsworth, 2000). The liability associated with task complexity is often exacerbated by time pressure, fatigue, and emotions such as fear or anger. These factors are endemic to policing and can undermine the ability to engage in complex or controlled thought. For example, a program of research by Payne and colleagues found that participants are more likely to mistakenly identify nongun objects as guns when the objects are paired with images of Black (rather than White) faces, but only when given a limited amount of time to respond (Payne, 2001; Payne, Lambert, and Jacoby, 2002).

A second (probably related) situational risk factor relevant in policing may be *environmental threat*, or the sense of danger created by the location in which an encounter occurs. In both studies of real-world police behavior and in laboratory simulations, poorer and more dangerous neighborhoods were associated with greater use of force (Terrill and Reisig, 2003; Correll et al., 2011).

A third situational factor relevant to policing may be *stereotype threat*, the concern with confirming or being negatively evaluated in terms of stereotypes about one's own group (Steele, 1992). While this phenomenon is usually studied with academically stigmatized groups in educational settings, there is a growing body of research suggesting that those concerned with being seen as criminal will respond with behaviors that objectively attract police suspicion (Najdowski, 2011; Najdowski, Bottoms, and Goff, 2015). Conversely, those concerned with being stereotyped as motivated by racial animus can respond negatively to individuals who evoke that concern (Frantz et al., 2004; Goff, Steele, and Davies, 2008)—a finding of potential concern for police officers in the current climate.

Fourth and finally, concerns with appearing racist, foolish, or otherwise being negatively evaluated can reduce executive functioning and increase intergroup negativity (Richeson and Shelton, 2007, 2013; Trawalter, Richeson, and Shelton, 2009).

In summary, while not yet specifically tested among police, social psychological research on risk factors for racially biased behavior suggest that police officers who are (1) working in an environment where they are interacting with non-Whites, (2) have plausible race-neutral reasons for the biased behavior, and (3) feel criticized or generally unappreciated, may be more likely to exhibit biased behavior against non-Whites. Further, there is evidence that people who hold relatively stronger racial animus toward non-Whites are more likely to behave differently toward non-Whites in both overt and subtle ways. In the policing context, this may inhibit de-escalation of an event and influence the perceived legitimacy of a police-citizen encounter, hypotheses that should be tested directly in field studies. Importantly, although dispositional differences robustly predict behavioral differences, they are often strongly moderated by situational factors. While the available research does not allow us to draw conclusions regarding proactive policing, future studies should examine these risk factors more directly.

Protective (bias-reducing) Factors for Biased Behavior

Research suggests that expertise and training may reduce the likelihood of bias occurring in particular situations. In general, individuals with more practice tend to be more likely to complete tasks accurately (e.g., MacLeod,

1998) and are less likely to engage in biased behavior (e.g., Kawakami, Dovidio, and van Kamp, 2005). Not surprisingly, practice on weapon identification can reduce racially biased behavior. For example, Plant and colleagues (Plant and Peruche, 2005; Plant, Peruche, and Butz, 2005) gave participants (including both student and police) a choice to shoot or not shoot a target person who was viewed on-screen accompanied by either a gun or another object. Over the course of the 160-trial task, the participants made racially biased shooting errors at first, but by the second half of the task, bias had decreased dramatically. Similarly, Correll and colleagues (2007), as noted earlier, compared police officers to community members in a videogame simulation. They observed that community members showed bias in their decisions to shoot but the police officers did not. A subsequent study of undergraduates in the laboratory demonstrated one possible reason why police (who have more expertise) tend to exhibit less bias and greater accuracy: undergraduates who practiced the simulation showed similar improvements in performance (Correll et al., 2007).

A second class of protective factors might be agency policies that directly address specific risks or that provide clear guidelines for behavior. For example, research has found that study participants demonstrate greater racial bias when they are forced to respond quickly and when they feel threatened. Policies that help address these vulnerabilities (e.g., more strongly encouraging officers to seek cover or increasing two-officer patrols) may help mitigate against these risk factors. In addition, clear guidelines about when and how to interact with members of the community may have the potential to reduce biased behavior by reducing discretion. Guidelines that clearly specify, for example, when a speeding car should be stopped might reduce the likelihood that officers will use race to inform their decisions.

Many of the studies to date have been conducted in the laboratory rather than assessing police officers acting in field settings, a limitation that make it difficult to draw conclusions regarding the ways and extent to which racial animus, whether acknowledged or not, may shape police behavior in practice. However, some risk factors for biased behavior may also be common to features of proactive policing. This suggests the importance of more direct research on the dispositional and situational factors that may influence whether police officers make biased decisions. It is also important to identify training programs that improve officer performance. There are no experimental studies of the effectiveness of "implicit bias training" in policing, for example, and the committee encourages further research in this area.

EVIDENCE FROM CRIMINOLOGY, ECONOMICS, AND SOCIOLOGY ON RACIAL BIAS IN POLICING

Like psychology, empirical research in criminology, economics, and sociology recognizes that the existence of disparities is not in and of itself evidence of racially biased behavior among police officers, nor is it evidence for the source (e.g., animus or statistical prediction or something else) for that bias. This section describes common strategies that have been used in these fields to estimate how police officers are using race in their decision-making process, focusing on a specific type of racial bias commonly called "racial profiling." Racial profiling usually refers to police decisions to engage in vehicle or pedestrian stops, searches, or arrests or to take other law enforcement actions based at least in part on a targeted individual's race, outside of the context in which officers target an individual because he satisfies a specific description of a criminal suspect.

Most of the empirical research on racial profiling does not address proactive policing specifically, though there are a few notable exceptions. Nevertheless, the research does consider profiling in the context of police stops, searches, and arrests, which is relevant insofar as proactive strategies, especially deterrence-based strategies, often promote increasing stops, searches, or arrests as a means to prevent crime. Nearly all the research on racial profiling, including evaluations of racial profiling in proactive policing strategies, evaluates the role of bias in police behavior using either a benchmarking approach or an outcome test. In the discussion and analysis that follows, the committee selectively reviews these two bodies of research. We highlight principal findings from some of the key studies in this area and also highlight the methodological shortcomings inherent to each methodological approach to identifying racial disparities in police–citizen interactions.

Comparisons of Racial Composition of Police–Citizen Interactions to Alternative Population Benchmarks

There are a number of studies that employ census data, driver's license data, or both to compare the racial composition of those stopped by the police to the racial composition of the local resident population, to the population of areas near roadways, or to the current population of drivers. A 2003 study of Minnesota compared the racial composition of police stops and searches to the racial composition of the driving-age population in 65 municipalities throughout the state and demonstrated that in nearly all localities, Black people were overrepresented and White people underrepresented among those stopped and searched by the police (Institute on

Race and Poverty, 2003).[8] A 2005 study of Illinois by the Northwestern University Center for Public Safety compared the racial composition of traffic stops in various localities throughout Illinois, as well as traffic stops statewide, to estimates of the racial composition of drivers in each locality and statewide (Weiss and Grumet-Morris, 2005). The authors found that across all localities, non-White drivers were only slightly more likely to be stopped than White drivers and that, in some localities (Chicago in particular), non-White drivers were less likely to be stopped by police. As one final example, a 2000 study by the Texas Department of Public Safety compared the racial composition of those stopped, cited, warned, and searched by the police to the racial composition of state residents. The analysis found that Black and Hispanic drivers were underrepresented among stopped drivers, among those cited, and among those receiving written warnings, but overrepresented among vehicle searches (Texas Department of Public Safety, 2000).

A series of studies attempts to refine the benchmarks to focus more specifically on the distribution of driver's licenses and on heterogeneity in miles driven, as well as the difference in the geographic distribution of driving behavior by race. Smith and colleagues (2004) analyzed stop data for the state of North Carolina and compared cross-city variation in the proportion of stops of Black drivers to three benchmarks: (1) the proportion of licensed drivers in the locality who are Black, (2) estimates from direct observations of those driving on streets and freeways of the proportion of these actual drivers who are Black, and (3) the proportion of auto accidents involving Black people. The findings showed higher stop rates relative to the benchmarks for Black drivers, with the disproportionality in stop rates increasing with the relative size of the Black driving population in each locality. Alpert, Dunham, and Smith (2007), in an analysis of Dade County, Florida, police, compared the racial composition of stops to the racial composition of observed traffic violators at key intersections and to the racial composition of the not-at-fault driver in two-vehicle crashes throughout the county. Whereas they found that Black drivers were only slightly overrepresented among those stopped, there were clearer and larger difference in post-stop treatment. Lamberth (1994) used traffic surveys conducted by the researcher to estimate the racial composition of drivers as well as the proportion of drivers that are exceeding the speed limit along the New Jersey Turnpike by at least 5 miles per hour. These estimates were then compared to the racial composition of those stopped by state troopers and to the racial composition of those arrested, using data culled from patrol and radio logs. The analysis found that Blacks were disproportionately rep-

---

[8] This study also compared racial disparities in whether searches uncovered contraband, a methodological approach we review in the next section.

resented among those stopped and arrested along the New Jersey Turnpike, relative to either the estimates of the racial composition of drivers or the observed racial composition of speeders.

Grogger and Ridgeway (2006) proposed an alternative benchmarking strategy that exploited differences in the level of ambient lighting and the consequent effect on officer ability to identify drivers' ethnicity/race. Using microdata on officer-initiated stops in Oakland, CA, they basically assessed whether Black drivers constituted a higher proportion of stops made during the day relative to those made during the night. The reasoning behind this comparison was that those stopped at night, "under the veil of darkness" and for whom officer could not assess race, provided an unbiased estimate of the racial composition of those violating traffic laws or being stopped for reasons independent of race. They found little evidence of a disparity and concluded that their test yielded little evidence of disparate treatment by the police.[9]

Stop, question, and frisk (SQF) was used in New York City as a proactive policing strategy in specific neighborhoods or to target crime hot spots (Gelman, Fagan, and Kiss, 2007; Weisburd, Telep, and Lawton, 2014). In a benchmarking study of this intervention, Ridgeway (2007) compared the composition of those stopped, questioned, and frisked by New York City police to the racial composition of crime suspect descriptions. This study also compared the behavior of individual officers to internal benchmarks constructed to account for differences in shift and patrol location. Ridgeway found that despite comprising the overwhelming share of stops (more than 80%), Black residents were underrepresented among stops relative to citizens' crime-suspect descriptions. The study also identified a small set of officers who stopped non-White people at very high rates relative to the constructed internal benchmark; it also identified cross-borough heterogeneity in the degree to which non-White people were overrepresented among those stopped by the police.

Gelman, Fagan, and Kiss (2007) provided an additional benchmarking study of SQF in New York City that used prior criminal activity as a benchmark. The authors employed stop-and-frisk data for New York City for the late 1990s to estimate count models at the precinct level. These models were then used to assess the degree to which non-Whites were stopped and frisked at rates disproportionate to prior-year arrests. They also assessed whether there was heterogeneity that varied systematically with precinct-level characteristics. For example, they assessed whether White people were more likely to be stopped in predominantly non-White precincts and vice

---

[9] One criticism of this research is that the location of the stop and the make and model of the vehicle may often be sufficient indicators of a non-White driver, given racial and ethnic income disparities and the racial residential patterns of Oakland, California, during the period studied.

versa. The findings indicate that Black people and Hispanic people were stopped at rates that were disproportionate to their arrest rates. There was some evidence that "being out of place" increases SQF for all races/ethnicities. This study also found evidence of lower hit rates (likelihood of arrest, conditional on SQF) for Black people and Hispanic people relative to White people (Gelman, Fagan, and Kiss, 2007), the interpretation of which will be discussed in detail in the next section. Studies like these use broad-area statistics to develop benchmarks. However, other research in New York City suggests that SQFs were highly concentrated on specific streets within neighborhoods, which raises questions regarding the ability to rely on the comparisons made using broad-area benchmarks (Weisburd, Telep, and Lawton, 2014).

Beckett and colleagues (2005) and Beckett, Nyrop, and Pfingst (2006) employed surveys of chronic drug users to estimate the racial composition of those engaged in drug delivery. These two studies were primarily interested in explaining the high proportions of Black people among those arrested in Seattle for drug offenses overall (Beckett et al., 2005) and for drug delivery offenses (Beckett, Nyrop, and Pfingst, 2006). The authors noted the relatively small Black population of Seattle (roughly 7% of the population) and the high proportion of Black people among drug arrestees (more than 50%), which often resulted from strategic and concentrated enforcement of drug laws. They used several sources to measure the composition of serious drug users and those engaged in drug delivery. First, they conducted a survey of participants in needle exchanges, recording the race/ethnicity of users, the drugs in the needles being exchanged, and the perceived race/ethnicity of the person from whom the exchanging person purchased or received drugs most recently. Second, they spent roughly 40 hours observing outdoor transactions in two prominent open air drug markets in Seattle, recording perceived race/ethnicity of buyers and sellers and the drugs being sold (inferred from the knowledge of key informants or in some instances from subjects attempting to sell the observer drugs). Third, the 2005 study incorporated information on the racial composition and specific substances used among those participating in publicly funded (either fully or partially) substance abuse treatment programs. Beckett and colleagues used these datasets to estimate the composition of users by substance (the 2005 study) and the racial composition of drug deliverers by substance (the 2006 study).

In these studies, White people constituted the overwhelming majority of heroin, meth, and MDMA users and deliverers in Seattle, while Blacks constituted the plurality of crack cocaine users and those involved in crack delivery. The authors estimated the proportion of street transactions involving each substance and found that the proportion of arrests involving crack cocaine exceeded by a fair amount the proportion of street transactions involving that drug. They also found that drug arrests involving crack yielded less in terms of confiscated product, money, and weapons. Buy-bust arrests were also less productive along these dimensions, relative to arrests of individuals in private spaces involving warrants. The disproportionate representation of Blacks among drug arrestees appeared to be due in large part to a focus on crack cocaine and a focus of resources on buy-busts occurring outside. The authors noted anecdotal evidence from buy-busts of a local prioritization of enforcement targeted toward crack cocaine, with undercover officers explicitly looking to buy crack and in some instances not buying heroin or meth when offered. They attributed this prioritization to a racialized script regarding what it means to be a drug addict and a drug offender and the ensuing direction of policing resources toward drug offenses committed by Black people, despite their minority status in the city and among drug users and deliveries not involving crack cocaine.

The conclusion from these Seattle studies has been called into question by Engel, Smith, and Cullen (2012). These authors analyzed the geographic distribution of drug arrests in Seattle for a later period than that studied by Beckett and colleagues (2005) and Beckett, Nyrop, and Pfingst (2006) and assessed how the geography of drug arrests compares to the geography of drug-related calls for service through the city's 911 system (as captured and recorded through the Seattle Police Department's computer-aided dispatch system). Engel, Smith, and Cullen (2012) also coded the suspect's race, as indicated from the narratives of calls for service, and compared the composition of described suspects to the composition of drug arrests. They found a tight association, across geographic units of varying levels of spatial disaggregation, between drug arrests, drug-related calls for services, and reported crimes. The authors also found close correspondence between the racial composition of drug arrests and the composition of suspect descriptions in 911 calls. Based on these findings, the authors contested the conclusion that the enforcement focus on crack cocaine or some other form of racialized framing of the local drug problem was driving racial disparities in arrests. Instead, these authors argued that the geography of police deployment driven by responses to calls for service explains enforcement priorities and that racial disproportionality was much less when benchmarked against suspect descriptions from the public. The authors left as an open question whether calls for service by the public are racially biased.

There are several notable differences between the Engel, Smith, and Cullen (2012) study and the research in Beckett et al. (2005) and Beckett, Nyrop, and Pfingst (2006) that make it difficult to draw head-to-head comparisons of the conclusions and findings. To start, the two sets of research teams seem to be asking different questions in their study designs. Beckett and colleagues essentially asked whether the racial composition of drug arrests matches the racial composition of those who violate drug law in Seattle (using rehab statistics, needle exchange surveys, and observation of drug market activity as benchmarks). Given that they found heavy overrepresentation of Black people among drug arrests, they then asked what policy and practice factors may be behind these disparities. Engel, Smith, and Cullen (2012), on the other hand, asked whether responsive deployment of police resources (to calls for service and crime rates) can explain the geography of arrests and whether the racial composition of suspect description from the public better match the racial composition of arrests. It is entirely plausible that both statistical associations are valid; namely, that (1) Black drug users and deliverers face a higher risk of arrest relative to White drug users and deliverers, and (2) the racial composition of reported suspects matches the racial composition of arrests. Hence, it is not clear that this more recent research contradicts the earlier findings by Beckett and colleagues, as it essentially asks and answers fundamentally different questions.[10]

With the exception of the benchmarking study of SQF and the drug enforcement study in Seattle, there are very few benchmarking studies relevant to proactive policing that assess whether specific policing efforts have disparate impacts on non-White communities. Employing standard benchmarking strategies to assess the outcomes of geographically focused and person-focused policing strategies would likely face particular difficulties. For example, defining the racial composition of individuals congregating on specific street corners that would be the target of proactive SQF or the racial composition of individuals who are candidates for lever-pulling strategies or strategic preemptive call-ins is likely impossible using standard administrative data or local-area data collected and published by the U.S. Census Bureau. In fact, the extensive field work and original data collection by Becket and colleagues in Seattle was intended primarily to overcome these data limitations.

---

[10] In her published reaction to Engel, Smith, and Cullen (2012), Beckett (2012) also raised several objections that are worth noting. First, the Seattle Police Department testified that calls for service were not used for deployment decisions during the time period under analysis in the earlier studies. Second, Engle and colleagues did not disaggregate arrests by drug type, and Beckett (2012) showed that the racial disparities in arrest rates can largely be attributed to the high proportion of arrests that were crack related (i.e., geography does not explain racial arrest disparities). Addressing the bivariate analysis showing the strong association between crime and drug arrest, Beckett (2012) raised concerns about possible reverse causality: to the extent that the police focus on specific areas to enforce drug law, they will also encounter and record more crime through their presence in the area. She even raised the concern that drug-related calls for service may be endogenous to enforcement policy, as the Seattle Police Department unveiled a drug offense monitoring system and actively encouraged the public to report drug activity into the CAD (computer-aided dispatch) system. Beckett (2012) also raised the possibility that the community outreach effort focused on neighborhoods where drug arrests were concentrated.

Outcome Tests for Racial Disparities in Treatment

As noted above, a second body of research employs outcome tests for unjustifiable racial disparities in police–citizen interactions. Outcome tests analyze the results of police–citizen interactions and infer racial bias from racial differences in the productivity of a police stop, usually measured by whether a search results in the detection of contraband. As noted earlier, the method of testing for biased behavior by testing for differences in outcomes has been extensively debated. Here, we review the key studies that have employed this strategy to study police practices in the United States. Again, while much of this research has focused on generating tests for racial profiling by the police in general, a few notable studies have applied the methods to study the fairness and efficiency of SQF as a proactive policing strategy.

Knowles, Persico, and Todd (2001) provided one of the earliest outcome test studies of police behavior. The authors employed data on police stops and searches by the Maryland State Police occurring along Interstate 95 during the 1990s and compared hit rates, using various definitions of contraband and guilt, by the race/ethnicity of the searched drivers. The principal findings from this study are that hit rates for searches involving Black drivers were equal to or higher than those involving White drivers (roughly 32% higher for the most inclusive definition). By contrast, hit rates for Hispanic drivers were very low: equal to roughly one-third those for Black and White drivers.

Sanga (2009) reanalyzed the dataset used in Knowles, Persico, and Todd (2001) by extending the analysis to all driver searches conducted by the Maryland State Police during the time period analyzed in the original study and extending the analysis through 2006. Note that the earlier study focused only on searches of drivers resulting from stops made along I-95, which constituted roughly 30 percent of all searches. Analysis of all searches yielded statistically significant differences in hit rates, with hit rates for Black searches 6 percentage points lower than those for Whites, during the period 1995–1999. Estimates using the extended period from 1995 through 2006 yielded even larger disparities, with Black hit rates 10 percentage points lower than White hit rates, suggesting that the overall disparity in hit rates increased in the latter part of the extended period. Similar to the original finding in Knowles, Persico, and Todd (2001), Sanga (2009) found very large Hispanic-White differentials in hit rates, with the Hispanic hit rate for the entire period approximately 30 percentage points lower than the hit rate resulting from searches of White drivers.

Ayres and Borowsky (2008) analyzed field development report data (completed after each motor vehicle stop or interaction with a citizen) for the Los Angeles Police Department for the period July 2003 through June 2004. The authors analyzed disparities in stop rates per 10,000 residents and in differences in the likelihood of being searched, asked to exit the car, or frisked conditional on being stopped, as well as racial disparities in a series of outcomes that included arrest, citation, and the detection of contraband, weapons, or drugs. Using reporting districts as the unit of observations, the authors found that controlling for geographic variation in crime rates, demographics, unemployment rates, and poverty does not explain racial disparities in the stops per 10,000 local residents. Two divisions in particular (Central and Hollywood) had stop rates that exceeded 10,000 per 10,000 Black residents The authors also found that Black residents who were stopped were more likely to be arrested, less likely to be cited, more likely to be asked to exit the vehicle, more likely to be frisked, and had lower hit rates relative to White residents. Similar disparities relative to White residents were found for Hispanic residents. They also performed tests of whether officer race mediated these disparities and found evidence of less biased behavior against non-White citizens by non-White officers.

Anwar and Fang (2006) developed a model of police stops and searches whereby officers develop a posterior likelihood of a successful hit and search all motorists where the expected net benefits are positive. In their model, officers are permitted to behave in a non-monolithic manner, in the sense that an officer is permitted to determine differential suspicion thresholds by motorist race. The authors were particularly interested in the infra-marginality problem that plagues outcomes tests of racial profiling, and they used their model to generate a sufficient but not necessary condition for evidence of racially biased treatment that in turn provides a low-powered empirical test for racial profiling. To be specific, their model implies that when officers do not engage in biased behavior, particularly biased behavior motived by statistical prediction, differences across officers of different racial groups in the propensity to stop or search motorists (conditional on motorist race) does not depend on the race of the motorist. In other words, if White officers stop White drivers at a higher rate relative to Black officers, the satisfaction of this condition would imply that White officers also stop Black motorists at a higher rate.

The authors used this model to analyze data on highway stops in Florida. They found that White officers searched individuals of all races at higher rates, followed by Hispanic officers, with Black officers third. Similarly, cross-officer-race disparities in hit rates yielded rankings that do not depend on the race of the motorist. However, the authors did find higher search rates for Black people, followed by Hispanic people and then White people, and lower hit rates for Hispanic people and Black people relative to White people. White officers searched all groups at the highest rates, but the differences by motorist race were largest for White officers, as were the hit rate differentials.

Antonovics and Knight (2009) analyzed data on police stops by the

Boston police department, focusing specifically on differences in the propensity to search motorists of different races, according to the race of the officer. They developed a simple model whereby heterogeneity by officer race in the costs of searching yields differences in the propensity to stop and search motorists of different races. Similar to previous work in this area, they formalized "taste-based" bias (animus-related biased behavior, in this committee's terminology) as a lower cost associated with stopping members of the biased-against group. The key prediction here is that to the extent that officer race interacts with motorist race in determining the likelihood that a stop results in a search, then there is a disparity in search costs that cannot be justified by statistical prediction in actual racial disparities in the propensity to offend. The authors' analysis found evidence of such an interaction effect, with Black officers more likely to search White motorists relative to White officers, and White officers more likely to search Black motorist relative to Black officers.

Several studies of the use of SQF employed outcome tests of racial bias. Persico and Coviello (2015) analyzed New York City data for the period 2003 to 2012. The principal strategy in this study was to assess whether Black and Latino people who were stopped by the police were less likely to be arrested than White people who were stopped by the police. The proposition here is that to the extent that an arrest is a signal of (accurate predictor for) actual law breaking, lower arrest rates for Black or Latino stops relative to White stops would be evidence of disparate and biased treatment of non-White people. The authors found that Black stops were less likely to result in an arrest relative to White stops and that the difference in arrest rates is statistically significant. However, controlling for precinct of arrest led to a higher conditional arrest rate for Black people. To be sure, the authors' conclusions are premised on the assumption that an arrest is a race-neutral gauge of suspect culpability. They offered evidence that, conditional on reported offense, Black people were only slightly more likely to be arrested than White people. However, to the extent that the reported offense is endogenous to the interaction between the officer and citizen (i.e., officers list more serious charges for people they wish to arrest), this evidence is of limited value. Moreover, given the enormous racial disparities in the frequency of coercive interactions with the police, one might expect that the SQF incidents involving Black and Latino people are more likely to be tense exchanges, with perhaps an elevated likelihood of escalation.

Goel, Rao, and Shroff (2016) analyzed racial disparities in the composition of police stops in New York City due to suspicion of criminal possession of a weapon. The authors used data on 760,000 such SQF incidents occurring between 2008 and 2012 to assess the productivity of such stops in terms of weapons recovered, racial disparities in productivity as measured by average hit rates, the degree to which these disparities are explained by localized (i.e., precinct level) variation in practice, and whether improvements in efficiency could reduce racial disparities in the incidents of these stops while still confiscating the majority of confiscated weapons.

The authors modeled the likelihood that an SQF incident results in a weapons seizure using the first 3 years of data. Their logistic model specification includes data on demographics (race, age, gender), physical characteristics (build, weight), time and day of the stop, precinct, a distance-weighted measure of the productivity of recent such stops, a complete set of precinct fixed effects, and full interactions between all terms. They estimated the parameters of their model using the 2008 through 2010 data and then used the trained model to estimate the ex ante likelihood of recovering a weapon for more recent years. The key innovation is that they used factors observed ex ante to the stop to predict the likelihood of discovering a weapon and used their trained model to estimate the complete distribution of the ex ante hit-rate probability across all stops occurring during the out-of-sample period.

Several findings resulted from this study. First, average hit rates were lower for Black people relative to White people, and there were large differences in the distribution of ex ante likelihood by race. Second, much of the racial disparity can be explained by variation in practice by precinct, though White hit rates were still higher within precincts. Third, the authors showed that the ex ante likelihood of recovering a weapon is very low for a large proportion of searches. They also showed that focusing on the subset of searches with high ex ante likelihood could greatly curtail the volume of searches while recovering nearly all of the weapons discovered through the less-focused SQF program (Goel, Rao, and Shroff, 2016).

A key issue left unanswered in this study concerns whether the hit rates are in part a function of the level of SQF activity. The authors estimated that the 6 percent of stops with the highest ex ante probabilities of uncovering weapons netted 50 percent of the weapons recovered. Similarly, 60 percent of stops generated 90 percent of the weapons recovered. These tabulations implicitly assume that the likelihood of carrying a weapon is not sensitive to the extent of SQF activity initiated by the police. To the extent that SQF deters the unlawful carrying of firearms, the ex ante probability distribution for weapons carrying estimated under conditions when SQF is used liberally may not match the comparable distribution in an environment when SQF is rarely used.

CONCLUSION

Concerns about racial bias, particularly bias driven by animus, loom large in discussions of policing today, and these concerns must be framed in the context of the history of the police as agents who sometimes enforced discriminatory laws and social norms, often through violence. The currently high levels of distrust in the police must be understood through this historical frame because that history continues to influence Black views about the police.

Having outlined this history, the committee also notes evidence that racial animus has become less central to American society and to policing relative to the 18th and 19th centuries. However, there are a number of indications that racial animus, and racially biased behavior in general, continue in more subtle forms, and some proactive strategies may have features that align with psychological risk factors for biased behavior by police officers. Because none of these areas in the psychological literature has tested how the observed laboratory effects may or not may not generalize to street-level policing decisions, the evidence from this field is not sufficient for the committee to draw any conclusions regarding its specific impacts on proactive policing. Nevertheless, the general evidence for the continuing existence of both negative racial attitudes, whether conscious or unacknowledged, and racially biased behavior support the importance of efforts to study the role of racial bias in contemporary police behavior generally and in proactive policing in particular.

Inferring the role of racial bias in contributing to disparate impacts is a challenging question for research. Existing research demonstrates that concentrated enforcement efforts in high-crime areas and on highly active individuals can lead to racial disparities in police–citizen interactions. One consequence of this geographic concentration is observable in the geographic concentrations of arrests, SQFs, and general police activity in non-White neighborhoods in many cities. From a statistical standpoint, this means that regression adjustment that accounts for local measured crime rates or that includes general spatial control variables—as in several studies that adjusted for precinct of arrest or patrol districts within jurisdiction—frequently generates findings of substantially reduced, or even eliminated, evidence of racial bias. But, as community advocates argued to the committee (see Appendix A), this does not address or respond to the fact that crime in these areas is itself an outcome of social forces that may have been generated by long-term inequalities and discrimination in non-White communities.

Studies that seek to benchmark citizen-police interactions against simple population counts or broad publicly available measures of criminal activity do not yield conclusive information regarding the potential for racial bias in proactive policing efforts. This statement is based on several facts. Proactive strategies tend to be geographically focused, sometimes person-focused, and often problem focused, where the definition of the problem is articulated a priori through some executive local analysis. Assessing disparate impact requires detailed information on the geography and nature of the strategy, in order to identify an appropriate benchmark. In addition, assessing whether the disparate impact is indicative of racial bias further requires localized knowledge of the relative importance of the problem at hand. For example, should the Seattle police focus more on crack cocaine, which tends to be sold and used by Black people, or heroin, which is relatively more likely to be used and sold by White people?

Although research that tests for differential outcomes of police–citizen interactions is potentially informative regarding the disparate impacts of proactive policing efforts, research on this issue tends to be undertheorized or defines the objectives of police so narrowly as to limit the ability to draw broad inferences from existing empirical findings. For example, the infra-marginality problem detailed early in this chapter (refer to Box 7-1) makes it difficult to conclude that there is no bias from a finding of equal hit rates across racial groups. If one's prior assumption is that non-White people tend to offend at a higher rate, a finding of lower hit rates for non-White searches might support the conclusion that bias, and potentially animus-driven bias, exists, though even this conclusion is conditional on several assumptions regarding the objectives pursued by the police and the responsiveness of individuals to the threat of being searched.

Some of the most compelling evidence on the potential impact of aggressive enforcement-based proactive policing and increased citizen–police contacts on racial outcomes relates to the use of SQF in New York City. This research seeks to model the probabilities that police suspicion of criminal possession of a weapon turns out to be justified, given the information available to officers when deciding whether to stop someone. This work has found substantial racial and ethnic disparities in the distribution of these probabilities, suggesting that police in New York City apply a lower threshold of suspicion to Black and Hispanic residents.

While this chapter has reviewed the psychological science related to police bias and detailed what researchers have discovered by examining stop rates and outcomes tests of police behaviors, there are a number of areas not engaged by this chapter. That is largely because scholarship of police behavior has disproportionately focused on crime and delinquency and less frequently on the racial causes and consequences of those behaviors. As a result, there simply is not much literature on the downstream consequences of police contact between communities and police. There is promising research on the negative consequences of police contact on institutional trust (Lerman and Weaver, 2014b; Jones, 2014; Weaver and Lerman, 2010) and racial identity development (Brunson, 2007; Brunson and Miller, 2005, 2006). But the evidence base is still thin regarding how police contact—much less proactive policing—may influence family dynamics, educational outcomes, employment, and housing decisions. Similarly, there are some studies exploring the link between racial residential segregation and police size (Kent and Jacobs, 2005; Stults and Baumer, 2007) and some work demonstrating the overrepresentation of Black faces in local news coverage of crime (even compared to actual rates of arrest) (Dixon and Linz, 2000a, 2000b) and how that coverage influences public opinion on what crime policy should be (Dixon, 2006, 2008a, 2008b; Dixon and Azocar, 2007). However, there is not a robust empirical literature exploring how racial attitudes or politics may causally influence police policy or officer decision making.

That the scholarship does not exist should not be taken to suggest either the presence or absence of racial disparities, racial bias, or racial animus. It should also not be taken to mean that the topics are unimportant; indeed, our review of ethnographic evidence and consultations with community groups (see Appendix A) suggests that these topics are central to fully quantifying the net social costs and benefits of proactive policing policies. However, the committee notes that even basic measures of the impact of police policies and practices on communities are undeveloped or nonexistent, relative to estimates of the impact of policing on crime. For example, there is no component of the Uniform Crime Reports that records officer-initiated stops or incidents of force, in aggregate or broken out by race. The National Incident Based Reporting System (NIBRS), which contains significantly more detail about police actions, crime, victims, and arrestees, currently does not cover police agencies operating in places where roughly 70 percent of the U.S. population lives, and it covers none of the nation's largest urban areas.[11] Further, while there are a number of well-developed estimates of the cost of crime (Heaton, 2010), the committee is unaware of any estimates of the costs of racial disparities in criminal justice contact, the costs of racial profiling or other racially biased behaviors by police, or the cost of racial animus in policing. For example, if place-based policing reduces the probability that most non-White people are subject to racial profiling but increases the rate at which non-White people in certain crime hot spots have unwanted police interactions that are perceived to be racially biased, does this increase or decrease social welfare? The committee is currently unaware of any quantitative metric for this issue. Until these basic measurement issues are addressed, any attempt to quantify the net social cost or benefit of policing policies will be necessarily inaccurate.

The committee calls for scholars to produce research that will expand the conceptual map of what causes police behavior; what the consequences of those behaviors are; and how race, gender, class, and other vulnerable identities may play a role in both. Ethnographic and qualitative evidence

---

[11] As of 2015, only one agency with a jurisdiction of more than 1 million people reported NIBRS data to the Federal Bureau of Investigation (the Fairfax County, Virginia, police department), and only 32 agencies with jurisdiction of more than 250,000 did so.

on community and citizen responses to policing should be used to develop hypotheses that can be rigorously tested with quantitative data. The current lack of such scholarship severely limits the ways in which evidence-based approaches to policing can address community concerns about group-based disparities.

The committee has drawn the following main conclusions regarding racial disparities in proactive policing:

CONCLUSION 7-1 There are likely to be large racial disparities in the volume and nature of police–citizen encounters when police target high-risk people or high-risk places, as is common in many proactive policing programs.

CONCLUSION 7-2 Existing evidence does not establish conclusively whether, and to what extent, the racial disparities associated with concentrated person-focused and place-based enforcement are indicators of statistical prediction, racial animus, implicit bias, or other causes. However, the history of racial injustice in the United States, in particular in the area of criminal justice and policing, as well as ethnographic research that has identified disparate impacts of policing on non-White communities, makes the investigation of the causes of racial disparities a key research and policy concern.

Taken in its totality, this chapter suggests the need for more systematic research in specific areas, including more research involving police officers acting in field settings (see Chapter 8). There are large disparities in all manner of interactions and outcomes with the police by race and ethnicity. Given the current state of the empirical evidence, it is difficult to infer the meaning of these disparities. But given the long history of policing bias against non-Whites, and especially Black Americans, it is clearly time for this question to be more carefully examined.

8

Conclusions and Implications for Policy and Research

Proactive policing is a relatively new phenomenon in the United States. It developed from a crisis in confidence in policing that began to emerge in the 1960s because of social unrest, rising crime rates, and growing skepticism regarding the effectiveness of standard approaches to policing. In response, beginning in the 1980s and 1990s, innovative police practices and policies that took a more proactive approach began to develop. In this report, the committee used the term "proactive policing" to refer to **all policing strategies that have as one of their goals the prevention or reduction of crime and disorder and that are not reactive in terms of focusing primarily on uncovering ongoing crime or on investigating or responding to crimes once they have occurred.** Specifically, the elements of proactivity include an emphasis on prevention, mobilizing resources based on police initiative, and targeting the broader underlying forces at work that may be driving crime and disorder. This contrasts with the standard model of policing, which involves an emphasis on reacting to particular crime events after they have occurred, mobilizing resources based on requests coming from outside the police organization, and focusing on the particulars of a given criminal incident.

Proactive policing in this report is distinguished from the everyday decisions of police officers to be proactive in specific situations and instead refers to a strategic decision by police agencies to use proactive police responses in a programmatic way to reduce crime. This report has documented that proactive policing strategies are used widely in the United States. They are not isolated programs used by a select group of agencies but rather a set of approaches that have spread across the landscape of policing.

The United States has once again been confronted by a crisis of confidence in policing. Instances of perceived or actual police misconduct have given rise to nationwide protests against unfair and abusive police practices. Although this report was not intended to respond directly to the crisis of confidence in policing that can be seen in the United States today, it is nevertheless important to consider how proactive policing strategies may bear upon this crisis. It is not enough to simply identify "what works" for reducing crime and disorder; it is also critical to consider issues such as how proactive policing affects the legality of policing, the evaluation of the police in communities, potential abuses of police authority, and the equitable application of police services in the everyday lives of citizens.

Proactive policing has taken a number of different forms over the past two decades, and these variants often overlap in practice. The four broad approaches to proactive policing described in this report are place-based interventions, problem-solving interventions, person-focused interventions, and community-based interventions (see Table 2-1 in Chapter 2). Place-based interventions capitalize on the growing research base that shows that crime is concentrated at specific places within a city as a means of more efficiently allocating police resources to reduce crime. Its main applications have been directed at microgeographic hot spots. Person-based interventions also capitalize on the concentration of crimes to proactively prevent crime, but in this case it is concentration among a subset of offenders. Person-based interventions focus on high-rate criminals who have been identified as committing a large proportion of the crime in a community. Problem-solving innovations focus on specific problems that are viewed as contributing to crime incidence and that can be ameliorated by the police. In this case, a systematic approach to solve problems is used to prevent future crime. Finally, community-based interventions emphasize the role of the community in doing something about crime problems. Community approaches look to strengthen collective efficacy in the community or to strengthen the bonds between the police and the community, as a way of enhancing informal social controls and increasing cooperation with the police, with the goal of preventing crime.

In this concluding chapter, the committee summarizes the main findings for each of the four areas on which the report has focused: law and legality, crime control, community impacts, and racial disparities and racially biased behavior. For each area, we list the main conclusions reached (the conclusions are numbered according to the report chapter in which they were developed) and then provide a final, summary discussion of the findings. We then turn to the broader policy implications of the report as a whole. Finally, we offer suggestions for filling research gaps in order to strengthen the knowledge base regarding proactive policing and its impacts.

LAW AND LEGALITY

CONCLUSION 3-1 Factual findings from court proceedings, federal investigations into police departments, and ethnographic and theoretical arguments support the hypothesis that proactive strategies that use aggressive stops, searches, and arrests to deter criminal activity may decrease liberty and increase violations of the Fourth Amendment and Equal Protection Clause; proactive policing strategies may also affect the Fourth Amendment status of policing conduct. However, there is not enough direct empirical evidence on the relationship between particular policing strategies and constitutional violations to draw any conclusions about the likelihood that particular proactive strategies increase or decrease constitutional violations.

CONCLUSION 3-2 Even when proactive strategies do not violate or encourage constitutional violations, they may undermine legal values, such as privacy, equality, and accountability. Empirical studies to date have not assessed these implications.

However effective a policing practice may be in preventing crime, it is impermissible if it violates the law. The most important legal constraints on proactive policing are the Fourth Amendment to the U.S. Constitution, the Equal Protection Clause (of the Fourteenth Amendment), and related statutory provisions.

Although proactive policing strategies do not inherently violate the Fourth Amendment, any proactive strategy could lead to Fourth Amendment violations to the degree that it is implemented by having officers engage in stops, searches, and arrests that violate constitutional standards. This risk is especially relevant for stop, question, and frisk (SQF); broken windows policing; and hot spots policing interventions if they use an aggressive practice of searches and seizures to deter criminal activity.

In addition, in conjunction with existing Fourth Amendment doctrine, proactive policing strategies may limit the effective strength or scope of constitutional protection or reduce the availability of constitutional remedies. For example, when departments identify "high crime areas" pursuant to place-based proactive policing strategies, courts may allow stops by officers of individuals within those areas that are based on less individualized behavior than they would require without the "high crime" designation. In this way, geographically oriented proactive policing may lead otherwise identical citizen-police encounters to be treated differently under the law.

The Equal Protection Clause guarantees equal and impartial treatment of citizens by government actors. It governs all policies, decisions, and acts taken by police officers and departments, including those in furtherance of proactive policing strategies. As a result, Equal Protection claims may arise with respect to any proactive policing strategy to the degree that it discriminates against individuals based on their race, religion, or national origin, among other characteristics. Since most policing policies today do not expressly target racial or ethnic groups, most Equal Protection challenges require proving discriminatory purpose in addition to discriminatory effect in order to establish a constitutional violation.

Specific proactive policing strategies such as SQF and "zero tolerance" versions of broken windows policing have been linked to violations of both the Fourth Amendment and the Equal Protection Clause by courts in private litigation and by the U.S. Department of Justice in its investigations of police departments. Ethnographic studies and theoretical arguments further support the idea that proactive strategies that use aggressive stops, searches, and arrests to deter criminal activity may decrease liberty and increase Fourth Amendment and Equal Protection violations. However, empirical evidence is insufficient—using the accepted standards of causality in social science—to support any conclusion about whether proactive policing strategies systematically promote or reduce constitutional violations. In order to establish a causal link, studies would ideally determine the incidence of problematic behavior by police under a proactive policy and compare that to the incidence of the same behavior in otherwise similar circumstances in which a proactive policy is not in place.

However, even when proactive strategies do not lead to constitutional violations, they may raise concerns about deeper legal values such as privacy, equality, autonomy, accountability, and transparency. Even procedural justice policing and community-oriented policing, neither of which are likely to violate legal constraints on policing (and, to the extent that procedural justice operates as intended, may make violations of law less likely), may, respectively, undermine the transparency about the status of police-citizen interactions and alter the structure of decision making and accountability in police organizations.

CRIME AND DISORDER

The available scientific evidence suggests that certain proactive policing strategies are successful in reducing crime and disorder. This important conclusion provides support for a growing interest among American police in innovating to develop effective crime prevention strategies. At the same time, there is substantial heterogeneity in the effectiveness of different proactive policing interventions in reducing crime and disorder. For some types of proactive policing, the evidence consistently points to effectiveness, but for others the evidence is inconclusive. Evidence in many cases is restricted to localized crime prevention impacts, such as specific places, or to specific individuals. There is relatively little evidence-based knowledge about whether and to what extent the approaches examined in this report will have crime prevention benefits at the larger jurisdictional level (e.g., a city as a whole, or even large administrative areas such as precincts within a city) or across all offenders. One key problem that needs to be examined in this regard, but which has not been studied so far, is the degree to which specific policing programs create "opportunity costs" in terms of the allocation of police or policing resources in other domains. Furthermore, the crime prevention outcomes that are observed are mostly observed in the short term, and the evidence seldom addresses long-term crime-prevention outcomes.

It is important to note here that, in practice, police departments typically implement crime-reduction programs that include elements typical of several prevention strategies, as those strategies are defined for this report (see Chapter 2). Given this hybridization of tactics in practice, the committee's review of the evidence was often hindered by the overlapping character of the real-world proactive policing interventions evaluated in many of the published research studies.

Place-Based Strategies

CONCLUSION 4-1 The available research evidence strongly suggests that hot spots policing strategies produce short-term crime-reduction effects without simply displacing crime into areas immediately surrounding targeted locations. Hot spots policing studies that do measure possible displacement effects tend to find that these programs generate a diffusion of crime-control benefits into immediately adjacent areas. There is an absence of evidence on the long-term impacts of hot spots policing strategies on crime and on possible jurisdictional outcomes.

CONCLUSION 4-2 At present, there are insufficient rigorous empirical studies on predictive policing to support a firm conclusion for or against either the efficacy of crime prediction software or the effectiveness of any associated police operational tactics. It also remains difficult to distinguish a predictive policing approach from hot spots policing at small geographic areas.

CONCLUSION 4-3 The results from studies examining the introduction of closed circuit television camera schemes are mixed, but they tend to show modest outcomes in terms of property crime reduction at high-crime places for passive monitoring approaches.

CONCLUSION 4-4 There are insufficient studies to draw conclusions regarding the impact of the proactive use of closed circuit television on crime and disorder reduction.

Policing has always had a geographic or place-based component, especially in how patrol resources are allocated for emergency response systems. However, over the past three decades scholars and the police have begun to recognize that crime is highly concentrated at specific places. Following this recognition, a series of place-based strategies have been developed in policing. In contrast to the focus of the standard model of policing, proactive place-based policing calls for a refocusing of policing on very small, "microgeographic" units of analysis, often termed "crime hot spots." A number of rigorous evaluations of hot spots policing programs, including a series of randomized controlled trials, have been conducted.

The available research evidence suggests that hot spots policing interventions generate statistically significant short-term crime-reduction impacts without simply displacing crime into areas immediately surrounding the targeted locations. Instead, hot spots policing studies that do measure possible displacement effects tend to find that these programs generate a diffusion-of-crime-control benefit into immediately adjacent areas. While the evidence base is strong for the benefits of hot spots policing in ameliorating local crime problems, there are no rigorous field studies of whether and to what extent this strategy will have jurisdictionwide impacts.

Predictive policing also takes a place-based approach, but it focuses greater concern on predicting the future occurrence of crimes in time and place. It relies upon sophisticated computer algorithms to predict changing patterns of future crime, often promising to be able to identify the exact locations where crimes of specific types are likely to occur next. While this approach has potential to enhance place-based crime prevention approaches, there are at present insufficient rigorous empirical studies to draw any firm conclusions about either the efficacy of crime prediction software or the effectiveness of any associated police operational tactics. Moreover, it remains difficult to distinguish the police actions used in a predictive policing approach from hot spots policing at small geographic areas.

Another technology relevant to improving police capacity for proactive intervention at specific places is closed circuit television (CCTV), which can be used either passively or proactively. The results from studies examining the introduction of CCTV camera schemes are mixed, but they tend to show modest outcomes in terms of property crime reduction at high-crime places for passive monitoring approaches. Again, the committee did not find evidence that would allow us to estimate whether CCTV implemented as a jurisdictionwide strategy would have meaningful impacts on crime in that jurisdiction. As far as the proactive use of CCTV is concerned, there are insufficient studies to draw conclusions regarding the impact of this strategy on crime and disorder.

Problem-Solving Strategies

CONCLUSION 4-5 There is a small group of rigorous studies of problem-oriented policing. Overall, these consistently show that problem-oriented policing programs lead to short-term reductions in crime. These studies do not address possible jurisdictional impacts of problem-oriented policing and generally do not assess the long-term impacts of these strategies on crime and disorder.

CONCLUSION 4-6 A small but rigorous body of evidence suggests that third party policing generates short-term reductions in crime and disorder; there is more limited evidence of long-term impacts. However, little is known about possible jurisdictional outcomes.

Problem-solving strategies such as problem-oriented policing and third party policing use an approach that seeks to identify causes of problems that engender crime incidents and draws upon innovative solutions to those problems to assess whether the solutions are effective. Problem-oriented policing uses a basic iterative process of problem identification, analysis, response, assessment, and adjustment of the response (often called the SARA [scanning, analysis, response, and assessment] model). This approach provides a framework for uncovering the complex mechanisms at play in crime problems and for developing tailored interventions to address the underlying conditions that cause crime problems in specific situations. Despite its popularity as a crime-prevention strategy, there are surprisingly few rigorous program evaluations of problem-oriented policing.

Much of the available evaluation evidence consists of non-experimental analyses that find strong associations between problem-oriented interventions and crime reduction. Program evaluations also suggest that it is difficult for police officers to fully implement problem-oriented policing. Many problem-oriented policing projects are characterized by weak problem analysis and a lack of non-enforcement responses to targeted problems. Nevertheless, even these limited applications of problem-oriented policing have been shown by rigorous evaluations to generate statistically significant short-term crime prevention impacts.

Third party policing draws upon the insights of problem solving, but also leverages "third parties" who are believed to offer significant new resources for preventing crime and disorder. Using civil ordinances and civil courts or the resources of private agencies, police departments engaged in third party policing recognize that much social control is exercised by institutions other than the police (e.g., public housing agencies, property owners, parents, health and building inspectors, and business owners) and that crime can be managed through coordination with agencies and in ways other than enforcement responses under the criminal law. Though there are only a small number of program evaluations, the impact of third party policing interventions on crime and disorder has been assessed using randomized controlled trials and rigorous quasi-experimental designs. The available evidence suggests that third party policing generates statistically significant crime- and disorder-reduction effects. Related programs that employ Business Improvement Districts also show crime-prevention outcomes with long-term impacts, though research designs have been less rigorous in establishing causality.

Person-Focused Strategies

CONCLUSION 4-7 Evaluations of focused deterrence programs show consistent crime control impacts in reducing gang violence, street crime driven by disorderly drug markets, and repeat individual offending. The available evaluation literature suggests both short-term and long-term areawide impacts of focused deterrence programs on crime.

CONCLUSION 4-8 Evidence regarding the crime-reduction impact of stop, question, and frisk when implemented as a general, citywide crime-control strategy is mixed.

CONCLUSION 4-9 Evaluations of focused uses of stop, question, and frisk (SQF) (combined with other self-initiated enforcement activities by officers), targeting places with violence or serious gun crimes and focusing on high-risk repeat offenders, consistently report short-term crime-reduction effects; jurisdictional impacts, when estimated, are modest. There is an absence of evidence on the long-term impacts of focused uses of SQF on crime.

In the standard model of policing, the primary goal of police was to identify and arrest offenders *after* crimes had been committed. But beginning in the early 1970s, research evidence began to suggest that the police could be more effective if they focused on a relatively small number of chronic offenders. These studies led to innovations in policing based on the logic that crime prevention outcomes could be enhanced by focusing policing efforts on the small number of offenders who account for a large proportion of crime.

Offender-focused deterrence strategies, also known as "pulling levers," attempt to deter crime among a particular offending population and are often implemented in combination with problem-solving tactics. Offender-focused deterrence allows police to increase the certainty, swiftness, and severity of punishment in innovative ways. These strategies seek to change offender behavior by understanding the underlying crime-producing dynamics and conditions that sustain recurring crime problems and by implementing a blended strategy of law enforcement, community mobilization, and social service actions.

A growing number of quasi-experimental evaluations suggest that focused deterrence programs generate statistically significant crime-reduction impacts. Robust crime-control impacts have been reported by controlled evaluations testing the effectiveness of focused deterrence programs in reducing gang violence and street crime driven by disorderly drug markets and by non-experimental studies that examine repeat individual offending. It is noteworthy that the size of the effects observed are large, though the committee observed that many of the largest impacts are in studies with evaluation designs that are less rigorous. The committee did not identify any randomized experiments in this program area. Nonetheless, many of the quasi-experiments have study designs that create highly credible equivalence between their treatment and comparison conditions, which supports interpreting their results as evidence of causation.

While SQF has long been a law enforcement tool of policing, the landmark 1968 Supreme Court decision *Terry v. Ohio* provided a set of standard criteria that facilitated its use as a strategy for crime control. According to that decision, police may stop a person based upon a "reasonable suspicion" that that person may commit or is in the process of committing a crime; if a separate "reasonable suspicion" that the person is armed exists, the police may conduct a frisk of the stopped individual. While this standard means that *Terry* stops could not be legally applied without reference to the behavior of the individual being stopped, interpretation of that behavior gave significant leeway to the police. As a proactive policing strategy, departments often employ SQF more expansively and to promote forward-looking, preventive ends.

Non-experimental analyses of SQF broadly applied across a jurisdiction show mixed findings. However, a separate body of controlled evaluation research (including randomized experiments) that examines the effectiveness of SQF and other self-initiated enforcement activities by officers in targeting places with serious gun crime problems and focusing on high-risk repeat offenders consistently reports statistically significant short-term crime reductions.

Community-Based Strategies

CONCLUSION 4-10 Existing studies do not identify a consistent crime-prevention benefit for community-oriented policing programs. However, many of these studies are characterized by weak evaluation designs.

CONCLUSION 4-11 At present, there are an insufficient number of rigorous empirical studies on procedural justice policing to draw a firm conclusion about its effectiveness in reducing crime and disorder.

CONCLUSION 4-12 Broken windows policing interventions that use aggressive tactics for increasing misdemeanor arrests to control disorder generate small to null impacts on crime.

CONCLUSION 4-13 Evaluations of broken windows interventions that use place-based, problem-solving practices to reduce social and physical disorder have reported consistent short-term crime-reduction impacts. There is an absence of evidence on the long-term impacts of these kinds of broken windows strategies on crime or on possible jurisdictional outcomes.

The committee also reviewed the crime-prevention impacts of interventions using a community-based crime prevention approach. Such strategies include community-oriented policing, broken windows policing, and procedural justice policing. The logic models informing these community-based strategies seek to enlist and mobilize people who are not police in the processes of policing. In this case, however, the focus is generally not on specific actors such as business or property owners (as in the case of third party policing) but on the community more generally. In some cases, community-based strategies rely on enhancing "collective efficacy," which is a community's ability to engage in collective action to do something about crime (e.g., community-oriented policing and broken windows policing). In other cases, community-based models seek to change community members' evaluations of the legitimacy of police actions (e.g., procedural justice policing) with the goal of increasing cooperation between the police and the public or encouraging law-abiding behavior. These goals are often intertwined in a real-world policing program.

As a proactive crime-prevention strategy, community-oriented policing tries to address and mitigate community problems (crime or otherwise) and, in turn, to build social resilience, collective efficacy, and empowerment to strengthen the infrastructure for the coproduction of safety and crime prevention. Community-oriented policing involves three core processes and structures: (1) citizen involvement in identifying and addressing public safety concerns; (2) the decentralization of decision making to develop responses to locally defined problems; and (3) problem solving. Problem solving and decentralization acquire a *community-oriented policing* character when these process elements are embedded in the community engagement (often called "partnership") element.

Although the committee identified a large number of studies of community-oriented policing programs, many of these programs were implemented in tandem with tactics typical of other approaches, such as problem solving. This was not surprising, given that basic definitions of community policing used by police departments often included problem solving as a key programmatic element. The studies also varied in their outcomes, reflecting the broad range of tactics and practices that are included in community-oriented policing programs, and many of the studies were characterized by weak evaluation designs. With these caveats, the committee did not identify a consistent crime prevention benefit for community-oriented policing programs.

Procedural justice policing seeks to impress upon citizens and the wider community that the police exercise their authority in legitimate ways. When citizens accord legitimacy to police activity, according to this logic model, they are more inclined to defer to police authority in instances of citizen-police interaction and to collaborate with police in the future, even to the extent of being more inclined not to violate the law. There is currently only a very small evidence base from which to support conclusions about the impact of procedural justice policing on crime prevention. Existing research does not support a conclusion that procedural justice policing impacts crime or disorder outcomes. At the same time, because the evidence base is small, the committee also cannot conclude that such strategies are ineffective.

Broken windows policing shares with community-oriented policing a concern for community welfare and envisions a role for police in finding ways to strengthen community structures and processes that provide a degree of immunity from disorder and crime in neighborhoods. Unlike the community-oriented policing strategy, it does not emphasize the coproductive collaborations of police and community as a mode of intervention; rather, it focuses on what police should do to establish conditions that allow "natural" community entities to flourish and promote neighborhood order and social/economic vitality. Implementations of broken windows interventions vary from informal enforcement tactics (warnings, rousting disorderly people) to formal or more intrusive ones (arrests, citations, stop and frisk), all of which are intended either to disrupt the forces of disorder before they overwhelm a neighborhood's capacity for order maintenance or to restore afflicted neighborhoods to a level where intrinsic community sources of order can manage it.

The impacts of broken windows policing are mixed across evaluations, again complicating the ability of the committee to draw strong inferences. However, the available program evaluations suggest that aggressive, misdemeanor arrest–based approaches to control disorder generate small to null impacts on crime. In contrast, controlled evaluations of place-based approaches that use problem-solving interventions to reduce social and physical disorder provide evidence of consistent crime-reduction impacts.

COMMUNITY IMPACTS

There is broad recognition that a positive community relationship with the police has value in its own right, irrespective of any influence it may have on crime or disorder. Democratic theories assert that the police, as an arm of government, are to serve the community and should be accountable to it in ways that elicit public approval and consent. Given this premise and the recent conflicts between the police and the public, the committee thought it very important to assess the impacts of proactive policing on issues, such as fear of crime, collective efficacy, and community evaluation of police legitimacy.

Place-Based, Problem-Solving, and Person-Focused Interventions

CONCLUSION 5-1 Existing research suggests that place-based policing strategies rarely have negative short-term impacts on community outcomes. At the same time, such strategies rarely improve community perceptions of the police or other community outcome measures. There is a virtual absence of evidence on the long-term and jurisdiction-level impacts of place-based policing on community outcomes.

CONCLUSION 5-2 Studies show consistent small-to-moderate, positive impacts of problem-solving interventions on short-term community satisfaction with the police. There is little evidence available on the long-term and jurisdiction-level impacts of problem-solving strategies on community outcomes.

CONCLUSION 5-3 There is little consistency found in the impacts of problem-solving policing on perceived disorder, quality of life, fear of crime, and police legitimacy, except for the near-absence of backfire effects. The lack of backfire effects suggests that the risk is low of harmful community effects from tactics typical of problem-solving strategies.

CONCLUSION 5-4 Studies evaluating the impact of person-focused strategies on community outcomes have a number of design limitations that prevent causal inferences to be drawn about program effects. However, the studies of citizens' personal experiences with person-focused strategies do show marked negative associations between exposure to stop, question, and frisk and proactive traffic enforcement approaches and community outcomes. The long-term and jurisdictionwide community consequences of person-focused proactive strategies remain untested.

Place-based, person-focused, and problem-solving interventions are distinct from community-based proactive strategies in that they do not directly seek to engage the public to enhance legitimacy evaluations and cooperation. In this context, the concerns regarding community outcomes for these approaches have often focused not on whether they improve community attitudes toward the police but rather on whether the focus on crime control leads inevitably to declines in positive community attitudes. Community-based strategies, in contrast, specifically seek to reduce fear, increase trust and willingness to intervene in community problems, and increase trust and confidence in the police.

A body of research evaluating the impact of place-based strategies on community attitudes is only now emerging; this research includes both quasi-experimental and experimental studies. However, the consistency of the findings suggests that place-based proactive policing strategies rarely have negative short-term impacts on community attitudes. At the same time, the evidence suggests that such strategies rarely improve community perceptions of the police or other community outcome measures. Moreover, existing studies have generally examined the broader community and not specific individuals who are the focus of place-based interventions at crime hot spots. As noted below, more aggressive policing tactics that are focused on individuals may have negative outcomes on those who have contact with the police. Existing studies also generally measure short-term changes, which may not be sensitive to communities that become the focus of long-term implementation of place-based policing. Finally, there has not been measurement of the impacts of place-based approaches on the broader community, extending beyond the specific focus of interventions.

The research literature on community impacts of problem-solving interventions is larger. Although much of the literature relies on quasi-experimental designs, a few well-implemented randomized experiments also provide information on community outcomes. Studies show consistent positive short-term impacts of problem-solving strategies on community satisfaction with the police. At the same time, however, the research base lacks estimates of larger jurisdictional impacts of these strategies.

Because problem-solving strategies are so often implemented in tandem with tactics typical of community-based policing (i.e., community engagement), it is difficult to determine what role the problem-solving aspect plays in community outcomes, compared to the impact of the community engagement element. Although this fact makes it difficult to draw strong conclusions about "what" is impacting community attitudes, as we note below, it may be that implementing multiple approaches in tandem can also have more positive outcomes for police agencies.

While there is evidence that problem-solving approaches increase community satisfaction with the police, we found little consistency in problem-solving policing's impacts on perceived disorder/quality of life, fear of crime, and police legitimacy. However, the near-absence of backfire (i.e., undesired negative) effects in the evaluations of problem-solving strategies suggests that the risk of harmful community effects from problem-solving strategies is low. As with place-based approaches, community outcomes generally do not examine people who have direct contact with the police, and measurement of impacts is local as opposed to jurisdictional.

The body of research evaluating the impact of person-focused strategies on community outcomes is relatively small, even in comparison with the evidence base on problem-solving and place-based strategies; the long-term community consequences of person-focused proactive strategies also remain untested. These studies involve qualitative or correlational designs that make it difficult to draw causal inferences about typical impacts of these strategies. Correlational studies do find strong negative associations between exposure to the strategy and the attitudes and orientations of individuals who are the subjects of aggressive law enforcement interventions (SQF and proactive traffic enforcement). Moreover, a number of ethnographic and survey-based studies have found negative outcomes, especially for Black and other non-White youth who are continually exposed to SQFs. The studies that measure the impact on the larger community show a more complicated and unclear pattern of outcomes.

Community-Based Interventions

CONCLUSION 6-1 Community-oriented policing leads to modest improvements in the public's view of policing and the police in the short term. (Very few studies of community-oriented policing have traced its long-term effects on community outcomes or its jurisdictionwide consequences.) These improvements occur with greatest consistency for measures of community satisfaction and less so for measures of perceived disorder, fear of crime, and police legitimacy. Evaluations of community-oriented policing rarely find "backfire" effects on community attitudes. Hence, the deployment of community-oriented policing as a proactive strategy seems to offer prospects for modest gains at little risk of negative consequences.

CONCLUSION 6-2 Due to the small number of studies, mixed findings, and methodological limitations, no conclusion can be drawn about the impact of community-oriented policing on collective efficacy and citizen cooperative behavior.

CONCLUSION 6-3 The committee is not able to draw a conclusion regarding the impacts of broken windows policing on fear of crime or collective efficacy. This is due in part to the surprisingly small number of studies that examine the community outcomes of broken windows policing and in part to the mixed effects observed.

CONCLUSION 6-4 In general, studies show that perceptions of procedurally just treatment are strongly and positively associated with subjective evaluations of police legitimacy and cooperation with the police. However, the research base is currently insufficient to draw conclusions about whether procedurally just policing causally influences either perceived legitimacy or cooperation.

CONCLUSION 6-5 Although the application of procedural justice concepts to policing is relatively new, there are more extensive literatures on procedural justice in social psychology, in management, and with other legal authorities such as the courts. Those studies are often designed in ways that make causal inferences more compelling, and results in those areas suggest that the application of procedural justice concepts to policing has promise and that further studies are needed to examine the degree to which the success of such strategies in those other domains can be replicated in the domain of policing.

The available empirical research on community-oriented policing's community effects focuses on citizen perceptions of police performance (in terms of what they do and the consequences for community disorder), satisfaction with police, and perceived police legitimacy. The evidence suggests that community-oriented policing leads to modest improvements in the community's view of policing and the police in the short term. This occurs with greatest consistency for measures of community satisfaction and less so for measures of perceived disorder, fear of crime, and perceived legitimacy. Evaluations of community-oriented policing rarely find "backfire" effects from the intervention on community attitudes. Therefore, the deployment of community-oriented policing as a proactive strategy seems to offer prospects of modest gains at little risk of negative consequences.

Broken windows policing is often evaluated directly in terms of its short-term crime control impacts. We have emphasized in this report that the logic model for broken windows policing seeks to alter the community's levels of fear and collective efficacy as a method of enhancing community social controls and reducing crime in the long run. While this is a key element of the broken windows policing model, the committee's review of the evidence found that these outcomes have seldom been examined. The evidence was insufficient to draw any conclusions regarding the impact of broken windows policing on community social controls. Studies of the impacts of broken windows policing on fear of crime do not support the model's claim that such programs will reduce levels of fear in the community, at least in the short run.

While there is a rapidly growing body of research on the community impacts of procedural justice policing, it is difficult to draw causal inferences from these studies. In general, the studies show that perceptions of procedurally just treatment are strongly correlated with subjective evaluations of police legitimacy. The extant research base on the impacts of procedural justice proactive policing strategies on perceived legitimacy and cooperation was insufficient for the committee to draw conclusions about whether procedurally just policing will improve community evaluations of police legitimacy or increase cooperation with the police.

Although this committee finding may appear at odds with a growing movement to encourage procedurally just behavior among the police, the committee thinks it is important to stress that a finding that there is insufficient evidence to support the expected outcomes of procedural justice policing is not the same as a finding that such outcomes do not exist. Moreover, although the application of procedural justice to policing is relatively new, there is a more extensive evidence base on procedural justice in social psychology and organizational management, as well as on procedural justice with other legal authorities such as the courts. Those studies are often designed in ways that make causal inferences more compelling, and results in those areas suggest meaningful impacts of procedural justice on the legitimacy of institutions and authorities involved. Thus, the application of procedural justice ideas to policing has promise, although further studies are needed to examine the degree to which the success of such implementations in other social contexts can be replicated in the arena of policing.

RACIAL BIAS AND DISPARITIES

CONCLUSION 7-1 There are likely to be large racial disparities in the volume and nature of police–citizen encounters when police target high-risk people or high-risk places, as is common in many proactive policing programs.

CONCLUSION 7-2 Existing evidence does not establish conclusively whether, and to what extent, the racial disparities associated with concentrated person-focused and place-based enforcement are indicators of statistical prediction, racial animus, implicit bias, or other causes. However, the history of racial injustice in the United States, in particular in the area of criminal justice and policing, as well as ethnographic research that has identified disparate impacts of policing on non-White communities, makes the investigation of the causes of racial disparities a key research and policy concern.

Concerns about racial bias loom especially large in discussions of policing. The interest of this report was to assess whether and to what extent proactive policing affects racial disparities in police–citizen encounters and racial bias in police behavior. Recent high-profile incidents of police shootings and abusive police–citizen interaction caught on camera have raised questions regarding basic fairness, racial discrimination, and the excessive use of force of all forms against non-Whites, and especially Blacks, in the United States. In considering these incidents, the committee stresses that the origins of policing in the United States are intimately interwoven with the nation's history of racial prejudice. Although in recent decades police have often made a strong effort to address racially biased behaviors, wide disparities remain in the extent to which non-White people and White people are stopped or arrested by police. Moreover, as our discussion of constitutional violations in Chapter 3 notes, the U.S. Department of Justice has identified continued racial disparities and biased behavior in policing in a number of major American police agencies.

As social norms have evolved to make overt expressions of bigotry less acceptable, psychologists have developed tools to measure more subtle factors underlying biased behavior. A series of studies suggest that negative racial attitudes may influence police behavior—although there is no direct research on proactive policing. There is a further growing body of research identifying how these psychological mechanisms may affect behavior and what types of situations, policies, or practices may exacerbate or ameliorate racially biased behaviors. In a number of studies, social psychologists have found that race may affect decision making, especially under situations where time is short and such decisions need to be made quickly. More broadly, social psychologists have identified dispositional (i.e., individual characteristics) and situational and environmental factors that are associated with higher levels of racially biased behavior.

Proactive strategies often facilitate increased officer contact with residents (particularly in high-crime areas), involve contacts that are often enforcement-oriented and uninvited, and may allow greater officer discretion compared to standard policing models. These elements align with broad categories of possible risk factors for biased behavior by police officers. For example, when contacts involve stops or arrests, police may be put in situations where they have to "think fast" and react quickly. Social psychologists have argued that such situations may be particularly prone to the emergence of what they define as implicit biases.

Relative to the research on the impact of proactive policing policies on crime, there is very little field research exploring the potential role that racially biased behavior plays in proactive policing. There is even less research on the ways that race may shape police policy or color the consequences of police encounters with residents. These research gaps leave police departments and communities concerned with bias in police behavior without an evidence base from which to make informed decisions. Because of these gaps, the committee was unable to draw any concrete conclusions about the role of biased behavior in proactive policing. Consequently, research on these topics is urgently needed both so that the field may better understand potential negative consequences of proactive policing and so that communities and police departments may be better equipped to align police behaviors with values of equity and justice.

Inferring the role of racial animus, statistical prediction, or other dispositional and situational risk factors in contributing to observed racial disparities is a challenging question for research. Although focused policing approaches may reduce overall levels of police intrusion, we also detailed in Chapter 7 the very large disparities in the stops and arrests of non-White, and especially Black Americans, and we noted that concentrating enforcement efforts in high-crime areas and on highly active individual offenders may lead to racial disparities in police–citizen interactions. Although these disparities are often much reduced when taking into account population benchmarks such as official criminality, the committee also noted that studies that seek to benchmark citizen–police interactions against simple population counts or broad, publicly available measures of criminal activity do not yield conclusive information regarding the potential for racially biased behavior in proactive policing efforts. Identifying an appropriate benchmark would require detailed information on the geography and nature of the proactive strategy, as well as localized knowledge of the relative importance of the problem. Such benchmarks are not currently available. The absence of such benchmarks makes it difficult to distinguish between accurate statistical prediction and racial profiling.

Some of the most illuminating evidence on the potential impact of proactive policing and increased citizen–police contacts on racial outcomes relates to the use of SQF in New York City. This research seeks to model the probabilities that police suspicion of criminal possession of a weapon turns out to be justified, given the information available to officers when deciding whether to stop someone. This work finds substantial racial and ethnic disparities in the distribution of these probabilities, suggesting that police in New York City apply lower thresholds of suspicion to blacks and Hispanics. We do not know whether this pattern exists in other settings.

Per the charge to the committee, this report reviewed a relatively narrow area of intersection between race and policing. This focus, though, is nested in a broader societal framework of possible disparities and biased behaviors across a whole array of social contexts. These can affect proactive policing in, for example, the distribution of crime in society and the extent of exposure of specific groups to police surveillance and enforcement. However, it was beyond the scope of this study to review them systematically in the context of the committee's work.

POLICY IMPLICATIONS

In its review of the evidence, the committee tried to identify the most credible evidence on whether particular types of proactive policing strategies have been shown to affect legality, crime, communities, racial disparities, and racially biased behavior. A strategy is said to have "impact" if it affects outcomes compared with what they would have been at that same time and place in the absence of the implementation of a specific strategy. The strongest evidence often derives from randomized field trials and natural experiments in the field, typically implemented through a change in the activities of a police department structured so as to create a credibly comparable control condition with which to compare the "treatment" condition. However, as we have emphasized throughout the report, other methodological approaches can also provide rigorous evidence for the types of outcomes that we have examined. In turn, ethnographic studies have provided important information for the committee in understanding the processes that lead to such outcomes. Nonetheless, the emphasis in many sections of our report is on the "internal validity" of the evaluation: how strong is the evidence that a particular treatment implemented in a particular place *caused* the observed impact? And this assessment of validity has important implications for the strength of policy recommendations that we can draw from our review.

We want to emphasize that even a well-designed experimental trial implemented with fidelity may yield biased effect estimates if the outcomes data are not reliable. Most of the studies of crime outcomes examined in this report used crime data collected by the police department that is responsible for implementing the program. With the exception of homicide and perhaps motor-vehicle theft, the police only know of a fraction of all serious crimes. Less than one-half of robberies, aggravated assaults, and burglaries are reported to the police, and of course, reporting is a precondition for inclusion in the departmental statistics. That fact does not negate the usefulness of these data in measuring impact, but it does compel consideration of whether the intervention is likely to affect the likelihood that a crime will be reported to and recorded by the police. For example, if a community-based policing intervention has the effects of both reducing crime and increasing the percentage of crimes reported to the police, the result might be that the latter will mask the former and obscure the crime-reduction effect. We note this possibility as a potential challenge to the internal validity of even well-designed and faithfully implemented experimental interventions, if they rely solely on police data.

Data that are collected by researchers may also have serious weaknesses. In some of the community surveys reviewed in this report, response rates were exceptionally low. A number of studies that we examined also used laboratory data; the laboratory environment allows a great deal of control over the research process but can be criticized as artificial and as a poor indicator of what actually happens in the field in policing.

More generally, we want to point to three specific limitations when it comes to the usefulness of this review in informing policy choice. First, the literature that we reviewed typically lacks much information on the magnitudes of the effects of the strategies evaluated. A clear demonstration that the "treatment effect" is greater than would be expected by chance—that is, that the estimated effect is statistically significantly different from zero—helps establish that the program "worked" but not that it was "worthwhile" from a policy perspective. A more complete evaluation would require a comparison of the estimated magnitude of the effect with an estimate of the costs of the program. How many serious crimes were prevented by the candidate program for every $100,000 worth of resources devoted to it, and what are the effects of removing that $100,000 from what it would otherwise have been used for? For a police chief or city mayor, resources are limited and must be accounted for in making well-informed choices about policing practice. This problem becomes even more difficult when one is trying to calculate costs and benefits for such outcomes as community satisfaction or perceived legitimacy. The literature rarely provides such a cost-effectiveness analysis, and hence this committee cannot provide policy prescriptions that would give specific advice about the costs or cost savings.

Second, and closely related, is that the evaluation evidence, because it typically does not account for cost, may actually provide a misleading impression of whether a program "worked"—whether in reducing crime or improving community attitudes for the entire jurisdiction—as opposed to having an effect only for the segment of the city represented by the treatment group. As we have noted throughout the report, most evaluations provide a local estimate of program impacts. They do not report how the program affected the jurisdiction overall. Absent such reports, or at least evidence-grounded estimates of jurisdiction-level impact, it is very difficult to provide guidance to police executives about how redeployment of resources will impact overall trends across a city. Since most of the evaluations we reviewed assess local impacts only, we often do not know what the impacts of a program will be on the broader community when a program is broadly applied, as opposed to when it is implemented on a small scale.

Third, a police chief who is considering adopting a particular innovation may be able to make a prediction about whether it will reduce crime or improve community attitudes, based on evaluations of one or more similar programs, but that prediction must always be hedged by the constraint that making inferences about "here and now" based on "there and then" is a tricky business. A well-known example comes from the "coerced abstinence" program for drug-involved convicts known as HOPE. The program originated and was carefully evaluated in courts in Honolulu, Hawaii, where it appeared very effective. It has been replicated a number of times on the mainland United States, with at best mixed results. The variability in results may reflect differences in the quality of implementation by the law enforcement agencies, the modal type of drug of abuse (which differs among jurisdictions), or other factors.[1] To the extent that programmatic effects are moderated by the characteristics of the target population and the implementing agency, then importing a program that appears promising into another setting can lead to disappointment. The uncertainties created by this "external validity" problem for evaluating field trials cannot be readily quantified. A common-sense view is that a single evaluation is not enough to establish a strong case for adoption in a different time and place and that understanding potential modifiers of the effects is important for evidence-based policy.

However, while acknowledging these caveats, the committee thinks that we can provide broad policy guidance regarding what the science of policing is today and how that might affect the choices that police executives make. Waiting until the evidence base is fully developed to draw from science in policy making is not only unrealistic—it also means that practitioners will not benefit from what is known already. Our report provides important knowledge for policing, knowledge that can help inform the debate about what the police should be doing. Nonetheless, as we have noted, there are important limitations in how existing knowledge can be used, and those limitations should be considered when drawing upon the science in this report.

A number of identifiable policing strategies provide evidence of consistent short-term crime-prevention benefits at the local level. These in-

---

[1] For a discussion of HOPE, see the special issue of *Criminology & Public Policy* (November 2016), Volume 15, Issue 4.

clude hot spots policing, problem-oriented policing, third party policing, SQF targeted to violent and gun-crime hot spots, focused deterrence, and problem-solving efforts incorporated in broken windows policing. What these approaches have in common is their effort to more tightly specify and focus police activities. Police executives who implement such strategies are drawing upon evidence-based approaches. At the same time, the ability to generalize from existing evaluations to the broader array of at least larger American cities is sometimes limited by the limited number and scope of studies that are available, though in the case of hot spots policing a larger number of studies across diverse contexts have been carried out. We also find that these strategies, with the important exception of SQF, do not lead to negative community outcomes. With the caveats noted above, it appears that crime-prevention outcomes can be obtained without this type of unintended negative consequence. Albeit preliminary, this finding reinforces the policy relevance of these evidence-based approaches.

At the same time, the results of our review suggest that police executives should not view certain proactive policing approaches as evidence based, at least at this time. For instance, SQF indiscriminately focused across a jurisdiction or broken windows policing programs relying on a generalized approach to misdemeanor arrests ("zero tolerance") have not shown evidence of effectiveness. This caveat, combined with research evidence that documents negative individual outcomes for people who are the subject of aggressive police enforcement efforts, even in the absence of clear causal interpretation, should lead police executives to exercise caution in adopting generalized, aggressive enforcement tactics. Moreover, our review of the constitutional basis for focusing police resources on people or places suggests that issues of legality are particularly relevant in the case of such strategies. Even in the case of focused programs for which there is evidence of crime-control success, when aggressive approaches such as SQF are employed, police executives must consider and actively try to prevent potential negative outcomes on the community and on legality, and they should cooperate with researchers attempting to quantify and evaluate these issues. This means not only that police executives should proceed with caution in adopting such strategies but also that agencies that are already applying them broadly and without careful focus should consider scaling down present efforts.

The committee's findings regarding community-based strategies raise important questions about whether such approaches will yield crime-prevention benefits. Many scholars and policy makers have sought to argue that community-oriented policing and procedural justice policing will yield not only better relations with the public but also greater crime control. We do not find consistent evidence for this proposition, and police executives

CONCLUSIONS AND IMPLICATIONS FOR POLICY AND RESEARCH 325

should be accordingly wary of implementing community-based strategies primarily as a crime-control approach.

The committee also concluded that community-oriented policing programs were likely to improve evaluations of the police, albeit modestly. Accordingly, if the policy goal of an agency is to improve its relationship with the communities it serves, then community-oriented policing is a promising strategy choice, although we are unable to offer a judgment on whether the benefits are sufficient to justify the expected costs. Our review of policing programs with a community-based approach also suggests that police executives may want to consider applying multiple strategies as a more general agency approach. The difficulty of distinguishing the effects of community-based and problem-solving approaches that are often implemented together has been noted numerous times in this report. However, we also think that better outcomes may be obtained when programs are hybridized across the approaches defined in this report. If, for example, an agency seeks to improve both crime prevention and community satisfaction with the police, it seems reasonable to combine practices typical of community-oriented policing with evidence-based crime-prevention practices typical of strategies such as hot spots policing or problem-oriented policing. This has already been done in problem-solving approaches that emphasize community engagement, where these dual benefits have been observed.

Existing studies do not provide evidence of crime prevention effectiveness in the case of proactive procedural justice policing. Accordingly, the committee believes that caution should be used in advocating for such approaches on the ground that they will reduce crime. At the same time, studies reviewed by the committee did not find that procedural justice policing has the expected positive community outcomes. Does this mean that police should not encourage procedural justice policing programs? We think that this would be a serious mistake for two reasons. The first is simply that procedural justice reflects the behavior of police that is appropriate in a democratic society. Procedural justice encourages democratic policing even if it may not change citizen attitudes. The second reason relates to the state of research in this area. While it is a mistake to draw strong conclusions that procedural justice policing will improve community members' evaluations of police legitimacy or cooperation with the police, it is equally wrong to draw the conclusion that it will not do so. Again, the evidence base here is too sparse to support either position.

RESEARCH GAPS

While there is a large body of evaluation research in policing today, as contrasted with two or three decades ago, the committee identified a number of key gaps in what is known about proactive policing. Filling such gaps in the evidence base is critical for developing the type of knowledge that, as we noted earlier, is necessary to inform policy decisions for policing. Policing in the United States represents a large commitment of public resources; it is estimated to cost federal, state, and local governments more than $125 billion per year (Kyckelhahn, 2015). Given that investment, the extent of the research gaps on proactive policing is surprising. For the police to take advantage of the revolution in police practices that proactive policing represents, they will need the help of the federal government and private foundations in answering a host of questions regarding effectiveness, community outcomes, legality, and racially biased behavior. The committee also noted an imbalance in the evidence base across the areas of the committee's charge. While far from complete, there is a large body of credible causal evidence on the impact of proactive policing on crime rates. However, social science research of a similar form on other equally important outcomes of policing is only beginning to occur.

We think it also important to note at the outset that more research needs to be focused on the standard model of policing. The 2004 National Research Council report, *Fairness and Effectiveness in Policing: The Evidence,* argued that there was little evidence supporting such standard police practices as random police patrol across large areas, follow-up investigations, and rapid response to citizen calls for service. However, a number of new studies have been carried out since the 2004 study, and this recent research suggests that the view of the standard model of policing in that report may need to be reassessed (see, e.g., Chaflin and McCrary, 2017; Evans and Owens, 2007; Cook, 2015). In order to estimate the benefits of proactive policing efforts, more information is needed on whether standard policing practices are generating crime-prevention benefits, as well as sustaining and perhaps improving the community's trust in and regard for the police.

Improving the Quality of Data and Research on Proactive Policing

Drawing conclusions about the efficacy of proactive policing strategies or about policing innovations more broadly is complicated by the absence of comprehensive data on police behavior in the field. Just because a policy has been formally adopted does not mean that officers on the beat behave according to the tenets of that policy. The impact of the adoption of a policy on any outcome is, essentially, a combination of the actual impact of a police agency adopting, for example, a place-based intervention, and the probability that officers actually implement this intervention as they engage in targeted patrol in particular places. Identifying ways to measure what police officers actually do is, therefore, a central problem for evaluating the impact of proactive policing strategies on crime, communities, and the legality of officer behavior.

To be useful for evaluating the impact of a proactive policing strategy on what officers do in the field, it is necessary for the data to, at minimum, measure officer behavior both before and after the policy change. Ideally, the data would span multiple agencies, thereby allowing for a more credible analysis of what officers might have done in the absence of the policy change. There have been some examples of efforts by governments to proactively develop such data sources. Such efforts include the Federal Bureau of Investigation's National Use-of-Force Data Collection project, the Police Data Initiative in the Office of Community Oriented Policing Services (COPS Office) in the U.S. Department of Justice, and the proactive efforts in California to require local agencies to report information on all stops to that state's Office of the Attorney General (CA AB 953).[2] Similarly, there are a number of academic and nonprofit efforts to augment police data collection efforts and thereby provide enhanced analytic capacity, such as the Center for Policing Equity's National Justice Database and the Stanford Open Policing Project.[3] Substantially more effort needs to be devoted to collecting reliable data on how proactive policing is carried out in the field.[4] Without the routine collection of such data, it is not possible to assess the prevalence and incidence of proactive policing or to characterize the content of such strategies.

The committee also noted more general weaknesses in existing studies that limit the conclusions that can be drawn. One important limitation is that proactive policing interventions often overlap in terms of the strategies represented by the elements of the intervention. For example, many place-based policing interventions include elements of a problem-solving approach, as do many community-based programs. While we recognize that the police and program developers are focused on crime prevention and not on identifying the specific components of a program that have impact, the mixing of elements from different approaches makes it extremely difficult to draw strong conclusions about which element(s) in a program had a crime-prevention impact. Therefore, it is very important in future research to develop study designs that allow identification of the specific mechanisms that produce impacts.

---

[2] See https://leginfo.legislature.ca.gov/faces/billNavClient.xhtml?bill_id=201520160AB953 [November 2016].

[3] See http://mashable.com/2017/02/23/google-racial-justice-commitment/#8KbrqmHvKkqj http://observer.com/2016/02/traffic-stops-database/ [November 2016].

[4] Interesting new opportunities for such data collection have been taken advantage of by researchers. For example, S. Weisburd (2016) used GPS data on exactly where police cars are in Dallas, Texas, at small intervals of time to draw inferences about the effectiveness of police patrol in small areas.

More generally, it is important for evaluations to focus on the underlying logic models that are proposed to account for (or promise) program impacts. Broken windows policing, for example, was conceived as a method for increasing community social controls in the long run. However, very few studies of broken windows policing actually examine how police activities in reducing disorder will impact such long-term attitudes. This is true for many of the proactive policing strategies examined in this report. Research funding agencies should require the incorporation of tests of the validity of underlying logic models in their study solicitations.

The focus on short-run, rather than long-run, impacts also pervades the evaluation of crime incidence, which is the most researched outcome the committee examined. Seldom do researchers look at program impacts extending for more than a year after program initiation, and only a handful of the studies identified by the committee look at crime prevention in the long run. While research indicates that many proactive practices seem to create a crime-reduction effect in the short term, the long-term impacts of these programs also should be an important focus of study. And whereas most of the available research that measures community effects does so over a relatively short term (a year or less), it is likely that community effects—especially those involving people who have little or no direct contact with the police—require much longer to register. Some research suggests that community effects are dynamic, but that research has generally not examined effects over several years. For all these reasons, more research is needed that tracks the effects of proactive policing over several years.

With regard to the types of research conducted, more implementation and process evaluations are needed to better understand the challenges of getting programs and policies translated into police practice, as well as to better understand the actual practices that are being evaluated in terms of community outcomes. The standardization of measures of implementation and dosage for specific strategies will improve the capacity of systematic reviews of these studies to interpret an array of findings. In turn, in many areas there is a need for more rigorous evaluation designs—and especially the development of well-implemented randomized trials.

In looking at the studies reviewed in this report, the committee notes that most are concentrated in large, urban jurisdictions. Smaller, suburban, and rural jurisdictions are understudied, but they should be included in the mix of funded evaluations. Community dynamics in such jurisdictions may vary in ways not revealed in the studies of larger communities. Evaluations should also control for the larger organizational context in which policing programs operate. Little is known about how the structure of a department and, for example, its management style affects its ability to develop and sustain proactive policing programs that reduce crime while enhancing the legitimacy and legality of police officers' actions. Further research is also needed on how these outcomes are affected by police oversight and accountability mechanisms, including review boards, lawsuits, data disclosure requirements, and the standardized collection of data on officer activities (as recommended above).

Finally, the committee notes the absence of rigorous research on training of police. Training has been shown to change behavior in other settings, particularly management. Police training programs for proactive policing are recent, and there is very little evidence at this time about their long-term effects. Several recent studies suggest that training programs can influence officers' attitudes toward, and behavior within, communities. Studies need to examine the impact of training on police officers' orientations and behaviors. Expanding the Census of Law Enforcement Training Academies, and in particular identifying which agencies hire graduates, as opposed to simply how many agencies, is a possible first step that would facilitate linking officer training to actual field outcomes. It is especially important for future research to evaluate which training approaches and methods prove most effective for imparting the necessary will and skill required to implement a given proactive strategy well.

Proactive Policing and the Law

There is less research on how proactive policies influence the legality of officer behavior than on how those policies affect crime or community perceptions of crime. One of the hurdles is the absence of a clear measure of what, exactly, constitutes legal behavior on an officer's part. Research on how to quantify the legality of police officer behavior in a way that is consistent with the law and lends itself to causal analysis is a necessary first step. Because of the complex issues involved, such research is likely to be most productive if conducted by members of the legal, social science, and police leadership communities in collaboration.

Researchers studying the impacts of proactive policies on citizen law-breaking, using experimental or quasi-experimental designs and administrative data, also should identify the relevant legal standards for officer behavior and include measures of officer behavior that are affected by these standards as one of their assessed outcomes. Ethnographic, qualitative, and mixed methods social science research, as well as legal scholarship, should inform how quantitative researchers conceptualize these measures. Given that officer law-breaking is as important, if not more so, in a general evaluation of such policies as undesirable behavior on the part of citizens, researchers who have access to administrative data that measure and make reliable legal judgments about officer behavior, including data collected by body-worn cameras, should include assessment of such outcomes in their analysis of the policies' impacts on crime by citizens.

Crime-Control Impacts of Proactive Policing

As noted above, while the committee has provided a series of conclusions regarding the crime- and disorder-control impacts of proactive policing, there are significant caveats that limited our ability to develop specific policy prescriptions. Given the importance of the policing enterprise and its impacts on U.S. society, we think that a major investment in research on proactive policing is warranted, with a complementary investment in assessing standard policing practices.

A better understanding is needed of the crime-prevention effects of proactive policing programs relative to each other and relative to such activities as crime investigation, response to 911 calls, and routine patrol. For example, which types of proactive activities create a greater deterrent effect in a crime hot spot: foot patrol, technological surveillance (such as CCTVs), problem-solving projects, enforcement activities, or situational crime-prevention strategies? Can gun crimes be best reduced through focused deterrence/pulling levers, pedestrian and traffic stops, or crime prevention through environmental design?

Equally important to the relative deterrent effect of proactive policing approaches are the social costs and collateral consequences of those approaches. At the most basic level, identifying other effects than crime reduction of proactive policing approaches—positive or negative—is needed. Once identified, measuring for these effects when testing for the crime prevention effects of proactive policing should be included in study designs.

A key issue in place-based studies is whether crime displaces to other areas. There is now a strong literature showing that immediate geographic displacement is not common, and studies instead point to a diffusion of crime control benefits to areas near targeted hot spots. However, little is known about displacement to more distal areas and whether such displacement affects the crime prevention benefits of place-based strategies. Study of distal displacement needs to be a central feature of the next generation of research on place-based policing. Most evaluations also provide only local estimates of impacts, and it is critical to examine whether place-based strategies implemented across cities will have jurisdictional impacts. Estimating the size of jurisdictional impacts for strategies such as hot spots policing is critical for police executives and policy makers as they consider the wider benefits of these approaches.

More research is also needed on how technology contributes to the crime prevention effects of proactive policing strategies. There has been relatively little research on the impacts of technology in policing beyond technical, efficiency, or process evaluations. More studies of the crime-control impacts of license plate readers, body-worn cameras, gun-shot detection technologies, forensic technologies, and CCTV are needed. Furthermore, the effectiveness of analytic technologies such as crime analysis and predictive policing software applications also remains under-researched. Given their increased use in proactive policing strategies, much more needs to be known.

To date, there are no rigorous outcome evaluations of law enforcement proactive interventions designed to reduce and prevent technology-related crime, such as cybercrime, fraud and theft using the Internet, or hacking. Proactive activities by federal agencies such as the Federal Bureau of Investigation or the U.S. Department of Homeland Security remain completely immune from public-domain evaluation in this and all other aspects of their proactive efforts.

Finally, it is important to determine whether community-oriented or procedural justice approaches can produce crime prevention effects. While improving citizen reaction to police activity is an important goal in and of itself, equally important—and connected to this goal—is the detection, prevention, reduction, and control of crime. Perhaps community-oriented or procedural justice approaches can be combined with other effective practices from the place-based, person-focused, or problem-solving approaches to attain both goals. But to date, the effectiveness of community-oriented and procedural justice interventions in crime control is uncertain.

Community Impacts of Proactive Policing

While there is broad recognition of the importance of community impacts of proactive policing strategies, there are only a few studies available on the community impacts of place-based and person-focused strategies, and the results for most types of outcomes are varied. A more extensive menu of observational, quasi-experimental, and experimental evaluations is needed. Systematic assessment of the contingent nature of outcomes is needed. Moreover, although a variety of logic models propose to account for the role that various community outcomes play in the process of affecting crime and disorder levels and community perceptions and behaviors, these logic models have not been subjected to rigorous empirical tests.

A gap noted throughout the research on community impacts is the lack of studies of the long-term effects of proactive strategies. Regardless of the rigor of the evaluation design in terms of inferring causal linkages between strategies and community outcomes, the extant literature provides only an ahistorical, incomplete, and potentially misleading perspective on what the consequences of proactive strategies will be. Future research should take into account both the long-term exposure of research subjects to proactive policing and the need to track the community consequences of those strategies over years, not months. Both variation in the accumulation of dosage over extended time and the consequences of this extended exposure are virtually unexplored. Whether and how much a pattern of consequences is sustained or decays is also important to know.

One approach to changing community perception of police legitimacy is to change police behavior during contacts with the public. There is considerable evidence in the social psychology literature suggesting that personal contacts can change attitudes. However, there is insufficient research on the likelihood that one personal contact with a police officer can change orientations that have built up over a lifetime, irrespective of how the police behave during that single contact. Studies of the impact of a single experience with the police on a person's general orientation toward the police are relatively few, and the results are mixed. Research is needed that tests the ability of a single interaction to shape general views about police legitimacy. This work needs to consider different types of encounters. It also needs to take account of characteristics of the person being stopped (race, age, gender, trust in the police) and that person's history of encounters with the police. Finally, there needs to be a broader consideration of impacts on communities and the inevitable interactions between what the police do in a community and how that activity affects the development trajectory of that community, not only with respect to crime but also for housing, economic development, and other social outcomes.

Racial Bias and Disparities in Proactive Policing

The committee believes that the area of racial disparity and racially biased behavior is a particularly important one for enhancing the rigor and quantity of research on proactive policing. The committee identified five areas where research is most urgently needed with regard to racially biased behavior and proactive policing: (1) psychological risk factors, (2) training on bias reduction, (3) attention to behavioral bias as an important outcome of research on crime reduction, (4) an emphasis on assessing "downstream" consequences of proactive policing on racial outcomes, and (5) an emphasis on "upstream" influences regarding how proactive policing approaches are adopted.

First, a focus is needed on the psychological mechanisms of racially biased police behavior in actual field contexts, not only in laboratory simulations. As we reviewed in Chapter 7, research in social psychology has identified a number of risk and protective factors that in laboratory settings are associated with either an increase or decrease in racially biased behaviors, even in subjects who do not appear to harbor racial animus. Many situations common in proactive policing map onto these factors. In spite of the potential relevance of the laboratory findings, there is virtually no evidence about whether or not police contexts or trainings produce sufficient protections against those risks in the field. A systematic approach to these risk factors in proactive policing would be an important step toward producing an evidence base for evaluating racial disparities in proactive policing.

Second, rigorous research is needed on whether police training in this area affects actual police behavior. Even though there have been large investments in police training to address racial bias and disparate treatment, there are at present no rigorous studies that inform these efforts.

Third, the incidence of racially biased behavior and of racial disparities in outcomes should become an important outcome metric for research on proactive policing. To date, outcome evaluations in policing have focused primarily on crime control and at times on community satisfaction or perceived legitimacy. Seldom have studies assessed racial outcomes of proactive policing, despite the fact that these outcomes constitute a key issue for policy in American society. Assessing disparate impacts in policing in an informative way will require spatially detailed demographic information about the population at risk of encountering the police when the policy is in place, in order to identify an appropriate benchmark and identify the marginal person affected by the policy. Until standardized metrics for measuring racially biased behavior are available, along with measures of the populations exposed to proactive policing policies, thorough assessments of proactive policing efforts will likely require formal empirical analysis, as well as qualitative and ethnographic analysis, of proactive strategies, their implementation, and their impacts.

Fourth, understanding the downstream consequences of racial disparities is an urgent research need. Does proactive policing have a long-term impact on racial disparities or race relations in communities? What are the costs of such impacts, and can and should they be compared to the crime-control benefits of proactive policing? As we argued in Chapter 7, proactive policing may lead to long-term decreases in inequalities in communities because of the benefits of lowered crime and related social consequences of crime. But little is known about such issues to date. To weigh these potential costs of proactive policing against the crime-reducing benefits, researchers must develop some metric for quantifying and estimating the cost of racial disparities, racially biased behavior, and racial animus. Survey techniques commonly used for cost-benefit research in environmental economics may be a useful guide.

Finally, the committee identified very little research on what drives law enforcement agencies to adopt proactive police policies. The history of criminal justice and law enforcement in the United States, along with ethnographic evidence on how police actions are perceived in communities, suggests that the role of race and ethnicity in the adoption of policing practices should be carefully assessed. However, scholars of proactive policing have yet to study carefully how race may influence the adoption of specific proactive policing policies. It is critically important to understand not only the impacts of proactive policing on racial outcomes but also how race may affect the adoption of specific types of proactive policing. This was a concern raised to us by representatives of such groups as The Movement for Black Lives and the NAACP Legal Defense and Educational Fund (see Chapter 7 and Appendix A). Are more aggressive proactive policing strategies more likely to be chosen when Black or disadvantaged communities are the focus of police enforcement? This question needs to be addressed systematically in future research.

THE FUTURE OF PROACTIVE POLICING

Proactive policing has become a key part of police efforts to do something about crime in the United States. This report supports the general conclusion that there is sufficient scientific evidence to support the adoption of some proactive policing practices. Proactive policing efforts that focus on high concentrations of crimes at places or among the high-rate subset of offenders, as well as practices that seek to solve specific crime-fostering problems, show consistent evidence of effectiveness without evidence of negative community outcomes. Community-based strategies have also begun to show evidence of improving the relations between the police and public. At the same time, there are significant gaps in the knowledge base that do not allow one to identify with reasonable confidence the long-term effects of proactive policing. For example, existing research provides little guidance as to whether police programs to enhance procedural justice will improve community perceptions of police legitimacy or community cooperation with the police.

Much has been learned over the past two decades about proactive policing programs. But now that scientific support for these approaches has accumulated, it is time for greater investment in understanding what is cost-effective, how such strategies can be maximized to improve the relationships between the police and the public, and how they can be applied in ways that do not lead to violations of the law by the police.

References

Abrams, D., and Hogg, M. (1988). Comments on the motivational status of self-esteem in social identity and intergroup discrimination. *European Journal of Social Psychology,* 18(4), 317–334.

Abuwala, R., and Farole, D. J. (2008). *The Effects of the Harlem Housing Court on Tenant Perceptions of Justice.* New York: Center for Court Innovation.

Achenbach, J., Wan, W., Berman, M., and Balingit, M. (2016). Five Dallas police officers were killed by a lone attacker, authorities say. *The Washington Post,* July 8. Available: https://www.washingtonpost.com/news/morning-mix/wp/2016/07/08/like-a-little-war-snipers-shoot-11-police-officers-during-dallas-protest-march-killing-five [September 2016].

Alexander, M. (2012). *The New Jim Crow: Mass Incarceration in the Age of Colorblindness.* New York: The New Press.

Allen, M. (2002). Community policing credited in NW Pasadena: King's Village to take down walls. *Pasadena Star-News,* October 14.

Alpert, G. P. (2016). Toward a national database of officer involved shootings: A long and winding road. *Criminology & Public Policy,* 15(1), 237–242.

Alpert, G. P., Dunham, R. G., and Smith, M. R. (2007). Investigating racial profiling by the Miami-Dade police department: A multimethod approach. *Criminology,* 6(1), 22–55.

Amodio, D. M., Devine, P. G., and Harmon-Jones, E. (2008). Individual differences in the regulation of intergroup bias: The role of conflict monitoring and neural signals for control. *Journal of Personality and Social Psychology,* 94, 60–74.

Andresen, M. A., and Malleson, N. (2011). Testing the stability of crime patterns: Implications for theory and policy. *Journal of Research in Crime & Delinquency,* 48(1), 58–82.

Angwin, J., Larson, J., Mattu, S., and Kirchner, L. (2016). *Machine Bias: There Is Software That Is Used across the County to Predict Future Criminals. And It Is Biased Against Blacks.* Available: https://www.propublica.org/article/machine-bias-risk-assessments-in-criminal-sentencing [April 2017].

Antonovics, K., and Knight, B. G. (2009). A new look at racial profiling: Evidence from the Boston Police Department. *Review of Economics and Statistics,* 91(1), 163–177.

Anwar, S., and Fang, H. (2006). An alternative test of racial prejudice in motor vehicle searches: Theory and evidence. *American Economic Review, 96*(1), 127–151.

Apel, R. (2016). On the deterrent effect of stop, question, and frisk. *Criminology & Public Policy, 15*(1), 57–66. doi: 10.1111/1745-9133.12175.

Armitage, R., and Monchuk, L. (2011). Sustaining the crime reduction impact of designing out crime: Re-evaluating the Secured by Design scheme 10 years on. *Security Journal, 24*(4), 320–343.

Augustyn, M. B. (2015). Updating perceptions of (in)justice. *Journal of Research in Crime & Delinquency, 53*(2), 1–32.

Ayres, I., and Borowsky, J. (2008). *A Study of Racially Disparate Outcomes in the Los Angeles Police Departments*. Los Angeles: American Civil Liberties Union of Southern California.

Baker, A., Goodman, J. D., and Mueller, B. (2015). Beyond the chokehold: The path to Eric Garner's death. *The New York Times*, June 13. Available: http://www.nytimes.com/2015/06/14/nyregion/eric-garner-police-chokehold-staten-island.html [April 2017].

Baker, T. (2016). Exploring the relationship of shared race/ethnicity with court actors, perceptions of court procedural justice, and obligation to obey among male. *Race and Justice, 7*(1), 87–102.

Baker, T. E., and Wolfer, L. (2003). The crime triangle: Alcohol, drug use, and vandalism. *Police Practice on Research: An International Journal, 4*(1), 47–61.

Balz, D., and Clement, S. (2014). On racial issues, America is divided both black and white and red and blue. *The Washington Post*, December 27. Available: https://www.washingtonpost.com/politics/on-racial-issues-america-is-divided-both-black-and-white-and-red-and-blue/2014/12/26/3d2964c8-8d12-11e4-a085-34e9b9f05a58_story.html [April 2017].

Bartik, T. J. (1991). *Who Benefits from State and Local Economic Development Policies?* Kalamazoo, MI: W. E. Upjohn Institute for Employment Research. doi:10.17848/9780585223940.

Bates, L., Allen, S., and Watson, B. (2016). The influence of the elements of procedural justice and speed camera enforcement on young novice driver self-reported speeding. *Accident Analysis & Prevention, 92*, 34–42. doi:10.1016/j.aap.2016.03.023.

Bayley, D. H. (1994). *Police for the Future*. New York: Oxford University Press.

Bayley, D. H. (2006). *Changing the Guard: Developing Democratic Police Abroad*. New York: Oxford University Press.

Becker, G. S. (1968). Crime and punishment: An economic approach. *Journal of Political Economy, 76*(2), 169–217.

Beckett, K. (2012). Race, drugs, and law enforcement: Toward equitable policing. *Criminology & Public Policy, 11*(4), 641–653.

Beckett, K., Nyrop, K., and Pfingst, L. (2006). Race, drug use and policing: Understanding disparities in drug delivery busts. *Criminology, 44*(1), 105–137.

Beckett, K., Nyrop, K., Pfingst, L., and Bowen, M. (2005). Drug use, drug possession arrests, and the question of race: Lessons from Seattle. *Social Problems, 52*(3), 419–441.

Bellin, J. (2014). The inverse relationship between the constitutionality and effectiveness of New York City "stop and frisk." *Boston University Law Review, 94*(5), 1495–1550.

Bennett, T. (1990). *Evaluating Neighborhood Watch*. Basingstoke, UK: Gower.

Berk, R. (2005). Knowing when to fold 'em: An essay on evaluating the impact of ceasefire, Compstat, and exile. *Criminology & Public Policy, 4*(3), 451–466.

Berk, R. (2010). Recent perspectives on the regression discontinuity design. In A. R. Piquero and D. Weisburd (Eds.), *Handbook of Quantitative Criminology* (pp. 563–579). New York: Springer.

Berk, R., and MacDonald, J. (2010). Policing the homeless: An evaluation of efforts to reduce homeless-related crime. *Criminology & Public Policy, 9*(4), 813–840.

Bichler, G., Schmerler, K., and Enriquez, J. (2013). Curbing nuisance motels: An evaluation of police as place regulators. *Policing: An International Journal of Police Strategies and Management, 36*(2), 437–462.

Bittner, E. (1970). *The Functions of the Police in Modern Society: A Review of Background Factors, Current Practices, and Possible Role Models.* Chevy Chase, MD: National Institute of Mental Health.

Bittner, E. (1983). Technique and the conduct of life. *Social Problems, 30*(3), 249–261. doi:10.2307/800351.

Black, D. (1971). The social organization of arrest. *Stanford Law Review, 23*(6), 1104–1109.

Blackmon, D. A. (2009). *Slavery by Another Name: The Re-enslavement of Black Americans from the Civil War to World War II.* New York: Anchor Books.

Blumenberg, B., Blom, B., and Artigiani, E. (1998). A co-production model of code enforcement and nuisance abatement. In L. Mazerolle and J. Roehl (Eds.), *Civil Remedies and Crime Prevention, Crime Prevention Studies* (vol. 9, pp. 261–290). Monsey, NY: Criminal Justice Press.

Blumstein, A., Farrington, D. P., and Moitra, S. (1985). Delinquency careers: Innocents, desisters, and persisters. In M. Tonry and N. Morris (Eds.), *Crime and Justice* (vol. 6, pp. 187–222). Chicago, IL: University of Chicago Press.

Bobo, L. D., and Johnson, D. (2004). A taste for punishment: Black and white Americans' views on the death penalty and the war on drugs. *Du Bois Review, 1*(1), 151–180.

Bodenhausen, G. V., and Lichtenstein, M. (1987). Social stereotypes and information processing strategies: The impact of task complexity. *Journal of Personality and Social Psychology, 52,* 871-888.

Bond, C. E. W., and Gow, D. J. (1995). *Toowoomba Beat Policing Pilot Project: Main Evaluation Report.* Brisbane, Australia: Queensland Criminal Justice Commission.

Bond, C. E. W., and Gow, D. J. (1996). Policing the beat: The experience in Toowoomba, Queensland. *Crime Prevention Studies, 6,* 153–173.

Bordua, D., and Reiss, A. (1966). Command, control, and charisma: Reflections on police bureaucracy. *American Journal of Sociology, 72*(1), 68–76.

Bottoms, A., and Tankebe, J. (2012). Beyond procedural justice: A dialogic approach to legitimacy in criminal justice. *Journal of Criminal Law & Criminology, 102*(1), 119–170.

Bradford, B. (2011). Voice, neutrality and respect: Use of victim support services, procedural justice, and confidence in the criminal justice system. *Criminology & Criminal Justice, 11*(4), 345–366.

Bradford, B., Quinton, P., Myhill, A., and Porter, G. (2014). Why do "the law" comply? Procedural justice, group identification and officer motivations in police organizations. *European Journal of Criminology, 11*(1), 110–131.

Bradford, B., Hohl, K., Jackson, J., and Macqueen, S. (2015). Obeying the rules of the road: Procedural justice, social identity, and normative compliance. *Journal of Contemporary Criminal Justice, 31*(2), 171–191.

Braga, A. A. (2001). The effects of hot spots policing on crime. *The ANNALS of the American Academy of Political and Social Science, 578*(1), 104–125.

Braga, A. A. (2008). *Problem-Oriented Policing and Crime Prevention* (2nd ed.). Boulder, CO: Lynne Rienner.

Braga, A. A. (2010). Setting a higher standard for the evaluation of problem-oriented policing initiatives. *Criminology & Public Policy, 9*(1), 173–182.

Braga, A. A. (2012). Getting deterrence right? Evaluation evidence and complementary crime control mechanisms. *Criminology & Public Policy, 11*(2), 201–210.

Braga, A. A., and Bond, B. J. (2008). Policing crime and disorder hot spots: A randomized controlled trial. *Criminology, 46*(3), 577–608.

Braga, A. A., and Bond, B. J. (2009). Community perception of police crime prevention efforts: Using interviews in small areas to evaluate crime reduction strategies. In J. Knutsson and N. Tilley (Eds.), *Evaluating Crime Reduction* (pp. 85–120). Monsey, NY: Criminal Justice Press.

Braga, A. A., and Weisburd, D. L. (2006). Problem-oriented policing: The disconnect between principles and practice. In D. L. Weisburd and A. A. Braga (Eds.), *Police Innovation: Contrasting Perspectives* (pp. 133–154). New York: Cambridge University Press.

Braga, A. A., and Weisburd, D. L. (2010). *Policing Problem Places: Crime Hot Spots and Effective Prevention*. New York: Oxford University Press.

Braga, A. A., and Weisburd, D. L. (2012). The effects of focused deterrence strategies on crime: A systematic review and meta-analysis of the empirical evidence. *Journal of Research in Crime & Delinquency*, 49(3), 323–358.

Braga, A. A., and Weisburd, D. L. (2014). Must we settle for less rigorous evaluations in large area-based crime prevention programs? Lessons from a Campbell review of focused deterrence. *Journal of Experimental Criminology*, 10(4), 573–597.

Braga, A. A., and Weisburd, D. L. (2015). Focused deterrence and the prevention of violent gun injuries: Practice, theoretical principles, and scientific evidence. *Annual Review of Public Health*, 36, 55–68. doi:10.1146/annurev-publhealth-031914-122444.

Braga, A. A., Weisburd, D. L., Waring, E. J., Mazerolle, L. G., Spelman, W., and Gajewski, F. (1999). Problem-oriented policing in violent crime places: A randomized controlled experiment. *Criminology*, 37(3), 541–580.

Braga, A. A., Kennedy, D. M., Waring, E. J., and Piehl, A. M. (2001). Problem-oriented policing, deterrence, and youth violence: An evaluation of Boston's Operation Ceasefire. *Journal of Research in Crime & Delinquency*, 38(3), 195–225.

Braga, A. A., Flynn, E., Kelling, G., and Cole, C. (2011). *Moving the Work of Criminal Investigators towards Crime Control*. Harvard Executive Session on Policing and Public Safety. Washington, DC: National Institute of Justice.

Braga, A. A., Apel, R., and Welsh, B. C. (2013). The spillover effects of focused deterrence on gang violence. *Evaluation Review*, 37(3/4), 314–342.

Braga, A. A., Hureau, D. M., and Papachristos, A. V. (2014). Deterring gang-involved gun violence: Measuring the impact of Boston's Operation Ceasefire on street gang behavior. *Journal of Quantitative Criminology*, 30(1), 113–139.

Braga, A. A., Papachristos, A. V., and Hureau, D. M. (2014). The effects of hot spots policing on crime: An updated systematic review and meta-analysis. *Justice Quarterly*, 31(4), 633–663.

Braga, A. A., Welsh, B. C., and Schnell, C. (2015). Can policing disorder reduce crime? A systematic review and meta-analysis. *Journal of Research in Crime and Delinquency*, 52(4), 567–588.

Braga, A. A., Weisburd, D. L., and Turchan, B. (forthcoming). Focused deterrence strategies and crime control: An updated systematic review and meta-analysis of the empirical evidence. *Criminology & Public Policy*, 17(1).

Branas, C. C., Kondo, M. C., Murphy, S. M., South, E. C., Polsky, D., and MacDonald, J. M. (2016). Urban blight remediation as a cost-beneficial solution to firearm violence. *American Journal of Public Health*, 106(12), 2158–2164.

Branch, T. (1998). *Pillar of Fire: America in the King Years 1963–65*. New York: Simon & Schuster.

Brandl, S. G., Frank, J., Worden, R. E., and Bynum, T. S. (1994). Global and specific attitude toward the police: Disentangling the relationship. *Justice Quarterly*, 11(1), 119–134.

Branscombe, N. R., Ellemers, N., Spears, R., and Doosje, B. (1999). The context and content of social identity threat. In N. Ellemers, R. Spears, and B. Doosje (Eds.), *Social Identity: Context, Commitment, Content* (pp. 35-58). Oxford, UK: Blackwell.

Brantingham, P. J., and Brantingham, P. L. (1982). *Environmental Criminology.* Beverly Hills, CA: SAGE.
Brantingham, P. L., and Brantingham, P. J. (1984). *Patterns in Crime.* New York: Macmillan.
Brantingham, P. L., and Brantingham, P. J. (1993). Environment, routine and situation: Toward a pattern theory of crime. *Advances in Criminological Theory,* 5, 259–294.
Brantingham, P. L., and Brantingham, P. J. (1999). Theoretical model of crime hot spot generation. *Studies Crime and Crime Prevention,* 8(1), 7–26.
Bratton, W., and Knobler, P. (1998). *Turnaround: How America's Top Cop Reversed the Crime Epidemic.* New York: Random House.
Brayne, S. (2014). Surveillance and system avoidance: Criminal justice contact and institutional attachment. *American Sociological Review,* 79(3), 367–391.
Breen, M. D. (1997). *Community Policing in Manchester, Connecticut: A Case Study.* Ph.D. Dissertation. Storrs, CT: University of Connecticut. Available: http://digitalcommons.uconn.edu/dissertations/AAI9737395 [April 2017].
Brickey, K. (1995). Criminal mischief: The federalization of American criminal law. *Hastings Law Journal,* 46, 1135.
Brondolo, E., ver Halen, N., Pencille, M., Beatty, D., and Contrada, R. (2009). Coping with racism: A selective review of the literature and a theoretical and methodological critique. *Journal of Behavioral Medicine,* 32(1), 64–88.
Brooks, R. R. W., and Rose, C. M. (2013). *Saving the Neighborhood: Racially Restrictive Covenants, Law, and Social Norms.* Cambridge, MA: Harvard University Press.
Brunson, R. K. (2007). "Police don't like black people": African-American young men's accumulated police experiences. *Criminology & Public Policy,* 6(1), 71–102.
Brunson, R. K., and Miller, J. (2006). Young black men and urban policing in the United States. *The British Journal of Criminology,* 46(4), 613–640.
Brunson, R. K., and Weitzer, R. (2007). Police relations with black and white youths in different urban neighborhoods. *Urban Affairs Review,* 44(6), 858–885.
Buchanan, L., Fessenden, F., Lai, K. K. R., Park, H., Parlapiano, A., Tse, A., Wallace, T., Watkins, D., and Yourish, K. (2015). Q&A: What happened in Ferguson? *The New York Times,* August 10. Available: http://www.nytimes.com/interactive/2014/08/13/us/ferguson-missouri-town-under-siege-after-police-shooting.html?_r=1 [April 17, 2017].
Buerger, M. E. (Ed.). (1994). *The Crime Prevention Handbook: Securing High Crime Locations.* Washington, DC: Crime Control Institute.
Buerger, M. E., and Mazerolle, L. G. (1998). Third party policing: A theoretical analysis of an emerging trend. *Justice Quarterly,* 15(2), 301–328.
Bylander, J. (2015). Civil unrest, police use of force, and the public's health. *Health Affairs,* 34(8), 1264–1268.
Cahill, M., Coggeshall, M., Hayeslip D., Wolff, A., Lagerson, E., Scott, M., Davies, E., Roland, K., and Decker, S. (2008). *Community Collaboratives Addressing Youth Gangs: Interim Findings from the Gang Reduction Program.* Washington, DC: Urban Institute Justice Policy Center.
Campbell, S. W. (2012). *The Slave Catchers: Enforcement of the Fugitive Slave Law, 1850–1860.* Chapel Hill, NC: UNC Press Books.
Capers, I. B. (2010). Rethinking the Fourth Amendment: Race, citizenship, and the equality principle. *Harvard Civil Rights-Civil Liberties Law Review,* 46, 10–15.
Capowich, G., and Roehl, J. (1994). Problem-oriented policing: Actions and effectiveness in San Diego. In D. Rosenbaum (Ed.), *The Challenge of Community Policing: Testing the Promises* (pp. 127–146). Thousand Oaks, CA: SAGE.
Casper, J. D., Tyler, T. R., and Fisher, B. (1988). Procedural justice in felony cases. *Law and Society Review,* 22(3), 483–508.

Cavanagh, C., and Cauffman, E. (2015). Viewing law and order: Mothers' and sons' justice system legitimacy attitudes and juvenile recidivism. *Psychology, Public Policy, and Law*, 21(4), 432–441.

Cella, M. (2004). Homicide drops steeply in D.C.: The city could finish the year with under 200 slayings for the first time since 1986. *The Washington Times*, June 27, p. A01.

Chadwick, B. (2017). *Law and Disorder: The Chaotic Birth of the NYPD*. New York: St. Martin's Press.

Chaflin, A., and McCrary, J. (2017). Are U.S. cities underpoliced? Theory and evidence. *The Review of Economics and Statistics*. doi:10.1162/REST_a_00694.

Chaiken, J. (1978). What is known about deterrent effects of police activities. In J. Cromer (Ed.), *Preventing Crime*. Beverly Hills, CA: SAGE.

Chang, C. (2015). *Relationships of Organizational Justice and Organizational Constraints with Performance: A Meta-Analysis*. Ph.D. Dissertation. Bowling Green, OH: Bowling Green University.

Chesluk, B. (2004). Visible signs of a city out of control: Community policing in New York City. *Cultural Anthropology*, 19(2), 250–275.

Chicago Community Policing Evaluation Consortium. (1995). *Community Policing in Chicago, Year Two: An Interim Report*. Chicago, IL: Illinois Criminal Justice Information Authority. Available: https://www.ncjrs.gov/pdffiles1/Digitization/156071NCJRS.pdf [April 2017].

Childress, S. (2016). The problem with "broken windows" policing. *Frontline*. June 28. Available: http://www.pbs.org/wgbh/frontline/article/the-problem-with-broken-windows-policing [July 2016].

Clancy, A., Hough, M., Aust, R., and Kershaw, C. (2001). *Crime, Policing and Justice: The Experience of Ethnic Minorities*. London, UK: Home Office.

Clarke, R. V. (1980). "Situational" crime prevention: Theory and practice. *British Journal of Criminology*, 20(2), 136–147.

Clarke, R. V. (1995). Situational crime prevention. *Crime and Justice*, 19, 91–150.

Clarke, R. V. (Ed.). (1997). *Situational Crime Prevention: Successful Case Studies* (2nd ed.). Albany, NY: Harrow & Heston.

Clarke, R. V. (1998). Defining police strategies: Problem solving, problem-oriented policing and community-oriented policing. In T. O'Connor and A. C. Grant (Eds.), *Problem-Oriented Policing: Crime-Specific Problems, Critical Issues, and Making POP Work* (pp. 315–329). Washington, DC: Police Executive Research Forum.

Clarke, R. V., and Cornish, D. (1985). Modeling offender's decisions: A framework for research and policy. *Crime & Justice*, 6, 147–185.

Clarke, R. V., and Eck, J. (2005). *Crime Analysis for Problem Solvers in 60 Small Steps*. Washington, DC: Office of Community Oriented Policing Services, U.S. Department of Justice.

Clarke, R. V., and Weisburd, D. (1994). Diffusion of crime control benefits: Observations on the reverse of displacement. In R. V. Clarke (Ed.), *Crime Prevention Studies* (vol. 2, pp. 165–182). Monsey, NY: Criminal Justice Press.

Cohen, L., and Felson, M. (1979). Social change and crime rate trends: A routine activity approach. *American Sociological Review*, 44(4), 588–608. Available: http://www.jstor.org/stable/2094589 [April 17, 2017].

Cohen, J., and Ludwig, J. (2003). Policing crime guns. In J. Ludwig and P. J. Cook (Eds.), *Evaluating Gun Policy: Effects on Crime and Violence* (pp. 217–239). Washington, DC: Brookings Institution Press.

Cohen-Charash, Y., and Spector, P. E. (2001). The role of justice in organizations: A meta-analysis. *Organizational Behavior and Human Decision Processes*, 86(2), 278–321.

Colb, S. F. (2001). Stopping a moving target. *Rutgers Race and the Law*, 3, 191–222.

Cole, N. D., and Latham, G. P. (1997). Effects of training in procedural justice on perceptions of disciplinary fairness by unionized employees and disciplinary subject matter experts. *Journal of Applied Psychology, 82*(5), 699–705.

Colgate-Love, M., Roberts, J., and Klingele, C. (2013). *Collateral Consequences of Criminal Convictions: Law, Policy and Practice*. Eagan, MN: NACDL Press and Thomson Reuters Westlaw.

Collins, P., Greene, J., Kane, R., Stokes, R., and Piquero, A. (1999). *Implementing Community Policing in Public Housing: Philadelphia's 11th Street Corridor Program*. Final Technical Report. Washington, DC: National Institute of Justice.

Colquitt, J. A., Conlon, D. E., Wesson, M. J., Porter, C. O., and Ng, K. Y. (2001). Justice at the millennium: A meta-analytic review of 25 years of organizational justice research. *Journal of Applied Psychology, 86*(3), 425–445.

Colquitt, J. A., Scott, B. A., Rodell, J. B., Long, D. M., Zapata, C. P., Conlon, D. E., and Wesson, M. J. (2013). Justice at the millennium, a decade later: A meta-analytic test of social exchange and affect-based perspectives. *Journal of Applied Psychology, 98*(2), 199–236.

Connell, N. M., Miggans, K., and McGloin, J. M. (2008). Can a community policing initiative reduce serious crime? A local evaluation. *Police Quarterly, 11*(2), 127–150.

Cook, P. J. (1979). The clearance rate as a measure of criminal justice system effectiveness. *Journal of Public Economics, 11*(1), 135–142.

Cook, P. J. (1986). The demand and supply of criminal opportunities. In M. Tonry and N. Morris (Eds.), *Crime and Justice: An Annual Review of Research* (vol. 7, pp. 1–28). Chicago, IL: University of Chicago Press.

Cook, P. J. (2011). Co-production in deterring crime. *Criminology & Public Policy, 10*(1), 103–108.

Cook, P. J. (2015). Will the current crisis in police legitimacy increase crime? Research offers a way forward. *Psychological Science in the Public Interest, 16*(3), 71–74.

Cook, P. J., and MacDonald, J. (2011). Public safety through private action: An economic assessment of BIDs. *The Economic Journal, 121*(552), 445–462.

Cook, T. D., and Campbell, D. T. (1979). *Quasi-Experimentation: Design & Analysis for Field Settings*. Chicago, IL: Rand McNally.

Cordner, G. W. (1998). Community policing: Elements and effects. In G. Alpert and A. Piquero (Eds.), *Community Policing: Contemporary Readings* (pp. 1–8). Prospect Heights, IL: Waveland.

Cordner, G. W. (2014). Community policing. In M. Reisig and R. Kane (Eds.), *The Oxford Handbook of Police and Policing* (pp. 148–171). New York: Oxford University Press.

Cordner, G. W., and Biebel, E. (2005). Problem-oriented policing in practice. *Criminology & Public Policy, 4*(2), 155–180.

Corman, H., and Mocan, N. (2005). Carrots, sticks, and broken windows. *Journal of Law and Economics, 48*(1), 235–266.

Cornish, D., and Clarke, R. V. (2003). Opportunities, precipitators, and criminal decisions: A reply to Wortley's critique of situational crime prevention. In N. Tilly (Ed.), *Evaluation for Crime Prevention* (vol. 16, pp. 41–96). Monsey, NY: Criminal Justice Press.

Correll, J., Park, B., Judd, C. M., and Wittenbrink, B. (2002). The police officer's dilemma: Using ethnicity to disambiguate potentially threatening individuals. *Journal of Personality and Social Psychology, 83*(6), 1314–1329.

Correll, J., Park, B., Judd, C. M., Wittenbrink, B., Sadler, M. S., and Keesee, T. (2007). Across the thin blue line: Police officers and racial bias in the decision to shoot. *Journal of Personality and Social Psychology, 92*(6), 1006–1023.

Correll, J., Wittenbrink, B., Park, B., Judd, C. M., and Goyle, A. (2011). Dangerous enough: Moderating racial bias with secondary threat cues. *Journal of Experimental Social Psychology*, 47, 184-189.

Corsaro, N., Hunt, E. D., Hipple, N. K., and McGarrell, E. F. (2012). The impact of drug market pulling levers policing on neighborhood violence. *Criminology & Public Policy*, 11(2), 167–199.

Critchley, T. A. (1972). *A History of Police in England and Wales*. Montclair, NJ: Patterson Smith.

Crow, W. J., and Bull, J. (1975). *Robbery Deterrence: An Applied Behavioral Science Demonstration: Final Report*. La Jolla, CA: Western Behavioral Science Institute.

Cullen, F. T. (2010). Cloward, Richard A.: The theory of illegitimate means. In F. T. Cullen and P. Wilcox (Eds.), *Encyclopedia of Criminological Theory* (pp. 167–170). Thousand Oaks, CA: SAGE.

Cunningham, W. A., Preacher, K. J., and Banaji, M. R. (2001). Implicit attitude measurement: Consistency, stability, and convergent validity. *Psychological Science*, 12, 163–170.

Curman, A. S., Andresen, M. A., and Brantingham, P. J. (2015). Crime and place: A longitudinal examination of street segment patterns in Vancouver, BC. *Journal of Quantitative Criminology*, 31(1), 127–147.

Dai, M., Frank, J., and Sun, I. (2011). Procedural justice during police-citizen encounters. *Journal of Criminal Justice*, 39(2), 159–168.

Damaska, M. (1975). Presentation of evidence and factfinding precision. *University of Pennsylvania Law Review*, 123(5), 1083–1106.

De Angelis, J., and Kupchik, A. (2007). Citizen oversight, procedural justice, and officer perceptions of the complaint investigation process. *Policing*, 30(4), 651–671.

De Angelis, J., and Kupchik, A. (2009). Ethnicity, trust, and acceptance of authority among police officers. *Journal of Criminal Justice*, 37(3), 273–279.

DeCremer, D., and Tyler, T. R. (2005). Managing group behavior: The interplay between procedural justice, sense of self, and cooperation. In M. Zanna (Ed.), *Advances in Experimental Social Psychology* (vol. 37, pp. 151–218). New York: Academic Press.

Desmond, M., and Valdez, N. (2013). Unpolicing the urban poor: Consequences of third-party policing for inner-city women. *American Sociological Review*, 78, 117–141.

Desmond, M., Papachristos, A. V., and Kirk, D. S. (2016). Police violence and citizen crime reporting in the black community. *American Sociological Review*, 81(5), 857-876.

Dewan, S., and Oppel, R. A. (2015). In Tamir Rice case, many errors by Cleveland police, then a fatal one. *The New York Times*, January 22. Available: http://www.nytimes.com/2015/01/23/us/in-tamir-rice-shooting-in-cleveland-many-errors-by-police-then-a-fatal-one.html?_r=0 [September 2016].

Dharmapala, D., and Ross, S. L. (2004). Racial bias in motor vehicle searches: Additional theory and evidence. *Contributions to Economic Analysis and Policy*, 3(1), 1–21.

Diggle, P. J., Chetwynd, A. G., Haggkvist, R., and Morris S. (1995). Second-order analysis of space-time clustering. *Statistical Methods in Medical Research*, 4(2), 124–136.

Dillon, P., and Emery, R. (1996). Divorce mediation and resolution of child custody disputes: Long-term effects. *The American Journal of Orthopsychiatry*, 66(1), 131–140.

DiLulio, Jr., J. (1995). The coming of the super-predators. *The Weekly Standard*, November 27. Available: http://www.weeklystandard.com/the-coming-of-the-super-predators/article/8160 [October 2017].

Dixon, T. L. (2006). Psychological reactions to crime news portrayals of Black criminals: Understanding the moderating roles of prior news viewing and stereotype endorsement. *Communication Monographs*, 73, 162-187.

Dixon, T. L. (2008a). Crime news and racialized beliefs: Understanding the relationship between local news viewing and perceptions of African Americans and crime. *Journal of Communication*, 58, 106-125.

Dixon, T. L. (2008b). Network news and racial beliefs: Exploring the connection between national television news exposure and stereotypical perceptions of African Americans. *Journal of Communication*, 58(2), 321-337.

Dixon, T. L., and Azocar, C. (2007). Priming crime and activating blackness: Understanding the psychological impact of the overrepresentation of African Americans as lawbreakers on television news. *Journal of Communication*, 57, 229-253.

Dixon, T. L., and Linz, D. G. (2000a). Overrepresentation and underrepresentation of African Americans and Latinos as lawbreakers on television news. *Journal of Communication*, 50(2), 131-154.

Dixon, T. L., and Linz, D. G. (2000b). Race and the misrepresentation of victimization on local television news. *Communication Research*, 27, 547-573.

Domonoske, C. (2016). After fatal police shooting, protest erupts in Charlotte, N.C. *NPR News*, September 21. Available: http://www.npr.org/sections/the two-way/2016/09/21/494844130/after-police-shooting-protesters-in-charlotte-n-c-shut-down-interstate [September 2016].

Donner, C., Maskaly, J., Fridell, L., and Jennings, W. G. (2015). Policing and procedural justice: A state-of-the-art review. *Policing*, 38(1), 153–172.

Douglas, W. O. (1960). Vagrancy and arrest on suspicion. *Yale Law Journal*, 70(1), 1–14.

Dovidio, J. F. (2001). On the nature of contemporary prejudice: The third wave. *Journal of Social Issues*, 57(4), 829–849.

Dovidio, J. F., and Gaertner, S. L. (2004). Aversive racism. *Advances in Experimental Social Psychology*, 36, 1–52.

Dovidio, J. F., Kawakami, K., and Gaertner, S. L. (2002). Implicit and explicit prejudice and interracial interaction. *Journal of Personality and Social Psychology*, 82(1), 62–68.

Dovidio, J. F., Gaertner, S. L., and Abad-Merino, S. (2017). Helping behavior and subtle discrimination. In E. van Leeuwen and H. Zagefka (Eds.), *Intergroup Helping: The Positive Side of Intergroup Behaviour*. Cham: Springer.

Dowdy, Z. (2004). Nearly 10 percent drop cited: Major crimes down in Suffolk. *Newsday*, November 19.

Dressler, W., Oths, K., and Gravlee, C. (2005). Race and ethnicity in public health research: Models to explain health disparities. *Annual Review of Anthropology*, 34, 231–252.

Dunford, B., and Devine, D. (1998). Employment at-will and employee discharge: A justice perspective on legal action following termination. *Personnel Psychology*, 51(4), 903–934.

Durlauf, S. N., and Nagin, D. S. (2011). Imprisonment and crime. *Criminology & Public Policy*, 10(1), 13–54.

Earley, C., and Lind, A. (1987). Procedural justice and participation in task selection: The role of control in mediating justice judgments. *Journal of Personality and Social Psychology*, 52(6), 1148–1160.

Eberhardt, J. L., Goff, P. A., Purdie, V. J., and Davies, P. G. (2004). Seeing black: Race, crime, and visual processing. *Journal of Personality and Social Psychology*, 87(6), 876–893.

Eck, J. E. (1983). *Solving Crime: A Study of the Investigation of Burglary and Robbery*. Washington, DC: Police Executive Research Forum.

Eck, J. E. (2006). Science, values, and problem-oriented policing: Why problem-oriented policing? In D. L. Weisburd and A. A. Braga (Eds.), *Police Innovation: Contrasting Perspectives* (pp. 117–132). New York: Cambridge University Press.

Eck, J. E., and Maguire, E. (2000). Have changes in policing reduced violent crime? In A. Blumstein and J. Wallman (Eds.), *The Crime Drop in America* (pp. 207–265). New York: Cambridge University Press.

Eck, J. E., and Maguire E. (2006). Have changes in policing reduced violent crime? An assessment of the evidence. In A. Blumstein and J. Wallman (Eds.), *The Crime Drop in America* (2nd ed., pp. 207–265). New York: Cambridge University Press.

Eck, J. E., and Spelman, W. (1987). *Problem-Solving: Problem-Oriented Policing in Newport News*. Washington, DC: Police Executive Research Forum.

Eck, J. E., and Wartell, J. (1998). Improving the management of rental properties with drug problems: A randomized experiment. *Crime Prevention Studies* (vol. 9, pp. 161–185). Monsey, NY: Criminal Justice Press.

Eck, J. E., and Weisburd, D. L. (1995). Crime places in crime theory. In. J. Eck and D. L. Weisburd (Eds.), *Crime and Place: Crime Prevention Studies* (pp. 1–34). Monsey, NY: Criminal Justice Press and the Police Executive Research Forum.

Ehrlich, I. (1973). Participation in illegitimate activities: A theoretical and empirical investigation. *Journal of Political Economy*, 81(3), 521–565.

Ekins, E. (2016). *Policing in America: Understanding Public Attitudes toward the Police*. Washington, DC: The Cato Institute. Available: https://object.cato.org/sites/cato.org/files/pubs/pdf/policing-in-america-1-3-17.pdf [April 2017].

Elliott, I., Thomas, S. D., and Ogloff, J. R. (2011). Procedural justice in contacts with the police: Testing a relational model of authority in a mixed methods study. *Psychology, Public Policy, and Law*, 17(4), 592–610.

Engel, R. S., Smith, M. R., and Cullen, F. T. (2012). Race, place, and drug enforcement: Reconsidering the impact of citizen complaints and crime rates on drug arrests. *Criminology & Public Policy*, 11(4), 603–635.

Epp, C. R., Maynard-Moody, S., and Haider-Markel, D. P. (2014). *Pulled Over: How Police Stops Define Race and Citizenship*. Chicago, IL: University of Chicago Press.

Equal Employment Opportunity Commission. (2016). *Advancing Diversity in Law Enforcement*. Washington, DC: U.S. Department of Justice.

Esbensen, F. (1987). Foot patrols: Of what value? *American Journal of Police*, 6(1), 45–65.

Evans, W., and Owens, E. (2007). COPS and crime. *Journal of Public Economics*, 91(1–2), 181–201.

Fagan, J. (2002). Policing guns and youth violence. *The Future of Children*, 12(2), 132–151.

Fagan, J., and Davies, G. (2000). Street stops and broken windows: Terry, race, and disorder in New York City. *Fordham Urban Law Journal*, 28(2), 457–504.

Fagan, J., and Davies, G. (2003). Policing guns: Order maintenance and crime control in New York. In B. Harcourt (Ed.), *Guns, Crime, and Punishment in America* (pp. 191–221). New York: New York University Press.

Fagan, J., and Geller, A. (2015). Following the script: Narratives of suspicion in Terry stops in street policing. *The University of Chicago Law Review*, 82(51), 51–88.

Fagan, J., and MacDonald, J. (2012). Policing, crime, and legitimacy in New York and Los Angeles: The social and political contexts of two historic crime declines. In D. Halle and A. Beveridge (Eds.), *New York and Los Angeles: The Uncertain Future* (pp. 219–262). New York: Oxford University Press.

Fagan, J., and Piquero, A. R. (2007). Rational choice and developmental influences on recidivism among adolescent felony offenders. *Journal of Empirical Legal Studies*, 4(4), 715–748.

Fagan, J., and Tyler, T. (2005). Legal socialization of children and adolescents. *Social Justice Research*, 18(3), 217–241.

Fagan, J., Geller, A., Davies, G., and West, V. (2010). Street stops and broken windows revisited: The demography and logic of proactive policing in a safe and changing city. In S. K. Rice and M. D. White (Eds.), *Race, Ethnicity, and Policing: New and Essential Readings* (pp. 309–348). New York: New York University Press.

Farmer, S. J., Beehr, T. A., and Love, K. G. (2003). Becoming an undercover police officer. *Journal of Organizational Behavior, 24*(4), 373–387.

Farole, D. J. (2007). *Public Perceptions of New York's Courts: The New York State Residents Survey.* New York: Center for Court Innovation.

Farrington, D. P., and West, D. J. (1993). Criminal, penal and life histories of chronic offenders: Risk and protective factors and early identification. *Criminal Behaviour and Mental Health, 3*(4), 492–523.

Fazio, R. H. (1995). Attitudes as object-evaluation associations: Determinants, consequences, and correlates of attitude accessibility. In R. E. Petty and J. A. Krosnick (Eds.), *Attitude Strength: Antecedents and Consequences* (pp. 247–282). Hillsdale, NJ: Lawrence Erlbaum Associates.

Fazio, R. H., Jackson, J. R., Dunton, B. C., and Williams, C. J. (1995). Variability in automatic activation as an unobtrusive measure of racial attitudes: A bona fide pipeline? *Journal of Personality and Social Psychology, 69*(6), 1013–1027.

Fein, S., and Spencer, S. J. (1997). Prejudice as self-image maintenance: Affirming the self through derogating others. *Journal of Personality and Social Psychology, 73*, 31-44.

Ferguson, A. G. (2011). Crime mapping and the fourth amendment: Redrawing "high crime areas." *Hastings Law Journal, 63*(1), 179–232.

Ferguson, A. G. (2012). Predictive policing and reasonable suspicion. *Emory Law Journal, 62*, 259–325.

Ferguson, A. G. (2015). Big data and predictive reasonable suspicion. *University of Pennsylvania Law Review, 163*, 327–410.

Fiedler, K., Messner, C., and Bluemke, M. (2006). Unresolved problems with the "I", the "A", and the "T": A logical and psychometric critique of the Implicit Association Test (IAT). *European Review of Social Psychology, 17*, 74–147.

Fogelson, R. M. (1977). *Big-City Police.* Cambridge, MA: Harvard University Press.

Foner, E. (1988). *Reconstruction: America's Unfinished Revolution, 1863–1877.* New York: Harper & Row.

Ford, C., and Airhihenbuwa, C. (2010). The public health critical race methodology: Praxis for antiracism research. *Social Science & Medicine, 71*(8), 1390–1398.

Forman, Jr., J. (2017). *Locking Up Our Own: Crime and Punishment in Black America.* New York: Farrar, Straus and Giroux.

Fortner, M. J. (2015). *Black Silent Majority: The Rockefeller Drug Laws and the Politics of Punishment.* Cambridge, MA: Harvard University Press.

Frantz, C. M., Cuddy, A. J. C., Burnett, M., Ray, H., and Hart, A. (2004). A threat in the computer: The Race Implicit Association Test as a stereotype threat experience. *Personality and Social Psychology Bulletin, 30*(12), 1611–1624.

Fratello, J., Rengifo, A., Trone, J., and Velazquez, B. (2013). *Coming of Age with Stop and Frisk: Experiences, Self-Perceptions, and Public Safety Implications.* New York: Vera Institute.

Freedman, M., and Owens, E. (2011). Low-income housing development and crime. *Journal of Urban Economics, 70*(2-3), 115–131.

Fuld, L. (1909) (reprinted 1971). *Police Administration: A Critical Study of Police Organisations in the United States and Abroad.* Montclair, NJ: Patterson Smith.

Gaertner, S. L., and Dovidio, J. F. (1986). *The Aversive Form of Racism.* Cambridge, MA: Academic Press.

Garcia, J. R. (1980). *Operation Wetback.* Westport, CT: Greenwood Press.

Garcia, J. J. L., and Sharif, M. Z. (2015). Black lives matter: A commentary on racism and public health. *American Journal of Public Health, 105*(8), E27–E30.

Garland, D. (2001a). *Mass Imprisonment: Social Causes & Consequences.* Thousands Oaks, CA: SAGE.

Garland, D. (2001b). *The Culture of Control: Crime and Social Order in Contemporary Society*. Chicago, IL: University of Chicago Press.

Garofalo, J. (1981). The fear of crime: Causes and consequences. *The Journal of Criminal Law & Criminology*, 72(2), 839–857.

Garofalo, J., and Laub, J. (1978). The fear of crime: Broadening our perspective. *Victimology*, 3(3/4), 242–253.

Gau, J. M., and Brunson, R. K. (2010). Procedural justice and order maintenance policing: A study of inner-city young men's perceptions of police legitimacy. *Justice Quarterly*, 27(2), 256–279.

Gau, J. M., and Brunson, R. K. (2015). Procedural injustice, lost legitimacy, and self-help: Young males' adaptations to perceived unfairness in urban policing tactics. *Journal of Contemporary Criminal Justice*, 31(2), 132–150.

Gee, G., and Ford, C. (2011). Structural racism and health inequities. *Du Bois Review*, 8(1), 115–132.

Geller, A., Fagan, J., Tyler, T., and Link, B. G. (2014). Aggressive policing and the mental health of young urban men. *American Journal of Public Health*, 104(12), 2321–2327.

Gelman, A., Fagan, J., and Kiss, A. (2007). An analysis of the New York City Police Department's "stop-and-frisk" policy in the context of claims of racial bias. *Journal of the American Statistical Association*, 102(479), 813–823.

Gerell, M. (2016). Hot spot policing with actively monitored CCTV cameras: Does it reduce assaults in public places? *International Criminal Justice Review*, 26(2), 187–201.

Giacomazzi, A. L. (1995). *Community Crime Prevention, Community Policing, and Public Housing: An Evaluation of a Multi-Level, Collaborative Drug-Crime Elimination Program in Spokane, Washington*. Ph.D. Dissertation. Pullman: Washington State University.

Giacomazzi, A., McGarrell, E., and Thurman, Q. (1998). *Community Crime Prevention, Community Policing, and Public Housing: An Evaluation of a Multi-Level, Collaborative Drug-Crime Elimination Program in Spokane, Washington*. Final Technical Report. Washington, DC: National Institute of Justice.

Gill, M., and Spriggs, A. (2005). *Assessing the Impact of CCTV*. London, UK: Research, Development and Statistics Directorate (Home Office).

Gill, C., Weisburd, D. L., Telep, C. W., Vitter, Z., and Bennett, B. (2014). Community-oriented policing to reduce crime, disorder and fear and increase satisfaction and legitimacy among citizens: A systematic review. *Journal of Experimental Criminology*, 10(4), 399–428.

Goel, S., Rao, J. M., and Shroff, R. (2016). Precinct or prejudice? Understanding racial disparities in New York City's stop and frisk policy. *The Annals of Applied Statistics*, 10(1), 365–394.

Goff, P. A. (2013). A measure of justice: What policing racial bias research reveals. In F. C. Harris and R. C. Lieberman (Eds.), *Beyond Discrimination: Racial Inequality in a Postracial Era* (pp. 157–185). New York: Russell Sage Foundation.

Goff, P. A. (2017). Evidence as a tool for racial justice. *Behavioral Science & Policy Journal*, 2(2).

Goff, P. A., and Godsil, R. (2017). The moral ecology of policing. In J. Jacobs and J. Jackson (Eds.), *The Routledge Handbook of Criminal Justice Ethics*. Abingdon: Routledge.

Goff, P. A., Steele, C. M., and Davies, P. G. (2008). The space between us: Stereotype threat and distance in interracial contexts. *Journal of Personality and Social Psychology*, 94(1), 91–107.

Goff, P. A., Epstein, L. M., and Reddy, K. S. (2013). Crossing the line of legitimacy: The impact of cross-deputization policy on crime reporting. *Psychology, Public Policy, and Law*, 19, 250–258.

Goldstein, H. (1979). Improving policing: A problem-oriented approach. *Crime & Delinquency*, 25(2), 236–258.

Goldstein, H. (1987). Toward community-oriented policing: Potential, basic requirements and threshold questions. *Crime & Delinquency*, 33(1), 6–30.
Goldstein, H. (1990). *Problem-Oriented Policing*. New York: McGraw-Hill.
Golembeski, C., and Fullilove, R. (2005). Criminal (in)justice in the city and its associated health consequences. *American Journal of Public Health*, 95(10), 1701–1706.
Goluboff, R. L. (2016). *Vagrant Nation: Police Power, Constitutional Change, and the Making of the 1960s*. New York: Oxford University Press.
Goode, E. (2012). Philadelphia defends policy on frisking, with limits. *New York Times*, July 11. Available: http://www.nytimes.com/2012/07/12/us/stop-and-frisk-controls-praised-in-philadelphia.html [December 2016].
Gorr, W. L., and Lee, Y. J. (2015). Early warning system for temporary crime hot spots. *Journal of Quantitative Criminology*, 31(1), 25–47.
Gottfredson, M. R., and Hirschi, T. (1990). *A General Theory of Crime*. Stanford, CA: Stanford University Press.
Gould, J., and Mastrofski, S. (2004). Suspect searches: Assessing police behavior under the U.S. Constitution. *Criminology & Public Policy*, 3(3), 315–362.
Governing. (2015). Diversity on the force: Where police don't mirror communities. *Governing*, September. Available: http://media.navigatored.com/documents/policediversityreport.pdf [April 2017].
Graham, D. (2016). The horror of the Baltimore Police Department: A Department of Justice report finds widespread constitutional violations, the targeting of African Americans, and a culture of retaliation. *The Atlantic*, August 10. Available: http://www.theatlantic.com/news/archive/2016/08/the-horror-of-the-baltimore-police-department/495329 [September 2016].
Grant, R. A. (2010). *Sir Robert Peel: The Life and Legacy*. New York: Palgrave.
Graziano, L. M., Rosenbaum, D. P., and Schuck, A. M. (2014). Building group capacity for problem-solving and police-community partnerships through survey feedback and training: A randomized controlled trial within Chicago's community policing program. *Journal of Experimental Criminology*, 10(1), 79–103.
Greenberg, J. (1990). Employee theft as a reaction to underpayment inequity: The hidden cost of pay cuts. *Journal of Applied Psychology*, 75(5), 561–568.
Greenberg, J. (1994). Using socially fair treatment to promote acceptance of a work site smoking ban. *Journal of Applied Psychology*, 79(2), 288–297.
Greene, J. R. (2000). *Community Policing in America: Changing the Nature, Structure, and Function of the Police* (vol. 3). Available: https://www.ncjrs.gov/criminal_justice2000/vol_3/03g.pdf [April 2017].
Greene, J. R., and Mastrofski, S. (Eds.). (1988). *Community Policing: Rhetoric or Reality*. New York: Praeger.
Greene, C., Sprott, J., Madon, N., and Jung, M. (2010). Punishing processes in youth court: Procedural justice, court atmosphere and youths' views of the legitimacy of the justice system. *Canadian Journal of Criminology and Criminal Justice*, 52(5), 527–544.
Greenwald, A. G., McGhee, D. E., and Schwartz, J. L. (1998). Measuring individual differences in implicit cognition: The implicit association test. *Journal of Personality and Social Psychology*, 74(6), 1464–1480.
Greenwald, A. G., Nosek, B. A., and Banaji, M. R. (2003). Understanding and using the Implicit Association Test: I. An improved scoring algorithm. *Journal of Personality and Social Psychology*, 85(2), 197-216.
Greenwald, A. G., Poehlman, T. A., Uhlmann, E. L., and Banaji, M. R. (2009). Understanding and Using the Implicit Association Test: III. Meta-analysis of predictive validity. *Journal of Personality and Social Psychology*, 97(1), 17-41.

Greenwood, P. W., Chaiken, J., Petersilia, M., and Prusoff, L. (1975). *Criminal Investigation Process, III: Observations and Analysis*. Santa Monica, CA: RAND.

Greenwood, P. W., Petersilia, M., and Chaiken, J. (1977). *The Criminal Investigation Process*. Lexington, MA: D.C. Heath.

Groff, E., Ratcliffe, J., Haberman, C., Sorg, E., Joyce, N., and Taylor, R. (2015). Does what police do at hot spots matter? The Philadelphia Policing Tactics Experiment, *Criminology*, 53(1), 23–53.

Grogger, J., and Ridgeway, G. (2006). Testing for racial profiling in traffic stops from behind the veil of darkness. *Journal of the American Statistical Association*, 101(475), 878–998.

Guerry, A. M. (2002) (original published 1833). *A Translation of Andre-Michel Guerry's Essay on the Moral Statistics of France*. Lewinston, NY: Edwin Mellen.

Haas, N., Van Craen, M., Skogan, W., and Fleitas, D. (2015). Explaining officer compliance: The importance of procedural justice and trust inside a police organization. *Criminology and Criminal Justice*, 15(4), 442–463.

Hagan, J., Shedd, C., and Payne, M. R. (2005). Race, ethnicity, and youth perceptions of criminal injustice. *American Sociological Review*, 70(3), 381–407.

Hahn, A., Judd, C. M., Hirsh, H. K., and Blair, I. V. (2014). Awareness of implicit attitudes. *Journal of Experimental Psychology. General*, 143(3), 1369–1392.

Haller, M. H. (1976). Historical roots of police behavior, Chicago 1895–1925. *Law and Society Review*, 10(2), 303–323.

Harcourt, B. E. (1998). Reflecting on the subject: A critique of the social influence conception of deterrence, the broken-windows theory, and order maintenance policing New York style. *Michigan Law Review*, 97(2), 291–389.

Harcourt, B. E. (2001). *Illusion of Order: The False Promise of Broken Windows Policing*. Cambridge, MA: Harvard University Press.

Harcourt, B. E. (2007). *Against Prediction: Profiling, Policing, and Punishing in an Actuarial Age*. Chicago, IL: University of Chicago Press.

Harcourt, B. E., and Ludwig, J. (2005). Broken windows: New evidence from New York City and a five-city social experiment. *University of Chicago Law Review*, 73, 271–320.

Harmon, R. (2012a). Limited leverage: Federal remedies and policing reform. *Saint Louis University Public Law Review*, 32, 33–57.

Harmon, R. (2012b). The problem of policing. *Michigan Law Review*, 110(5), 761–818.

Harmon, R. (2015). Federal programs and the real costs of policing. *New York University Law Review*, 90, 870–960.

Harmon, R. (2017). Police consent decrees: Evaluating and improving structural reform in police departments. *Criminology & Public Policy*, 16(2), 617–627.

Harris, C. J., and Worden, R. E. (2014). The effects of sanctions on police misconduct. *Crime & Delinquency*, 60(8), 1258–1288.

Harris, D. A. (1998). Particularized suspicion, categorical judgments: Supreme Court rhetorical versus lower court reality under *Terry v. Ohio*. *St. John's Law Review*, 72(3), 975–1024.

Hart, A. J., Whalen, P. J., Shin, L. M., McInerney, S. C., Fischer, H., and Rauch, S. L. (2000). Differential response in the human amygdala to racial outgroup vs. ingroup face stimuli. *Neuroreport*, 11(11), 2351–2354.

Hasisi, B., and Weisburd, D. L. (2011). Going beyond ascribed identities: The importance of procedural justice in airport security screening in Israel. *Law & Society Review*, 45(4), 867–892.

Hayden, R., and Anderson, J. (1979). On the evaluation of procedural systems in laboratory experiments. *Law and Human Behavior*, 3(1/2), 21–38.

Heaton, P. (2010). *Hidden in Plain Sight: What Cost-of-Crime Research Can Tell Us About Investing in Police.* Santa Monica, CA: RAND. Available: http://www.rand.org/pubs/occasional_papers/OP279.html [October 2017].

Heffernan, W. C., and Lovely, R. W. (1991). Evaluating the fourth amendment exclusionary rule: The problem of police compliance with the law. *University of Michigan Journal of Law Reform, 24*(2), 311–369.

Higginson, A., and Mazerolle, L. (2014). Legitimacy policing of places: The impact on crime and disorder. *Journal of Experimental Criminology, 10*(4), 429–457.

Higgs, R. (1977). *Competition and Coercion: Blacks in the American Economy, 1865–1914.* Cambridge, MA: Cambridge University Press.

Hinds, L. (2007). Building police-youth relationships: The importance of procedural justice. *National Association of Youth Justice, 7*(3), 195–209.

Hinds, L. (2009). Youth, police legitimacy, and informal contact. *Journal of Police and Criminal Psychology, 24*(1), 10–21.

Hinds, L., and Murphy, K. (2007). Public satisfaction with police: Using procedural justice to improve police legitimacy. *The Australian & New Zealand Journal of Criminology, 40*(1), 27–42.

Hinkle, J. C. (2013). The relationship between disorder, perceived risk and collective efficacy: A look into the indirect pathways of the broken windows thesis. *Criminal Justice Studies, 26*(4), 408–432.

Hinkle, J. C., and Weisburd, D. L. (2008). The irony of broken windows policing: A microplace study of the relationship between disorder, focused police crackdowns and fear of crime. *Journal of Criminal Justice, 36*(6), 503–512.

Hinton, E. (2016a). *From the War on Poverty to the War on Crime: The Making of Mass Incarceration in America.* Cambridge, MA: Harvard University Press.

Hinton, E. (2016b). *The Broader Context of Race and Policing in America.* Paper prepared for the Committee on Proactive Policing—Effects on Crime, Communities, and Civil Liberties, Washington, DC, National Academies of Sciences, Engineering, and Medicine.

Hipple, N. K., Gruenewald, J., and McGarrell, E. F. (2014). Restorativeness, procedural justice, and defiance as predictors of reoffending of participants in family group conferences. *Crime & Delinquency, 60*(8), 1131–1157.

Hirschi, T. (1969). *Causes of Delinquency.* Berkeley: University of California Press.

Holzer, H. J., Raphael, S., and Stoll, M. A. (2006). Perceived criminality, criminal background checks, and the racial hiring practices of employers. *Journal of Law and Economics, 49*(2), 451–480.

Houlden, P., LaTour, S., Walker, L., and Thibaut, J. (1978). Preference for modes of dispute resolution as a function of process and decision control. *Journal of Experimental Social Psychology, 14*(1), 13–30.

Howell, J. C., Krisberg, B., Hawkins, J. D., and Wilson, J. (Eds). (1995). *Serious, Violent, and Chronic Juvenile Offenders: A Sourcebook.* Thousand Oaks, CA: SAGE.

Hunt, P., Saunders, J., and Hollywood, J. S. (2014). *Evaluation of the Shreveport Predictive Policing Experiment.* Santa Monica, CA: RAND.

Hunter, A. (1978). *Symbols of Incivility: Social Disorder and Fear of Crime in Urban Neighborhoods.* Paper presented at the Annual Meeting of the American Society of Criminology Dallas, TX, November.

Hutzel, E., and MacGregor, M. (1933). *The Policewoman's Handbook.* New York: Columbia University Press.

Ingram, T. (2014). *Dixie Highway: Road Building and the Making of the Modern South, 1900–1930.* Chapel Hill: University of North Carolina Press.

Institute on Race and Poverty. (2003). *Minnesota Racial Profiling Study.* Minneapolis: University of Minnesota.

Ito, T. A., Friedman, N. P., Bartholow, B. D., Correll, J., Loersch, C., Altamirano, L. J., and Miyake, A. (2015). Toward a comprehensive understanding of executive cognitive function in implicit racial bias. *Journal of Personality and Social Psychology, 108*(2), 187.

Jackman, T. (2016). U.S. police chiefs group apologizes for "historical mistreatment" of minorities. *Washington Post*, October 17. Available: https://www.washingtonpost.com/news/true-crime/wp/2016/10/17/head-of-u-s-police-chiefs-apologizes-for-historic-mistreatment-of-minorities/?utm_term=.80737fda0070 [January 2017].

Jackson, J., Bradford, B., Hough, M., Myhill, Q. P., and Tyler, T. R. (2012). Why do people comply with the law? Legitimacy and the influence of legal institutions. *British Journal of Criminology, 52*(6), 1051–1071.

Jackson, J., Huq, A. Z., Bradford, B., and Tyler, T. R. (2013). Monopolizing force? Police legitimacy and public attitude acceptability of violence. *Psychology, Public Policy, and Law, 19*, 479–497.

James, L., James, S. M., and Vila, B. J. (2016). The reverse racism effect: Are cops more hesitant to shoot black than white suspects?. *Criminology & Public Policy, 15*(2), 457–479.

James, L., Klinger, D., and Vila, B. (2014). Racial and ethnic bias in decisions to shoot seen through a stronger lens: Experimental results from high-fidelity laboratory simulations. *Journal of Experimental Criminology, 10*(3), 323–340.

James, L., Vila, B., and Daratha, K. (2013). Results from experimental trials testing participant responses to white, Hispanic, and black suspects in high-fidelity deadly force judgment and decision-making simulations. *Journal of Experimental Criminology, 9*(2), 189–212.

Jeffery, C. R. (1971). *Crime Prevention through Environmental Design*. Beverly Hills, CA: SAGE.

Jesilow, P., Meyer, J., Parsons, D., and Tegeler, W. (1998). Evaluating problem-oriented policing: A quasi-experiment. *Policing: An International Journal of Police Strategies & Management, 21*(3), 449–464.

Joh, E. E. (2017). The undue influence of surveillance technology companies on policing. *New York University Law Review Online*. Available: https://papers.ssrn.com/sol3/papers.cfm?abstract_id=2924620 [October 2017].

Johnson, R., and Raphael, S. (2009). The effects of male incarceration dynamics on acquired immune deficiency syndrome infection rates among African American women and men. *Journal of Law and Economics, 52*(2), 251–293.

Johnson, S. D., Bowers, K. J., Birks, D., and Pease, K. (2009). Predictive mapping of crime by ProMap: Accuracy, units of analysis and the environmental backcloth. In D. L. Weisburd, W. Bernasco, and G. J. N. Bruinsma (Eds.), *Putting Crime in Its Place: Units of Analysis in Geographic Criminology* (pp. 171–198). New York: Springer-Verlag.

Jonathan-Zamir, T., and Weisburd, D. L. (2013). The effects of security threats on antecedents of police legitimacy: Findings from a quasi-experiment in Israel. *Journal of Research in Crime & Delinquency, 50*(1), 3–32.

Jonathan-Zamir, T., Mastrofski, S. D., and Moyal, S. (2015). Measuring procedural justice in police-citizen encounters, *Justice Quarterly*, 845–871.

Jones, C. (2001). Invited commentary: "Race," racism, and the practice of epidemiology. *American Journal of Epidemiology, 154*(4), 299–304.

Jones, J. M. (2015). In U.S., confidence in police lowest in 22 years. *Gallup*, June 19. Available: http://www.gallup.com/poll/183704/confidence-police-lowest-years.aspx [April 2017].

Jones, N. (2014). "The regular routine": Proactive policing and adolescent development among young, poor black men. *New Directions for Child and Adolescent Development, 143*, 33–54.

Jones-Brown, D., Stoudt, B. G., and Moran, K. (2013). *Stop, Question and Frisk Policing Practices in New York City: A Primer (Revised)*. New York: John Jay College of Criminal Justice. Available: http://www.atlanticphilanthropies.org/app/uploads/2015/09/SQF_Primer_July_2013.pdf [April 2017].

Justice, B., and Meares, T. L. (2014). How the criminal justice system educates citizens. *The ANNALS of the American Academy of Political and Social Science*, 651(1), 159–177.

Kaeble, D., Maruschak, L., and Bonczar, T. P. (2015). *Probation and Parole in the United States, 2014*. Washington, DC: Bureau of Justice Statistics, U.S. Department of Justice, and Office of Justice Programs. Available: https://www.bjs.gov/content/pub/pdf/ppus14.pdf [April 2017].

Kahn, K. B., and Davies, P. G. (2011). Differentially dangerous? Phenotypic racial stereotypicality increases implicit bias among ingroup and outgroup members. *Group Processes & Intergroup Relations*, 14(4), 569–580.

Kahn, K. B., Goff, P. A., Lee, J. K., and Motamed, D. (2016). Protecting whiteness: White phenotypic racial stereotypicality reduces police use of force. *Social Psychological and Personality Science*, 7(5), 403–411.

Kane, R. J. (2005). Compromised police legitimacy as a predictor of violent crime in structurally disadvantaged communities. *Criminology*, 43(2), 469–498.

Kansas City Police Department. (1977). *Response Time Analysis*. Kansas City, MO: Kansas City Police Department.

Kawakami, K., Dovidio, J. F., and van Kamp, S. (2005). Kicking the habit: Effects of nonstereotypic association training and correction processes on hiring decisions. *Journal of Experimental Social Psychology*, 41(1), 68–75.

Keizer, K., Lindenberg, S., and Steg, L. (2008). The spreading of disorder. *Science*, 322(5908), 1681–1685.

Kelling, G. L. (1999). *"Broken Windows" and Police Discretion*. Washington, DC: National Institute of Justice.

Kelling, G. L., and Coles, C. (1996). *Fixing Broken Windows: Restoring Order and Reducing Crime in Our Communities*. New York: The Free Press.

Kelling, G. L., and Moore, M. H. (1988). From political to reform to community: The evolving strategy of the police. In J. R. Greene and S. D. Mastrofski (Eds.), *Community Policing: Rhetoric or Reality?* (pp. 3–25). New York: Praeger.

Kelling, G. L., Pate, A., Dieckman, D., and Brown, C. E. (1974). *The Kansas City Preventive Patrol Experiment: Technical Report*. Washington, DC: Police Foundation.

Kelling, G. L., and Sousa, W. H. (2001). *Do Police Matter? An Analysis of the Impact of New York City's Police Reforms*. Civic Report No. 22. New York: Manhattan Institute for Policy Research.

Kennedy, D. M. (1997). Pulling levers: Chronic offenders, high-crime settings, and a theory of prevention. *Valparaiso University Law Review*, 31(2), 449–484.

Kennedy, D. M., and Wong, S. L. (2009). *The High Point Drug Intervention Strategy*. Washington, DC: U.S. Department of Justice.

Kennedy, D. M., Piehl, A. M., and Braga, A. A. (1996). Youth violence in Boston: Gun markets, serious youth offenders, and a use-reduction strategy. *Law and Contemporary Problems*, 59(1), 147–196.

Kennedy, L. W., Caplan, J. M., and Piza, E. (2011). Risk clusters, hotspots, and spatial intelligence: Risk terrain modeling as an algorithm for police resource allocation strategies. *Journal of Quantitative Criminology*, 27(3), 339–362.

Kent, S. L., and Jacobs, D. (2005). Minority threat and police strength from 1980 to 2000: A fixed-effects analysis of nonlinear and interactive effects in large U.S. cities. *Criminology*, 43(3), 731–760.

Kerner Commission. (1968). *Report of the National Advisory Commission on Civil Disorders*. New York: Bantam Books.

Kim, W. C., and Mauborgne, R. A. (1993). Procedural justice, attitudes, and subsidiary top management compliance with multinationals' corporate strategic decisions. *Academy of Management, 36*(3), 502–526.

Kitzmann, K. M., and Emery, R. E. (1993). Procedural justice and parents' satisfaction in a field study of child custody dispute resolution. *Law and Human Behavior, 17*(5), 553–567.

Kitzmann, K. M., and Emery, R. E. (1994). Child and family coping one year after mediated and litigated child custody disputes. *Journal of Family Psychology, 8*(2), 150–159.

Klinger, D. A. (2004). Environment and organization: Reviving a perspective on the police. *The ANNALS of the American Academy of Political and Social Science, 593*(1), 119–136.

Klockars, C. B. (1985). *The Idea of Police*. Beverly Hills, CA: SAGE.

Klockars, C. B. (1988). The rhetoric of community policing. In J. R. Greene and S. D. Mastrofski (Eds.), *Community Policing: Rhetoric or Reality* (pp. 239–258). New York: Praeger.

Kneebone, E., and Raphael, S. (2011). *City and Suburban Crime Trends in Metropolitan America*. Washington, DC: The Brookings Institution.

Knowles, J., Persico, N., and Todd, P. (2001). Racial bias in motor vehicle searches: Theory and evidence. *Journal of Political Economy, 109*(1), 203–229.

Kochel, T. R. (2011). Constructing hot spots policing: Unexamined consequences for disadvantaged populations and for police legitimacy. *Criminal Justice Policy Review, 22*(3), 350–374.

Kochel, T. R. (2012). Can police legitimacy promote collective efficacy? *Justice Quarterly, 29*(3), 384–419.

Kochel, T. R., and Weisburd, D. L. (2017). Assessing community consequences of implementing hot spots policing in residential areas: Findings from a randomized field trial. *Journal of Experimental Criminology*, 1–28.

Kochel, T. R., Wilson, D. B., and Mastrofski, S. D. (2011). The effect of suspect race on police officers' arrest decisions. *Criminology, 49*(2), 473–512.

Koivisto, S., and Lipponen, J. (2015). A leader's procedural justice, respect and extra-role behavior: The roles of leader in-group prototypicality and identification. *Social Justice Research, 28*(2), 187–206.

Koper, C. S. (1995). Just enough police presence: Reducing crime and disorderly behavior by optimizing patrol time in crime hotspots. *Justice Quarterly, 12*(4), 649–672.

Koper, C. S. (2014). Assessing the practice of hot spots policing: Survey results from a national convenience sample of local police agencies. *Journal of Contemporary Criminal Justice, 30*(2), 123–146.

Koper, C. S., and Mayo-Wilson, E. (2006). Police crackdowns on illegal gun carrying: A systematic review of their impact on gun crime. *Journal of Experimental Criminology, 2*(2), 227–261.

Koper, C. S., and Mayo-Wilson, E. (2012). Police strategies to reduce illegal possession and carrying of firearms: Effects on gun crime. *Campbell Systematic Reviews, 11*.

Koper, C. S., Hoffmaster, D., Luna, A., McFadden, S., and Woods, D. (2010). *Developing a St. Louis Model for Reducing Gun Violence: A Report from the Police Executive Research Forum to the St. Louis Metropolitan Police Department*. Washington, DC: Police Executive Research Forum.

Koper, C. S., Woods, D. J., and Isom, D. (2016). Evaluating a police-led community initiative to reduce gun violence in St. Louis. *Police Quarterly, 19*(2), 115–149.

Kyckelhahn, T. (2015). *Justice Expenditure and Employment Extracts, 2012—Preliminary.* Washington, DC: Bureau of Justice Statistics. Available: https://www.bjs.gov/index.cfm?ty=pbdetail&iid=5239 [January 2017].

LaFree, G. (1998). *Losing Legitimacy: Street Crime and the Decline of Social Institutions in America.* Boulder, CO: Westview Press.

Lai, C. K., Marini, M., Lehr, S. A., Cerruti, C., Shin, J.-E. L., Joy-Gaba, J. A., Ho, A. K., Teachman, B. A., Wojcik, S. P., Koleva, S. P., Frazier, R. S., Heiphetz, L., Chen, E. E., Turner, R. N., Haidt, J., Kesebir, S., Hawkins, C. B., Schaefer, H. S., Rubichi, S., Sartori, G., Dial, C. M., Sriram, N., Banaji, M. R., and Nosek, B. A. (2014). Reducing implicit racial preferences: I. A comparative investigation of 17 interventions. *Journal of Experimental Psychology: General, 143*(4), 1765–1785. doi:10.1037/a0036260.

Lamberth, J. C. (1994). *Revised Statistical Analysis of the Incidence of Police Stops and Arrests of Black Drivers/Travelers on the New Jersey Turnpike between Exits or Interchanges 1 and 3 from the Years 1988 through 1991.* Technical Report. Philadelphia, PA: Temple University, Department of Psychology.

Langan, P. A. (1995). *The Racial Disparity in U.S. Drug Arrests.* Washington, DC: U.S. Department of Justice.

Langton, L., and Durose, M. (2013). *Police Behavior during Traffic and Street Stops, 2011.* Washington, DC: U.S. Department of Justice, Bureau of Justice Statistics.

Larsen, T. (2016). *Convict Lease in the American South and the Margins of Corruption.* Manuscript, University of Colorado Boulder.

Larson, R. C., and Cahn, M. F. (1985). *Synthesizing and Extending the Results of Police Patrols.* Washington, DC: U.S. Government Printing Office.

LaTour, S. (1978). Determinations of participant and observer satisfaction with adversary and inquisitorial modes of adjudication. *Journal of Personality and Social Psychology, 36*(12), 1531–1545.

La Vigne, N. G., Lowry, S. S., Markman, J. A., and Dwyer, A. M. (2011). *Evaluating the Use of Public Surveillance Cameras for Crime Control and Prevention.* Washington, DC: Urban Institute.

La Vigne, N. G., Lachman, P., Rao, S., and Matthews, A. (2014). *Stop and Frisk: Balancing Crime Control with Community Relations.* Washington, DC: Office of Community Oriented Policing Services. Available: http://www.urban.org/sites/default/files/alfresco/publication-pdfs/413258-Stop-and-Frisk-Balancing-Crime-Control-with-Community-Relations.pdf [December 2016].

Lee, Y., Eck, J., and Corsaro, N. (2016). Conclusions from the history of research into the effects of police force size on crime—1968 through 2013: A historical systematic review. *Journal of Experimental Criminology, 12*(3), 431–451.

Lee, J., Shaver, J., Lai, K. K. R., and Petersen, M. (2016). Scenes and voices from the protests in Charlotte. *The New York Times,* September 22. Available: http://www.nytimes.com/interactive/2016/09/22/us/charlotte-police-shooting-protest.html?rref=collection%2Ftimestopic%2FPolice%20Brutality%20and%20Misconduct&action=click&contentCollection=timestopics&region=stream&module=stream_unit&version=latest&contentPlacement=34&pgtype=collection&_r=0 [September 2016].

LeFlouria, T. L. (2015). *Chained in Silence: Black Women and Convict Labor in the New South.* Chapel Hill: University of North Carolina Press.

Lerman, A. E., and Weaver, V. (2014a). *Arresting Citizenship: The Democratic Consequences of American Crime Control.* Chicago, IL: University of Chicago Press.

Lerman, A. E., and Weaver, V. (2014b). Staying out of sight? Concentrated policing and local political action. *The ANNALS of the American Academy of Political and Social Science, 651*(1), 202–219.

Leventhal, G. S. (1980). What should be done with equity theory?: New approaches to the study of fairness in social relationships. In K. Gergen, M Greenberg, and R. Willis (Eds.), *Social Exchange* (pp. 27–55). New York: Plenum Press.

Levett, A. E. (1975). *Centralization of City Police in the Nineteenth Century United States.* Ph.D. Dissertation. Ann Arbor: University of Michigan

Levine, J. P. (1975). Ineffectiveness of adding police to prevent crime. *Public Policy*, 23(4), 523–545.

Lewis, T., Everson-Rose, S., Powell, L., Matthews, K., Brown, C., and Karavolos, K. (2006). Chronic exposure to everyday discrimination and coronary artery calcification in African-American women: The SWAN Heart Study. *Psychosomatic Medicine*, 68(3), 362–368.

Lichtenstein, A. (1993). Good roads and chain gangs in the progressive South: "The negro convict is a slave." *The Journal of Southern History*, 59(1), 85–110.

Lichtenstein, A. (1996). *Twice the Work of Free Labor: The Political Economy of Convict Labor in the New South.* Brooklyn, NY: Verso.

Lind, E. A., Thibaut, J., and Walker, L. (1973). Discovery and presentation of evidence in adversary and nonadversary proceedings. *Michigan Law Review*, 71(6), 1129–1144.

Lind, E. A., Erickson, B. E., Friedland, N., and Dickenberger, M. (1978). Reactions to procedural models for adjudicative conflict resolution: A cross-national study. *Journal of Conflict Resolution*, 22(2), 318–341.

Lind, E. A., and Tyler, T. R. (1988). *The Social Psychology of Procedural Justice.* New York: Plenum Press.

Lind, E. A., Kulik, C. T., Ambrose, M., and de Vera Park, M. (1993). Individual and corporate dispute resolution. *Administrative Science Quarterly*, 38(2), 224–251.

Lind, E. A., Greenberg, J., Scott, K., and Welchans, T. D. (2000). The winding road from employee to complainant: Situational and psychological determinants of wrongful-termination claims. *Administrative Science Quarterly*, 45(3), 557–590.

Lindsay, B., and McGillis, D. (1986). Citywide community crime prevention: An assessment of the Seattle program. In D. Rosenbaum (Ed.), *Community Crime Prevention: Does It Work?* (pp. 46–67). Beverly Hills, CA: SAGE.

Link, B. G., and Phelan, J. C. (1995). Social conditions as fundamental causes of disease. *Journal of Health and Social Behavior*, 35, 80–94.

Lipsey, M. W., and Wilson, D. B. (2001). *Practical Meta-Analysis.* Thousand Oaks, CA: SAGE.

Loewen, J. W. (2005). *Sundown Towns: A Hidden Dimension of American Racism.* New York: The New Press.

Lofstrom, M., and Raphael, S. (2016). Crime, the criminal justice system, and socioeconomic inequality. *Journal of Economic Perspectives*, 30(2), 103–126.

Lowrey, B., Maguire, E., and Bennett, R. (2016). Testing the effects of procedural justice and overaccommodation in traffic stops: A randomized experiment. *Criminal Justice and Behavior*, 43(10), 1430–1449.

Ludwig, J. (2005). Better gun enforcement, less crime. *Criminology & Public Policy*, 4(4), 677–716. doi:10.1111/j.1745-9133.2005.00352.x.

Ludwig, J., Kling, J. R., and Mullainathan, S. (2011). Mechanism experiments and policy evaluations. *Journal of Economic Perspectives*, 25(3), 17–38.

Lum, C., and Koper, C. S. (2017). *Evidence-Based Policing: Translating Research into Practice.* New York: Oxford University Press.

Lum, C., and Nagin, D. S. (2017). Reinventing American policing. *Crime and Justice*, 46(1), 339–393.

Lum, C., Koper, C. S., and Telep, C. W. (2011). The evidence-based policing matrix. *Journal of Experimental Criminology*, 7(1), 3–26.

Lum, C., Koper, C. S., and Willis, J. (2016). Understanding the limits of technology's impact on police effectiveness. *Police Quarterly, 20*(2), 135–163. Available: http://journals.sagepub.com/doi/abs/10.1177/1098611116667279 [April 2017].

Lum, C., Hibdon, J., Cave, B., Koper, C. S., and Merola, L. (2011). License plate reader (LPR) police patrols in crime hot spots: An experimental evaluation in two adjacent jurisdictions. *Journal of Experimental Criminology, 7*(4), 321–345.

Lytle, D. J. (2014). The effects of suspect characteristics: A meta-analysis. *Journal of Criminal Justice, 42*(6), 589–597.

Ma, B., Liu, S., and Liu, D. (2014). The impact of organizational identification on the relationship between procedural justice and employee work outcomes. *Social Behavior and Personality: An International Journal, 42*(3), 437–444.

Ma, D. S., and Correll, J. (2011). Target prototypicality moderates racial bias in the decision to shoot. *Journal of Experimental Social Psychology, 47*, 391–396.

MacCoun, R. J. (2005). Voice, control, and belonging: The double-edged sword of procedural fairness. *Annual Review of Law and Social Sciences, 1*, 171–201.

MacCoun, R. J., Lind, E. A., Hensler, D. R., Bryant, D. L., and Ebener, P. A. (1988). *Alternative Adjudication*. Santa Monica, CA: RAND.

Machin, S., and Olivier, M. (2011). Crime and police resources: The street crime initiative. *Journal of the European Economic Association, 9*(4), 678–701.

MacLeod, C. M. (1998). Training on integrated versus separated Stroop tasks: The progression of interference and facilitation. *Memory & Cognition, 26*(2), 201–211.

MacQueen, S., and Bradford, B. (2015). Enhancing public trust and police legitimacy during road traffic encounters: Results from a randomized controlled trial in Scotland. *Journal of Experimental Criminology, 11*(3), 419–443.

MacQueen, S., and Bradford, B. (2017). Where did it all go wrong? Implementation failure—and more—in a field experiment of procedural justice policing. *Journal of Experimental Criminology, 13*(3), 321–345. doi:10.1007/s11292-016-9278-7.

Macrae, C. N., Bodenhausen, G. V, Milne, A. B., and Jetten, J. (1994). Out of mind but back in sight: Stereotypes on the rebound. *Journal of Personality and Social Psychology, 67*(5), 808–817.

Maguire, E. R., and Mastrofski, S. D. (2000). Patterns of community policing in the United States. *Police Quarterly, 3*(1), 4–45.

Mancini, M. J. (1996). *One Dies, Get Another: Convict Leasing in the American South, 1866–1928*. Columbia: University of South Carolina Press.

Manning, P. K. (2010). *Democratic Policing in a Changing World*. Boulder, CO: Paradigm.

Manski, C. F. (2006). Search profiling with partial knowledge of deterrence. *The Economic Journal, 116*(515), 385–401.

Mastrofski, S. D. (2015). Police CEOs: Agents of change? *The Police Chief, 82*(11), 52–54.

Mastrofski, S. D., and Fridell, L. (n.d.). *Police Departments' Adoption of Innovative Practice*. National Police Research Platform. Available: http://static1.1.sqspcdn.com/static/f/733761/26580910/1443907094233/Department+Characteristics+Survey.pdf?token=1xxue9jmC71p%2BeA7gpKCf2WEf7U%3D [January 2016].

Mastrofski, S. D., and Uchida, C. D. (1993). Transforming the police. *Journal of Research in Crime & Delinquency, 30*(3), 330–358.

Mastrofski, S. D., and Willis, J. J. (2010). Police organization continuity and change: Into the twenty-first century. *Crime and Justice: A Review of Research, 39*(1), 55–144.

Mastrofski, S. D., Worden, R. E., and Snipes, J. P. (1995). Law enforcement in a time of community policing. *Criminology, 33*(4), 539–563.

Mastrofski, S. D., Snipes, B., and Supina, A. E. (1996). Compliance on demand: The public's response to specific police requests. *Journal of Research in Crime & Delinquency, 33*(3), 269–305.

Mastrofski, S. D., Jonathan-Zamir, T., Moyal, S., and Willis, J J. (2016). Predicting procedural justice in police-citizen encounters. *Criminal Justice and Behavior, 43*(1), 119–139.

Mayhew, H. (1968) (original work 1862). *London Labour and the London Poor.* New York: Dover.

Mazerolle, L., and Ransley, J. (2006). The case for third-party policing. In D. L. Weisburd and A. A. Braga (Eds.), *Police Innovation: Contrasting Perspectives* (pp. 191–206). New York: Cambridge University Press.

Mazerolle, L., and Roehl, J. (1999). *Controlling Drug and Disorder Problems: Oakland's Beat Health Program.* Research in Brief. Washington, DC: National Institute of Justice. Available: https://www.ncjrs.gov/pdffiles1/175051.pdf [September 2016].

Mazerolle, L., Price, J., and Roehl, J. (2000). Civil remedies and drug control: A randomized field trial in Oakland, CA. *Evaluation Review, 24*(2), 212–241.

Mazerolle, L., Bennett, S., Davis, J., Sargeant, E., and Manning, M. (2012a). Legitimacy in policing: A systematic review. *Campbell Systematic Reviews, 9.*

Mazerolle, L., Bennett, S., Antrobus, E., and Eggins, E. (2012b). Procedural justice, routine encounters and citizen perceptions of police: Main findings from the Queensland Community Engagement Trial (QCET). *Journal of Experimental Criminology, 8*(4), 343–367.

Mazerolle, L., Bennett, S., Davis, J., Sargeant, E., and Dunning, M. (2013a). Procedural justice and police legitimacy: A systematic review of the research. *Journal of Experimental Criminology, 9*(3), 245–274.

Mazerolle, L., Antrobus, E., Bennett, S., and Tyler, T. R. (2013b). Shaping citizen perceptions of police legitimacy: A randomized field trial of procedural justice. *Criminology, 51*(1), 33–63.

Mazerolle, L., Sargeant, E., Cherney, A., Bennett, S., Murphy, K., Antrobus, E., and Martin, P. (2014). *Procedural Justice and Legitimacy in Policing.* New York: Springer.

McCluskey, J. D. (2003). *Police Requests for Compliance: Coercive and Procedurally Just Tactics.* New York: LFB Scholarly.

McConnell, A. R., and Leibold, J. M. (2001). Relations among the Implicit Association Test, discriminatory behavior, and explicit measures of racial attitudes. *Journal of Experimental Social Psychology, 37*(5), 435–442.

McCoy, D. C., Raver, C. C., and Sharkey, P. (2015). Children's cognitive performance and selective attention following recent community violence. *Journal of Health and Social Behavior, 56*(1), 19–36. doi:10.1177/0022146514567576.

McCrary, J. (2007). The effect of court-ordered hiring quotas on the composition and quality of police.*American Economic Review, 97*(1): 318–353.

McCurdy, A., and Bradley, M. (2013). Procedural justice: High expectations. *COPS Office, Community Policing Dispatch, 6*(9). Available: http://cops.usdoj.gov/html/dispatch/09-2013/procedural_justice_high_expectations.asp [September 2016].

McGarrell, E. F., Giacomazzi, A. L., and Thurman, Q. C. (1999). Reducing disorder, fear, and crime in public housing: A case study of place specific crime prevention. *Justice Research and Policy, 1*(2), 61–88.

McGarrell, E. F., Chermak, S., Weiss, A., and Wilson, J. (2001). Reducing firearms violence through directed police patrol. *Criminology & Public Policy, 1*(1), 119–148.

McGarrell, E. F., Chermak S., Wilson, J., and Corsaro, N. (2006). Reducing homicide through a "lever-pulling" strategy. *Justice Quarterly, 23*(2), 214–231.

McLaughlin, K., Hatzenbuelher, M., and Keyes, K. (2010). Responses to discrimination and psychiatric disorders among black, Hispanic, female, and lesbian, gay, and bisexual individuals. *American Journal of Public Health, 100*(8), 1477–1484.

McLean, K., and Wolfe, S. E. (2016). A sense of injustice loosens the moral bind of law: Specifying the links between procedural injustice, neutralizations and offending. *Criminal Justice and Behavior, 43*(1), 27–44.

McLean, S. J., Worden, R. E., and Kim, M. S. (2013). Here's looking at you: An evaluation of public CCTV cameras and their effects on crime and disorder. *Criminal Justice Review, 38*(3), 303–334.

McMahon, J., Garner, J., Davis, R., and Kraus, A. (2002). *How to Correctly Collect and Analyze Racial Profiling Data: Your Reputation Depends on It!.* Final Project Report for Racial Profiling Data Collection and Analysis. Washington, DC: U.S. Government Printing Office. Available: https://cops.usdoj.gov/html/cd_rom/inaction1/pubs/HowToCorrectlyCollectAnalyzeRacialProfilingData.pdf [April 2017].

Meares, T. L. (1998). Symposium on race and criminal law: Place and crime. *Chicago-Kent Law Review, 73*, 467–473. Available: http://chicagounbound.uchicago.edu/cgi/viewcontent.cgi?article=2643&context=journal_articles [October 2017].

Meares, T. L. (2006). Third-party policing: A critical view. In D. L. Weisburd and A. A. Braga (Eds.), *Police Innovation: Contrasting Perspectives* (pp. 207–224). New York: Cambridge University Press.

Meares, T. L. (2013). *The Good Cop: Knowing the Difference between Lawful or Effective Policing and Rightful Policing—and Why It Matters.* Faculty Scholarship Series 4661. Available: http://digitalcommons.law.yale.edu/fss_papers/4661 [April 2017].

Meares, T. L. (2014). The law and social science of stop and frisk. *Annual Review of Law and Social Science, 10*(1), 335–352.

Meares, T. L. (2015). Programming errors: Understanding the constitutionality of stop-and-frisk as a program, not an incident. *The University of Chicago Law Review*, 159–179.

Meares, T. L., Tyler, T. R., and Gardener, J. (2016). Lawful or fair?: How cops and laypeople perceive good policing. *Journal of Criminology and Criminal Law, 105*(2), 297–344.

Miller, D. (2001). Disrespect and the experience of injustice. *Annual Review of Psychology, 52*, 527–553.

Miller, J., and D'Souza, A. (2016). Indirect effects of police searches on community attitudes to the police: Resentment or reassurance? *British Journal of Criminology, 56*(3), 456–478.

Miller, J., Bland, N., and Quinton, P. (2000). *The Impact of Stops and Searches on Crime and the Community.* London, UK: Home Office, Policing and Reducing Crime Unit, Research, Development and Statistics Directorate.

Miller, W. R. (1975). Police authority in London and New York City, 1830–1870. *Journal of Social History, 8*(2), 81–101.

Miller, W. R. (1977). *Cops and Bobbies: Police Authority in New York and London, 1830–1870.* Chicago, IL: University of Chicago Press.

Minneapolis Medical Research Foundation, Inc. (1976). Critiques and commentaries on evaluation research activities—Russell Sage reports. *Evaluation, 3*(1–2), 115–118.

Mohler, G. O., Short, M. B., Brantingham, P. J., Schoenberg, F. P., and Tita, G. E. (2011). Self-exciting point process modeling of crime. *Journal of the American Statistical Association, 106*(493), 100–108.

Mohler, G. O., Short, M. B., Malinowski, S., Johnson, M., Tita, G. E., Bertozzi, A., and Brantingham, J. (2015). Randomized controlled field trials of predictive policing. *Journal of the American Statistical Association, 110*(512), 1399–1411.

Monkkonen, E. H. (1981). *Police in Urban America, 1860–1920.* Cambridge, UK: Cambridge University Press.

Morin, R., Parker, K., Stepler, R., and Mercer, A. (2017). *Behind the Bridge.* Washington, DC: Pew Research Center. Available: http://www.pewsocialtrends.org/2017/01/11/behind-the-badge [April 2017].

Mueller, B., and Baker, A. (2014). 2 N.Y.P.D. officers killed in Brooklyn ambush; suspect commits suicide. *The New York Times*, December 20. Available: http://www.nytimes.com/2014/12/21/nyregion/two-police-officers-shot-in-their-patrol-car-in-brooklyn.html [September 2016].

Muir, W. K., Jr. (1977). *Police Streetcorner Politicians.* Chicago, IL: University of Chicago Press.

Muniz, A. (2012). Disorderly community partners and broken windows policing. *Ethnography, 13*(3), 330–351.

Muniz, A. (2014). Maintaining racial boundaries: Criminalization, neighborhood context, and the origins of gang injunctions. *Social Problems, 61*(2), 216–236.

Murphy, K. (2005). Regulating more effectively: The relationship between procedural justice, legitimacy, and tax non-compliance. *Journal of Law and Society, 32*(4), 562–589.

Murphy, K. (2013). Does procedural justice matter to youth? Comparing adults' and youths' willingness to collaborate with police. *Policing & Society, 25*(1), 53–76.

Murphy, K., Hinds, L., and Fleming, J. (2008). Encouraging public cooperation and support for police. *Policing & Society, 18*(2), 136–155.

Myhill, A., and Bradford, B. (2012). Can police enhance confidence in improving quality of service? *Policing & Society, 22*(4), 397–425.

Myhill, A., and Quinton, P. (2011). *It's a Fair Cop? Police Legitimacy, Public Cooperation and Crime Reduction.* London, UK: National Policing Improvement Agency.

Nagin, D. S. (2013). Deterrence in the 21st century. In M. Tonry (Ed.), *Crime and Justice in America, 1975–2015* (vol. 42). Chicago, IL: University of Chicago Press.

Nagin, D. S., and Telep, C. W. (2017). Procedural justice and legal compliance. *Annual Review of Law and Social Science, 13.* doi:10.1146/annurev-lawsocsci-110316-113310.

Nagin, D. S., and Weisburd, D. L. (2013). Evidence and public policy: The example of evaluation research in policing. *Criminology & Public Policy, 12*(4), 651–679.

Nagin, D. S., Solow, R. M., and Lum, C. (2015). Deterrence, criminal opportunities, and police. *Criminology, 53*(1), 74–100.

Najdowski, C. J. (2011). Stereotype threat in criminal interrogations: Why innocent Black suspects are at risk for confessing falsely. *Psychology, Public Policy, and Law, 17,* 562–591.

Najdowski, C. J., Bottoms, B. L., and Goff, P. A. (2015). Stereotype threat and racial differences in citizens' experiences of police encounters. *Law and Human Behavior, 39*(5), 463–477.

Nakamura, S., Somemura, H., Sasaki, N., Yamamoto, M., Tanaka, M., and Tanaka, K. (2016). Effect of management training in organizational justice: A randomized controlled trial. *Industrial Health, 54*(3), 263–271.

National Academies of Sciences, Engineering, and Medicine (2016). *The Economic and Fiscal Consequences of Immigration.* Panel on the Economic and Fiscal Consequences of Immigration. F. D. Blau and C. Mackie (Eds.). Committee on National Statistics, Division of Behavioral and Social Sciences and Education. Washington, DC: The National Academies Press.

National Institute on Drug Abuse. (2016). *Cocaine.* Available: https://www.drugabuse.gov/publications/research-reports/cocaine [January 2017].

National Research Council. (2004). *Fairness and Effectiveness in Policing: The Evidence.* Committee to Review Research on Police Policy and Practices. W. Skogan and K. Frydl (Eds.). Committee on Law and Justice, Division of Behavioral and Social Sciences and Education. Washington, DC: The National Academies Press.

National Research Council. (2005). *Firearms and Violence: A Critical Review.* Committee to Improve Research Information and Data on Firearms. C. F. Wellford, J. V. Pepper, and C. V. Petrie (Eds.). Committee on Law and Justice, Division of Behavioral and Social Sciences and Education. Washington, DC: The National Academies Press.

Neely, J. H. (1977). Semantic priming and retrieval from lexical memory: Roles of inhibitionless spreading activation and limited-capacity attention. *Journal of Experimental Psychology: General, 106,* 226–254.

Nestler, E. J. (2005). The neurobiology of cocaine addiction. *Science & Practice Perspectives*, 3(1), 4–10.
Newman, O. (1972). *Defensible Space: Crime Prevention through Urban Design*. New York: Macmillan.
Nolan, K., and Chokshi, N. (2016). Milwaukee shaken by eruption of violence after shooting by police. *The New York Times*, August 14. Available: http://www.nytimes.com/2016/08/15/us/milwaukee-shaken-by-eruption-of-violence-after-shooting-by-police.html?rref=collection%2Ftimestopic%2FPolice%20Brutality%20and%20Misconduct&action=click&contentCollection=timestopics&region=stream&module=stream_unit&version=latest&contentPlacement=117&pgtype=collection&mtrref=www.nytimes.com&gwh=FE4315E43E2B8EFE1E20D24CEF79511C&gwt=pay [September 2016].
Nordberg, A., Crawford, M., Praetorius, R., and Smith Hatcher, S. (2015). Exploring minority youths' police encounters: A qualitative interpretive meta-synthesis. *Child and Adolescent Social Work Journal*, 33(2), 137–149.
Norman, J. (2009). Seen and not heard: Young people's perceptions of the police. *Policing*, 3(4), 364–372.
North, D. C. (1981). *Structure and Change in Economic History*. New York: W. W. Norton.
Nosek, B. A., and Banaji, M. R. (2001). The go/no-go association task. *Social Cognition*, 19(6), 625–666.
Nosek, B. A., Greenwald, A. G., and Banaji, M. R. (2007). The Implicit Association Test at age 7: A methodological and conceptual review. In J. A. Bargh (Ed.), *Automatic Processes in Social Thinking and Behavior* (pp. 265–292). New York: Psychology Press.
O'Flaherty, B. (2015). *The Economics of Race in the United States*. Cambridge, MA: Harvard University Press.
Oliver, M. (2017) *August Vollmer: The Father of American Policing*. Durham, NC: Carolina Academic Press.
Oswald, F. L., Mitchell, G., Blanton, H., Jaccard, J., and Tetlock, P. E. (2013). Predicting ethnic and racial discrimination: A meta-analysis of IAT criterion studies. *Journal of Personality and Social Psychology*, 105(2), 171-192.
Oswald, F. L., Mitchell, G., Blanton, H., Jaccard, J., and Tetlock, P. E. (2015). Using the IAT to predict ethnic and racial discrimination: Small effect sizes of unknown societal significance. *Journal of Personality and Social Psychology*, 108(4), 562-571.
Owens, E. G., Weisburd, D. L., Alpert, G., and Amendola, K. L. (2016). *Promoting Police Integrity through Early Engagements and Procedural Justice in the Seattle Police Department*. Washington, DC: National Institute of Justice, U.S. Department of Justice.
Pager, D. (2003). The mark of a criminal record. *American Journal of Sociology*, 108(5), 937–975.
Papachristos, A. V., Meares, T. L., and Fagan, J. (2007). Attention felons: Evaluating Project Safe neighborhoods in Chicago. *Journal of Empirical Legal Studies*, 4(2), 223–250.
Parks, R. B., Mastrofski, S. D., DeJong, C., and Gray, M. K. (1999). How officers spend their time with the community. *Justice Quarterly*, 16(3), 483–518.
Pate, A., Bowers, R., and Parks, R. (1976). *Three Approaches to Criminal Apprehension in Kansas City: An Evaluation Report*. Washington, DC: Police Foundation.
Pate, A. M., and Skogan, W. (1985). *Coordinated Community Policing: The Newark Experience*. Technical Report. Washington, DC: Police Foundation.
Pate, A. M., Lavrakas, P. J., Wycoff, M. A., Skogan, W. G., and Sherman, L. W. (1985a). *Neighborhood Police Newsletters: Experiments in Newark and Houston*. Technical Report. Washington, DC: Police Foundation.

Pate, A. M., Skogan, W. G., Wycoff, M. A., and Sherman, L.W. (1985b). *Coordinated Community Policing: The Newark Experience.* Technical Report. Washington, DC: Police Foundation.

Pate, A. M., Skogan, W. G., Wycoff, M., and Sherman, L. W. (1985c). *Reducing the "Signs of Crime:" The Newark Experience.* Washington, DC: Police Foundation.

Pate, A. M., Wycoff, M. A., Skogan, W. G., and Sherman, L. W. (1986). *Reducing Fear of Crime in Houston and Newark: A Summary Report.* Washington, DC: Police Foundation.

Pate, A. M., McPherson, M., and Silloway, G. (1987). *The Minneapolis Community Crime Prevention Experiment: Draft Evaluation Report.* Washington, DC: Police Foundation.

Paternoster, R., Brame, R., Bachman, R., and Sherman, L. (1997). Do fair procedures matter? The effect of procedural justice on spouse abuse. *Law & Society Review, 31*(1), 163–204.

Payne, B. K. (2001). Prejudice and perception: The role of automatic and controlled processes in misperceiving a weapon. *Journal of Personality and Social Psychology, 81*(2), 181–192.

Payne, B. K. (2005). Conceptualizing control in social cognition: How executive functioning modulates the expression of automatic stereotyping. *Journal of Personality and Social Psychology, 89*(4), 488–503.

Payne, E. (2014). NBA and NFL players join demonstrations against police violence. *CNN*, December 9. Available: http://www.cnn.com/2014/12/09/us/athletes-police-protest [September 2016].

Payne, B. K., Lambert, A. J., and Jacoby, L. L. (2002). Best laid plans: Effects of goals on accessibility bias and cognitive control in race-based misperceptions of weapons. *Journal of Experimental Social Psychology, 38*(4), 384–396.

Perea, J. F., Delgao, R., Harris, A. P., Stefanic, J., and Wildman, S. M. (2014). *Race and Races: Cases and Resources for a Diverse America* (3rd ed.). St. Paul, MN: West Academic Press.

Perry, W. L., McInnis, B., Price, C. C., Smith, S. C., and Hollywood, J. S. (2013). *Predictive Policing: The Role of Crime Forecasting in Law Enforcement Operations.* Washington, DC: RAND.

Persico, N., and Coviello, D. (2015). An economic analysis of black–white disparities in NYPD's Stop and Frisk Program. *Journal of Legal Studies, 44*(2), 315–360.

Phelps, E. A., O'Connor, K. J., Cunningham, W. A., Funayama, E. S., Gatenby, J. C., Gore, J. C., and Banaji, M. R. (2000). Performance on indirect measures of race evaluation predicts amygdala activation. *Journal of Cognitive Neuroscience, 12*(5), 729–738.

Pickett, J. T. (2017). Methodological myths and the role of appeals in criminal justice journals: The case of response rates. *ACJS Today, 43*(3), 61–66.

Piehl, A. M., Cooper, S. J., Braga, A. A., and Kennedy, D. M. (2003). Testing for structural breaks in the evaluation of programs. *Review of Economics and Statistics, 85*(3), 550–558.

Pierce, G. L., Spaar, S., and Briggs, L. R. (1988). *The Character of Police Work: Strategic and Tactical Implications.* Boston, MA: Center for Applied Social Research, Northeastern University.

Piquero, A. R., Gomez-Smith, Z., and Langton, L. (2004). Discerning unfairness when others may not: Low self-control and unfair sanction perceptions. *Criminology, 42*(3), 699–733.

Piza, E. L., Caplan, J. M., and Kennedy, L. W. (2014). Is the punishment more certain? An analysis of CCTV detections and enforcement. *Justice Quarterly, 31*(6), 1015–1043.

Piza, E., Caplan, J. M., Kennedy, L. W., and Gilchrist, A. M. (2015). The effects of merging proactive CCTV monitoring with directed police patrol: A randomized controlled trial. *Journal of Experimental Criminology, 11*(1), 43–69.

Plant, E. A., and Peruche, B. M. (2005). The consequences of race for police officers' responses to criminal suspects. *Psychological Science, 16*(3), 180–183.

Plant, E. A., Devine, P. G., and Peruche, M. B. (2010). Routes to positive interracial interactions: Approaching egalitarianism or avoiding prejudice. *Personality and Social Psychology Bulletin, 36*(9), 1135–1147.

Plant, E. A., Peruche, B. M., and Butz, D. A. (2005). Eliminating automatic racial bias: Making race non-diagnostic for responses to criminal suspects. *Journal of Experimental Social Psychology, 41*(2), 141–156.

Police Executive Research Forum. (2008). Violent crime in America: What we know about hot spots enforcement. *Critical Issues in Policing*. Washington, DC: Police Executive Research Forum. Available: http://www.policeforum.org/assets/docs/Critical_Issues_Series/violent%20crime%20in%20america%20-%20what%20we%20know%20about%20hot%20spots%20enforcement%202008.pdf [January 2016].

Police Executive Research Forum. (2014). *Future Trends in Policing*. Washington, DC: U.S. Department of Justice, Office of Community Oriented Policing Services.

Police Foundation. (1981). *The Newark Foot Patrol Experiment*. Washington, DC: Police Foundation. Available: https://www.policefoundation.org/wp-content/uploads/2015/07/144273499-The-Newark-Foot-Patrol-Experiment.pdf [July 2017].

President's Commission on Law Enforcement and Administration of Justice. (1967). *The Challenge of Crime in a Free Society*. Washington, DC: U.S. Government Printing Office.

President's Task Force on 21st Century Policing. (2015). *Final Report of the President's Task Force on 21st Century Policing*. Washington, DC: Office of Community Oriented Policing Services.

Press, S. J. (1971). *Some Effects of an Increase in Police Manpower in the 20th Precinct of New York City*. New York: New York City Rand Institute.

Quetelet, M. A. (1842). *Treatise on Man*. Edinburgh, UK: William and Robert Chambers.

Quillian, L., and Pager, D. (2001). Black neighbors, higher crime? The role of racial stereotypes in evaluations of neighborhood crime. *American Journal of Sociology, 107*(3), 717–767.

Quinton, P., and Morris, J. (2008). *Neighbourhood Policing: Impact of Piloting and Early National Implementation*. London, UK: Home Office.

Rankin, R. E., and Campbell, D. T. (1955). Galvanic skin response to Negro and white experimenters. *The Journal of Abnormal and Social Psychology, 51*(1), 30–33.

Ransom, R. L., and Sutch, R. (1977). *One Kind of Freedom: The Economic Consequences of Emancipation*. Cambridge, UK: Cambridge University Press.

Raphael, S., and Stoll, M. A. (2013). *Why Are So Many Americans in Prison?* New York: Russell Sage Foundation.

Rashbaum, W. (2003). Mayor extending focus on crime hot spots. *The New York Times*, July 2.

Ratcliffe, J. H. (2006). *Video Surveillance of Public Places*. Washington, DC: Center for Problem Oriented Policing.

Ratcliffe, J. H. (2014). What is the future . . . of predictive policing? *Translational Criminology*, 4–5.

Ratcliffe, J. H., Taniguchi, T., and Taylor, R. B. (2009). The crime reduction effects of public CCTV cameras: A multi-method spatial approach. *Justice Quarterly, 26*(4), 746–770.

Ratcliffe, J. H., Taniguchi, T., Groff, E. R., and Wood, J. D. (2011). The Philadelphia Foot Patrol Experiment: A randomized controlled trial of police patrol effectiveness in violent crime hotspots. *Criminology, 49*(3), 795–831.

Ratcliffe, J., Groff, E., Sorg, E., and Haberman, C. (2015). Citizens' reactions to hot spots policing: Impacts on perceptions of crime, disorder, safety, and police. *Journal of Experimental Criminology, 11*(3), 393–417.

Read, T., and Tilley, N. (2000). *Not Rocket Science? Problem-Solving and Crime Reduction*. Crime Reduction Research Series, Paper No. 6. London, UK: Home Office Policing and Reducing Crime Unit.

Reaves, B. (2010). *Local Police Departments, 2007*. Washington, DC: U.S. Department of Justice, Bureau of Justice Statistics.

Reaves, B. (2015). *Local Police Departments, 2013: Personnel, Policies, and Practices*. Washington, DC: U.S. Department of Justice, Bureau of Justice Statistics.

Reisig, M. D. (2010). Community and problem oriented policing. *Crime and Justice*, 39(1), 1–53.

Reisig, M. D., and Lloyd, C. (2009). Procedural justice, police legitimacy, and helping the police fight crime: Results from a survey of Jamaican adolescents. *Police Quarterly*, 12(1), 42–62.

Reisig, M. D., Bratton, J., and Gertz, M. (2007). The construct validity and refinement of process-based policing measures. *Criminal Justice and Behavior*, 34(8), 1005–1028.

Reisig, M. D., Tankebe, J., and Mesko, G. (2014). Compliance with the law in Slovenia: The role of procedural justice and police legitimacy. *European Journal of Criminal Policy and Research*, 20(2), 259–276.

Reiss, A. J., Jr. (1971). *The Police and the Public*. New Haven, CT: Yale University Press.

Reiss, A. J. (1973). How much "police brutality" is there? In S. M. David and P. E. Peterson (Eds.), *Urban Politics and Public Policy: The City in Crisis* (pp. 269-286). New York: Praeger.

Reiss, A. J., Jr. (1992). Police organization in the twentieth century. In M. Tonry and N. Morris (Eds.), *Modern Policing* (vol. 15, pp. 50–97). Chicago, IL: Chicago University Press.

Reiss, A. J., Jr., and Bordua, D. (1967). *Environment and organization*. In D. Bordua (Ed.), *The Police: Six Sociological Essays* (pp. 25–55). New York: John Wiley.

Reiss, A. J., and Tonry, M. (1986). *Communities and Crime* (vol. 8). Chicago, IL: The University of Chicago Press.

Renauer, B. C. (2007). Is neighborhood policing related to informal social control? *Policing: An International Journal of Police Strategies and Management*, 30(1), 61–81.

Repetto, T. (1976). Crime prevention and the displacement phenomenon. *Crime & Delinquency*, 22(2), 166–177.

Richeson, J. A., and Shelton, J. N. (2003). When prejudice does not pay: Effects of interracial contact on executive function. *Psychological Science*, 14(3), 287–290.

Richeson, J. A., and Shelton, J. N. (2005). Thin slices of racial bias. *Journal of Nonverbal Behavior*, 29, 75–86.

Richeson, J. A., and Shelton, J. N. (2007). Negotiating interracial interactions. *Current Directions in Psychological Science*, 16, 316–320.

Richeson, J. A., and Shelton, J. N. (2012). Stereotype threat in interracial interactions. In M. Inzlicht and T. Schmader (Eds.), *Stereotype Threat: Theory, Process, and Application*. (pp. 231- 245). Oxford University Press.

Richeson, J. A. and Sommers, S. R. (2016). Race relations in the 21st century. *Annual Review of Psychology*, 67, 439-463.

Richter, M., König, C. J., Koppermann, C., and Schilling, M. (2016). Displaying fairness while delivering bad news: Testing the effectiveness of organizational bad news training in the layoff context. *Journal of Applied Psychology*.

Ridgeway, G. (2007). *Analysis of Racial Disparities in the New York Police Department's Stop, Question, and Frisk Practices*. Document No. TR-534-NYCPF. Santa Monica, CA: RAND.

Robertson, A., McMillan, L., Godwin, J., and Deuchar, R. (2014). *The Scottish Police and Citizen Engagement (SPACE) Trial: Final Report*. Glasgow, UK: Glasgow Caledonian University.

Robinson, M. D., Schmeichel, B. J., and Inzlicht, M. (2010). A cognitive control perspective of self-control strength and its depletion. *Social and Personality Psychology Compass*, 4(3), 189–200.

Roehl, J. (1998). Civil remedies for controlling crime: The role of community organizations. In L. Mazerolle and J. Roehl (Eds.), *Civil Remedies and Crime Prevention, Crime Prevention Studies* (vol. 9, pp. 241–260). Monsey, NY: Criminal Justice Press.

Rogers, C. (2002). *Community Safety and Zero Tolerance: A Study of Partnership Policing*. Ph.D. Dissertation. Pontypridd, UK: University of Glamorgan.

Rogers, E. (2003). *Diffusion of Innovations* (5th ed.). New York: Free Press.

Roncek, D. (2000). Schools and crime. In V. Goldsmith, P. McGuire, J. Mollenkopf, and T. Ross (Eds.), *Analyzing Crime Patterns Frontiers of Practice* (pp. 153–166). Thousand Oaks, CA: SAGE.

Rosenbaum, D. P. (Ed.). (1994). *The Challenge of Community Policing: Testing the Promises*. Thousand Oaks, CA: SAGE.

Rosenbaum, D. P. (2006). The limits of hot spots policing. In D. L. Weisburd and A. A. Braga (Eds.), *Police Innovation: Contrasting Perspectives* (pp. 245–266). New York: Cambridge University Press.

Rosenbaum, D. P., and Lawrence, D. S. (2013). *Teaching Respectful Police-Citizen Encounters and Good Decision Making: Results of a Randomized Control Trial with Police Recruits*. Washington, DC: National Police Research Platform.

Rosenbaum, P. R., and Rubin, D. B. (1983). The central role of the propensity score in observational studies for causal effects. *Biometrika*, 70(1), 41–55.

Rosenbaum, D. P., Schuck, A. M., Costello, S. K., Hawkins, D. F., and Ring, M. K. (2005). Attitudes toward the police: The effects of direct and vicarious experience. *Police Quarterly*, 8(3), 343–365.

Rosenfeld, R., and Fornango, R. (2014). The impact of police stops on precinct robbery and burglary rates in New York City, 2003–2010. *Justice Quarterly*, 31(1), 96–122.

Rosenfeld, R., Deckard, M., and Blackburn, E. (2014). The effects of directed patrol and self-initiated enforcement on firearm violence: A randomized controlled study of hot spot policing. *Criminology*, 52(3), 428–449. doi:10.1111/1745-9125.12043.

Rosenfeld, R., Fornango, R., and Baumer, E. (2005). Did Ceasefire, Compstat, and Exile reduce homicide? *Criminology & Public Policy*, 4(3), 419–450. doi:10.1111/j.1745-9133.2005.00310.x.

Rosenfeld, R., Fornango, R., and Rengifo, A. (2007). The impact of order maintenance policing on New York City robbery and homicide rates: 1988–2001. *Criminology*, 45(2), 355–384. doi:10.1111/j.1745-9125.2007.00081.x.

Roth, J. A., Roehl, J., and Johnson, C. C. (2004). Trends in adaptation of community policing. In W. G. Skogan (Ed.), *Community Policing: Can It Work* (pp. 3–29). Belmont, CA: Wadsworth.

Roush, C. (2012). Comment, quis ipsos custodes? Limits on widespread surveillance and intelligence gathering by local law enforcement after 9/11. *Marquette Law Review*, 96(1), 315.

Ruggles, S., Genadek, K., Goeken, R., Grover, J., and Sobek, M. (2015). *Integrated Public Use Microdata Series: Version 6.0* [dataset]. Minneapolis: University of Minnesota.

Sabath, M., and Carter, H. (2000). *Evaluation of Efforts to Strengthen Police–Resident Relations in El Centro, California: A Final Report*. No. NCJ 181051. Washington, DC: U.S. Department of Justice, Office of Justice Programs, National Institute of Justice.

Sahin, N. M. (2014). *Legitimacy, Procedural Justice and Police-Citizen Encounters: A Randomized Controlled Trial of the Impact of Procedural Justice on Citizen Perceptions of the Police During Traffic Stops in Turkey*. Ph.D. Dissertation. Newark: Rutgers, The State University of New Jersey.

Sahin, N. M., Braga, A. A., Apel, R., and Brunson, R. K. (2016). The impact of procedurally-just policing on citizen perceptions of police during traffic stops: The Adana Randomized Controlled Trial. *Journal of Quantitative Criminology*, 1–26.

Sampson, R. J. (2002). Transcending tradition: New directions in community research, Chicago style. *Criminology, 40*(2), 213–230.

Sampson, R. J. (2011). The community. In J. Q. Wilson and J. Petersilia (Eds.), *Crime and Public Policy* (2nd ed., pp. 210–236). New York: Oxford University Press.

Sampson, R. J. (2012). When things aren't what they seem: Context and cognition in appearance-based regulation. *Harvard Law Review Forum, 125*(1), 97–107.

Sampson, R. J., and Lauritsen, J. L. (1997). Racial and ethnic disparities in crime and criminal justice in the United States. *Crime and Justice, 21*, 311–374.

Sampson, R. J., and Raudenbush, S. W. (1999). Systematic social observation of public spaces: A new look at disorder in urban neighborhoods. *American Journal of Sociology, 105*(3), 603–651.

Sampson, R. J., and Raudenbush, S. W. (2004). Seeing disorder: Neighborhood stigma and the social construction of "broken windows." *Social Psychology Quarterly, 67*(4), 319–342.

Sampson, R. J., Raudenbush, S., and Earls, F. (1997). Neighborhoods and violent crime: A multilevel study of collective efficacy. *Science, 277*(5328), 918–924.

Sanga, S. (2009). Reconsidering racial bias in motor vehicle searches: Theory and evidence. *Journal of Political Economy, 117*(6), 1155–1159.

Santos, R. (2014). The effectiveness of crime analysis for crime reduction: Cure or diagnosis? *Journal of Contemporary Criminal Justice, 30*(2), 147–168.

Sargeant, E., Wickes, R., and Mazerolle, L. (2013). Policing community problems: Exploring the role of formal social control in shaping collective efficacy. *Australian and New Zealand Journal of Criminology, 46*(1), 70–87.

Saunders, J., Lundberg, R., Braga, A. A., Ridgeway, G., and Miles, J. (2015). A synthetic control approach to evaluating place-based crime interventions. *Journal of Quantitative Criminology, 31*(3), 413–434.

Schaefer, B., and Hughes, T. (2016). *Honing Interpersonal Necessary Tactics (H.I.N.T.): An Evaluation of Procedural Justice Training.* Available: https://louisville.edu/spi/news/LMPDHoningInterpersonalNecessaryTacticsTrainingEvaluation.pdf [July 2016].

Schnebly, S. (2008). The influence of community-oriented policing on crime-reporting behavior. *Justice Quarterly, 25*(2), 223–251.

Schnelle, J., Kirchner, R. E., Jr., Casey, J. D., Uselton, P. H., Jr., and McNees, M. P. (1977). Patrol evaluation research: A multiple-baseline analysis of saturation police patrolling during day and night hours. *Journal of Applied Behavior Analysis, 10*(1), 33–40.

Schoenfeld, H. (2014). The delayed emergence of penal modernism in Florida. *Punishment & Society, 16*(3), 258–284.

Schwartz, J. C. (2010). Myths and mechanics of deterrence: The role of lawsuits in law enforcement decisionmaking. *UCLA Law Review, 57*, 1023.

Schwartz, J. C. (2014). Police indemnification. *New York University Law Review, 89*(3), 885–1005. Available: http://www.nyulawreview.org/sites/default/files/pdf/NYULawReview-89-3-Schwartz.pdf [April 22, 2017].

Scott, J. D. (2002). Assessing the relationship between police–community coproduction and neighborhood-level social capital. *Journal of Contemporary Criminal Justice, 18*(2), 147–166.

Scrivner, E., and Stephens, D. (2015). *Community Policing in the New Economy.* Washington, DC: Office of Community Oriented Policing Services.

Sears, D. O. (1988). Symbolic racism. In P. A. Katz and D. A. Taylor (Eds.), *Eliminating Racism: Profiles in Controversy* (pp. 53–84). Boston, MA: Springer.

Segrave, M., and Collins, L. (2004). *Evaluation of a Suburban Crime Prevention Team.* Report No. 14. Canberra, Australia: Australian Institute of Criminology.

Sekhon, N. S. (2011). Redistributive policing. *Journal of Criminal Law and Criminology, 101*(4), 1171–1226.

Sharkey, P., and Torrats-Espinosa, G. (2017). The effect of violent crime on economic mobility. *Journal of Urban Economics*, 102, 22–23.

Sharkey, P., Schwartz, A. E., Ellen, I. E., and Lacoe, J. (2014). High stakes in the classroom, high stakes on the street: The effects of community violence on students' standardized test performance. *Sociological Science*, 1, 199–220. doi:10.15195/v1.a14.

Shaw, J. (1995). Community policing against guns: Public opinion of the Kansas City gun experiment. *Justice Quarterly*, 12(4), 695–710.

Shedd, C. (2015). *Unequal City: Race, Schools, and Perceptions of Injustice*. New York: Russell Sage Foundation.

Shelton, J. N., and Richeson, J. A. (2005). Intergroup contact and pluralistic ignorance. *Journal of Personality and Social Psychology*, 88, 91–107.

Shelton, J. N., and Richeson, J. A. (2006). Interracial interactions: A relational approach. In M. P. Zanna (Ed.), *Advances in Experimental Social Psychology* (vol. 38, pp. 121-181). New York: Academic Press.

Shelton, J. N., and Richeson, J. A. (2014). Interacting across racial lines. In. J. F. Dovidio and J. Simpson (Eds.), *APA Handbook of Personality & Social Psychology: Group Processes*. Washington, DC: APA Books.

Shelton, J. N., Richeson, J. A., and Vorauer, J. D. (2006). Threatened identities and interethnic interactions. *European Review of Social Psychology*, 17, 321–358.

Sherman, L. W. (1997). Policing for crime prevention. In L. W. Sherman, D. Gottfredson, D. MacKenzie, J. Eck, P. Reuter, and S. Bushway (Eds.), *Preventing Crime: What Works, What Doesn't, What's Promising*. Washington, DC: National Institute of Justice, U.S. Department of Justice.

Sherman, L. W. (2017). *Foreword to August Vollmer: The Father of American Policing*. Durham, NC: Carolina Academic Press.

Sherman, L. W., and Eck, J. (2002). Policing for prevention. In L. W. Sherman, D. Farrington, B. C. Welsh, and D. L. MacKenzie (Eds.), *Evidence Based Crime Prevention* (pp. 295–329). New York: Routledge.

Sherman, L. W., and Weisburd, D. L. (1995). General deterrent effects of police patrol in crime "hot-spots": A randomized controlled trial. *Justice Quarterly*, 12(4), 626–648.

Sherman, L. W., Buerger, M., and Gartin, P. (1989). *Repeat Call Address Policing: The Minneapolis RECAP Experiment*. Washington, DC: Crime Control Institute.

Sherman, L. W., Shaw, J., and Rogan, D. (1995). The Kansas City Gun Experiment. *NIJ Research in Brief*, January. Available: https://www.ncjrs.gov/pdffiles/kang.pdf [March 2016].

Sherman, L. W., Schmidt, J. D., Rogan, D. P., and Smith, D. A. (1992). The variable effects of arrest on criminal careers: The Milwaukee Domestic Violence Experiment. *Journal of Criminal Law and Criminology*, 83(1), 137–169.

Sherman, L. W., Farrington, D. P., Welsh, B. C., and MacKenzie, D. L. (Eds.). (2002). *Evidence-Based Crime Prevention*. New York: Routledge.

Shute, S., Hood, R., and Seemungal, F. (2005). *A Fair Hearing? Ethnic Minorities in the Criminal Courts*. Cullompton, UK: Willan.

Sidanius, J., and Pratto, F. (1999). *Social Dominance: An Intergroup Theory of Social Hierarchy and Oppression*. New York: Cambridge University Press.

Sidanius, J., and Pratto, F. (2001). *Social Dominance: An Intergroup Theory of Social Hierarchy and Oppression*. Cambridge, MA: Cambridge University Press.

Sidanius, J., Liu, J. H., Shaw, J. S., and Pratto, F. (1994). Social dominance orientation, hierarchy attenuators, and hierarchy enhancers: Social dominance theory and the criminal justice system. *Journal of Applied Social Psychology*, 24(4), 338–366.

Sim, J. J., Correll, J., and Sadler, M. S. (2013). Understanding police and expert performance when training attenuates (vs. exacerbates) stereotypic bias in the decision to shoot. *Personality and Social Psychology Bulletin*, *39*(3), 291–304.

Skarlicki, D., and Latham, G. (1996). Increasing citizenship behavior within a labor union: A test of organizational justice theory. *Journal of Applied Psychology*, *81*(2), 161–169.

Skarlicki, D., and Latham, G. (1997). Leadership training in organizational justice to increase citizenship behavior within a labor union: A replication. *Personnel Psychology*, *50*(3), 617–633.

Sklansky, D. A. (2005). Not your father's police department: Making sense of the new demographics of law enforcement criminology. *Journal of Criminal Law and Criminology*, *96*, 1209–1244.

Skogan, W. G. (1986). Fear of crime and neighborhood change. *Crime and Justice*, *8*.

Skogan, W. G. (1988). Disorder, crime and community decline. In M. Shaw and T. Hope (Eds.), *Communities and Crime Reduction* (pp. 48–61). London, UK: Her Majesty's Stationery Office.

Skogan, W. G. (1990). *Disorder and Decline: Crime and the Spiral of Decay in American Cities*. New York: Free Press.

Skogan, W. G. (1992). *Impact of Policing on Social Disorder: Summary of Findings*. Washington, DC: U.S. Department of Justice, Office of Justice Programs.

Skogan, W. G. (1994). *Contacts between Police and Public: Findings from the 1992 British Crime Survey*. London, UK: Her Majesty's Stationery Office.

Skogan, W. G. (2006a). Asymmetry in the impact of encounters with police. *Policing and Society*, *16*(2), 99–126.

Skogan, W. G. (2006b). *Police and Community in Chicago: A Tale of Three Cities*. New York: Oxford University Press.

Skogan, W. G. (2006c). The promise of community policing. In D. L. Weisburd and A. A. Braga (Eds.), *Police Innovation: Contrasting Perspectives* (pp. 27–43). New York: Cambridge University Press.

Skogan, W. G. (2009). Concern about crime and confidence in the police: Reassurance or accountability? *Police Quarterly*, *12*(3), 301–318.

Skogan, W. G., and Antunes, G. E. (1979). Information, apprehension, and deterrence: Exploring the limits of police productivity. *Journal of Criminal Justice*, *7*(3), 217–241.

Skogan, W. G., and Hartnett, S. M. (1997). *Community Policing, Chicago Style*. New York: Oxford University Press.

Skogan, W. G., and Steiner, L. (2004). *Community Policing in Chicago, Year Ten: An Evaluation of Chicago's Alternative Policing Strategy*. Chicago, IL: Chicago Community Policing Evaluation Consortium Program.

Skogan, W. G., Hartnett, S. M., DuBois, J., Comey, J. T., Kaiser, M., and Lovig, J. H. (1999). *On the Beat: Police and Community Problem Solving*. Boulder, CO: Westview.

Skogan, W. G., Van Craen, M., and Hennessy, C. (2015). Training police for procedural justice. *Journal of Experimental Criminology*, *11*(3), 319–334.

Skolnick, J. H., and Bayley, D. H. (1986). *The New Blue Line. Police Innovation in Six American Cities*. New York: The Free Press.

Slocum, L. A., Taylor, T. J., Brick, B. T., and Esbensen, F. A. (2010). Neighborhood structural characteristics, individual-level attitudes, and youths' crime reporting intentions. *Criminology*, *48*(4), 1063–1100. doi:10.1111/j.1745-9125.2010.00212.x.

Smith, B. W., Novak, K. J., and Frank, J. (2001). Community policing and the work routines of street-level officers. *Criminal Justice Review*, *26*(1), 17–37.

Smith, D., and Purtell, R. (2008). *Does Stop and Frisk Stop Crime?* Draft paper presented at the Annual Research Conference of the Association of Public Policy and Management, Los Angeles, CA, November.

Smith, G. J. D. (2004). Behind the screens: Examining constructions of deviance and informal practices among CCTV control room operators in the UK. *Surveillance & Society*, 2(2/3), 376–395.

Smith, W. R., Tomaskovic, D., Zingraff, M. T., Mason, M. H., Warren, P. Y., and Pfaff Wright, C. (2004). *The North Carolina Traffic Study*. Document No. 204021. Available: https://www.ncjrs.gov/pdffiles1/nij/grants/204021.pdf [April 2017].

Snyder, H. N. (2011). *Arrest in the United States, 1980–2009*. Washington, DC: Bureau of Justice Statistics.

Solum, L. B. (2004). Procedural justice. *Southern California Law Review*, 78(1), 181–322.

Sommers, S. R., and Ellsworth, P. C. (2000). Race in the courtroom: Perceptions of guilt and dispositional attributions. *Personality and Social Psychology Bulletin*, 26, 1367–1379.

Sorg, E. T., Haberman, C. P., Ratcliffe, J. H., and Groff, E. R. (2013). Foot patrol in violent crime hot spots: Longitudinal impacts of deterrence and post-treatment effects of displacement. *Criminology*, 51(1), 65–101.

Sparrow, M. K. (2016). *Handcuffed: What Holds Policing Back, and the Keys to Reform*. Washington, DC: Brookings Institution Press.

Sparrow, M. K., Moore, M. H., and Kennedy, D. M. (1992). *Beyond 911: A New Era for Policing*. New York: Basic Books.

Spelman, W., and Brown, D. K. (1981). *Calling the Police: A Replication of the Citizen Reporting Component of the Kansas City Response Time Analysis*. Washington, DC: Police Executive Research Forum.

Spelman, W., and Brown, D. K. (1984). *Calling the Police: Citizen Reporting of Serious Crime*. Washington, DC: Police Executive Research Forum.

Stangor, C., and Crandall, C. (Eds.). (2013). *Stereotyping and Prejudice*. New York: Psychology Press.

Steele, C. M. (1992). Race and the schooling of Black Americans. *The Atlantic Monthly*, 269(4), 68–78.

Steffens, L. (1931). *The Autobiography of Lincoln Steffens*. New York: Chautauqua Press.

Stott, C., Hoggett, J., and Pearson, G. (2012). Keeping the peace: Social identity, procedural justice and the policing of football crowds. *British Journal of Criminology*, 52(2), 381–399.

Stoud, B. G., Fine, M., and Fox, M. (2011). *Growing Up Policed in the Age of Aggressive Policing Policies*. New York: John Jay College of Criminal Justice.

Stults, B., and Baumer, E. (2007). Racial context and police force size: Evaluating the empirical validity of the minority threat perspective. *American Journal of Sociology*, 113(2), 507–546.

Stuntz, W. J. (2002). Local policing after the terror. *Yale Law Journal*, 111(8).

Sunshine, J., and Tyler, T. R. (2003). The role of procedural justice and legitimacy in shaping public support for policing. *Law & Society Review*, 37(3), 513–548.

Sykes, G. M., and Matza, D. (1957). Techniques of neutralization: A theory of delinquency. *American Sociological Review*, 22(6), 664–670.

Tankebe, J. (2013). Viewing things differently: The dimensions of public perceptions of police legitimacy. *Criminology*, 51(1), 103–136.

Taxman, F. S., and Gordon, J. A. (2009). Do fairness and equity matter? An examination of organizational justice among correctional officers in adult prisons. *Criminal Justice and Behavior*, 36(7), 695–711.

Taylor, R. B. (2001). *Breaking Away from Broken Windows*. Boulder, CO: Westview.

Taylor, R. B. (2006). Incivilities reduction policing, zero tolerance, and the retreat from coproduction: Weak foundations and strong pressures. In D. L. Weisburd and A. A. Braga (Eds.), *Police Innovation: Contrasting Perspectives* (pp. 98–116). New York: Cambridge University Press.

Taylor, R. B., and Lawton, B. A. (2012). An integrated contextual model of confidence in local police. *Police Quarterly, 1*(4), 414–445.

Taylor, B., Koper, C., and Woods, D. (2011). A randomized controlled trial of different policing strategies at hot spots of violent crime. *Journal of Experimental Criminology, 7*(2), 149–181.

Telep, C. W., Mitchell, R., and Weisburd, D. L. (2014). How much time should the police spend at crime hot spots? Answers from a police agency directed randomized field trial in Sacramento, California. *Justice Quarterly, 31*(5), 905–933.

Terkel, A. (2013). Ray Kelly on stop and frisk: "No question" violent crime will rise if program is stopped. *The Huffington Post*, August 18. Available: http://www.huffingtonpost.com/2013/08/18/ray-kelly-stop-and-frisk_n_3776035.html [September 2016].

Terrill, W., and Mastrofski, S., (2002.) Situational and officer based determinants of police coercion. *Justice Quarterly, 19*, 215–248.

Terrill, W., and Reisig, M. D. (2003). Neighborhood context and police use of force. *Journal of Research in Crime and Delinquency, 40*(3), 291–321.

Texas Department of Public Safety. (2000). *Traffic Stop Data Report*. Austin: Texas Department of Public Safety. Available: https://www.dps.texas.gov/director_staff/public_information/trafrep2q00.pdf [April 2017].

Thibaut, J., and Walker, L. (1975). *Procedural Justice: A Psychological Analysis*. Hillsdale, NJ: Lawrence Erlbaum Associates.

Thibaut, J., Friedland, N., and Walker, L. (1974). Compliance with rule: Some social determinants. *Journal of Personality and Social Psychology, 30* 6), 782–801.

Thibaut, J., Walker, L., and Lind, E. A. (1972). Adversary presentation and bias in legal decision making. *Harvard Law Review, 86*(2), 386–401.

TIME. (1996). Finally, we're winning the war against crime. Here's why. *TIME*, January 15. Available: http://content.time.com/time/covers/0,16641,19960115,00.html [April 2017].

Toby, J. (1957). Social disorganization and stake in conformity: Complementary factors in the predatory behavior of hoodlums. *Journal of Criminal Law, Criminology, and Police Science, 48*(1), 12–17.

Tonry, M. (1995). *Malign Neglect: Race, Crime, and Punishment in America*. New York: Oxford University Press.

Tonry, M., and Melewski, M. (2008). The malign effects of drug and crime control policies on black Americans. *Crime and Justice, 37*, 1–44.

Tor, A., Gazal-Ayal, O., and Garcia, S. M. (2010). Fairness and the willingness to accept plea bargain offers. *Journal of Empirical Legal Studies, 7*(1), 97–116. doi:10.1111/j.1740-1461.2009.01171.x.

Trawalter, S., Richeson, J. A., and Shelton, J. N. (2009). Predicting behavior during interracial interactions: A stress and coping approach. *Personality and Social Psychology Review, 13*, 243–268.

Tremblay, M., Cloutier, J., Simard, G., Chenevert, D., and Vandenberghe, C. (2010). The role of HRM practices, procedural justice, organizational support and trust in organization commitment and in-role and extra-role performance. *International Journal of Human Resource Management, 21*(3), 405–433.

Trinkner, R., Tyler, T. R., and Goff, P. A. (2016). Justice from within: The relations between a procedurally just organizational climate and police organizational efficiency, endorsement of democratic policing, and officer well-being. *Psychology, Public Policy, and Law, 22*(2), 158–172.

Trojanowicz, R., and Bucqueroux, B. (1994). *Community Policing: How to Get Started*. Cincinnati, OH: Anderson.

Tso, G. (2016). Police brutality is not invisible. *The Hill, Congress Blog*, January 14. Available: http://thehill.com/blogs/congress-blog/civil-rights/265795-police-brutality-is-not-invisible [July 2016].

Tuffin, R., Morris, J., and Poole, A. (2006). *An Evaluation of the Impact of the National Reassurance Policing Programme*. Home Office Research Study 296. Available: https://www.gov.uk/government/uploads/system/uploads/attachment_data/file/115825/hors296.pdf [April 2017].

Tyler, T. R. (1987). The psychology of dispute resolution: Implications for the mediation of disputes by third parties. *Negotiation Journal*, 3, 367–374.

Tyler, T. R. (1988). What is procedural justice?: Criteria used by citizens to assess the fairness of legal procedures. *Law and Society Review*, 22(1), 103–135.

Tyler, T. R. (1989). The quality of dispute resolution processes and outcomes: Measurement problems and possibilities. *Denver University Law Review*, 66, 419–436.

Tyler, T. R. (1990). *Why People Obey the Law*. New Haven, CT: Yale University Press.

Tyler, T. R. (2000). Social justice: Outcome and procedure. *International Journal of Psychology*, 35(2), 117–125.

Tyler, T. R. (2001). Public trust and confidence in legal authorities: What do majority and minority group members want from the law and legal institutions? *Behavioral Sciences and the Law*, 19(2), 215–235.

Tyler, T. R. (2003). Procedural justice, legitimacy, and the effective rule of law. In M. Tonry (Ed.), *Crime and Justice* (vol. 30, pp. 431–505). Chicago, IL: University of Chicago Press.

Tyler, T. R. (2004). Enhancing police legitimacy. *The ANNALS of the American Academy of Political and Social Science*, 593(1), 84–99.

Tyler, T. R. (2006). *Why People Obey the Law*. Princeton, NJ: Princeton University Press.

Tyler, T. R. (2009). Legitimacy and criminal justice: The benefits of self-regulation. *Ohio State Journal of Criminal Law*, 7, 307–359.

Tyler, T. R. (2011). *Why People Cooperate: The Role of Social Motivations*. Princeton, NJ: Princeton University Press.

Tyler, T. R., and Blader, S. L. (2000). *Cooperation in Groups: Procedural Justice, Social Identity, and Behavioral Engagement*. Philadelphia, PA: Psychology Press.

Tyler, T. R., and Blader, S. L. (2005). Can businesses effectively regulate employee conduct? The antecedents of rule following in work settings. *The Academy of Management Journal*, 48(6), 1143–1158.

Tyler, T. R., and Fagan, J. (2008). Legitimacy and cooperation: Why do people help the police fight crime in their communities? *Ohio State Journal of Criminal Law*, 6, 230–274. Available: http://moritzlaw.osu.edu/osjcl/Articles/Volume6_1/Tyler-Fagan-PDF.pdf [April 2017].

Tyler, T. R., and Huo, Y. (2002). *Trust in the Law: Encouraging Public Cooperation with the Police and Courts*. New York: Russell Sage Foundation.

Tyler, T. R., and Jackson, J. (2014). Popular legitimacy and the exercise of legal authority: Motivating compliance, cooperation and engagement. *Psychology, Public Policy and Law*, 20(1), 78–95.

Tyler, T. R., and Lind, E. A. (1992). A relational model of authority in groups. In M. Zanna (Ed.), *Advances in Experimental Social Psychology* (vol. 25, pp. 115–191). San Diego, CA: Academic Press.

Tyler, T. R., and Wakslak, C. J. (2004). Profiling and police legitimacy: Procedural justice, attributions of motive, and acceptance of police authority. *Criminology*, 42(2), 253–282.

Tyler, T. R., Casper, J. D., and Fisher, B. (1989). Maintaining allegiance toward political authorities. *American Journal of Political Science*, 33(3), 629–652.

Tyler, T. R., Callahan, P. E., and Frost, J. (2007). Armed, and dangerous (?): Motivating rule adherence among agents of social control. *Law & Society Review*, 41(2), 457–492.

Tyler, T. R., Sherman, L., Strang, H., Barnes, G. C., and Woods, D. (2007). Reintegrative shaming, procedural justice, and recidivism: The engagement of offenders' psychological mechanisms in the Canberra RISE drinking-and-driving experiment. *Law & Society Review*, 41(3), 553–586.

Tyler, T. R., Schulhofer, S. J., and Huq, A. Z. (2010). Legitimacy and deterrence effects in counter-terrorism policing. *Law & Society Review*, 44(2), 365–402.

Tyler, T. R., Fagan, J., and Geller, A. (2014). Street stops and police legitimacy: Teachable moments in young urban men's legal socialization. *Journal of Empirical Legal Studies*, 11(4), 751–785.

Tyler, T. R., Goff, P. A., and MacCoun, R. J. (2015). The impact of psychological science on policing in the United States: Procedural justice, legitimacy, and effective law enforcement. *Psychological Science in the Public Interest*, 16(3), 75–109.

Tyler, T. R., Jackson, J., and Mentovich, A. (2015). The consequences of being an object of suspicion: Potential pitfalls of proactive police contact. *Journal of Empirical Legal Studies*, 12(4), 602–636.

Uchida, C. (2009). *A National Discussion on Predictive Policing: Defining Our Terms and Mapping Successful Implementation Strategies*. Washington, DC: U.S. Department of Justice, National Institute of Justice.

U.S. Department of Justice. (2011). *Investigation of the New Orleans Police Department*. Washington, DC: Author. Available: https://www.nlg-npap.org/sites/default/files/DOJInvestigation%20NOLA.pdf [April 2017].

U.S. Department of Justice. (2014). *Uniform Crime Reporting Program Data: Police Employee (LEOKA) Data, 2014*. Federal Bureau of Investigation. ICPSR36395-v1. Ann Arbor, MI: Inter-university Consortium for Political and Social Research [distributor], 2016-03-24. Available: https://doi.org/10.3886/ICPSR36395.v1 [November 2017].

U.S. Department of Justice. (2016). *Investigation of the Baltimore City Police Department*. Washington, DC: Author. Available: https://www.justice.gov/opa/file/883366/download [April 2017].

USA Today. (2016). Rallies continue across USA protesting shootings by police. *USA Today*, July 11. Available: http://www.usatoday.com/story/news/nation-now/2016/07/10/tensions-flare-nationwide-against-prayers-and-protests-police-shootings/86913818 [September 2016].

Van Damme, A., Pauwels, L., and Svensson, R. (2015). Why do Swedes cooperate with the police? A SEM analysis of Tyler's procedural justice model. *European Journal on Criminal Policy and Research*, 21(1), 15–33.

Velez, M. B. (2001). The role of public social control in urban neighborhoods: A multilevel analysis of victimization risk. *Criminology*, 39(4), 837–864.

Voigt, R., Camp, N. C., Prabhakaran, V., Hamilton, W. L., Hetey, R. C., Griffiths, C. M., Jurgens, D., Jurafsky, D., and Eberhardt, J. L. (2017). Language from police body camera footage shows racial disparities in officer respect. *Proceedings of the National Academy of Sciences of the United States of America*, 114(25), 6521–6526.

Vollmer, A. (1936) (reprinted 1971). *The Police and Modern Society*. Berkeley: University of California Press.

Vollmer, A., and Parker, A. E. (1937). *Crime, Crooks & Cops*. New York: Funk and Wagnall's.

Vorauer, J. D., and Kumhyr, S. (2001). Is this about you or me? Self versus other-directed judgments and feelings in response to intergroup interaction. *Personality and Social Psychology Bulletin*, 27, 706–719.

Vorauer, J. D., Hunter, A. J., Main, K. J., and Roy, S. (2000). Metastereotype activation: Evidence from indirect measures for specific evaluative concerns experienced by members of dominant groups in intergroup interaction. *Journal of Personality and Social Psychology*, 78, 690–707.

Vorauer, J. D., Main, K. J., and O'Connell, G. B. (1998). How do individuals expect to be viewed by members of lower status groups? Content and implications of meta-stereotypes. *Journal of Personality and Social Psychology, 75*, 917–937.

Walker, L., Latour, S., Lind, E. A., and Thibaut, J. (1974). Reactions of participants and observers to modes of adjudication. *Journal of Applied Social Psychology, 4*(4), 295–310.

Walker, S. (1977). *A Critical History of Police Reform: The Emergence of Professionalism.* Lexington, MA: Lexington Books.

Walker, S. (1998). *Popular Justice: A History of American Criminal Justice* (2nd ed.). New York: Oxford University Press.

Walker, S. (2016). The History of Proactive Policing in the U.S. Paper prepared for the Committee on Proactive Policing—Effects on Crime, Communities, and Civil Liberties, Washington, DC, National Academies of Sciences, Engineering, and Medicine.

Walker, S., Spohn, C., and DeLone, M. (2007). *The Color of Justice: Race, Ethnicity, and Crime in America* (4th ed.). Belmont, CA: Wadsworth.

Wallace, D., Papachristos, A. V., Meares, T., and Fagan J. (2016). Desistance and legitimacy: The impact of offender notification meetings on recidivism among high risk offenders. *Justice Quarterly, 33*(7), 1237–1264.

Ward, J. T., Nobles, M. R., Lanza-Kaduce, L., Levett, L. M., and Tillyer, R. (2011). Caught in their own speed trap: The intersection of speed enforcement policy, police legitimacy, and decision acceptance. *Police Quarterly, 14*(3), 251–276.

Watson, A. C., and Angell, B. (2013). The role of stigma and uncertainty in moderating the effect of procedural justice on cooperation and resistance in police encounters with persons with mental illnesses. *Psychology, Public Policy, and Law, 19*(1), 30–39.

Weaver, V. M., and Lerman, A. E. (2010). Political consequences of the carceral state. *American Political Science Review, 104*(4), 817–833.

Wegener, D. T., and Petty, R. E. (1997). The flexible correction model: The role of naive theories of bias in bias correction. *Advances in Experimental Social Psychology, 29*, 141–208.

Weisburd, D. L. (2008). Place-based policing. *Ideas in American Policing*, No. 9. Washington, DC: Police Foundation. Available: https://www.policefoundation.org/wp-content/uploads/2015/06/Weisburd-2008-Place-Based-Policing.pdf [August 2016].

Weisburd, D. L. (2015). The law of crime concentration and the criminology of place. *Criminology 53*(2), 133–157.

Weisburd, D. L. (2016). Does hot spots policing inevitably lead to unfair and abusive police practices, or can we maximize both fairness and effectiveness in the new proactive policing? *The University of Chicago Legal Forum, 2016*(1), Article 16. Available: http://chicagounbound.uchicago.edu/cgi/viewcontent.cgi?article=1578&context=uclf [April 2017].

Weisburd, D. L., and Amram, S. (2014). The law of concentrations of crime at place: The case of Tel Aviv-Jaffa. *Police Practice and Research, 15*(2), 101–114.

Weisburd, D. L., and Braga, A. A. (2006a). Hot spots policing as a model for police innovation. In D. L. Weisburd and A. A. Braga (Eds.), *Police Innovation: Contrasting Perspectives* (pp. 225–244). New York: Cambridge University Press.

Weisburd, D. L., and Braga, A. A. (2006b). Introduction: Understanding police innovation. In D. L. Weisburd and A. A. Braga (Eds.), *Police Innovation: Contrasting Perspectives* (pp. 1–26). New York: Cambridge University Press.

Weisburd, D. L., and Braga, A. A. (Eds.). (2006c). *Police Innovation: Contrasting Perspectives.* New York: Cambridge University Press.

Weisburd, D. L., and Eck, J. (2004). What can police do to reduce crime, disorder, and fear? *The ANNALS of the American Academy of Political and Social Science, 593*(1), 42–65.

Weisburd, D. L., and Green, L. (1995). Policing drug hotspots: The Jersey City drug market analysis experiment. *Justice Quarterly, 12*(4), 711–735.

Weisburd, D. L., and Greenspan, R. (2000). Police attitudes toward abuse of authority: Findings from a national study. *National Institute of Justice Research in Brief*. Washington, DC: National Institute of Justice.

Weisburd, D. L., and McEwen, J. T. (Eds.). (1997). *Crime Mapping and Crime Prevention*. Monsey, NY: Willow Tree Press.

Weisburd, D. L., and Telep, C. W. (2010). The efficiency of place-based policing. *Journal of Police Studies*, 17, 247–262.

Weisburd, D. L., Davis, M., and Gill, C. (2015). Increasing collective efficacy and social capital at crime hot spots: New crime control tools for police. *Policing*, 9(3), 265–274.

Weisburd, D. L., Eck, J. E., Hinkle, J. C., and Telep, C. W. (2008). Effects of problem-oriented policing on crime and disorder. *Campbell Collaboration Library of Systematic Reviews*. Available: http://www.campbellcollaboration.org/library.php [October 2017].

Weisburd, D. L., Groff, E. R., and Yang, S.-M. (2012). *The Criminology of Place: Street Segments and Our Understanding of the Crime Problem*. New York: Oxford University Press.

Weisburd, D. L., Maher, L., and Sherman, L. (1992). Contrasting crime general and crime specific theory: The case of hot spots of crime. In F. Adler and W. S. Laufer (Eds.), *Advances in Criminological Theory* (vol. 4, pp. 45–70). New Brunswick, NJ: Transaction.

Weisburd, D. L., McElroy, J., and Hardyman, P. (1988). Challenges to supervision in community policing: Observations on a pilot project. *American Journal of Police*, 7(2), 29–50.

Weisburd, D. L., Morris, N. A., and Groff, E. R. (2009). Hot spots of juvenile crime: A longitudinal study of street segments in Seattle, Washington. *Journal of Quantitative Criminology*, 25, 443–467.

Weisburd, D. L., Morris, N. A., and Ready, J. (2008). Risk-focused policing at places: An experimental evaluation. *Justice Quarterly*, 25(1), 163–200.

Weisburd, D. L., Telep, C. W., and Lawton, B. A. (2014) Could innovations in policing have contributed to the New York City crime drop even in a period of declining police strength?: The case of stop, question and frisk as a hot spots policing strategy. *Justice Quarterly*, 31(1), 129–153.

Weisburd, D. L., Mastrofski, S., McNally, A. M., Greenspan, R., and Willis, J. (2003). Reforming to preserve: Compstat and strategic problem solving in American policing. *Criminology & Public Policy*, 2(3), 421–456. doi:10.1111/j.1745-9133.2003.tb00006.x.

Weisburd, D. L., Bushway, S., Lum, C., and Yang, S.-M. (2004). Trajectories of crime at place: A longitudinal study of street segments in the city of Seattle. *Criminology*, 42(2), 283–322.

Weisburd, D. L., Mastrofski, S. D., Willis, J. J., and Grenspan, R. (2006a). Changing everything so that everything can remain the same: Compstat and American policing. In D. L. Weisburd and A. A. Braga (Eds.), *Police Innovation: Contrasting Perspectives* (pp. 284–304). Cambridge, UK: Cambridge University Press.

Weisburd, D. L., Wyckoff, L., Ready, J., Eck, J. E., Hinkle, J. C., and Gajewski, F. (2006b). Does crime just move around the corner?: A controlled study of spatial displacement and diffusion of crime control benefits. *Criminology*, 44(3), 549–591.

Weisburd, D. L., Telep, C. W., Hinkle, J. C., and Eck, J. E. (2008). *The Effects of Problem-Oriented Policing on Crime and Disorder*. Document No. 224990. Available: https://www.ncjrs.gov/pdffiles1/nij/grants/224990.pdf [April 2017].

Weisburd, D. L., Telep, C. W., Hinkle, J. C., and Eck, J. E. (2010). Is problem-oriented policing effective in reducing crime and disorder? Findings from a Campbell systematic review. *Criminology & Public Policy*, 9(1), 139–172.

Weisburd, D. L., Hinkle, J. C., Famega, C., and Ready, J. (2011). The possible "backfire" effects of hot spot policing: An experimental assessment of impacts on legitimacy, fear and collective efficacy. *Journal of Experimental Criminology*, 7(4), 297–320.

Weisburd, D. L., Hinkle, J. C., Braga, A. A., and Wooditch, A. (2015). Understanding the mechanisms underlying broken windows policing: The need for evaluation evidence. *Journal of Research in Crime & Delinquency*, 52(4), 589–608.

Weisburd, D. L., Wooditch, A., Weisburd, S., and Yang, S.-M. (2016). Do stop, question, and frisk practices deter crime? Evidence at micro units of space and time. *Criminology & Public Policy*, 15(1), 31–56.

Weisburd, D. L., Braga, A. A., Groff, E. R., and Wooditch, A. (2017). Can hot spot policing reduce crime in urban areas? An agent-based simulation. *Criminology*, 55(1), 137–173.

Weisburd, S. (2016). *Police Presence, Rapid Response Rates, and Crime Prevention*. Available: https://econ.tau.ac.il/sites/economy.tau.ac.il/files/media_server/Economics/PDF/seminars%202016-17/Sarit%20Weisburd_Police%20Presence%2C%20Rapid%20Response%20Rates%2C%20and%20Crime.pdf [October 2017].

Weiss, A., and Grumet-Morris, A. (2005). *Illinois Traffic Stop Statistics Act Report for the Year 2004*. Technical Report. Evanston, IL: Northwestern University Center for Public Safety.

Weitzer, R., and Tuch, S. A. (2002). Perceptions of racial profiling: Race, class and personal experience. *Criminology*, 40(2), 435–456. doi:10.1111/j.1745-9125.2002.tb00962.x.

Welsh, B. C., and Farrington, D. P. (2008). Effects of closed circuit television surveillance on crime. *Campbell Systematic Reviews*, 73.

Wemmers, J. A., Van der Leeden, R., and Steensma, H. (1995). What is procedural justice: Criteria used by Dutch victims to assess the fairness of criminal justice procedures. *Social Justice Research*, 8(4), 329–350.

Wemmers, J. M. (1996). *Victims in the Criminal Justice System: A Study into the Treatment of Victims and Its Effect on Their Attitudes and Behavior*. Ph.D. Dissertation. Available: https://www.wodc.nl/binaries/ov-1996-05-full-tekst_tcm28-78069.pdf [April 2017].

Wemmers, J. M. (2013). Victims' experiences in the criminal justice system and their recovery from crime. *International Review of Victimology*, 19(3), 221–233.

Western, B. (2006). *Punishment and Inequality in America*. New York: Russell Sage Foundation.

Wheller, L., Quinton, P., Fildes, A., and Mills, A. (2013). *The Greater Manchester Police Procedural Justice Training Experiment*. Coventry, UK: College of Policing.

White, M. D., Mulvey, P., and Dario, L. M. (2016). Arrestees' perceptions of the police: Exploring procedural justice, legitimacy, and willingness to cooperate with police across offender types. *Criminal Justice and Behavior*, 43(3), 343–364.

Wilcox, P., Land, K. C., and Hunt, S. C. (2003). *Criminal Circumstance: A Dynamic Multi-contextual Criminal Opportunity Theory*. New York: Walter de Gruyster.

Williams, T. (2003). NYC crime rate drops again in 2002. *The Associated Press State & Local Wire*, June 16.

Williams, D., and Mohammed, S. (2013). Racism and health: Pathways and scientific evidence. *American Behavioral Scientist*, 57(8), 1152–1173.

Williams, H. L., and Murphy, P. V. (1990). *The Evolving Strategy of Police: A Minority View. Perspectives on Policing*. Washington, DC: National Institute of Justice. Available: https://www.ncjrs.gov/pdffiles1/nij/121019.pdf [April 2017].

Willis, J. J. (2014). A recent history of the police. In M. D. Reisig and R. J. Kane (Eds.), *The Oxford Handbook of Police and Policing* (pp. 3–33). New York: Oxford University Press.

Willis, J. J., Mastrofski, S. D., and Weisburd, D. L. (2007). Making sense of Compstat: A theory-based analysis of organizational change in three police departments. *Law & Society Review*, 41(1), 147–188.

Wilson, D. B. (n.d.). *Meta-Analysis Stuff*. Available: http://mason.gmu.edu/~dwilsonb/ma.html [October 2017].

Wilson, J. Q. (1968). *Varieties of Police Behavior: The Management of Law and Order in Eight Communities*. Cambridge, MA: Harvard University Press.

Wilson, J. Q., and Kelling, G. (1982). Broken windows: The police and neighborhood safety. *The Atlantic Monthly*, 249(3), 29–38.

Wolfe, S. E., and Piquero, A. (2011). Organizational justice and police misconduct. *Criminal Justice and Behavior*, 38(4), 332–353.

Wolfe, S. E., Nix, J., Kaminski, R., and Rojek, J. (2016). Is the effect of procedural justice on police legitimacy invariant? Testing the generality of procedural justice and competing antecedents of legitimacy. *Journal of Quantitative Criminology*, 32(2), 253–282.

Wolfgang, M. E., Figlio, R. M., and Sellin, T. (1972). *Delinquency in a Birth Cohort*. Chicago, IL: University of Chicago Press.

Wood, S. (2001). Region's crime drops 20% in 5 years: Community policing and enforcement of quality of life laws credited. *The Times Union (Albany, NY)*, October 29.

Wooditch, A., and Weisburd, D. L. (2016). Using space-time analysis to evaluate criminal justice programs: An application to stop-question-frisk practices. *Journal of Quantitative Criminology*, 32(2), 191–213.

Worden, R. E., and McLean, S. J. (2014). *Assessing Police Performance in Citizen Encounters: Police Legitimacy and Management Accountability*. Washington, DC: National Institute of Justice, U.S. Department of Justice.

Worden, R. E., and McLean, S. J. (2016). Measuring, managing, and enhancing procedural justice in policing: Promise and pitfalls. *Criminal Justice Police Review*. Available: http://journals.sagepub.com/doi/pdf/10.1177/0887403416662505 [October 2017].

Worden, R. E., and McLean, S. J. (2017a). *Mirage of Police Reform: Procedural Justice and Police Legitimacy*. Oakland: University of California Press.

Worden, R. E., and McLean, S. J. (2017b). Research on police legitimacy: The state of the art. *Policing: An International Journal of Police Strategy and Management*, 40(3), 480–513. doi:10.1108/PIJPSM-05-2017-0062.

Wycoff, M. A., and Skogan, W. G. (1993). *Community Policing in Madison: Quality from the Inside Out. An Evaluation of Implementation and Impact*. NCJ 144390. Washington, DC: National Institute of Justice.

Wycoff, M., Pate, A. M., Skogan, W., and Sherman, L. W. (1985). *Citizen Contact Patrol in Houston: Executive Summary*. Washington, DC: Police Foundation.

Yang, S. M. (2010). Assessing the spatial-temporal relationship between disorder and violence. *Journal of Quantitative Criminology*, 26(1), 139–163.

Youmans, S. (2000). Police: More officers, community efforts extend crime decline. *The Associated Press State & Local Wire*, May 9.

Zimbardo, P. G. (1969). The human choice: Individuation, reason, and order versus deindividuation, impulse, and chaos. *Nebraska Symposium on Motivation*, 17, 237–307.

Zimbardo, P. G., and Ebbesen, E. B. (1969). *Influencing Attitudes and Changing Behavior*. Reading, MA: Addison Wesley.

Appendix A

Perspectives from the Field

During the course of this study, the committee gathered information through public information-gathering roundtables and webinars. The purpose of these activities was to explore topics and issues relevant to the study charge from the perspective of the police carrying out proactive policing and the perspective of the communities that experience proactive policing. These sessions informed the committee's deliberations and served as a valuable complement to the committee's other information-gathering activities and approaches.

The Police Practitioner Roundtable and the Community Perspective Roundtable were held during the open session of the committee meeting April 4–5, 2016, in Washington, DC. The webinars with Alicia Garza and Brittany N. Packnett were held June 22 and June 24, 2016, respectively.

POLICE PRACTITIONER ROUNDTABLE

Participants: Chief Art Acevado (Austin, TX)
Chief Debora Black (Glendale, AZ)
Chief Jane Castor (retired) (Tampa, FL)
Sheriff Bob Gualtieri (Pinellas County, FL)
Commissioner Robert Haas (Cambridge, MA)
Superintendent Ronal Serpas (retired) (New Orleans, LA)

Moderator: Jim Bueermann (Police Foundation), committee member

The roundtable began by noting that police officers today are better trained, better equipped, better educated, and more professional than they have ever been before. According to Sheriff Gualtieri, law enforcement has undergone enormous changes in his 35-year career. Law enforcement officers and departments have not been afraid to accept change or adopt new, innovative styles of policing. Among these innovations are proactive policing strategies, which Chief Black described as becoming more prominent within the past 10 years.

In defining proactive policing, the police practitioners agreed that, to them, proactive policing aims to prevent crime as opposed to responding to crime after the fact. In this way, proactive policing is everything that is not reactive policing and includes problem-oriented policing, predictive policing, and community outreach and engagement. Proactive policing reflects an expansion from the traditional bounds of policing, according to Commissioner Haas, and because of this expansion, it necessarily relies on community support for its success.

Given the nature of proactive policing strategies, the police practitioners agreed that controlling crime while also enhancing community trust and confidence was a key goal and that the activities undertaken as part of a proactive policing strategy should be guided by community concerns. To this end, Chief Castor noted that the mission of her department is to reduce crime and improve quality of life through partnerships with all citizens. This mission prioritizes cooperation with the community and guides the actions of all her officers. Similarly, proactive policing, according to Superintendent Serpas, has been "a way of increasing our savings account of citizens' support and trust because we were actively finding out what they wanted us to fix."

Community trust and support is also built through accountability. Should mistakes happen, Sheriff Gualtieri said, the community has to know that law enforcement leadership is going to do the right thing and hold people accountable. Part of proactive policing, then, is not only to know what the limits of the law and the police department's policies are but also to exercise independent judgment and discretion within those limits in ways that are mindful of the department's mission and in accord with the desires of the community.

Another aspect of building community trust and support, according to the police practitioners, was having an open and honest conversation with communities about the police department's activities and priorities. The police practitioners noted that sometimes this means having difficult conversations and telling communities things they do not want to hear. Chief Acevado noted that many of his resources are distributed to low-income and predominately Black neighborhoods. The department's annual racial profiling report typically says that they disproportionately stop Blacks as compared to Whites. However, Chief Acevado said, "We put officers where they are needed. I will not apologize because I make it a priority for young boys and girls of color. . . . I believe they should have the same right to go to the neighborhood park, to their grandma's house, or to the little market on the corner." The police practitioners agreed that opening lines of communication enables the police and communities to have a better understanding of where each is coming from, resulting in better outcomes and better use of resources.

When choosing to implement a particular proactive policing strategy, the police practitioners noted that a number of considerations influence their decision. For instance, Chief Black noted that an ideal strategy would be fact based and data driven and capitalize on partnerships with the community and other governmental and nongovernmental partners. The strategy should also include evaluable measures of success, such as declining crime rates or neighborhood satisfaction. The police practitioners also agreed that any proactive strategy that they consider implementing has to be in line with their organizational values. According to Chief Black, "[If] it doesn't adhere to the very high standards and expectations that we have of our officers and how they will perform, not only within the law, but with issues of respect, compassion, and absolute full regard for human dignity, then it never gets off the ground." Chief Acevedo expanded on this point, using stop, question, and frisk (SQF) programs as an example: "Most communities and most Americans are not going to support or tolerate that kind of tactic. For me, part of being proactive means understanding the collective mind-set of values, the expectations, and the strategies that the folks we serve expect from us."

The police practitioners also discussed how, after a proactive policing strategy is implemented, law enforcement agencies typically measure its effectiveness. They all agreed that reduction in crime is a readily available and important metric. However, the participants also noted that community satisfaction is an important measure of effectiveness and can be assessed through citizen satisfaction surveys or other methods. Chief Black suggested that policing has further room to evolve in this area, saying that crime rates do not always tell the whole picture and that it is necessary to look at the conditions and impressions of neighborhoods to understand the department's effectiveness. Commissioner Haas reiterated this notion and challenged his colleagues in the field to think beyond the traditional measures.

In their concluding remarks, the police practitioners stressed that, in the end, what matters most is not what they are doing, but how they are doing it. Law enforcement will be judged by whether they are being professional, respectful, and granting people their dignity and whether, in doing so, they are following the Constitution, state laws, and departmental policies.

COMMUNITY PERSPECTIVES ROUNDTABLE

Participants: John DeTaeye, Collaborative Solutions for Communities
Jin Hee Lee, NAACP Legal Defense and Educational Fund
Joseph Lipari, Citizen Review Board, Syracuse, NY
Julia Ryan, Local Initiatives Support Corporation

Moderator: Phillip Atiba Goff (John Jay College of Criminal Justice; Center for Policing Equity), committee member

As in the Police Practitioner Roundtable, the community perspectives roundtable participants began by defining proactive policing. According to the community representatives, proactive policing encompasses everything that is not reactive, and it comes in two distinct forms: those strategies that are community-focused, and those that are more aggressive and enforcement-based. The representatives agreed that the second type is more problematic and more likely to lead to complaints and constitutional violations. For example, Ms. Lee noted that proactive policing strategies that attempt to predict criminal behavior may easily lead to stereotyping of groups or neighborhoods, and Mr. Lipari pointed out that most of the complaints that he sees at the Citizen Review Board in Syracuse, New York, come from incidents arising from a proactive policing interaction.

The community representatives also discussed the impact of proactive policing on police-community relations. They agreed that proactive policing can, at times, lead to a deterioration of trust between the community and police. Ms. Lee noted that some strategies create hostility with people in the community who are not engaged in criminal activity but are nonetheless targeted and presumed to be criminals.

This distrust is often deeply rooted. Referring to Black communities in particular, Ms. Lee discussed the history of discrimination against Blacks by law enforcement. This history leads to skepticism of how police as an institution treat certain communities, and when incidents of misconduct occur, they are not seen by many in the community as aberrations but rather as another example in a long history of mistreatment. This mistrust is further amplified when individual officers are seen as not being held accountable for their actions, thereby delegitimizing the system. Although in some cases individual officers are held accountable and face repercussions, for many in the community there is little hope that any larger reform measure in the police agency will be undertaken.

The roundtable also discussed whether proactive policing has been successful. They agreed that police should not be judged solely on crime statistics. Mr. DeTaeye indicated that, for many people in the neighborhoods where he works, their assessment of proactive policing has been that it "is not helping us" and in some places "is hurting us and killing us." However, this does not mean that communities do not want police presence and protection. According to Mr. Lipari, "I wouldn't say that people in these communities don't want that service. . . . They want effective, Constitutional policing that doesn't infringe on their liberty." The roundtable participants also agreed that there is often dissatisfaction with the services that the police offer, as well as a disconnect between what the police officers provide and what the community wants from the police.

Policing operates within a broader social context, and the community representatives stressed that in many of the neighborhoods in which they work there is no access to jobs, education, or affordable housing. They said that the communities where the questions about policing are most fraught are the same communities that have been failed by every other system in government and that these communities lack capacity, adequate resources, and support. Mr. De Taeye noted that, to the people with whom he works, it seems that the only response from the government to these issues is to send the police. He said communities often ask, "Why is it that the police are the only government entity that we see when we are asking for help?" Ms. Ryan, discussing the mission of policing, said that though these other social issues are not the sole responsibility of the police, the police can do more than make arrests and undertake enforcement activities. The police play an important role in many cross-sector efforts and should be guided by a mission to make neighborhoods safe, high-quality places to live, whether that is through partnerships with the housing, small business, education, or health sectors. Mr. Lipari agreed, stressing that the police cannot be the only ones to address these larger problems and must work in concert with other agencies and stakeholders. Emphasizing the distinction between the police and other social service agencies, Ms. Lee noted that law enforcement has the power and authority to enforce laws. It is very different for a police officer as opposed to a social worker to be involved in something—because the police have the power to arrest, there are risks for those with whom they engage.

The community representatives also discussed their assessment of police-community relations currently and whether they have seen a change since the shooting of Michael Brown in Ferguson, Missouri, in August 2014. Ms. Ryan noted that her organization, Local Initiative Support Corporation, has been working in this field for more than 35 years, and many issues are the same. However, whereas one used to be able to resolve issues and break down barriers of distrust through conversations between the police and community members, those conversations have been tenser since August 2014. The community leaders who fostered these relationships in the past are "tired" and find it more and more difficult to build bridges between a distrustful community and law enforcement. Mr. Lipari said that he believed there were more complaints now arising from incidents in which a citizen took a more confrontational attitude toward an officer. He noted that educating citizens about their rights and how to interact with officers is important in this new environment. Ms. Lee said that post-Ferguson activism has largely been driven by a need or demand for dignity. She noted that many Black people experience proactive policing as an affront to dignity and as a loss of liberty. That is, they do not "feel comfortable moving around, whether it's to and from your neighborhood or going to see friends, because you are afraid that you might have this kind of interaction with a police officer."

The roundtable participants concluded by stressing the diversity of the communities they represent. They agreed that the term "community" should be used loosely and to encompass a diversity of groups and diversity within groups, who have a variety of needs. Ms. Lee challenged the group to "talk about the people, the members of the community who have been the most victimized by whatever aggressive policing has existed in whatever jurisdiction."

COMMUNITY PERSPECTIVES—BLACK LIVES MATTER (PART I)

Participant: Alicia Garza, National Domestic Workers Alliance

Moderator: Phillip Atiba Goff (John Jay College of Criminal Justice; Center for Policing Equity), committee member

Ms. Garza, a co-creator of #BlackLivesMatter, spoke about a "re-imagined" vision of policing. Such a vision would, she said, empower people to solve problems and limit the distance between the police and the community. She noted the need for officers to live in the communities they serve. For example, she said, most of the officers in Oakland, California, do not live in the city. As a result, they are predisposed to the idea that Oakland is a dangerous community, and this bias affects the way officers police the community. Ms. Garza also emphasized that police reforms should establish practices for taking into account existing biases and for collecting data on racial and ethnic disparities in police contact. Mechanisms for accountability, oversight, and transparency, as well as improved training and mental health services and support for police officers, are also critical.

Ms. Garza said this "new vision" of policing was necessary because of the many harms that policing has inflicted on communities. One harm, she noted, was the discrepancy in responses between affluent and poor communities. This inconsistency—more aggressive enforcement in poor communities—further exacerbates the existing problem of Blacks and Hispanics having greater contact with the criminal justice system. With regard to proactive policing generally, Ms. Garza described the consequences as varying by place. In New York City, for example, she said, the SQF program was implemented to promote redevelopment in neighborhoods to "make space" for new people of higher socioeconomic status. Ms. Garza explained that the individuals who live in these communities have been harmed by such aggressive police tactics in which "people of color are labeled as problems." She questioned the wisdom of such strategies and urged the police to consider the real problems that need to be addressed in these communities.

Discussing changes in the dynamics between the police and communities in the past 5 years, Ms. Garza said that she has seen an uptick in advocacy that demands quality of life for communities. This advocacy has seen fruitful gains. For example, there have been a number of criminal justice reforms passed in state legislatures, and some localities have seen policing reforms implemented. However, she has also witnessed worsened relationships between the police and communities, and she noted that there has been an increase in surveillance of community activists. With growing distrust on both sides, she said, there needs to "be a real reckoning before we can transform the police." Despite this growing distrust, Ms. Garza was optimistic that both the police and community want reforms and can work together to achieve changes. She said that key questions to keep in mind during such a process are "How do we properly train police officers to solve problems in communities without criminalizing the people in those communities?" and "What are the tools of policing, and are they appropriate to solve the present problems?"

COMMUNITY PERSPECTIVES—BLACK LIVES MATTER (PART II)

Participant: Brittany N. Packnett, Teach for America

Moderator: Phillip Atiba Goff (John Jay College of Criminal Justice; Center for Policing Equity), committee member

According to Ms. Packnett, police-community interactions tend to happen either through an incident that mobilizes activists and communities or through interactions between activists and police after such incidents have occurred. She said the former tend to occur as a result of unlawful stops or disproportionate responses from the police during lawful stops, with the killings of Michael Brown, Eric Garner, and Tamir Rice falling into the latter category. Ms. Packnett regarded these interactions as "attempts to control young people in certain environments" and noted a troubling trend toward increasingly aggressive interactions between the police and young people in spaces where young people are supposed to feel safe, such as schools. Ms. Packnett said that, in response to incidents that galvanize a community response, she has witnessed a militarization of the police and use of proactive policing to surveil activists and community members, noting that proactive policing is "just another lever for the police to control the community."

Describing the experiences of individuals targeted by proactive policing, Ms. Packnett said that it is important to remember that policing does not exist in a vacuum. She said that, for many individuals in Black communities, proactive policing tactics like SQF do not feel neutral, considering the disparities that exist throughout the broader criminal justice system. Individuals feel targeted because they are poor or because they live in certain neighborhoods, and to their dismay the government (as represented by the police) seems to be doing little to address the root causes of the societal ills that plague their neighborhoods. To them, Ms. Packnett said, the government, through proactive policing, is privileging a criminal justice response over addressing the real problems facing their communities. She asked, "Why not proactive jobs, or proactive education?" Ms. Packnett also discussed how individuals in Black communities internalize the effects of proactive policing and racism and, in doing so, internalize their oppression. This process, she said, makes it seem normal that young children are placed in handcuffs or that police officers are in schools. According to Ms. Packnett, it "deprives individuals of the ability to dream and imagine a different way."

Similarly, Ms. Packnett said, efforts to build trust between the police and communities alone are not enough. Before trust can be built, she said, communities need to experience justice first. Procedural justice policing, for example, is worthwhile in that it promotes professional decorum, but if the stop itself was suspect, then to many in the community it does not matter how procedurally just the interaction was. In this way, according to Ms. Packnett, procedural justice policing is simply transactional and is not a substitute for social justice.

Describing her vision of policing, Ms. Packnett said that police are public servants and that the most important proactive tactic they could undertake would be to listen. She said that listening would require the police to recognize the validity of the distrust and trauma that has affected communities and to pay attention to the voices of marginalized people.

Ms. Packnett also emphasized that there are deep divisions within Black communities. This diversity within communities leads to various needs and desires, and because of this, she said, the police need to make deliberate efforts to interact not only with older members of communities but also with the young people who are most directly affected by proactive policing tactics. In conclusion, Ms. Packnett emphasized the need to validate people's lived experiences as real data and to empower people on the ground to keep using their voices.

Appendix B

Biographical Sketches of Committee Members

David Weisburd (*Chair*) is a professor of criminology, law, and society and executive director of the Center for Evidence-Based Crime Policy at George Mason University, the Walter E. Meyer professor of law and criminal justice at the Hebrew University Faculty of Law, Jerusalem, and senior science advisor at the Police Foundation, Washington, DC. He is an elected fellow of the American Society of Criminology and the Academy of Experimental Criminology and a member of the Office of Justice Programs Science Advisory Board, the Campbell Collaboration Crime and Justice Group, and the Scientific Commission of the International Society of Criminology. He is also a National Associate of the National Research Council. Dr. Weisburd is author or editor of more than 25 books and more than 175 scientific articles covering a wide range of criminal justice research topics, including crime at place, white collar crime, policing, and criminal justice statistics and social deviance. He received the 2010 Stockholm Prize in Criminology; the Sutherland (2014) and Vollmer (2017) Awards from the American Society of Criminology; and the Campbell Collaboration's Boruch Award for Distinctive Research Contributions to Policy (2014). In 2015, he received the Israel Prize. His Ph.D. is in sociology from Yale University.

Hassan Aden has more than 28 years of law enforcement service and is founder of the Aden Group. He previously was director of research and programs at the International Association of Chiefs of Police (IACP). Prior to that, he was chief of police with the Greenville (NC) Police Department and served 26 years in the Alexandria (VA) Police Department, rising to deputy chief of police. His expertise covers the administrative, investigative, and operational aspects of policing, and he has successfully dealt with issues of crime control policies and strategic planning. While chief of police in Greenville, he and his staff were deeply committed to community partnerships aimed at reducing crime and improving the city's quality of life. Due to his commitment to the continued professionalization of policing, he serves as commissioner for the Commission on Accreditation for Law Enforcement Agencies. He is an active member of the Police Executive Research Forum and a senior executive fellow with the Police Foundation, Washington, D.C. He is a graduate of, and earned an MPA certificate from American University's Institute for the Study of Public Policy Implementation. He also holds an M.P.A. degree from American University's School of Public Affairs.

Anthony A. Braga is a distinguished professor and the director of the School of Criminology and Criminal Justice at Northeastern University. In his research, Professor Braga collaborates with criminal justice, social service, and community-based organizations to address illegal access to firearms, reduce gang and group-involved violence, and control crime hot spots. His work with the Boston Police Department on its Safe Street Teams Program received the 2011 Excellence in Law Enforcement Research Award from the International Association of Chiefs of Police. He also received the U.S. Attorney General's Award for Outstanding Contributions to Community Partnerships for Public Safety in 2009 and the U.S. Department of Justice Project Safe Neighborhoods' Distinguished Service by a Research Partner Award in 2010. Dr. Braga is an elected fellow of the American Society of Criminology. He is also a past president and fellow of the Academy of Experimental Criminology and the 2014 recipient of its Joan McCord Award recognizing his commitment to advancing randomized controlled experiments. He received his M.P.A. from Harvard University and his Ph.D. in criminal justice from Rutgers University.

Jim Bueermann is president of the Police Foundation, a national, nonpartisan, nonprofit organization dedicated to supporting innovation and improvement in policing. Mr. Bueermann worked for the Redlands, California, Police Department for 33 years, serving in every unit within the department. He was appointed chief of police and director of Housing, Recreation and Senior Services in 1998. He retired in June 2011. As chief, he developed a holistic approach to community policing and problem solving that consolidated housing and recreation services into the police department and was based on risk and protective factor research into adolescent problem prevention. This strategy was recognized as one of the country's 25 most innovative programs in the 2000 Innovations in American Government program sponsored by Harvard's Kennedy School. He was the first police chief to be inducted as an honorary fellow in the Academy of Experimental Criminology and into the halls of fame at George Mason University's Center for Evidence Based Crime Policy and the School of Behavioral Science at California State University, San Bernardino. He is on policing advisory boards at Cambridge University, George Mason University, John Jay College, and the Council for State Governments and works in evidence-based policing, innovative technologies, and prisoner reentry. He was an executive fellow with the National Institute of Justice and a senior fellow at George Mason University. He is a graduate of California State University, San Bernardino; the University of Redlands; the FBI National Academy; and the California Command College.

Philip J. Cook is Sanford professor emeritus of public policy and professor of economics and sociology at Duke University. He has conducted research on various aspects of public health policy, social policy, and crime and criminal justice, with a sustained focus on gun violence and gun policy. His methodological contributions include the development and first use of the "diff-in-diff" panel regression method of policy evaluation (with George Tauchen, 1982) and the development of the conceptual foundations for valuing lives and other irreplaceable entities (with Daniel Graham, 1976). He serves as co-organizer of the Workshop on the Economics of Crime of the National Bureau of Economic Research. His current work focuses on underground gun markets, economics of crime prevention, truancy prevention, determinants of academic achievement, and alcohol control policy. His 1996 book with Robert H. Frank, *The Winner-Take-All Society*, was named a *New York Times* Notable Book of the Year and is available in six languages. He is an elected member of the National Academy of Medicine and an honorary fellow of the American Society of Criminology and the Academy of Experimental Criminology. His Ph.D. is in economics from the University of California, Berkeley.

Phillip Atiba Goff is the Franklin A. Thomas professor in policing equity at John Jay College of Criminal Justice. He is cofounder and president of the Center for Policing Equity (CPE) and an expert in contemporary forms of racial bias and discrimination, as well as the intersections of race and gender. His work has explored ways in which racial prejudice is not a necessary precondition for racial discrimination, demonstrating that contextual factors can facilitate racially unequal outcomes. He recently became one of three CPE principal investigators for the U.S. Department of Justice's National Initiative for Building Community Trust and Justice. This initiative will contribute information to another major CPE project, the National Justice Database: the first national database on racial disparities in police stops and use of force. His model of evidence-based approaches to fairness has been supported with grants from federal agencies and multiple major foundations, as well as the Major Cities Chiefs Association and the NAACP Legal Defense Fund. He was a witness for the President's Task Force on 21st Century Policing and has presented before members of Congress and congressional panels, Senate press briefings, and White House advisory councils.

Rachel A. Harmon is the F.D.G. Ribble professor of law at the University of Virginia. Her research focuses on the legal regulation of law enforcement. She serves as associate reporter on the American Law Institute's recently announced project on police investigations. From 1998 to 2006, she was a prosecutor in the U.S. Department of Justice; after working in the U.S. Attorney's Office in the Eastern District of Virginia, she worked in the Civil Rights Division, Criminal Section, prosecuting hate crimes and official misconduct cases, many of which involved excessive force or sexual abuse by police officers. Prior to that, she clerked for Judge Guido Calabresi of the U.S. Court of Appeals for the Second Circuit and Justice Stephen Breyer of the U.S. Supreme Court. She has an M.Sc. in political theory and an M.Sc. in political sociology, both with distinction, from the London School of Economics and a J.D. from Yale Law School.

Amelia Haviland is as an associate professor with the Heinz College. Previously she was a senior statistician at the RAND Corporation. Her awards include the Anna Loomis McCandless Chair, a Thomas Lord Distinguished Scholar Award (Institute for Civil Justice, RAND), a MacArthur Fellowship for Younger Scholars (MacArthur Research Network on Social Interactions and Economic Inequality), and a Wray Jackson Smith Scholarship (Section on Government Statistics, American Statistical Association). Her research focuses on causal analysis with observational data and analysis of longitudinal and complex survey data applied to policy issues in health and criminology. She recently led a research team assessing the effects of high deductible account–based health insurance plans on health care costs, use, and disparities. Other health policy work involves assessing mechanisms for health disparities for Medicare recipients and exploring connections between patient safety and recent reductions in medical malpractice claims. Her work in criminology includes methodological work extending group-based trajectory modeling to address causal questions related to the effect of gang membership on violent delinquency. Her work has been published in peer-reviewed journals of psychology, human resource management, criminology, public health and services, and health economics. She received a Ph.D. in statistics and public policy from Carnegie Mellon University.

Cynthia Lum is professor in the Department of Criminology, Law and Society at George Mason University and director of its Center for Evidence-Based Crime Policy. She researches primarily in the area of policing, evidence-based crime policy, and evaluation research. Her work has included evaluations of policing interventions and police technology, understanding the translation into practice and receptivity of research in policing, and assessing security efforts of federal agencies. With Dr. Christopher Koper, she has developed the Evidence-Based Policing Matrix and its associated demonstration projects, which are translation tools designed to help police practitioners incorporate research into their strategic and tactical portfolio. She is a member of the Standing Committee on Traffic Law Enforcement, Transportation Research Board (National Academies of Sciences), the Research Advisory Committee of the International Association of Chiefs of Police, the International Advisory Committee of the Scottish Institute for Police Research, the Board of Trustees for the Pretrial Justice Institute, and a Fulbright specialist. She is the founding editor of *Translational Criminology* and the Springer Series on Translational Criminology. Dr. Lum holds a Ph.D. in criminology and criminal justice from the University of Maryland at College Park and was formerly a police officer and detective.

Charles F. Manski has been Board of Trustees professor in economics at Northwestern University since 1997. He previously was a faculty member at the University of Wisconsin–Madison, Hebrew University of Jerusalem, and Carnegie Mellon University. His research spans econometrics, judgment and decision, and the analysis of public policy. He is author of six monographs on methodological issues in statistical treatment of research questions in the social sciences and econometrics, as well as coauthor or coeditor on other books. He was coeditor of the Econometric Society Monograph Series, member of the editorial board of the *Annual Review of Economics*, and associate editor of the *Annals of Applied Statistics, Journal of Economic Perspectives, Econometrica*, the *Journal of the American Statistical Association*, and *Transportation Science*. He was director of the Institute for Research on Poverty (1988–1991) and chaired the Board of Overseers of the Panel Study of Income Dynamics (1994–1998). He is an elected fellow of the Econometric Society, American Economic Association, American Statistical Association, American Academy of Arts and Sciences, American Association for the Advancement of Science, and the British Academy, as well as an elected member of the National Academy of Sciences. He received his B.S. and Ph.D. in economics from the Massachusetts Institute of Technology.

Stephen Mastrofski is University Professor in the Department of Criminology, Law and Society and director of the Center for Justice Leadership and

Management at George Mason University. His research interests include police discretion, police organizations and their reform, and systematic field-observation methods in criminology. For several years, he led a team of researchers supporting and evaluating the transformation of the Trinidad and Tobago Police Service. Current research projects include measuring the quality of street-level policing and assessing police organization development and change. He has served on editorial boards of seven criminology and criminal justice journals and currently serves on the boards of two international policing journals. He was a visiting fellow at the National Institute of Justice and the Office of Community Oriented Policing and has consulted for a variety of public and private organizations. In 2000, he received the O.W. Wilson Award from the Academy of Criminal Justice Sciences for education, research, and service on policing. In 2008, he and coauthors received the Law and Society Association's article prize. He is an elected fellow of the American Society of Criminology and received the Lifetime Achievement Award from the Division of Policing of the American Society of Criminology. His Ph.D. in political science is from the University of North Carolina at Chapel Hill.

Tracey L. Meares is the Walton Hale Hamilton professor of law at Yale University. Previously, she was Max Pam professor of law and director of the Center for Studies in Criminal Justice at the University of Chicago Law School. At both law schools, she was the first African American woman to be granted tenure. Before entering academia, she clerked for the Honorable Harlington Wood, Jr., of the U.S. Court of Appeals for the Seventh Circuit and was an honors program trial attorney in the Antitrust Division of the U.S. Department of Justice. In 2010, she was named by the Attorney General to the Department of Justice's newly created Science Advisory Board. In 2014, President Obama named her to the President's Task Force on 21st Century Policing. Her teaching and research interests focus on criminal procedure and criminal law policy, with particular emphasis on empirical investigation of these subjects. She has written widely on these topics in both the academic and trade press and has engaged in action-oriented research projects in Chicago, Northern California, and several sites across New York State, focused on violence reduction through legitimacy-enhancing strategies. She codirects the Justice Collaboratory at Yale Law School, which with two other institutions has a central role in a new federal initiative to build trust and confidence in the criminal justice system. She has a B.S. in general engineering from the University of Illinois and a J.D. from the University of Chicago Law School.

Daniel S. Nagin is Teresa and H. John Heinz III university professor of public policy and statistics at the Heinz College, Carnegie Mellon University.

His research focuses on the evolution of criminal and antisocial behaviors over the life course, the deterrent effect of criminal and noncriminal penalties on illegal behaviors, and the development of statistical methods for analyzing longitudinal data. He is an elected fellow of the American Society of Criminology, American Association for the Advancement of Science, and American Academy of Political and Social Science and the recipient of the American Society of Criminology's Edwin H. Sutherland Award in 2006, the Stockholm Prize in Criminology in 2014, Carnegie Mellon University's Alumni Distinguished Achievement Award in 2016, and the National Academy of Sciences Award for Scientific Reviewing in 2017.

Emily Owens is an associate professor at the University of California, Irvine. Previously, she was at Cornell University in policy and management. She studies a wide range of topics in the economics of crime, including policing, sentencing, and the impact of local public policies on criminal behavior. She focuses primarily on the effect of government regulations on crime, which includes studying how government policies affect the prevalence of criminal activity, as well as the structure and response of the criminal justice system. Her current research includes projects on police training and performance, alcohol regulation, immigration policy, and economic development programs. She has a B.S. in applied math and economics from Brown University and an M.A. and Ph.D. in economics from the University of Maryland.

Steven Raphael is a professor of public policy at University of California, Berkeley. His research focuses on the economics of low-wage labor markets, housing, and the economics of crime and corrections. His most recent research focuses on the social consequences of the large increases in U.S. incarceration rates. He also works on immigration policy, research questions pertaining to various aspects of racial inequality, the economics of labor unions, social insurance policies, homelessness, and low-income housing. He is coauthor of *Why Are so Many Americans in Prison?* and *The New Scarlet Letter? Negotiating the U.S. Labor Market with a Criminal Record*. He is editor in chief of *Industrial Relations* and a research fellow at the University of Michigan National Poverty Center, the University of Chicago Crime Lab, IZA (Bonn, Germany), and the Public Policy Institute of California. He holds a Ph.D. in economics from the University of California, Berkeley.

Jerry Ratcliffe is a professor in the Department of Criminal Justice at Temple University. He directs the university's Center for Security and Crime Science and is a member of the Science Advisory Board for the Office of Justice Programs in the U.S. Department of Justice. Previously, he was a police officer with London's Metropolitan Police for more than a decade. His research focuses on evidence-based policing, the analysis and reduction of crime and harm, and criminal intelligence. Across these areas, he has published more than 70 research articles and six books. Dr. Ratcliffe's current projects include a SMART Policing Initiative collaboration with the Philadelphia Police Department and as coprincipal investigator on the Philadelphia Predictive Policing Experiment, the largest randomized field experiment in predictive policing to date. He has twice received the Professional Service Award from the International Association of Law Enforcement Intelligence Analysts and, in 2010, was awarded the Law Enforcement Intelligence Unit's Distinguished Service Award for continued dedication and outstanding contributions to the law enforcement community. He sits on the executive advisory board for the FBI's National Academy. He received his Ph.D. from the University of Nottingham.

Tom Tyler is the Macklin Fleming professor of law and professor of psychology at Yale Law School, as well as a professor in the Yale School of Management. Previously, he was a university professor at New York University, where he taught in both the psychology department and the law school. Before that, he taught at the University of California, Berkeley, and Northwestern University. His research explores the role of justice in shaping people's relationships with groups, organizations, communities, and societies, in particular examining the role of judgments about the justice or injustice of group procedures in shaping legitimacy, compliance, and cooperation. Dr. Tyler is the author of several monographs on why people cooperate, why they obey the law, and legitimacy in criminal justice. He was awarded the Harry Kalven prize for "paradigm shifting scholarship in the study of law and society" by the Law and Society Association in 2000. In 2012, he received a Lifetime Achievement Award for innovative research on social justice from the International Society for Justice Research. He holds a B.A. in psychology from Columbia University and an M.A. and Ph.D. in social psychology from the University of California, Los Angeles.